CHILTON BOOK COMPANY

REPAIR MANUAL

HONDA 1973 to 1988

All U.S. and Canadian models of Accord • Accord CVCC • Civic •
Civic CVCC • CRX • Prelude

D1312615

President GARY R. INGERSOLL
Senior Vice President, Book Publishing and Research RONALD A. HOXTER
Publisher KERRY A. FREEMAN, S.A.E.
Editor-in-Chief DEAN F. MORGANTINI, S.A.E.
Senior Editor RICHARD J. RIVELE, S.A.E.

CHILTON BOOK COMPANY
Radnor, Pennsylvania
19089

CONTENTS

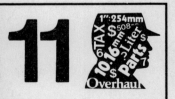

SAFETY NOTICE

Proper service and repair procedures are vital to the safe, reliable operation of all motor vehicles, as well as the personal safety of those performing repairs. This book outlines procedures for servicing and repairing vehicles using safe, effective methods. The procedures contain many NOTES, CAUTIONS and WARNINGS which should be followed along with standard safety procedures to eliminate the possibility of personal injury or improper service which could damage the vehicle or compromise its safety.

It is important to note that repair procedures and techniques, tools and parts for servicing motor vehicles, as well as the skill and experience of the individual performing the work vary widely. It is not possible to anticipate all of the conceivable ways or conditions under which vehicles may be serviced, or to provide cautions as to all of the possible hazards that may result. Standard and accepted safety precautions and equipment should be used during cutting, grinding, chiseling, prying, or any other process that can cause material removal or projectiles.

Some procedures require the use of tools specially designed for a specific purpose. Before substituting another tool or procedure, you must be completely satisfied that neither your personal safety, nor the performance of the vehicle will be endangered.

Although the information in this guide is based on industry sources and is as complete as possible at the time of publication, the possibility exists that the manufacturer made later changes which could not be included here. While striving for total accuracy, Chilton Book Company cannot assume responsibility for any errors, changes, or omissions that may occur in the compilation of this data.

PART NUMBERS

Part numbers listed in this reference are not recommendations by Chilton for any product by brand name. They are references that can be used with interchange manuals and aftermarket supplier catalogs to locate each brand supplier's discrete part number.

SPECIAL TOOLS

Special tools are recommended by the vehicle manufacturer to perform their specific job. Use has been kept to a minimum, but where absolutely necessary, they are referred to in the text by the part number of the tool manufacturer. These tools can be purchased, under the appropriate part number, from your Honda dealer or regional distributor or an equivalent tool can be purchased locally from a tool supplier or parts outlet. Before substituting any tool for the one recommended, read the SAFETY NOTICE at the top of this page.

ACKNOWLEDGMENTS

Chilton Book Company expresses its appreciation to the Honda Motor Company, Dearborn, Michigan for their generous assistance.

Manufactured in the United States of America
    567890   87654321

Chilton's Repair Manual: Honda 1973–88
ISBN 0-8019-7840-8
Library of Congress Catalog Card No. 87-47936

General Information and Maintenance

1

HOW TO USE THIS BOOK

Chilton's Repair & Tune-Up Guide for Honda models is intended to teach you more about the inner workings of your car and save you money on its upkeep. The first two chapters will be used the most, since they contain maintenance and tune-up information and procedures. The following chapters concern themselves with the more complex systems. Operating systems from engine through brakes are covered to the extent that we feel the average do-it-yourselfer should get involved as well as more complex procedures that will benefit both the advanced do-it-yourselfer mechanic as well as the professional. This book will explain such things as rebuilding the transaxle and it should be advised that the expertise required, and the investment in special tools makes this task uneconomical and unpractical for the novice mechanic. We will also tell you how to change your own brake pads and shoes, replace spark plugs, perform routine maintenance, and many more jobs that will save you money, give you personal satisfactions, and help you avoid problems.

A secondary purpose of this book is a reference guide for owners who want to understand their Honda and/or their mechanics better. In this case, no tools at all are required. Knowing just what a particular repair job requires in parts and labor time will allow you to evaluate whether or not you're getting a fair price quote and help decipher itemized bills from a repair shop.

Before attempting any repairs or service on your Honda, read through the entire procedure outlined in the appropriate chapter. This will give you the overall view of what tools and supplies will be required. There is nothing more frustrating than having to walk to the bus stop on Monday morning because you were short one gasket on Sunday afternoon. So read ahead and plan ahead. Each operation should be approached logically and all procedures thoroughly understood before attempting any work. Some special tools that may be required can often be rented from local automotive jobbers or places specializing in renting tools and equipment. Check the yellow pages of your phone book.

All chapters contain adjustments, maintenance, removal and installation procedures, and overhaul procedures. When overhaul is not considered practical, we tell you how to remove the failed part and, then, how to install the new or rebuilt replacement. In this way, you at least save the labor costs. Backyard overhaul of some components (such as the alternator or water pump) is just not practical, but the removal and installation procedure is often simple and well within the capabilities of the average Honda owner.

Two basic mechanic's rules should be mentioned here. First, whenever the LEFT side of the Honda or engine is referred to, it is meant to specify the DRIVER'S side of the Honda. Conversely, the RIGHT side of the Honda means the PASSENGER'S side. Second, all screws and bolts are removed by turning counterclockwise, and tightened by turning clockwise.

Safety is always the most important rule. Constantly be aware of the dangers involved in working on or around an automobile and take proper precautions to avoid the risk of personal injury or damage to the Honda. See the section in this chapter, Servicing Your Vehicle Safely, and the SAFETY NOTICE on the acknowledgment page before attempting any service procedures and pay attention to the instructions provided. There are 3 common mistakes in mechanical work:

1. Incorrect order of assembly, disassembly or adjustment. When taking something apart or putting it together, doing things in the wrong order usually just costs you extra time; how-

ever, it CAN break something. Read the entire procedure before beginning disassembly. Do everything in the order in which the instructions say you should do it, even if you can't immediately see a reason for it. When you're taking apart something that is very intricate (for example a carburetor), you might want to draw a picture of how it looks when assembled at one point in order to make sure you get everything back in its proper position. We will supply exploded views whenever possible, but sometimes the job requires more attention to detail than an illustration provides. When making adjustments (especially tune-up adjustments), do them in order. One adjustment often affects another and you cannot expect satisfactory results unless each adjustment is made only when it cannot be changed by any other.

2. Overtorquing (or undertorquing) nuts and bolts. While it is more common for overtorquing to cause damage, under torquing can cause a fastener to vibrate loose and cause serious damage, especially when dealing with aluminum parts. Pay attention to torque specifications and utilize a torque wrench in assembly. If a torque figure is not available remember that, if you are using the right tool to do the job, you will probably not have to strain yourself to get a fastener tight enough. The pitch of most threads is so slight that the tension you put on the wrench will be multiplied many times in actual force on what you are tightening. A good example of how critical torque is can be seen in the case of spark plug installation, especially where you are putting the plug into an aluminum cylinder head. Too little torque can fail to crush the gasket, causing leakage of combustion gases and consequent overheating of the plug and engine parts. Too much torque can damage the threads or distort the plug, which changes the spark gap at the electrode. Since more and more manufacturers are using aluminum in their engine and chassis parts to save weight, a torque wrench should be in any serious do-it-yourselfer's tool box.

3. There are many commercial chemical products available for ensuring that fasteners won't come loose, even if they are not torqued just right (a very common brand is Loctite®). If you're worried about getting something together tight enough to hold, but loose enough to avoid mechanical damage during assembly, one of these products might offer substantial insurance. Read the label on the package and make sure the product is compatible with the materials, fluids, etc. involved before choosing one.

4. Crossthreading. This occurs when a part such as a bolt is screwed into a nut or casting at the wrong angle and forced, causing the threads to become damaged. Crossthreading is more likely to occur if access is difficult. It helps to clean and lubricate fasteners, and to start threading with the part to be installed going straight in, using your fingers. If you encounter resistance, unscrew the part and start over again at a different angle until it can be inserted and turned several times without much effort. Keep in mind that many parts, especially spark plugs, use tapered threads so that gentle turning will automatically bring the part you're threading to the proper angle if you don't force it or resist a change in angle. Don't put a wrench on the part until it's been turned in a couple of times by hand. If you suddenly encounter resistance and the part has not seated fully, don't force it. Pull it back out and make sure it's clean and threading properly.

Always take your time and be patient; once you have some experience, working on your Honda will become an enjoyable hobby.

TOOLS AND EQUIPMENT

Naturally, without the proper tools and equipment it is impossible to properly service your vehicle. It would be impossible to catalog each tool that you would need to perform each or every operation in this book. It would also be unwise for the amateur to rush out and buy an expensive set of tools on the theory that he may need one or more of them at sometime.

The best approach is to proceed slowly, gathering together a good quality set of those tools that are used most frequently. Don't be misled by the low cost of bargain tools. It is far better to spend a little more for better quality. Forged wrenches, 6 or 12 point sockets and fine tooth ratchets are by far preferable to their less expensive counterparts. As any good mechanic can tell you, there are few worse experiences than trying to work on a Honda with bad tools. Your monetary savings will be far outweighed by frustration and mangled knuckles.

Certain tools, plus a basic ability to handle tools, are required to get started. A basic mechanics tool set, a torque wrench, and, for later models, a Torx® bits set. Torx® bits are hexlobular drivers which fit both inside and outside on special Torx® head fasteners used in various places on Honda vehicles.

Begin accumulating those tools that are used most frequently; those associated with routine maintenance and tune-up.

In addition to the normal assortment of screwdrivers and pliers you should have the following tools for routine maintenance jobs (your Honda, uses metric fasteners):

1. Metric wrenches, sockets and combination open end/box end wrenches in sizes from 3mm

to 19mm; and a spark plug socket $^{13}\!/_{16}''$). If possible, buy various length socket drive extensions. One break in this department is that the metric sockets available in the U.S. will all fit the ratchet handles and extensions you may already have (¼", ⅜", and ½" drive).

2. Jackstands for support.

3. Oil filter wrench.

4. Oil filter spout for pouring oil.

5. Grease gun for chassis lubrication.

6. Hydrometer for checking the (old style) battery.

7. A container for draining oil.

8. Many rags for wiping up the inevitable mess.

In addition to the above items there are several others that are not absolutely necessary but handy to have around. These include oil-absorbing material, a transmission funnel and the usual supply of lubricants, antifreeze and fluids, although these can be purchased as needed. This is a basic list for routine maintenance, but only your personal needs and desires can accurately determine your list of necessary tools.

The second list of tools is for tune-ups. While the tools involved here are slightly more sophisticated, they need not be outrageously expensive. There are several inexpensive tach/dwell meters on the market that are every bit as good for the average mechanic as a $100.00 professional model. Just be sure that it goes to at least 1,200-1,500 rpm on the tach scale and that it works on 4 cylinder engines. A basic list of tune-up equipment could include:

1. Tach/dwell meter.

2. Spark plug wrench.

3. Timing light (a DC light that works from the Honda's battery is best, although an AC light that plugs into 110V house current will suffice at some sacrifice in brightness).

4. Wire spark plug gauge/adjusting tools.

5. Set of feeler blades.

Here again, be guided by your own needs. A feeler blade will set the point gap as easily as dwell meter will read dwell, but slightly less accurately. And since you will need a tachometer anyway ... well, make your own decision.

In addition to these basic tools, there are several other tools and gauges you may find useful. These include:

1. A compression gauge. The screw-in type is slower to use, but eliminates the possibility of a faulty reading due to escaping pressure.

2. A manifold vacuum gauge.

3. A test light.

4. An induction meter. This is used for determining whether or not there is current in a wire. These are handy for use if a wire is broken somewhere in a wiring harness.

As a final note, you will probably find a torque wrench necessary for all but the most basic work. The beam type models are perfectly adequate, although the newer click (breakaway) type are more precise and you don't have to crane your neck to see a torque reading in awkward situations. The breakaway torque wrenches are more expensive and should be recalibrated periodically.

Torque specification for each fastener will be given in the procedure in any case that a specific torque value is required. If no torque specifications are given, use the following values as a guide, based upon fastener size:

Bolts marked 6T

6mm bolt/nut: 5-7 ft. lbs.

8mm bolt/nut: 12-17 ft. lbs.

10mm bolt/nut: 23-34 ft. lbs.

12mm bolt/nut: 41-59 ft. lbs.

14mm bolt/nut: 56-76 ft. lbs.

Bolts marked 8T

6mm bolt/nut: 6-9 ft. lbs.

8mm bolt/nut: 13-20 ft. lbs.

10mm bolt/nut: 27-40 ft. lbs.

12mm bolt/nut: 46-69 ft. lbs.

14mm bolt/nut: 75-101 ft. lbs.

NOTE: *Special tools are occasionally necessary to perform a specific job or are recommended to make a job easier. Their use has been kept to a minimum. When a special tool is indicated, it will be referred to by manufacturer's part number, and, where possible, an illustration of the tool will be provided so that an equivalent tool may be used.*

Some special tools are available commercially from major tool manufacturers. Others can be purchased through your Honda dealer.

SERVICING YOUR VEHICLE SAFELY

It is virtually impossible to anticipate all of the hazards involved with automotive maintenance and service, but care and common sense will prevent most accidents.

The rules of safety for mechanics range from "don't smoke around gasoline," to "use the proper tool for the job." The trick to avoiding injuries is to develop safe work habits and take every possible precaution.

Dos

• Do keep a fire extinguisher and first aid kit within easy reach.

• Do wear safety glasses or goggles when cutting, drilling or prying, even if you have 20-20 vision. If you wear glasses for the sake of vision, they should be made of hardened glass that can also serve as safety glasses, or wear safety goggles over your regular glasses.

• Do shield your eyes whenever you work around the battery. Batteries contain sulphuric acid; in case of contact with the eyes or skin, flush the area with water or a mixture of water and baking soda and get medical attention immediately.

• Do use safety stands for any under-car service. Jacks are for raising vehicles; safety stands are for making sure the vehicle stays raised until you want it to come down. Whenever the vehicle is raised, block the wheels remaining on the ground and set the parking brake.

• Do use adequate ventilation when working with any chemicals. Like carbon monoxide, the asbestos dust resulting from brake lining wear can be poisonous in sufficient quantities.

• Do disconnect the negative battery cable when working on the electrical system. The primary ignition system can contain up to 40,000 volts.

• Do follow manufacturer's directions whenever working with potentially hazardous materials. Both brake fluid and antifreeze are poisonous if taken internally.

• Do properly maintain your tools. Loose hammerheads, mushroomed punches and chisels, frayed or poorly grounded electrical cords, excessively worn screwdrivers, spread wrenches (open end), cracked sockets, slipping ratchets, or faulty droplight sockets can cause accidents.

• Do use the proper size and type of tool for the job being done.

• Do when possible, pull on a wrench handle rather than push on it, and adjust your stance to prevent a fall.

• Do be sure that adjustable wrenches are tightly adjusted on the nut or bolt and pulled so that the face is on the side of the fixed jaw.

• Do select a wrench or socket that fits the nut or bolt. The wrench or socket should sit straight, not cocked.

• Do strike squarely with a hammer — avoid glancing blows.

• Do set the parking brake and block the drive wheels if the work requires that the engine be running.

Don'ts

• Don't run an engine in a garage or anywhere else without proper ventilation — EVER! Carbon monoxide is poisonous; it takes a long time to leave the human body and you can build up a deadly supply of it in your system by simply breathing in a little every day. You may not realize you are slowly poisoning yourself. Always use power vents, windows, fans or open the garage doors.

• Don't work around moving parts while wearing a necktie or other loose clothing. Short sleeves are much safer than long, loose sleeves and hard-toed shoes with neoprene soles protect your toes and give a better grip on slippery surfaces. Jewelry such as watches, fancy belt buckles, beads or body adornment of any kind is not safe working around a vehicle. Long hair should be hidden under a hat or cap.

• Don't use pockets for toolboxes. A fall or bump can drive a screwdriver deep into you body. Even a wiping cloth hanging from the back pocket can wrap around a spinning shaft or fan.

• Don't smoke when working around gasoline, cleaning solvent or other flammable material.

• Don't smoke when working around the battery. When the battery is being charged, it gives off explosive hydrogen gas.

• Don't use gasoline to wash your hands; there are excellent soaps available. Gasoline may contain lead, and lead can enter the body through a cut, accumulating in the body until you are very ill. Gasoline also removes all the natural oils from the skin so that bone-dry hands will suck up oil and grease.

• Don't service the air conditioning system unless you are equipped with the necessary tools and training. The refrigerant, R-12, is extremely cold and when exposed to the air, will instantly freeze any surface it comes in contact with, including your eyes. Although the refrigerant is normally non-toxic, R-12 becomes a deadly poisonous gas in the presence of an open flame. One good whiff of the vapors from burning refrigerant can be fatal.

• Don't use screwdrivers for anything other than driving screws! A screwdriver used as a prying tool can snap when you least expect it, causing injuries. At the very least, you'll ruin a good screwdriver.

• Don't use a bumper jack (that little ratchet, scissors, or pantograph jack supplied with the vehicle) for anything other than changing a flat! These jacks are only intended for emergency use out on the road; they are NOT designed as a maintenance tool. If you are serious about maintaining your vehicle yourself, invest in a hydraulic floor jack of at least 1½ ton capacity, and at least two sturdy jackstands.

HISTORY

This repair manual for Honda's covers all the various model changes from 1973 through 1988. These are broken into four model groups, Civic, CRX, Accord, and Prelude. It should be noted that for purposes of this book the CRX has been combined with the Civic models except where noted. There have been four major design changes for the Civic models, two for the CRX, three for the Accord, and three for the Prelude.

- Civic 1st generation: 1973-79
- Civic 2nd generation: 1980-83
- Civic 3rd generation: 1984-87
- Civic 4th generation: 1988
- CRX 1st generation: 1984-87
- CRX 2nd generation: 1988
- Accord 1st generation: 1976-81
- Accord 2nd generation: 1982-85
- Accord 3rd generation: 1986-88
- Prelude 1st generation: 1979-82
- Prelude 2nd generation: 1983-87
- Prelude 3rd generation: 1988

SERIAL NUMBER IDENTIFICATION

Vehicle Identification (Chassis) Number

Vehicle identification numbers are mounted on the top edge of the instrument panel and are visible from the outside. In addition, there is a Vehicle/Engine Identification plate under the hood on the hood mounting bracket on models built in 1974-78. On 1979-88 models, there are also identification plates located on the firewall and the rear door jamb of the driver's door.

The chassis number and engine number are both stamped on the tag under the hood

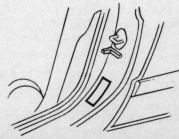

The chassis number on 1980 and later models is located on the rear door jamb of the driver's side door

Engine Serial Number

The engine serial number is stamped into the clutch casing on all vehicles. The first three (1973-86) or five (1987-88) digits indicate engine model identification. The remaining numbers refer to production sequence. This same number is also stamped onto the Vehicle/Engine Identification plate mounted on the hood bracket.

Transaxle Serial Number

The transaxle serial number is stamped on the top of the transaxle/clutch case.

ROUTINE MAINTENANCE

Air Cleaner

REMOVAL AND INSTALLATION

The air cleaner element, housed above or to one side of the carburetor/throttle body, must be replaced every 12,000 miles (1973-74 models), 15,000 miles (1975-80 models), or 30,000 miles (1980-88 models).

1. To remove, unscrew the wing nut(s), bolts and/or spring clips from the air cleaner cover; on some models, it may be necessary to also remove a standard nut.
2. Remove the air cleaner cover and the air cleaner element.
3. Using a clean rag, clean out the air cleaner housing.

Air cleaner element replacement—Carbureted engines typical

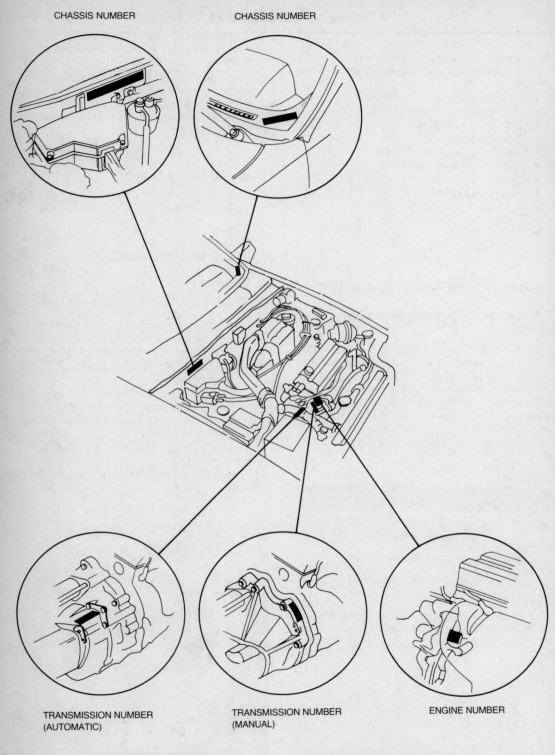

CHASSIS NUMBER

CHASSIS NUMBER

TRANSMISSION NUMBER
(AUTOMATIC)

TRANSMISSION NUMBER
(MANUAL)

ENGINE NUMBER

Chassis number
Chassis number
Automatic transaxle number

Manual transaxle number
Engine number

View of the identification number locations

Engine Identification

Year	Model	Engine Displacement cc/liter	Engine Series Identification	No. of Cylinders	Fuel System
1973	Civic	1170/1.2	EB1	4	2 bbl.
1974	Civic 1200	1237/1.2	EB2	4	2 bbl.
1975	Civic 1200	1237/1.2	EB2	4	2 bbl.
	Civic CVCC	1487/1.5	ED1	4	3 bbl.
	Civic Wgn.	1487/1.5	ED3	4	3 bbl.
1976	Civic 1200	1237/1.2	EB2	4	2 bbl.
	Civic CVCC	1487/1.5	ED3	4	3 bbl.
	Civic Wgn.	1487/1.5	ED4	4	3 bbl.
	Accord	1600/1.6	EF1	4	3 bbl.
1977	Civic 1200	1237/1.2	EB2	4	2 bbl.
	Civic CVCC	1487/1.5	ED3	4	3 bbl.
	Civic Wgn.	1487/1.5	ED4	4	3 bbl.
	Accord	1600/1.6	EF1	4	3 bbl.
1978	Civic 1200	1237/1.2	EB2	4	2 bbl.
	Civic 1200	1237/1.2	EB3	4	2 bbl.
	Civic CVCC	1487/1.5	ED3	4	3 bbl.
	Civic Wgn.	1487/1.5	ED4	4	3 bbl.
	Accord	1600/1.6	EF1	4	3 bbl.
1979	Civic 1200	1237/1.2	EB2	4	2 bbl.
	Civic 1200	1237/1.2	EB3	4	2 bbl.
	Civic CVCC	1487/1.5	ED3	4	3 bbl.
	Civic Wgn.	1487/1.5	ED4	4	3 bbl.
	Accord	1751/1.8	EK1	4	3 bbl.
	Prelude	1751/1.8	EK1	4	3 bbl.
1980	Civic 1300	1335/1.3	EJ1	4	3 bbl.
	Civic CVCC	1487/1.5	EM1	4	3 bbl.
	Accord	1751/1.8	EK1	4	3 bbl.
	Prelude	1751/1.8	EK1	4	3 bbl.
1981	Civic 1300	1335/1.3	EJ1	4	3 bbl.
	Civic 1500	1487/1.5	EM1	4	3 bbl.
	Accord	1751/1.8	EK1	4	3 bbl.
	Prelude	1751/1.8	EK1	4	3 bbl.
1982	Civic 1300	1335/1.3	EJ1	4	3 bbl.
	Civic 1500	1487/1.5	EM1	4	3 bbl.
	Accord	1751/1.8	EK1	4	3 bbl.
	Prelude	1751/1.8	EK1	4	3 bbl.
1983	Civic 1300	1335/1.3	EJ1	4	3 bbl.
	Civic 1500	1487/1.5	EM1	4	3 bbl.
	Accord	1751/1.8	EK1	4	3 bbl.
	Prelude	1829/1.8	ES1	4	Dual Sidedraft

Engine Identification (cont.)

Year	Model	Engine Displacement cc/liter	Engine Series Identification	No. of Cylinders	Fuel System
1984	Civic/CRX, 1.3	1342/1.3	EV1	4	3 bbl.
	Civic/CRX, HF, 1.5	1488/1.5	EW1	4	3 bbl.
	Accord	1829/1.8	ES2	4	3 bbl.
	Prelude	1829/1.8	ES1	4	Dual Sidedraft
1985	Civic/CRX, 1.3	1342/1.3	EV1	4	3 bbl.
	Civic/CRX, HF, 1.5	1488/1.5	EW1	4	3 bbl.
	Civic/CRX, Si	1488/1.5	EW3	4	PGM-FI
	Accord	1829/1.8	ES2	4	3 bbl.
	Accord SE-i	1829/1.8	ES3	4	PGM-FI
	Prelude	1829/1.8	ET2	4	Dual Sidedraft
1986	Civic/CRX, 1.3	1342/1.3	EV1	4	3 bbl.
	Civic/CRX, HF, 1.5	1488/1.5	EW1	4	3 bbl.
	Civic/CRX, Si	1488/1.5	EW4	4	PGM-FI
	Accord	1955/2.0	BS	4	2 bbl.
	Accord LX-i	1955/2.0	BT	4	PGM-FI
	Prelude	1829/1.8	ET2	4	Dual Sidedraft
	Prelude Si	1955/2.0	BT	4	PGM-FI
1987	Civic/CRX, 1.3	1342/1.3	D13A2	4	2 bbl.
	Civic/CRX, HF, 1.5	1488/1.5	D15A2	4	2 bbl.
	Civic/CRX, Si	1488/1.5	D15A3	4	PGM-FI
	Accord	1955/2.0	A20A1	4	2 bbl.
	Accord LX-i	1955/2.0	A20A3	4	PGM-FI
	Prelude	1829/1.8	A18AI	4	Dual Sidedraft
	Prelude Si	1955/2.0	A20A3	4	PGM-FI
1988	Civic	1493/1.5	D15B1	4	DP-FI
	Civic/CRX	1493/1.5	D15B2	4	DP-FI
	Civic/CRX, HF	1493/1.5	D15B6	4	MP-FI
	Civic/CRX, Si	1590/1.6	D16A6	4	PGM-FI
	Accord, DX/LX	1955/2.0	A20A1	4	2 bbl.
	Accord LX-i	1955/2.0	A20A3	4	PGM-FI
	Prelude	1955/2.0	B20A3	4	Dual Sidedraft
	Prelude Si	1955/2.0	B20A5	4	PGM-FI

CVCC: Controlled Vortex Combustion Chamber
DP-FI: Dual-Point Fuel Injection
MP-FI: Multi-Point Fuel Injection
PGM-FI: Programmed Fuel Injection

4. Using a new air cleaner element, reverse the removal procedures.

NOTE: *Air cleaner elements are not interchangeable, although they may appear to be. Make sure you have the proper element for the year and model.*

Fuel Filter

All vehicles use a disposable type fuel filter which cannot be disassembled for cleaning. On 1973-74 models, the recommended replacement interval is 24,000 miles. On 1975-81 mod-

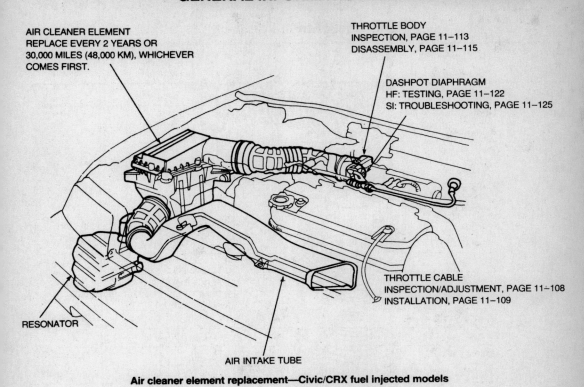

AIR CLEANER ELEMENT
REPLACE EVERY 2 YEARS OR
30,000 MILES (48,000 KM), WHICHEVER
COMES FIRST.

THROTTLE BODY
INSPECTION, PAGE 11–113
DISASSEMBLY, PAGE 11–115

DASHPOT DIAPHRAGM
HF: TESTING, PAGE 11–122
SI: TROUBLESHOOTING, PAGE 11–125

THROTTLE CABLE
INSPECTION/ADJUSTMENT, PAGE 11–108
INSTALLATION, PAGE 11–109

RESONATOR

AIR INTAKE TUBE

Air cleaner element replacement—Civic/CRX fuel injected models

AIR CLEANER ELEMENT
REPLACE EVERY 2 YEARS OR 30,000 MILES (48,000 KM),
WHICHEVER COMES FIRST.

AIR CLEANER COVER

AIR CLEANER CASE

FAST IDLE VALVE
INSPECTION,
PAGE 11–100
THROTTLE BODY
INSPECTION PAGE 11–98
DISASSEMBLY, PAGE 11–99
THROTTLE CABLE
INSPECTION/ADJUSTMENT,
PAGE 11–97
REPLACEMENT, PAGE 11–97

RESONATOR

DASHPOT DIAPHRAGM
TEST, PAGE 11–101

Air cleaner element replacement—Prelude fuel injected models 1986–87

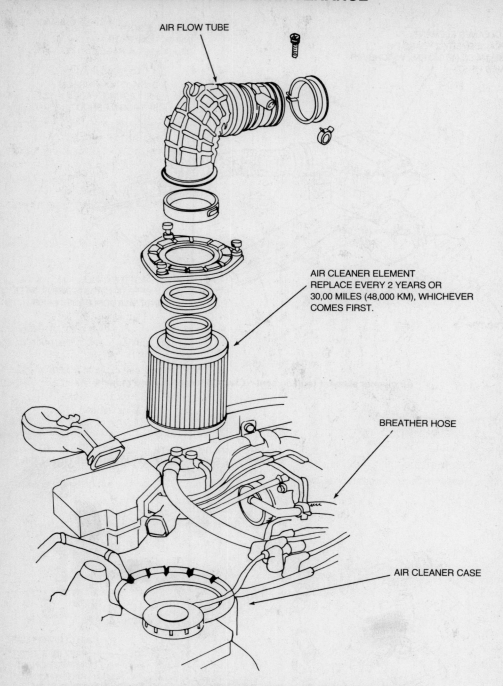

AIR FLOW TUBE

AIR CLEANER ELEMENT
REPLACE EVERY 2 YEARS OR
30,00 MILES (48,000 KM), WHICHEVER
COMES FIRST.

BREATHER HOSE

AIR CLEANER CASE

Air cleaner element replacement—Prelude DOHC fuel injected model 1988

els, the filter is replaced after the first 15,000 miles, and every 30,000 miles thereafter. On 1982-88 models, the filter is replaced at 60,000 miles. Honda recommends that all rubber fuel hoses be replaced at the same time.

CAUTION: *Before disconnecting any fuel lines, be sure to open the gas tank filler cap to*

relieve any pressure in the system. If this is not done, you may run the risk of being squirted with gasoline.

On 1975 CVCC Sedan models, the filter is located beneath a special access cover under the rear seat on the driver's side. The rear seat can be removed after removing the bolt at the rear

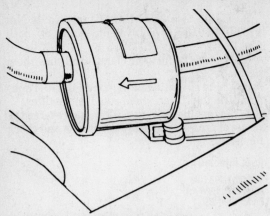

Fuel filter—non-CVCC Civic (arrow)

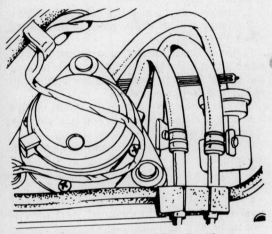

CVCC sedan fuel pump and filter location

center of the cushion and then pivoting the seat forward from the rear.

REMOVAL AND INSTALLATION

Carbureted

CIVIC 1973-75 — 1237CC (AIR) ENGINES

The filter, together with the electric fuel pump, are located in the recess.

1. Remove the four screws retaining the access cover to the floor and remove the cover.
2. Pinch the lines shut, loosen the hose clamps and remove the filter.
3. To install, use a new filter and reverse the removal procedures.

ACCORD (WAGON)
1976-81 CVCC
1975-81 PRELUDE

The filter is located under the rear of the vehicle, in front of the spare tire, together with the electrical fuel pump.

1. Raise and support the rear of the vehicle.
2. Clamp off the fuel lines on both sides of the fuel filter.
3. Loosen the hose clamps and work the hoses off by twisting, taking note of which hose is the inlet and which is the outlet.
4. Remove the fuel filter.

NOTE: *Some replacement filters have an arrow embossed or printed on the filter body, in which case you want to install the new filter with the arrow pointing in the direction of fuel flow.*

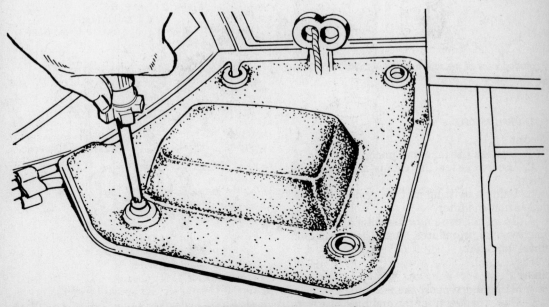

CVCC sedan fuel filter access plate

Accord and Prelude fuel filter location (arrow) —wagon similar

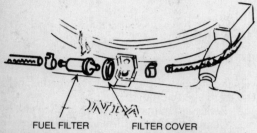

FUEL FILTER   FILTER COVER

Exploded view of the front fuel filter—carbureted Civics—1984—88

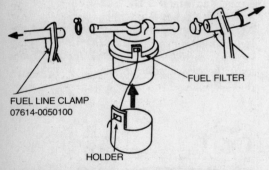

FUEL FILTER

FUEL LINE CLAMP
07614-0050100

HOLDER

Exploded view of the rear fuel filter—Civic 1982—87— Carbureted

1982-88 ALL MODELS

Front

1. Depress the tang and unclip the filter.
2. Loosen the fuel line clamps and slide them back.
3. Using a twisting motion, remove the fuel lines from the filter.
4. To install, use a new fuel filter and reverse the removal procedures. Start the engine and check for leaks.

Rear

1. Raise and support the rear of the vehicle.
2. Push the fuel filter tab and release it from the holder.

3. Using two Fuel Line Clamp tools No. 07614-0050100 or equivalent, clamp off both fuel lines.
4. Loosen the fuel line clamps and slide them back.
5. Using a twisting motion, pull the fuel lines from the fuel filter, then, remove the filter.
6. To install, use a new filter and reverse the removal procedures. Start the engine and check for leaks.

Fuel Injected

ACCORD 1985-88
PRELUDE 1986-88
CIVIC 1986-88

The fuel filter is located in the engine compartment.
1. Disconnect the negative battery terminal.
2. Using a shop cloth, place it under and around the fuel filter.
3. Using 6mm wrench, slowly turn the service bolt (on top of the fuel filter), while holding the special banjo bolt with another wrench, to reduce the fuel pressure.
NOTE: *When the bleeding fuel filter, always replace washer between the bolt and the special banjo bolt.*
4. Remove the banjo bolts and washers from the fuel filter.
5. Remove the fuel filter clamp bolt and the filter.
6. To install, use a new filter, washers and reverse the removal procedures. Start the engine and check for leaks.

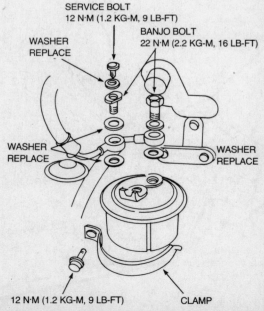

SERVICE BOLT
12 N·M (1.2 KG-M, 9 LB-FT)

BANJO BOLT
22 N·M (2.2 KG-M, 16 LB-FT)

WASHER
REPLACE

WASHER
REPLACE

WASHER
REPLACE

12 N·M (1.2 KG-M, 9 LB-FT)   CLAMP

Exploded view of the fuel injection filter—Accord and Prelude 1986—88

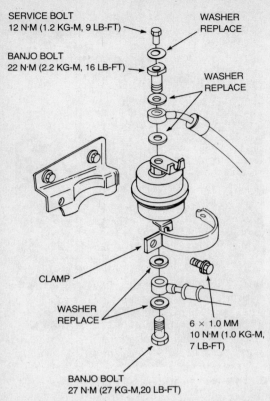

SERVICE BOLT
12 N·M (1.2 KG-M, 9 LB-FT)

WASHER
REPLACE

BANJO BOLT
22 N·M (2.2 KG-M, 16 LB-FT)

WASHER
REPLACE

CLAMP

WASHER
REPLACE

6 × 1.0 MM
10 N·M (1.0 KG-M,
7 LB-FT)

BANJO BOLT
27 N·M (27 KG-M,20 LB-FT)

Exploded view of the fuel injection filter—Civic 1986–88

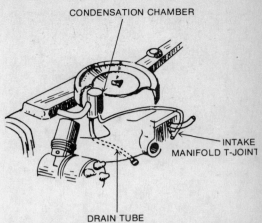

CONDENSATION CHAMBER

INTAKE
MANIFOLD T-JOINT

DRAIN TUBE

Typical PCV system component location. 1973 model shown

Remove this Phillips head screw to disconnect the condensation chamber from the air cleaner

Removing the air cleaner housing bolts from the engine

Positive Crankcase Ventilation (PCV)

The Honda is equipped with a Positive Crankcase Ventilation (PCV)system in which blow-by gas is returned to the combustion chamber through the intake manifold and/or the air cleaner.

REMOVAL AND INSTALLATION

1. On 1973-75 models, squeeze the lower end of the drain tube and drain any oil or water which may have collected. Maintenance intervals are every 15,000 miles (1973-79 miles) and 60,000 miles (1980-88 models). On 1976-82 models, remove the tube, invert and drain it; after all condensation has been drained, reinstall it.

2. Make sure that the intake manifold T-joint is clear. You first have to remove the air cleaner to where the joint is located. To clear the joint, pass the shank end of a drill of 0.9mm diameter through both ends (both orifices) of the joint.

3. Check for loose, disconnected or deteriorated tubes and replace if necessary. Make sure the hoses are clean inside, cleaning them with a safe solvent, if necessary. If the system has a

1976 and later drain tube location. Disconnect the tube from the condensation chamber and invert it to drain

Evaporative canister

1975 and later CVCC PCV system orifice location

condensation chamber attached to the bottom of the air cleaner, unscrew and remove the chamber, clean and replace it; when removing the top gasket from the chamber, note the angle of installation. Reinstall it in the same position to provide proper airflow.

4. The 1983-88 models use a regular PCV valve. Check the valve by pulling it out of the valve cover with the engine idling. Cover the open end of the valve with your finger so airflow is stopped. If the valve clicks, it is OK; if not, replace it.

For further information on the servicing of

Honda emission control components, check Chapter 4.

Evaporative Charcoal Canister

The charcoal canister is part of the Evaporative Emission Control System. This system prevents the escape of raw gasoline vapors from the fuel tank and carburetor.

The charcoal canister is designed to absorb fuel vapors under certain conditions. For a more detailed description, see Chapter 4.

The canister is a coffee can-sized object located in the engine compartment. Label the hoses leading to the canister before disconnecting them, then, remove the old canister from its mounting bracket and discard it. Install the new canister and connect the hoses as before.

SERVICING

Maintenance on the canister consists of testing and inspection at 12,000 mile intervals (1973-74 models), 15,000 mile intervals (1975-80 models) and replacement at 24,000 miles (1973-74 models) or 30,000 miles (1975-80 models). On the 1981-88 models, the canister does not require periodic replacement. The entire system requires a careful operational check with a vacuum gauge at 60,000 miles, however. See Chapter 4 for testing procedures.

Battery

FLUID LEVEL (EXCEPT MAINTENANCE FREE BATTERIES)

Check the battery electrolyte level at least once a month, or more often in hot weather or during periods of extended car operation. The level can be checked through the case on translucent polypropylene batteries; the cell caps must be removed on other models. The electrolyte level in each cell should be kept filled to the split ring inside, or the line marked on the outside of the case.

If the level is low, add only distilled water, or colorless, odorless drinking water, through the opening until the level is correct. Each cell is completely separate from the others, so each must be checked and filled individually.

If water is added in freezing weather, the car should be driven several miles to allow the water to mix with the electrolyte. Otherwise, the battery could freeze.

SPECIFIC GRAVITY (EXCEPT MAINTENANCE-FREE BATTERIES)

At least once a year, check the specific gravity of the battery. It should be between 1.20 in.Hg and 1.26 in.Hg at room temperature.

The specific gravity can be check with the use of an hydrometer, an inexpensive instrument available from many sources, including auto parts stores. The hydrometer has a squeeze bulb at one end and a nozzle at the other. Bat-

Checking the battery electrolyte level

tery electrolyte is sucked into the hydrometer until the float is lifted from its seat. The specific gravity is then read by noting the position of the float. Generally, if after charging, the specific gravity between any two cells varies more than 50 points (0.50), the battery is bad and should be replaced.

It is not possible to check the specific gravity in this manner on sealed (maintenance free) batteries. Instead, the indicator built into the top of the case must be relied on to display any signs of battery deterioration. If the indicator is dark, the battery can be assumed to be OK. If the indicator is light, the specific gravity is low, and the battery should be charged or replaced.

CABLES AND CLAMPS

Once a year, the battery terminals and the cable clamps should be cleaned. Loosen the clamps and remove the cables, negative cable first. On batteries with posts on top, the use of a puller specially made for the purpose is recommended. These are inexpensive, and available in auto parts stores. Side terminal battery cables are secured with a bolt.

Clean the cable lamps and the battery terminal with a wire brush, until all corrosion, grease, etc., is removed and the metal is shiny. It is especially important to clean the inside of the clamp thoroughly, since a small deposit of foreign material or oxidation there will prevent a sound electrical connection and inhibit either starting or charging. Special tools are available for cleaning these parts, one type for conventional batteries and another type for side terminal batteries.

Before installing the cables, loosen the battery hold down clamp or strap, remove the battery and check the battery tray. Clear it of any debris, and check it for soundness. Rust should be wire brushed away, and the metal given a coat of anti-rust paint. Replace the battery and tighten the hold down clamp or strap securely,

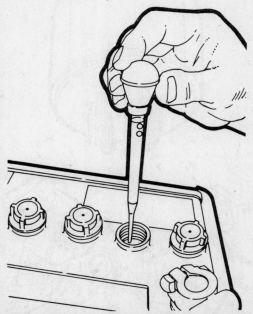

An inexpensive hydrometer will quickly test the state of charge of the battery

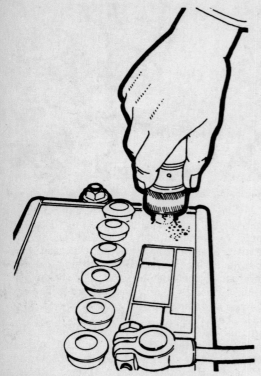

Cleaning the battery post with a wire brush

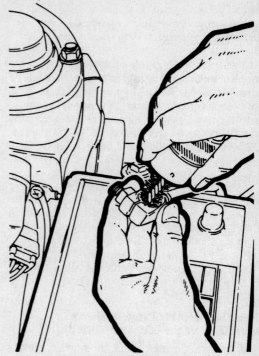

Cleaning the terminal ends of the cable with a wire cleaner

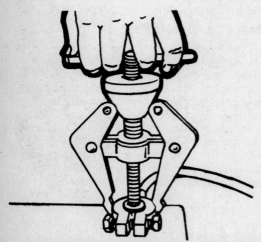

Top terminal battery cables can be removed with a puller available at most parts stores

but be careful not to over tighten, which will crack the battery case.

After the clamps and terminals are clean, re-install the cables, negative cable last; do not hammer on the clamps to install. Tighten the clamps securely, but do not distort them. Give the clamps and terminals a thin external coat of grease after installation, to retard corrosion.

Check the cables at the same time that the

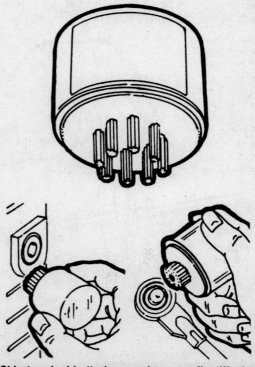

Side terminal batteries require a small, stiff wire brush for cleaning terminals are cleaned. If the cable insulation is cracked or broken, or if the ends are frayed, the cable should be replaced with a new cable of the same length and gauge.

CAUTION: *Keep flame or sparks away from the battery; it gives off explosive hydrogen gas. Battery electrolyte contains sulphuric acid. If you should splash any on your skin or in your eyes, flush the affected area with plenty of clear water. If it lands in your eyes, get medical help immediately.*

Belts

INSPECTION

On the 1973-79 models, adjust the drive belt(s) after the first 3,000 miles, afterwards, inspect the belt(s) every 12,000 miles/12 months for evidence of wear such as cracking, fraying and/or incorrect tension; on the 1980-88 models, inspect the drive belt(s) every 30,000 miles/24 months. Determine the belt tension at a point halfway between the pulleys by pressing on the belt with moderate thumb pressure. The belt should deflect about ¼" over a 7-10" span or ½" over a 13-16" span, at this point. If the deflection is found to be too much or too little, perform the tension adjustments.

CHECKING AND ADJUSTING TENSION

Before adjusting, inspect the belt to see that it is not cracked or worn. Be sure that its surfaces are free of grease and oil.

1. Push down on the belt halfway between pulleys with moderate force. The belt should deflect approximately ½". Deflection should be slightly less with a new belt as tension is lost rapidly for the first ½ hour or so of operation.

2. If the belt tension requires adjustment, loosen the adjusting link bolt and move the alternator with a pry bar positioned against the front of the alternator housing. On 1983-88 models, loosen the top mounting bolt and then turn the adjusting nut outboard of the alterna-

Check the belt tension midway between the two pulleys

Loosen the pivot bolt before loosening the adjusting bolt

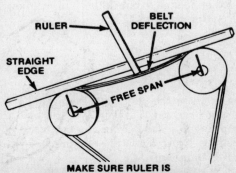

RULER — BELT DEFLECTION

STRAIGHT EDGE

FREE SPAN

MAKE SURE RULER IS PERPENDICULAR TO STRAIGHT EDGE

Measuring belt deflection

HOW TO SPOT WORN V-BELTS

V-Belts are vital to efficient engine operation—they drive the fan, water pump and other accessories. They require little maintenance (occasional tightening) but they will not last forever. Slipping or failure of the V-belt will lead to overheating. If your V-belt looks like any of these, it should be replaced.

This belt has deep cracks, which cause it to flex. Too much flexing leads to heat build-up and premature failure. These cracks can be caused by using the belt on a pulley that is too small. Notched belts are available for small diameter pulleys.

Cracking or weathering

Oil and grease on a belt can cause the belt's rubber compounds to soften and separate from the reinforcing cords that hold the belt together. The belt will first slip, then finally fail altogether.

Softening (grease and oil)

Glazing is caused by a belt that is slipping. A slipping belt can cause a run-down battery, erratic power steering, overheating or poor accessory performance. The more the belt slips, the more glazing will be built up on the surface of the belt. The more the belt is glazed, the more it will slip. If the glazing is light, tighten the belt.

Glazing

The cover of this belt is worn off and is peeling away. The reinforcing cords will begin to wear and the belt will shortly break. When the belt cover wears in spots or has a rough jagged appearance, check the pulley grooves for roughness.

Worn cover

This belt is on the verge of breaking and leaving you stranded. The layers of the belt are separating and the reinforcing cords are exposed. It's just a matter of time before it breaks completely.

Separation

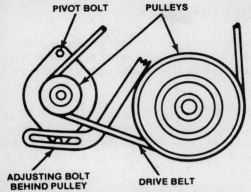

Some accessories can be moved only if the pivot bolt is loosened

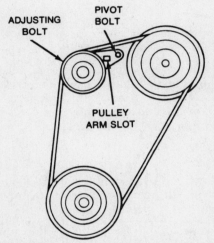

Some pulleys have a rectangular slot to aid in moving the accessory

tor. This will reposition the alternator without prying.

3. When the belt tension is correct tighten the upper mounting bolt to about 16 ft. lbs. Recheck the tension, correcting the adjustment if necessary.

NOTE: *Do not apply pressure to any other part of the alternator.*

REMOVAL AND INSTALLATION

1. Loosen the component-to-mounting bracket bolts.
2. Rotate the component to relieve the tension on the drive belt.
3. Slip the drive belt from the component pulley and remove it from the engine.

NOTE: *If the engine uses more than one belt, it may be necessary to remove other belts that are in front of the one being removed.*

4. To install, reverse the removal procedures. Adjust the component drive belt tension to specifications.

Hoses

The upper/lower radiator hoses and all heater hoses should be checked for deterioration, leaks and loose hose clamps every 15,000 miles/12 months (1973-79) or 30,000 miles/24 months (1980-88).

REMOVAL AND INSTALLATION

1. Drain the cooling system.

CAUTION: *When draining the coolant, keep in mind that cats and dogs are attracted by the ethylene glycol antifreeze, and are quite likely to drink any that is left in an uncovered container or in puddles on the ground. This will prove fatal in sufficient quantities. Always drain the coolant into a sealable container. Coolant should be reused unless it is contaminated or several years old.*

2. Loosen the hose clamps at each end of the hose.
3. Working the hose back and forth, slide it off it's connection, then, install a new hose, if necessary.

NOTE: *When replacing the heater hoses, maintain a 1½" clearance from any surface.*

4. To install, reverse the removal procedures. Refill the cooling system.

NOTE: *Draw the hoses tight to prevent sagging or rubbing against other components; route the hoses through the clamps as installed originally. Always make sure that the hose clamps are beyond the component bead and placed in the center of the clamping surface before tightening them.*

Air Conditioning System
SAFETY WARNINGS

Because of the importance of the necessary safety precautions that must be exercised when working with air conditioning systems and R-12 refrigerant, a recap of the safety precautions are outlined.

● Avoid contact with a charged refrigeration system, even when working on another part of the air conditioning system or vehicle. If a heavy tool comes into contact with a section of copper tubing or a heat exchanger, it can easily cause the relatively soft material to rupture.

● When it is necessary to apply force to a fitting which contains refrigerant, as when checking that all system couplings are securely tightened, use a wrench on both parts of the fitting involved, if possible. This will avoid putting torque on the refrigerant tubing. It is advisable, when possible, to use tube or line wrenches when tightening these flare nut fittings.

● DO NOT attempt to discharge the system

HOW TO SPOT BAD HOSES

Both the upper and lower radiator hoses are called upon to perform difficult jobs in an inhospitable environment. They are subject to nearly 18 psi at under hood temperatures often over 280°F., and must circulate nearly 7500 gallons of coolant an hour—3 good reasons to have good hoses.

Swollen hose

A good test for any hose is to feel it for soft or spongy spots. Frequently these will appear as swollen areas of the hose. The most likely cause is oil soaking. This hose could burst at any time, when hot or under pressure.

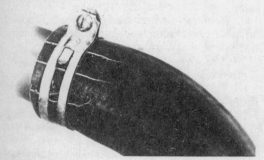

Cracked hose

Cracked hoses can usually be seen but feel the hoses to be sure they have not hardened; a prime cause of cracking. This hose has cracked down to the reinforcing cords and could split at any of the cracks.

Frayed hose end (due to weak clamp)

Weakened clamps frequently are the cause of hose and cooling system failure. The connection between the pipe and hose has deteriorated enough to allow coolant to escape when the engine is hot.

Debris in cooling system

Debris, rust and scale in the cooling system can cause the inside of a hose to weaken. This can usually be felt on the outside of the hose as soft or thinner areas.

by merely loosening a fitting or removing the service valve caps and cracking these valves. Precise control is possible only when using the service gauges. Place a rag under the open end of the center charging hose while discharging the system to catch any drops of liquid that might escape. Wear protective gloves when connecting or disconnecting service gauge hoses.

- Discharge the system only in a well ventilated area, as high concentrations of the gas can exclude oxygen and act as an anesthetic. When leak testing or soldering, this is particularly important, as toxic gas is formed when R-12 contacts any flame.

- Never start a system without first verifying that both service valves are back-seated (if equipped) and that all fittings throughout the system are snugly connected.

- Avoid applying heat to any refrigerant line or storage vessel. Charging may be aided by using water heated to less than 125°F to warm the refrigerant container. Never allow a refrigerant storage container to sit out in the sun or near any other heat source, such as a radiator.

- Always wear goggles when working on a system to protect the eyes. If refrigerant contacts the eyes, it is advisable in all cases to see a physician as soon as possible.

- Frostbite from liquid refrigerant should be treated by first gradually warming the area with cool water, then, gently apply petroleum jelly. A physician should be consulted.

- Always keep the refrigerant drum fittings capped when not in use. Avoid any sudden shock to the drum, which might occur from dropping it or from banging a heavy tool against it. Never carry a drum in the passenger compartment of a vehicle.

- Always completely discharge the system before painting the vehicle (if paint is to be baked on), or before welding anywhere near the refrigerant lines.

NOTE: *Any repair work to an air conditioning system should be left to a professional. DO NOT, under any circumstances, attempt to loosen or tighten any fitting or perform any work other than that outlined here.*

SYSTEM INSPECTION

Checking For Oil Leaks

Refrigerant leaks show up as oily areas on the various components because the compressor oil is transported around the entire system along with the refrigerant. Look for oily spots on all the hoses and lines, especially on the hose and tubing connections. If there are oily deposits, the system may have a leak, have it checked by a qualified repairman.

NOTE: *A small area of oil on the front of the*

compressor is normal and no cause for alarm.

Checking The Compressor Belt

Refer to the Drive Belt section in this Chapter.

Keep The Condenser Clear

Periodically inspect the front of the condenser for bent fins or foreign material (dirt, buts, leaves, etc.). If any cooling fins are bent, straighten them carefully with needlenosed pliers. You can remove any debris with a stiff bristle brush or hose.

Operate The Air Conditioning System Periodically

A lot of air conditioning problems can be avoided by simply running the air conditioner at least once a week regardless of the season. Simply let the system run for a least 5 minutes a week (even in the winter) and you'll keep the internal parts lubricated as well as preventing the hoses from hardening.

Leak Testing the System

There are several methods of detecting leaks in an air conditioning system; among them, the two most popular are (1) halide leak detection or the open flame method and (2) electronic leak detector.

The Halide Leak Detection tool No. J-6084 or equivalent, is a torch like device which produces a yellow-green color when refrigerant is introduced into the flame at the burner. A purple or violet color indicates the presence of large amounts of refrigerant at the burner.

An Autobalance Refrigerant Leak Detector tool No. J-29547 or equivalent, is a small portable electronic device with an extended probe. With the unit activated, the probe is passed along those components of the system which contain refrigerant. If a leak is detected, the

The sight glass is located on top of the receiver-drier

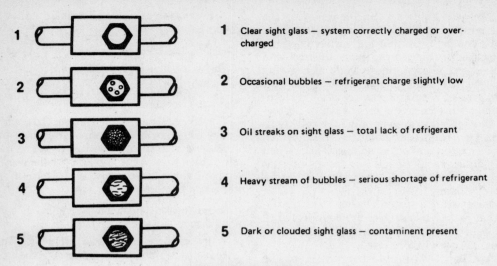

1 Clear sight glass — system correctly charged or over-charged

2 Occasional bubbles — refrigerant charge slightly low

3 Oil streaks on sight glass — total lack of refrigerant

4 Heavy stream of bubbles — serious shortage of refrigerant

5 Dark or clouded sight glass — contaminent present

Sight glass inspection

unit will sound an alarm signal or activate a display signal depending on the manufacturer's instructions as the design and function of the detection may vary significantly.

CAUTION: *Care should be taken to operate either type of detector in well ventilated areas, so as to reduce the chance of personal injury, which may result from coming in contact with poisonous gases produced when R-12 is exposed to flame or electric spark.*

GAUGE SETS (USE)

Most of the service work performed in air conditioning requires the use of a set of two gauges, one for the high (head) pressure side of the system, the other for the low (suction) side.

The low side gauge records both pressure and vacuum. Vacuum readings are calibrated from 0-30 in.Hg and the pressure graduations read from 0-60 psi.

The high side gauge measures pressure from 0-600 psi.

Both gauges are threaded into a manifold that contains two hand shut-off valves. Proper manipulation of these valves and the use of the attached test hoses allow the user to perform the following services:

1. Test high and low side pressures.
2. Remove air, moisture and/or contaminated refrigerant.
3. Purge the system of refrigerant.
4. Charge the system with refrigerant.

The manifold valves are designed so they have no direct effect on the gauge readings but serve only to provide for or cut off the flow of refrigerant through the manifold. During all testing and hook-up operations, the valves are kept in a Closed position to avoid disturbing the re-

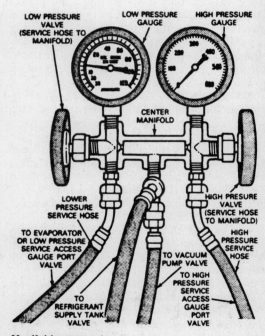

Manifold gauge set

frigeration system. The valves are Opened ONLY to purge the system of refrigerant or to charge it.

When purging the system, the center hose is uncapped at the lower end and both valves are cracked (Opened) slightly. This allows the refrigerant pressure to force the entire contents of the system out through the center hose. During charging, the valve on the high side of the manifold is Closed and the valve on the low side is cracked (Opened). Under these conditions, the low pressure in the evaporator will draw re-

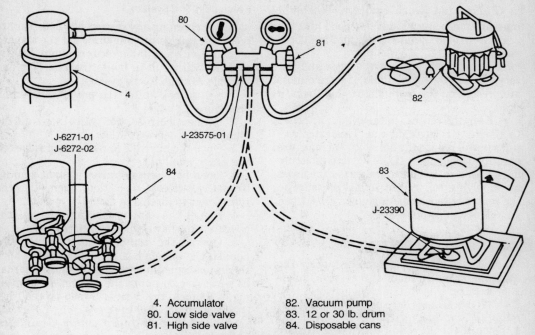

4. Accumulator
80. Low side valve
81. High side valve
82. Vacuum pump
83. 12 or 30 lb. drum
84. Disposable cans

View of the A/C charging gauges

frigerant from the relatively warm refrigerant storage container into the system.

Service Valves

For the user to diagnose an air conditioning system, he or she must gain entrance to the system in order to observe the pressures; the type of terminal for this purpose is the Schrader valve.

The Schrader valve is similar to a tire valve stem and the process of connecting the test hoses is the same as threading a hand pump outlet hose to a bicycle tire. As the test hose is threaded to the service port the valve core is depressed, allowing the refrigerant to enter the test hose outlet. Removal of the test hose automatically closes the system.

Extreme caution must be observed when removing the test hoses from the Schrader valves as some refrigerant will normally escape, usually under high pressure; observe safety precautions.

Using The Manifold Gauges

The following are step-by-step procedures to guide the user to the correct gauge usage.

CAUTION: *Wear goggles or face shield during all testing operations. Backseat hand shut-off type service valves.*

1. Remove the caps from the high and low side service ports. Make sure both gauge valves are Closed.

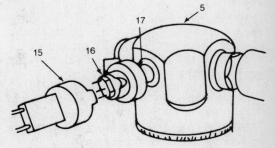

5. Accumulator
15. Electrical connector
16. Pressure cycling switch adjusting screw
17. "Schrader" type valve

View of the A/C accumulator with the Schrader valve

2. Connect the low side test hose to the service valve that leads to the evaporator (located between the evaporator outlet and the compressor).

3. Attach the high side test hose to the service valve that leads to the condenser.

4. Mid-position the hand shutoff type service valves.

5. Start the engine allow it to warm-up. All testing and charging of the system should be done after the engine and system has reached normal operating temperatures (except when using certain charging stations).

6. Adjust the air conditioner controls to Max. Cold.

7. Observe the gauge readings. When the gauges are not being used it is a good idea to:

  a. Keep both hand valves in the Closed position.

  b. Attach both ends of the high and low service hoses to the manifold, if extra outlets are present on the manifold or plug them (if not).

  c. Keep the center charging hose attached to an empty refrigerant can. This extra precaution will reduce the possibility of moisture entering the gauges. If the air and moisture have gotten into the gauges, purge the hoses by supplying refrigerant under pressure to the center hose with both gauge valves Open and all openings plugged.

DISCHARGING THE SYSTEM

When it is necessary to remove (purge) the refrigerant pressurized in the system, follow this procedure:

CAUTION: *Be sure to perform this operation in a well ventilated area.*

1. Operate the air conditioner for at least 10 minutes.

2. Attach the gauges, turn Off the engine and the air conditioner.

3. Place a container or rag at the outlet of the center charging hose on the gauge. The refrigerant will be discharged there and this precaution will avoid its uncontrolled exposure.

4. Open the low side hand valve on the gauge, slightly.

5. Open the high side hand valve, slightly.

NOTE: *Too rapid a purging process will be identified by the appearance of an oily foam. If this occurs, close the hand valves a little more until this condition stops.*

6. Close both hand valves on the gauge set when the pressures read 0 psi and all the refrigerant has left the system.

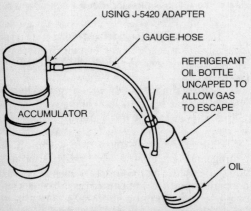

USING J-5420 ADAPTER

GAUGE HOSE

REFRIGERANT OIL BOTTLE UNCAPPED TO ALLOW GAS TO ESCAPE

ACCUMULATOR

OIL

Discharging the A/C system without using a charging station

Evacuating The System

Before charging any system it is necessary to purge the refrigerant and draw out the trapped moisture with a suitable vacuum pump. Failure to do so will result in ineffective charging and possible damage to the system.

Use this hook-up for the proper evacuation procedure:

1. Connect both service gauge hoses to the high and low service outlets.

2. Open the high and low side hand valves on the gauge manifold.

3. Open both service valves a slight amount (from the back seated position), then, allow the refrigerant to discharge from the system.

4. Install the center charging hose of the gauge set to the vacuum pump.

5. Operate the vacuum pump for at least one hour. If the system has been subjected to open conditions for a prolonged period of time, it may be necessary to pump the system down overnight. Refer to the System Sweep procedure.

NOTE: *If the low pressure gauge does not show at least 28 in.Hg within 5 minutes, check the system for a leak or loose gauge connectors.*

6. Close the had valves on the gauge manifold.

7. Turn Off the pump.

8. Observe the low pressure gauge to determine if the vacuum is holding. A vacuum drop may indicate a leak.

System Sweep

An efficient vacuum pump can remove all the air container in a contaminated air conditioning system very quickly, because of its vapor state. Moisture, however, is far more difficult to remove because the vacuum must force the liquid to evaporate before it will be able to be removed from the system. If the system has become severely contaminated, as it might become after all the charge was lost in conjunction with vehicle accident damage, moisture removal is extremely time consuming. A vacuum pump could remove all of the moisture only if it were operated for 12 hours or more.

Under these conditions, sweeping the system with refrigerant will speed the process of moisture removal considerably. To sweep, follow the following procedure:

1. Connect the vacuum pump to the gauges, operate it until the vacuum ceases to increase, then, continue the operation for ten or more minutes.

2. Charge the system with 50% of its rated refrigerant capacity.

3. Operate the system at fast idle for 10 minutes.

Troubleshooting Basic Air Conditioning Problems

Problem	Cause	Solution
There's little or no air coming from the vents (and you're sure it's on)	• The A/C fuse is blown • Broken or loose wires or connections • The on/off switch is defective	• Check and/or replace fuse • Check and/or repair connections • Replace switch
The air coming from the vents is not cool enough	• Windows and air vent wings open • The compressor belt is slipping • Heater is on • Condenser is clogged with debris • Refrigerant has escaped through a leak in the system • Receiver/drier is plugged	• Close windows and vent wings • Tighten or replace compressor belt • Shut heater off • Clean the condenser • Check system • Service system
The air has an odor	• Vacuum system is disrupted • Odor producing substances on the evaporator case • Condensation has collected in the bottom of the evaporator housing	• Have the system checked/repaired • Clean the evaporator case • Clean the evaporator housing drains
System is noisy or vibrating	• Compressor belt or mountings loose • Air in the system	• Tighten or replace belt; tighten mounting bolts • Have the system serviced

Sight glass condition
  Constant bubbles, foam or oil streaks
  Clear sight glass, but no cold air
  Clear sight glass, but air is cold
  Clouded with milky fluid
	
	• Undercharged system
	
	• No refrigerant at all
	• System is OK
	• Receiver drier is leaking dessicant
		
		• Charge the system
		
		• Check and charge the system
		
		• Have system checked

Large difference in temperature of lines	• System undercharged	• Charge and leak test the system
Compressor noise	• Broken valves • Overcharged • Incorrect oil level • Piston slap • Broken rings • Drive belt pulley bolts are loose	• Replace the valve plate • Discharge, evacuate and install the correct charge • Isolate the compressor and check the oil level. Correct as necessary. • Replace the compressor • Replace the compressor • Tighten with the correct torque specification
Excessive vibration	• Incorrect belt tension • Clutch loose • Overcharged • Pulley is misaligned	• Adjust the belt tension • Tighten the clutch • Discharge, evacuate and install the correct charge • Align the pulley
Condensation dripping in the passenger compartment	• Drain hose plugged or improperly positioned • Insulation removed or improperly installed	• Clean the drain hose and check for proper installation • Replace the insulation on the expansion valve and hoses
Frozen evaporator coil	• Faulty thermostat • Thermostat capillary tube improperly installed • Thermostat not adjusted properly	• Replace the thermostat • Install the capillary tube correctly • Adjust the thermostat
Low side low—high side low	• System refrigerant is low • Expansion valve is restricted	• Evacuate, leak test and charge the system • Replace the expansion valve
Low side high—high side low	• Internal leak in the compressor—worn	• Remove the compressor cylinder head and inspect the compressor. Replace the valve plate assembly if necessary. If the compressor pistons, rings or

Troubleshooting Basic Air Conditioning Problems (cont.)

Problem	Cause	Solution
Low side high—high side low (cont.)		cylinders are excessively worn or scored replace the compressor
	• Cylinder head gasket is leaking	• Install a replacement cylinder head gasket
	• Expansion valve is defective	• Replace the expansion valve
	• Drive belt slipping	• Adjust the belt tension
Low side high—high side high	• Condenser fins obstructed	• Clean the condenser fins
	• Air in the system	• Evacuate, leak test and charge the system
	• Expansion valve is defective	• Replace the expansion valve
	• Loose or worn fan belts	• Adjust or replace the belts as necessary
Low side low—high side high	• Expansion valve is defective	• Replace the expansion valve
	• Restriction in the refrigerant hose	• Check the hose for kinks—replace if necessary
	• Restriction in the receiver/drier	• Replace the receiver/drier
	• Restriction in the condenser	• Replace the condenser
Low side and high side normal (inadequate cooling)	• Air in the system	• Evacuate, leak test and charge the system
	• Moisture in the system	• Evacuate, leak test and charge the system

4. Discharge the system.

5. Repeat (twice) the process of charging to 50% capacity, running the system for ten minutes, then, discharge it for a total of three sweeps.

6. Replace the drier.

7. Pump the system down as in Step 1.

8. Charge the system.

CHARGING

CAUTION: *Never attempt to charge the system by opening the high pressure gauge control while the compressor is operating. The compressor accumulating pressure can burst the refrigerant container, causing severe personal injuries.*

1. Start the engine, operate it with the choke Open and normal idle speed, then, position the air conditioning control lever Off.

2. Using a drum or 14 oz. cans of refrigerant, in the inverted position, allow about 1 lb. of refrigerant to enter the system through the low side service fitting on the accumulator.

3. After the 1 lb. of refrigerant enters the system, position the control lever to Normal (the compressor will engage) and the blower motor on Hi speed; this operation will draw the remainder of the refrigerant into the system.

NOTE: *To speed up the operation, position a fan in front of the condenser; the lowering of the condenser temperature will allow refrigerant to enter the system faster.*

4. When the system is charged, turn Off the refrigerant source and allow the engine to run for 30 seconds to clear the lines and gauges.

5. With the engine running, remove the hose adapter from the accumulator service fitting (unscrew the hose quickly to prevent refrigerant from escaping).

CAUTION: *Never remove the gauge line from the adapter when the line is connected to the system; always remove the line adapter from the service fitting first.*

6. Replace the accumulator protective caps and turn the engine Off.

7. Using a leak detector, inspect the air conditioning system for leaks. If a leak is present, repair it.

Windshield Wipers
REPLACING WIPER BLADES

For maximum effectiveness and longest element lift, the windshield and wiper blades should be kept clean. Dirt, tree sap, road tar and etc. will cause streaking, smearing and blade deterioration, if left on the glass. It is advisable to wash the windshield carefully with a commercial glass cleaner at least once a month. Wipe off the rubber blades with the wet rag, afterwards.

If the blades are found to be cracked, broken or torn, they should be replaced immediately. Replacement intervals will vary with usage, although ozone deterioration usually limits blade life to about one year. If the wiper pattern is smeared, streaked or if the blade chatters across the glass, the elements should be re-

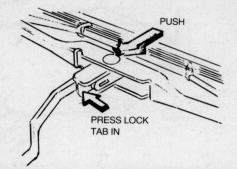

Detaching the wiper blade assembly at the arm (Civic)

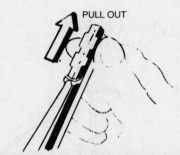

Release the retainer at the end of the blade by depressing the two halves of the clip

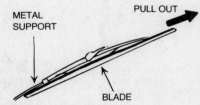

Slide the blade out as shown

placed. It is easiest and most sensible to replace the elements in pairs.

1. To replace the blade elements, detach the wiper blade assembly from the arm or raise the wiper arm assemblies.

2. On some models, press together the two sides of the metal locking tab at one end of the assembly and slide the blade out. On other models, simply separate the rubber element from the wiper blade.

3. Using a new rubber element, reverse the removal procedures.

NOTE: *If using the locking tab type, slide the blade in until the locking click is heard.*

Tires and Wheels

TIRE INFLATION

Tire inflation is the most ignored item of auto maintenance. Gasoline mileage can drop as much as 0.8% for every 1 psi of under inflation.

Two items should be a permanent fixture in every glove compartment: a tire pressure gauge and a tread depth gauge. Check the tire pressure (including the spare) regularly with a pocket type gauge. Kicking the tires won't tell you a thing, and the gauge on the service station air hose is notoriously inaccurate.

A plate located on the left door will tell the proper pressure for the tires. Ideally, inflation pressure should be checked when the tires are cool. When the air becomes heated it expands and the pressure increases. Every 10°F rise (or drop) in temperature means a difference of 1 psi, which also explains why the tire appears to lose air on a very cold night. When it is impossible to check the tires **Cold**, allow for pressure build-up due to heat. If the **Hot** pressure exceeds the **Cold** pressure by more than 15 psi, reduce vehicle speed, load or both. Otherwise internal heat is created in the tire. When the heat approaches the temperature at which the tire was cured, during manufacture, the tread can separate from the body.

CAUTION: *Never counteract excessive pressure build-up by bleeding off air pressure (letting some air out). This will only further raise the tire operating temperature.*

Before starting a long trip with lots of luggage, you can add about 2-4 psi to the tires to make them run cooler but never exceed the maximum inflation pressure on the side of the tire.

TIRE DESIGN

For maximum satisfaction, tires should be used in sets of five. Mixing of different types (radial, bias-belted, fiberglass belted) should be avoided.

Conventional bias tires are constructed so that the cords run bead-to-bead at an angle. This type of construction gives rigidity to both tread and sidewall.

Bias-belted tires are similar in construction to conventional bias ply tires. Belts run at an angle and also at a 90° angle to the bead, as in the radial tire. Tread life is improved considerably over the conventional bias tire. The radial tire differs in construction but instead of the carcass plies running at an angle of 90° to each other, they run at an angle of 90° to the bead. This gives the tread a great deal of flexibility and accounts for the characteristic bulge associated with radial tires.

If radial tires are used, tire sizes and wheel diameters should be selected to maintain ground clearance and tire load capacity equivalent to the minimum specified tire. Radial tires should always be used in sets of five but in an emergency, radial tires can be used with caution on the rear axle only. If this is done, both tires on the rear should be of radial design.

CAUTION: *Radial tires should never be used on only the front axle.*

Snow tires should not be operated at sustained speeds over 70 mph.

On four wheel drive vehicles, all tires must be of the same size, type and tread pattern, to provide even traction on loose surfaces, to prevent driveline bind when conventional four wheel drive is used and to prevent excessive wear on the center differential with full time four wheel drive.

TREAD DEPTH

All tires made since 1968, have 8 built-in tread wear indicator bars that show up as $\frac{1}{2}''$ wide smooth bands across the tire when $\frac{1}{16}''$ of tread remains. The appearance of tread wear indicators means that the tires should be replaced. In fact, many states have laws prohibiting the use of tires with less than $\frac{1}{16}''$ tread.

You can check your own tread depth with an inexpensive gauge or by using a Lincoln head penny. Slip the Lincoln penny into several tread grooves. If you can see the top of Lincoln's head in 2 adjacent grooves, the tires have less than $\frac{1}{16}''$ tread left and should be replaced. You can measure snow tires in the same manner by using the "tails" side of the Lincoln penny. If you can see the top of the Lincoln memorial, it's time to replace the snow tires.

TIRE ROTATION

Tires must be rotated periodically to equalize wear patterns that vary with a tire's position on the vehicle. Tires will also wear in an uneven way as the front steering/suspension system wears to the point where the alignment should be reset. Rotating the tires will ensure maximum life for the tires as a set, as you will not have to discard a tire early due to wear on only part of the tread.

The cardinal rule to follow with radials is to make sure that they always roll in the same direction. This means that a tire used on the left side of the vehicle must not be switched to the right side and vice-versa. If a tire or tires is removed from a running position on the vehicle for a time for use as a spare or because of seasonal use of snow tires, make sure to clearly mark the wheel as to the side of the vehicle it was used on and to observe the mark when reinstalling the tire(s).

NOTE: *Recently the cardinal rule has been re-written and tire manufacturers have begun recommending cross rotating radials. The best recommendation I can make, if your're not sure, is to check with the tire man-*

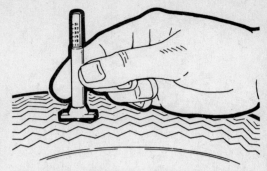

Using a depth gauge to determine tread depth

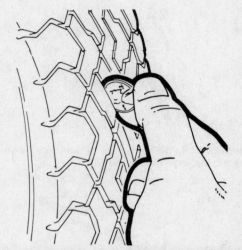

Using a Lincoln penny to determine tread depth. If the top of Lincoln's head is visible, in 2 adjacent grooves, replace the tire

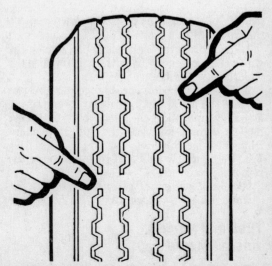

Since 1968 wear indicators have been built into tires. When these bands become visible on the tire's surface, replace the tire

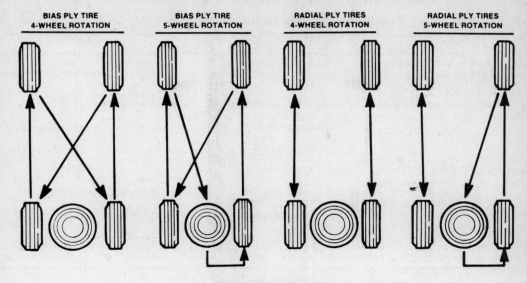

Tire rotation diagrams

ufacturer of the tires currently on your Honda.

TIRE STORAGE

Store the tires at proper inflation pressure if they are mounted on wheels. All tires should be kept in a cool, dry place. If they are stored in the garage or basement, do not let them stand on a concrete floor, set them on strips of wood.

FLUIDS AND LUBRICANTS

Fuel and Engine Oil Recommendations

FUEL

All 1973-79 Hondas are designed to run on regular gasoline. High octane (premium) gasoline is not required. This is permitted because

Troubleshooting Basic Wheel Problems

Problem	Cause	Solution
The car's front end vibrates at high speed	• The wheels are out of balance • Wheels are out of alignment	• Have wheels balanced • Have wheel alignment checked/adjusted
Car pulls to either side	• Wheels are out of alignment • Unequal tire pressure • Different size tires or wheels	• Have wheel alignment checked/adjusted • Check/adjust tire pressure • Change tires or wheels to same size
The car's wheel(s) wobbles	• Loose wheel lug nuts • Wheels out of balance • Damaged wheel • Wheels are out of alignment • Worn or damaged ball joint • Excessive play in the steering linkage (usually due to worn parts) • Defective shock absorber	• Tighten wheel lug nuts • Have tires balanced • Raise car and spin the wheel. If the wheel is bent, it should be replaced • Have wheel alignment checked/adjusted • Check ball joints • Check steering linkage • Check shock absorbers
Tires wear unevenly or prematurely	• Incorrect wheel size • Wheels are out of balance • Wheels are out of alignment	• Check if wheel and tire size are compatible • Have wheels balanced • Have wheel alignment checked/adjusted

Troubleshooting Basic Tire Problems

Problem	Cause	Solution
The car's front end vibrates at high speeds and the steering wheel shakes	• Wheels out of balance • Front end needs aligning	• Have wheels balanced • Have front end alignment checked
The car pulls to one side while cruising	• Unequal tire pressure (car will usually pull to the low side) • Mismatched tires • Front end needs aligning	• Check/adjust tire pressure • Be sure tires are of the same type and size • Have front end alignment checked
Abnormal, excessive or uneven tire wear See "How to Read Tire Wear"	• Infrequent tire rotation • Improper tire pressure • Sudden stops/starts or high speed on curves	• Rotate tires more frequently to equalize wear • Check/adjust pressure • Correct driving habits
Tire squeals	• Improper tire pressure • Front end needs aligning	• Check/adjust tire pressure • Have front end alignment checked

Tire Size Comparison Chart

"Letter" sizes			Inch Sizes	Metric-inch Sizes		
"60 Series"	"70 Series"	"78 Series"	1965–77	"60 Series"	"70 Series"	"80 Series"
		Y78-12	5.50-12, 5.60-12 6.00-12	165/60-12	165/70-12	155-12
		W78-13 Y78-13	5.20-13 5.60-13 6.15-13	165/60-13 175/60-13 185/60-13	145/70-13 155/70-13 165/70-13	135-13 145-13 155-13, P155/80-13
A60-13 B60-13	A70-13 B70-13	A78-13 B78-13	6.40-13 6.70-13 6.90-13	195/60-13 205/60-13	175/70-13 185/70-13	165-13 175-13
C60-13 D60-13 E60-13	C70-13 D70-13 E70-13	C78-13 D78-13 E78-13	7.00-13 7.25-13 7.75-13	215/60-13	195/70-13	185-13 195-13
			5.20-14 5.60-14 5.90-14	165/60-14 175/60-14	145/70-14 155/70-14	135-14 145-14
A60-14	A70-14 B70-14 C70-14	A78-14 B78-14 C78-14	6.15-14 6.45-14 6.95-14	185/60-14 195/60-14 205/60-14	165/70-14 175/70-14 185/70-14	155-14 165-14 175-14
D60-14 E60-14 F60-14 G60-14 H60-14 J60-14 L60-14	D70-14 E70-14 F70-14 G70-14 H70-14 J70-14 L70-14	D78-14 E78-14 F78-14, F83-14 G77-14, G78-14 H78-14 J78-14	7.35-14 7.75-14 8.25-14 8.55-14 8.85-14 9.15-14	215/60-14 225/60-14 235/60-14 245/60-14 255/60-14 265/60-14	195/70-14 200/70-14 205/70-14 215/70-14 225/70-14 235/70-14	185-14 195-14 205-14 215-14 225-14
	A70-15	A78-15	5.60-15	185/60-15	165/70-15	155-15
B60-15 C60-15	B70-15 C70-15 D70-15	B78-15 C78-15 D78-15	6.35-15 6.85-15	195/60-15 205/60-15	175/70-15 185/70-15	165-15 175-15
E60-15 F60-15 G60-15 H60-15 J60-15	E70-15 F70-15 G70-15 H70-15 J70-15 K70-15	E78-15 F78-15 G78-15 H78-15 J78-15	7.35-15 7.75-15 8.15-15/8.25-15 8.45-15/8.55-15 8.85-15/8.90-15 9.00-15	215/60-15 225/60-15 235/60-15 245/60-15 255/60-15 265/60-15	195/70-15 205/70-15 215/70-15 225/70-15 235/70-15 245/70-15	185-15 195-15 205-15 215-15 225-15 230-15
L60-15	L70-15 M70-15	L78-15, L84-15 M78-15 N78-15	9.15-15			235-15 255-15

Note: Every size tire is not listed and many size comparisons are approximate, based on load ratings. Wider tires than those supplied new with the vehicle, should always be checked for clearance.

the engines uses the CVCC combustion system, thereby avoiding the catalytic converter. The octane number is used as a measure of the anti-knock properties of a gasoline and the use of a higher octane gasoline than that which is necessary to prevent engine knock is simply a waste of money. If your Honda does knock (usually heard as a pinging noise), it is probably a matter of improper ignition timing, in which case you should check Chapter 2 for the proper adjustment procedure. You might also want to check that the EGR system is functioning properly (see Chapter 4).

The 1980-88 models use a catalytic converter even if the engine uses the CVCC system. This is because of increasingly stringent emissions standards. While unleaded gas is usually more expensive than leaded, there are many side benefits, including better fuel economy, less dirt in the engine oil and longer exhaust system life. Since the use of leaded fuel will damage the catalytic converter, it *does not pay* to attempt to bypass the narrow filler opening for the fuel tank and run the vehicle on leaded fuel. Little more than a single tankful will render the converter ineffective and may cause it to clog the exhaust system and affect engine operation.

You should be careful to use quality fuels having an octane rating of 86 when measured by the R/M method, which averages "Research" and "Motor" octane ratings. Too low an octane rating will produce combustion knock, which will prove to be damaging to the engine over a long period. Always buy fuel from a reputable dealer, preferably where a regular volume is pumped so that the fuel is always fresh.

OIL

When using engine oil, there are two types of ratings with which you should be familiar: vis-

Typical oil rating location on can

Lubricant Specifications

Engine Oil	6000 mile motor oil (MS or SE sequence tested)

Single Viscosity Oils	
When outside temperature is consistently	Use SAE Viscosity Number
−4°F to +32°F	10W
+32°F to +59°F	20W-20
+59°F to +86°F	30
Above 86°F	40

Multiviscosity Oils	
Above 5°F	10W/40
+5°F to +86°F	10W/30
Above 32°F	20W/40
	20W/50
Manual Transmission and Differential Gear Oil	Use engine oil according to the above specifications
Automatic Transmission	Automatic Transmission Fluid—Dexron® type

Oil pan drain plug location

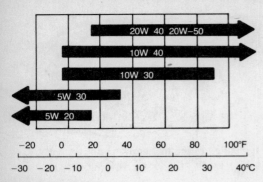

Oil viscosity chart

cosity and service (quality). There are several service ratings, resulting from tests established by the American Petroleum Institute. Use only SE rated oil or SF (for better fuel economy). SF oil passes SE requirements and also reduces fuel consumption. No other service ratings are acceptable.

Oil can be purchased with two types of viscosity ratings, single and multi-viscosity. Oil viscosity ratings are important because oil tends to thin out at high temperatures while getting too thick and stiff at low temperatures. Single viscosity oil, designated by only one number (SAE 30), varies in viscosity or thickness, a great deal over a wide range of temperatures. The single rating number comes from the fact that the oil is basically a single, straight grade of petroleum. A multi-viscosity oil rating is given as two numbers (for example: SAE 10W-40, the **W** standing for **winter**). Multi-viscosity oils slow changes in viscosity with temperature. These changes occur with changes in engine temperature conditions, such as cold starts versus eventual engine warm-up and operation. The double designation refers to the fact that the oil behaves like straight 10W oil at 0°F and like straight 40W oil at 200°F. The desirable advantage of multi-viscosity oil is that it can maintain adequate thickness at high engine operating temperatures (when oil tends to get too thin) while it resists the tendency to thicken at very low temperatures. A straight 30 oil gets so thick near 0°F. that the engine will usually not crank fast enough to start. Because of its versatility, a multi-viscosity oil would be the more desirable choice.

When adding oil, try to use the same brand that's in the crankcase since not all oils are completely compatible with each other.

Engine

OIL LEVEL CHECK

Checking the oil level is one of the simplest and most important checks. It should be done FREQUENTLY because low oil level can lead to oil pan or even engine overheating and eventual starvation of the oil pump. This can mean inadequate lubrication and *immediate, severe* engine damage. Because oil consumption patterns of an engine can change quickly and unexpectedly due to leakage or changes in the weather, check the oil every time you stop for fuel.

NOTE: *If the engine has been running, allow it to rest for a few minutes until the oil accumulates in the sump, before checking the oil level.*

1. Raise the hood, pull the oil dipstick from the engine and wipe it clean.
2. Insert the dipstick into the engine until it is fully seated, then, remove it and check the reading.

NOTE: *The oil level on all Hondas should register within the crosshatch design on the dipstick or between the two lines, depending on the type of stick.*

3. Oil is added through the capped opening of the rocker arm cover. Do not add oil if the level is significantly above the lower line or lower edge of the crosshatch. If the level is near or below the crosshatch or lower line, ADD oil but do not overfill. The length covered by the crosshatching on the dipstick is roughly equivalent to one quart of oil.

NOTE: *Refer to the "Engine Oil and Fuel Recommendations" in this section for the proper viscosity oil to use.*

4. If oil has been added, replace the dipstick and recheck the level. It is important to avoid overfilling the crankcase because doing so will cause the oil to foam due to the motion of the crankshaft, affecting lubrication and may also harm the engine oil seals.

OIL AND FILTER CHANGE

After the initial 600 miles oil and filter change, the oil should be changed every 3,000 miles/3 months (severe conditions), 5,000 miles/6 months (1973-79) or 7,500 miles/6 months (1980-88), whichever comes first. The oil filter should be changed at every oil change! Remember the "You can pay me now or pay me later" commercials you've seen on TV? If your going to skimp on anything, do let it be your intervals for changing oil. Be certain to use a high quality oil and filter.

1. Before changing the oil, see that the vehicle is situated on a flat surface with the engine warmed; warm oil will flow more freely from the oil pan.
2. Turn the engine Off, open the hood and remove the oil filler cap from the top of the engine valve cover.

CAUTION: *Hot oil can burn you. Keep an in-*

ward pressure on the plug until the last thread is cleared, then, quickly remove it.

3. Place a container under the oil pan; large enough to catch the oil. A large, flat drain pan is the most desirable.

CAUTION: *The EPA warns that prolonged contact with used engine oil may cause a number of skin disorders, including cancer! You should make every effort to minimize your exposure to used engine oil. Protective gloves should be worn when changing the oil. Wash your hands and any other exposed skin areas as soon as possible after exposure to used engine oil. Soap and water, or waterless hand cleaner should be used.*

4. Remove the oil drain plug and allow the oil to drain completely. When the oil has finished draining, install the drain plug tight enough to prevent oil leakage, use a new washer (if necessary) on the plug.

NOTE: *Only oil filters which have an integral by-pass should be used when replacing the filter. Also note that before removing the filter it is advisable to have an oil filter wrench which is inexpensive and makes the job much easier.*

5. Move the oil drain pan under the oil filter; the filter retains some oil which will drain when it is removed.

6. Using an oil filter wrench, loosen the filter, then, unscrew it by hand.

7. Using a clean cloth, wipe the filter mounting surface of the cylinder block. Apply a thin coat of clean oil to the new filter gasket and install the filter.

NOTE: *Hand-tighten the filter only; DO NOT use a wrench for tightening. If the filter has instruction printed on it as to how far it should be tightened (for example ½ or ¾ turn), mark the filter, then, tighten it accordingly.*

8. Remove the drain pan from under the engine.

9. Add the correct amount of recommended oil into the oil filler hole on top of the valve cover. Be sure that the oil level registers near the full line on the oil dipstick.

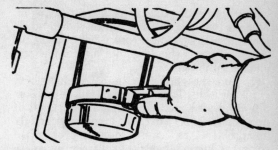

Remove the oil filter with a strap wrench

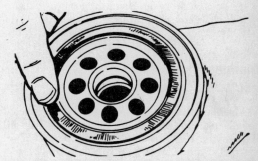

Lubricate the gasket on the new filter with clean engine oil. A dry gasket may not make a good seal and will allow the filter to leak

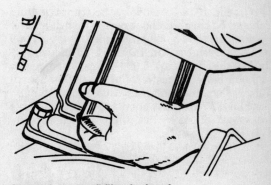

Install the new oil filter by hand

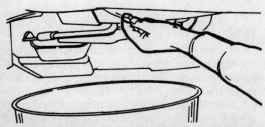

By keeping inward pressure on the plug as you unscrew it, oil won't escape past the threads

Add oil through the capped opening in the cylinder head cover

10. Replace the filler cap, start the engine without touching the accelerator pedal and allow it to idle. The oil pressure light on the instrument panel should go out after a few seconds of running.

11. Run the engine for a 1-2 minutes and check for leaks. Turn the engine Off, then, after a few minutes, recheck the oil level; add oil (if necessary). Be sure to check for oil leaks and fix any problems, as this is a common problem on early production models using the Japanese filter.

NOTE: *If the filter leaks lightly, gently turn it just a bit more but don't turn it really tight. If it still leaks, try another filter.*

12. Recheck and/or refill the engine with oil.

Manual Transaxles

FLUID RECOMMENDATIONS

All manual transaxles use engine oil labeled for SE use. On the 1973-79 models, use 10W-40 oil. On the 1980-88 models 10W-30 or 10W-40 viscosity; the 10W-40 viscosity is the safer recommendation, especially driving frequency is at high speeds for prolonged periods in hot weather.

LEVEL CHECK

On the 1973-74 models, the transaxle fluid should be checked about once a month and replaced the first 3,000 miles, then, every 24,000 miles thereafter. On the 1975-79 models, replace the fluid at 15,000 miles, then, every 30,000 miles thereafter. On the 1980-88 models, replace the fluid every 30,000 miles.

The 1973-75 4-speed transaxle, uses a threaded dipstick with a crosshatch pattern.

Manual transmission drain plug location—automatic similar

The dipstick is located beneath the battery. To check the fluid level, remove the dipstick, wipe it off and reinsert it *without turning it inward.* That is, make sure the threads on the dipstick itself are sitting on top of the threads in the transaxle housing. Approximately ¾ qt. will bring the fluid level from the ADD (lower) to the FULL (upper) line.

1976-77 Models

On the 1976-77 models, a special check bolt in the side of the transaxle is used.

1. To check the fluid level, turn the check bolt outward until fluid begins to flow from the transaxle or several turns, *stopping the flat side of the bolt facing upwards.*

2. If fluid runs out, retighten the check bolt; if not, loosen the filler cap and pour oil in slowly until it begins to run out via the level check bolt. Then, tighten the bolt and filler cap.

All Other Models

1. Remove the oil level check bolt from the side of the transaxle. If oil runs out, retighten the bolt.

2. Loosen the filler cap and pour oil in slowly until it begins to run out via the level check bolt, then, tighten the bolt and filler cap.

DRAIN AND REFILL

1. Raise and support the front of the vehicle.

2. Place a fluid catch pan under the transaxle.

3. Remove the upper and lower plugs, then, drain the fluid.

4. Using a new washer, install the bottom plug. Refill the transaxle, until the oil is level with the upper filler plug hole.

Automatic Transaxles

FLUID RECOMMENDATIONS

All Hondamatics use Dexron®II automatic transmission fluid. Only Dexron®II is available today. It replaces straight Dexron® fluid which is the actual recommendation for older models and can be mixed with it.

LEVEL CHECK

On the 1973-74 models, the transaxle fluid should be checked about once a month and replaced after the first 3,000 miles (every 24,000 miles thereafter). On the 1975-79 models, replace the fluid at 15,000 miles, then, every 30,000 miles thereafter. On the 1980-88 models, replace the fluid every 30,000 miles.

The 1973-75 Hondamatic automatic transaxle, uses a threaded dipstick with a crosshatch pattern. The dipstick is located beneath the battery. To check the fluid level, remove the dipstick, wipe it clean and reinsert it *without turning it inward.* That is, make sure the threads on the dipstick itself are sitting on top of the threads in the transaxle housing. Approximately ¾ qt. will bring the fluid level from the ADD (lower) to the FULL (upper) line.

The fluid level is checked with the engine running. It is also necessary to warm up the transaxle by driving the vehicle a few miles, starting and stopping frequently.

1. Park the vehicle on level ground and let the engine idle with the transaxle in **Park**.

2. Unscrew the dipstick, wipe it clean and reinsert it. DO NOT SCREW IT IN, as this would result in an erroneous reading.

3. Using Dexron®II automatic transmission fluid, top off the transaxle, as necessary; add the fluid, if necessary, in small amounts, taking care not to overfill.

4. Recheck the transaxle oil level.

DRAIN AND REFILL

1. Drive the vehicle to bring the transaxle fluid up to operating temperatures.

2. Raise and support the front of the vehicle.

3. Place a fluid catch pan under the transaxle.

4. Remove the drain plug, located on the bottom of the transaxle housing, and drain the transaxle.

5. Using a new washer, install the drain plug. Using Dexron®II automatic transmission fluid refill the transaxle using the transaxle fluid dipstick hole or filler cap, until fluid reaches the Full mark on the dipstick; DO NOT overfill the transaxle.

NOTE: *Be sure that the quantity of fluid you add is always slightly less than the specified quantity, due to the remaining fluid left in the transaxle housing recesses.*

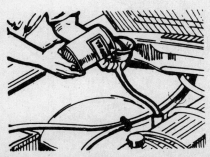

Fill the transmission with the required amount of fluid. Do not overfill. Start the engine and run the selector through all the shift points. Check the fluid and add as necessary

Transfer Case

The transfer case (4WD Wagon) is an integral part of the transaxle housing. No fluid check, drain or refill is necessary or possible.

Drive Axle — 4WD Wagon
FLUID RECOMMENDATIONS

The rear drive axle requires Hypoid gear oil API GL-5; use SAE 90 for temperatures above 41°F or SAE 80 for temperatures below 41°F. Replace the fluid every 30,000 miles or 24 months.

LEVEL CHECK

1. Raise and support the vehicle on a level plane.

2. Remove the oil filler plug from the drive axle housing.

3. Check that the oil is level with the bottom edge of the filler hole; if not, add oil.

NOTE: *If the oil level is low, inspect the companion flange and drive axle housing for signs of leakage.*

4. Using a new aluminum washer, install the filler plug. Torque the plug to 33 ft. lbs.

DRAIN AND REFILL

1. Raise and support the vehicle on a level plane.

2. Place a drain pan under the drive axle housing.

3. Remove the oil filler and drain plugs from the drive axle housing, then, allow the drive axle to drain.

4. Using a new aluminum washer, install the drain plug. Torque the plug to 33 ft. lbs.

5. Using fresh gear oil, pour it through the filler hole until it is level with the bottom edge of the filler hole.

6. Using a new aluminum washer, install the filler plug. Torque the plug to 33 ft. lbs.

Cooling System
FLUID RECOMMENDATIONS

Use a quality, ethylene-glycol based engine coolant specifically recommended for use with vehicles utilizing aluminum engine parts that are in contact with the coolant. Note that some coolants, although labeled for use in such vehicles, actually may fail to provide effective corrosion protection; if necessary, consult a professional mechanic. It is best to buy a top quality product that is known to work effectively under such conditions. Always add coolant mixed with the proper amount of clean water. Never add either water or coolant alone. Mix the coolant at a 50:50 ratio, unless this will not provide sufficient freeze protection. Consult the chart on the antifreeze container and utilize the proportions recommended for the lowest expected temperatures in your area.

LEVEL CHECK

To check the coolant level, simply discern whether the coolant is up to the **FULL** line on the expansion tank. Add coolant to the expansion tank if the level is low, being sure to mix it with clean water. Never add cold water or coolant to a hot engine as damage to both the cooling system and the engine could result.

The radiator cap should be removed only for the purpose of cleaning or draining the system.

CAUTION: *The cooling system is under pressure when Hot. Removing the radiator cap when the engine is warm or overheated will cause coolant to spill or shoot out, possibly causing serious burns. The system should be allowed to cool before attempting removal of the radiator cap or hoses.*

NOTE: *If any coolant spills on painted portions of the body, rinse it off immediately.*

DRAIN AND REFILL

The radiator coolant should be changed every 24,000 miles (1973-74 models), 30,000 miles (1975-80 models) or 45,000 miles (1981-88 models); thereafter, replace every 24 months or 30,000 miles. When following this procedure, be sure to follow the same precautions as detailed in the **Coolant Level** section.

1. Remove the radiator cap.
2. Slide a fluid catch pan under the radiator. Loosen the drain bolt at the base of the radiator and drain the radiator. If equipped, loosen the drain bolt on the drain cock on the side of the block.

CAUTION: *When draining the coolant, keep in mind that cats and dogs are attracted by the ethylene glycol antifreeze, and are quite likely to drink any that is left in an uncovered container or in puddles on the ground. This will prove fatal in sufficient quantity. Always drain the coolant into a sealable container. Coolant should be reused unless it is contaminated or several years old.*

3. Drain the coolant in the reservoir tank by unclipping and disconnecting the hose.

NOTE: *In cold weather the thermostat may be closed; it may be necessary to remove the thermostat to completely drain the engine.*

4. Mix a solution of 50% ethylene glycol (designed for use in aluminum engines) and 50% clean water. Use a stronger solution, as specified on the antifreeze container, if the climate in your area demands it. Tighten the drain bolt(s) and refill the radiator all the way to the

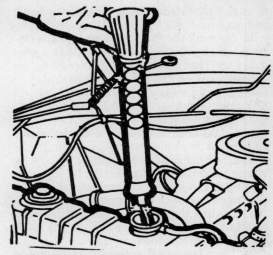

Testing coolant condition with a tester

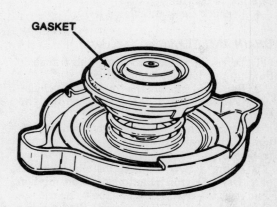

GASKET

Checking the radiator cap gasket for cracks or wear

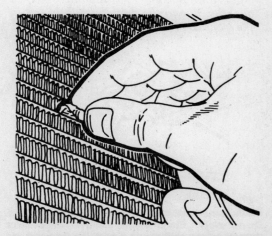

Keep the radiator fins clear of debris for maximum cooling

filler mouth. Reconnect the overflow tank connecting tube.

5. Loosen the cooling system bleed bolt to purge air from the system. When coolant flows out of the bleed port, close the bolt and refill the radiator with coolant up to the mouth.

6. To purge any air trapped in other parts of the cooling system, set the heater control to **Hot**, start the engine, set it to fast idle and allow it to reach normal operating temperatures. DO NOT tighten the radiator cap and leave the heater control in the **Hot** position. When the engine reaches normal operating temperatures, top off the radiator and keep checking until the level stabilizes; then, refill the coolant reservoir to the **Full** mark and make sure that the radiator cap is properly tightened.

FLUSHING AND CLEANING THE SYSTEM

1. Refer to the "Thermostat, Removal and Installation" procedures in Chapter 3 and remove the thermostat from the engine.

2. Using a high pressure water hose, force fresh water into the thermostat housing opening, allowing the water to back-flush into the engine, heater and radiator. Back-flush the system until the water flowing from the radiator hose is clear.

3. After cleaning, reverse the removal procedures. Refill the cooling system with fresh coolant.

Brake and Clutch Master Cylinder
FLUID RECOMMENDATIONS

Use only DOT 3 or DOT 4 specification brake fluid from a tightly sealed container. If you are unsure of the condition of the fluid (whether or not it has been tightly sealed), use new fluid rather than taking a chance of introducing moisture into the system. It is critically important that the fluid meet the specification so the heat generated by modern disc brakes will not cause it to boil and reduce braking performance. Fluid must be moisture free for the same reason.

LEVEL CHECK

Brake and clutch master cylinder fluid level should be checked every few weeks for indication of leaks or low fluid level due to normal wear of the brake lining. Infrequent topping-off will be required in normal use because of this wear.

On all Hondas there is a fill line on the brake fluid reservoir(s) as well as an arrow on the reservoir cap(s) which should face forward when installed. When adding brake fluid, the following precautions should be observed:

1. Use only recommended brake fluid: DOT 3 or DOT 4; SAE J 1703b HD type.

2. Never reuse brake fluid and never use fluid that is dirty, cloudy or has air bubbles.

3. Store brake fluid in a clean dry place in the original container. Cap tightly and do not puncture a breather hole in the container.

4. Carefully remove any dirt from around the master cylinder reservoir cap before opening.

5. Take special care not to spill the fluid. The painted surface of the vehicle will be damaged by brake fluid.

Power Steering Pump
FLUID RECOMMENDATIONS

Only genuine Honda power steering fluid or a known equivalent may be used when adding fluid. Honda says that ATF or fluids manufactured for use in other brands of vehicles by their manufacturers or independents are not compatible with the Honda power steering system. The use of any other fluid will cause the seals to swell and create leaks.

RESERVOIR LEVEL CHECK

The fluid in the power steering reservoir should be checked every few weeks for indications of leaks or low fluid level. Check the fluid with the engine cold and the vehicle parked on a level spot. The level should be between the upper and lower marks. Fluid need not be added right away unless it has dropped almost to the lower mark. DO NOT overfill the reservoir.

Manual Steering gear
INSPECTION

The manual steering used on Hondas is of the rack and pinion design. This unit is packed with grease and therefore does not require a periodic fluid level check. However, inspect the box and associated rubber boot-type seals for obvious grease leaks or torn boots for 1973-78 models: 5,000 miles, then, at every 10,000 mile increments; for the 1979 models: 5,000 miles, 15,000 miles, then, at 15,000, then, at every 15,000 mile increments; for 1980-88 models: 15,000 miles, 30,000 miles, then, at 30,000 mile increments. Make repairs as necessary.

FLUID RECOMMENDATIONS

Repack with about 2 oz. of multipurpose grease.

Chassis Greasing

All the suspension fittings on the Hondas covered by this guide are permanently lubricated. However, at the time when the steering box is inspected for grease leakage (see the item directly above), inspect the suspension and steering joints for grease leakage and/or torn rubber boots and make repairs as necessary.

Body Lubrication

Lubricate all locks and hinges with multipurpose grease every 6000 miles or 6 months.

Rear Wheel Bearings — 2WD Only

To check the wheel bearings for basic problems, jack up each wheel to clear the ground. Hold the wheel and shake it to check the bearings for any play. Also rotate the wheel to check for any roughness. If any play is felt or there is noticeable roughness, the bearing may have to be replaced. Hondas use various types of front wheel bearing arrangements all of which require detailed procedures to adjust or replace. Adjust the bearing; then, if play is still present, replace the bearing.

NOTE: *Over tightening the spindle nuts will cause excessive bearing friction and will result in rough wheel rotation and eventual bearing failure. Therefore, follow the procedures given in Chapter 8 exactly, using the proper procedures and tools.*

REMOVAL PACKING AND INSTALLATION

CAUTION: *Brake shoes contain asbestos, which has been determined to be a cancer causing agent. Never clean the brake surfaces with compressed air! Avoid inhaling any dust from any brake surface! When cleaning brake surfaces, use a commercially available brake cleaning fluid.*

All Except Civic (1984-88), Prelude (1984-88) and Accord (1986-88)

1. Slightly loosen the rear wheel lug nuts. Raise and support the rear of the vehicle.
2. Release the parking brake. Remove the rear wheel assembly.
3. Remove the rear wheel grease cap, the cotter pin, the spindle nut retainer, the spindle nut, the thrust washer and the outer wheel bearing.
4. Pull the brake drum from the wheel spindle.
5. Using a hammer and a drift punch, drive the outer bearing race from the hub.

NOTE: *When removing the bearing races, use a criss-cross pattern to avoid cocking the race in the hub bore.*

6. Turn the hub over and drive the inner bearing race and grease seal from the hub; discard the grease seal.
7. Using solvent, clean the bearings, races

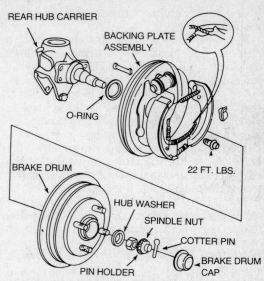

Exploded view of the rear bearing hub assembly—all except Civic (1984-88), Prelude (1984-88) and Accord (1986-88)

and the hub. Using compressed air, blow dry the components.

8. Using the Bearing Driver tool No. 07949-6110000, 07749-0010000 or equivalent, and the Driver Attachment tool No. 07946-6920100 or equivalent, drive the bearing races into the hub until they seat against the shoulders.

9. Using Multipurpose grease, pack the wheel hub and the wheel bearings, also, lightly coat the lips of the grease seal. Install the inner bearing into the hub.

10. Using a mallet, tap the grease seal (using a criss-cross method) into the rear of the hub until it is flush with it.

11. To install the hub, reverse the removal procedures. To adjust the spindle nut, perform the following procedures:

 a. Rotate the brake drum and torque the spindle nut to 4 ft. lbs.

 b. Loosen the spindle nut and retorque to 3 ft. lbs.

 c. Install the spindle nut retainer and align a slot with the hole in the spindle.

NOTE: *If the cotter pin holes do not align, tighten the nut slightly until they do.*

 d. Using a new cotter pin, install it through the spindle nut retainer.

12. To complete the installation, fill the grease cap with multi-purpose grease and reverse the removal procedures.

Prelude (1984-88)

1. Slightly loosen the rear wheel lug nuts. Raise and support the rear of the vehicle.
2. Release the parking brake. Remove the rear wheel assembly.

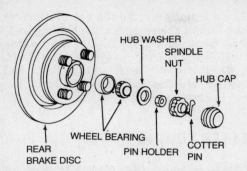

Exploded view of the rear bearing hub assembly—
Prelude (1984–88)

3. If equipped, remove the caliper shield. Disconnect the parking brake cable from the caliper. Remove the caliper-to-bracket bolts and suspend the caliper on a wire; do not disconnect the brake hose.

4. Remove the caliper bracket mounting bolts and the bracket.

5. Remove the grease cap, the cotter pin, the spindle nut retainer, the spindle nut, the thrust washer and the outer bearing. Pull the rear disc brake hub assembly from the spindle.

6. Using a hammer and a drift punch, drive the outer bearing race from the hub.

NOTE: *When removing the bearing races, use a criss-cross pattern to avoid cocking the race in the hub bore.*

7. Turn the hub over and drive the inner bearing race and grease seal from the hub; discard the grease seal.

8. Using solvent, clean the bearings, races and the hub. Using compressed air, blow dry the components.

9. Using the Bearing Driver tool No. 07749-0010000 or equivalent, and the Driver Attachment tool No. 07946-6920100 or equivalent, drive the bearing races into the hub until they seat against the shoulders.

10. Using Multipurpose grease, pack the wheel hub and the wheel bearings, also, lightly coat the lips of the grease seal. Install the inner bearing into the hub.

11. Using a mallet, tap the grease seal (using a criss-cross method) into the rear of the hub until it is flush with it.

12. To install the hub, reverse the removal procedures. To adjust the spindle nut, perform the following procedures:

a. Rotate the brake disc and torque the spindle nut to 18 ft. lbs.

b. Loosen the spindle nut and retorque to 18 ft. lbs.

c. Loosen the spindle nut and retorque to 4 ft. lbs.

d. Install the spindle nut retainer and align a slot with the hole in the spindle.

NOTE: *If the cotter pin holes do not align, tighten the nut slightly until they do.*

e. Using a new cotter pin, install it through the spindle nut retainer.

13. To complete the installation, fill the grease cap with multi-purpose grease and reverse the removal procedures. Torque the caliper bracket mounting bolts to 28 ft. lbs. and the caliper-to-bracket bolts to 17 ft. lbs. Reconnect the parking brake cable to the caliper.

1984-88 Civic
1986-88 Accord

1. Slightly loosen the rear wheel lug nuts. Raise and support the rear of the vehicle.

2. Release the parking brake. Remove the rear wheel assembly.

3. Remove the brake drum , the hub cap, the spindle nut, the thrust washer and the wheel hub unit.

4. Disconnect and plug the brake tube at the trailing arm connection.

5. Remove the stabilizing arm control plate nuts and the control arm.

6. Remove the backing plate-to-swing bearing housing unit nuts and the backing plate.

7. Remove the swing bearing housing unit-to-axle beam nuts and the swing bearing housing unit.

8. Using a hydraulic press and the Hub Disassembly/Assembly Base A tool No. 07965-6340301 or equivalent, press the rear wheel spindle from the swing bearing housing.

9. Using a Bearing Remover tool, press the inner bearing race from the wheel spindle.

NOTE: *The swing bearing housing unit is a*

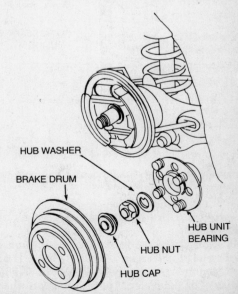

Exploded view of the rear bearing hub assembly—
Civic (1984–88) and Accord (1986–88)

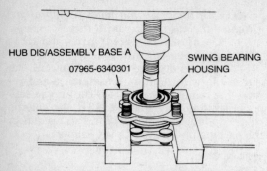

Removing the swing bearing housing unit from the spindle—Civic (1984–88) and Accord (1986–88)

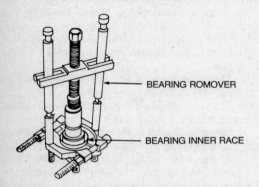

Removing the bearing race from the spindle—Civic (1984–88) and Accord (1986–88)

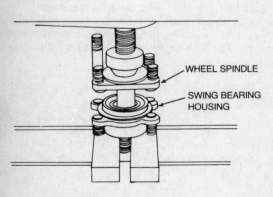

SPECIAL TOOL:
HUB DIS/ASSEMBLY BASE A 07965-6340301

Installing the swing bearing housing unit onto the spindle—Civic (1984–88) and Accord (1986–88)

sealed unit and must be replaced as an assembly.

10. Using a new swing bearing housing unit, a hydraulic press and the Hub Disassembly/Assembly Base A tool No. 07965-6340301 or equivalent, press the rear wheel spindle into the swing bearing housing until it seat against the shoulder.

11. To install, reverse the removal procedures. Torque the swing bearing housing unit-to-axle beam nuts to 33 ft. lbs., the backing plate-to-swing bearing housing unit to 33 ft. lbs., stabilizer control arm nuts to 29 ft. lbs. and the wheel hub-to-spindle nut to 134 ft. lbs. Bleed the brake system.

TRAILER TOWING

NOTE: *Although Honda's can be used for light trailer hauling, it is generally considered not to be a good choice in heavy applications.*

General Recommendations

Your car was primarily designed to carry passengers and cargo. It is important to remember that towing a trailer will place additional loads on your vehicle's engine, drive train, steering, braking and other systems. However, if you find it necessary to tow a trailer, using the proper equipment is a must.

Local laws may require specific equipment such as trailer brakes or fender mounted mirrors. Check your local laws.

Trailer Weight

The weight of the trailer is the most important factor. A good weight-to-horsepower ratio is about 35:1, 35 lbs. of GCW (Gross Combined Weight) for every horsepower your engine develops. Multiply the engine's rated horsepower by 35 and subtract the weight of the car passengers and luggage. The result is the approximate ideal maximum weight you should tow, although a a numerically higher axle ratio can help compensate for heavier weight.

Hitch Weight

Figure the hitch weight to select a proper hitch. Hitch weight is usually 9-11% of the trailer gross weight and should be measured with the trailer loaded. Hitches fall into three types: those that mount on the frame and rear bumper or the bolt-on or weld-on distribution type used for larger trailers. Axle mounted or clamp-on bumper hitches should never be used.

Check the gross weight rating of your trailer. Tongue weight is usually figured as 10% of gross trailer weight. Therefore, a trailer with a maximum gross weight of 2,000 lb. will have a maximum tongue weight of 200 lb. Class I trailers fall into this category. Class II trailers are those with a gross weight rating of 2,000-3,500 lb., while Class III trailers fall into the 3,500-6,000 lb. category. Class IV trailers are those over 6,000 lb. and are for use with fifth wheel trucks, only.

When you've determined the hitch that you'll need, follow the manufacturer's installation instructions, exactly, especially when it comes to fastener torques. The hitch will subjected to a lot of stress and good hitches come with hardened bolts. Never substitute an inferior bolt for a hardened bolt.

Cooling
ENGINE

One of the most common, if not THE most common, problems associated with trailer towing is engine overheating.

If you have a standard cooling system, without an expansion tank, you'll definitely need to get an aftermarket expansion tank kit, preferably one with at least a 2 quart capacity. These kits are easily installed on the radiator's overflow hose, and come with a pressure cap designed for expansion tanks.

Another helpful accessory is a Flex Fan. These fan are large diameter units are designed to provide more airflow at low speeds, with blades that have deeply cupped surfaces. The blades then flex, or flatten out, at high speed, when less cooling air is needed. These fans are far lighter in weight than stock fans, requiring less horsepower to drive them. Also, they are far quieter than stock fans.

If you do decide to replace your stock fan with a flex fan, note that if your car has a fan clutch, a spacer between the flex fan and water pump hub will be needed.

Aftermarket engine oil coolers are helpful for prolonging engine oil life and reducing overall engine temperatures. Both of these factors increase engine life.

While not absolutely necessary in towing Class I and some Class II trailers, they are recommended for heavier Class II and all Class III towing.

Engine oil cooler systems consist of an adapter, screwed on in place of the oil filter, a remote filter mounting and a multi-tube, finned heat exchanger, which is mounted in front of the radiator or air conditioning condenser.

TRANSMISSION

An automatic transmission is usually recommended for trailer towing. Modern automatics have proven reliable and, of course, easy to operate, in trailer towing.

The increased load of a trailer, however, causes an increase in the temperature of the automatic transmission fluid. Heat is the worst enemy of an automatic transmission. As the temperature of the fluid increases, the life of the fluid decreases.

It is essential, therefore, that you install an automatic transmission cooler.

The cooler, which consists of a multi-tube, finned heat exchanger, is usually installed in front of the radiator or air conditioning compressor, and hooked inline with the transmission cooler tank inlet line. Follow the cooler manufacturer's installation instructions.

Select a cooler of at least adequate capacity, based upon the combined gross weights of the car and trailer.

Cooler manufacturers recommend that you use an aftermarket cooler in addition to, and not instead of, the present cooling tank in your radiator. If you do want to use it in place of the radiator cooling tank, get a cooler at least two sizes larger than normally necessary.

NOTE: *A transmission cooler can, sometimes, cause slow or harsh shifting in the transmission during cold weather, until the fluid has a chance to come up to normal operating temperature. Some coolers can be purchased with or retrofitted with a temperature bypass valve which will allow fluid flow through the cooler only when the fluid has reached operating temperature, or above.*

Handling A Trailer

Towing a trailer with ease and safety requires a certain amount of experience. It's a good idea to learn the feel of a trailer by practicing turning, stopping and backing in an open area such as an empty parking lot.

PUSHING AND TOWING

If your Honda's rear axle is operable, you can tow your vehicle with the rear wheels on the ground. Due to its front wheel drive, the Honda is a relatively easy vehicle to tow with the front wheels up. Before doing so, you should release the parking brake.

If the rear axle is defective, the vehicle must then be towed with the rear wheels off the ground. Before attempting this, a dolly should be placed under the front wheels. If a dolly is not available, and you still have to tow it with the rear wheels up, then you should first shift the transaxle into Neutral and then lock the steering wheel so that the front wheels are pointing straight ahead. In such a position, the vehicle must not be towed at speeds above 35 mph or for more than short distances (50 miles). *It's critically important that you observe these limitations to prevent damage to your transaxle due to inadequate lubrication.*

JUMP STARTING A DEAD BATTERY

The chemical reaction in a battery produces explosive hydrogen gas. This is the safe way to jump start a dead battery, reducing the chances of an accidental spark that could cause an explosion.

Jump Starting Precautions

1. Be sure both batteries are of the same voltage.
2. Be sure both batteries are of the same polarity (have the same grounded terminal).
3. Be sure the vehicles are not touching.
4. Be sure the vent cap holes are not obstructed.
5. Do not smoke or allow sparks around the battery.
6. In cold weather, check for frozen electrolyte in the battery. Do not jump start a frozen battery.
7. Do not allow electrolyte on your skin or clothing.
8. Be sure the electrolyte is not frozen.
CAUTION: *Make certain that the ignition key, in the vehicle with the dead battery, is in the OFF position. Connecting cables to vehicles with on-board computers will result in computer destruction if the key is not in the OFF position.*

Jump Starting Procedure

1. Determine voltages of the two batteries; they must be the same.
2. Bring the starting vehicle close (they must not touch) so that the batteries can be reached easily.
3. Turn off all accessories and both engines. Put both cars in Neutral or Park and set the handbrake.
4. Cover the cell caps with a rag—do not cover terminals.
5. If the terminals on the run-down battery are heavily corroded, clean them.
6. Identify the positive and negative posts on both batteries and connect the cables in the order shown.
7. Start the engine of the starting vehicle and run it at fast idle. Try to start the car with the dead battery. Crank it for no more than 10 seconds at a time and let it cool off for 20 seconds in between tries.
8. If it doesn't start in 3 tries, there is something else wrong.
9. Disconnect the cables in the reverse order.
10. Replace the cell covers and dispose of the rags.

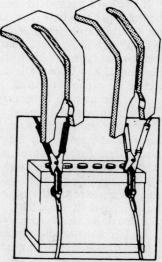

Side terminal batteries occasionally pose a problem when connecting jumper cables. There frequently isn't enough room to clamp the cables without touching sheet metal. Side terminal adaptors are available to alleviate this problem and should be removed after use.

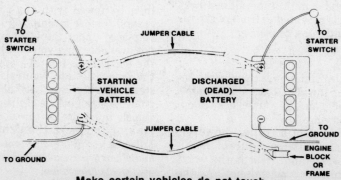

Make certain vehicles do not touch

This hook-up for negative ground cars only

JUMP STARTING

Hondas equipped with a manual transaxle can be push-started. Make sure that the bumpers match as otherwise a damaged bumper and/or fender could result from push-starting. To push-start your Honda, turn the ignition switch **ON**, push the clutch in, and select 2nd or 3rd gear. Depress the accelerator pedal to set the choke as you normally would, *then, release it.* As the vehicle picks up speed (10-15 mph), slowly release the clutch pedal until the engine fires up.

If your vehicle is equipped with an automatic transaxle, it cannot be push-started. Shifting the transaxle into gear has absolutely no effect until the transmission oil pump, driven by the engine, begins to run.

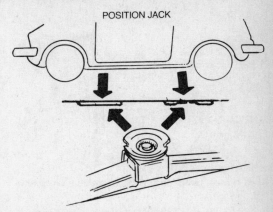

Jacking locations for the 1975 Civic

JACKING

Your Honda comes equipped with a scissors jack. This jack is fine for changing a flat tire or other operations where you do not have to go beneath the vehicle. There are four lifting points where this jack may be used: one behind each front wheel well and one in front of each rear wheel well in reinforced sheet metal brackets beneath the rocker panels.

A more convenient way of jacking is the use of a garage or floor jack. You may use the floor jack beneath any of the four scissors jacking points or you can raise either the entire front or entire rear of the vehicle using the special jacking brackets beneath the front center or rear

The correct method of raising the Honda with a garage hoist

Reinforced lifting point on the side of the Honda (arrow)

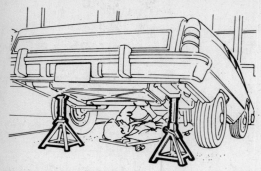

Always use jackstands when working under the car

center of the vehicle. On station wagon models, the rear of the vehicle may be jacked beneath the center of the rear axle beam.

The following safety points cannot be overemphasized:

• Always block the opposite wheel or wheels to keep the vehicle from rolling off the jack.

• When raising the front of the vehicle, firmly apply the parking brake.

• When raising the rear of the vehicle, place the transaxle in Low or Reverse gear.

• Always use jack stands to support the vehicle when you are working underneath. Place the stands beneath the scissors jacking brackets. Before climbing underneath, rock the vehicle a bit to make sure it is firmly supported.

If you are going to have your Honda serviced on a garage hoist, make sure the four hoist platform pads are placed beneath the scissors jacking brackets. These brackets are reinforced and will support the weight of the entire vehicle.

Maintenance Intervals Chart

Intervals are for number of months or thousands of miles, whichever comes first

Operation	'73–'79	'80–'88
Engine Oil/Filter Change	5	7.5 ①
Air Cleaner (Replace)	15	30
PCV Valve/Fixed Orifice (Clean/Inspect)	15	30
Adjust Valve Lash	15	15
Replace Spark Plugs	15	30
Fuel Filter (Replace)	15, 45, etc.	60
Check Ignition Timing, Replace Points (If applicable)	15	60
Adjust Belt Tension, Inspect Belts	15	30
Change Transaxle Fluid (Manual)	15, 45, etc.	30
Change Transaxle Fluid (Automatic)	15, 45, etc.	15, 45, etc.
Inspect Brakes	10 ②	7.5 ③

① Change oil every 3,000 miles/3 months when driving mostly short trips, in cold weather, or very dusty conditions

② On 1973–79 models, adjust rear brakes every 5,000 miles or 5 months, whichever comes first. Honda recommends that calipers be inspected for proper operation every 5,000 miles/5 months. Remember that state law may specify more frequent inspection.

③ Figure applies to front brakes. Inspect rear brakes every 15,000 miles or 15 months. Remember that state law may specify more frequent inspection.

Capacities

Year	Model	Engine Displacement cc	Engine Crankcase With Filter	Engine Crankcase Without Filter	Transmission (pts.) 4-Spd	Transmission (pts.) 5-Spd	Transmission (pts.) Auto. ①	Drive Axle (pts.)	Fuel Tank (gal.)	Cooling System (qts.)
1973	Civic	1170	3.8	3.2	5.2	—	5.2	—	10.0	4.2
1974	Civic 1200	1237	3.8	3.2	5.2	—	5.2	—	10.0	4.2
1975	Civic 1200	1237	3.8	3.2	5.2	—	5.2	—	10.6	4.2
	Civic CVCC	1487	3.8	3.2	5.2	5.2	5.2	—	10.6 ⑪	4.2
1976	Civic 1200	1237	3.8	3.2	5.2	—	5.2	—	10.0	4.2
	Civic CVCC	1487	3.8	3.2	5.2	5.2	5.2	—	10.6 ⑪	4.2
	Accord	1600	3.8	3.2	5.2	5.2	5.2	—	13.2	4.2

Capacities (cont.)

Year	Model	Engine Displacement cc	Engine Crankcase		Transmission (pts.)			Drive Axle (pts.)	Fuel Tank (gal.)	Cooling System (qts.)
			With Filter	Without Filter	4-Spd	5-Spd	Auto.①			
1977	Civic 1200	1237	3.8	3.2	5.2	—	5.2	—	10.6	4.2
	Civic CVCC	1487	3.8	3.2	5.2	5.2	5.2	—	10.6⑪	4.2
	Accord	1600	3.8	3.2	5.2	5.2	5.2	—	13.2	4.2
1978	Civic 1200	1237	3.8	3.2	5.2	—	5.2	—	10.6	4.2
	Civic CVCC	1487	3.8	3.2	5.2	5.2	5.2	—	10.6⑪	4.2
	Accord	1600	3.8	3.2	5.2	5.2	5.2	—	13.2	4.2
1979	Civic 1200	1237	3.8	3.2	5.2	—	5.2	—	10.6	4.8
	Civic CVCC	1487	3.8	3.2	5.2	5.6	5.2	—	10.6⑪	4.8
	Accord	1751	3.8	3.2	5.2	5.2	5.2	—	13.2	6.4
	Prelude	1751	3.8	3.2	5.2	5.2	5.2	—	13.2	6.0
1980	Civic 1300	1335	3.8	3.2	4.8	5.2	5.2	—	10.8	5.2
	Civic CVCC	1487	3.8	3.2	4.8	5.2	5.2	—	10.8	5.2
	Accord	1751	3.8	3.2	5.0	5.0	5.2	—	13.2	6.4
	Prelude	1751	3.8	3.2	5.0	5.0	5.2	—	13.2	6.0
1981	Civic	1335 1487	3.8	3.2	5.2	5.2	5.2	—	10.8②	4.8③
	Accord	1751	3.8	3.2	5.0	5.0	5.2	—	13.2	6.4
	Prelude	1751	3.7	3.2	5.0	5.0	5.2	—	13.2	6.0
1982	Civic	1335 1487	3.7	3.2	5.2	5.2	5.2	—	10.8②	4.8③
	Accord	1751	3.7	3.2	5.0	5.0	5.2	—	15.8②	6.0
	Prelude	1751	3.7	3.2	5.0	5.0	5.2	—	13.2	6.0
1983	Civic	1335 1487	3.7	3.2	5.2	5.2	5.2	—	10.4②	4.8③
	Accord	1751	3.7	3.2	5.0	5.0	6.0	—	15.8	6.0
	Prelude	1829	3.7	3.2	—	5.0	5.8	—	15.9	6.3
1984	Civic/CRX	1342 1488	3.7	3.2	5.0	5.0	6.0	—	11.9④	4.8⑤
	Accord	1829	3.7	3.2	—	5.0	6.0	—	15.8	6.4
	Prelude	1829	3.7	3.2	—	5.0	5.8	—	15.9	6.3⑥
1985	Civic/CRX	1342 1488	3.7	3.2	5.0	5.0	6.0	—	11.9④	4.8⑤
	Accord	1829	3.7	3.2	—	5.0	6.0	—	15.8	6.4
	Prelude	1829	3.7	3.2	—	5.0	5.8	—	15.9	6.3⑥
1986	Civic/CRX	1342 1488	3.7	3.2	5.0	5.0	5.0⑦	⑨	11.9④	4.8⑤
	Accord	1955	3.7	3.2	—	5.0	5.2	—	15.9	5.2⑧
	Prelude	1829 1955	3.7	3.2	—	5.0	5.8	—	15.9	6.3⑥
1987	Civic/CRX	1342 1488	3.7	3.2	5.0	5.0	5.0⑦	⑨	11.9④	4.8③
	Accord	1955	3.7	3.2	—	5.0	5.2	—	15.9	5.2⑧

Capacities (cont.)

Year	Model	Engine Displacement cc	Engine Crankcase		Transmission (pts.)			Drive Axle (pts.)	Fuel Tank (gal.)	Cooling System (qts.)
			With Filter	Without Filter	4-Spd	5-Spd	Auto. ①			
1987	Prelude	1829 1955	3.7	3.2	—	5.0	5.8	—	15.9	6.3 ⑥
1988	Civic/CRX	1493 1590	3.7	3.2	—	5.0	5.0	—	11.9 ⑩	5.8
	Accord	1955	3.7	3.2	—	5.0	6.0	—	15.9	5.8
	Prelude	1955	4.1	3.6	4.0	4.0	6.0	—	15.9	8.2

① Does not include torque converter.
② 4-dr. sedan: 12.1
③ 1335cc: 4.0
④ 4-dr.: 12.1
  CRX: 10.8
  CRX HF: 10.0
  CRX Si: 11.9
⑤ 1342cc: 3.6
⑥ Auto. Trans.: 7.1
⑦ CRX: 6.0
⑧ Auto. Trans.: 5.8
⑨ 4wd: 2.5
⑩ HF: 10.6
⑪ Station Wagon: 11.0

Engine Performance and Tune-Up

TUNE-UP PROCEDURES

The procedures in this section are specifically intended for your Honda and intended to be as basic and complete as possible.

Spark Plugs

NOTE: *The spark plugs should be replaced every 15,000 miles (1973-79) or 30,000 miles (1980-88).*

Most people know that the spark plug ignites the air/fuel mixture in the cylinder, which in turn forces the piston downward, turning the crankshaft. This action turns the drivetrain (clutch, transaxle, drive axles) and moves the vehicle. What many people do not know, however, is that spark plugs should be chosen according to the type of driving done. The plug with a long insulator nose retains heat long enough to burn off oil and combustion deposits under light engine load conditions. A short-nosed plug dissipates heat rapidly and prevents pre-ignition and detonation under heavily

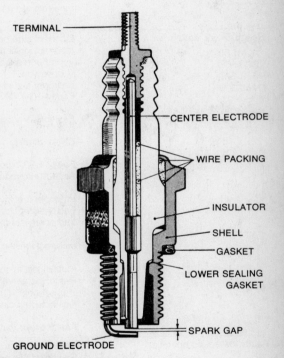

TERMINAL

CENTER ELECTRODE

WIRE PACKING

INSULATOR

SHELL

GASKET

LOWER SEALING GASKET

SPARK GAP

GROUND ELECTRODE

Spark plug cross-section

loaded conditions. Under normal driving conditions, a standard plug is just fine.

Spark plug life is largely governed by operating conditions and varies accordingly. To ensure peak performance, inspect the plugs at least every 6,000 miles on vehicles burning leaded fuel and every 10,000-15,000 miles on vehicles running exclusively on unleaded fuel and having electronic ignition. Faulty or excessively worn plugs should be replaced immediately. It is also helpful to check plugs for types of deposit and degree of electrode wear, as an indication of engine operating condition. Excessive or oily deposits could be an indication of real engine trouble, it would be wise to

Underhood emissions control sticker containing tune-up information

Troubleshooting Engine Performance

Problem	Cause	Solution
Hard starting (engine cranks normally)	• Binding linkage, choke valve or choke piston	• Repair as necessary
	• Restricted choke vacuum diaphragm	• Clean passages
	• Improper fuel level	• Adjust float level
	• Dirty, worn or faulty needle valve and seat	• Repair as necessary
	• Float sticking	• Repair as necessary
	• Faulty fuel pump	• Replace fuel pump
	• Incorrect choke cover adjustment	• Adjust choke cover
	• Inadequate choke unloader adjustment	• Adjust choke unloader
	• Faulty ignition coil	• Test and replace as necessary
	• Improper spark plug gap	• Adjust gap
	• Incorrect ignition timing	• Adjust timing
	• Incorrect valve timing	• Check valve timing; repair as necessary
Rough idle or stalling	• Incorrect curb or fast idle speed	• Adjust curb or fast idle speed
	• Incorrect ignition timing	• Adjust timing to specification
	• Improper feedback system operation	• Refer to Chapter 4
	• Improper fast idle cam adjustment	• Adjust fast idle cam
	• Faulty EGR valve operation	• Test EGR system and replace as necessary
	• Faulty PCV valve air flow	• Test PCV valve and replace as necessary
	• Choke binding	• Locate and eliminate binding condition
	• Faulty TAC vacuum motor or valve	• Repair as necessary
	• Air leak into manifold vacuum	• Inspect manifold vacuum connections and repair as necessary
	• Improper fuel level	• Adjust fuel level
	• Faulty distributor rotor or cap	• Replace rotor or cap
	• Improperly seated valves	• Test cylinder compression, repair as necessary
	• Incorrect ignition wiring	• Inspect wiring and correct as necessary
	• Faulty ignition coil	• Test coil and replace as necessary
	• Restricted air vent or idle passages	• Clean passages
	• Restricted air cleaner	• Clean or replace air cleaner filler element
	• Faulty choke vacuum diaphragm	• Repair as necessary
Faulty low-speed operation	• Restricted idle transfer slots	• Clean transfer slots
	• Restricted idle air vents and passages	• Clean air vents and passages
	• Restricted air cleaner	• Clean or replace air cleaner filter element
	• Improper fuel level	• Adjust fuel level
	• Faulty spark plugs	• Clean or replace spark plugs
	• Dirty, corroded, or loose ignition secondary circuit wire connections	• Clean or tighten secondary circuit wire connections
	• Improper feedback system operation	• Refer to Chapter 4
	• Faulty ignition coil high voltage wire	• Replace ignition coil high voltage wire
	• Faulty distributor cap	• Replace cap
Faulty acceleration	• Improper accelerator pump stroke	• Adjust accelerator pump stroke
	• Incorrect ignition timing	• Adjust timing
	• Inoperative pump discharge check ball or needle	• Clean or replace as necessary
	• Worn or damaged pump diaphragm or piston	• Replace diaphragm or piston

Troubleshooting Engine Performance (cont.)

Problem	Cause	Solution
Faulty acceleration (cont.)	• Leaking carburetor main body cover gasket	• Replace gasket
	• Engine cold and choke set too lean	• Adjust choke cover
	• Improper metering rod adjustment (BBD Model carburetor)	• Adjust metering rod
	• Faulty spark plug(s)	• Clean or replace spark plug(s)
	• Improperly seated valves	• Test cylinder compression, repair as necessary
	• Faulty ignition coil	• Test coil and replace as necessary
	• Improper feedback system operation	• Refer to Chapter 4
Faulty high speed operation	• Incorrect ignition timing	• Adjust timing
	• Faulty distributor centrifugal advance mechanism	• Check centrifugal advance mechanism and repair as necessary
	• Faulty distributor vacuum advance mechanism	• Check vacuum advance mechanism and repair as necessary
	• Low fuel pump volume	• Replace fuel pump
	• Wrong spark plug air gap or wrong plug	• Adjust air gap or install correct plug
	• Faulty choke operation	• Adjust choke cover
	• Partially restricted exhaust manifold, exhaust pipe, catalytic converter, muffler, or tailpipe	• Eliminate restriction
	• Restricted vacuum passages	• Clean passages
	• Improper size or restricted main jet	• Clean or replace as necessary
	• Restricted air cleaner	• Clean or replace filter element as necessary
	• Faulty distributor rotor or cap	• Replace rotor or cap
	• Faulty ignition coil	• Test coil and replace as necessary
	• Improperly seated valve(s)	• Test cylinder compression, repair as necessary
	• Faulty valve spring(s)	• Inspect and test valve spring tension, replace as necessary
	• Incorrect valve timing	• Check valve timing and repair as necessary
	• Intake manifold restricted	• Remove restriction or replace manifold
	• Worn distributor shaft	• Replace shaft
	• Improper feedback system operation	• Refer to Chapter 4
Misfire at all speeds	• Faulty spark plug(s)	• Clean or replace spark plug(s)
	• Faulty spark plug wire(s)	• Replace as necessary
	• Faulty distributor cap or rotor	• Replace cap or rotor
	• Faulty ignition coil	• Test coil and replace as necessary
	• Primary ignition circuit shorted or open intermittently	• Troubleshoot primary circuit and repair as necessary
	• Improperly seated valve(s)	• Test cylinder compression, repair as necessary
	• Faulty hydraulic tappet(s)	• Clean or replace tappet(s)
	• Improper feedback system operation	• Refer to Chapter 4
	• Faulty valve spring(s)	• Inspect and test valve spring tension, repair as necessary
	• Worn camshaft lobes	• Replace camshaft
	• Air leak into manifold	• Check manifold vacuum and repair as necessary
	• Improper carburetor adjustment	• Adjust carburetor
	• Fuel pump volume or pressure low	• Replace fuel pump
	• Blown cylinder head gasket	• Replace gasket
	• Intake or exhaust manifold passage(s) restricted	• Pass chain through passage(s) and repair as necessary
	• Incorrect trigger wheel installed in distributor	• Install correct trigger wheel

Troubleshooting Engine Performance (cont.)

Problem	Cause	Solution
Power not up to normal	• Incorrect ignition timing	• Adjust timing
	• Faulty distributor rotor	• Replace rotor
	• Trigger wheel loose on shaft	• Reposition or replace trigger wheel
	• Incorrect spark plug gap	• Adjust gap
	• Faulty fuel pump	• Replace fuel pump
	• Incorrect valve timing	• Check valve timing and repair as necessary
	• Faulty ignition coil	• Test coil and replace as necessary
	• Faulty ignition wires	• Test wires and replace as necessary
	• Improperly seated valves	• Test cylinder compression and repair as necessary
	• Blown cylinder head gasket	• Replace gasket
	• Leaking piston rings	• Test compression and repair as necessary
	• Worn distributor shaft	• Replace shaft
	• Improper feedback system operation	• Refer to Chapter 4
Intake backfire	• Improper ignition timing	• Adjust timing
	• Faulty accelerator pump discharge	• Repair as necessary
	• Defective EGR CTO valve	• Replace EGR CTO valve
	• Defective TAC vacuum motor or valve	• Repair as necessary
	• Lean air/fuel mixture	• Check float level or manifold vacuum for air leak. Remove sediment from bowl
Exhaust backfire	• Air leak into manifold vacuum	• Check manifold vacuum and repair as necessary
	• Faulty air injection diverter valve	• Test diverter valve and replace as necessary
	• Exhaust leak	• Locate and eliminate leak
Ping or spark knock	• Incorrect ignition timing	• Adjust timing
	• Distributor centrifugal or vacuum advance malfunction	• Inspect advance mechanism and repair as necessary
	• Excessive combustion chamber deposits	• Remove with combustion chamber cleaner
	• Air leak into manifold vacuum	• Check manifold vacuum and repair as necessary
	• Excessively high compression	• Test compression and repair as necessary
	• Fuel octane rating excessively low	• Try alternate fuel source
	• Sharp edges in combustion chamber	• Grind smooth
	• EGR valve not functioning properly	• Test EGR system and replace as necessary
Surging (at cruising to top speeds)	• Low carburetor fuel level	• Adjust fuel level
	• Low fuel pump pressure or volume	• Replace fuel pump
	• Metering rod(s) not adjusted properly (BBD Model Carburetor)	• Adjust metering rod
	• Improper PCV valve air flow	• Test PCV valve and replace as necessary
	• Air leak into manifold vacuum	• Check manifold vacuum and repair as necessary
	• Incorrect spark advance	• Test and replace as necessary
	• Restricted main jet(s)	• Clean main jet(s)
	• Undersize main jet(s)	• Replace main jet(s)
	• Restricted air vents	• Clean air vents
	• Restricted fuel filter	• Replace fuel filter
	• Restricted air cleaner	• Clean or replace air cleaner filter element
	• EGR valve not functioning properly	• Test EGR system and replace as necessary
	• Improper feedback system operation	• Refer to Chapter 4

Gasoline Engine Tune-Up Specifications

Year	Model	Engine Displacement (cc)	Spark Plugs Type	Gap (in.)	Ignition Timing (deg.) MT	AT	Compression (psi)	Fuel Pump (psi)	Idle Speed (rpm) MT	AT	Valve Clearance In.[13]	Ex.
1973	Civic	1170	B-6ES	.030 [14]	TDC [1]	TDC [1]	N.A.	2.5	750–850	700–800	0.005–0.007	0.005–0.007
1974	Civic 1200	1237	B-6ES	.030 [14]	5B [1]	5B [1]	N.A.	2.5	750–850	700–800	0.004–0.006	0.004–0.006
1975	Civic 1200	1237	B-6ES	.030 [14]	7B [1]	7B [1]	N.A.	2.5	750–850	700–800	0.004–0.006	0.004–0.006
	Civic CVCC	1487	B-6ES	.030 [14]	TDC	3A	N.A.	2.5	800–900	700–800	0.005–0.007	0.005–0.007
1976	Civic 1200	1237	B-6ES	.030 [14]	7B [1]	7B [1]	N.A.	2.5	750–850	700–800	0.004–0.006	0.004–0.006
	Civic CVCC	1487	B-6ES	.030 [14]	2B [15]	2B [16]	N.A.	2.5	800–900	700–800	0.005–0.007	0.005–0.007
	Accord	1600	B-6ES	.030 [14]	6B	2B	N.A.	2.5	800–900	700–800	0.005–0.007	0.005–0.007
1977	Civic 1200	1237	B-6ES	.030 [14]	7B [1]	7B [1]	N.A.	2.5	750–850	700–800	0.004–0.006	0.004–0.006
	Civic CVCC	1487	B-6ES	.030 [14]	2B [15]	2B [16]	N.A.	2.5	800–900	700–800	0.005–0.007	0.005–0.007
	Accord	1600	B-6ES	.030 [14]	6B	2B	N.A.	2.5	800–900	700–800	0.005–0.007	0.005–0.007
1978	Civic 1200	1237	B-6ES	.030 [14]	7B [1]	7B [1]	N.A.	2.5	750–850	700–800	0.004–0.006	0.004–0.006
	Civic CVCC	1487	B-6ES	.030 [14]	2B [15]	2B [16]	N.A.	2.5	800–900	700–800	0.005–0.007	0.005–0.007
	Accord	1600	B-6ES	.030 [14]	6B	2B	N.A.	2.5	800–900	700–800	0.005–0.007	0.005–0.007
1979	Civic 1200	1237	B-6ES	.030 [14]	2B [1]	2B [1]	N.A.	2.5	650–750	600–700	0.004–0.006	0.004–0.006
	Civic CVCC	1487	B-6EB	.030 [14]	2B	6B	N.A.	2.5	650–750	600–700	0.005–0.007	0.007–0.009
	Accord	1751	B-7EB	.030	6B [17]	4B [18]	190	2.5	650–750 [1]	650–750 [2]	0.005–0.007	0.010–0.012
	Prelude	1751	B-7EB	.030	6B [17]	4B [18]	190	2.5	650–750 [1]	650–750 [2]	0.005–0.007	0.010–0.012
1980	Civic 1300	1335	B6EB-11	.042	2B [3]	TDC	180	2.5	700–800 [1]	700–800 [2]	0.005–0.007	0.007–0.009
	Civic CVCC	1487	B7EB-11	.042	15B [19]	TDC	180	2.5	700–800	700–800	0.005–0.007	0.007–0.009
	Accord	1751	B-7EB	.030	4B	TDC	190	2.5	750–850 [1]	750–850 [2]	0.005–0.007	0.010–0.012
	Prelude	1751	B-7EB	.030	4B	TDC	190	2.5	750–850 [1]	750–850 [2]	0.005–0.007	0.010–0.012
1981	Civic	1487	B6EB-11	.042	10B	2A	180	2.5	700–800 [1]	700–800 [2]	0.005–0.007	0.007–0.009

Gasoline Engine Tune-Up Specifications (cont.)

Year	Model	Engine Displacement (cc)	Spark Plugs Type	Gap (in.)	Ignition Timing (deg.) MT	Ignition Timing (deg.) AT	Compression (psi)	Fuel Pump (psi)	Idle Speed (rpm) MT	Idle Speed (rpm) AT	Valve Clearance In.[13]	Valve Clearance Ex.
1981	Civic 1300	1335	B6EB-11	.042	2B [3]	—	180	2.5	700– 800 [1]	—	0.005– 0.007	0.007– 0.009
	Accord	1751	B6EB-L11	.042	TDC [8]	TDC	190	2.5	750– 850 [1]	750– 850 [2]	0.005– 0.007	0.010– 0.012
	Prelude	1751	B6EB-L11	.042	TDC [8]	TDC	190	2.5	750– 850 [1]	750– 850 [2]	0.005– 0.007	0.010– 0.012
1982	Civic 1300	1335	BR6EB-11	.042	20B [3]	—	210	2.5	650– 750 [1]	—	0.005– 0.007	0.007– 0.009
	Civic 1500	1487	BR6EB-11	.042	18B [3]	18B [3]	190	2.5	650– 750 [1]	650– 750 [2]	0.005– 0.007	0.007– 0.009
	Accord	1751	BR6EB-L11	.042	16B [5]	16B	190	2.5	750– 850 [1]	750– 850 [2]	0.005– 0.007	0.010– 0.012
	Prelude	1751	BR6EB-L11	.042	12B [6]	16B	190	2.5	700– 800 [1]	700– 800 [2]	0.005– 0.007	0.010– 0.012
1983	Civic 1300	1335	BR6EB-11	.042	18B [7][3]	—	210	2.5	600– 750 [1]	—	0.005– 0.007	0.007– 0.009
	Civic 1500	1487	BR6EB-11	.042	18B [3]	18B [3]	210	2.5	650– 750 [1]	650– 750 [2]	0.005– 0.007	0.007– 0.009
	Accord	1751	BR6EB-L11	.042	16B [5][3]	16B [3]	195	2.5	700– 800 [1]	650– 750 [2]	0.005– 0.007	0.010– 0.012
	Prelude	1829	BUR6EB-11	.042	10B [5][3]	12B [3]	215	2.5	750– 850 [1]	700– 800 [2]	0.005– 0.007	0.010– 0.012
1984	Civic/ CRX 1.3	1342	BUR6EB-11	.042	21B [11]	—	220	3.0	650– 750	—	0.007– 0.009	0.009– 0.011
	Civic/ CRX 1.5	1488	BUR6EB-11	.042	20B [11]	15B [11]	210	3.0	650– 750	650– 750	0.007– 0.009	0.009– 0.011
	Accord	1829	BUR6EB-11	.042	22B [3]	18B [3]	210	2.5	700– 800	650– 750	0.005– 0.007	0.010– 0.012
	Prelude	1829	BPR6EY-11	.042	20B [3]	12B [3]	210	2.5	750– 850	750– 850	0.005– 0.007	0.010– 0.012
1985	Civic/ CRX 1.3	1342	BUR5EB-11	.042	21B [6][11]	—	225	3.0	650– 750	—	0.007– 0.009	0.009– 0.011
	Civic/ CRX 1.5	1488	BUR5EB-11	.042	20B [11]	15B [11]	210	3.0	650– 750	650– 750	0.007– 0.009	0.009– 0.011
	Civic/ CRX HF	1488	BUR4EB-11	.042	21B [6]	— [11]	210	3.0	650– 750	650– 750	0.007– 0.009	0.009– 0.011
	Civic/ CRX Si	1488	BPR6EY-11	.042	16B [5][11]	—	190	35	550– 650	—	0.007– 0.009	0.009– 0.011

Gasoline Engine Tune-Up Specifications (cont.)

Year	Model	Engine Displacement (cc)	Spark Plugs Type	Gap (in.)	Ignition Timing (deg.) MT	Ignition Timing (deg.) AT	Compression (psi)	Fuel Pump (psi)	Idle Speed (rpm) MT	Idle Speed (rpm) AT	Valve Clearance In.⑬	Valve Clearance Ex.
1985	Accord	1829	BUR5EB-11	.042	22B ③	18B ⑨	190 ③	2.5	700– 800	650– 750	0.005– 0.007	0.010– 0.012
	Accord SE-i	1829	BPR6EY-11	.042	18B ③	18B ③	200	35	700– 800	700– 800	0.005– 0.007	0.010– 0.012
	Prelude	1829	BPR6EY-11	.042	20B ③	12B ③	200	2.5	750– 850	750– 850	0.005– 0.007	0.012– 0.012
1986	Civic/ CRX 1.3	1342	BUR4EB-11	.042	21B ⑥⑪	—	225	3.0	650– 750	—	0.007– 0.009	0.009– 0.011
	Civic/ CRX 1.5	1488	BUR4EB-11	.042	20B ⑪	15B ⑩⑪	200	3.0	650– 750	650– 750	0.007– 0.009	0.009– 0.011
	Civic/ CRX HF	1488	BUR4EB-11	.042	21B ⑥⑪	—	190	3.0	650– 750	650– 750	0.007– 0.009	0.009– 0.011
	Civic/ CRX Si	1488	BPR6EY-11	.042	16B ⑤⑪	—	190	35	700– 800	—	0.007– 0.009	0.009– 0.011
	Accord	1955	BPR5EY-11	.042	24B ③⑫	15B ③	200	3.0	700– 800	650– 750	0.005– 0.009	0.010– 0.012
	Accord LX-i	1955	BPR5EY-11	.042	15B ③	15B ③	210	35	700– 800	700– 800	0.005– 0.007	0.010– 0.012
	Prelude	1829	BPR6EY-11	.042	20B ③	12B ③	200	2.5	750– 850	750– 850	0.005– 0.007	0.010– 0.012
	Prelude Si	1955	BPR5EY-11	.042	15B ③	15B ③	210	35	700– 800	700– 800	0.005– 0.007	0.010– 0.012
1987	Civic/ CRX 1.3	1342	BUR4EB-11	.042	21B ⑥⑪	—	225	3.0	650– 750	—	0.007– 0.009	0.009– 0.011
	Civic/ CRX 1.5	1488	BUR4EB-11	.042	20B ⑪	15B ⑩⑪	200	3.0	650– 750	650– 750	0.007– 0.009	0.009– 0.011
	Civic/ CRX HF	1488	BUR4EB-11	.042	26B ⑥⑪	—	164	3.0	650– 750	650– 750	0.007– 0.009	0.009– 0.011
	Civic/ CRX Si	1488	BPR6EY-11	.042	16B ⑤⑪	—	156	35	700– 800	—	0.007– 0.009	0.011– 0.011
	Accord	1955	BPR5EY-11	.042	24B ③⑫	15B ③	171	3.0	700– 800	650– 750	0.005– 0.007	0.010– 0.012
	Accord LX-i	1955	BPR5EY-11	.042	15B ③	15B ③	178	35	700– 800	700– 800	0.005– 0.007	0.010– 0.012
	Prelude	1829	BPR6EY-11	.042	20B ③	12B ③	156	2.5	750– 850	750– 850	0.005– 0.007	0.010– 0.012
	Prelude Si	1955	BPR5EY-11	.042	15B ③	15B ③	178	35	700– 800	700– 800	0.005– 0.007	0.010– 0.012
1988	Civic/ CRX HF, 1.5	1493	BCPR6E-11	.042	14B	14B	185	35	600– 700	700– 800	0.005– 0.007	0.007– 0.009
	Civic/CRX Std., 1.5	1493	BCPR6E-11	.042	18B	18B	185	35	700– 700	700– 800	0.007– 0.009	0.009– 0.011
	Civic/CRX Si, 1.6	1590	BCPR6E-11	.042	18B	18B	185	35	700– 800	700– 800	0.007– 0.009	0.009– 0.011
	Accord DX/LX	1955	BPR5EY-11	.042	24B ⑫	15B ③	171	3.0	800– 850	700– 800	0.005– 0.007	0.010– 0.012

Gasoline Engine Tune-Up Specifications (cont.)

Year	Model	Engine Displacement (cc)	Spark Plugs Type	Gap (in.)	Ignition Timing (deg.) MT	AT	Compression (psi)	Fuel Pump (psi)	Idle Speed (rpm) MT	AT	Valve Clearance In.⑬	Ex.
1988	Accord LX-i	1955	BPR5EY-11	.042	15B ③	15B ③	178	35	750–800	750–800	0.005–0.007	0.010–0.012
	Prelude	1955	BCPR5E-11	.042	20B	12B	156	2.5	800–850	750–800	0.005–0.007	0.010–0.012
	Prelude Si	1955	BCPR6EY-11	.042	15B	15B	178	35	750–800	750–800	0.003–0.005	0.006–0.008

NOTE: The underhood specifications sticker often reflects tune-up changes made in production. Sticker figures must be used if they disagree with those in this chart.

TDC Top Dead Center
B Before top dead center
A After top dead center
— Not applicable
NA Not available
① In neutral, with headlights on
② In drive range, with headlights on
③ Aim timing light at red mark on fly wheel or torque converter drive plate with the distributor vacuum hose connected at the specified idle speed.
④ Wagon/Sedan: 4B, Calif-2A
⑤ Calif: 12B
⑥ Std.: Calif: 16B
  MT: 20B, AT: 15B
⑦ 4 speed: 20B
⑧ Aim timing light at white mark
⑨ California models: 18B
⑩ Models w/power steering: 17B
⑪ Aim timing light at red mark on crankshaft pulley
⑫ Calif:20B
⑬ Auxiliary valve, all except 1342cc and 1488cc: 0.005–0.007
  1342cc and 1488cc: 0.007–0.009
⑭ Ignition point: gap: .020
        dwell: 49–55
⑮ Sedan with 5 speed from engine number 2500001 and up: 6B
⑯ Station Wagon: TDC
⑰ California and high altitude: TDC
⑱ California and high altitude: 2B
⑲ Station Wagon 49 states: 10B

investigate the problem thoroughly and make sure the cause is found and corrected.

REMOVAL AND INSTALLATION

1. Place a piece of masking tape around each spark plug wire and number it according to its corresponding cylinder.

2. Pull the wires from the spark plugs, grasping the wire by the end of the rubber boot and twisting off.

NOTE: *Avoid spark plug removal while the engine is Hot. Since the cylinder head spark plug threads are aluminum, the spark plug becomes tight due to the different coefficients of heat expansion. If a plug is too tight to be removed even while the engine is Cold, apply a solvent around the plug followed with an application of oil once the solvent has penetrated the threads. Do this only when the engine is* **Cold**.

3. Loosen each spark plug with a $^{13}/_{16}$″ spark plug socket. When the plug has been loosened a few turns, stop to clean any material from around the spark plug holes; compressed air is preferred. If air is not available, simply use a rag to clean the area.

NOTE: *In no case should foreign matter be allowed to enter the cylinders. Severe damage could result.*

4. Remove and inspect the spark plugs; if necessary, clean them.

5. To install, oil the spark plug threads and hand tighten them into the cylinder head. Torque the spark plugs into the cylinder head to 13 ft. lbs.

NOTE: *It's a good idea to apply an anti-seize*

When removing spark plug wires, always pull on the plug boot, never on the wire itself

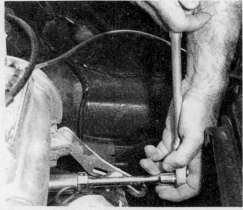

Keep the socket straight on the plug to avoid breaking the insulator. A ratchet with a flexible head is helpful

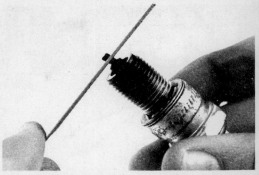

Use a small file to clean and square up the electrode if the plug is still usable

When gapping plugs, new or used, make sure the wire gauge passes through the gap with just a slight drag. Don't use a flat feeler gauge

Bend the side electrode carefully using a spark plug gapping tool

compound on the threads of the spark plugs before installing them. *DO NOT over-tighten them because of the aluminum cylinder heads.*

6. Connect the wires to the plugs, making sure that each is securely fitted.

INSPECTION AND CLEANING

Before attempting to clean and re-gap plugs be sure that the electrode ends are not worn or damaged and that the insulators (the white porcelain covering) are not cracked; replace the plug if this condition exists.

NOTE: *For further information on spark*

plug problems, refer to the color insert of *Spark Plug Analysis* in this book.

Clean reusable plugs with a small file or a wire brush. The plug gap should be checked and readjusted, if necessary, by bending the ground electrode with a spark plug gapping tool.

NOTE: *DO NOT use a flat gauge to check plug gap. An incorrect reading will result; use a wire gauge only. Also, replace the plugs one at a time, keeping the ignition wires connected to those plugs you're not working on. This will avoid confusion about how to recon-*

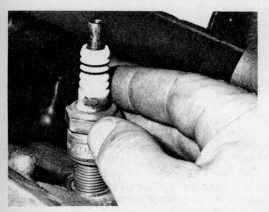

Always start the plugs by hand to avoid crossthreading them

nect the plug wires according to the firing order.

Spark Plug Wires

Spark plug wires do a critical job for your vehicle's ignition system. They transmit the very, very tiny amounts of current that fire the spark plugs at an extremely high voltage. Voltage is high at the plugs because the spark must actually leap the plug gap, something which requires tremendous electrical pressure or **voltage**. Electricity has great difficulty in traveling through air or air/fuel mixture. In fact, the mixture will not transmit electricity at all in its natural state. The tremendous voltage at the plug's center electrode actually pumps electrons into the air, **ionizing** it before the spark can travel to the ground electrode. The required voltage is especially high because of the pressure generated in the cylinders during the compression stroke.

Since the coil's ability to increase the voltage in the ignition system is traded in direct proportion for decreased amperage or current flow, there is little room for loss of current due to poor ignition wires. To make matters worse, the high voltage existing throughout the wires naturally tends to create a corona effect and loss of both current and voltage.

All this is worth knowing for one simple reason, it pays to buy quality ignition wires with a metallic conductor and it pays to inspect wires frequently for either cracked or brittle insulation. A most common symptom of ignition wires that are starting to give out is poor performance or difficult starting in wet weather that improves after the engine warms up or when the weather clears. You can confirm this problem by watching the engine run in the dark. If you see a lot of blue sparking around the wires, replace them. At this time, it is also a

good idea to inspect the distributor cap and rotor, replace them, if there is any sign of cracking or carbon **tracking**. These are paths of burnt plastic, usually beginning at a crack or groove, where sparks may have been leaping from the center of the cap to ground.

Note too that you may be able to improve ignition performance by purchasing either resistor wires or resistor spark plugs for improved performance of your radio. You do not need to purchase components with the **resistor** designation in both cases!

If you have an ignition problem that seems to come and go, yet the insulation on the outside of the ignition wires is still good, it may pay to have your vehicle run on an ignition scope or diagnostic system. The scope readings will sometimes reveal high resistance in the conductor at the center of each wire. You can also use an ohmmeter to measure the resistance of the wire from end to end; it should not exceed 25,000Ω.

Ignition wires are most easily replaced one at a time. Make sure to very carefully insert wires all the way into the cap and onto the ends of the plugs; make sure all insulator boots are installed all the way onto the cap or plugs.

Firing Orders

NOTE: *To avoid confusion, remove and tag the wires one at a time, for replacement.*

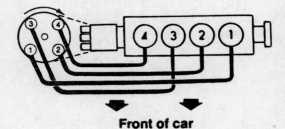

Front of car

1829cc—1984 Accord & 1985 Accord SE-i
1342cc & 1488cc—1984–87 Civic
Firing Order: 1-3-4-2
Distributor rotation—clockwise

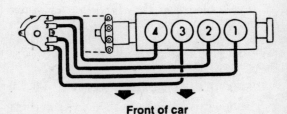

Front of car

1829cc—1985 Accord (carbureted) &
1983–87 Prelude
1955cc—1986–88 Accord & Prelude
Firing Order: 1-3-4-2
Distributor rotation—clockwise

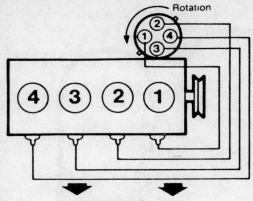

Front of car

1170cc & 1237cc Civic
Firing Order: 1-3-4-2
Distributor Rotation—Counter-clockwise

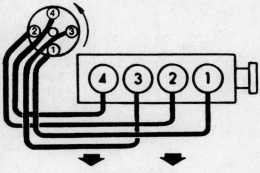

Front of car

1335cc—1980–83 Civic
1487cc—1980–83 Civic
1751cc—1979–83 Accord
        1979–83 Prelude
Firing Order: 1-3-4-2
Distributor rotation—counter-clockwise

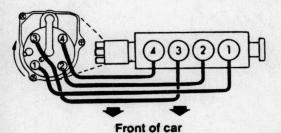

Front of car

1493cc & 1590 cc—1988 Civic
Firing Order: 1-3-4-2
Distributor rotation—clockwise

Breaker Points and Condenser

The points and condenser function as a circuit breaker for the primary circuit of the ignition system. They are used on 1973-79 models, which do not have a catalytic converter. The ignition coil must boost the 12V of electrical pressure supplied to it by the battery to about 20,000V in order to fire the spark plugs. To do this, the coil depends on the points and condenser for assistance.

The coil has a primary and a secondary circuit. When the ignition key is turned to the **ON** position, the battery supplies voltage to the primary side of the coil which passes the voltage on to the points. The points are connected to ground to complete the primary circuit. As the cam in the distributor turns, the points open and the primary circuit collapses. The magnetic force in the primary circuit of the coil cuts through the secondary circuit and increases the voltage in the secondary circuit to a level that is sufficient to fire the spark plugs. When the points open, the electrical charge contained in the primary circuit collapses, energizing the secondary circuit. If this electrical charge was not transferred elsewhere, the material on the contacts of the points would melt and that all-important gap between the contacts would start to change. If this gap is not maintained, the points will not break the primary circuit abruptly enough. If the primary circuit is not broken properly, the secondary circuit will not have enough voltage to fire the spark plugs. Enter the condenser.

The function of the condenser is to absorb the excessive voltage from the coil which jumps across the points when they open. This prevents the points from becoming pitted or burned.

There are two ways to check breaker point gap: with a feeler gauge or with a dwell meter. Either way the points are set, you are adjusting the amount of time (in degrees of distributor rotation) that the points remain open. If the points are adjusted with a feeler gauge, you are setting the maximum amount the points will open when the rubbing block on the points is on a high point of the distributor cam. When you adjust the points with a dwell meter, you are measuring the number of degrees (of distributor cam rotation) that the points will remain closed before they start to open as the distributor cam approaches the rubbing block of the points.

If you still do not understand how the points function, take a friend, go outside and remove the distributor cap from your engine. Have your friend operate the starter (make sure the transaxle is not in gear) as you look at the exposed parts of the distributor.

NOTE: *There are two rules that should always be followed when adjusting or replacing points. The points and condenser are a matched set; never replace one without*

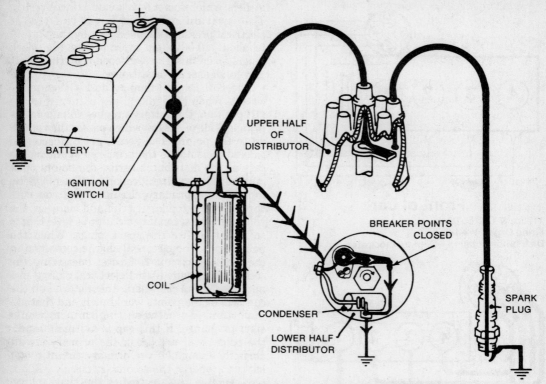

Primary side of ignition circuit is energized when breaker points are closed

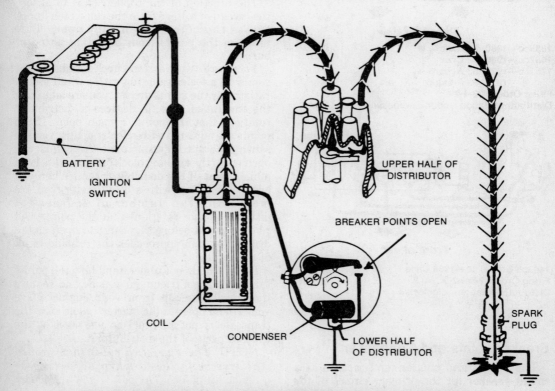

Secondary side of ignition circuit is energized when breaker points are open

replacing the other. *If the points are adjusted, the timing must also be adjusted.*

INSPECTION

1. Disconnect the high tension wire from the coil.

2. Unfasten the two retaining clips to remove the distributor cap.

3. Remove the rotor from the distributor shaft by pulling it straight up. Examine the condition of the rotor. If it is cracked or the metallic tip is excessively burned, replace it.

4. Pry the breaker points open with a screwdriver and examine the condition of the contact points. If the points are excessively worn, burned or pitted, they should be replaced.

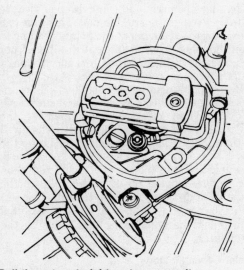

Pull the rotor straight up to remove it

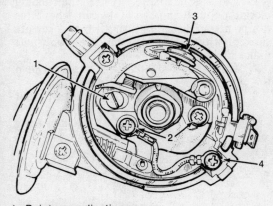

1. Point gap adjusting screw
2. Breaker point retaining screws
3. Primary lead wire connection
4. Ground wire connection

Distributor breaker plate details—all except CVCC Hondamatic. Notice that the rubbing block is on the high spot of the cam lobe

NOTE: *Contact points which have been used for several thousand miles will have a gray, rough surface but this is not necessarily an indication that they are malfunctioning. The roughness between the points matches so that a large contact area is maintained.*

5. If the points are in good condition, polish them with a point file.

NOTE: *DO NOT use emery cloth or sandpaper as they may leave particles on the points which could cause them to arc.*

After polishing the points, refer to the section following the breaker point replacement procedures for proper adjustment. If the points need replacing, refer to the following procedure.

REMOVAL AND INSTALLATION

1. Remove the small nut from the terminal screw located in the side of the distributor housing and remove the nut, screw, condenser wire and primary wire from the terminal. Remove the terminal from the slot in the distributor housing.

2. Remove the screw(s) which attaches the condenser to the outside of the distributor housing (most models) or to the breaker plate inside the distributor (CVCC Hondamatic models) and the condenser.

3. Using a Phillips head screwdriver, remove the ground wire-to-breaker point assembly screw and lift the end of the ground wire out of the way.

4. Remove the two the point assembly-to-breaker plate screws and the point assembly.

NOTE: *When removing or installing the point assembly screws, use a magnetic or locking screwdriver; trying to locate one of these tiny screws after you have dropped it can be an excruciating affair.*

Primary wire removal

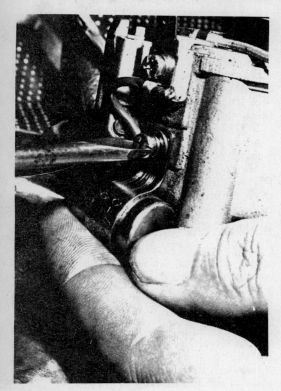

Condenser removal

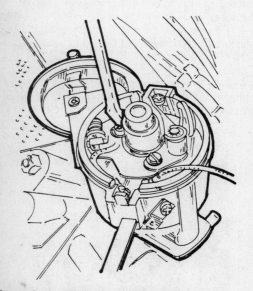

Removing point set retaining screws

5. Wipe all dirt and grease from the distributor plate and cam with a lint-free cloth. Apply a small amount of heat resistant lubricant to the distributor cam. Although the lube is supplied with most breaker point kits, you can buy it at any auto store if necessary.

6. Properly position the new points on the breaker plate of the distributor and secure with the two point screws. Attach the ground wire, with its screw, to the breaker plate assembly. Screw the condenser to its proper position on the distributor housing or breaker plate.

7. Fit the terminal into the distributor housing notch, attach the condenser and primary wires to the terminal screw, then, fasten with the nut.

DWELL ADJUSTMENT

Dwell or cam angle refers to the amount of time the points remain closed and is measured in degrees of distributor rotation. Dwell will vary according to the point gap, since dwell is a function of point gap. If the point gap is too wide, they open gradually, and dwell angle (the time they remain closed) is small. This wide gap causes excessive arcing at the points, leading to point burning. The insufficient dwell does not give the coil sufficient time to build up maximum energy, so coil output decreases.

If the point gap is too small, dwell is increased, the idle becomes rough and starting is difficult. When setting points, remember: the wider the point opening, the smaller the dwell or the smaller the point opening, the larger the dwell. When connecting a dwell meter, connect one negative lead (black) to a good ground on the engine and the positive lead (red) to the negative or distributor side of the coil. This terminal is easy to find, look for the terminal which has the small wire that leads to the distributor.

Feeler Gauge Method

1. Rotate the crankshaft pulley until the point gap is at its greatest (where the rubbing block is on the high point of the cam lobe). This can be accomplished by using either a remote starter switch or by rotating the crankshaft pulley by hand.

2. Using a 0.018-0.022″ feeler gauge between the points, a slight drag should be felt.

3. If no drag is felt or the feeler gauge cannot

Crankshaft pulley bolt access window—CVCC models

Rotating crankshaft pulley by hand

be inserted, loosen, but do not remove the two breaker point set screws.

4. Adjust the points as follows:

a. Using a screwdriver, insert it through the hole in the breaker point assembly and into the notch provided on the breaker plate.

b. Twist the screwdriver to open or close the points.

c. When the correct gap has been obtained, retighten the point set screws.

5. Recheck the point gap to be sure that it did not change when the breaker point attaching screws were tightened.

6. Align the rotor with the distributor shaft and push the rotor onto the shaft until it is fully seated.

7. Reinstall the distributor cap and the coil high tension wire.

Dwell Meter Method

1. Install a dwell/tach according to the manufacturer's instructions. See the preceding section for instructions on connecting the dwell meter.

2. Warm the engine and read the dwell meter; running at the specified idle speed.

3. If the point dwell is not within specifications, turn the engine **OFF** and adjust the point

Closeup of the points showing the rubbing block exactly on one of a high spot of the cam

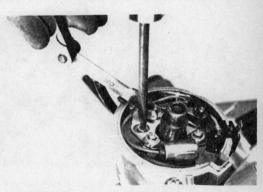

Adjusting point gap with feeler gauge

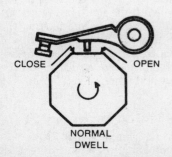
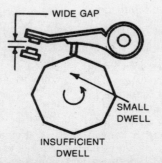
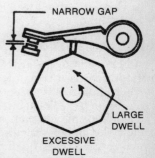

Dwell angle as a function of point gap

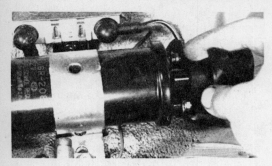

Ignition coil primary terminals

Taking a dwell reading. Notice the ground wire location

gap. Remember, increasing the point gap decreases the dwell angle and vice-versa.

4. Check the dwell reading again and adjust it as required.

Electronic Ignition

All 1980-88 vehicles are equipped with a magnetic pulse type electronic ignition system. This system eliminates the points and condenser, it requires no periodic maintenance.

The electronic ignition system uses a magnetic pulse/igniter distributor and a conventional ignition coil. The distributor cap, rotor, advance mechanism (vacuum and centrifugal) and secondary ignition wires are also of standard design. The distributor contains the stator, reluctor and pulse generator (pick-up coil) and igniter assembly.

During operation, the teeth of the reluctor align with the stator, a signal is generated by the pulse generator (pick-up coil) and sent to the igniter (module). The module, upon receiving the signal, opens the primary of the ignition coil. As the primary magnetic field collapses, a high voltage surge is developed in the secondary windings of the coil. This high voltage surge travels from the coil to the distributor cap and rotor through the secondary ignition wires to the spark plugs.

NOTE: *The electronic ignition system on your Honda requires special handling. Unlike conventional ignition systems, it is very sensitive to abrupt changes in voltage or voltage applied in the wrong direction electrically. Observe the precautions listed below to prevent expensive system damage!*

1. Always disconnect the battery cables before doing repair work on the electronic ignition system.

2. Always double check the markings on the battery and the routing of the cables before making connections, especially if the battery has been removed and might have been reinstalled in the opposite position. Hooking the battery connections up backwards will cause current to flow through the electronic ignition system in an improper way and may immediately damage it. Be careful, also when jumping the vehicle's battery with another for the same reasons.

3. Do not allow the wires connected to the pulse generator to touch other ignition wiring connections.

4. Abnormal voltage pulses may damage the system. Therefore, be sure to disconnect the battery before doing any work on the vehicle that is of an electrical nature. This includes charging the battery and replacing small bulbs.

5. Connect any electrical tachometer to the negative (−) terminal of the ignition coil − *not to any other connection!*.

6. Always double check any connection (you are making) involving the ignition system before reconnecting the battery and putting the system into operation.

7. When cranking the engine for compression testing or similar purposes, disconnect the coil wire at the distributor.

RELUCTOR GAP ADJUSTMENT

1. Remove the distributor cap and the rotor.

2. Turn the crankshaft to align the reluctor points with the stator ends.

3. Using a non-metallic feeler gauge, check

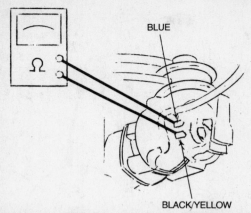

When cranking the engine for a compression test, disconnect the coil wire at the distributor to protect the ignition system

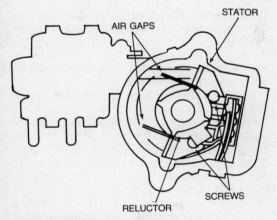

Inspecting the reluctor-to-stator air gaps

the air reluctor-to-stator air gaps; they must be equal.

4. To adjust, loosen the stator-to-distributor screws, adjust the stator-to-reluctor air gaps and tighten the screws.

5. Recheck the air gaps.

PARTS REPLACEMENT

Retailers are offer Tune-Up kits consisting of a pick-up coil, igniter unit (if used), reluctor, rotor and distributor cap.

Reluctor

1. Disconnect the negative battery terminal.
2. Remove the distributor cap and the rotor.
3. Using two medium pry bars, pry the reluctor from the distributor shaft; be careful not to damage the reluctor or stator.

NOTE: *When installing the reluctor, be sure the manufacturer's number is facing upward.*

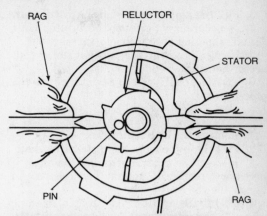

Removing the reluctor from the distributor

4. To install, push the reluctor onto the distributor shaft. When installing the reluctor roll pin, be sure to position the pin gap facing away from the distributor shaft.

Pickup Coil

1. Refer to the Reluctor Removal and Installation procedures in this section and remove the reluctor.
2. Disconnect the electrical connector from the pickup coil.
3. Remove the pickup coil-to-distributor screws and pull the pickup coil from the distributor.
4. To install, use a new pickup coil (if necessary) and reverse the removal procedures.

Igniter Unit

On the Accord (1983-88), Prelude (1983-88) and Civic (1986-88), fuel injected engines, Toyo Denso introduced an igniter unit which is installed on the side of the distributor housing.

1. Disconnect the negative battery terminal.
2. Remove the igniter cover-to-distributor screws and the cover.

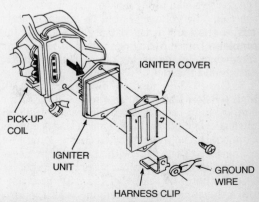

Removing the igniter unit from the distributor—Toyo Denso model

3. Pull the igniter unit from the distributor.

4. If necessary, perform the Igniter Unit Troubleshooting procedures in this section.

5. Using silicone grease, apply it to the connector housing.

6. To install, reverse the removal procedures.

Rotor

1. Remove the distributor cap.

2. Pull the rotor from the distributor shaft.

3. Inspect the rotor burns and damage; if necessary, replace it. It may be necessary to lightly file the tip.

4. To install, apply a light coat of silicone grease to the rotor tip, align the rotor with the distributor shaft and push it into place and reverse the removal procedures.

TROUBLESHOOTING

Troubleshooting the electronic ignition system is a simple procedure. Use a quality electrical multimeter — a tester which will measure voltage and resistance precisely.

1. To verify that the electronic ignition system is malfunctioning, first carefully pull the coil wire out of the coil. Then, hold the wire so that the metal parts of the coil tower and wire are ¼" apart. Have someone crank the engine with the ignition switch so the ignition will be turned **ON**. If there is spark, the electronic ignition system is working, proceed with routine checks for spark at the plugs and inspection of the ignition wires, cap and rotor to be certain the rest of the ignition system is operable. If there is a large, fat spark, reconnect the coil high tension wire securely; if there is no spark or if the spark is weak, proceed with the tests below.

2. With the ignition switch still **ON**, switch the multimeter into the 12V range. Connect the ground (black) lead of the meter to a good, clean ground that is not covered with paint. Connect the positive lead to the positive (+) terminal of the coil. The voltage should be approximately 12V — the same as the battery. If not, look for problems in the wiring connector at the coil or somewhere in the wiring between the ignition switch and the coil.

3. On 1973-85 models, disconnect the coil high tension lead, this time at the distributor end. (Skip to the next step for testing 1986-88 models). Ground the high tension lead securely. Connect the voltmeter across the (+) and (−) connectors of the coil, with the black or negative lead at the (−) connector. Set the meter on a scale that will read less than 5V precisely. Have someone crank the engine with the key; the reading must be 1-3V. If the reading is within the specified range, check the coil primary

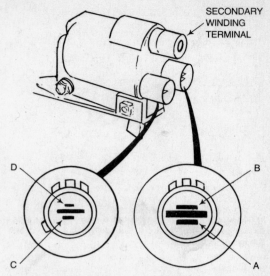

SECONDARY WINDING TERMINAL

On '86 models, the primary winding terminals are identified as shown for testing coil resistance. See the text.

and secondary resistance as in Step 4. Otherwise, proceed with Step 5.

4. On all models, turn the ignition switch **OFF**. Set your meter to read resistance (Ohms). Choose a scale that will measure the resistance specified effectively. Make sure the coil is at approximately 70°F (21°C). On 1986-88 models, disconnect the coil high tension wire and the two primary connectors. On all models, connect the two meter probes to the two primary (small) terminals of the coil. On 1973-85 models, these are the two small connectors that use nuts to retain the coil wires. On 1986-88 models, these are marked **A** and **D** in the illustration. Read the resistance; it must be 1.0-1.3Ω (1980), 1.06-1.24Ω (1981-85) or 1,215-1,485Ω (1986-88). Now read the secondary resistance. Connect the meter probes between the (+) primary terminal and the large, secondary connector — the coil tower on all models 1973-85. On 1986-88 models, connect the ohmmeter between the **A** terminal and the coil tower or **Secondary Winding Terminal** (both are shown in the illustration). This resistance must be 7,400-11,000Ω on models (1973-85). On 1986-88 models, it must be 11,074-11,526Ω. On 1986-88 coils, read the resistance between **B** and **D** terminals, also. It should be approximately 2,200Ω. If any test is failed, replace the coil. If all tests were passed, check the spark plug wire resistance by disconnecting each wire at both ends and connecting a probe from the meter to either end of the wire. Resistance must be no more than 25,000Ω. Otherwise, the wire must be replaced. Remember to check the coil-to-distributor wire as well as the individual

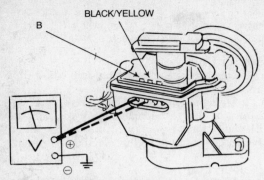

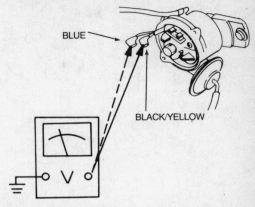

On the Toyo Denso type distributor for models up to 1985, measure the voltage at each of the terminals on the left side; the igniter unit continuity is measured between the same two terminals. The Blue is on the left and the Black/Yellow is the next one over, going to the right. On '86 and later fuel injected models, the locations are different. Note the locations of the Blue and Black/Yellow wires before disconnecting them.

View of the igniter unit lead wires—Hitachi

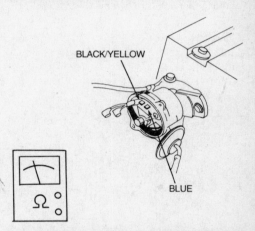

View of the igniter unit termianls—Hitachi

plug wires. Check the wires one at a time to avoid mixing up the firing order.

5. Note the locations for the blue and black/yellow connectors. Disconnect the lead wires from the igniter unit. Turn the ignition switch **ON**. Measure voltage between the blue wire and a good, clean ground. Do the same for the black/yellow wire. In both cases, battery voltage MUST be present at both connectors. Otherwise, trace the wiring back through the ignition switch to find the problem. Turn the ignition switch **OFF**. Now, measure the resistance in the igniter with the meter set to the **R x 100** scale. Connect the positive probe onto the black/yellow distributor terminal and the negative onto the blue distributor terminal. There must be continuity. Now, reverse the probes so that the positive probe is on the blue terminal and the negative probe is on the black/yellow. There must be NO continuity with the probes in this position. If the continuity test is failed either way, replace the igniter. On 1986-88 models with fuel injection, you can also test the pick-up coil resistance. Proceed with Step 6.

6. Connect the ohmmeter probes between the blue wire and green wire distributor terminals. Pick-up coil resistance must be approximately 750Ω. Otherwise, replace the pick-up coil.

DIAGNOSIS AND TESTING

Igniter Unit Test

1983-88 ACCORD AND PRELUDE (WITH HITACHI TYPE)
1984-85 CIVIC
1986-87 CIVIC (WITH CARBURETED ENGINE)

1. Disconnect lead wires from igniter unit.
2. Using a voltmeter, check the voltage be-

tween blue wire and body ground, then, black/yellow wire to body ground, with ignition switch **ON**. There should be battery voltage.

3. If no voltage, check wiring to igniter unit.
4. Using a ohmmeter, set the scale on the **R x 100** position, disconnect the lead wires and check the continuity.
5. Place the positive (red) probe on the black/yellow wire terminal and negative (black) probe on the blue wire terminal; no continuity should be read on ohmmeter.
6. Place the positive (red) probe on the blue wire terminal and negative (black) probe on the black/yellow wire terminal; continuity should be read on the ohmmeter.
7. If ohmmeter readings are not as specified in Steps 5 and 6, replace igniter unit.

1983-85 ACCORD
1983-86 PRELUDE (WITH TOYO DENSO TYPE)
1986 CIVIC (WITH FUEL INJECTION ENGINE)

Igniter Unit

1. Disconnect lead wires from igniter unit.
2. Using a voltmeter, check the voltage be-

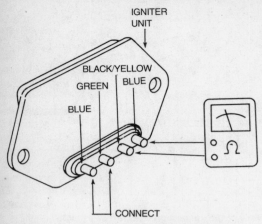

View of the igniter unit lead wires—Toyo denso

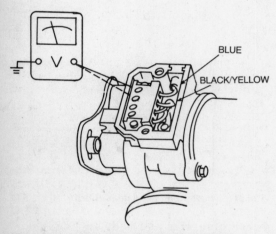

View of the igniter unit terminals—Toyo Denso

tween the blue wire and ground, then, the black/yellow wire to ground, with the ignition switch **ON**; there should be battery voltage.

3. If no voltage, check wiring to igniter unit.

Pick-up Coil

1. Using an ohmmeter, set the scale on the **R x 100** position, disconnect the lead wires and check the continuity between the igniter unit terminals.

2. Place probes of meter to black/yellow wire terminal and blue wire terminal. No continuity should be read on ohmmeter.

3. Reverse the meter probes. Continuity should be read on ohmmeter.

NOTE: *Polarity may change with different meters. Determine polarity of your ohmmeter before conducting this test.*

4. If ohmmeter readings are not as specified in Steps 2 and 3, replace igniter unit.

1986-88 ACCORD
1987-88 CIVIC (WITH FUEL INJECTED ENGINE)
1987-88 PRELUDE (WITH TOYO DENSO TYPE)

Igniter Unit

1. Remove igniter cover and pull out igniter unit.

2. Using a voltmeter, check the voltage between the **Bu^1** terminal and **ground**, then, the **Bl/Y** wire terminal and **ground**, with ignition switch **ON**; battery voltage should be present.

Pick-up Coil

1. Using an ohmmeter, measure the resistance between the **G** and **Bu^2** terminals on pick-up coil. Pick-up coil resistance should be approximately 750Ω @ 70°F (21°C); replace the pick-up coil if resistance is not within specifications.

NOTE: *Resistance will vary with coil temperature.*

2. Using an ohmmeter, set the dial on the **R x 100** scale.

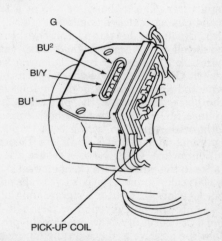

View of the pickup coil terminal locations

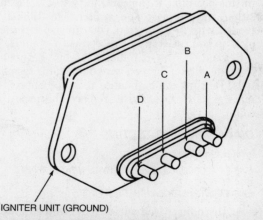

View of the igniter unit terminal locations

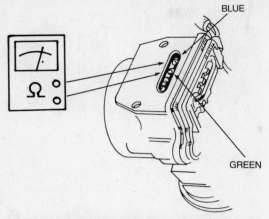

BLUE

GREEN

Testing the pickup coil—Civic—fuel injected

3. Check the continuity between the **A** and **B** terminals; there should be continuity in only one direction.

4. Adjust the ohmmeter to the **R x 100,000** scale.

5. Connect the positive (red) probe to the **D** terminal and the negative (black) probe to **ground**; the reading should be 50,000Ω or more @ 70°F (21°C).

NOTE: *The resistance will vary with the temperature.*

6. To install, apply silicone grease to the igniter connector housing and reverse the removal procedures.

Pick-up Coil Test

1985-88 CIVIC WITH FUEL INJECTED ENGINE

1. Using an ohmmeter, connect the probes to blue and green wire terminals and measure resistance. Resistance should be approximately 750Ω @ 70°F (21°C).

2. If not to specifications, check and/or replace as necessary.

Distributor Top End Inspection

1984-88 ACCORD, PRELUDE AND CIVIC

1. Check to be sure that air gaps are equal.

2. If necessary, back off screws and move stator as required to adjust.

3. Check for rough or pitted rotor and cap terminals.

4. Scrape or file off carbon deposits. Smooth rotor terminal with an oil stone or No. 600 sandpaper if rough.

5. Apply a thin coat of silicone grease to tip of rotor.

Ignition Timing

Ignition timing is the measurement, in degrees of crankshaft rotation, at the instant the spark plugs in the cylinders fire, in relation to the location of the piston, while the piston is on its compression stroke.

Ideally, the air/fuel mixture in the cylinder will be ignited (by the spark plug) and just beginning its rapid expansion as the piston passes top dead center (TDC) of the compression stroke. If this happens, the piston will be beginning the power stroke just as the compressed (by the movement of the piston) and ignited (by the spark plug) air/fuel mixture starts to expand. The expansion of the air/fuel mixture will force the piston down on the power stroke and turn the crankshaft.

It takes a fraction of a second for the spark from the plug to completely ignite the mixture in the cylinder. Because of this, the spark plug must fire before the piston reaches TDC, if the mixture is to be completely ignited as the piston passes TDC. This measurement is given in degrees (of crankshaft rotation) before the piston reaches top dead center (BTDC). If the ignition timing setting is 6° BTDC, this means that the spark plug must fire at a time when the piston for that cylinder is 6° BTDC of its compression stroke. However, this only holds true while your engine is at idle speed.

As you accelerate from idle, the speed of your engine (rpm) increases. The increase in rpm means that the pistons are now traveling up and down much faster. Because of this, the spark plugs will have to fire even sooner if the mixture is to be completely ignited as the piston passes TDC. To accomplish this, the distributor incorporates means to advance the timing of the spark as engine speed increases.

The distributor has two means of advancing the ignition timing. One is called centrifugal advance and is actuated by weights in the distributor. The other is called vacuum advance and is controlled in that large circular housing on the side of the distributor.

In addition, some Honda distributors have a vacuum retard mechanism which is contained in the same housing on the side of the distributor as the vacuum advance. Models having two hoses going to the distributor vacuum housing have both vacuum advance and retard. The function of this mechanism is to regulate the timing of the ignition spark under certain engine conditions. This causes more complete burning of the air/fuel mixture in the cylinder and consequently lowers exhaust emissions.

If ignition timing is set too far advanced (BTDC), the ignition and burning of the air/fuel mixture in the cylinder will try to oppose the motion of the piston in the cylinder while it is still traveling upward. This causes engine **ping**. If the ignition timing is too far retarded (after, or ATDC), the piston will have already started down on the power stroke when the air/fuel mixture ignites and expands. This will cause the piston to be forced down with much less potency. This will result in rough engine performance and lack of power and gas mileage.

CHECKING AND ADJUSTING

Honda recommends that the ignition timing be checked at 12,000 mile intervals (1973-74), 15,000 mile intervals (1975-78) or when problems are suspected (1979-82). On 1983-88 models, check the timing and adjust (if necessary) every 60,000 miles.

NOTE: *If the vehicle is equipped with a conventional ignition system, the timing should always be adjusted after installing new points or adjusting the dwell angle.*

On all non-CVCC engines (including fuel injection engines) and the 1342cc & 1488cc CVCC engines, the timing marks are located on the crankshaft pulley, with a pointer on the timing belt cover. All are visible from the driver's side of the engine compartment. On all CVCC engines except the 1342cc & 1488cc, the timing marks are located on the flywheel (manual transaxle) or torque converter drive plate (automatic transaxle), with a pointer on the rear of the cylinder block. All are visible from the front right side of the engine compartment after removing a special rubber access plug in the timing mark window. In all cases, the timing is checked with the engine warmed to operating temperature (176°F [80°C]), idling in Neutral (manual transaxle) or Drive (automatic transaxle), and with all vacuum hoses connected.

1. Stop the engine and install a tachometer to the engine. The positive lead connects to the distributor side terminal of the ignition coil and the negative lead to a good ground, such as an engine bolt.

NOTE: *On some models you will have to pull back the rubber ignition coil cover to reveal the terminals.*

2. Following the manufacturers instructions, install a timing light to the engine. The positive and negative leads connect to their corresponding battery terminals and the spark plug lead to No. 1 spark plug. The No. 1 spark plug is the one at the driver's side of the engine compartment.

3. Make sure that all wires are clear of the cooling fan and hot exhaust manifolds.

4. Set the parking brake and block the front wheels. Start the engine. Check that the idle speed is set to specifications with the transaxle in **Neutral** (manual transaxle) or **Drive** (automatic transaxle).

5. If the distributor is equipped with a vacuum advance mechanism, disconnect the hos-

Timing marks on the non-CVCC engines. The white mark is TDC

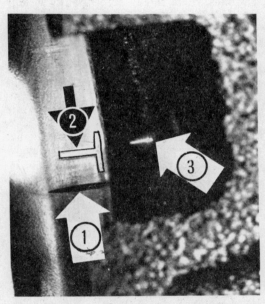

View of the typical timing marks (thru 1981)—all engines except 1342cc and 1488cc Arrow "1" is the red notch, which is the ignition timing mark Arrow "2" is the TDC mark. The "T" has been outlined for clarity in this picture Arrow "3" is the ignition pointer

e(s), plug it (them) and reinstall on the vacuum advance.

NOTE: *Any engine speed other than specified, the distributor advance or retard mechanisms will actuate, leading to an erroneous timing adjustment.*

6. Point the timing light at the timing marks.

NOTE: *On Non-CVCC and 1342cc & 1488cc CVCC engines, align the pointer with the* **F** *or* **red** *notch on the crankshaft pulley. On CVCC engines except 1342cc & 1488cc, align* the pointer with the red notch on the flywheel or torque converter drive plate (except on vehicles where the timing specification is TDC in which case the **T** or **white** notch is used).

7. If necessary to adjust the timing, loosen the distributor holddown (clamp) bolt(s) and/or nut, then, slowly rotate the distributor in the required direction while observing the timing marks.

CAUTION: *DO NOT grasp the top of the distributor cap while the engine is running, as you might get a nasty shock. Instead, grab the distributor housing to rotate.*

8. To complete the adjustment operation, tighten the holddown bolt, taking care not to disturb the adjustment. If equipped with a vacuum advance mechanism, unplug and reinstall the hose(s).

NOTE: *Some models are equipped with two bolts, others are equipped with a bolt and a nut, which may be loosened to adjust ignition timing. If there is a smaller bolt on the underside of the distributor swivel mounting plate, it should not be loosened, unless you cannot obtain a satisfactory adjustment using the upper bolt. Its purpose is to provide an extra*

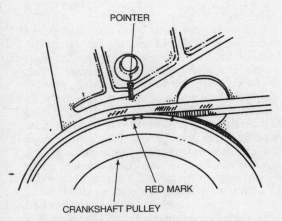

View of the timing marks—1342cc and 1488cc engines

Loosen this distributor hold-down (clamp) bolt to rotate the distributor for ignition timing adjustments

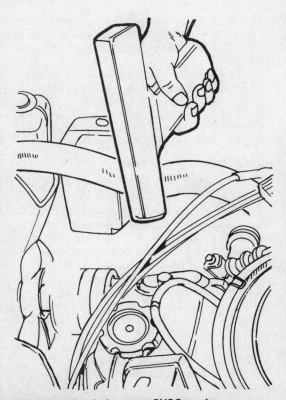

Checking the timing on a CVCC engine

If the timing cannot be adjusted within the range of the upper (larger) clamp bolt, this smaller one can be loosened to provide extra adjustment

Distributor rotor at no. 1 piston Top Dead Center (TDC) position

range of adjustment, such as in cases where the distributor was removed and then installed one tooth off.

Valve Arrangements

All valves are identified, starting from the front (camshaft sprocket) of the engine to the rear; Intake — I, Exhaust — E and Auxiliary — A.

Non-CVCC (1973-78)

Right Side: **I-I-I-I** (front-to-rear)
Left Side: **E-E-E-E** (front-to-rear)

Accord (1976-81), Civic CVCC (1975-83) and Prelude (1979-81)

Right Side: **I-E-E-I-I-E-E-I** (front-to-rear)
Left Side: **A-A-A-A** (front-to-rear)

Civic (1984-88) and Civic CRX (1985-88)

Right Side: **I-I-I-I-I-I-I-I** (front-to-rear)
Left Side: **A-E-E-A-A-E-E-A** (front-to-rear)

Accord (1982-83) and Prelude (1982)

Right Side: **E-I-E-I-I-E-I-E** (front-to-rear)
Left Side: **A-A-A-A** (front-to-rear)

Accord (1984-85) and Prelude (1983)

Right Side: **I-I-I-I-I-I-I-I** (front-to-rear)
Left Side: **A-E-A-E-E-A-E-A** (front-to-rear)

Accord (1986-88) and Prelude (1984-88)

Right Side: **I-I-I-I-I-I-I-I** (front-to-rear)
Left Side: **E-E-E-E** (front-to-rear)

Valve Lash

Valve adjustment is one factor which determines how far the intake and exhaust valves will open into the cylinder. If the valve clear-ance is too large, part of the lift of the camshaft will be used up in removing the excessive clearance, thus the valves will not be opened far enough. This condition has several effects. The valve train components will emit a tapping noise as they take up the excessive clearance and also as they shut very abruptly. Also, the engine will perform poorly, as the valves will not cause the engine to breathe in the normal manner. Finally, the carburetor will produce a richer than normal mixture, increasing emissions and, possibly, fouling spark plugs over a great length of time.

If the valve clearance is too small, the intake and exhaust valves will not fully seat on the cylinder head when they close. When a valve seats on the cylinder head it does two things: it seals the combustion chamber so none of the gases in the cylinder can escape and it cools itself by transferring some of the heat it absorbed from the combustion process through the cylinder head and into the engine cooling system. Also, the change in valve timing that occurs will lean out the mixture, causing hesitation and possible burning of the valves. Therefore, if the valve clearance is too small, the engine will run poorly (due to gases escaping from the combustion chamber and lean mixture) and the valves will tend to overheat and warp (since they cannot transfer heat unless they are touching the seat in the cylinder head).

Honda recommends that the valve clearance be checked at 12,000 mile intervals (1973-74 models) or 15,000 mile intervals (1975-88 models).

NOTE: *While all valve adjustments must be as accurate as possible, it is better to have the valve adjustment slightly loose than slightly tight, as burned valves may result from overly tight adjustments. Valves that are only slightly loose will not damage the engine.*

Non-CVCC Models — 1973-78

1. Adjust the valves when the engine is **Cold** (100°F [38°C] or less).

2. Remove the valve cover and align the TDC (Top Dead Center) mark on the crankshaft pulley with the index mark on the timing belt cover. The TDC notch is the one immediately following the 5° BTDC (red) notch used for setting ignition timing.

3. When the No. 1 cylinder is at TDC on the compression stroke, check and adjust the following valves (numbered from the crankshaft pulley end of the engine):

Intake — Nos. 1 and 2 cylinders
Exhaust — Nos. 1 and 3 cylinders

To adjust the valves, perform the following procedures:

a. Using a feeler gauge, check the valve clearance between the tip of the rocker arm

Valve adjustment—CVCC and non-CVCC models

Adjusting auxiliary valve clearance—CVCC models

and the top of the valve; there should be a slight drag on the feeler gauge.

b. If there is no drag or the gauge cannot be inserted, loosen the valve adjusting screw locknut.

c. Using a screwdriver, turn the adjusting screw to obtain the proper clearance.

d. Hold the adjusting screw and tighten the locknut.

e. Recheck the clearance before reinstalling the valve cover.

4. Rotate the crankshaft 360°, position the No. 4 piston on TDC its compression stroke, then, check and/or adjust the following valves by performing the procedures in Step 3.

Intake – Nos. 3 and 4 cylinders.

Exhaust – Nos. 2 and 4 cylinders.

5. To install the valve cover, use a new gasket, sealant (if necessary) and reverse the removal procedures.

CVCC Models

1975-78

The engine must be **Cold** (cylinder head temperature below 100°F [38°C]) before performing this procedure.

1. Remove the valve cover.

2. From the front of the engine, take a look at the forward face of the camshaft timing belt gear. When the No. 1 cylinder is at Top Dead Center (TDC), the keyway for the woodruff key retaining the timing gear to the camshaft will be facing upward. On 1976-78 models, the word **UP** will be at the top of the gear. Double-check this by checking the distributor rotor position. Using a piece of chalk or crayon, mark the No. 1 spark plug wire position on the distributor cap; then, remove the cap and check that the rotor faces that mark.

3. With the No. 1 cylinder at the TDC of it compression stroke, adjust the following valves (numbered from the crankshaft pulley end of the engine):

Intake – Nos. 1 and 2 cylinders.

Auxiliary – Nos. 1 and 2 cylinders.

Exhaust – Nos. 1 and 3 cylinders.

Adjust the valves as follows:

a. Using a feeler gauge, position it between the tip of the rocker arm and the top of the valve; there should be a slight drag on the feeler gauge.

b. If there is no drag or if the gauge cannot

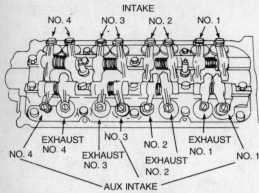

Location of the intake, exhaust and auxiliary valves on the CVCC engines—others are similar

be inserted, loosen the valve adjusting screw locknut.

c. Using a screwdriver, turn the adjusting screw to obtain the proper clearance.

d. Hold the adjusting screw and tighten the locknut.

e. Recheck the clearance before reinstalling the valve cover.

4. Rotate the crankshaft 360° to position the No. 4 cylinder on the TDC of its compression stroke; this will correspond to an 180° movement of the distributor rotor and camshaft timing gear. The rotor will now be pointing opposite the mark made for the No. 1 cylinder. The camshaft timing gear keyway or **UP** mark will now be at the bottom (6 o'clock position). Adjust the remaining valves:

Intake — Nos. 3 and 4 cylinders.
Auxiliary Intake — Nos. 3 and 4 cylinders.
Exhaust — Nos. 2 and 4 cylinders.

1979-88 EXCEPT THE 1955cc DOHC ENGINE

Be aware the engines for this time period vary in the location of the intake, exhaust and auxiliary (intake) valves (see valve arrangements). Exhaust valves align with the exhaust manifold tubes and the intake valves with intake tubes.

NOTE: *The valves cannot be adjusted until*

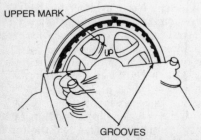

UPPER MARK

GROOVES

Positioning the camshaft to adjust the valves for No 1 cylinder—1979–88 engines

the engine has cooled to below 100°F (38°C).

1. Remove the valve cover.

2. Using a wrench on the crankshaft pulley bolt, rotate the crankshaft until the No. 1 cylinder is on TDC of its compression stroke; the **UP**, round mark or semicircular cut in the bottom of the opening on the rear of the camshaft pulley aligns with the small mark on the rear of the timing belt housing and the two TDC marks on the rear of the pulley align with the cylinder head surface.

3. To double check the engine's position, perform the following procedures:

a. Remove the distributor cap; the distributor rotor should align with the No. 1 plug wire.

b. Adjust all of the valves for No. 1 cylinder.

NOTE: *On 1984-88 Civics intake (and auxiliary) valves are adjusted to 0.18-0.23mm and the exhaust valve is adjusted to 0.23-0.28mm (Std and Si) or 0.18-0.23mm (HF). On 1979-83 Civics, the intake and auxiliary valves are adjusted to 0.13-0.18mm and exhaust valves to 0.18-0.23mm. On Preludes and Accords, the intakes are adjusted to 0.13-0.18mm and the exhausts to 0.25-0.30mm.*

c. Loosen the locknut. Using a flat feeler gauge, place it between the top of the valve and the adjusting stud. If the clearance is under, rotate the stud outward with a screwdriver until the blade can be inserted between the two items, then, tighten the stud very gently just until it touches the gauge. A slight drag on the gauge should be felt by moving the gauge in and out — it must not be pinched between the two parts. Hold the position of the stud with a screwdriver, then, tighten the locknut securely but not extremely tight — 14 ft. lbs. is the recommended torque (10 ft. lbs. for the auxiliary valve, which are smaller). Slide the gauge in and out to make sure the required clearance has been maintained. If not, readjust the valve. Repeat the procedure for the remaining No. 1 cylinder valves.

NOTE: *As the work progresses, keep double checking that you are using the proper gauge for the type of valve being adjusted.*

4. Rotate the crankshaft counterclockwise 180° (the camshaft turns 90°). Now, the TDC groove on the outer edge of the camshaft pulley should be aligned with the indentation on the timing belt cover. The distributor rotor will point to the No. 3 cylinder plug wire; the No. 3 cylinder should be on TDC of its compression stroke. Perform the same adjustment procedures as you did for the No. 1 cylinder.

NOTE: *On the Civic 1342cc engines, there is no TDC groove. For these engines, perform* the same adjustment procedures as you did for the No. 1 cylinder.

5. Rotate the crankshaft counterclockwise 180°. Now the TDC grooves will again be visible and the distributor rotor will point to No. 4 cylinder's plug wire. The No. 4 cylinder should be at the TDC of its compression stroke. Perform the same adjustment procedures as you did for the No. 1 cylinder.

6. Rotate the crankshaft counterclockwise 180°, until the mark on the rear of the pulley aligns with the indentation on the belt cover and the distributor rotor points to No. 2 plug wire. The **UP** mark should also be visible, on the left side of the camshaft pulley. Perform the same adjustment procedures as you did for the No. 1 cylinder.

NOTE: *On the Civic 1342cc engines, the TDC groove on the camshaft sprocket will be aligned with the indentation on the timing belt cover.*

7. To install the valve cover, use a new gasket, sealant (if necessary) and reverse the removal procedures. On late model Civics and CRX, torque in sequence, turning the screws two turns at a time. Torque to 9 ft. lbs. For high valve covers, which use just two, crown type nuts, torque them evenly in several stages to 7 ft. lbs.

1955cc Dual Overhead Cam Engine

NOTE: *The valves should be adjusted cold when the cylinder head temperature is less than 100°F (38°C). Adjustment is the same for the intake and exhaust valves.*

1. Remove the valve cover as outlined through out this section. Remove the distributor cap.

2. Set the number one cylinder (piston) at top dead center (TDC). The **UP** marks on the pulleys should be at the top, and the TDC grooves on the back side of the pulley should align with the cylinder head surface. The distributor rotor should be pointing towards the number one spark plug wire.

3. At this point the valves on the number one cylinder can be adjusted.

NOTE: *To adjust the valves loosen the locknut and turn the adjusting screw until the proper flat feeler gauge slides back and forth with a slight amount of drag (0.08-0.13mm on intake and 0.15-0.20mm on exhaust). Hold the adjusting screw and tighten the locknut. Recheck the valve clearance again. Repeat this adjustment as necessary.*

4. Rotate the crankshaft 180° counterclockwise (the cam pulley will turn 90°). The **UP** marks should be at the exhaust side. The distributor rotor should point to the number three

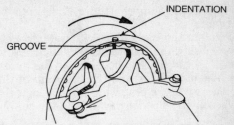

Positioning the camshaft to adjust the valves for No 3 cylinder—1979–88 engines

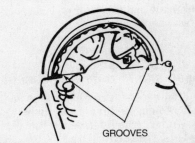

Positioning the camshaft to adjust the valves for No 4 cylinder—1979–88 engines

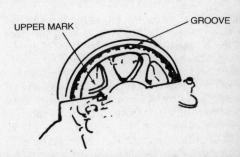

Positioning the camshaft to adjust the valves for No 2 cylinder—1979–88 engines

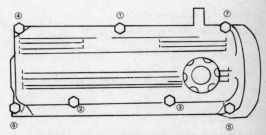

On the Civic and CRX, tighten the valve cover bolts in the order shown to 9 ft. lbs.

spark plug wire. At this point the valves on number three cylinder can be adjusted.

5. Rotate the crankshaft 180° counterclockwise to bring the number four piston up to TDC. Both **UP** marks should be at the bottom and the distributor rotor should point to the number four spark plug wire. At this point the

valves on the number four cylinder can be adjusted.

6. Rotate the crankshaft 180° counterclockwise to bring the number two cylinder up to TDC. The **UP** marks should be at the intake side. The distributor rotor should point at the number two spark plug wire. At this point the valves on the number two cylinder can be adjusted.

7. Once all the valves have been adjusted and rechecked, replace the valve cover gaskets with new gaskets and reinstall the valve covers on the engine. Also reinstall the distributor cap. Start the engine and check for oil leaks, be sure to road test the vehicle.

Idle Speed and Mixture Adjustment

This section contains only adjustments which apply to engine tune-up — namely, idle speed and mixture adjustments (on earlier models). Descriptions of the carburetors/throttle bodies used and complete adjustment procedures can be found in Chapter 5.

Idle speed and mixture adjustment is the last step in any tune-up. Prior to making the final carburetor adjustments, make sure that the spark plugs, points and condenser (if used), dwell angle, ignition timing and valve clearance have all been checked, serviced and adjusted (if necessary). If any of these tune-up items have been overlooked, it may be difficult to obtain a proper adjustment.

NOTE: *All adjustments must be made with the engine fully warmed to operating temperatures.*

CARBURETED MODELS

Civic 1170cc — Hitachi 2-bbl (1973)

1. Set the parking brake and block the front wheels.

2. Turn the headlights **ON** and the cooling fan **OFF**.

3. From the radiator base, on the engine side, disconnect the electrical leads from either the cooling fan motor or the thermoswitch (screwed into the base of the radiator).

4. If equipped with a manual transaxle, position the shift selector in **Neutral**; if equipped with a Hondamatic transaxle, position the shift selector **gear 1**.

5. From the carburetor, remove the limiter cap and turn the idle mixture screw counterclockwise, until engine speed drops, then, turn the idle speed screw in the reverse direction (clockwise) until the engine reaches its highest

rpm; if the idle speed is higher than specifications, repeat Steps 2 and 5.

6. Continue to turn the idle mixture screw clockwise to obtain the specified rpm drop:
4-speed — 40 rpm.
Hondamatic — 20 rpm.

7. Replace the limiter cap and reconnect the cooling fan lines.

Non-CVCC Civic — Hitachi 2-bbl (1974-77)

1. Set the parking brake and block the front wheels.

2. Turn the headlights **ON** and the radiator cooling fan **OFF**. To make sure that the cooling fan is turned **OFF** while you are making your adjustments, disconnect the fan leads.

CAUTION: *DO NOT leave the cooling fan leads disconnected for any longer than necessary, as the engine may overheat.*

3. If equipped with a manual transaxle, position the shift selector in **Neutral**; if equipped with a Hondamatic transaxle, position in shift selector in **gear 1**.

4. From the carburetor, remove the plastic limiter cap from the idle mixture screw.

5. Using a tachometer, connect it to the engine with the positive lead connected to the distributor side (terminal) of the coil and the negative lead to a good ground. On 1976 models, disconnect the breather hose from the valve cover.

6. Start the engine. To adjust, turn the mixture screw (turn counterclockwise to richen), then, the idle speed screw for the best quality idle at 870 rpm (manual transaxle) or 770 rpm (automatic transaxle in gear).

7. Turn the idle mixture screw (clockwise), until the idle speed drops to 800 rpm (manual transaxle) or 750 rpm (automatic transaxle in gear).

8. Replace the limiter cap, connect the cooling fan and disconnect the tachometer.

CVCC Models — Keihin 3-bbl (1977-79)

1. Apply the parking brake and block the front wheels.

2. Start the engine and allow it to reach normal operating temperatures, the cooling fan should turn **ON**.

NOTE: *If the fan does not turn **ON**, load the electrical system (for purposes of adjusting the idle speed), by turning the high speed heater blower **ON** instead. Do not have both the cooling fan and heater blower operating simultaneously, as this will load the engine too much and lower the idle speed abnormally.*

3. Turn the headlights **ON**. Position the transaxle's shift selector in **Neutral** (manual transaxle) or in **2nd (Hi) Gear** (Hondamatic).

Idle speed and mixture screw locations on the Keihin 3-bbl carburetor used on the CVCC engines. Arrow 1 is the idle speed screw, and arrow 2 is the mixture screw. The 2-bbl carburetor used on the non-CVCC engines is similar

4. Using a tachometer, connect it to the engine with the positive lead connected to the distributor side (terminal) of the coil and the negative lead to a good ground.

5. Remove the plastic cap from the idle mixture screw. Start the engine and rotate the idle mixture screw counterclockwise (rich), until the highest rpm is achieved. Then, adjust the idle speed screw to 910 rpm (manual transaxle) or 810 rpm (automatic transaxle in 2nd gear).

6. Finally, lean out the idle mixture (turn mixture screw clockwise) until the idle speed drops to 700 rpm (manual transaxle) or 650 rpm (automatic transaxle in 2nd gear).

NOTE: *If the idle speed cannot be adjusted properly, check and/or adjust the throttle cable.*

7. Replace the limiter cap (make sure the pointer is facing 180° away from the boss on the carburetor base) and disconnect the tachometer.

Carbureted Engines (1980-88)

Changes in the carburetors have made the adjustment of the idle mixture impossible without a propane enrichment system not available to the general public. The idle speed may be adjusted as follows:

1. Operate the engine until normal operating temperatures are reached.

2. Remove the vacuum hose from the intake air control diaphragm and clamp the hose end.

3. Using a tachometer, connect it to the engine.

4. With the headlights, heater blower, rear window defroster, cooling fan and air conditioner **OFF**, adjust the idle speed by turning the throttle stop screw to the rpm listed in the **Tune-Up Specifications** or underhood sticker.

CVCC Models — Keihin 3-bbl (1980-82)

NOTE: *This procedure requires a propane enrichment kit, and, for California cars, a special tool for fuel/air mixture adjustment.*

1. Start the engine and warm it up to normal operating temperature. The cooling fan will come on.

2. Remove the vacuum tube from the intake air control diaphragm and plug the tube end.

3. Connect a tachometer.

4. Check the idle speed with the headlights, cooling fan and air conditioner OFF. Adjust the idle speed if necessary, by turning the throttle stop screw. Idle speed should be set to the specifications found in the Tune-Up Specifications Chart or on the emission control decal in the engine compartment.

5. Remove the air cleaner intake tube from the air duct on the radiator bulkhead.

6. Insert the tube of the propane enrichment kit into the intake tube about 4 inches.

7. With the engine idling, depress the push button on top of the propane device, then slowly open the propane control valve to obtain maximum engine speed. Engine speed should increase as the percentage of injected propane increases.

NOTE: *Open the propane control valve slowly; a sudden burst of propane may stall the engine.*

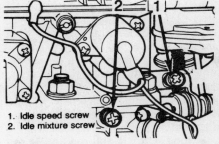

1. Idle speed screw
2. Idle mixture screw

Idle speed and mixture screws—Keihin 3 bbl carburetor

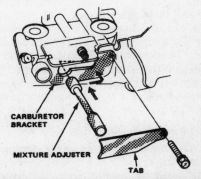

CARBURETOR BRACKET

MIXTURE ADJUSTER

TAB

Using special tool for mixture adjustment on California models

a. If the engine speed does not increase, the mixture screw is improperly adjusted. Go to Step 8.

b. If the engine speed increase, go to Step 9.

8. Lean out the mixture until the idle speed (with propane on) increases. On California cars remove the screws on the right side of the carburetor then swing the tab out of the way. Insert the mixture adjuster all the way to the right and slip it onto mixture the screw. Turn the mixture screw clockwise to lean out the mixture as required.

NOTE: *49 States models still have the normal mixture screw. No special tools are required for mixture adjustment.*

a. If the speed increase matched the specification, go to Step 11.

b. If the speed increase is out of specification, go to Step 9.

9. Check the speed increase against the specifications. If adjustment is required, adjust the engine speed to the propane enriched maximum rpm by turning the mixture screw. Turn it clockwise to increase; counterclockwise to decrease. Again, adjust the propane control valve for maximum engine speed.

10. Close the propane control valve and recheck the idle speed.

NOTE: *Run the engine at 2500 rpm for 10 seconds to stabilize the condition.*

a. If the idle speed is as specified (Step 4) go to Step 12.

b. If the idle speed is not as specified (Step 4), go to Step 11.

11. Recheck the idle speed and, if necessary, adjust it by turning the throttle stop screw, then repeat Steps 7-10.

12. Remove the propane enrichment kit and reconnect the air cleaner intake tube on the radiator bulkhead.

13. On 49 States cars, install the limiter cap with the pointer 180° away from the boss on the carburetor body. On California cars, remove the mixture adjuster, then push the tab back into place and install the screw.

14. If the car is equipped with air conditioning, recheck the idle speed with the air conditioning on. The speed should still be within specifications. If the speed is outside the specification, remove the rubber cap on the idle boost diaphragm and adjust it by turning the adjusting screw.

CVCC Models — Keihin 3-bbl (1983 Models)

NOTE: *This procedure requires a propane enrichment kit.*

1. Start the engine and warm it up to normal operating temperature. The cooling fan will come on.

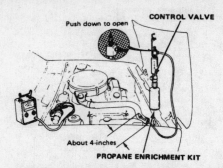

Mixture adjustment using propane enrichment method

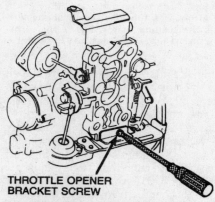

Accord and Civic throttle opener bracket location

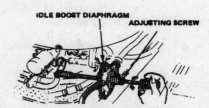

Adjusting idle boost diaphragm

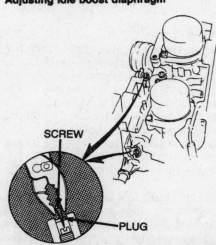

1983 and later Prelude mixture screw plug removal

2. Remove the vacuum hose from the intake air control diaphragm and clamp the hose end.

3. Connect a tachometer to the engine as per the manufacturer's instructions.

4. Check the idle speed with the headlights, heater blower, rear window defroster, cooling fan and the air conditioner OFF. Idle speed should be set to specifications according to the Tune-Up Specifications Chart or the emission control decal in the engine compartment.

5. Adjust the idle speed if necessary with the throttle stop screw.

   a. On the Prelude with automatic transmission, remove the frequency solenoid valve **A** and the control valve **A**. Disconnect the vacuum tubes and connect the lower hose to the air control valve **A**.

   b. On the Accord with automatic transmission, remove the air filter from the frequency solenoid valve **C** and plug the opening in the solenoid valve. On all models, insert the tube of the propane enrichment kit into the air intake tube about 4 inches.

6. With the engine idling, depress the push button on top of the propane device, then slowly open the propane control valve to obtain maximum engine speed. Engine speed should increase as the percentage of the propane injected goes up.

NOTE: *Open the propane control valve slowly; a sudden burst of propane may stall the engine.*

   a. If the engine speed increases, go to Step 13.

   b. If the engine speed does not increase, the mixture screw is improperly adjusted; go to Step v.

7. Remove the air cleaner. Disconnect the vacuum hose from the fast idle unloader. Remove the bolts holding the throttle opener bracket to the rear edge of the carburetor.

8. On the Accord and Civic models, remove the carburetor nuts and washers. Remove the brake booster hose and throttle cable from their brackets. Lift the carburetor off the studs and tilt it backwards. Remove the throttle opener screw and bracket.

9. Remove the mixture adjusting screw cap from the throttle opener bracket. Reinstall the bracket. Using new O-rings on the insulator and new gaskets on the heat shield, install the carburetor.

10. Reconnect the vacuum hose to the fast idle unloader.

11. Install the air cleaner, start the engine and warm it to normal operating temperature. The cooling fan will come on.

12. Disconnect and plug the vacuum hose from the intake air control diaphragm.

13. On the Prelude models, label and disconnect all the lines from the carburetors. Disconnect the throttle cable and the vacuum hose from the throttle opener diaphragm. Disconnect the automatic choke lead. Drain the coolant and disconnect hoses. Remove the carburetors.

CAUTION: *When draining the coolant, keep in mind that cats and dogs are attracted by the ethylene glycol antifreeze, and are quite likely to drink any that is left in an uncovered container or in puddles on the ground. This will prove fatal in sufficient quantity. Always drain the coolant into a sealable container. Coolant should be reused unless it is contaminated or several years old.*

14. Place a drill stop on a 3mm drill bit, 3mm from end. Drill through the center of the mixture screw plug. Screw a 5mm sheet metal screw into the plug. Grab the screw head with a pair of pliers and remove the plug. Reinstall the carburetors in the reverse order of removal and refill the cooling system.

15. On all models, install the propane enrichment kit and recheck the maximum propane enriched rpm. If the enriched rpm is too low, lean out the mixture. If it is too high, enrich the mixture. Turn the mixture screw clockwise to increase rpm; counterclockwise to decrease rpm.

16. Run the engine for about 10 seconds to stabilize the mixture. Close the propane control valve and recheck the idle speed. Repeat the procedure until the idle rpm is correct. Remove the propane enrichment kit and reconnect the air cleaner intake tube.

Keihin 2-bbl (1984-88 Civic, 1984-85 Accord & 1986-89 Accord with Manual Transmission)

NOTE: *This procedure requires a propane enrichment kit.*

1. Place the vehicle in the Park or neutral position, apply the emergency brake and block the drive wheels. Start the engine and warm it up to normal operating temperature. The cooling fan should come on.

2. Remove (the number 8) vacuum hose from the intake air control diaphragm and clamp the hose end.

3. Connect a suitable tachometer to the engine using the manufacturers instructions.

4. Check the idle speed with all the accessories turned off. Adjust the idle speed by turning the throttle stop screw, if necessary.

5. Disconnect the air cleaner intake tube from the air duct on the radiator bulkhead.

6. Insert the hose from the propane kit into the intake tube approximately 4 inches.

NOTE: *Be sure that the propane bottle has an adequate supply of gas before before going any further with this procedure.*

7. With the engine idling, depress the push button on top of the propane device, then slowly open the propane control valve to obtain the maximum engine speed. The engine speed should increase as the percentage of propane injected goes up.

NOTE: *Open the propane control valve slowly, because a sudden burst of propane may cause the engine to stall.*

8. The engine idle speed should increase as follows:

● 1984-88 Civic 1488cc (except the HF) with manual transmission − 100 ± 25 rpm.
● 1984-88 Civic 1488cc (except the HF) with automatic transmission − 50 ± 20 rpm.
● 1984-85 Accord with manual transmission 100 ± 25 rpm.
● 1984-85 Accord with automatic transmission 50 ± 20 rpm.
● 1986 Accord with manual transmission 35 ± 20 rpm.
● 1986-89 Accord with manual transmission 50 ± 20 rpm.

9. If the engine speed increases according to specifications, remove the propane kit, all test equipment and reconnect all disconnected vacuum hoses. If the engine speed fails to increase as specified, go on with the following steps.

10. Disconnect the vacuum hose to the fast idle unloader. Pull the throttle cable out of the bracket.

11. Remove the carburetor nuts and washers and bolts securing the steel tubing vacuum manifold. Lift the carburetor clear off the studs, then tilt it backward to obtain the access to the throttle controller bracket screws.

12. Remove the throttle controller bracket. Remove the mixture adjusting screw hole cap from the throttle controller bracket and then reinstall the bracket.

13. Reinstall the carburetor, reconnect the vacuum hose to the fast idle unloader. Reinstall the air cleaner.

14. Start the engine and let it warm up to normal operating temperature, the cooling fan will come on.

15. Remove the vacuum hose from the intake air control diaphragm and clamp the hose end. Reinstall the propane enrichment kit and recheck the maximum propane enrichment rpm.

16. If the propane enriched speed is to low, the mixture is rich. Turn the mixture screw a ¼ turn clockwise and recheck.

17. If the propane enriched speed is to high, the mixture is lean. Turn the mixture screw a ¼ turn counterclockwise and recheck.

18. Close the propane control valve and recheck the idle speed. Be sure to run the engine at 2500 rpm for 10 seconds to stabilize the idle condition.

19. If the engine speed is set to specifications, remove the propane enrichment kit, all test equipment and reconnect all vacuum hoses and the air cleaner intake tube.

20. If the engine speed is not set to specifications, recheck the engine speed and if necessary adjust by turning the throttle stop screw, then repeat Steps 14-19.

21. Reinstall the mixture adjusting screw hole cap. Check the idle controller booster speed, if so equipped.

NOTE: *There is no idle controller on: automatic transmission vehicles without air conditioning and power steering. On vehicles except the 1488cc automatic transmissions and power steering, check the idle speed with the headlights on and the heater blower set on high (III). On 1488cc models with automatic transmission and equipped with power steering, check the idle speed with the steering turned fully to the right or left.*

22. Adjust the idle speed, if necessary by turning the idle control screw.

NOTE: *On Civic models with power steering, when adjusting the idle speed, disconnect the power steering oil pressure switch wires and connect the wire terminals with a jumper wire to operate the idle controller. Keep the steering wheel pointed straight ahead.*

23. If equipped with air conditioning, make a second check with the air conditioning on. Adjust the speed if necessary by turning the adjusting screw on the idle boost diaphragm.

NOTE: *Some 1984 Accord models may develop a stalling problem at idle. The probable cause of this stalling, is a sticking slow mixture cut-off solenoid. If this is the case the solenoid should be removed and replaced with the updated type of solenoid.*

Keihin 2-bbl (1986-89 Accord with Automatic Transmission)

1. Place the vehicle in the Park or neutral position, apply the emergency brake and block the drive wheels. Start the engine and warm it up to normal operating temperature. The cooling fan should come on.

2. Remove vacuum hose from the intake air control diaphragm and clamp the hose end.

3. Connect a suitable tachometer to the engine using the manufacturers instructions.

4. Remove air filter from frequency solenoid valve **C** and plug opening in solenoid valve.

5. With no engine load, lower idle speed as much as possible by turning throttle stop screw.

6. Adjust idle speed by turning idle control screw to 600 ± 50 rpm (630 ± 50 on 1987-89 models.

7. With headlights and rear defroster on, and heater blower to maximum, adjust idle speed by turning adjusting screw **A**. Idle should be 600 ± 50 rpm on 1986 models and 700 ± 50 on 1987-89 models.

8. If equipped with air conditioning, adjust idle speed by turning adjusting screw **B** to 700 ± 50 rpm with air conditioning on.

9. With no engine load, remove inside vacuum hose from idle boost throttle controller and plus hose.

10. Adjust idle speed by turning throttle stop screw to 700 ± 50 rpm (650 ± 50 rpm at high altitude).

11. Disconnect hose from frequency solenoid valve **A** and connect to air control valve A.

12. Check maximum engine speed by propane enrichment method (see Accord with manual transmission), rpm increase should be 135 ± 25 rpm.

13. If engine speed does not increase per specification, adjust enriched speed by turning mixing screw.

14. Stop engine. Close propane control valve, remove all plugs, and reconnect all hoses.

15. Restart engine and recheck idle speed.
NOTE: *Raise engine speed to 2500 rpm 2 or 3 times in 10 seconds, and then check idle speed. Idle speed should be 700 ± 50 rpm on 1986 models and 730 ± 50 on 1987-89 models.*

16. Recheck idle speed with headlights, heater blower and rear window defroster on. Idle speed should be 700 ± 50 rpm.

17. Recheck idle speed with automatic transmission lever in gear. Idle speed should be 700 ± 50 rpm.

18. Recheck idle speed with air conditioning on and with shift lever in PARK or NEUTRAL position. Idle speed should be 750 ± 50 rpm.

19. Recheck idle speed with air conditioning on and in gear. Idle should be 750 ± 50 rpm.

20. If idle speed does not reach specified idle speeds in Steps 15 through 19, inspect idle control system.

Keihin Dual Sidedraft (1983-89 Prelude)

NOTE: *This procedure requires a propane enrichment kit. Check that carburetors are synchronized properly before making idle speed and mixture inspection. It will also be necessary to remove the ECU fuse from the fuse box for at least 10 seconds to reset the control unit, after this procedure is complete.*

1. Start engine and warm up to normal operating temperature. Cooling fan will come on.

2. Remove vacuum hose from intake air control diaphragm and clamp hose end.

3. Connect tachometer. Check that the fast idle lever is not seated against the fast idle cam.
NOTE: *If the fast idle lever is seated against the fast idle cam, it may be necessary to replace the left carburetor.*

4. Check idle speed with all accessories turned off. Idle speed should be 800 ± 50 rpm (750 ± 50 rpm on automatic transmission in gear). Adjust idle speed, if necessary, by turning throttle stop screw.
NOTE: *If the idle speed is excessively high, check the throttle control.*

5. On automatic cars only, remove attaching bolt, then remove frequency solenoid valve A and air control valve A. Disconnect the two prong connector from the EACV and disconnect the hose from the vacuum hose manifold, then cap the hose end.

6. Disconnect vacuum tubes and connect lower hose to air control valve A. Disconnect the vacuum hose from the air conditioning idle boost throttle controller. Disconnect the air cleaner intake tube from the air intake duct.

7. Insert propane enrichment hose into opening of intake tube about 4".
NOTE: *Not necessary to disconnect intake tube. Opening for the tube is just behind right headlight. Check that propane bottle has adequate gas before beginning test.*

8. With engine idling, depress push button on top of propane device, then slowly open propane control valve to obtain maximum engine speed. Engine speed should increase as percentage of propane injected goes up.
NOTE: *Open propane control valve slowly. Sudden burst of propane may stall engine.*

9. Propane enrichment maximum rpm:
- 1983-86 manual transmission — 45 ± 25 rpm.
- 1983-86 automatic transmission — 110 ± 25 rpm (in D3 or D4).
- 1987 manual transmission — 65 ± 20 rpm.
- 1987 automatic transmission — 130 ± 25 rpm (in D3 or D4).
- 1988-89 manual transmission — 170 ± 20 rpm.
- 1988-89 automatic transmission — 50 ± 10 rpm.

10. If engine speed does not increase per specification, remove carburetor.

11. Place a drill stop on a 1/8" drill bit, then drill through center of mixture screw hole plug.
NOTE: *If drilled deeper than this measurement, damage to mixture adjusting screw may result from bit. On the later models, remove the mixture adjusting screw hole caps, by pulling them straight out.*

12. Screw a 5mm sheet metal screw into hole plug.

13. Grab screw head with a pair of pliers and remove hole plug.

14. Reinstall carburetor.

15. Start engine and warm up to normal operating temperature. Cooling fan will come on.

16. Recheck maximum propane enriched rpm. If mixture is rich, turn both mixture screws ¼ turn counterclockwise.

17. Close propane control valve.

18. Run engine at 2500 rpm for 1800 seconds to stabilize mixture conditions, then check idle speed. Adjust idle speed, if necessary.

19. On 1984-86 models, remove propane enrichment kit and reconnect intake air control diaphragm hose. Install new plugs into idle mixture screw holes.

20. On 1987-89 models, disconnect #5 vacuum hose from air suction valve and plug hose.

21. Disconnect upper #22 vacuum hose from air leak solenoid valve at air jet controller stay, and plug end of hose, than connect a vacuum gauge to solenoid valve.

22. With engine idling, depress push button on top of propane device, then slowly open propane control valve and check vacuum. Vacuum should be available.

23. If no vacuum, inspect air leak solenoid valve.

24. Inspect thermovalve **C**.

25. Remove propane enrichment kit and reconnect connector.

26. Install new plugs into idle mixture screw holes.

NOTE: *Some 1984-85 Prelude models may experience hesitation on acceleration before the engine has reached normal operating temperature. This can be corrected by installing a cold driveability kit from the manufacturer so as to hold a full vacuum advance when the engine is cold.*

Tailpipe Emission Inspection
CARBURETED MODELS

1. Perform Steps 1-2 of the Propane Enrichment Procedure as outlined in this section. If necessary adjust the idle speed. On Accord and Civic models, disconnect the air cleaner intake tube from the air duct on the radiator bulkhead.

2. Warm up and calibrate the CO meter according to the manufacturer's instructions.

3. Check the idle CO with the headlights, heater blower, rear window defroster, cooling fan and the air conditioner off. The CO reading should be 0.1% maximum. If the CO level is correct go to Step 4. If the CO level is not correct, remove the idle mixture plug as described in the Propane Enrichment Procedure and adjust the

mixture screws to obtain the proper CO meter reading.

4. Recheck the idle speed and adjust it if necessary by turning the throttle stop screw. Recheck the CO level adjust if necessary. On Prelude models, check and adjust the propane enriched rpm according to Step 10 of the Propane Enrichment Procedure above.

FUEL INJECTED MODELS

NOTE: *The idle mixture is electronically controlled on the fuel injected models and is not adjustable.*

1985 Accord and 1985-87 Civic

1. Start engine and warm up to normal operating temperature; cooling fan will come on.

2. Connect a suitable tachometer using the manufacturers instructions.

3. Check idle speed with all accessories off.
NOTE: *To prevent idle control system from operating pinch vacuum hose (#10 on 1985-87 Civic and #27 on 1985 Accord).*

4. Idle speed should be 750 ± 50 rpm (in neutral). Adjust idle speed, if necessary, by turning idle adjusting screw, check fast idle valve.

5. Check idle controller boosted speed with air conditioning on. Idle speed should be:
- 1985-87 Civic — 750 ± 50 rpm (in neutral).
- 1985 Accord — 800 ± 50 rpm (in neutral).

6. Adjust idle speed, if necessary, by turning adjusting screw **B**.

1986-87 Accord and Prelude

1. Start engine and warm up to normal operating temperature; cooling fan will come on twice.

2. Connect tachometer.

3. Disconnect upper vacuum hose of idle control solenoid valve (between valve and intake manifold) from intake manifold.

4. Cap end of hose and intake manifold.

5. With all accessories off, check idle speed. Idle speed should be 750 ± 50 rpm (in neutral). Adjust idle speed, if necessary, by turning idle adjusting screw.

6. Check idle speed with heater fan switch at HI and air conditioning on. Idle speed should be 750 ± 50 rpm (in neutral)›. Adjust idle speed, if necessary, by turning adjusting bolt on air conditioning idle boost valve.

7. After adjustment, connect idle control solenoid valve vacuum hose.

8. On automatic transmission model, after adjusting idle speed, check that it remains with-

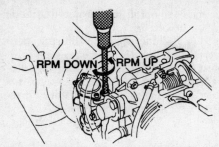

Fuel injection idle speed adjustment screw—1488cc and 1829cc engines

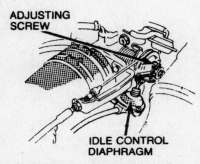

Fuel injection secondary idle speed adjustment—1488 & 1829cc engines

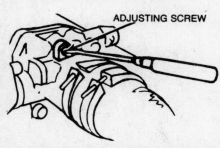

Fuel injection idle speed adjustment screw—1955cc engine

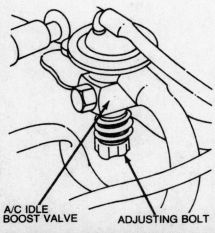

Fuel injection secondary idle speed adjustment—1955cc engine

in specified limit when shifted in gear. Idle speed should be 750 ± 50 rpm.

9. Check idle speed with all accessories on and air conditioning off. Idle should remain 750 ± 50 rpm.

1988 All Models

1. Start engine and warm up to normal operating temperature; cooling fan will come on twice.

2. Connect tachometer.

3. Disconnect the two prong connector on the EACV, which is located near the throttle body.

4. Set the steering in the straight forward position and check the idle speed with all the accessories in the OFF position. The idle speed should be as follows:

- Civic models – 625 ± 50 rpm manual transmission.
- Civic models – 625 ± 50 rpm automatic transmission in PARK.
- Accord & Prelude – 650 ± 50 rpm manual transmission.
- Accord & Prelude – 650 ± 50 rpm automatic transmission in PARK.

5. if the idle speed is out of specifications, adjust it by turning the idle adjusting screw, located on the throttle body.

NOTE: *If the idle speed is excessively high, be sure to check the throttle control system, if so equipped.*

6. Reconnect the two prong connector to the EACV, then remove the hazard fuse (the number 11, 10A fuse on the Accord and Prelude) in the main fuse box for 10 seconds to reset the ECU.

7. Set the steering in the straight forward position and check the idle speed with all the accessories in the OFF position. The idle speed should be as follows:

- Civic models – 725 ± 50 rpm manual transmission.
- Civic models – 725 ± 50 rpm automatic transmission in PARK.
- Accord & Prelude – 750 ± 50 rpm manual transmission.
- Accord & Prelude – 750 ± 50 rpm automatic transmission in PARK.

8. Idle the engine for at least one minute with all the accessories on. If the vehicle is equipped with an automatic transmission, block the drive wheels, apply the emergency brake and place it gear. The idle speed should now be as follows:

- Civic models – 780 ± 50 rpm manual transmission.
- Civic models – 780 ± 50 rpm automatic transmission in DRIVE.

- Accord & Prelude — 750 ± 50 rpm manual transmission.
- Accord & Prelude — 750 ± 50 rpm automatic transmission in PARK.

9. Idle the engine for at least one minute with the heater fan switch on the HI position and the air conditioner on. The idle speed should be as follows:

- Civic models — 780 ± 50 rpm manual transmission.
- Civic models — 780 ± 50 rpm automatic transmission in DRIVE.
- Accord & Prelude — 750 ± 50 rpm manual transmission.
- Accord & Prelude — 750 ± 50 rpm automatic transmission in PARK.

10. After the idle speed has been set and re-checked, turn off the engine and remove all test equipment.

ENGINE ELECTRICAL

Ignition Coil
TESTING
1973-85

1. Turn the ignition switch **OFF**.
2. Disconnect the primary and the secondary wiring connectors from the ignition coil.
3. Using an ohmmeter, inspect the resistance between the primary terminals; the resistance should be 3.42-4.18Ω @ 70°F (1973-75), 1.35-1.65Ω @ 70°F (1976-78), 1.78-2.08Ω @ 70°F (1979-80) or 1.06-1.24Ω @ 70°F (1981-85). If the resistance specification is not meet, replace the ignition coil.

NOTE: *The resistance will vary with the coil's temperature.*

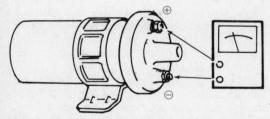

Testing the primary winding resistance of the ignition coil

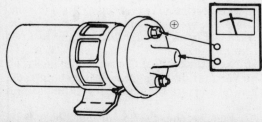

Testing the secondary winding resistance of the ignition coil

4. Using an ohmmeter, inspect the resistance between the primary positive (+) terminal and the **secondary** wiring terminal; the resistance should be 6,400-9,600Ω @ 70°F (1973-75), 8,000-12,000Ω @ 70°F (1976-78), 8,800-13,200Ω @ 70°F (1979-80) or 7,400-11,000Ω @ 70°F (1981-85). If the resistance specification is not meet, replace the ignition coil.

1986-88

1. Turn the ignition switch **OFF**.
2. Disconnect the primary and the secondary wiring connectors from the ignition coil.
3. Using an ohmmeter, inspect the resistance between the primary terminals **A** and **D**; the resistance should be 1.2-1.5Ω @ 70°F (20°C). If the resistance specification is not meet, replace the ignition coil.

NOTE: *The resistance will vary with the coil's temperature.*

4. Using an ohmmeter, inspect the resistance between the primary terminal **A** and **sec-**

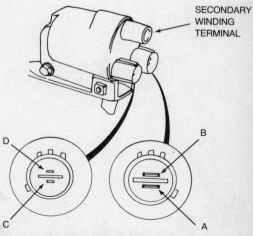

Identification of the ignition coil terminals—1986–88

ondary wiring terminal; the resistance should be 11,074-11,526Ω @ 70°F (20°C). If the resistance specification is not meet, replace the ignition coil.

5. Using an ohmmeter, inspect the resistance between the primary terminals **B** and **D**; the resistance should be approximately 2,200Ω @ 70°F (20°C). If the resistance specification is not meet, replace the ignition coil.

REMOVAL AND INSTALLATION

1. Turn the ignition switch **OFF**.
2. Disconnect the primary and the secondary wiring connectors from the ignition coil.
3. Remove the ignition coil-to-mount screws and the coil from the vehicle.
4. To install, reverse the removal procedures.

Distributor

The distributor is bevel gear driven by the camshaft on 1973-83 engines except Prelude. On the 1983 Prelude and all 1984-88 engines, the distributor is driven directly by the camshaft.

All distributors utilize centrifugal advance mechanisms to advance ignition timing as engine speed increases. Centrifugal advance is controlled by a pair of weights located under the breaker plate. As the distributor shaft spins faster, the weights are affected by centrifugal force and move away from the shaft, advancing the timing.

In addition, all distributors use some kind of

Honda distributor. Note the helical teeth on the drive gear (arrow)

vacuum ignition control, although this varies from model to model.

Vacuum advance works as follows: When the engine is operating under low load conditions (light acceleration), the vacuum diaphragm moves the breaker plate in the opposite direction of distributor rotation, thereby advancing the timing.

Vacuum retard, on the other hand, is actuated when the engine is operating under high vacuum conditions (deceleration or idle), and moves the breaker plate in the same direction of rotation as the distributor, thereby retarding the spark. On models equipped with both vacuum advance and retard, both these ignition characteristics are true. You can always tell a dual diaphragm distributor by its two hoses.

REMOVAL AND INSTALLATION
Breaker Point Type
ENGINE UNDISTURBED

1. Disconnect the negative battery terminal from the battery.
2. Disconnect the high tension (distributor-to-coil) lead and the primary leads, then, move them out of the way.
3. At the distributor cap, unsnap the retaining clamps. Remove the distributor cap and move it out of the way.
4. To position the No. 1 piston at the TDC of its compression stroke, perform the following procedures:

    a. Locate the No. 1 spark plug wire position on the distributor cap and align the cap with the housing.

    b. Using a piece of chalk, mark the No. 1 cylinder position on the distributor housing.

    c. Using a wrench on the crankshaft pulley, rotate the crankshaft until the distributor rotor aligns with the mark on the distributor housing.

5. Using a piece of chalk, mark distributor rotor-to-housing position and the distributor housing-to-engine position. When this is done, the mark on the distributor housing should be aligned with the rotor tip and the engine block mark.

NOTE: *This aligning procedure is very important because the distributor must be reinstalled in the exact location from which it was removed, if correct ignition timing is to be maintained.*

6. Note the position of the vacuum line(s) on the vacuum diaphragm with masking tape, then, disconnect the line(s) from the vacuum unit.

7. Remove the distributor holddown bolts and the distributor from the engine.

WARNING: *DO NOT disturb the engine*

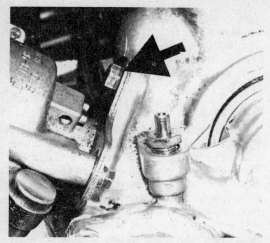

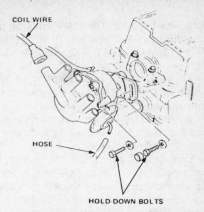

COIL WIRE

HOSE

HOLD-DOWN BOLTS

Exploded view of the distributor (1983–88—carbureted engine—Accord and Prelude

CVCC distributor hold-down bolt; non-CVCC similar

while the distributor is removed. If you attempt to start the engine with the distributor removed, you will have to retime the engine.

8. To install, place the rotor on the distributor shaft and align the tip of the rotor with the line that you made on the distributor housing.

9. With the rotor and housing aligned, insert the distributor into the engine while aligning the mark on the housing with the mark on the block or extension housing.

NOTE: *Since the distributor pinion gear has helical teeth, the rotor will turn slightly as the distributor gear meshes with the camshaft gear. Allow for this when installing the distributor by aligning the mark on the distributor with the mark on the block but positioning the tip of the rotor slightly to the side of the mark on the distributor.*

10. When the distributor is fully seated in the engine, install and tighten the distributor holddown bolts.

11. To complete the installation, reverse the removal procedures. If necessary, refer to Chapter 2 to check and/or adjust the ignition timing.

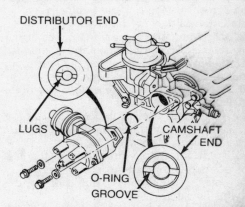

DISTRIBUTOR END

LUGS

CAMSHAFT END

O-RING GROOVE

Exploded view of the distributor used on 1342cc, 1488cc and 1829cc carbureted engines

INSTALLATION WHEN ENGINE HAS BEEN DISTURBED

If the engine was cranked with the distributor removed, it will be necessary to retime the engine. If you have installed the distributor incorrectly and you have found that, for that reason, the engine will not start, remove the distributor from the engine and start from scratch.

1. To position the engine on the correct firing position, perform the following procedures:

   a. Remove the No. 1 spark plug from the engine.

   b. Using a clean rag, insert it into the spark plug hole.

   c. Using a wrench on the crankshaft pulley bolt, rotate the engine until the compression blows the rag from the No. 1 cylinder. Check and/or align the engine's timing mark(s); this is the TDC of the No. 1 cylinder's compression stroke.

2. Align the rotor with the No. 1 cylinder position on the distributor housing.

3. Carefully insert the distributor into the cylinder head opening with the holddown bolt

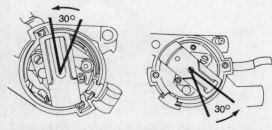

30°

30°

Upon installation the rotor will turn 30 degrees. Allow for this when installing the distributor. The figure on the left shows a typical installation for cars with manual transaxle; the one on the right shows installation for cars with automatic transaxle

slot aligned with the distributor mounting hole in the cylinder head, then, secure the plate at the center of the adjusting slot. The rotor head must face No. 1 cylinder.

NOTE: *Since the distributor pinion gear has helical teeth, the rotor will turn slightly as the gear on the distributor meshes with the gear on the camshaft. Allow for this when installing the distributor by positioning the tip of the rotor to the side of the protrusion.*

4. To complete the installation, reverse the removal procedures. If necessary, refer to Chapter 2 to check and/or adjust the ignition timing. Inspect and adjust the point gap.

Electronic Ignition Type

1. Using masking tape, remove the spark plug wires from the cap and number them for installation as they are removed.

2. Disconnect the vacuum hoses, the primary wire and the high tension wire. If equipped with fuel injection, remove and the four prong connector from the crank angle sensor.

3. Remove the holddown bolt(s) and pull the distributor from the head.

NOTE: *On the Prelude and Accord with fuel injection, there are two bolts; on the CRX with fuel injection, there are three bolts.*

4. Crank the engine until No. 1 piston is at TDC of its compression stroke.

5. Using a new O-ring, install it on the distributor housing.

6. On the 1984-88 models, the distributor drive gear remains engaged when the distributor is removed. To install, align the distributor and turn the shaft until the drive locks and the distributor seats in the cylinder head.

7. On the 1973-83 models, align the raised mark on the lower part of the distributor housing with the punch mark on the distributor gear shaft. Insert the distributor into the head and the rotor will turn to No. 1 firing position.

Then, on all models, loosely install the holddown bolt(s). Tighten the bolt(s) temporarily and replace the cap.

8. Connect all wires and hoses.

9. Start the engine and adjust the ignition timing.

Alternator

The alternator converts the mechanical energy which is supplied by the drive belt into electrical energy by electromagnetic induction. When the ignition switch is turned **ON**, current flows from the battery, through the charging system light or ammeter, to the voltage regulator and finally to the alternator. When the engine is started, the drive belt turns the rotating field (rotor) in the stationary windings (stator), inducing alternating current. This alternating current is converted into usable direct current by the diode rectifier. Most of this current is used to charge the battery and power the electrical components of the vehicle. A small part is returned to the field windings of the alternator enabling it to increase its output. When the current in the field windings reaches a predetermined control voltage, the voltage regulator grounds the circuit, preventing any further increase. The cycle is continued so that the voltage remains constant.

CVCC alternator mounting

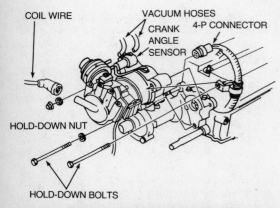

COIL WIRE   VACUUM HOSES   CRANK ANGLE SENSOR   4-P CONNECTOR

HOLD-DOWN NUT

HOLD-DOWN BOLTS

Exploded view of the distributor (1985–88)—fuel injected engine—Accord and Prelude—Civic is similar

On early non-CVCC models, the alternator is located beneath the distributor toward the rear of the engine compartment. On all other models, the alternator is located near the No. 1 spark plug at the front of the engine compartment. On models equipped with air conditioning, the alternator is mounted on a special vibration absorbing bracket at the driver's side of the engine compartment.

PRECAUTIONS

1. Observe the proper polarity of the battery connections by making sure that the positive (+) and negative (−) terminal connections are not reversed. Misconnection will allow current to flow in the reverse direction, resulting in damaged diodes and an overheated wire harness.

2. Never ground or short out any alternator or alternator regulator terminals.

3. Never operate the alternator with any of its or the battery's leads disconnected.

4. Always remove the battery or disconnect its output lead while charging it.

5. Always disconnect the ground cable when replacing any electrical components.

6. Never subject the alternator to excessive heat or dampness.

7. Never use arc welding equipment with the alternator connected.

REMOVAL AND INSTALLATION

1. Disconnect the negative (−) battery terminal.

2. Disconnect the wire(s) and/or harness connector from the rear of the alternator.

3. Remove the alternator-to-bracket bolts, the V-belt and the alternator assembly from the engine.

Alternator mounting—CVCC models with air conditioning

Alternator wiring connections—CVCC shown

4. To install, reverse the removal procedure. Adjust the alternator belt tension according to the "Belt Tension Adjustment" section below. Torque the lower alternator-to-bracket bolt(s) to 33 ft. lbs. and the upper adjusting nut/bolt to 17 ft. lbs.

BELT TENSION ADJUSTMENT

The initial inspection and adjustment to the alternator drive belt should be performed after the first 3,000 miles or if the alternator has been moved for any reason. Afterwards, you should inspect the belt tension every 12,000 miles (1973-78), 15,000 miles (1977-79) or 30,000 miles (1980-88). Before adjusting, inspect the belt to see that it is not cracked or worn. Be sure that its surfaces are free of grease and oil.

1. Push down on the belt halfway between pulleys with a force of about 24 lbs. The belt should deflect 12-17mm.

2. If the belt tension requires adjustment, loosen the adjusting link bolt and move the alternator with a pry bar positioned against the front of the alternator housing.

WARNING: *Do not apply pressure to any other part of the alternator.*

3. After obtaining the proper tension, tighten the adjusting link. Do not overtighten the belt; damage to the alternator bearings could result.

Regulator

The regulator is a device which controls the output of the alternator. If the regulator did not limit the voltage output of the alternator, the excessive output could burn out components of the electrical system, as well as the alternator itself. On 1984-88 models, use a regulator that is integral with the alternator and requires no separate service.

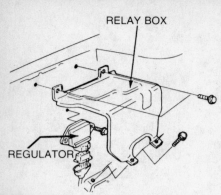

1982–83 Accord voltage regulator mounting

REMOVAL AND INSTALLATION

All except 1982-83 Accord

The regulator is inside the engine compartment, attached to the right fenderwell just above the battery.

1. Disconnect the negative (−) terminal from the battery.
2. Remove and label the regulator terminal lead wires to avoid confusion during installation.
3. Remove the regulator retaining bolts and the regulator from the vehicle.
4. To install, reverse the removal procedure.

1982-83 Accord

1. Disconnect the negative (−) terminal from the battery.
2. Remove the four main fuse plate retaining bolts and the main fuse plate to gain access to the solid state regulator.
3. Remove the regulator terminal plug from the regulator.
4. Unscrew the regulator retaining bolts and remove the regulator from the vehicle.
5. To install, reverse the removal procedure.

Battery

REMOVAL AND INSTALLATION

The battery is located in the engine compartment on all models.

1. Make sure the ignition switch is turned **OFF**.
2. Disconnect the negative battery cable (1st), then, the positive cable from the battery.
3. Remove the battery holddown clamp nuts, the clamp and the battery from the vehicle.
4. To install, reverse the removal procedures; be sure the battery is seated correctly on the battery tray.

NOTE: *Before installing the battery, it would be a wise idea to clean the battery posts and the terminal connectors.*

5. Install the positive battery cable (1st), then, the negative battery cable. Coat the battery terminals with a non-metallic grease; this will keep the terminals from oxidizing.

Starter

The starter is located on the firewall side of the engine block, adjacent to the flywheel or torque converter housing. On 1170cc and

Troubleshooting Basic Charging System Problems

Problem	Cause	Solution
Noisy alternator	• Loose mountings • Loose drive pulley • Worn bearings • Brush noise • Internal circuits shorted (High pitched whine)	• Tighten mounting bolts • Tighten pulley • Replace alternator • Replace alternator • Replace alternator
Squeal when starting engine or accelerating	• Glazed or loose belt	• Replace or adjust belt
Indicator light remains on or ammeter indicates discharge (engine running)	• Broken fan belt • Broken or disconnected wires • Internal alternator problems • Defective voltage regulator	• Install belt • Repair or connect wiring • Replace alternator • Replace voltage regulator
Car light bulbs continually burn out— battery needs water continually	• Alternator/regulator overcharging	• Replace voltage regulator/alternator
Car lights flare on acceleration	• Battery low • Internal alternator/regulator problems	• Charge or replace battery • Replace alternator/regulator
Low voltage output (alternator light flickers continually or ammeter needle wanders)	• Loose or worn belt • Dirty or corroded connections • Internal alternator/regulator problems	• Replace or adjust belt • Clean or replace connections • Replace alternator or regulator

1237cc models, use a direct drive type starter, while the CVCC uses a gear reduction starter. Otherwise, the two units are similar in operation and service. Both starters are 4-pole, series wound, DC units to which an outboard solenoid is mounted. When the ignition switch is turned to the start position, the solenoid armature is drawn in, engaging the starter pinion with the flywheel. When the starter pinion and flywheel are fully engaged, the solenoid armature closes the main contacts for the starter, causing the starter to crank the engine. When the engine starts, the increased speed of the flywheel causes the gear to overrun the starter clutch and rotor. The gear continues in full mesh until the ignition is switched from the start to the on position, interrupting the starter current. The shift lever spring then returns the gear to its neutral position.

REMOVAL AND INSTALLATION

1. Disconnect the negative battery terminal and the starter motor cable at the positive terminal.

2. Disconnect the starter motor cable from the motor.

3. Remove the starter motor by loosening the two attaching bolts. On CVCC models, the bolts attach from opposing ends of the starter.

4. To install, reverse the removal procedures. Torque the starter-to-engine bolts to 29-36 ft. lbs. and make sure that all wires are securely connected.

STARTER DRIVE REPLACEMENT

Hitachi And Nippondenso Direct Drive Types

1. Remove the solenoid by loosening and removing the attaching bolts.

2. Remove the two brush holder plate retaining screws from the rear cover. Also pry off the rear dust cover along with the clip and thrust washer(s).

3. Remove the two through-bolts from the rear cover and lightly tap the rear cover with a mallet to remove it.

4. Remove the four carbon brushes from the brush holder and the brush holder.

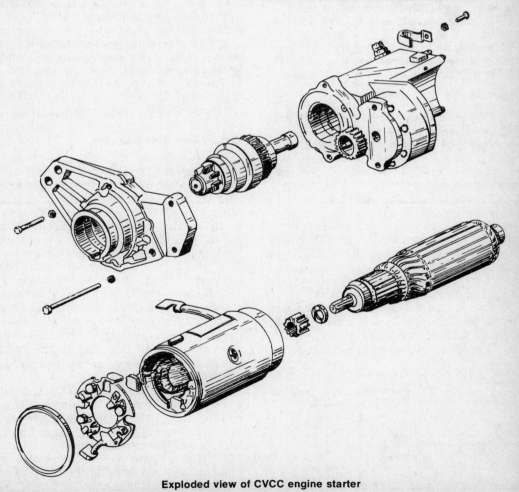

Exploded view of CVCC engine starter

CVCC starter showing rear bolt (arrow)

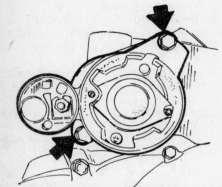

Non-CVCC engine starter showing mounting bolts (arrows)

5. Separate the yoke from the case. The yoke is provided with a hole for positioning, into which the gear case lock pin is inserted.

6. Pull the yoke assembly from the gear case, being sure to carefully detach the shift lever from the pinion.

7. Remove the armature unit from the yoke casing and the field coil.

8. To remove the pinion gear from the armature, first set the armature on end with the pinion end facing upward and pull the clutch stop collar downward toward the pinion. Remove the pinion stop clip, then, pull the pinion stop and gears from the armature shaft as a unit.

9. To assemble and install the starter motor, reverse the disassembly and removal procedures. Be sure to install new clips, be careful of the installation direction of the shift lever.

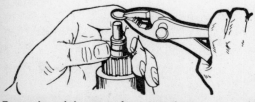

Removing pinion gear from armature

Nippondenso Reduction Gear Type

These starters come in 1.0 and 1.4 KW sizes and are used on various models, the larger power rating on the 1500 and larger engines. They may be identified in two ways. This starter uses a double reduction set of pinion gears and has a very wide reduction gear housing. Also, its solenoid is housed entirely within the housing of the starter, rather than in an externally visible unit.

1. Remove the solenoid end cover. Pull out the solenoid. There is a spring on the shaft and a steel ball at the end of the shaft.

2. Remove the through bolts retaining the end frame to the motor and solenoid housing.

3. Remove the end frame. The over-running clutch assembly complete with drive gear can be removed. The idler and motor pinion gears can be removed separately. The idler gear retains five steel roller bearings.

4. The clutch assembly is held together by a circlip. Push down on the gear against the spring inside the clutch assembly and remove the circlip with a circlip expander. Slide the stopper ring, gear, spring and washer out of the clutch assembly.

5. To assemble, reverse the disassembly procedures. The stopper ring is installed with the smaller end with the lip towards the clutch. Be sure that the steel ball is in place at the end of the solenoid shaft. Grease all sliding surfaces of the solenoid before reassembly.

Mitsuba Gear Reduction Type

This starter may be distinguished from the Nipopondenso gear reduction starter in two ways. First, the armature drives the overrunning clutch directly using a very small pinion rather than through a double reduction, making the gear housing cover much narrower than it is on the Nippondenso. Secondly, the solenoid housing forms an obvious bulge that is separate from the field winding housing. It is used on late model 1300-1500 and larger engines.

1. Remove the three solenoid retaining screws from the front of the gear housing cover. First, shift the solenoid away from the plane of the armature to disengage it from the solenoid lever, then, remove it and its gasket. Remove any remaining screws attaching the gear housing cover to the gear housing.

2. Loosen the through bolts retaining the end frame and armature housing to the gear housing, then, pull off the gear housing cover and gear housing, leaving the armature, brushes and bearings assembled.

3. From the rear, remove the three screws retaining the gear housing cover to the gear housing. Remove the gear housing cover. Now

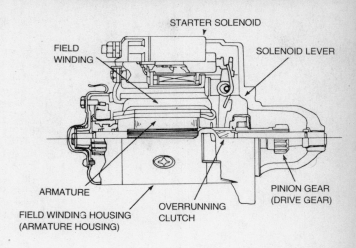

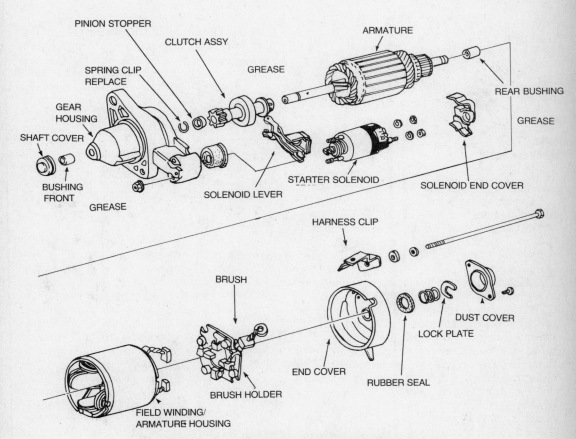

Exploded view of the Nippondenso direct-drive starter motor

remove the over-running clutch assembly complete with drive gear and the solenoid lever. Be careful not to dislodge and loose the labyrinth tube and it rubber seal.

4. Check the clutch assembly by moving the clutch along the shaft. If movement is not free and smooth or if the clutch does not positively prevent rotation in the counterclockwise direction (looking at the pinion gear end), replace the clutch assembly.

5. To assemble, reverse the disassembly procedures. Grease all sliding surfaces of the solenoid lever before reassembly, using mobydenum disulphide grease.

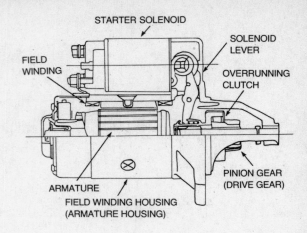

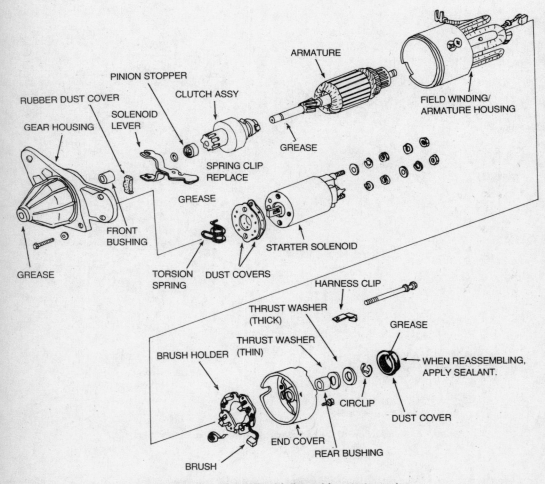

Exploded view of the Hitachi direct-drive starter motor

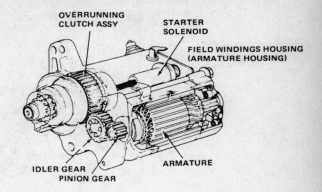

OVERRUNNING
CLUTCH ASSY

STARTER
SOLENOID

FIELD WINDINGS HOUSING
(ARMATURE HOUSING)

IDLER GEAR
PINION GEAR

ARMATURE

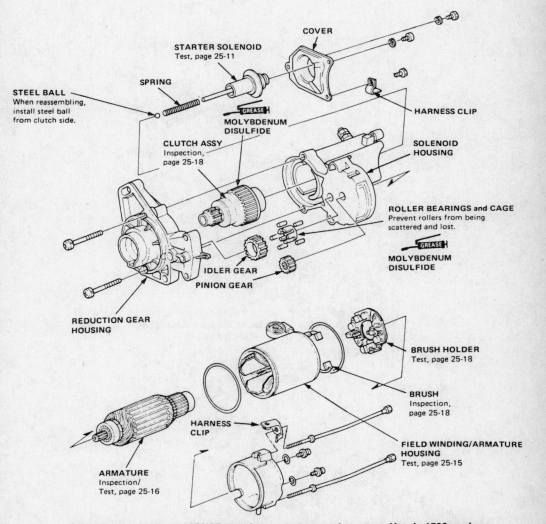

COVER

STARTER SOLENOID
Test, page 25-11

SPRING

STEEL BALL
When reassembling,
install steel ball
from clutch side.

GREASE
MOLYBDENUM
DISULFIDE

HARNESS CLIP

CLUTCH ASSY
Inspection,
page 25-18

SOLENOID
HOUSING

ROLLER BEARINGS and CAGE
Prevent rollers from being
scattered and lost.

GREASE
MOLYBDENUM
DISULFIDE

IDLER GEAR

PINION GEAR

REDUCTION GEAR
HOUSING

BRUSH HOLDER
Test, page 25-18

BRUSH
Inspection,
page 25-18

HARNESS
CLIP

FIELD WINDING/ARMATURE
HOUSING
Test, page 25-15

ARMATURE
Inspection/
Test, page 25-16

Exploded view of the 1.4 KW Nippondenso starter, used on many Honda 1500 engines

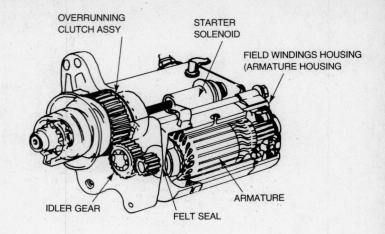

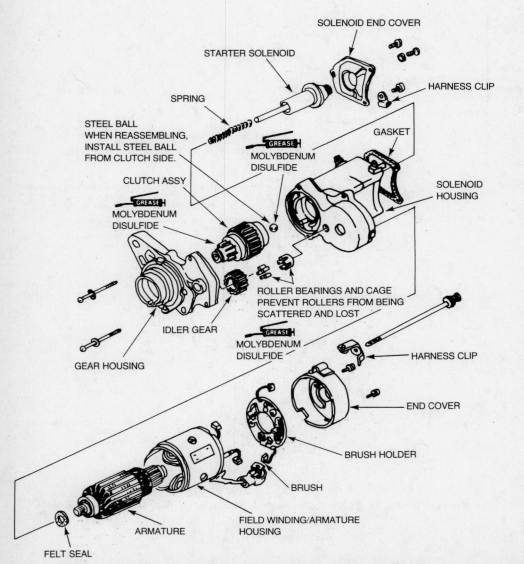

Exploded view of the Nippondenso gear reduction starter motor

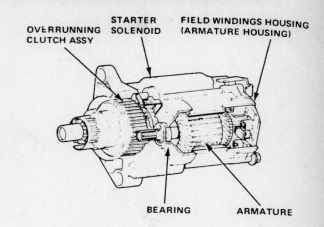

OVERRUNNING CLUTCH ASSY
STARTER SOLENOID
FIELD WINDINGS HOUSING (ARMATURE HOUSING)
BEARING
ARMATURE

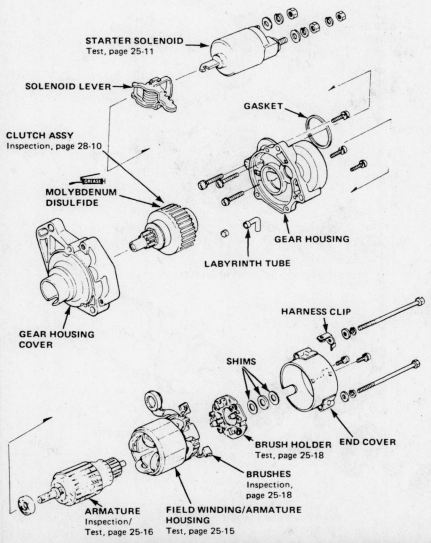

STARTER SOLENOID
Test, page 25-11

SOLENOID LEVER

CLUTCH ASSY
Inspection, page 28-10

MOLYBDENUM DISULFIDE

GEAR HOUSING COVER

GASKET

GEAR HOUSING

LABYRINTH TUBE

HARNESS CLIP

SHIMS

BRUSH HOLDER
Test, page 25-18

END COVER

BRUSHES
Inspection,
page 25-18

ARMATURE
Inspection/
Test, page 25-16

FIELD WINDING/ARMATURE HOUSING
Test, page 25-15

Exploded view of the 1.0 KW Mitsuba starter, used on 1300-1500 engines

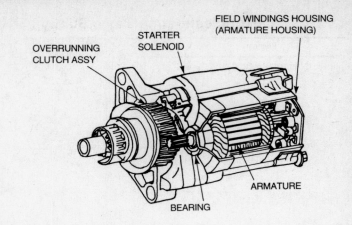

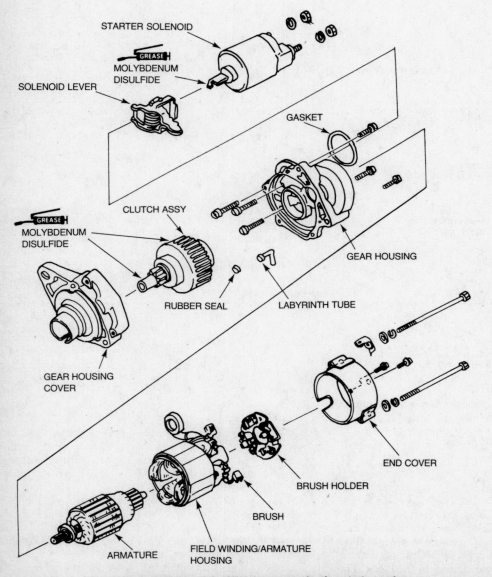

Exploded view of the Mitsuba gear reduction starter motor

Troubleshooting Basic Starting System Problems

Problem	Cause	Solution
Starter motor rotates engine slowly	• Battery charge low or battery defective	• Charge or replace battery
	• Defective circuit between battery and starter motor	• Clean and tighten, or replace cables
	• Low load current	• Bench-test starter motor. Inspect for worn brushes and weak brush springs.
	• High load current	• Bench-test starter motor. Check engine for friction, drag or coolant in cylinders. Check ring gear-to-pinion gear clearance.
Starter motor will not rotate engine	• Battery charge low or battery defective	• Charge or replace battery
	• Faulty solenoid	• Check solenoid ground. Repair or replace as necessary.
	• Damage drive pinion gear or ring gear	• Replace damaged gear(s)
	• Starter motor engagement weak	• Bench-test starter motor
	• Starter motor rotates slowly with high load current	• Inspect drive yoke pull-down and point gap, check for worn end bushings, check ring gear clearance
	• Engine seized	• Repair engine
Starter motor drive will not engage (solenoid known to be good)	• Defective contact point assembly	• Repair or replace contact point assembly
	• Inadequate contact point assembly ground	• Repair connection at ground screw
	• Defective hold-in coil	• Replace field winding assembly
Starter motor drive will not disengage	• Starter motor loose on flywheel housing	• Tighten mounting bolts
	• Worn drive end busing	• Replace bushing
	• Damaged ring gear teeth	• Replace ring gear or driveplate
	• Drive yoke return spring broken or missing	• Replace spring
Starter motor drive disengages prematurely	• Weak drive assembly thrust spring	• Replace drive mechanism
	• Hold-in coil defective	• Replace field winding assembly
Low load current	• Worn brushes	• Replace brushes
	• Weak brush springs	• Replace springs

ENGINE MECHANICAL

Design

The engines used in the Honda Civic, Accord and Prelude are water cooled, overhead cam, transversely mounted, inline four cylinder powerplants. They can be divided into two different engine families; CVCC and non-CVCC.

The non-CVCC engines have been offered in two different displacements; 1170cc (1973 only), and 1237cc (1974-79). These engines are somewhat unusual in that both the engine and the cylinder head are aluminum. The cylinder head is a crossflow design. The block uses sleeved cylinder liners and a main bearing girdle to add rigidity to the block. The engine uses five main bearings.

The CVCC (Compound Vortex Controlled Combustion) engine is unique in that its cylinder head is equipped with three valves per cylinder, instead of the usual two. Besides the intake and exhaust valve, each cylinder has an auxiliary intake valve which is much smaller than the regular intake valve. This auxiliary intake valve has its own separate precombustion chamber (adjacent to the main chamber with a crossover passage), its own intake manifold passages and carburetor circuit.

Briefly, what happens is this; at the beginning of the intake stroke, a small but very rich mixture is introduced into the precombustion chamber, while next door in the main combustion chamber, a large but very lean mixture makes its debut. At the end of the compression stroke, ignition occurs. The spark plug, located in the precombustion chamber, easily ignites the rich auxiliary mixture and this ignition spreads out into the main combustion chamber, where the large lean mixture is ignited. This two-stage combustion process allows the engine to operate efficiently with a much leaner overall air/fuel ratio. So, whereas the 1975 and later non-CVCC engines require a belt driven air injection system to control pollutants, the CVCC accomplishes this internally and gets better gas mileage.

On the 1983-88 models, Honda decided to improve engine breathing by replacing the single large main intake valve with a pair of smaller ones. This allows a much greater total intake valve area than a single valve and it also permits intake valve timing to be staggered slightly. This gave Honda engineers a unique opportunity to design air swirl into the combustion process. Such swirl not only tends to reduce engine knock but improves combustion speed and therefore engine efficiency, especially at low speeds. These engines retain the auxiliary intake valve on the exhaust side of the head.

All of the latest Honda engines have substituted fuel injection for carburetion. In the interests of retaining the efficiency, power and emissions benefits the two-valve intake system provides, they retain it. The CVCC system has been deleted, however, on the fuel injected engines. This is because fuel injection, by providing the charge directly to the port of each cylinder and utilizing greater pressure than a carburetor, permits the engine to run on leaner

mixtures. This makes the CVCC system unnecessary.

Engine Overhaul Tips

Most engine overhaul procedures are fairly standard. In addition to specific parts replacement procedures and complete specifications for your individual engine, this chapter also is a guide to accepted rebuilding procedures. Examples of standard rebuilding practices are shown and should be used along with specific details concerning your particular engine.

Competent and accurate machine shop services will ensure maximum performance, reliability and engine life. Procedures marked with the symbol shown above should be performed by a competent machine shop and are provided so that you will be familiar with the procedures necessary to a successful overhaul.

In most instances, it is more profitable for the do-it-yourself mechanic to remove, clean and inspect the component, buy the necessary parts and deliver these to a shop for actual machine work.

On the other hand, much of the rebuilding work (crankshaft, block, bearings, pistons, rods and other components) is well within the scope of the do-it-yourself mechanic.

Tools

The tools required for an engine overhaul or parts replacement will depend on the depth of your involvement. With a few exceptions, they will be the tools found in a mechanic's tool kit (see Chapter 1). More indepth work will require any or all of the following:
- a dial indicator (reading in thousandths) mounted on a universal base
- micrometers and telescope gauges
- jaw and screw-type pullers
- scraper
- valve spring compressor
- ring groove cleaner
- piston ring expander and compressor
- ridge reamer
- cylinder hone or glaze breaker
- Plastigage®
- engine stand

Use of most of these tools is illustrated in this chapter. Many can be rented for a one-time use from a local parts jobber or tool supply house specializing in automotive work.

Occasionally, the use of special tools is called for. See the information on Special Tools and the Safety Notice in the front of this book substituting another tool.

Inspection Techniques

Procedures and specifications are given in this chapter for inspecting, cleaning and assess-

Frontal view of CVCC engine

ing the wear limits of most major components. Other procedures such as Magnaflux® and Zyglo® can be used to locate material flaws and stress cracks. Magnaflux® is a magnetic process applicable only to ferrous materials. The Zyglo® process coats the material with a fluorescent dye penetrant and can be used on any material. Check for suspected surface cracks can be more readily made using spot check dye. The dye is sprayed onto the suspected area, wiped off and the area sprayed with a developer. Cracks will show up brightly.

Overhaul Tips

Aluminum has become extremely popular for use in engines, due to its low weight. Observe the following precautions when handling aluminum parts:

• Never hot tank aluminum parts (the caustic hot-tank solution will eat the aluminum).

• Remove all aluminum parts (identification tag, etc.) from engine pats prior to hot-tanking.

• Always coat threads lightly with engine oil or anti-seize compounds before installation, to prevent seizure.

• Never over-torque bolts or spark plugs, especially in aluminum threads.

Stripped threads in any component can be repaired using any of several commercial repair kits (Heil-Coil®, Microdot®, Keenserts®, etc.).

When assembling the engine, any parts that will be in frictional contact must be prelubed to provide lubrication at initial start-up. Any product specifically formulated for this purpose can be used but engine oil is not recommended as a prelube.

When semi-permanent (locked, but removable) installation of bolts or nuts is desired, threads should be cleaned and coated with Loctite® or other similar, commercial non-hardening sealant.

Repairing Damaged Threads

Several methods of repairing damaged threads are available. Heli-Coil® (shown here), Keenserts® and Microdot® are among the most widely used. All involved basically the same principle — drilling out stripped threads, tapping the hole and installing a pre-wound insert — making welding, plugging and oversize fasteners unnecessary.

Two types of thread repair inserts are usually supplied: a standard type for most Inch Coarse, Inch Fine, Metric Coarse and Metric Fine thread sizes and a spark plug type to fit most spark plug port sizes. Consult the individual manufacturer's catalog to determine exact applications. Typical thread repair kits will contain a selection of prewound threaded inserts, a

tap (corresponding to the outside diameter threads of the insert) and an installation tool. Spark plug inserts usually differ because they require a tap equipped with pilot threads and a combined reamer/tap section. Most manufacturers also supply blister-packed thread repair inserts separately in addition to a master kit containing a variety of taps and inserts plus installation tools.

Before effecting a repair to a threaded hole, remove any snapped, broken or damaged bolts or studs. Penetrating oil can be used to free frozen threads; the offending item can be removed with locking pliers or with a screw or stud extractor. After the hole is clear, the thread can be repaired, as follows:

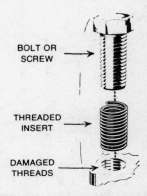

Damaged bolt holes can be repaired with thread repair inserts

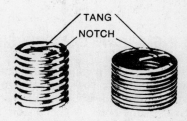

Standard thread repair insert (left) and spark plug thread insert (right)

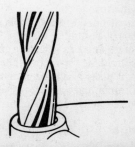

Drill out the damaged threads with specified drill. Drill completely through the hole or to the bottom of a blind hole

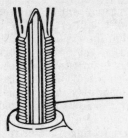

With the tap supplied, tap the hole to receive the thread insert. Keep the tap well oiled and back it out frequently to avoid clogging the threads

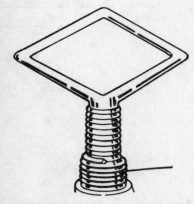

Screw the threaded insert onto the installation tool until the tang engages the slot. Screw the insert into the tapped hole until it is ¼–½ turn below the top surface. After installation break off the tang with a hammer and punch

CHECKING ENGINE COMPRESSION

A noticeable lack of engine power, excessive oil consumption and/or poor fuel mileage measured over an extended period are all indicators of internal engine wear. Worn piston rings, scored or worn cylinder bores, blown head gaskets, sticking or burnt valves and worn valve seats are all possible culprits here. A check of each cylinder's compression will help you locate the problems.

As mentioned in the "Tools and Equipment" section of Chapter 1, a screw-in type compression gauge is more accurate than the type you simply hold against the spark plug hole, although it takes slightly longer to use. It's worth it to obtain a more accurate reading. Follow the procedures below for gasoline engines.

Gasoline Engines

1. Warm the engine to normal operating temperatures.

2. Remove all spark plugs.

3. Disconnect the high tension lead from the ignition coil.

4. On carbureted vehicles, fully open the throttle either by operating the carburetor throttle linkage by hand or by having an assistant "floor" the accelerator pedal. On the fuel injected vehicles, disconnect the cold start valve and all injector connections.

5. Screw the compression gauge into the No. 1 spark plug hole until the fitting is snug.

NOTE: *Be careful not to crossthread the plug hole. On aluminum cylinder heads use extra care, as the threads in these heads are easily ruined.*

6. Ask an assistant to depress the accelerator pedal fully on both carbureted and fuel injected vehicles. Then, while you read the compression gauge, ask the assistant to crank the engine two or three times in short bursts using the ignition switch.

7. Read the compression gauge at the end of each series of cranks and record the highest of these readings. Repeat this procedure for each of the engine's cylinders. Compare the highest reading of each cylinder to the compression pressure specifications in the "Tune-Up Specifications" chart in Chapter 2. The specs in this chart are maximum values.

NOTE: *A cylinder's compression pressure is usually acceptable if it is not less than 80% of maximum. The difference between each cylinder should be no more than 12-14 pounds.*

8. If a cylinder is unusually low, pour a tablespoon of clean engine oil into the cylinder through the spark plug hole and repeat the compression test. If the compression comes up after adding the oil, it appears that the cylinder's piston rings or bore are damaged or worn. If the pressure remains low, the valves may not be seating properly (a valve job is needed) or the head gasket may be blown near that cylinder. If compression in any two adjacent cylinders is low and if the addition of oil doesn't help the compression, there is leakage past the head gas-

The screw-in type compression gauge is more accurate

Standard Torque Specifications and Fastener Markings

In the absence of specific torques, the following chart can be used as a guide to the maximum safe torque of a particular size/grade of fastener.

- There is no torque difference for fine or coarse threads.
- Torque values are based on clean, dry threads. Reduce the value by 10% if threads are oiled prior to assembly.
- The torque required for aluminum components or fasteners is considerably less.

U.S. Bolts

SAE Grade Number	1 or 2			5			6 or 7		
Number of lines always 2 less than the grade number.									
Bolt Size (Inches)—(Thread)	Maximum Torque			Maximum Torque			Maximum Torque		
	Ft./Lbs.	Kgm	Nm	Ft./Lbs.	Kgm	Nm	Ft./Lbs.	Kgm	Nm
¼—20	5	0.7	6.8	8	1.1	10.8	10	1.4	13.5
—28	6	0.8	8.1	10	1.4	13.6			
⁵⁄₁₆—18	11	1.5	14.9	17	2.3	23.0	19	2.6	25.8
—24	13	1.8	17.6	19	2.6	25.7			
³⁄₈—16	18	2.5	24.4	31	4.3	42.0	34	4.7	46.0
—24	20	2.75	27.1	35	4.8	47.5			
⁷⁄₁₆—14	28	3.8	37.0	49	6.8	66.4	55	7.6	74.5
—20	30	4.2	40.7	55	7.6	74.5			
½—13	39	5.4	52.8	75	10.4	101.7	85	11.75	115.2
—20	41	5.7	55.6	85	11.7	115.2			
⁹⁄₁₆—12	51	7.0	69.2	110	15.2	149.1	120	16.6	162.7
—18	55	7.6	74.5	120	16.6	162.7			
⁵⁄₈—11	83	11.5	112.5	150	20.7	203.3	167	23.0	226.5
—18	95	13.1	128.8	170	23.5	230.5			
¾—10	105	14.5	142.3	270	37.3	366.0	280	38.7	379.6
—16	115	15.9	155.9	295	40.8	400.0			
⁷⁄₈—9	160	22.1	216.9	395	54.6	535.5	440	60.9	596.5
—14	175	24.2	237.2	435	60.1	589.7			
1—8	236	32.5	318.6	590	81.6	799.9	660	91.3	894.8
—14	250	34.6	338.9	660	91.3	849.8			

Metric Bolts

Relative Strength Marking	4.6, 4.8			8.8		
Bolt Markings						
Bolt Size Thread Size x Pitch (mm)	Maximum Torque			Maximum Torque		
	Ft./Lbs.	Kgm	Nm	Ft./Lbs.	Kgm	Nm
6 x 1.0	2–3	.2–.4	3–4	3–6	.4–.8	5–8
8 x 1.25	6–8	.8–1	8–12	9–14	1.2–1.9	13–19
10 x 1.25	12–17	1.5–2.3	16–23	20–29	2.7–4.0	27–39
12 x 1.25	21–32	2.9–4.4	29–43	35–53	4.8–7.3	47–72
14 x 1.5	35–52	4.8–7.1	48–70	57–85	7.8–11.7	77–110
16 x 1.5	51–77	7.0–10.6	67–100	90–120	12.4–16.5	130–160
18 x 1.5	74–110	10.2–15.1	100–150	130–170	17.9–23.4	180–230
20 x 1.5	110–140	15.1–19.3	150–190	190–240	26.2–46.9	160–320
22 x 1.5	150–190	22.0–26.2	200–260	250–320	34.5–44.1	340–430
24 x 1.5	190–240	26.2–46.9	260–320	310–410	42.7–56.5	420–550

ket. Oil and coolant water in the combustion chamber can result from this problem. There may be evidence of water droplets on the engine dipstick when a head gasket has blown.

Engine

REMOVAL AND INSTALLATION

WARNING: *If any repair operation requires the removal of a component of the air conditioning system (on vehicles equipped), do not disconnect the refrigerant lines. If it is impossible to move the component out of the way with the lines attached, have the air conditioning system evacuated by a trained serviceman. The air conditioning system contains freon under pressure. This gas can be very dangerous. Therefore, under no circumstances should an untrained person attempt to disconnect the air conditioner refrigerant lines.*

1170 and 1237cc Civic

1. Raise and support the front of the vehicle with safety stands.

2. Remove the front wheels.

CAUTION: *The EPA warns that prolonged contact with used engine oil may cause a number of skin disorders, including cancer! You should make every effort to minimize your exposure to used engine oil. Protective gloves should be worn when changing the oil. Wash your hands and any other exposed skin areas as soon as possible after exposure to used engine oil. Soap and water, or waterless hand cleaner should be used.*

3. Drain the oil from the engine and transaxle. Place a clean container under the radiator and drain the cooling system.

4. Remove the front turn signal lights and grille.

CAUTION: *When draining the coolant, keep in mind that cats and dogs are attracted by the ethylene glycol antifreeze, and are quite likely to drink any that is left in an uncovered container or in puddles on the ground. This will prove fatal in sufficient quantity. Always drain the coolant into a sealable container. Coolant should be reused unless it is contaminated or several years old.*

5. Remove the hood support bolts and the hood. Remove the fan shroud, if equipped.

Troubleshooting Engine Mechanical Problems

Problem	Cause	Solution
External oil leaks	• Fuel pump gasket broken or improperly seated	• Replace gasket
	• Cylinder head cover RTV sealant broken or improperly seated	• Replace sealant; inspect cylinder head cover sealant flange and cylinder head sealant surface for distortion and cracks
	• Oil filler cap leaking or missing	• Replace cap
	• Oil filter gasket broken or improperly seated	• Replace oil filter
	• Oil pan side gasket broken, improperly seated or opening in RTV sealant	• Replace gasket or repair opening in sealant; inspect oil pan gasket flange for distortion
	• Oil pan front oil seal broken or improperly seated	• Replace seal; inspect timing case cover and oil pan seal flange for distortion
	• Oil pan rear oil seal broken or improperly seated	• Replace seal; inspect oil pan rear oil seal flange; inspect rear main bearing cap for cracks, plugged oil return channels, or distortion in seal groove
	• Timing case cover oil seal broken or improperly seated	• Replace seal
	• Excess oil pressure because of restricted PCV valve	• Replace PCV valve
	• Oil pan drain plug loose or has stripped threads	• Repair as necessary and tighten
	• Rear oil gallery plug loose	• Use appropriate sealant on gallery plug and tighten
	• Rear camshaft plug loose or improperly seated	• Seat camshaft plug or replace and seal, as necessary
	• Distributor base gasket damaged	• Replace gasket

Troubleshooting Engine Mechanical Problems (cont.)

Problem	Cause	Solution
Excessive oil consumption	• Oil level too high	• Drain oil to specified level
	• Oil with wrong viscosity being used	• Replace with specified oil
	• PCV valve stuck closed	• Replace PCV valve
	• Valve stem oil deflectors (or seals) are damaged, missing, or incorrect type	• Replace valve stem oil deflectors
	• Valve stems or valve guides worn	• Measure stem-to-guide clearance and repair as necessary
	• Poorly fitted or missing valve cover baffles	• Replace valve cover
	• Piston rings broken or missing	• Replace broken or missing rings
	• Scuffed piston	• Replace piston
	• Incorrect piston ring gap	• Measure ring gap, repair as necessary
	• Piston rings sticking or excessively loose in grooves	• Measure ring side clearance, repair as necessary
	• Compression rings installed upside down	• Repair as necessary
	• Cylinder walls worn, scored, or glazed	• Repair as necessary
	• Piston ring gaps not properly staggered	• Repair as necessary
	• Excessive main or connecting rod bearing clearance	• Measure bearing clearance, repair as necessary
No oil pressure	• Low oil level	• Add oil to correct level
	• Oil pressure gauge, warning lamp or sending unit inaccurate	• Replace oil pressure gauge or warning lamp
	• Oil pump malfunction	• Replace oil pump
	• Oil pressure relief valve sticking	• Remove and inspect oil pressure relief valve assembly
	• Oil passages on pressure side of pump obstructed	• Inspect oil passages for obstruction
	• Oil pickup screen or tube obstructed	• Inspect oil pickup for obstruction
	• Loose oil inlet tube	• Tighten or seal inlet tube
Low oil pressure	• Low oil level	• Add oil to correct level
	• Inaccurate gauge, warning lamp or sending unit	• Replace oil pressure gauge or warning lamp
	• Oil excessively thin because of dilution, poor quality, or improper grade	• Drain and refill crankcase with recommended oil
	• Excessive oil temperature	• Correct cause of overheating engine
	• Oil pressure relief spring weak or sticking	• Remove and inspect oil pressure relief valve assembly
	• Oil inlet tube and screen assembly has restriction or air leak	• Remove and inspect oil inlet tube and screen assembly. (Fill inlet tube with lacquer thinner to locate leaks.)
	• Excessive oil pump clearance	• Measure clearances
	• Excessive main, rod, or camshaft bearing clearance	• Measure bearing clearances, repair as necessary
High oil pressure	• Improper oil viscosity	• Drain and refill crankcase with correct viscosity oil
	• Oil pressure gauge or sending unit inaccurate	• Replace oil pressure gauge
	• Oil pressure relief valve sticking closed	• Remove and inspect oil pressure relief valve assembly
Main bearing noise	• Insufficient oil supply	• Inspect for low oil level and low oil pressure
	• Main bearing clearance excessive	• Measure main bearing clearance, repair as necessary

Troubleshooting Engine Mechanical Problems (cont.)

Problem	Cause	Solution
Main bearing noise (cont.)	• Bearing insert missing • Crankshaft end play excessive • Improperly tightened main bearing cap bolts • Loose flywheel or drive plate • Loose or damaged vibration damper	• Replace missing insert • Measure end play, repair as necessary • Tighten bolts with specified torque • Tighten flywheel or drive plate attaching bolts • Repair as necessary
Connecting rod bearing noise	• Insufficient oil supply • Carbon build-up on piston • Bearing clearance excessive or bearing missing • Crankshaft connecting rod journal out-of-round • Misaligned connecting rod or cap • Connecting rod bolts tightened improperly	• Inspect for low oil level and low oil pressure • Remove carbon from piston crown • Measure clearance, repair as necessary • Measure journal dimensions, repair or replace as necessary • Repair as necessary • Tighten bolts with specified torque
Piston noise	• Piston-to-cylinder wall clearance excessive (scuffed piston) • Cylinder walls excessively tapered or out-of-round • Piston ring broken • Loose or seized piston pin • Connecting rods misaligned • Piston ring side clearance excessively loose or tight • Carbon build-up on piston is excessive	• Measure clearance and examine piston • Measure cylinder wall dimensions, rebore cylinder • Replace all rings on piston • Measure piston-to-pin clearance, repair as necessary • Measure rod alignment, straighten or replace • Measure ring side clearance, repair as necessary • Remove carbon from piston
Valve actuating component noise	• Insufficient oil supply • Push rods worn or bent • Rocker arms or pivots worn • Foreign objects or chips in hydraulic tappets • Excessive tappet leak-down • Tappet face worn • Broken or cocked valve springs • Stem-to-guide clearance excessive • Valve bent • Loose rocker arms • Valve seat runout excessive • Missing valve lock • Push rod rubbing or contacting cylinder head • Excessive engine oil (four-cylinder engine)	• Check for: (a) Low oil level (b) Low oil pressure (c) Plugged push rods (d) Wrong hydraulic tappets (e) Restricted oil gallery (f) Excessive tappet to bore clearance • Replace worn or bent push rods • Replace worn rocker arms or pivots • Clean tappets • Replace valve tappet • Replace tappet; inspect corresponding cam lobe for wear • Properly seat cocked springs; replace broken springs • Measure stem-to-guide clearance, repair as required • Replace valve • Tighten bolts with specified torque • Regrind valve seat/valves • Install valve lock • Remove cylinder head and remove obstruction in head • Correct oil level

Troubleshooting the Cooling System

Problem	Cause	Solution
High temperature gauge indication— overheating	• Coolant level low	• Replenish coolant
	• Fan belt loose	• Adjust fan belt tension
	• Radiator hose(s) collapsed	• Replace hose(s)
	• Radiator airflow blocked	• Remove restriction (bug screen, fog lamps, etc.)
	• Faulty radiator cap	• Replace radiator cap
	• Ignition timing incorrect	• Adjust ignition timing
	• Idle speed low	• Adjust idle speed
	• Air trapped in cooling system	• Purge air
	• Heavy traffic driving	• Operate at fast idle in neutral intermittently to cool engine
	• Incorrect cooling system component(s) installed	• Install proper component(s)
	• Faulty thermostat	• Replace thermostat
	• Water pump shaft broken or impeller loose	• Replace water pump
	• Radiator tubes clogged	• Flush radiator
	• Cooling system clogged	• Flush system
	• Casting flash in cooling passages	• Repair or replace as necessary. Flash may be visible by removing cooling system components or removing core plugs.
	• Brakes dragging	• Repair brakes
	• Excessive engine friction	• Repair engine
	• Antifreeze concentration over 68%	• Lower antifreeze concentration percentage
	• Missing air seals	• Replace air seals
	• Faulty gauge or sending unit	• Repair or replace faulty component
	• Loss of coolant flow caused by leakage or foaming	• Repair or replace leaking component, replace coolant
	• Viscous fan drive failed	• Replace unit
Low temperature indication— undercooling	• Thermostat stuck open	• Replace thermostat
	• Faulty gauge or sending unit	• Repair or replace faulty component
Coolant loss—boilover	• Overfilled cooling system	• Reduce coolant level to proper specification
	• Quick shutdown after hard (hot) run	• Allow engine to run at fast idle prior to shutdown
	• Air in system resulting in occasional "burping" of coolant	• Purge system
	• Insufficient antifreeze allowing coolant boiling point to be too low	• Add antifreeze to raise boiling point
	• Antifreeze deteriorated because of age or contamination	• Replace coolant
	• Leaks due to loose hose clamps, loose nuts, bolts, drain plugs, faulty hoses, or defective radiator	• Pressure test system to locate source of leak(s) then repair as necessary
	• Faulty head gasket	• Replace head gasket
	• Cracked head, manifold, or block	• Replace as necessary
	• Faulty radiator cap	• Replace cap
Coolant entry into crankcase or cylinder(s)	• Faulty head gasket	• Replace head gasket
	• Crack in head, manifold or block	• Replace as necessary
Coolant recovery system inoperative	• Coolant level low	• Replenish coolant to FULL mark
	• Leak in system	• Pressure test to isolate leak and repair as necessary
	• Pressure cap not tight or seal missing, or leaking	• Repair as necessary
	• Pressure cap defective	• Replace cap
	• Overflow tube clogged or leaking	• Repair as necessary
	• Recovery bottle vent restricted	• Remove restriction

Troubleshooting the Cooling System (cont.)

Problem	Cause	Solution
Noise	· Fan contacting shroud	· Reposition shroud and inspect engine mounts
	· Loose water pump impeller	· Replace pump
	· Glazed fan belt	· Apply silicone or replace belt
	· Loose fan belt	· Adjust fan belt tension
	· Rough surface on drive pulley	· Replace pulley
	· Water pump bearing worn	· Remove belt to isolate. Replace pump.
	· Belt alignment	· Check pulley alignment. Repair as necessary.
No coolant flow through heater core	· Restricted return inlet in water pump	· Remove restriction
	· Heater hose collapsed or restricted	· Remove restriction or replace hose
	· Restricted heater core	· Remove restriction or replace core
	· Restricted outlet in thermostat housing	· Remove flash or restriction
	· Intake manifold bypass hole in cylinder head restricted	· Remove restriction
	· Faulty heater control valve	· Replace valve
	· Intake manifold coolant passage restricted	· Remove restriction or replace intake manifold

NOTE: *Immediately after shutdown, the engine enters a condition known as heat soak. This is caused by the cooling system being inoperative while engine temperature is still high. If coolant temperature rises above boiling point, expansion and pressure may push some coolant out of the radiator overflow tube. If this does not occur frequently it is considered normal.*

Troubleshooting the Serpentine Drive Belt

Problem	Cause	Solution
Tension sheeting fabric failure (woven fabric on outside circumference of belt has cracked or separated from body of belt)	· Grooved or backside idler pulley diameters are less than minimum recommended	· Replace pulley(s) not conforming to specification
	· Tension sheeting contacting (rubbing) stationary object	· Correct rubbing condition
	· Excessive heat causing woven fabric to age	· Replace belt
	· Tension sheeting splice has fractured	· Replace belt
Noise (objectional squeal, squeak, or rumble is heard or felt while drive belt is in operation)	· Belt slippage	· Adjust belt
	· Bearing noise	· Locate and repair
	· Belt misalignment	· Align belt/pulley(s)
	· Belt-to-pulley mismatch	· Install correct belt
	· Driven component inducing vibration	· Locate defective driven component and repair
	· System resonant frequency inducing vibration	· Vary belt tension within specifications. Replace belt.
Rib chunking (one or more ribs has separated from belt body)	· Foreign objects imbedded in pulley grooves	· Remove foreign objects from pulley grooves
	· Installation damage	· Replace belt
	· Drive loads in excess of design specifications	· Adjust belt tension
	· Insufficient internal belt adhesion	· Replace belt
Rib or belt wear (belt ribs contact bottom of pulley grooves)	· Pulley(s) misaligned	· Align pulley(s)
	· Mismatch of belt and pulley groove widths	· Replace belt
	· Abrasive environment	· Replace belt
	· Rusted pulley(s)	· Clean rust from pulley(s)
	· Sharp or jagged pulley groove tips	· Replace pulley
	· Rubber deteriorated	· Replace belt

Troubleshooting the Serpentine Drive Belt (cont.)

Problem	Cause	Solution
Longitudinal belt cracking (cracks between two ribs)	• Belt has mistracked from pulley groove	• Replace belt
	• Pulley groove tip has worn away rubber-to-tensile member	• Replace belt
Belt slips	• Belt slipping because of insufficient tension	• Adjust tension
	• Belt or pulley subjected to substance (belt dressing, oil, ethylene glycol) that has reduced friction	• Replace belt and clean pulleys
	• Driven component bearing failure	• Replace faulty component bearing
	• Belt glazed and hardened from heat and excessive slippage	• Replace belt
"Groove jumping" (belt does not maintain correct position on pulley, or turns over and/or runs off pulleys)	• Insufficient belt tension	• Adjust belt tension
	• Pulley(s) not within design tolerance	• Replace pulley(s)
	• Foreign object(s) in grooves	• Remove foreign objects from grooves
	• Excessive belt speed	• Avoid excessive engine acceleration
	• Pulley misalignment	• Align pulley(s)
	• Belt-to-pulley profile mismatched	• Install correct belt
	• Belt cordline is distorted	• Replace belt
Belt broken (Note: identify and correct problem before replacement belt is installed)	• Excessive tension	• Replace belt and adjust tension to specification
	• Tensile members damaged during belt installation	• Replace belt
	• Belt turnover	• Replace belt
	• Severe pulley misalignment	• Align pulley(s)
	• Bracket, pulley, or bearing failure	• Replace defective component and belt
Cord edge failure (tensile member exposed at edges of belt or separated from belt body)	• Excessive tension	• Adjust belt tension
	• Drive pulley misalignment	• Align pulley
	• Belt contacting stationary object	• Correct as necessary
	• Pulley irregularities	• Replace pulley
	• Improper pulley construction	• Replace pulley
	• Insufficient adhesion between tensile member and rubber matrix	• Replace belt and adjust tension to specifications
Sporadic rib cracking (multiple cracks in belt ribs at random intervals)	• Ribbed pulley(s) diameter less than minimum specification	• Replace pulley(s)
	• Backside bend flat pulley(s) diameter less than minimum	• Replace pulley(s)
	• Excessive heat condition causing rubber to harden	• Correct heat condition as necessary
	• Excessive belt thickness	• Replace belt
	• Belt overcured	• Replace belt
	• Excessive tension	• Adjust belt tension

6. Remove the air cleaner case and air intake pipe at the air cleaner.

7. Disconnect the battery and engine ground cables at the battery and the valve cover.

8. Disconnect the hose from the fuel vapor storage canister at the carburetor.

9. Disconnect the fuel line at the fuel pump. NOTE: *Plug the line so that gas does not siphon from the tank.*

10. Disconnect the lower coolant hose from the water pump connecting tube and the upper hose from the thermostat cover.

11. Disconnect the following control cables and wires from the engine:

a. Throttle and choke cables from the carburetor.

b. Clutch cable from the release arm.

c. Ignition coil wires from the distributor.

General Engine Specifications

Year	Model	Engine Displacement (cc)	Net Horsepower (@ rpm)	Net Torque (@ rpm)	Bore x Stroke (in.)	Compression Ratio	Oil Pressure (@ rpm)
1973	Civic	1170	50 @ 5000	59 @ 3000	2.76 x 2.99	8.3:1	55 @ 5000
1974	Civic 1200	1237	63 @ 5000	77 @ 3000	2.83 x 3.23	7.9:1	55 @ 5000
1975	Civic 1200	1237	63 @ 5000	77 @ 3000	2.83 x 3.23	7.9:1	55 @ 5000
	Civic CVCC	1487	52 @ 5000	68 @ 3000	2.91 x 3.41	8.0:1	55 @ 5000
1976	Civic 1200	1237	63 @ 5000	77 @ 3000	2.83 x 3.23	7.9:1	55 @ 5000
	Civic CVCC	1487	52 @ 5000	68 @ 3000	2.91 x 3.41	7.9:1	55 @ 5000
	Accord	1600	68 @ 5000	85 @ 3000	2.91 x 3.66	8.2:1	55 @ 5000
1977	Civic 1200	1237	63 @ 5000	77 @ 3000	2.83 x 3.23	7.9:1	55 @ 5000
	Civic CVCC	1487	52 @ 5000	68 @ 3000	2.91 x 3.41	7.9:1	55 @ 5000
	Accord	1600	68 @ 5000	85 @ 3000	2.91 x 3.66	8.2:1	55 @ 5000
1978	Civic 1200	1237	63 @ 5000	77 @ 3000	2.83 x 3.23	7.9:1	55 @ 5000
	Civic CVCC	1487	52 @ 5000	68 @ 3000	2.91 x 3.41	7.9:1	55 @ 5000
	Accord	1600	68 @ 5000	85 @ 3000	2.91 x 3.66	8.2:1	55 @ 5000
1979	Civic 1200	1237	63 @ 5000	77 @ 3000	2.83 x 3.23	7.9:1	55 @ 5000
	Civic CVCC	1487	52 @ 5000	68 @ 3000	2.91 x 3.41	7.9:1	55 @ 5000
	Accord	1751	72 @ 4500	94 @ 3000	3.03 x 3.70	8.0:1	55 @ 5000
	Prelude	1751	72 @ 4500	94 @ 3000	3.03 x 3.70	8.0:1	55 @ 5000
1980	Civic 1300	1335	68 @ 5000	77 @ 3000	2.83 x 3.23	7.9:1	55 @ 5000
	Civic CVCC	1487	52 @ 5000	68 @ 3000	2.91 x 3.41	7.9:1	55 @ 5000
	Accord	1751	72 @ 4500	94 @ 3000	3.03 x 3.70	8.0:1	55 @ 5000
	Prelude	1751	72 @ 4500	94 @ 3000	3.03 x 3.70	8.0:1	55 @ 5000
1981	Civic 1300	1335	60 @ 5500	68 @ 4000	2.83 x 3.23	7.9:1	50 @ 2000
	Civic 1500	1487	63 @ 5000	77 @ 3000	2.91 x 3.41	9.9:1	50 @ 2000
	Accord	1751	72 @ 4500	94 @ 3000	3.03 x 3.70	8.8:1	50 @ 2000
	Prelude	1751	72 @ 4500	94 @ 3000	3.03 x 3.70	8.8:1	50 @ 2000
1982	Civic 1300	1335	60 @ 5500	68 @ 4000	2.83 x 3.23	9.3:1	50 @ 2000
	Civic 1500	1487	63 @ 5000	77 @ 3000	2.91 x 3.41	9.3:1	50 @ 2000
	Accord	1751	72 @ 4500	94 @ 3000	3.03 x 3.70	8.8:1	50 @ 2000
	Prelude	1751	72 @ 4500	94 @ 3000	3.03 x 3.70	8.8:1	50 @ 2000
1983	Civic 1300	1335	60 @ 5500	68 @ 4000	2.83 x 3.23	9.3:1	50 @ 2000
	Civic 1500	1487	63 @ 5000	77 @ 3000	2.91 x 3.41	9.3:1	50 @ 2000
	Accord	1751	75 @ 4500	96 @ 3000	3.03 x 3.70	8.8:1	50 @ 2000
	Prelude	1829	100 @ 5000	104 @ 4000	3.15 x 3.58	9.4:1	60 @ 1500
1984	Civic/CRX, 1.3	1342	60 @ 5500	73 @ 3500	2.91 x 3.02	10.0:1	50 @ 2000
	Civic/CRX HF, 1.5	1488	76 @ 6000	84 @ 3500	2.91 x 3.42	9.2:1	55 @ 2000
	Accord	1829	86 @ 5800	99 @ 3500	3.15 x 3.58	9.0:1	50 @ 2000
	Prelude	1829	100 @ 5500	104 @ 4000	3.15 x 3.58	9.1:1	60 @ 1500
1985	Civic/CRX, 1.3	1342	60 @ 5500	73 @ 3500	2.91 x 3.02	10.0:1	50 @ 2000
	Civic/CRX, 1.5	1488	76 @ 6000	84 @ 3500	2.91 x 3.42	9.2:1	55 @ 2000
	Civic/CRX, HF	1488	65 @ 5500	81 @ 3500	2.91 x 3.42	9.2:1	50 @ 2000

General Engine Specifications (cont.)

Year	Model	Engine Displacement (cc)	Net Horsepower (@ rpm)	Net Torque (@ rpm)	Bore x Stroke (in.)	Compression Ratio	Oil Pressure (@ rpm)
1985	Civic/CRX, Si	1488	91 @ 5500	93 @ 4500	2.91 x 3.41	8.7:1	50 @ 2000
	Accord	1829	86 @ 5800	99 @ 3500	3.15 x 3.58	9.0:1	50 @ 2000
	Accord SE-i	1829	101 @ 5800	108 @ 2500	3.15 x 3.58	8.8:1	50 @ 2000
	Prelude	1829	100 @ 5500	104 @ 4000	3.15 x 3.58	9.1:1	55 @ 2000
1986	Civic/CRX, 1.3	1342	60 @ 5500	73 @ 3500	2.91 x 3.02	10.0:1	50 @ 2000
	Civic/CRX, 1.5	1488	70 @ 6000	84 @ 3500	2.91 x 3.41	9.2:1	50 @ 2000
	Civic/CRX, HF	1488	58 @ 4500	80 @ 2500	2.91 x 3.41	8.7:1	50 @ 2000
	Civic/CRX, Si	1488	91 @ 5500	93 @ 4500	2.91 x 3.41	8.7:1	50 @ 2000
	Accord	1955	98 @ 5500	110 @ 3500	3.25 x 3.58	9.1:1	55 @ 2000
	Accord LX-i	1955	110 @ 5500	114 @ 4500	3.25 x 3.58	8.8:1	55 @ 2000
	Prelude	1829	100 @ 5500	107 @ 4000	3.15 x 3.58	9.1:1	50 @ 2000
	Prelude Si	1955	110 @ 5500	114 @ 4500	3.25 x 3.58	8.8:1	50 @ 2000
1987	Civic/CRX, 1.3	1392	60 @ 5500	73 @ 3500	2.91 x 3.07	10.0:1	50 @ 2000
	Civic/CRX, 1.5	1488	76 @ 6000	84 @ 3500	2.91 x 3.41	9.2:1	50 @ 2000
	Civic/CRX, HF	1488	58 @ 4500	80 @ 2500	2.91 x 3.41	9.6:1	50 @ 2000
	Civic/CRX, Si	1488	91 @ 5500	93 @ 4500	2.91 x 3.41	8.7:1	50 @ 2000
	Accord	1955	98 @ 5500	109 @ 3500	3.25 x 3.58	9.1:1	55 @ 2000
	Accord LX-i	1955	110 @ 5500	114 @ 4500	3.25 x 3.58	8.8:1	55 @ 2000
	Prelude	1829	100 @ 5500	107 @ 4000	3.15 x 3.58	9.1:1	50 @ 2000
	Prelude Si	1955	110 @ 5500	114 @ 4500	3.25 x 3.58	8.8:1	50 @ 2000
1988	Civic, 1.5	1493	70 @ 5500	83 @ 3000	2.95 x 3.33	9.6:1	50 @ 2000
	Civic/CRX, HF	1493	62 @ 5500	83 @ 3000	2.95 x 3.33	9.6:1	50 @ 2000
	Civic/CRX, 1.5	1493	92 @ 6000	89 @ 4500	2.95 x 3.33	9.2:1	50 @ 2000
	Civic/CRX Si	1590	105 @ 6000	98 @ 5000	2.95 x 3.54	9.1:1	50 @ 2000
	Accord	1955	98 @ 5500	109 @ 3500	2.25 x 3.58	9.1:1	55 @ 2000
	Accord LX-i	1955	110 @ 5500	114 @ 4500	3.25 x 3.58	9.3:1	55 @ 2000
	Prelude	1955	100 @ 5500	107 @ 4000	3.19 x 3.74	9.1:1	50 @ 2000
	Prelude Si	1955	110 @ 5500	114 @ 4500	3.18 x 3.74	9.0:1	50 @ 2000

Crankshaft and Connecting Rod Specifications

All measurements are given in inches

Year	Engine Displacement cc	Crankshaft				Connecting Rod		
		Main Brg. Journal Dia.	Main Brg. Oil Clearance	Shaft End-play	Thrust on No.	Journal Diameter	Oil Clearance	Side Clearance
1973	1170	1.9685–1.9673	0.0009–0.0017	0.0039–0.0138	3	1.5736–1.5748	0.0008–0.0015	0.0079–0.0177
1974	1237	1.9685–1.9673	0.0009–0.0017	0.0039–0.0138	3	1.5736–1.5748	0.0008–0.0015	0.0059–0.0118
1975	1237	1.9685–1.9673	0.0009–0.0017	0.0039–0.0138	3	1.5736–1.5748	0.0008–0.0015	0.0059–0.0118

Crankshaft and Connecting Rod Specifications (cont.)

All measurements are given in inches

Year	Engine Displacement cc	Crankshaft				Connecting Rod		
		Main Brg. Journal Dia.	Main Brg. Oil Clearance	Shaft End-play	Thrust on No.	Journal Diameter	Oil Clearance	Side Clearance
1975	1487	1.9687–1.9697	0.0010–0.0021	0.0039–0.0138	3	1.6525–1.6535	0.0008–0.0015	0.0059–0.0118
1976	1237	1.9685–1.9673	0.0009–0.0017	0.0039–0.0138	3	1.5736–1.5748	0.0008–0.0015	0.0059–0.0118
	1487	1.9687–1.9697	0.0010–0.0021	0.0039–0.0138	3	1.6525–1.6535	0.0008–0.0015	0.0059–0.0118
	1600	1.9687–1.9697	0.0010–0.0021	0.0039–0.0138	3	1.6525–1.6535	0.0008–0.0015	0.0059–0.0118
1977	1237	1.9685–1.9673	0.0009–0.0017	0.0039–0.0138	3	1.5736–1.5748	0.0008–0.0015	0.0059–0.0118
	1487	1.9687–1.9697	0.0010–0.0021	0.0039–0.0138	3	1.6525–1.6535	0.0008–0.0015	0.0059–0.0118
	1600	1.9687–1.9697	0.0010–0.0021	0.0039–0.1038	3	1.6525–1.6535	0.0008–0.0015	0.0059–0.0118
1978	1237	1.9685–1.9673	0.0009–0.0017	0.0039–0.0138	3	1.5736–1.5748	0.0008–0.0015	0.0059–0.0118
	1487	1.9687–1.9697	0.0010–0.0021	0.0039–0.0138	3	1.6525–1.6535	0.0008–0.0015	0.0059–0.0118
	1600	1.9687–1.9697	0.0010–0.0021	0.0039–0.0138	3	1.6525–1.6535	0.0008–0.0015	0.0059–0.0118
1979	1237	1.9687–1.9697	0.0009–0.0017	0.0040–0.0140	3	1.5739–1.5748	0.0008–0.0015	0.0059–0.0118
	1487	1.9687–1.9697	0.0010–0.0022	0.0040–0.0140	3	1.6526–1.6535	0.0008–0.0015	0.006–0.012
	1751	1.9687–1.9697	0.0010–0.0022	0.0040–0.0140	3	1.6525–1.6535	0.0008–0.0015	0.006–0.012
1980	1335	1.9687–1.9697	0.0010–0.0022	0.0040–0.0140	3	1.5739–1.5748	0.0008–0.0015	0.006–0.012
	1487	1.9687–1.9697	0.0010–0.0022	0.0040–0.0140	3	1.6526–1.6535	0.0008–0.0015	0.006–0.012
	1751	1.9687–1.9697	0.0010–0.0022	0.0040–0.0140	3	1.6525–1.6535	0.0008–0.0015	0.006–0.012
1981	1335	1.9676–1.9685	0.0009–0.0017	0.0040–0.0140	3	1.5739–1.5748	0.0008–0.0015	0.006–0.012
	1487	1.9687–1.9803	0.0010–0.0022	0.0040–0.0140	3	1.6525–1.6535	0.0008–0.0015	0.006–0.012
	1751	1.9687–1.9697	0.0010–0.0022	0.0040–0.0140	3	1.6525–1.6535	0.0008–0.0015	0.006–0.012
1982	1335	1.9676–1.9685	0.0009–0.0017	0.0040–0.0140	3	1.5739–1.5748	0.0006–0.0015	0.006–0.012
	1487	1.9687–1.9803	0.0010–0.0022	0.0040–0.0140	3	1.6525–1.6535	0.0008–0.0015	0.006–0.012
	1751	1.9687–1.9697	0.0010–0.0022	0.0040–0.0140	3	1.6525–1.6535	0.0008–0.0015	0.006–0.012
1983	1335	1.9676–1.9685	0.0009–0.0017	0.0040–0.0140	3	1.5739–1.5748	0.0008–0.0015	0.006–0.012
	1487	1.9687–1.9803	0.0010–0.0022	0.0040–0.0140	3	1.6525–1.6535	0.0008–0.0015	0.006–0.012

Crankshaft and Connecting Rod Specifications (cont.)

All measurements are given in inches

Year	Engine Displacement cc	Crankshaft				Connecting Rod		
		Main Brg. Journal Dia.	Main Brg. Oil Clearance	Shaft End-play	Thrust on No.	Journal Diameter	Oil Clearance	Side Clearance
1983	1751	1.9687–1.9697	0.0010–0.0022	0.0040–0.0140	3	1.6525–1.6535	0.0008–0.0015	0.006–0.012
	1829	1.9687–1.9697	0.0010–0.0022	0.0040–0.0140	3	1.7707–1.7717	0.0006–0.0015	0.006–0.012
1984	1342	1.7707–1.7717	0.0009–0.0017	0.0040–0.0140	3	1.4951–1.4961	0.0008–0.0015	0.006–0.012
	1488	1.9676–1.9685	0.0009–0.0017	0.0040–0.0140	3	1.6526–1.6535	0.0008–0.0015	0.006–0.012
	1829	1.9673–1.9683	0.0010–0.0022	0.0040–0.0140	3	1.7707–1.7717	0.0006–0.0015	0.006–0.012
1985	1342	1.7707–1.7717	0.0009–0.0017	0.0040–0.0140	3	1.4951–1.4961	0.0008–0.0015	0.006–0.012
	1488	1.9676–1.9685	0.0009–0.0017	0.0040–0.0140	3	1.6526–1.6535	0.0008–0.0015	0.006–0.012
	1829	1.9673–1.9683	0.0010–0.0022	0.0040–0.0140	3	1.7707–1.7717	0.0006–0.0015	0.006–0.012
1986	1342	1.7707–1.7717	0.0009–0.0017	0.0040–0.0140	3	1.4951–1.4961	0.0008–0.0015	0.006–0.012
	1488	1.9676–1.9685	0.0009–0.0017	0.0040–0.0140	3	1.6526–1.6535	0.0008–0.0015	0.006–0.012
	1829	1.9673–1.9683	0.0010–0.0022 ①	0.0040–0.0140	3	1.7707–1.7717	0.0008–0.0015	0.006–0.012
1987	1342	1.7707–1.7717	0.0009–0.0017	0.0040–0.0140	3	1.4951–1.4961	0.0008–0.0015	0.006–0.012
	1488	1.9676–1.9685	0.0009–0.0017	0.0040–0.0140	3	1.6526–1.6535	0.0008–0.0015	0.006–0.012
	1829	1.9673–1.9683 ②	0.0010–0.0022 ①	0.0040–0.0140	3	1.7707–1.7717	0.0006–0.0015	0.006–0.012
	1955	1.9673–1.9683 ②	0.0010–0.0022 ①	0.0040–0.0140	3	1.7707–1.7717	0.0006–0.0015	0.006–0.012
1988	1493	1.7707–1.7718	0.0010–0.0017	0.0040–0.0140	3	③	0.0008–0.0015	0.006–0.012
	1590	2.1644–2.1654	0.0010–0.0017	0.0040–0.0140	3	1.7707–1.7717	0.0008–0.0015	0.006–0.012
	1955 Accord	②	0.0010–0.0022 ①	0.0040–0.0140	3	1.7707–1.7717	0.0008–0.0015	0.006–0.012
	1955 Prelude	2.1644–2.1654	0.0010–0.0017 ④	0.0040–0.0140	3	1.7707–1.7717	0.0010–0.0017	0.006–0.012
	1955 Prelude Si	2.1644–2.1654	0.0010–0.0017 ④	0.0040–0.0140	3	1.8888–1.8900	0.0010–0.0017	0.006–0.012

① No. 3: 0.0013–0.0024
② Accord: No 1: 1.9676–1.9685
   No. 3: 1.9671–1.9680
   No. 2, 4, 5: 1.9673–1.9683

③ Exc. HF: 1.5739–1.5748
   HF: 1.4951–1.4961
④ No. 3: 0.0012–0.0019

Torque Specifications
All readings in ft. lbs.

Year	Engine Displacement cc	Cylinder Head Bolts ①	Main Bearing Bolts	Rod Bearing Bolts	Crankshaft Pulley Bolts	Flywheel Bolts	Manifold		Spark Plugs
							Intake	Exhaust	
1973	1170	④	27–31	18–21	34–38	34–38	13–17	13–17	15
1974	1237	37–42	27–31	18–21	34–38	34–38	13–17	13–17	15
1975	1237	37–42	27–31	18–21	34–38	34–38	13–17	13–17	15
	1487	40–47	30–35	18–21	34–38	34–38	15–18	15–18	15
1976	1237	37–42	27–31	18–21	34–38	34–38	13–17	13–17	15
	1487	40–47	30–35	18–21	34–38	34–38	15–18	15–18	15
	1600	40–47	30–35	18–21	34–38	34–38	15–18	15–18	15
1977	1237	37–42	27–31	18–21	34–38	34–38	13–17	13–17	15
	1487	40–47	30–35	18–21	34–38	34–38	15–18	15–18	15
	1600	40–47	30–35	18–21	34–38	34–38	15–18	15–18	15
1978	1237	37–42	27–31	18–21	34–38	34–38	13–17	13–17	15
	1487	40–47	30–35	18–21	34–38	34–38	15–18	15–18	15
	1600	40–47	30–35	18–21	34–38	34–38	15–18	15–18	15
1979	1237	37–42	27–31	18–21	34–38	34–38	13–17	13–17	15
	1487	33	29	21	61	51	18	18	15
	1751	43	48	23	61	51	18	18	15
1980	1335	43	29–33	21	80	51	18	18	13
	1487	43	29–33	21	80	51	18	18	13
	1751	43	48	23	80	51	18	18	13
1981	1335	43	29–33	21	80	51	18	18	13
	1487	43	29–33	21	80	51	18	18	13
	1751	43	48	23	83	51	18	18	13
1982	1335	43	29–33	21	80	51	18	18	13
	1487	43	29–33	21	80	51	18	18	13
	1751	43	48	21	80	51	18	18	13
1983	1335	43	29–33	21	80	51	18	18	13
	1487	43	29–33	21	80	51	18	18	13
	1751	43	48	21	80	51	18	18	13
	1829	49	48	23	83	76 ②	16	22	13
1984	1342	43	33	20	83	76 ②	16	23	13
	1488	43	33	20	83	76 ②	16	23	13
	1829	49	48	23	83	76 ②	16	22	13
1985	1342	43	33	20	83	76 ②	16	23	13
	1488	43	33	20	83	76 ②	16	23	13
	1829	49	48	23	83	76 ②	16	22	13
1986	1342	43	33	20	83	76 ②	16	23	13
	1488	43	33	20	83	76 ②	16	23	13
	1829	49	48	23	83	76 ②	16	22	13
	1955	49	48	23	83	76 ②	16	22	13

Torque Specifications (cont.)
All readings in ft. lbs.

Year	Engine Displacement cc	Cylinder Head Bolts ①	Main Bearing Bolts	Rod Bearing Bolts	Crankshaft Pulley Bolts	Flywheel Bolts	Manifold		Spark Plugs
							Intake	Exhaust	
1987	1342	43	33	20	83	76 ②	16	23	13
	1488	43	33	20	83	76 ②	16	23	13
	1829	49	48	23	83	76 ②	16	22	13
	1955	49	48	23	83	76 ②	16	22	13
1988	1493	49	48	23	83	87 ②	25	25	13
	1590	49	48	23	83	87 ②	25	25	13
	1955	49	49	23	83	76 ②	20	23	13
	1955 ③	49	49	33	83	76 ②	16	26	13

① 2-Step procedure; see text
② Auto Trans: 54
③ DOHC: Double overhead cam engine
④ To engine number EB 1-1019949: 30–35 ft. lbs.
  From engine number EB 1-1019950: 37–42 ft. lbs.

Valve Specifications

Year	Engine Displacement (cc)	Seat Angle (deg.)	Face Angle (deg.)	Spring Test Pressure (lbs.)	Spring Installed Height (in.)	Stem-to-Guide Clearance in. ①		Stem Diameter in. ①	
						In.	Ex.	In.	Ex.
1973	1170	45	45	NA	⑭	0.005–0.007	0.005–0.007	0.2591–0.2594	0.2579–0.2583
1974	1237	45	45	NA	⑭	0.005–0.007	0.005–0.007	0.2591–0.2594	0.2579–0.2583
1975	1237	45	45	NA	⑭	0.005–0.007	0.005–0.007	0.2591–0.2594	0.2579–0.2583
	1487	45	45	NA	⑬	0.0004–0.0016	0.0020–0.0031	0.2592–0.2596	0.2580–0.2584
1976	1237	45	45	NA	⑭	0.005–0.007	0.005–0.007	0.2591–0.2594	0.2579–0.2583
	1487	45	45	NA	⑬	0.0004–0.0016	0.0020–0.0031	0.2592–0.2596	0.2580–0.2584
	1600	45	45	NA	⑬	0.0004–0.0016	0.0020–0.0031	0.2592–0.2596	0.2580–0.2584
1977	1237	45	45	NA	⑭	0.005–0.007	0.005–0.007	0.2591–0.2594	0.2579–0.2583
	1487	45	45	NA	⑬	0.0004–0.0016	0.0020–0.0031	0.2592–0.2596	0.2580–0.2584
	1600	45	45	NA	⑬	0.0004–0.0016	0.0020–0.0031	0.2592–0.2596	0.2580–0.2584
1978	1237	45	45	NA	⑭	0.005–0.007	0.005–0.007	0.2591–0.2594	0.2579–0.2583
	1487	45	45	NA	⑬	0.0004–0.0016	0.0020–0.0031	0.2592–0.2596	0.2580–0.2584
	1600	45	45	NA	⑬	0.0004–0.0016	0.0020–0.0031	0.2592–0.2596	0.2580–0.2584

Valve Specifications (cont.)

Year	Engine Displacement (cc)	Seat Angle (deg.)	Face Angle (deg.)	Spring Test Pressure (lbs.)	Spring Installed Height (in.)	Stem-to-Guide Clearance in. ①		Stem Diameter in. ①	
						In.	Ex.	In.	Ex.
1979	1237	45	45	NA	⑭	0.005–0.007	0.005–0.007	0.2591–0.2594	0.2579–0.2583
	1487	45	45	NA	⑫	0.0004–0.0016	0.0020–0.0031	0.2592–0.2596	0.2580–0.2584
	1751	45	45	NA	⑪	0.001–0.002	0.002–0.004	0.2748–0.2751	0.2732–0.2736
1980	1335	45	45	NA	②	0.0008–0.0020	0.0008–0.0037	0.2591–0.2594	0.2574–0.2578
	1487	45	45	NA	②	0.0008–0.0020	0.0008–0.0037	0.2591–0.2594	0.2574–0.2578
	1751	45	45	NA	⑪	0.001–0.002	0.002–0.004	0.2748–0.2751	0.2732–0.2736
1981	1335	45	45	NA	②	0.0008–0.0020	0.0008–0.0037	0.2591–0.2594	0.2574–0.2578
	1487	45	45	NA	②	0.0008–0.0020	0.0008–0.0037	0.2591–0.2594	0.2574–0.2578
	1751	45	45	NA	③	0.001–0.002	0.002–0.004	0.2748–0.2751	0.2732–0.2736
1982	1335	45	45	NA	②	0.0008–0.0020	0.0025–0.0037	0.2591–0.2594	0.2574–0.2578
	1487	45	45	NA	②	0.0008–0.0020	0.0025–0.0037	0.2591–0.2594	0.2574–0.2578
	1751	45	45	NA	③	0.001–0.002	0.002–0.004	0.2748–0.2751	0.2732–0.2736
1983	1335	45	45	NA	②	0.0008–0.0020	0.0025–0.0037	0.2591–0.2594	0.2574–0.2578
	1487	45	45	NA	②	0.0008–0.0020	0.0025–0.0037	0.2591–0.2594	0.2574–0.2578
	1751	45	45	NA	③	0.001–0.002	0.002–0.004	0.2748–0.2751	0.2732–0.2736
	1829	45	45	NA	④	0.001–0.002	0.002–0.004	0.2591–0.2594	0.2736–0.2736
1984	1342	45	45	NA	⑤	0.001–0.002	0.002–0.003	0.2591–0.2594	0.2579–0.2583
	1488	45	45	NA	⑤	0.001–0.002	0.002–0.003	0.2591–0.2594	0.2579–0.2583
	1829	45	45	NA	④	0.001–0.002	0.002–0.004	0.2591–0.2594	0.2732–0.2736
1985	1342	45	45	NA	1.896 ⑥	0.001–0.002	0.002–0.003	0.2591–0.2594	0.2579–0.2583
	1488	45	45	NA	1.896 ⑥	0.001–0.002	0.002–0.003	0.2591–0.2594	0.2579–0.2583
	1829	45	45	NA	④	0.001–0.002	0.002–0.004	0.2591–0.2594	0.2732–0.2736
1986	1342	45	45	NA	1.896 ⑥	0.001–0.002	0.002–0.003	0.2591–0.2594	0.2579–0.2583
	1488	45	45	NA	1.896 ⑥	0.001–0.002	0.002–0.003	0.2591–0.2594	0.2579–0.2583

Valve Specifications (cont.)

Year	Engine Displacement (cc)	Seat Angle (deg.)	Face Angle (deg.)	Spring Test Pressure (lbs.)	Spring Installed Height (in.)	Stem-to-Guide Clearance in. ①		Stem Diameter in. ①	
						In.	Ex.	In.	Ex.
1986	1829	45	45	NA	⑦	0.001–0.002	0.002–0.004	0.2591–0.2594	0.2732–0.2736
	1955	45	45	NA	⑦	0.001–0.002	0.002–0.004	0.2591–0.2594	0.2732–0.2736
1987	1342	45	45	NA	⑤	0.001–0.002	0.002–0.003	0.2591–0.2594	0.2579–0.2583
	1488	45	45	NA	⑤	0.001–0.002	0.002–0.003	0.2591–0.2594	0.2579–0.2583
	1829	45	45	NA	⑦	0.001–0.002	0.002–0.004	0.2591–0.2594	0.2732–0.2736
	1955	45	45	NA	⑦	0.001–0.002	0.002–0.004	0.2591–0.2594	0.2732–0.2736
1988	1493	45	45	NA	⑧	0.001–0.002	0.002–0.003	0.2157–0.2161	0.2147–0.2150
	1590	45	45	NA	⑨	0.001–0.002	0.002–0.003	0.2157–0.2161	0.2147–0.2150
	1955	45	45	NA	⑦	0.001–0.002	0.002–0.004	0.2591–0.2594	0.2732–0.2736
	1955 ⑩	45	45	NA	1.683	0.001–0.002	0.002–0.003	0.2591–0.2594	0.2579–0.2583

NA Not Available
① Jet Valve: 0.0009–0.0023
② 1335cc, 1487cc:
  Intake & Exhaust inner: 1.402
  Intake & Exhaust outer: 1.488
  Auxiliary: 0.906
③ 1751cc:
  Intake & Exhaust inner: 1.402
  Intake & Exhaust outer: 1.488
  Auxiliary: 0.984
④ 1829cc, 1955cc:
  Intake: 1.660
  Exhaust inner: 1.460
  Exhaust outer: 1.670
  Auxiliary: 0.984 carbureted
⑤ 1342cc, 1488cc:
  Intake: 1.660
  Exhaust: 1.690
  Auxiliary: 0.980 carbureted
⑥ Auxiliary: 1.311
⑦ Intake: 1.913
  Exhaust: 1.876
⑧ 1493cc:
  Intake: 1.8498–1.8880
  Exhaust: 1.9278–1.9463

⑨ 1590cc:
  Intake: 1.8498–1.8683
  Exhaust: 1.9278–1.9263
⑩ DOHC: Double Overhead Cam Engine
⑪ 1751cc: (1979–80)
  Intake inner: 1.000
  Exhaust inner: 1.031
  Intake outer: 1.094
  Exhaust outer: 1.109
  Auxiliary: 0.875
⑫ 1487cc: (1979)
  Intake inner: 1.401
  Exhaust inner: 1.358
  Intake outer: 1.488
  Exhaust outer: 1.437
  Auxiliary: 0.906
⑬ 1487cc, 1600cc: (1975–78)
  Inner: 1.358
  Outer: 1.437
  Auxiliary: 0.906
⑭ 1170cc, 1237cc: (1973–79)
  Inner: 1.6535
  Outer: 1.5728

Piston and Ring Specifications

All measurements are given in inches.

Year	Engine Displacement cc	Piston Clearance	Ring Gap		Ring Side Clearance			
			Top Compression	Bottom Compression	Oil Control	Top Compression	Bottom Compression	Oil Control
1973	1170	0.0012–0.0039	0.008–0.016	0.008–0.016	0.008–0.035	0.0008–0.0018	0.0008–0.0018	Snug

Piston and Ring Specifications (cont.)

All measurements are given in inches.

Year	Engine Displacement cc	Piston Clearance	Ring Gap		Ring Side Clearance			Oil Control
			Top Compression	Bottom Compression	Oil Control	Top Compression	Bottom Compression	
1974	1237	0.0012–0.0039	0.010–0.016	0.010–0.016	0.011–0.034	0.0008–0.0018	0.0008–0.0018	Snug
1975	1237	0.0012–0.0039	0.010–0.016	0.010–0.016	0.011–0.034	0.0008–0.0018	0.0008–0.0018	Snug
	1487	0.0012–0.0039	0.008–0.016	0.008–0.016	0.008–0.035	0.0008–0.0018	0.0008–0.0018	Snug
1976	1237	0.0012–0.0039	0.010–0.016	0.010–0.016	0.011–0.034	0.0008–0.0018	0.0008–0.0018	Snug
	1487	0.0012–0.0039	0.008–0.016	0.008–0.016	0.008–0.035	0.0008–0.0018	0.0008–0.0018	Snug
	1600	0.0012–0.0039	0.008–0.016	0.008–0.016	0.008–0.035	0.0008–0.0018	0.0008–0.0018	Snug
1977	1237	0.0012–0.0039	0.010–0.016	0.010–0.016	0.011–0.034	0.0008–0.0018	0.0008–0.0018	Snug
	1487	0.0012–0.0039	0.008–0.016	0.008–0.016	0.008–0.035	0.0008–0.0018	0.0008–0.0018	Snug
	1600	0.0012–0.0039	0.008–0.016	0.008–0.016	0.008–0.035	0.0008–0.0018	0.0008–0.0018	Snug
1978	1237	0.0012–0.0039	0.010–0.016	0.010–0.016	0.011–0.034	0.0008–0.0018	0.0008–0.0018	Snug
	1487	0.0012–0.0039	0.008–0.016	0.008–0.016	0.008–0.035	0.0008–0.0018	0.0008–0.0018	Snug
	1600	0.0012–0.0039	0.008–0.016	0.008–0.016	0.008–0.035	0.0008–0.0018	0.0008–0.0018	Snug
1979	1237	0.0012–0.0039	0.010–0.016	0.010–0.016	0.011–0.034	0.0008–0.0018	0.0008–0.0018	Snug
	1487	0.0012–0.0060	0.008–0.016	0.008–0.016	0.008–0.035	0.0008–0.0018	0.0008–0.0018	Snug
	1751	0.0008–0.0028	0.006–0.014	0.006–0.014	0.012–0.035	0.0008–0.0018	0.0008–0.0018	Snug
1980	1335	0.0004–0.0020	0.006–0.014	0.006–0.014	0.012–0.035	0.0008–0.0018	0.0008–0.0018	Snug
	1487	0.0004–0.0020	0.006–0.014	0.006–0.014	0.012–0.035	0.0008–0.0018	0.0008–0.0018	Snug
	1751	0.0008–0.0028	0.006–0.014	0.006–0.014	0.012–0.035	0.0008–0.0018	0.0008–0.0018	Snug
1981	1335	0.0004–0.0020	0.006–0.014	0.006–0.014	0.012–0.035	0.0008–0.0018	0.0008–0.0018	Snug
	1487	0.0004–0.0020	0.006–0.014	0.006–0.014	0.012–0.035	0.0008–0.0018	0.0008–0.0018	Snug
	1751	0.0008–0.0028	0.006–0.014	0.006–0.014	0.012–0.035	0.0008–0.0018	0.0008–0.0018	Snug
1982	1335	0.004–0.0020	0.006–0.014	0.006–0.014	0.012–0.035	0.0012–0.0024	0.0012–0.0024	Snug
	1487	0.0004–0.0020	0.006–0.014	0.006–0.014	0.012–0.035	0.0012–0.0020	0.0012–0.0020	Snug
	1751	0.0004–0.0024	0.006–0.014	0.006–0.014	0.012–0.035	0.0008–0.0018	0.0008–0.0018	Snug

Piston and Ring Specifications (cont.)

All measurements are given in inches.

Year	Engine Displacement cc	Piston Clearance	Ring Gap		Ring Side Clearance			
			Top Compression	Bottom Compression	Oil Control	Top Compression	Bottom Compression	Oil Control
1983	1335	0.0004–0.0020	0.006–0.014	0.006–0.014	0.012–0.035	0.0012–0.0024	0.0012–0.0024	Snug
	1487	0.0004–0.0020	0.006–0.014	0.006–0.014	0.012–0.035	0.0012–0.0020	0.0012–0.0020	Snug
	1751	0.0004–0.0024	0.006–0.014	0.006–0.014	0.012–0.035	0.0008–0.0018	0.0008–0.0018	Snug
	1829	0.0008–0.0016	0.008–0.014	0.008–0.014	0.008–0.035	0.0008–0.0018	0.0008–0.0018	Snug
1984	1342	0.0004–0.0020	0.006–0.014	0.006–0.014	0.006–0.024	0.0012–0.0024	0.0012–0.0022	Snug
	1488	0.0004–0.0020	0.006–0.014	0.006–0.014	0.006–0.024	0.0012–0.0024	0.0012–0.0022	Snug
	1829	0.0008–0.0016	0.008–0.014	0.008–0.014	0.008–0.035	0.0008–0.0018	0.0008–0.0018	Snug
1985	1342	0.0004–0.0020	0.006–0.014	0.006–0.014	0.006–0.014	0.0012–0.0024	0.0012–0.0024	Snug
	1488	0.0004–0.0020	0.006–0.014	0.006–0.014	0.006–0.014	0.0012–0.0024	0.0012–0.0024	Snug
	1829	0.0008–0.0016	0.008–0.014	0.008–0.014	0.008–0.035	0.0008–0.0018	0.0008–0.0018	Snug
1986	1342	0.004–0.0020	0.006–0.014	0.006–0.014	0.008–0.024	0.0012–0.0024	0.0012–0.0022	Snug
	1488	0.0004–0.0020	0.006–0.014	0.006–0.014	0.008–0.024	0.0012–0.0024	0.0012–0.0022	Snug
	1829	0.0008–0.0016	0.008–0.014	0.008–0.014	0.008–0.035	0.0008–0.0018	0.0008–0.0018	Snug
	1955	0.0008–0.0016	0.008–0.014	0.010–0.015	0.008–0.020	0.0012–0.0022	0.0012–0.0022	Snug
1987	1342	0.0004–0.0020	0.006–0.014	0.006–0.014	0.008–0.024	0.0012–0.0024	0.0012–0.0022	Snug
	1488	0.0004–0.0020	0.006–0.014	0.006–0.014	0.008–0.024	0.0012–0.0024	0.0012–0.0022	Snug
	1829	0.0008–0.0016	0.008–0.014	0.008–0.014	0.008–0.035	0.0008–0.0018	0.0008–0.0018	Snug
	1955	0.0008–0.0016	0.008–0.014	0.008–0.014	0.008–0.020	0.0012–0.0024	0.0012–0.0024	Snug
1988	1493	0.0004–0.0016	0.006–0.014	0.006–0.014	0.008–0.024	0.0012–0.0024	0.0012–0.0022	Snug
	1590	0.0004–0.0016	0.006–0.014	0.006–0.014	0.008–0.024	0.0012–0.0024	0.0012–0.0022	Snug
	1955	0.0008–0.0016	0.008–0.014	0.016–0.022	0.008–0.028 [1]	0.0012–0.0024	0.0012–0.0024	Snug

[1] Carbureted Engine: 0.008–0.020

d. Starter motor positive battery cable connection and solenoid wire.

e. Back-up light switch and the TCS (Transmission Controlled Spark) switch wires from the transmission casing.

f. Speedometer and tachometer cables.

WARNING: *When removing the speedometer cable from the transaxle, it is not necessary to remove the entire cable holder. Remove the end boot (gear holder seal) and the cable retaining clip, then, pull the cable out of the holder. In no way should you disturb the holder unless it is absolutely necessary!*

The holder consists of three pieces: the holder, collar and a dowel pin. The dowel pin indexes the holder and collar and is held in place by the bolt that retains the holder. If the bolt is removed and the holder rotated, the dowel pin can fall into the transmission case, necessitating transaxle disassembly to remove the pin. To insure that this does not happen when the holder must be removed, do not rotate the holder more than 30° in either direction when removing it. Once removed, make sure that the pin is still in place. Use the same precaution when installing the holder.

g. Alternator wire and wire harness connector.

h. The wires from both water temperature thermal switches on the intake manifold.

i. Cooling fan connector and radiator thermoswitch wires.

j. Oil pressure sensor.

k. On 1975-76 models, vacuum hose to throttle opener at opener and vacuum hose

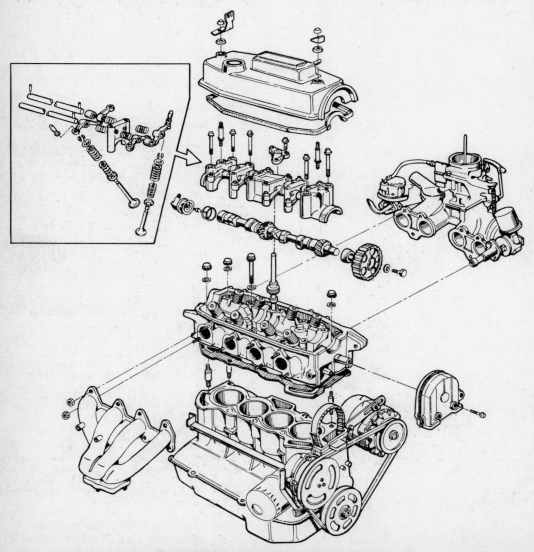

Exploded view of 1170 1237, 1335 cc engine

from carburetor insulator to throttle opener.

l. On 1976-77 models, bypass valve assemble and bracket.

NOTE: *It would be a good idea to tag all of these wires to avoid confusion during installation.*

12. Disconnect the heater hose by removing the **H** connector from the two hoses in the firewall.

13. Remove the engine torque rod from the engine and firewall.

14. Remove the starter motor.

15. Remove the radiator from the engine compartment.

16. Remove the exhaust pipe-to-manifold clamp.

17. Remove the exhaust pipe flange nuts and lower the exhaust pipe.

18. Using a Ball Joint Remover tool No. 07941-6340000 or equivalent, disconnect the left and right lower control arm ball joints from the steering knuckle.

19. Hold the brake disc, then, pull the both halfshafts from the differential case.

20. Depending on the transaxle used, perform the following procedures:

a. Manual transaxle: Using a drift punch, drive out the gearshift rod pin (8mm) and disconnect the rod at the transaxle case.

NOTE: *Do not disconnect the shift lever end of the gearshift rod and extension.*

b. Hondamatic only: Disconnect shift cable from the console and the cooler line from the transaxle.

21. If equipped with a manual transaxle, disconnect the gearshift extension from the engine.

22. Install two engine hanger bolts in the torque rod bolt hole and the bolt hole to the left of the distributor. Install a lift chain on the hanger bolts and lift the engine, slightly, to take the load off the engine mounts.

23. When the engine is properly supported, remove the two center mount bracket nuts.

24. On the 1973-74 models, remove the center beam.

25. Remove the left engine mount.

26. Lift the engine out slowly, taking care not to allow the engine to damage other parts of the vehicle.

27. To install, reverse the removal procedure. Pay special attention to the following points:

a. Lower the engine into position and install the left mount. On 1973-74 models, install the center beam with the front end between the stabilizer bar and frame; DO NOT attach mounting bolts at this time.

NOTE: *On 1973-74 models, be sure that the lower mount has the mount stop installed between the center beam and the rubber mount.*

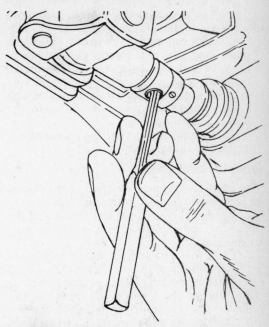

Driving gearshift rod pin out using pin driver

Center mount nut locations (arrows)

b. Align the center mount studs with the beam, then, tighten the nuts several turns (just enough to support the beam). On 1973-74 models, attach the rear end of the center beam to the subframe.

c. On 1973-74 models, attach the front end of the center beam. Torque the center beam bolts but do not tighten the lower mount nuts. Lower the engine so it rests on the lower mount. Torque the lower mount nuts.

d. Use a new shift rod pin.

e. After installing the halfshafts, attempt to move the inner joint housing in and out of the transaxle housing. If it moves easily, the driveshaft end clips should be replaced.

f. Make sure that the control cables and wires are connected properly.

g. When connecting the heater hoses, the upper hose goes to the water pump connecting pipe and the lower hose to the intake manifold.

h. Refill the engine, transaxle and cooling system with their respective fluids to the proper levels.

i. On Hondamatic vehicles, check and/or adjust the shift cable.

1335 and 1487cc Civic

1. Raise and support the front of the vehicle on jackstands. Remove both front wheels.

2. Remove the headlight rim screws and the rims. On 1980-82 models, remove the battery, tray and mount.

3. Open the hood and disconnect both parking light connectors. Remove the parking light bolts, backing plate and the parking lights.

4. Remove the lower grille molding, the grille-to-vehicle retaining bolts and the grille.

5. Disconnect and remove the windshield washer hose from the underside of the hood.

6. Disconnect the negative battery cable and the transaxle bracket-to-body ground cable.

7. Remove the upper torque (engine locating) arm.

8. Disconnect the vacuum hose from the power brake booster, thermosensors **A** and **B** at their wiring connectors and the coolant temperature gauge sending unit wire.

CAUTION: *When draining the coolant, keep in mind that cats and dogs are attracted by the ethylene glycol antifreeze, and are quite likely to drink any that is left in an uncovered container or in puddles on the ground. This will prove fatal in sufficient quantity. Always drain the coolant into a sealable container. Coolant should be reused unless it is contaminated or several years old.*

9. Drain the cooling system. After all coolant has drained, install the drain bolt fingertight.

10. Disconnect all four coolant hoses. Disconnect cooling fan motor connector and the temperature sensor. Remove the radiator hose to the overflow tank.

11. If equipped with a Hondamatic, remove both ATF cooler line bolts.

NOTE: *Save the washers from the cooler line banjo connectors and replace if damaged.*

12. Remove the radiator.

13. Label and disconnect the starter motor wires. Remove the starter-to-engine bolts (one from each end of the starter) and the starter.

14. Label and disconnect the spark plug wires from the plugs. Remove the distributor cap and scribe the position of the rotor on the side of the distributor housing. Remove the top distributor swivel bolt and the distributor (the rotor will rotate 30° as the drive gear is beveled).

15. If equipped with a manual transaxle, remove the C-clip retaining the clutch cable at the firewall. To remove the end of the clutch cable from the clutch release arm and bracket: First, pull up on the cable, then, push it out to release it from the bracket. Remove the end from the release arm.

16. Disconnect the backup light switch wires. Disconnect the control valve vacuum hose, the air intake hose and the preheat air intake hose. Disconnect the air bleed valve hose from the air cleaner. Label and disconnect all remaining vacuum hoses from the underside of the air cleaner. Remove the air cleaner.

17. Label and disconnect all remaining emission control vacuum hoses from the engine. Disconnect the emission box wiring connector and remove the black emission box from the firewall.

18. Remove the engine mount heat shield.

19. Disconnect the engine-to-body ground strap at the valve cover.

20. Disconnect the alternator wiring connector and oil pressure sensor leads.

Thermosensors and coolant temperature sending unit locations. Arrow 1 is the temperature sending unit, arrow 2 is thermosensor "A", and arrow 3 is the thermosensor "B"

Emission control black box—1976 type shown

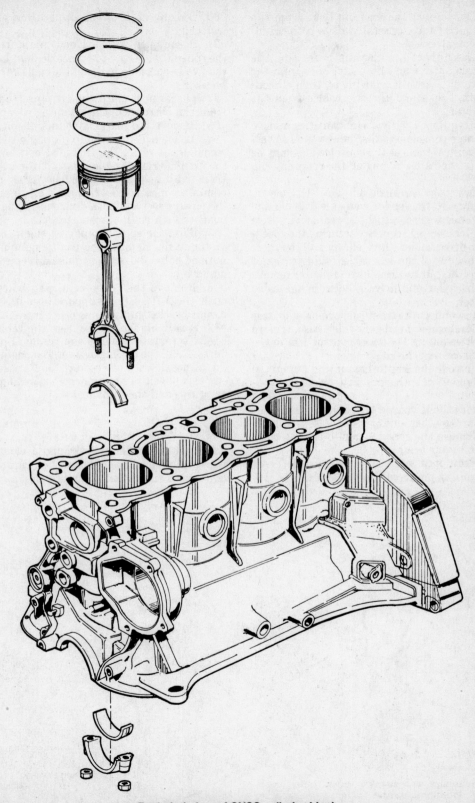

Exploded view of CVCC cylinder block

21. Disconnect the vacuum hose from the start control and electrical leads to both cut-off solenoid valves.

22. Disconnect the vacuum hose from the charcoal canister and both fuel lines from the carburetor. Mark the adjustment, then, disconnect the choke and throttle cables from the carburetor.

23. If equipped with a Hondamatic, remove the center console and disconnect the gear selector control cable at the console. This may be accomplished after removing the retaining clip and pin.

24. Drain the transaxle oil.

25. Remove the fender well shield under the right fender, exposing the speedometer drive cable. Remove the set screw securing the speedometer drive holder, then, slowly pull the cable assembly out of the transaxle, taking care not to drop the pin or drive gear. Finally, remove the pin, collar and drive gear from the cable assembly.

26. Disconnect the front suspension stabilizer bar from its mounts on both sides. Also, remove the bolt retaining the lower control arm to the sub-frame on both sides.

27. Remove the forward mounting nut on the radius rod from both sides. Pry the constant velocity joint out about ½ in. and pull the stub axle out of the transaxle case; repeat this procedure for the other side.

28. Remove the center beam-to-chassis bolts and the center beam.

29. If equipped with a manual transaxle, drive the retaining pin from the shift linkage.

30. Disconnect the lower torque arm from the transaxle.

31. If equipped with a Hondamatic, remove the control cable stay-to-transaxle bolt. Loosen the two U-bolt nuts and pull the cable out of its housing.

32. Disconnect the exhaust pipe from the manifold. Disconnect the retaining clamp also.

33. Remove the rear engine mount nut.

34. Attach a lifting hoist to the engine. Honda recommends using the threaded bolt holes at the extreme right and left ends of the cylinder head (with special hardened bolts) as lifting points, as opposed to wrapping a chain around the entire block and risk damaging some components such as the carburetor, etc.

35. Raise the engine to place a slight tension on the chain. Remove the front engine mount nut and bolts. Raise the engine and remove the mount.

36. Remove the three retaining bolts and push the left engine support into its shock mount bracket to the limit of its travel.

37. Slowly lift the engine from the vehicle.

38. To install, reverse the removal procedures. Refill the cooling system, the engine and the transaxle with the correct fluids. Start the engine, allow it to reach normal operating temperatures and check for leaks.

1342 and 1488cc Civic

1. Apply the parking brake and place blocks behind the rear wheels. Raise the front of the vehicle and support it on jackstands.

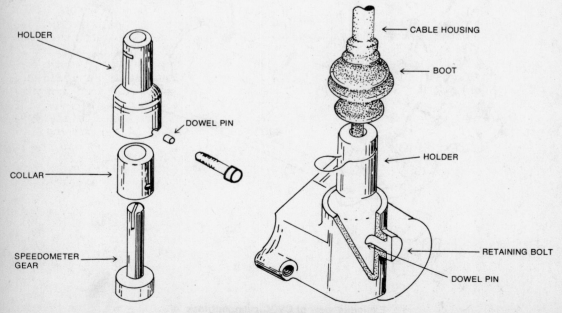

HOLDER

DOWEL PIN

COLLAR

SPEEDOMETER GEAR

CABLE HOUSING

BOOT

HOLDER

RETAINING BOLT

DOWEL PIN

Speedometer cable removal

2. Disconnect both battery cables from the battery. Remove the battery and the battery tray from the engine compartment.

3. Using a scratch awl, scribe a line where the hood brackets meet the inside of the hood; this will help realign the hood during the installation. Remove the hood-to-bracket bolts and the hood.

4. Remove the engine and wheelwell splash shields.

CAUTION: *The EPA warns that prolonged contact with used engine oil may cause a number of skin disorders, including cancer! You should make every effort to minimize your exposure to used engine oil. Protective gloves should be worn when changing the oil. Wash your hands and any other exposed skin areas as soon as possible after exposure to used engine oil. Soap and water, or waterless hand cleaner should be used.*

5. Drain the fluids from the engine, the radiator and the transaxle.

NOTE: *Removal of the filler plug or cap will speed the draining process.*

CAUTION: *When draining the coolant, keep in mind that cats and dogs are attracted by the ethylene glycol antifreeze, and are quite likely to drink any that is left in an uncovered container or in puddles on the ground. This will prove fatal in sufficient quantity. Always drain the coolant into a sealable container. Coolant should be reused unless it is contaminated or several years old.*

6. If equipped with a carburetor, perform the following procedures:

    a. Disconnect and label all hoses leading to the air cleaner.

    b. Remove the air cleaner cover and filter.

    c. Remove the air cleaner holddown bolts. Lift the air cleaner, then, disconnect the temperature sensor wire, the remaining two hoses and the air cleaner.

7. If equipped with fuel injection, perform the following procedures:

    a. Disconnect the air intake duct and vacuum hose.

    b. While holding the top of the fuel filter stationary with an open-end wrench, loosen the center service bolt with a box wrench; place a shop rag over the area so that any fuel spray will be absorbed. Carefully and slowly loosen the top service bolt, of the fuel filter, one turn.

    c. Disconnect the fuel return hose from the pressure regulator. Remove the fuel return hose bolt and the hose.

    d. From directly under the air cleaner outlet, disconect the electrical harness connector. Disconnect the electrical harness cable from the fuse box.

    e. Remove the front panel-to-valve cover ground cable.

    f. Disconnect the brake booster vacuum hose.

    g. If equipped with air conditioning, disconnect the idle control solenoid valve.

    h. Loosen the throttle cable locknut and the adjusting nut, then, slip the end of the cable from the bracket and the accelerator linkage.

NOTE: *When removing the throttle cable, be sure not to use pliers and perform the work carefully so not to bend the cable. If you should bend the cable, be sure to replace it.*

    i. Disconnect the No. 1 control box connector, (this control box is in front of the shock tower on the driver's side), then, lift the control box from its retaining bracket and support it next to the engine.

    j. Disconnect the two engine harness connectors. These are made of white plastic and are located near the brake fluid reservoir.

    k. Remove the distributor. Label and disconnect the radiator and heater hoses from the engine, leaving the heater valve cable in position.

8. If equipped with a carburetor, disconnect the following hoses and wires:

    a. The engine compartment sub-harness connector

    b. The engine secondary cable

    c. The brake booster vacuum hose

    d. If equipped with air conditioning, remove the idle control solenoid hoses from the valve and the valve.

9. Disconnect the control box connector(s). Remove the control box(s) from the bracket(s) and allow it (them) hang next to the engine.

10. Disconnect the purge control solenoid valve vacuum hose from the charcoal canister.

11. If equipped, remove the air jet controller.

12. Loosen the throttle cable locknut and adjusting nut, then, slip the cable end from the throttle bracket.

13. Disconnect the fuel hose from the fuel pump. Remove the fuel pump cover and the pump.

14. Label and remove the spark plug wires. Remove the distributor from the engine.

15. Remove the radiator and heater hoses from the engine.

NOTE: *Label the heater hoses so they will be reinstalled in their original locations.*

16. If equipped with a manual transaxle, perform the following procedures:

    a. Disconnect the ground cable from the transaxle.

    b. Loosen the clutch cable adjusting nut, then, remove the cable from the release arm.

c. From the clutch housing, disconnect the shift lever torque rod.

d. Slide the shift rod pin retainer out of the way. Using a pin punch, drive the pin out and remove the shift rod.

17. If equipped with a Hondamatic, perform the following procedures:

a. Remove the oil cooler hoses from the transaxle, allow the fluid to drain from the hoses, then, secure the hoses out of the way near the radiator.

b. From the inside of the vehicle, remove the center console.

c. Position the shift lever in Reverse, then, remove the lock pin from the end of the shift cable.

d. Unbolt and remove the shift cable holder.

e. Disconnect the throttle control cable from the throttle lever. Loosen the lower locknut on the throttle cable bracket and remove the cable from the bracket.

NOTE: *Do not move the upper locknut as it will change the transaxle shift points.*

17. Remove the speedometer cable clip and pull the cable from the holder.

NOTE: *Do not remove the holder from the transaxle for it may cause the speedometer gear to fall into the transaxle.*

18. Using penetrating oil, squirt it on the exhaust header pipe nuts, then, remove the nuts and pipe.

19. If working on a 4WD Wagon, perform the following procedures:

a. Using a crayon or paint, mark the driveshaft-to-transaxle flange.

b. Remove the driveshaft-to-transaxle flange bolts and disconnect the driveshaft from the transaxle.

20. To remove the halfshafts on all models, perform the following procedures:

a. Remove the jackstands and lower the vehicle. Loosen the 32mm spindle nuts with a socket. Raise the vehicle and resupport on jackstands.

b. Remove the front wheel spindle nut.

c. Place a floor jack under the lower control arm, then, remove the ball joint cotter pin and nut.

NOTE: *Be certain the lower control arm is positioned securely on top of the floor jack so that it doesn't suddenly jump or spring off when the ball joint remover is used.*

d. Using a Ball Joint Remover tool or equivalent, separate the ball joint from the front hub.

e. Slowly, lower the floor jack to lower the control arm. Pull the hub outward and off the halfshaft.

f. Using a small pry bar, pry out the in-

board CV-joint approximately ½" to release the spring clip from the groove in the transaxle.

g. Pull the halfshaft out of the transaxle case.

21. Using a lifting sling, attach it to the engine block, then, raise the hoist to remove the slack from the chain.

22. Remove the rear transaxle mount bracket. Remove bolts from the front transaxle mount and the engine side mount.

23. If equipped with air conditioning, perform the following procedures:

a. Loosen the belt adjusting bolts and remove the belt.

b. Remove the air conditioning compressor bolts, then, wire it up out of the way on the front beam.

NOTE: *DO NOT disconnect the air conditioning freon lines; the compressor can be moved without discharging the system.*

c. Remove the lower compressor mounting bracket.

24. Disconnect the alternator wiring harness connectors. Remove the alternator belt. Remove the alternator mounting bolts and the alternator.

25. Check that the engine and transaxle are free of any hoses or electrical connectors.

26. Slowly raise and remove the engine from the vehicle.

27. To install, reverse the removal procedures. Pay special attention to the following:

a. Torque the engine mounting bolts in the proper sequence.

(WAGON 4WD)
②TIGHTEN SNUG ONLY
⑧8 × 1.25 MM
43 N·M (4.3 KG-M, 31 LB. FT.)

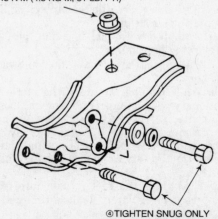

④TIGHTEN SNUG ONLY
⑦12 × 1.25 MM
65 N·M (6.5 KG-M, 47 LB. FT.)

Torque sequence for the engine mounts on CRX. Civic similar.

b. Be sure that the spring clip on the end of each halfshaft "clicks" into the transaxle.

NOTE: *Always use new spring clips upon installation.*

c. Bleed the air from the cooling system.

d. Adjust the belt(s) tension and the throttle cable tension.

e. Check and/or adjust the clutch pedal free play.

f. If equipped with a fuel injected engine, be sure to check carefully for fuel leaks because of the complexity of the system and its higher operating pressures. Do this by turning the ignition switch on three times for several seconds prior to cranking the engine.

1493cc and 1590cc Civic

NOTE: *Make sure that all jacks and jack stands are placed properly and hoist brackets are are attached to the correct positions on the engine. Always apply the parking brake and block the rear wheels so the vehicle will not roll off the support stands and possible fall on you while underneath the vehicle. Be sure to have everything that is needed to perform this job on hand before attempting this procedure. Be sure to use fender covers to avoid damaging any painted surfaces.*

1. Apply the parking brake and place blocks behind the rear wheels. Raise the front of the car and support it on jackstands.

2. Disconnect the battery cables from the battery. Remove the battery, and then remove the battery tray from the engine compartment.

3. Scribe a line where the hood brackets meet the inside of the hood. This will help re-align the hood during installation.

4. Disconnect the windshield washer fluid tubes. Unbolt and remove the hood.

5. Remove the engine and wheelwell splash shields.

CAUTION: *When draining the coolant, keep in mind that cats and dogs are attracted by the ethylene glycol antifreeze, and are quite likely to drink any that is left in an uncovered container or in puddles on the ground. This will prove fatal in sufficient quantity. Always drain the coolant into a sealable container. Coolant should be reused unless it is contaminated or several years old.*

6. Drain the oil from the engine, the coolant from the radiator, and the transmission oil from the transmission.

NOTE: *Removal of the filler plug or cap will speed the draining process.*

CAUTION: *The EPA warns that prolonged contact with used engine oil may cause a number of skin disorders, including cancer! You should make every effort to minimize your exposure to used engine oil. Protective gloves should be worn when changing the oil. Wash your hands and any other exposed skin areas as soon as possible after exposure to used engine oil. Soap and water, or waterless hand cleaner should be used.*

7. Remove the air intake duct and the front air intake duct.

8. Relieve the fuel pressure from the fuel system, by slowly loosening the service bolt (banjo bolt) on the fuel filler approximately one turn.

NOTE: *Do not smoke while working on the fuel system. Keep any and all open flames away from the work area. Before disconnecting any fuel lines, the fuel pressure should be relieved as described above. Place a suitable shop towel over the fuel filler to prevent the pressurized fuel from spraying over the engine.*

9. Disconnect and tag the engine compartment harness connectors, battery wires and transmission ground cable.

10. Remove the throttle cable by loosening the luck nut and the throttle cable adjust nut, then slip the throttle cable end out of the throttle bracket and accelerator linkage. Be sure not to bend the cable when removing it. Do not use pliers to remove the cable from the linkage. Always replaced a kinked cable with a new one.

11. Disconnect and tag the engine wire connectors and spark plug wires. Bring the engine up to TDC on the number one cylinder. Mark the distributor in relation with the engine block. Remove the distributor caps and bolts, then remove the distributor assembly from the cylinder head.

12. Disconnect the radiator hoses and heater hoses. Disconnect the transmission fluid cooler lines. Remove the speedometer cable.

NOTE: *Do not remove the speedometer cable holder, because the speedometer gear may fall into the transmission housing.*

13. Disconnect and tag the alternator wiring, remove the alternator adjusting bolts, mounting bolts and belt. Remove the alternator from the vehicle.

14. Loosen the air conditioning belt adjust bolt and the idler puller nut. Remove the compressor mounting bolts. Disconnect the air conditioning suction and discharge lines, only if it is necessary. Lift the compressor out of the bracket with the air conditioning hoses attached and wire the compressor to the front beam of the vehicle.

NOTE: *If it is necessary to remove the air conditioning suction and discharge lines, discharge the refrigerant from the air conditioning system. Be sure to discharge the refrigerant into a suitable container and be sure to wear safety goggles and gloves.*

15. On vehicles equipped with automatic transmissions, proceed as follows:

   a. Remove the header pipe, header pipe bracket, torque converter cover and shift control cable holder.

   b. Remove the shift control cable by removing the cotter pin, control pin and control lever roller from the control lever.

16. On vehicles equipped with manual transmissions, remove the shift lever torque rod, shift rod and clutch cable. On reassembly, slide the retainer back into place after driving in the spring pin.

17. Remove the wheelwell splash shields and engine splash shields. Remove the right and left drive (halfshafts) from the transmission and cover the shafts with a plastic bag so as to prevent the oil from spilling over the work area. Be sure to coat all precision finished surfaces with clean engine oil or grease.

18. Attach a suitable chain hoist to the engine block hoist brackets and raise the hoist just enough to remove the slack from the chain. To attach the rear engine chain, remove the plastic radiator hose bracket and hook the chain to the top of the clutch cable bracket.

19. Remove the rear transmission mount bracket. Remove the bolts from the front transmission bolt mount. Remove the bolts from the engine side mount. Remove the bolts from the engine side transmission mounts.

20. Check that the engine/transaxle assembly are completely free of vacuum, fuel, coolant hoses and electrical wires.

21. Slowly raise the engine approximately 6 inches and stop. Check again that the engine/transaxle assembly are completely free of vacuum, fuel, coolant hoses and electrical wires.

22. Raise the engine/transaxle assembly all the way up and out of the vehicle, once it is clear from the vehicle, lower the assembly into a suitable engine stand.

23. Installation is the reverse order of the removal procedure. Use the following steps to aid in the installation procedure.

24. Torque the engine mount bolts in the following sequence; be sure to replace the rear transmission bolt and the front transmission bolt with new bolts:

   a. Side transmission mount: 40 ft. lbs.

   b. Rear transmission mount bracket: 43 ft. lbs.

   c. Front transmission mount: 43 ft. lbs.

   d. Engine side mount: 40 ft. lbs.

NOTE: *Failure to tighten the bolts in the proper sequence can cause excessive noise and vibration and reduce bushing life. Be sure to check that the bushings are not twisted or offset.*

25. Check that the spring clip on the end of each driveshaft clicks into place. Be sure to use new spring clips on installation.

26. After assembling the fuel line parts, turn the ignition switch (do not operate the starter) to the ON position so that the fuel pump is operated for approximately two seconds so as to pressurize the fuel system. Repeat this procedure two or three times and check for a possible fuel leak.

27. Bleed the air from the cooling system at the bleed bolt with the heater valve open.

28. Adjust the throttle cable tension, install the air conditioning compressor and belt and adjust all belt tensions. Adjust the clutch cable free play and check that the transmission shifts into gear smoothly.

29. Clean the battery posts and cable terminals and reassemble, then apply grease to prevent corrosion. Check the ignition timing.

30. Install the speedometer cable, be sure to align the tab on the cable end with the slot holder. Install the clip so the bent leg is on the groove side. After installing, pull the speedometer cable to make sure it is secure.

1600cc Accord
1751cc Accord/Prelude

1. Disconnect the negative battery terminal.

2. Drain the cooling system, the engine and transaxle of fluids.

CAUTION: *When draining the coolant, keep in mind that cats and dogs are attracted by the ethylene glycol antifreeze, and are quite likely to drink any that is left in an uncovered container or in puddles on the ground. This will prove fatal in sufficient quantity. Always drain the coolant into a sealable container. Coolant should be reused unless it is contaminated or several years old.*

The EPA warns that prolonged contact with used engine oil may cause a number of skin disorders, including cancer! You should make every effort to minimize your exposure to used engine oil. Protective gloves should be worn when changing the oil. Wash your hands and any other exposed skin areas as soon as possible after exposure to used engine oil. Soap and water, or waterless hand cleaner should be used.

3. Raise and support the front of the vehicle, then, remove the front wheels.

4. Remove the air cleaner.

5. Remove the following wires and hoses:

   a. The coil wire and the ignition primary wire from the distributor.

   b. The engine subharness and the starter wires; mark the wires before removal to ease installation.

c. The vacuum tube from the brake booster.

d. On Hondamatic models, remove the ATF cooler hose from the transaxle.

e. The engine ground cable.

f. Alternator wiring harness.

g. Carburetor solenoid valve connector.

h. Carburetor fuel line.

i. On 1981-82 models with California and high altitude equipment, disconnect the hoses from the air controller.

6. Remove the choke and throttle cables.

7. Remove the radiator and heater hoses.

8. Remove the emission control "black box".

9. Remove the clutch slave cylinder with the hydraulic line attached.

10. Remove the speedometer cable. Pull the wire clip from the housing and the cable from the housing: DO NOT, under any circumstances, remove the housing from the transaxle.

11. Using an engine hoist, raise the engine slightly to remove the slack from the chain.

12. To disconnect the right or left lower ball joints and the tie rod ends, perform the following procedures:

a. Remove the cotter pin and nut from the ball joint(s) and the tie rod end(s).

b. Using a Ball Joint Remover tool or equivalent, separate the ball joint(s) and tie rod(s) from the steering knuckle.

c. An alternative method is to leave the ball joints connected, then, remove the lower control arm inner bolts and the radius rods from the lower control arms.

13. To remove the halfshafts from the transaxle, pry the snapring from the groove in the end of the shaft. While holding the steering knuckle, pull the halfshaft from the knuckle.

14. Remove the center engine mount.

15. Remove the shift rod positioner from the transaxle case.

16. Using a Pin Punch, drive the pin from the shift rod.

17. If equipped with a Hondamatic, remove the control cable from the transaxle.

18. Disconnect the exhaust pipe from the exhaust manifold.

19. Remove the three engine support bolts and push the left engine support into the shock mount bracket.

20. Remove the front and rear engine mounts.

21. Carefully, raise and remove the engine from the vehicle.

22. To install, reverse the removal procedures. Make sure the halfshaft clip seats in the transaxle groove; failure to do so could lead to the halfshaft disengaging from the transaxle while you are driving! Bleed the air from the cooling system. Adjust the throttle and choke cable tension. Check and/or adjust the clutch

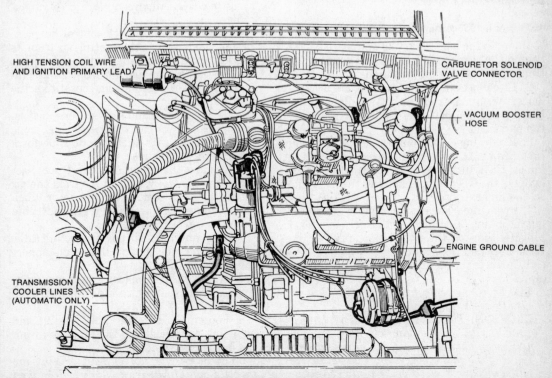

Accord and Prelude component removal points

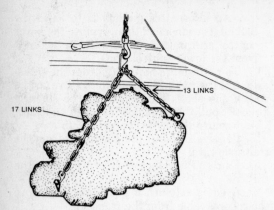

Accord and Prelude engine removal. Note the chain positioning

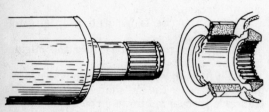

Accord and Prelude driveshaft removal

for the correct free play. Make sure that the transaxle shifts properly.

1829cc and 1955cc Accord/Prelude

1. Apply the parking brake and place blocks behind the rear wheels. Raise and support the front of the vehicle on jackstands.

2. Disconnect the negative, then, the positive battery terminals from the battery. Remove the battery and the battery tray from the engine compartment.

3. If working on a Prelude, remove the knob caps covering the headlight manual retracting knobs, then, turn the knobs to bring the headlights to the ON position. Remove the five grille screws and the grille.

4. From under the engine, remove the splash guard. Using a scratch awl, mark the hood hinge outline on the hood, then, remove the hood bolts and the hood.

5. Remove the oil filler cap and drain the engine oil.

NOTE: *When replacing the drain plug be sure to use a new washer.*

CAUTION: *The EPA warns that prolonged contact with used engine oil may cause a number of skin disorders, including cancer! You should make every effort to minimize your exposure to used engine oil. Protective gloves should be worn when changing the oil.*

Wash your hands and any other exposed skin areas as soon as possible after exposure to used engine oil. Soap and water, or waterless hand cleaner should be used.

6. Remove the radiator cap, then, open the radiator drain petcock and drain the coolant from the radiator.

CAUTION: *When draining the coolant, keep in mind that cats and dogs are attracted by the ethylene glycol antifreeze, and are quite likely to drink any that is left in an uncovered container or in puddles on the ground. This will prove fatal in sufficient quantity. Always drain the coolant into a sealable container. Coolant should be reused unless it is contaminated or several years old.*

7. Remove the transaxle filler plug, then, remove the drain plug and drain the transaxle.

8. If equipped with a carburetor, perform the following procedures:

a. Label and remove the coil wires and the engine secondary ground cable located on the valve cover.

b. Remove the air cleaner cover and filter.

c. For the Accord models, remove the air intake ducts, the air cleaner nuts/bolts, the air control valve and the air cleaner.

d. Loosen the throttle cable locknut and adjusting nut, then, slip the cable end from the carburetor linkage.

NOTE: *Be careful not to bend or kink the throttle cable. Always replace a damaged cable.*

e. Disconnect the No. 1 control box connector, then, remove the control box from its bracket and allow it hang next to the engine.

f. Disconnect the fuel line from the fuel filter and the solenoid vacuum hose from the charcoal canister.

g. For California and high altitude models, remove the air jet controller.

9. If equipped with fuel injection, perform the following procedures:

a. Remove the air intake duct. Disconnect the cruise control vacuum tube from the air intake duct and remove the resonator tube.

b. Remove the secondary ground cable from the top of the engine.

c. Disconnect the air box connecting tube. Unscrew the tube clamp bolt and disconnect the emission tubes.

d. Remove the air cleaner case mounting nuts and remove the air cleaner case assembly.

e. Loosen the throttle cable locknut and adjusting nut, then, slip the cable end from the bracket and linkage.

NOTE: *Be careful not to bend or kink the throttle cable. Always replace a damaged cable.*

f. Disconnect the following wires:
- The ground cable from the fuse box.
- The engine compartment subharness connector and clamp.
- The high tension wire and ignition primary leaks from the coil.
- The radio condenser connector from the coil.

g. To relieve the fuel pressure, perform the following procedures:
- Using a shop rag, place it over the fuel filter to absorb any gasoline which may be sprayed on the engine.
- Slowly loosen the service bolt approximately one full turn; this will relieve any pressure in the system.
- Using a new sealing washer, retighten the service bolt.

h. Disconnect the fuel return hose from the pressure regulator. Remove the banjo nut, then, the fuel hose.

i. Disconnect the vacuum hose from the brake booster.

10. Label and disconnect the radiator and heater hoses from the engine.

11. If equipped with an automatic transaxle, disconnect the oil cooler hoses from the trans-

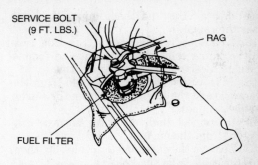

Relieving the fuel system pressure—fuel injection

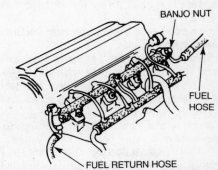

Disconnecting the fuel hoses—fuel injection

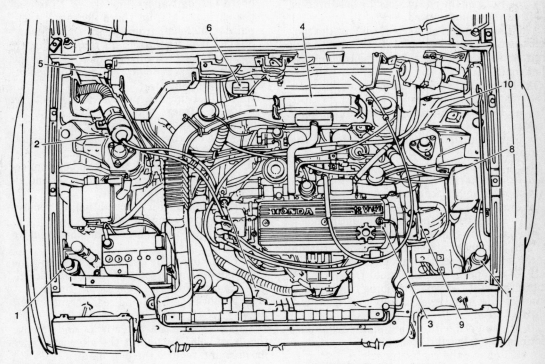

① Headlight retracting knobs
② Ignition coil wires
③ Secondary ground cable
④ Air cleaner assembly
⑤ No. 1 control box connector
⑥ Charcoal canister
⑦ Air bleed bolt for cooling system
⑧ No. 2 control box connector
⑨ Air chamber location (if so equipped)
⑩ Air jet controller location (if so equipped)

Component removal points on 1983 and later Prelude 1829cc

axle and drain the fluid, then, support the hoses near the radiator.

12. If equipped with a manual transaxle, loosen the clutch cable adjusting nut and remove the clutch cable from the release arm.

13. Disconnect the battery cable from the transaxle and the starter cable from the starter motor terminal.

14. Disconnect both electrical harness connectors from the engine.

15. Remove the speedometer cable clip, then, pull the cable from the holder.

NOTE: *DO NOT remove the holder as the speedometer gear may drop into the transaxle.*

16. If equipped with power steering perform the following procedures:

a. Remove the speed sensor-to-transaxle bolt and the sensor complete with the hoses.

NOTE: *Do not disconnect the hoses from the speed sensor, for power steering fluid will flow from it.*

b. Remove the power steering pump adjusting bolt, mounting bolt and the V-belt.

c. Without disconnecting the hoses, pull the pump away from its mounting bracket and position it out of the way.

d. Remove the power steering hose bracket from the cylinder head.

17. If working on an Accord, remove the center beam beneath the engine. Loosen the radius rod nuts to aid in the later removal of the halfshafts.

18. If equipped with air conditioning, perform the following procedures:

a. Remove the compressor clutch lead wire.

b. Loosen the belt adjusting bolt and the drive belt.

NOTE: *DO NOT remove the air conditioner hoses. The air conditioner compressor can be moved without discharging the air conditioner system.*

c. Remove the compressor mounting bolts, then, lift the compressor out of the bracket, with the hoses attached, and support it on the front bulkhead with a piece of wire.

19. If equipped with a manual transaxle, remove the shift rod yoke attaching bolt and disconnect the shift lever torque rod from the clutch housing.

20. If equipped with an automatic transaxle, perform the following procedures:

a. Remove the center console.

b. Place the shift lever in Reverse, then, remove the lock pin from the end of the shift cable.

c. Remove the shift cable mounting bolts and the shift cable holder.

d. Remove the throttle cable from the throttle lever. Loosen the lower locknut, then, remove the cable from the bracket.

NOTE: *DO NOT loosen the upper locknut as it will change the transaxle shift points.*

21. Disconnect the right and left lower ball joints and the tie rod ends.

22. To remove the halfshafts, perform the following procedures:

a. Remove the jackstands and lower the vehicle. Using a 32mm socket, loosen the spindle nuts. Raise and support the vehicle on jackstands.

b. Remove the front wheel and the spindle nut.

c. For the Prelude models, remove the damper fork and damper pinch bolts.

d. Remove the ball joint bolt and separate the ball joint from the front hub (Accord) or lower control arm (Prelude).

e. Disconnect the tie rods from the steering knuckles.

f. For the Accord models, remove the sway bar bolts.

g. Pull the front hub outward and off the halfshafts.

h. Using a small pry bar, pry out the inboard CV-joint approximately ½" to release the spring clip from the differential, then, pull the halfshaft from the transaxle case.

NOTE: *When installing the halfshaft, insert the shaft until the spring clip clicks into the groove. Always use a new spring clip when installing halfshafts.*

23. On fuel injected models, disconnect the sub-engine harness connectors and clamp.

24. Remove the exhaust header pipe.

25. Attach a chain hoist to the engine and raise it slightly to remove the slack.

26. Disconnect the No. 2 control box connector, lift the control box off of its bracket and allow it hang next to the engine.

27. If equipped with air conditioning, remove the idle control solenoid valve.

28. If equipped with an air chamber, remove it.

29. From under the air chamber, remove the three engine mount bolts, then, push the engine mount into the engine mount tower.

30. Remove the front and rear engine mount nuts.

31. Loosen the alternator bolts and remove the drive belt. Disconnect the alternator wire harness and remove the alternator.

32. At the engine, remove the bolt from the rear torque rod, then, loosen the bolt in the frame mount, swing the rod up and out of the way.

33. Carefully raise the engine from the vehi-

cle, checking that all wires and hoses have been removed from the engine/transaxle, then, remove it from the vehicle.

34. To install the engine, reverse the removal procedures and make the following checks:

    a. Torque the engine mounting bolts in the proper sequence.

    b. Bleed the air from the cooling system.

    c. Adjust the clutch pedal free play.

    d. Adjust the throttle cable tension.

    e. Make sure the transaxle shifts properly.

Rocker Arm Cover

REMOVAL AND INSTALLATION

1. On some models, it will be necessary to remove the air cleaner assembly.

2. Remove the ground cable, the spark plug wires (if necessary) and the throttle cable (if necessary) from the rocker arm cover.

3. If equipped, remove the PCV hose from the rocker arm cover.

4. Remove the rocker arm cover-to-cylinder head nuts, the washer/grommet assemblies and the rocker arm cover.

NOTE: *If the cover is difficult to remove, use a mallet to bump it loose.*

5. Using a putty knife, clean the gasket mounting surfaces.

6. To install, use a new gasket, sealant (if necessary) and reverse the removal procedures. Torque the rocker arm cover-to-cylinder head nuts to 7 ft. lbs.

Rocker Arms/Shafts

The rocker arms and shafts are an assembly; they must be removed from the engine as a unit.

REMOVAL AND INSTALLATION

All except 1342cc & 1488cc Engines (1984-87)

Refer to the "Camshaft, Removal and Installation" procedures in this section, for the camshaft can be removed with the removal of the rocker arm/shaft/holder assemblies.

1342cc & 1488cc Engines (1984-87)

1. Refer to the "Rocker Arm Cover, Removal and Installation" procedures in this section and remove the rocker arm cover.

2. Rotate the crankshaft until the No. 1 cylinder is on the TDC of its compression stroke.

3. Loosen the rocker arm lock nuts and back off the adjusting screws; this will make removal easier.

4. Remove the rocker arm shaft-to-cylinder head bolts; start removing the bolts (in a crisscross manner) from the outer edges and work toward the center holder. Lift the rocker arm/shaft assemblies from the cylinder head.

NOTE: *When removing or disassembling the rocker arm/shaft assemblies, be sure to keep them in order for reinstallation.*

5. Using a putty knife, clean the gasket mounting surfaces. Using a clean shop rag, wipe all of the mounting surfaces clean.

NOTE: *If the rocker arm/shaft holders (No. 1 and 5) have been removed (from the outer ends), replace them by installing liquid gasket between the holders and the cylinder head.*

6. To install, use a new gasket, sealant (if necessary) and reverse the removal procedures. Torque each rocker arm/shaft-to-cylinder head bolts, two turns at a time, in sequence (from the center to the outer edges), to 16 ft. lbs. Adjust the valve clearances. Start the engine and check for oil leaks.

Thermostat

On 1170 and 1237cc vehicles, the thermostat is located on the intake manifold, under the air cleaner nozzle, so you will first have to remove the air cleaner housing. On the CVCC and late model engines, it is located at the right rear of the distributor housing.

REMOVAL AND INSTALLATION

1. Place a clean drain pan under the radiator, remove the drain plug from the radiator and drain the coolant into the pan.

CAUTION: *When draining the coolant, keep in mind that cats and dogs are attracted by the ethylene glycol antifreeze, and are quite likely to drink any that is left in an uncovered container or in puddles on the ground. This will prove fatal in sufficient quantity. Always*

Thermostat housing and bleed bolt location— CVCC models

FUEL-INJECTED ENGINE:

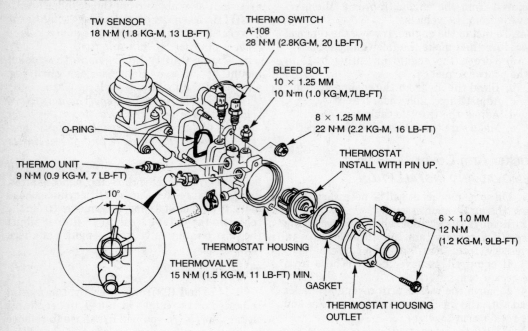

CARBURETED ENGINE:

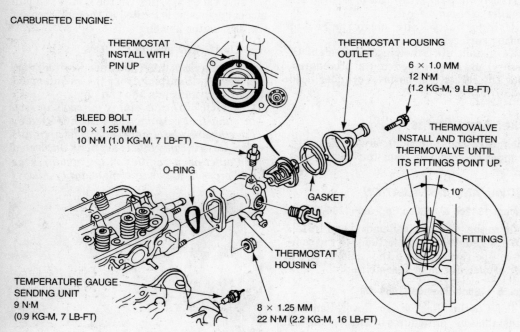

Exploded view of the thermostat housing—Accord and Prelude

drain the coolant into a sealable container. Coolant should be reused unless it is contaminated or several years old.

2. Remove the thermostat cover-to-thermostat housing bolts, the cover, the gasket and the thermostat.

3. Using a putty knife, clean the gasket mounting surfaces.

NOTE: *If the thermostat is equipped with a pin valve, be sure to install the thermostat with the pin facing upward.*

4. To install, use a new thermostat (if neces-

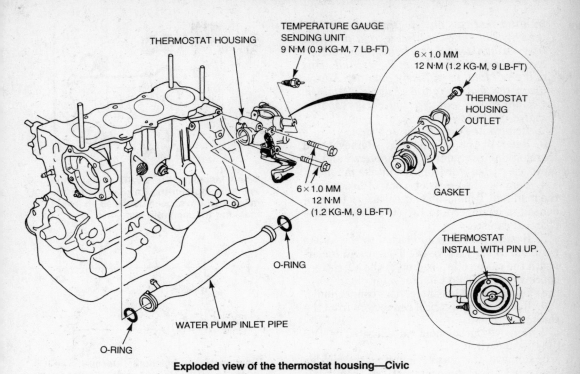

Exploded view of the thermostat housing—Civic

Thermostat housing and bleed bolt location—
non-CVCC models

Installing the thermostat with the pin valve facing upward

sary), gasket, O-ring (if used), sealant (if necessary) and reverse the removal procedures. Always install the spring end of the thermostat
facing the engine. Torque the thermostat cover-
to-thermostat housing bolts to 7 ft. lbs. (1973-
78) or 9 ft. lbs. (1979-88). Bleed the cooling
system.

Intake Manifold

REMOVAL AND INSTALLATION

Carbureted Models

NON-CVCC ENGINES

1. Place a clean pan under the radiator, remove the drain plug and drain the cooling
system.

CAUTION: *When draining the coolant, keep*

in mind that cats and dogs are attracted by the ethylene glycol antifreeze, and are quite likely to drink any that is left in an uncovered container or in puddles on the ground. This will prove fatal in sufficient quantity. Always drain the coolant into a sealable container. Coolant should be reused unless it is contaminated or several years old.

2. Remove the air cleaner and case.

3. Refer to the "Carburetor, Removal and Installation" procedures in Chapter 5 and remove the carburetor from the intake manifold.

4. Remove the emission control hoses from the manifold T-joint; one hose leads to the condensation chamber and the other leads to the charcoal canister.

5. Remove the hose connected to the intake manifold directly above the T-joint and underneath the carburetor, leading to the air cleaner check valve (refer to Chapter 5 for diagrams of the various emission control hose connections).

6. Remove the electrical connectors from the thermoswitches.

7. Remove the solenoid valve located next to the thermoswitch.

8. Remove the intake manifold-to-cylinder head nuts in a crisscross pattern, beginning from the center and moving out to both ends, then, remove the manifold.

9. Using a putty knife, clean the gasket mounting surfaces of the manifold and the cylinder head.

10. If the intake manifold is to be replaced, transfer all necessary components to the new manifold.

11. To install, use new gaskets, sealant (if necessary) and reverse the removal procedure, being sure to observe the following points:

   a. Apply a water-resistant sealer to the new intake manifold gasket before positioning it in place.

   b. Be sure all hoses are properly connected.

   c. Tighten the manifold attaching nuts in the reverse order of removal.

1342cc, 1488cc, 1829cc AND 1955cc ENGINES

1. Position a clean drain pan under the radiator, remove the drain plug and drain the cooling system.

CAUTION: *When draining the coolant, keep in mind that cats and dogs are attracted by the ethylene glycol antifreeze, and are quite likely to drink any that is left in an uncovered container or in puddles on the ground. This will prove fatal in sufficient quantity. Always drain the coolant into a sealable container. Coolant should be reused unless it is contaminated or several years old.*

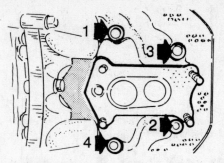

When installing the CVCC combination manifold, tighten the four bolts after the manifolds have been installed to avoid cracking the manifold ears

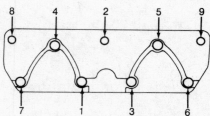

Combination manifold torque sequence—1978–79 1487cc, 1979 1751cc, 1980 1751cc (exc. Calif.), and 1980 1335cc engines

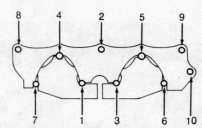

Combination manifold torque sequence—1980–81 1487cc, 1981 1335cc, 1980 1751cc (Calif.), and all 1981 1751cc engines

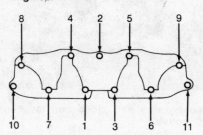

Combination manifold torque sequence—1982–83 1751cc engine

2. Remove the air cleaner and housing from the carburetor(s).

3. Remove the air valve, the EGR valve, the air suction valve and the air chamber (if equipped).

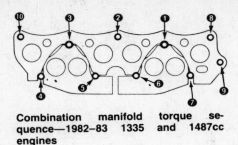

Combination manifold torque sequence—1982–83 1335 and 1487cc engines

4. Label and disconnect any electrical connectors from the carburetor(s) and intake manifold.

5. Disconnect the fuel line(s) from the carburetor. Disconnect the throttle cable from the carburetor.

6. Remove the carburetor(s) from the intake manifold.

7. Remove the intake manifold-to-cylinder head nuts (using a crisscross pattern), beginning from the center and moving out to both ends, then remove the manifold.

8. Using a putty knife, clean the gasket mounting surfaces.

9. If the intake manifold is to be replaced, transfer all the necessary components to the new manifold.

10. To install, use new gaskets, sealant (if necessary) and reverse the removal procedures. Tighten the nuts in a crisscross pattern in 2-3

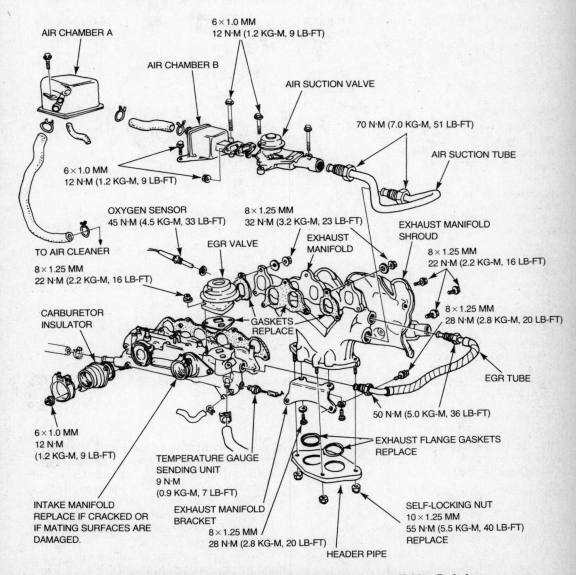

Exploded view of the carbureted intake and exhaust manifolds—Prelude

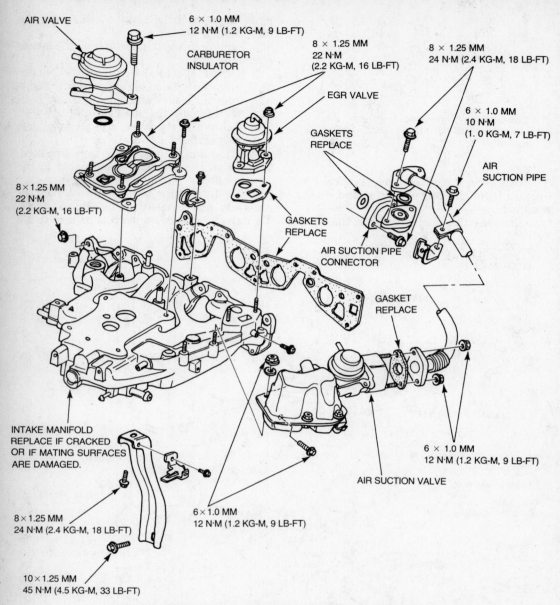

AIR VALVE

6 × 1.0 MM
12 N·M (1.2 KG-M, 9 LB-FT)

CARBURETOR
INSULATOR

8 × 1.25 MM
22 N·M
(2.2 KG-M, 16 LB-FT)

8 × 1.25 MM
24 N·M (2.4 KG-M, 18 LB-FT)

EGR VALVE

6 × 1.0 MM
10 N·M
(1. 0 KG-M, 7 LB-FT)

GASKETS
REPLACE

AIR
SUCTION PIPE

8 × 1.25 MM
22 N·M
(2.2 KG-M, 16 LB-FT)

GASKETS
REPLACE

AIR SUCTION PIPE
CONNECTOR

GASKET
REPLACE

INTAKE MANIFOLD
REPLACE IF CRACKED
OR IF MATING SURFACES
ARE DAMAGED.

6 × 1.0 MM
12 N·M (1.2 KG-M, 9 LB-FT)

AIR SUCTION VALVE

8 × 1.25 MM
24 N·M (2.4 KG-M, 18 LB-FT)

6 × 1.0 MM
12 N·M (1.2 KG-M, 9 LB-FT)

10 × 1.25 MM
45 N·M (4.5 KG-M, 33 LB-FT)

Exploded view of the carbureted intake manifold—Civic Si and CRX

steps, starting with the inner nuts. Be sure all hoses and wires are correctly connected. Start the engine and check for leaks.

Fuel Injected Models

1. Position a clean catch pan under the radiator, remove the radiator drain plug and drain the cooling system to a level below the intake manifold. Disconnect the cooling hoses from the intake manifold.

CAUTION: *When draining the coolant, keep in mind that cats and dogs are attracted by the ethylene glycol antifreeze, and are quite likely to drink any that is left in an uncovered container or in puddles on the ground. This will prove fatal in sufficient quantity. Always drain the coolant into a sealable container. Coolant should be reused unless it is contaminated or several years old.*

2. Label and disconnect the vacuum hoses and electrical connectors; for example crank angle sensor wiring and manifold absolute

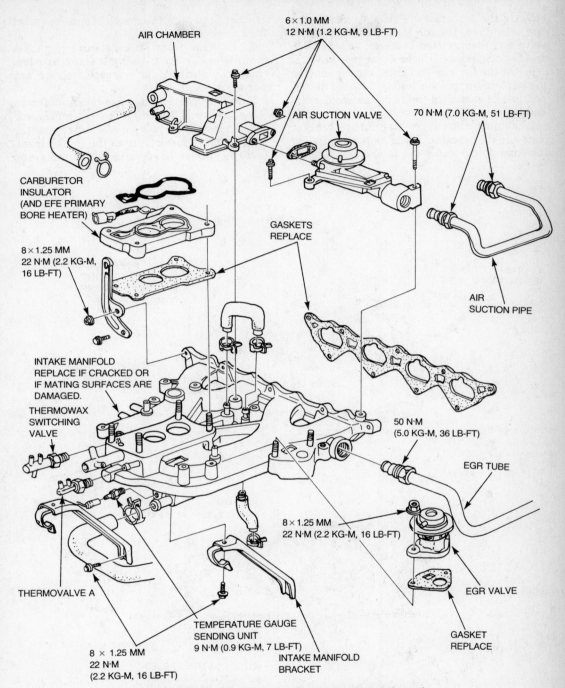

6 × 1.0 MM
12 N·M (1.2 KG-M, 9 LB-FT)

AIR CHAMBER

AIR SUCTION VALVE

70 N·M (7.0 KG-M, 51 LB-FT)

CARBURETOR
INSULATOR
(AND EFE PRIMARY
BORE HEATER)

GASKETS
REPLACE

8 × 1.25 MM
22 N·M (2.2 KG-M,
16 LB-FT)

AIR
SUCTION PIPE

INTAKE MANIFOLD
REPLACE IF CRACKED OR
IF MATING SURFACES ARE
DAMAGED.

THERMOWAX
SWITCHING
VALVE

50 N·M
(5.0 KG-M, 36 LB-FT)

EGR TUBE

8 × 1.25 MM
22 N·M (2.2 KG-M, 16 LB-FT)

THERMOVALVE A

TEMPERATURE GAUGE
SENDING UNIT
9 N·M (0.9 KG-M, 7 LB-FT)

EGR VALVE

8 × 1.25 MM
22 N·M
(2.2 KG-M, 16 LB-FT)

INTAKE MANIFOLD
BRACKET

GASKET
REPLACE

Expoded view of the carbureted intake manifold—Accord

presssure sensor vacuum lines. On the Accord and Prelude, disconnect the electrical connector from the EGR valve.

3. Relieve the fuel pressure before starting to break the fuel line connections.

4. Refer to the "Throttle Body, Removal and Installation" procedures in Chapter 5 and remove the throttle body. Refer to the same chapter and remove the fuel injector manifold pipe and injectors.

5. On the Accords and Preludes, remove the fast idle valve, the air bleed valve, the EGR valve and their related brackets. On the CRX and Civic Si, remove the breather pipe bracket.

6. On the Civic Si and CRX, the manifold is in two pieces (upper and lower). Remove the upper intake manifold-to-lower manifold bolts and upper manifold.

7. Remove the intake manifold-to-bracket bolts and the brackets. While supporting the intake manifold, remove the intake manifold-to-

cylinder head nuts, the manifold and the gasket from the cylinder head.

8. Using a putty knife, clean the gasket mounting surfaces. Using a straight edge, check the surfaces for warpage; replace any warped parts.

NOTE: *If the cylinder head/manifold mating surface is warped, it must be machined.*

9. To install, use new gaskets and reverse the removal procedures. Torque the intake manifold-to-cylinder head nuts (alternately and

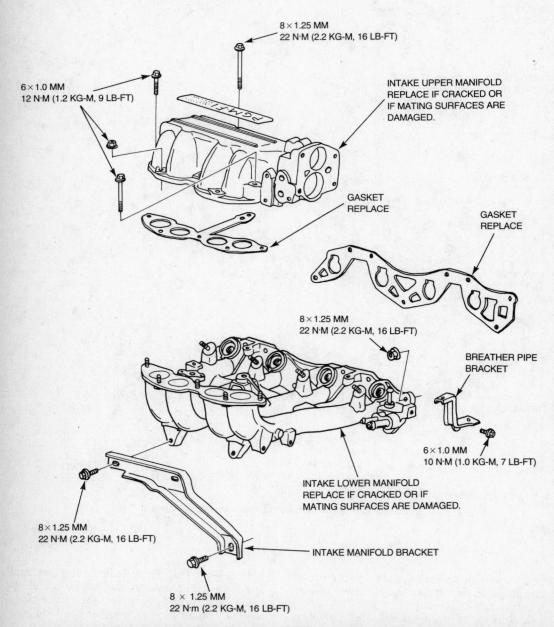

Exploded view of the two-piece intake manifold—Civic Si and CRX—fuel injected

evenly) to 16 ft. lbs. Torque the lower bracket-to-engine bolt to 33 ft. lbs. (Civic Si and CRX) and upper bracket-to-manifold bolt 16 ft. lbs. (Civic Si and CRX) or 18 ft. lbs. (Accord and Prelude).

10. On the Civic Si and CRX, torque the upper manifold-to-lower manifold nuts/bolts (evenly and alternately) to 16 ft. lbs. (large engine side bolt) and 9 ft. lbs. (forward side nuts/bolts).

11. To complete the installation, reverse the removal procedures. Refill and bleed the cooling system. Before starting the engine, turn the ignition switch ON and check for fuel leaks. Start the engine, allow it reach normal operating temperatures and check for leaks.

Exhaust Manifold

REMOVAL AND INSTALLATION

Carbureted Engines

NON-CVCC MODELS

WARNING: *Do not perform this operation on a warm or hot engine.*

1. Remove the front grille.
2. Remove the three exhaust pipe-to-manifold nuts and disconnect the exhaust pipe from the manifold.

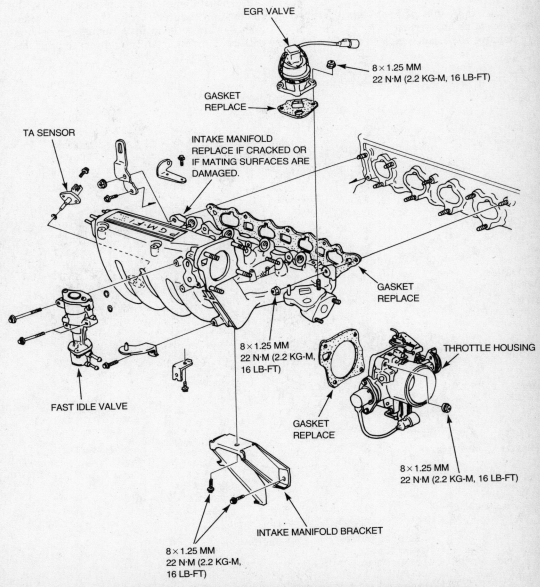

Exploded view of the fuel injected intake manifold—Accord and Prelude

3. On 1975 and later models, disconnect the air injection tubes from the exhaust manifold, then, remove the air injection manifold.

4. Remove the hot air cover-to-exhaust manifold bolts and the cover.

5. Using a criss-cross pattern (starting from the center), remove the exhaust manifold-to-cylinder head nuts and the manifold.

6. Using a putty knife, clean the gasket mounting surfaces.

7. To install, use new gaskets and reverse the removal procedure. Torque the exhaust manifold-to-cylinder head nuts (using ½ the torquing pressure) in the reverse order of removal.

1342cc, 1488cc, 1829cc AND 1955cc Engines

WARNING: *Do not perform this operation on a warm or hot engine.*

1. Remove the header pipe or catalytic converter-to-exhaust manifold nuts and separate the pipe from the manifold.

2. Disconnect and remove the oxygen sensor (if equipped).

3. If equipped, remove the EGR and the air suction tubes from the exhaust manifold.

4. Remove the exhaust manifold shroud.

5. Remove the exhaust manifold bracket bolts.

6. Using a criss-cross pattern (starting from the center), remove the exhaust manifold-to-cylinder head nuts, the manifold and the gaskets (discard them).

7. Using a putty knife, clean the gasket mounting surfaces.

8. To install, use new gaskets and reverse the removal procedure. Torque the exhaust manifold-to-cylinder head nuts (using a criss-cross pattern, starting from the center) to 23 ft. lbs.

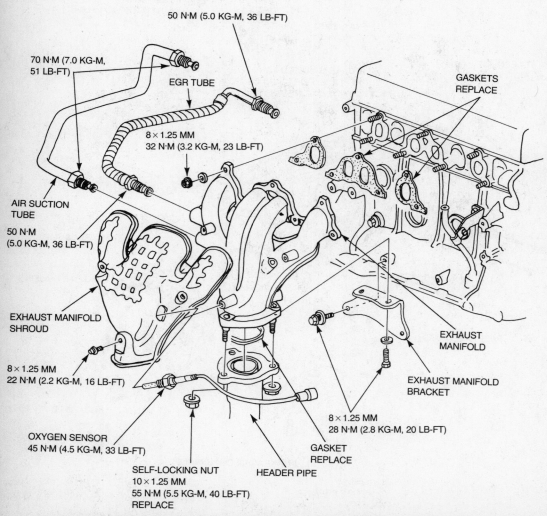

50 N·M (5.0 KG-M, 36 LB-FT)

70 N·M (7.0 KG-M, 51 LB-FT)

EGR TUBE

GASKETS REPLACE

8 × 1.25 MM
32 N·M (3.2 KG-M, 23 LB-FT)

AIR SUCTION TUBE

50 N·M
(5.0 KG-M, 36 LB-FT)

EXHAUST MANIFOLD SHROUD

EXHAUST MANIFOLD

EXHAUST MANIFOLD BRACKET

8 × 1.25 MM
22 N·M (2.2 KG-M, 16 LB-FT)

8 × 1.25 MM
28 N·M (2.8 KG-M, 20 LB-FT)

OXYGEN SENSOR
45 N·M (4.5 KG-M, 33 LB-FT)

GASKET REPLACE

SELF-LOCKING NUT
10 × 1.25 MM
55 N·M (5.5 KG-M, 40 LB-FT)
REPLACE

HEADER PIPE

Exploded view of the carbureted exhaust manifold—Accord and Prelude—fuel injected is similar

and the header pipe-to-exhaust manifold nuts to 40 ft. lbs., the oxygen sensor-to-exhaust manifold to 33 ft. lbs. Start the engine and check for exhaust leaks.

Fuel Injected Engines

NOTE: *Remove the exhaust manifold only when the engine is Cold.*

1. Remove the front grille for access. Discon-nect the electrical connector from the oxygen sensor and remove the sensor from the exhaust manifold. On the Accords and Preludes, discon-nect the EGR tube from the exhaust manifold.

2. Remove and discard the header pipe-to-ex-haust manifold nuts. Disconnect the header pipe and discard the gasket.

3. Remove the shroud-to-exhaust manifold bolt and the shroud. Remove the exhaust mani-

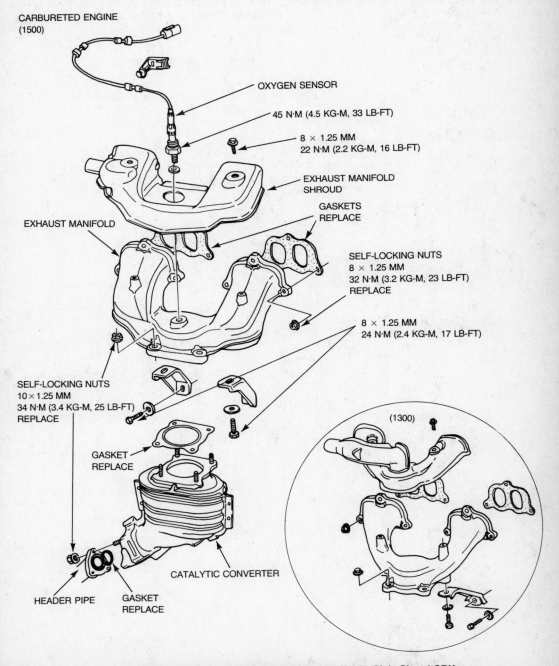

CARBURETED ENGINE
(1500)

OXYGEN SENSOR

45 N·M (4.5 KG-M, 33 LB-FT)

8 × 1.25 MM
22 N·M (2.2 KG-M, 16 LB-FT)

EXHAUST MANIFOLD
SHROUD

GASKETS
REPLACE

EXHAUST MANIFOLD

SELF-LOCKING NUTS
8 × 1.25 MM
32 N·M (3.2 KG-M, 23 LB-FT)
REPLACE

8 × 1.25 MM
24 N·M (2.4 KG-M, 17 LB-FT)

SELF-LOCKING NUTS
10 × 1.25 MM
34 N·M (3.4 KG-M, 25 LB-FT)
REPLACE

(1300)

GASKET
REPLACE

CATALYTIC CONVERTER

HEADER PIPE   GASKET
REPLACE

Exploded view of the carbureted exhaust manifold—Civic Si and CRX

fold bracket-to-engine bolts. Remove the exhaust manifold-to-cylinder head nuts/washers, the manifold and the gaskets (discard them).

4. Using a putty knife, clean the gasket mounting surfaces. Using a straightedge, inspect for warping; replace any warped parts. If the cylinder head/manifold mating surface is warped, it must be machined.

5. To install, use new gaskets, header pipe nuts (Accord and Prelude) and reverse the removal procedures.

NOTE: *There are three gaskets (Accord and Prelude) or two (Civic Si and CRX).*

6. Torque the exhaust manifold-to-cylinder head nuts to 23 ft. lbs., the header pipe-to-exhaust manifold nuts to 40 ft. lbs. (Accord and Prelude) or 25 ft. lbs. (Civic Si and CRX), the manifold bracket-to-engine bolts to 20 ft. lbs. (Accord and Prelude) or 33 ft. lbs. (Civic Si and CRX), the oxygen sensor-to-exhaust manifold to 33 ft. lbs. and the EGR tube-to-exhaust manifold to 36 ft. lbs. (Accord and Prelude).

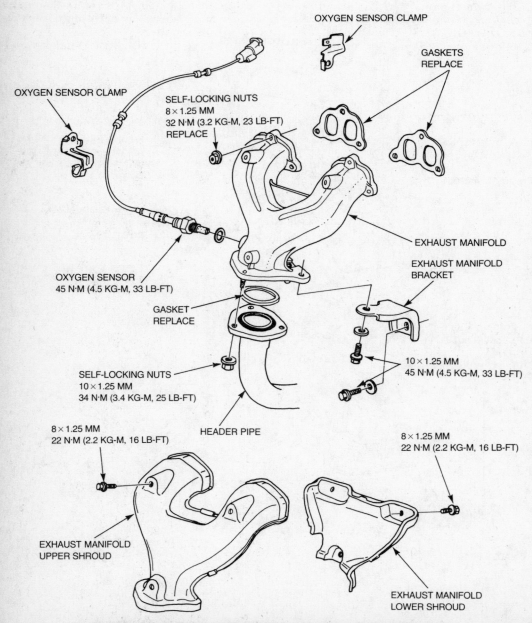

Exploded view of the fuel injected exhaust manifold—Civic Si and CRX

Combination Manifold — CVCC Models

REMOVAL AND INSTALLATION

1335cc, 1487cc and 1751cc Engines

1. Place a clean drain pan under the radiator, remove the drain plug and drain the cooling system. Disconnect coolant hose(s) from the intake manifold coolant hoses.

CAUTION: *When draining the coolant, keep in mind that cats and dogs are attracted by the ethylene glycol antifreeze, and are quite likely to drink any that is left in an uncovered container or in puddles on the ground. This will prove fatal in sufficient quantity. Always drain the coolant into a sealable container.*

Coolant should be reused unless it is contaminated or several years old.

2. Remove the air cleaner assembly.

3. Label and disconnect all vacuum hoses and electrical connectors from the carburetor.

4. Disconnect the fuel hose(s) and the throttle cable from the carburetor.

5. Remove the carburetor-to-intake manifold nuts and the carburetor.

6. Remove the upper heat shield. Loosen, but do not remove the four (1300cc) or two (1500cc) intake manifold-to-exhaust manifold bolts.

7. Remove the header pipe-to-exhaust manifold nuts (discard them), separate the header pipe from the exhaust manifold and discard the exhaust flange gasket.

8. Remove the combination manifold-to-cyl-

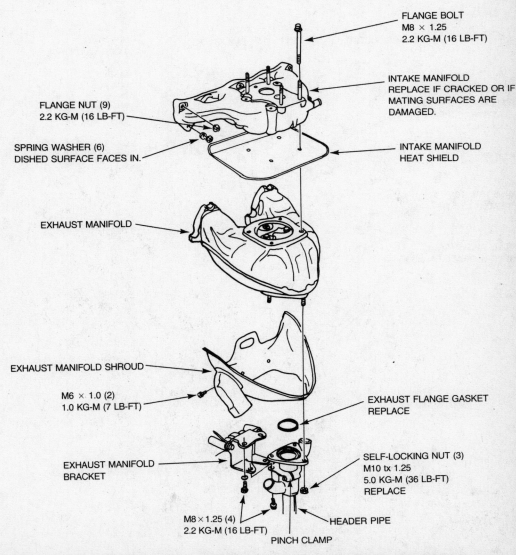

FLANGE BOLT
M8 × 1.25
2.2 KG-M (16 LB-FT)

INTAKE MANIFOLD
REPLACE IF CRACKED OR IF
MATING SURFACES ARE
DAMAGED.

FLANGE NUT (9)
2.2 KG-M (16 LB-FT)

SPRING WASHER (6)
DISHED SURFACE FACES IN.

INTAKE MANIFOLD
HEAT SHIELD

EXHAUST MANIFOLD

EXHAUST MANIFOLD SHROUD

M6 × 1.0 (2)
1.0 KG-M (7 LB-FT)

EXHAUST FLANGE GASKET
REPLACE

EXHAUST MANIFOLD
BRACKET

SELF-LOCKING NUT (3)
M10 tx 1.25
5.0 KG-M (36 LB-FT)
REPLACE

M8 × 1.25 (4)
2.2 KG-M (16 LB-FT)

HEADER PIPE

PINCH CLAMP

Exploded view of the combination manifold assembly—CVCC 1335cc engine

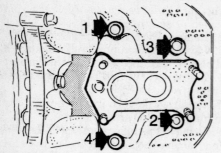

When reinstalling the combination manifold on CVCC models, tighten these four bolts *after* the manifolds have been attached to the engine. You'll crack the manifold ears if you tighten them beforehand

inder head nuts/washers and the manifold assembly from the cylinder head.

9. Remove the intake manifold-to-exhaust manifold bolts and separate the manifolds.

10. Using a putty knife, clean the gasket mounting surfaces.

11. To install, use new gaskets and reverse the removal procedures. The thick washers used beneath the cylinder head-to-manifold retaining nuts must be installed with the dished (concave), side toward the engine. Torque the combination manifold-to-cylinder head nuts (in a circular pattern from the center to the ends) to 16 ft. lbs., the intake manifold-to-exhaust manifold bolts to 16 ft. lbs. and the header pipe-to-exhaust manifold nuts to 36 ft. lbs. Check

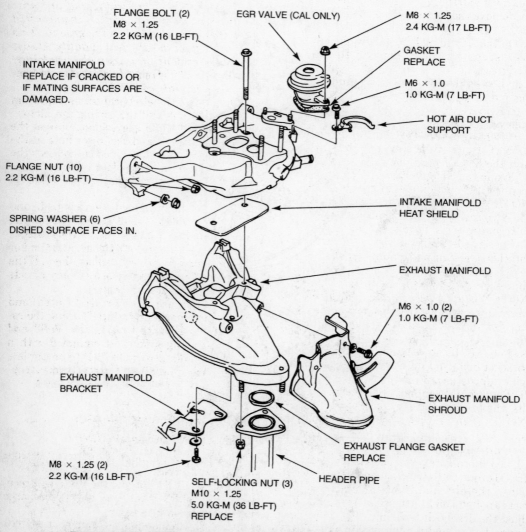

FLANGE BOLT (2)
M8 × 1.25
2.2 KG-M (16 LB-FT)

EGR VALVE (CAL ONLY)

M8 × 1.25
2.4 KG-M (17 LB-FT)

GASKET
REPLACE

INTAKE MANIFOLD
REPLACE IF CRACKED OR
IF MATING SURFACES ARE
DAMAGED.

M6 × 1.0
1.0 KG-M (7 LB-FT)

HOT AIR DUCT
SUPPORT

FLANGE NUT (10)
2.2 KG-M (16 LB-FT)

INTAKE MANIFOLD
HEAT SHIELD

SPRING WASHER (6)
DISHED SURFACE FACES IN.

EXHAUST MANIFOLD

M6 × 1.0 (2)
1.0 KG-M (7 LB-FT)

EXHAUST MANIFOLD
BRACKET

EXHAUST MANIFOLD
SHROUD

M8 × 1.25 (2)
2.2 KG-M (16 LB-FT)

EXHAUST FLANGE GASKET
REPLACE

SELF-LOCKING NUT (3)
M10 × 1.25
5.0 KG-M (36 LB-FT)
REPLACE

HEADER PIPE

Exploded view of the combination manifold assembly—CVCC 1487 cc engine

and/or adjust the choke and throttle linkage. Bleed the cooling system.

Air Conditioning Compressor
REMOVAL AND INSTALLATION

1. Operate the engine at idle speed and turn ON the air conditioning system for a few minutes.

2. Turn OFF the air conditioning system and the engine. Disconnect the negative battery terminal from the battery and the clutch wire from the air conditioning compressor.

3. Refer to "Discharging the System" procedures in Chapter 1 and very slowly discharge the air conditioning system.

4. On the Civic models, remove the left front under cover and the engine lower grille cowling, then, remove the receiver from the connecting lines.

5. On the Accord and Prelude equipped with power steering, perform the following procedures:

    a. Loosen the power steering pump adjusting and mounting bolts.

    b. Remove the drive belt from the pump's pulley.

    c. Remove the power steering pump and support it out of the way; DO NOT disconnect the hoses from the pump.

6. From the air conditioning compressor, disconnect the suction and discharge hoses.

NOTE: *When disconnecting the hoses from the compressor, be sure to plug the openings to keep dirt and moisture out of the system.*

7. Loosen the air conditioning compressor-to-bracket adjusting and mounting bolts/nut(s), then, remove the drive belt from the compressor.

NOTE: *On the Accord and Prelude, it may be necessary to remove the air conditioning cooling fan shroud and fan with the mounting frame.*

8. Remove the air conditioning compressor-to-bracket bolts and set the compressor on the engine support beam.

9. Remove the compressor bracket-to-engine bolts, the bracket and the compressor.

NOTE: *If installing a new compressor, install 1 oz. of refrigerant oil through the suction fitting of the compressor.*

10. To install, reverse the removal procedures. Torque the bracket-to-engine bolts to 34 ft. lbs., the air conditioning compressor-to-bracket bolts to 35 ft. lbs. or nut(s) to 32 ft. lbs. Adjust the drive belt tension to $5/16''$ deflection. Charge the air conditioning system and test its performance.

Radiator

The Honda employs water-cooling for engine heat dissipation. Air is forced through the radiator by an electric fan which is, in turn, activated by a water temperature sensor screwed into the base of the radiator.

CAUTION: *DO NOT attempt to open the cooling system when the engine is Hot; the system will be under high pressure and scalding may occur.*

REMOVAL AND INSTALLATION

NOTE: *When removing the radiator, take care not to damage the core and fins.*

1. Position a clean drain pan under the radiator, open the drain plug, remove the radiator cap and drain the cooling system.

CAUTION: *When draining the coolant, keep in mind that cats and dogs are attracted by the ethylene glycol antifreeze, and are quite likely to drink any that is left in an uncovered container or in puddles on the ground. This will prove fatal in sufficient quantity. Always drain the coolant into a sealable container. Coolant should be reused unless it is contaminated or several years old.*

2. Disconnect the electrical connectors from the thermo-switch and the cooling fan motor.

3. Disconnect the upper coolant hose at the upper radiator tank and the lower hose at the water pump connecting pipe. Disconnect the overflow hose from the coolant tank.

4. Remove the turn signals (Civic 1973-77) and front grille.

5. Remove the radiator-to-chassis bolts and the radiator with the fan attached. The fan can be easily unbolted from the back of the radiator.

6. Inspect the hoses for damage, leaks and/or deterioration; if necessary, replace them. If the radiator fins are clogged, wash off any insects or dirt with low pressure water.

7. To install, use new O-rings (if used) and reverse the removal procedure. Torque the radiator-to-chassis bolts to 7 ft. lbs. Refill and bleed the cooling system; if equipped with a coolant reservoir, be sure to fill it to proper level. Start the engine, allow it to reach normal operating temperatures and check for leaks.

Air Conditioning Condenser
REMOVAL AND INSTALLATION

1. Disconnect the negative battery terminal from the battery.

2. Refer to "Discharging the System" procedures in Chapter 1 and very slowly discharge the air conditioning system.

3. On the Prelude models, remove the front grille and the upper radiator frame bolts, then,

slightly move the frame to obtain access to the condenser.

4. On the Accord models, remove the hood lock brace bolts and position the brace on the engine; DO NOT disconnect the hood opener cable from the hood lock.

5. On the Civic models, perform the following procedures:

a. Remove the front bumper.

b. Disconnect the aluminum receiver line from the copper receiver line and the sight glass.

c. Remove the discharge hose clamp (from the base of the condenser) and the discharge hose from the condenser.

d. Disconnect the electrical connector from the condenser fan.

6. Disconnect and plug the refrigerant lines from the condenser.

NOTE:Be careful not to damage the condenser fins and tubes.

7. Remove the condenser from the vehicle.

8. On the Civic models, remove the condenser fan from the condenser (if necessary).

NOTE: *If installing a new condenser, pour 10mL of refrigerant oil in it.*

9. To install, reverse the removal procedures. Torque the condenser mounting bolts to 12 ft. lbs. Charge the air conditioning system. Test the performance of the air conditioning system.

Water Pump

REMOVAL AND INSTALLATION

All except 1342cc, 1488cc, 1493cc and 1590cc Engines

1. Place a clean drain pan under the radiator, remove the drain plug (from the front side of the engine block and the drain the cooling system to a level below the water pump.

CAUTION: *When draining the coolant, keep in mind that cats and dogs are attracted by the ethylene glycol antifreeze, and are quite likely to drink any that is left in an uncovered container or in puddles on the ground. This will prove fatal in sufficient quantity. Always drain the coolant into a sealable container. Coolant should be reused unless it is contaminated or several years old.*

2. If the water pump and alternator operate from the same drive belt, loosen the alternator bolts, move the alternator toward the cylinder block and remove the drive belt.

3. Remove the pulley-to-water pump bolts and the pulley.

4. Remove the water pump-to-engine bolts and the pump together with the pulley and the O-ring seal.

5. Using a putty knife, clean the gasket mounting surfaces.

6. To install, use a new O-ring (or gasket)

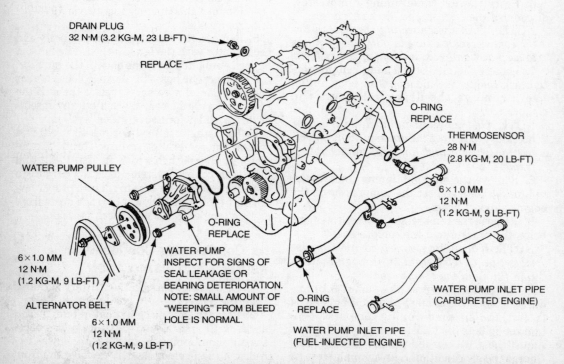

DRAIN PLUG
32 N·M (3.2 KG-M, 23 LB-FT)
REPLACE

O-RING
REPLACE

THERMOSENSOR
28 N·M
(2.8 KG-M, 20 LB-FT)

WATER PUMP PULLEY

6 × 1.0 MM
12 N·M
(1.2 KG-M, 9 LB-FT)

O-RING
REPLACE

WATER PUMP
INSPECT FOR SIGNS OF
SEAL LEAKAGE OR
BEARING DETERIORATION.
NOTE: SMALL AMOUNT OF
"WEEPING" FROM BLEED
HOLE IS NORMAL.

6 × 1.0 MM
12 N·M
(1.2 KG-M, 9 LB-FT)

ALTERNATOR BELT

6 × 1.0 MM
12 N·M
(1.2 KG-M, 9 LB-FT)

O-RING
REPLACE

WATER PUMP INLET PIPE
(FUEL-INJECTED ENGINE)

WATER PUMP INLET PIPE
(CARBURETED ENGINE)

Exploded view of the water pump—all engines, except 1342cc, 1488cc, 1493cc, and 1590cc engines

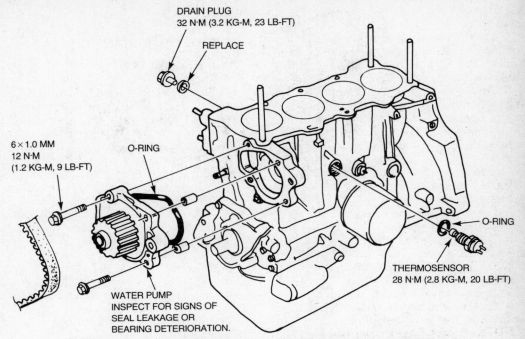

DRAIN PLUG
32 N·M (3.2 KG-M, 23 LB-FT)

REPLACE

6 × 1.0 MM
12 N·M
(1.2 KG-M, 9 LB-FT)

O-RING

O-RING

THERMOSENSOR
28 N·M (2.8 KG-M, 20 LB-FT)

WATER PUMP
INSPECT FOR SIGNS OF
SEAL LEAKAGE OR
BEARING DETERIORATION.

Exploded view of the water pump—1342cc, 1488cc, 1493cc, and 1590cc engines

and reverse the removal procedures. Torque the water pump-to-engine bolts to 9 ft. lbs. and the pulley-to-water pump bolts to 9 ft. lbs. Adjust the drive belt tension. Refill and bleed the cooling system. Operate the engine to normal operating temperatures and check for leaks.

1342cc, 1488cc, 1493cc and 1590cc Engines

1. Place a clean drain pan under the radiator, remove the drain plug (from the front side of the engine block) and the drain the cooling system to a level below the water pump.

CAUTION: *When draining the coolant, keep in mind that cats and dogs are attracted by the ethylene glycol antifreeze, and are quite likely to drink any that is left in an uncovered container or in puddles on the ground. This will prove fatal in sufficient quantity. Always drain the coolant into a sealable container. Coolant should be reused unless it is contaminated or several years old.*

2. Refer to the "Timing Belt, Removal and Installation" procedures in this section and remove the timing belt.

3. Remove the water pump-to-engine bolts and the water pump from the engine.

4. Using a putty knife, clean the gasket mounting surfaces.

5. To install, use new O-ring (or gasket) and reverse the removal procedures. Check and/or adjust the engine timing. Refill and bleed the

cooling system. Operate the engine to normal operating temperatures and check for leaks.

Cylinder Head

NOTE: *You will need a 12 point socket to remove and install the head bolts on the CVCC engine.*

PRECAUTIONS

● To prevent warping, the cylinder head should be removed when the engine is Cold.

● Remove oil, scale or carbon deposits accumulated from each part. When decarbonizing take care not to score or scratch the mating surfaces.

● After washing the oil holes or orifices in each part, make sure they are not restricted by blowing out with compressed air.

● If the parts will not be reinstalled immediately after washing, spray the parts with a rust preventive to protect from corrosion.

REMOVAL AND INSTALLATION

1170cc, 1237cc, 1335cc, 1487cc and 1600cc Engines — Civic

NOTE: *If the engine has already been removed from the vehicle, begin with Step 13 of the following procedure.*

1. Of the Civic (1973-77) models, remove the

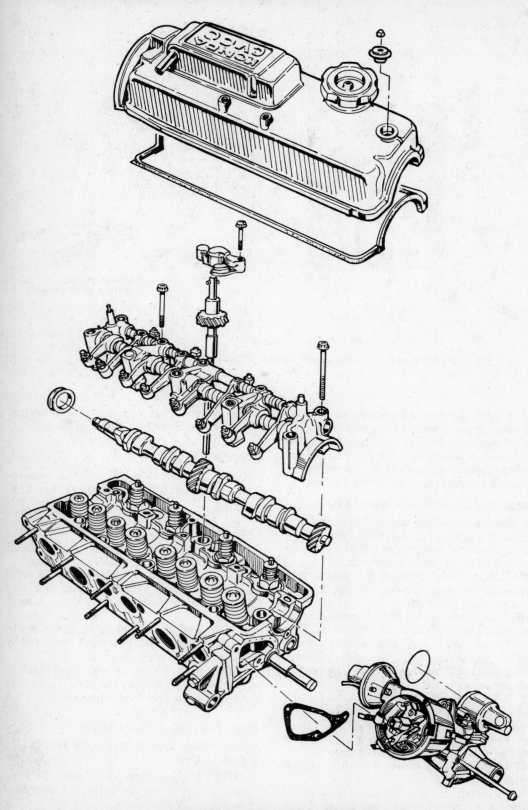

Exploded view of CVCC cylinder head

turn signals, grille and hood. Disconnect the negative battery terminal.

2. Place a clean drain pan under the radiator, remove radiator cap, the drain plug (from the front side of the engine block, if equipped) and the drain the cooling system.

CAUTION: *When draining the coolant, keep in mind that cats and dogs are attracted by the ethylene glycol antifreeze, and are quite likely to drink any that is left in an uncovered container or in puddles on the ground. This will prove fatal in sufficient quantity. Always drain the coolant into a sealable container. Coolant should be reused unless it is contaminated or several years old.*

3. Disconnect the upper radiator hose from the thermostat housing.

4. On CVCC models, remove distributor cap, ignition wires and primary wire. Loosen the alternator bracket and remove the upper mounting bolt from the cylinder head.

5. Remove the air cleaner housing.

6. Disconnect the charcoal canister-to-carburetor tube from the canister.

7. Disconnect the throttle and choke control cables. Label and disconnect all vacuum hoses.

8. Disconnect the heater hose from the intake manifold.

9. Disconnect the electrical connectors from both thermo-switches.

10. Disconnect the fuel line from the carburetor.

11. On the CVCC models, disconnect the temperature gauge sending unit wire, idle cut-off solenoid valve and the primary/main cut-off solenoid valve.

12. Remove the engine torque rod from the engine. Disconnect the exhaust pipe from the exhaust manifold.

13. Remove the valve cover-to-cylinder head bolts and the valve cover.

14. Remove the upper timing belt cover-to-engine bolts and the cover.

15. Rotate the crankshaft to position the No. 1 piston to the TDC of its compression stroke; to do this, align the notch next to the red notch used for setting ignition timing, with the index mark on the timing belt cover (1170cc and 1237cc) or the rear of engine block (CVCC).

16. Loosen, but do not remove, the timing belt adjusting bolt and pivot bolt.

17. On 1170cc and 1237cc models, remove the camshaft pulley bolt. Do not let the woodruff key fall inside the timing cover. Using the Pulley Removal tool No. 07935-6110000 or equivalent, remove the pulley.

Disassembled CVCC cylinder head showing major components

Timing belt pivot and adjustment bolts

Closeup of non-CVCC engine crankshaft showing gear removed, with woodruff key remaining

WARNING: *Use care when handling the timing belt. Do not use sharp instruments to remove the belt. Do not get oil or grease on the belt. Do not bend or twist the belt more than 90°.*

18. If equipped with a 1170cc or 1237cc engine, perform the following procedures:

a. Remove the fuel pump and distributor.

b. Remove the oil pump gear holder, then, the pump gear and shaft.

19. Remove the cylinder head bolts in the reverse order of the torquing sequence; the No. 1 cylinder head bolt is hidden under the oil pump.

20. Remove the cylinder head with the carburetor and manifolds attached.

21. If necessary, remove the intake and exhaust manifolds from the cylinder head.

NOTE: *After removing the cylinder head, cover the engine with a clean cloth to prevent materials from getting into the cylinders.*

22. Using a putty knife, clean the gasket mounting surfaces.

23. To install, use new gaskets and reverse the removal procedures, being sure to pay attention to the following points.

a. Be sure that No. 1 cylinder is at TDC of its compression stroke.

b. Use a new head gasket and make sure the head, engine block and gasket are clean.

c. The cylinder head aligning dowel pins should be in their proper place in the block before installing the cylinder head.

d. Using the torquing sequence, torque the head bolts according to the diagram. On the 1335cc and 1487cc engines, torque the cylinder head-to-engine bolts in two steps: to 22 ft. lbs., then, to 43 ft. lbs., in sequence each time.

e. After the head bolts have been tightened, install the woodruff key and camshaft pulley (if removed) and torque the pulley bolt

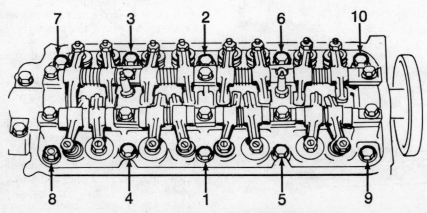

1342 and 1488cc cylinder head torque sequence

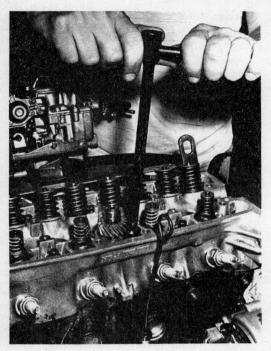

Cylinder head bolt removal. The rocker arms have been removed for clarity

according to specification. On the non-CVCC engines, align the marks on the camshaft pulley so they are parallel with the top of the head and the woodruff key is facing upwards; on the CVCC engines, the word **UP** should be facing upward and the mark on the cam gear should be aligned with the arrow on the cylinder head.

f. After installing the pulley (if removed), install the timing belt. Be careful not to disturb the timing position already set when installing the belt.

Hidden bolt next to oil pump gear (arrow)

1342cc and 1488cc Engines — Civic

1. Disconnect the negative battery terminal.
2. Place a clean drain pan under the radiator, remove the radiator cap, the drain plug (from the front side of the engine block, if equipped) and the drain the cooling system.
CAUTION: *When draining the coolant, keep in mind that cats and dogs are attracted by the ethylene glycol antifreeze, and are quite likely to drink any that is left in an uncovered container or in puddles on the ground. This will prove fatal in sufficient quantity. Always drain the coolant into a sealable container. Coolant should be reused unless it is contaminated or several years old.*
3. To remove the air cleaner, perform the following procedures:
    a. Remove the air cleaner cover and filter.
    b. Disconnect the hot and cold air intake ducts, then, remove the air chamber hose.
    c. Remove the 3 bolts holding the air cleaner.
    d. Lift the air cleaner housing, then, remove the remaining hoses and the air temperature sensor wire.
    e. Remove the air cleaner.
4. On fuel injected models, relieve the fuel pressure using the following procedures:
    a. Slowly loosing the service bolt on top of the fuel filter about one turn.
NOTE: *Place a rag under the filter during this procedure to prevent fuel from spilling onto the engine.*
    b. Disconnect the fuel return hose from the pressure regulator. Remove the special nut and then, remove the fuel hose.
5. Remove the brake booster vacuum tube from the intake manifold.
6. Remove the engine ground wire from the valve cover and disconnect the wires from the fuel cut-off solenoid valve, the automatic choke and the thermosensor.
7. Disconnect the fuel lines.
8. Label and disconnect the spark plug wires from the spark plugs, then, remove the distributor assembly.
9. Disconnect the throttle cable from the carburetor or throttle body.
10. Disconnect the hoses from the charcoal canister and from the No. 1 control box at the tubing manifold.
11. For California or high altitude models, disconnect the air jet controller.
12. If equipped with air conditioning, disconnect the idle control solenoid hoses.
13. Disconnect the upper radiator heater and bypass hoses.
14. On fuel injected models, disconnect the engine sub harness connectors and the follow-

ing couplers from the head and the intake manifold.

- The four injector couplers
- The TA sensor connector
- The ground connector
- The TW sensor connector
- The throttle sensor connector
- The crankshaft angle sensor coupler

15. Remove the thermostat housing-to-intake manifold hose.

16. Disconnect the oxygen sensor coupler.

17. Remove the exhaust manifold bracket and manifold bolts, then, remove the manifold.

18. Remove the bolts from the intake manifold and bracket.

19. Disconnect the breather chamber-to-intake manifold hose.

20. Remove the valve and timing belt covers.

21. Loosen the timing belt tensioner adjustment bolt, then, remove the belt.

22. Remove the cylinder head bolts in the reverse order given in the head bolt torque sequence.

NOTE: *Loosen the bolts ⅓ of a turn each time and repeat the sequence to prevent cylinder head warpage.*

23. Carefully remove the cylinder head from the engine.

24. Using a putty knife, clean the gasket mounting surfaces.

25. To install, use new gaskets and reverse the removal procedures, being sure to pay attention to the following points:

a. Be sure the No. 1 cylinder is at top dead center and the camshaft pulley **UP** mark is on the top before positioning the head in place.

b. The cylinder head dowel pins and oil control jet must be aligned.

c. Tighten the cylinder head bolts in two progressive steps as shown in the torque sequence diagram. First, to 22 ft. lbs. in sequence, then, to 43 ft. lbs. in the same sequence.

d. On the 1342cc engine, torque the valve cover two turns at a time (in the sequence shown) to 9 ft. lbs.

e. After installation, check to see that all hoses and wires are installed correctly.

1493cc and 1590cc Engines — Civic

NOTE: *To avoid damaging the cylinder head, wait until the coolant temperature drops below 100°F before loosening the retaining bolts. Be sure to inspect the timing belt before removing the cylinder head. Turn the crankshaft pulley so that the number one cylinder is at top dead center. Mark all emission hoses before disconnecting them. This procedure should make it possible to remove the cylinder head without removing the engine from the vehicle.*

1. Disconnect the negative battery cable. Drain the cooling system into a suitable container.

CAUTION: *When draining the coolant, keep in mind that cats and dogs are attracted by the ethylene glycol antifreeze, and are quite likely to drink any that is left in an uncovered container or in puddles on the ground. This will prove fatal in sufficient quantity. Always drain the coolant into a sealable container. Coolant should be reused unless it is contaminated or several years old.*

2. Remove the brake booster vacuum hose from the brake master power booster. Remove the engine secondary ground cable from the valve cover.

3. Remove the air intake hose and the air chamber. relieve the fuel pressure as outlined

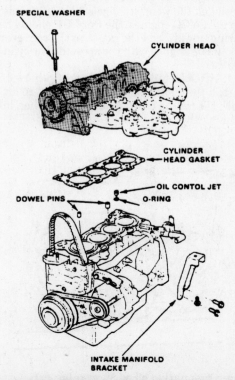

Cylinder head removal – 1988 Civic

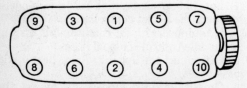

Cylinder head torque sequence for all engines—except the 1342cc, 1488cc, 1829cc and 1955cc engines

in this section. Disconnect the fuel hoses and fuel return hose.

4. Remove the air intake hose and resonator hose. Disconnect the throttle cable at the throttle body (Automatic Transmission only).

5. Disconnect the charcoal canister hose at the throttle valve.

6. Disconnect the following engine wire connectors from the cylinder head and the intake manifold:

a. 14 prong connector from the main wiring harness.

b. EACV connector.

c. Intake air temperature sensor connector.

d. Throttle angle sensor connector.

e. Injector connectors.

f. Ignition coil from the distributor.

g. Top dead center/crank sensor connector from the distributor.

h. Coolant temperature gauge sender connector.

i. Coolant temperature sensor connector.

j. Oxygen sensor.

7. Disconnect the vacuum hoses and the water bypass hoses from the intake manifold and throttle body.

8. Remove the upper radiator hose and the heater hoses from the cylinder head.

9. Remove the PCV hose, charcoal canister hose and vacuum hose from the intake manifold, and remove the vacuum hose from the brake master power booster.

10. Loosen the air conditioning idler pulley and remove the air conditioning belt. Remove the alternator belt.

11. Remove the intake manifold bracket. Remove the exhaust manifold bracket, then remove the header pipe.

12. Remove the exhaust manifold shroud, then remove the exhaust manifold.

13. Mark the position of the distributor in relation to the engine block, remove and tag the spark plug wires and remove the distributor assembly.

14. Remove the valve cover. Remove the timing belt cover.

15. Mark the direction of rotation on the timing belt. Loosen the timing belt adjust bolt, then remove the timing belt from the camshaft pulley.

NOTE: *Do not crimp or bend the timing belt more than 90° or less than 25mm in diameter (width).*

16. Remove the cylinder head bolts. Once the bolts are all removed, remove the cylinder head (along with the intake manifold) from the engine. Remove the intake manifold from the cylinder head.

17. Install the cylinder head in the reverse order of the removal procedure. Be sure to use the following steps as a guide to aid in the installation procedure:

a. Always use a new head gasket.

b. Be sure the cylinder head and the engine block surfaces are clean, level and straight.

c. Be sure the **UP** mark on the timing belt pulley is at the top.

d. Install the intake manifold and tighten the nuts in a criss-cross pattern in two or three steps (17 ft. lbs.) begining with the inner nuts.

e. Be sure the cylinder head dowel pins and control jet are aligned.

f. Install the bolts that secure the intake manifold to its bracket but do not tighten them at this point.

g. Position the cam correctly (as outlined in this section) and install the cylinder head bolts.

h. Tighten the cylinder head bolts in two steps. On the first step tighten all the bolts in the proper sequence to 22 ft. lbs. On the final step, using the same sequence, tighten the bolts to 49 ft. lbs.

i. On the Standard and Si models, install the exhaust manifold and tighten the nuts in a criss cross pattern in two or three steps (25 ft. lbs.) begining with the inner nuts.

j. On the HF models, install catalytic con-

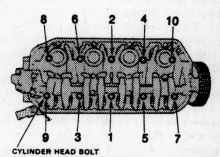

CYLINDER HEAD BOLT

Cylinder head torque sequence—1493cc and 1590cc engines

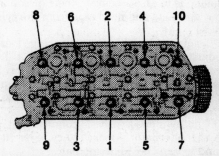

Cylinder head torque sequence—1493cc and 1590cc HF engines

verter to the exhaust manifold, then install the exhaust manifold assembly (25 ft. lbs.)

k. Install the header pipe onto the exhaust manifold. Tighten the bolts to the intake manifold bracket. Install the header pipe on to its bracket.

18. After the installation procedure is complete, check that all tubes, hoses and connectors are installed correctly. Adjust the valve timing as outlined in this section.

1751cc Engine — Accord and Prelude

WARNING: *The cylinder head temperature must be below 100°F.*

1. Disconnect the negative battery terminal from the battery.

2. Place a clean drain pan under the radiator, remove the drain plug and the radiator cap, then, drain the cooling system.

CAUTION: *When draining the coolant, keep in mind that cats and dogs are attracted by the ethylene glycol antifreeze, and are quite likely to drink any that is left in an uncovered container or in puddles on the ground. This will prove fatal in sufficient quantity. Always drain the coolant into a sealable container. Coolant should be reused unless it is contaminated or several years old.*

3. Label and disconnect the vacuum hoses from the air cleaner.

4. Disconnect the electrical connectors from the thermosenser temperature gauge sending unit, idle cut-off solenoid valve, primary/main cut-off solenoid valve and the automatic choke.

5. Disconnect the fuel lines and throttle cable from the carburetor(s).

6. Label and disconnect all emission hoses from the carburetor, then, remove the carburetor.

7. Label and disconnect the electrical connectors wires and hoses from the distributor, then, remove the distributor.

8. Remove the coolant hoses from the cylinder head.

9. Loosen the exhaust manifold-to-engine bracket bolts to ease assembly, then, disconnect the hot air ducts and head pipe from the cylinder head.

10. If equipped with power steering, loosen the adjustment bolt and remove the belt. Disconnect and plug the hoses/fittings to prevent contamination. Remove the pump-to-engine bolts and swing the pump to the right side of the engine.

11. If not equipped with air conditioning, remove the alternator bracket-to-cylinder head bolt and loosen the adjusting bolt.

12. If equipped with air conditioning, remove the alternator and bracket from the engine.

13. Disconnect the brake booster vacuum hose from the one-way valve.

14. Remove the valve cover and upper timing belt cover.

15. Loosen the timing belt pivot and adjusting bolts, then, slide the belt from the pulley.

16. Remove the oil pump gear cover and pull the oil pump shaft out of the cylinder head.

17. Remove the head bolts in sequence working from the outer ends, toward the center; this is the reverse of the torquing sequence. To prevent warpage, loosen the bolts ⅓ turn (in sequence) until they are loose.

18. Carefully lift the cylinder head from the engine block.

19. Using a putty knife, clean the gasket mounting surfaces.

20. To install, use new gaskets, seals and reverse the removal procedures. Make sure the head dowel pins are aligned. Make sure that the **UP** mark on the timing belt pulley is at the top. Torque the cylinder head bolts in two equal steps to 43 ft. lbs.

1829cc and 1955cc Engines except DOHC Engine — Accord and Prelude

WARNING: *The cylinder head temperature must be below 100°F.*

1. Disconnect the negative battery terminal from the battery.

2. Place a clean drain pan under the radiator, remove the drain plug and the radiator cap, then, drain the cooling system.

CAUTION: *When draining the coolant, keep in mind that cats and dogs are attracted by the ethylene glycol antifreeze, and are quite likely to drink any that is left in an uncovered container or in puddles on the ground. This will prove fatal in sufficient quantity. Always drain the coolant into a sealable container. Coolant should be reused unless it is contaminated or several years old.*

3. Remove the vacuum hose from the brake booster and the air intake ducts from the air cleaner case.

4. If equipped with fuel injection, relieve the fuel pressure using the following procedures:

a. Place a rag under the fuel filter to prevent fuel from spilling onto the engine.

b. Slowly loosen the service bolt (on top of the fuel filter) about one turn.

c. Disconnect the fuel return hose from the pressure regulator. Remove the banjo nut and the fuel hose; be sure to replace the washers.

5. Remove the secondary ground cable from the valve cover.

6. Label and disconnect the hoses from the air cleaner.

Cleaning the block mating surface of all traces of old gasket material

7. On carburetor models, disconnect the wires from the thermosenser temperature gauge sending unit, idle cut-off solenoid valve, primary/main cut-off solenoid valve and the automatic choke.

8. Disconnect the throttle cable from the carburetor or throttle body.

9. Label and disconnect all emission hoses from the carburetor, then, remove the carburetor.

10. Label and disconnect electrical connectors and hoses from the distributor, then, remove the distributor.

11. On fuel injected models, label and discon-

Cleaned block surface ready for head gasket

Head gasket positioning. Make sure all passages align with holes in the gasket

nect the following sub harness connectors and couplers from the cylinder head and intake manifold:
- The four injector couplers
- The TA sensor connector
- The ground connector located near the fuel pipe
- The throttle sensor connector
- The TW sensor connector
- The crankshaft angle sensor coupler
- The EGR valve connector
- The 4-wire harness clamps
- The oxygen sensor connector

12. On carbureted models, disconnect the following items:

   a. Disconnect the No. 1 control box emission hoses from the tubing manifold.

   b. Disconnect the air jet controller hoses.

13. Remove the coolant hoses from the cylinder head.

14. If equipped with power steering, perform the following procedures:

   a. Remove the pump bracket from the cylinder head.

   b. Remove the hose clamp bolt from the cylinder head.

   c. Remove the power steering pump bracket from the cylinder head.

15. If equipped with air conditioning, disconnect the idle control solenoid hoses.

16. If equipped with cruise control, remove the cruise control actuator.

17. Remove the exhaust header pipe nuts, the header pipe bracket and pull the pipe away from the exhaust manifold.

18. Remove the air cleaner base mount bolts.

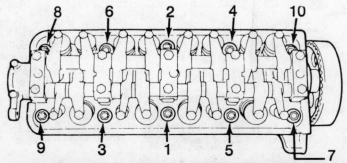

Cylinder head bolt torque sequence—1829cc and 1955cc engines

Disconnect the intake manifold-to-breather chamber hose.

19. Remove the valve cover and the upper timing belt cover.

20. Loosen the tensioner adjusting bolt and remove the timing belt.

NOTE: *When removing the timing belt, DO NOT bend the belt to less than 25mm diameter.*

21. Remove the cylinder head-to-engine bolts, in sequence working from the ends, toward the center; this is performed in the reverse order of the torquing sequence.

22. Remove the cylinder head from the engine, the exhaust manifold from the cylinder head, the air cleaner base from the intake manifold and the intake manifold from the cylinder head.

23. Using a putty knife, clean the gasket mounting surfaces. Inspect the parts for damage, replace them if necessrary.

24. To install, use new gaskets, seals and reverse the removal procedures. Make sure the head dowel pins are aligned. Make sure that the **UP** (fuel injected) or **Round** (carbureted) mark on the timing belt pulley is at the top position. Torque the cylinder head bolts in two equal steps to 49 ft. lbs. Check and/or adjust the valve timing. Refill the cooling system. Start the engine, allow it to reach normal operating temperatures and check for leaks.

1955cc Dual Overhead Cam Engine (DOHC engine)

NOTE: *The cylinder head temperature must be below 38°C. Inspect the timing belt before removing the cylinder head. Turn the flywheel so that number one piston is at top dead center. Be sure to tag all wires and emission hoses as they are removed or disconnected.*

1. Disconnect the battery ground cable.
2. Drain the cooling system.

CAUTION: *When draining the coolant, keep in mind that cats and dogs are attracted by the ethylene glycol antifreeze, and are quite likely to drink any that is left in an uncovered container or in puddles on the ground. This will prove fatal in sufficient quantity. Always drain the coolant into a sealable container. Coolant should be reused unless it is contaminated or several years old.*

3. Remove the brake booster vacuum hose from the intake manifold.

4. Remove the engine secondary ground cable from the valve cover. Disconnect the radio condenser connector and the ignition coil wire.

5. Remove the air cleaner assembly. Relieve the fuel pressure as previously outlined in this section.

6. Disconnect the fuel lines and fuel return line. Remove the air intake hose and the resonator hose. Disconnect the throttle cable at the throttle body.

7. Disconnect the throttle control cable at the throttle body, on vehicles with automatic transaxle. Disconnect the charcoal canister hose at the throttle valve.

8. Disconnect and tag all the necessary wire harness connectors from the cylinder head. Remove the emission control box and vacuum tank, then disconnect the two connectors. Do not remove the emission hoses.

9. Remove the upper radiator hose. Remove the heater hoses from the cylinder head. Remove the water bypass hoses from the water pump inlet pipe.

10. Remove the power steering pump belt and the alternator belt. Also remove the air conditioning belt if so equipped.

11. Disconnect the inlet hose from the power steering pump and remove the power steering pump from the cylinder head. Remove the alternator assembly as well.

NOTE: *When the power steering hose is disconnected, the fluid will flow out, so cover the alternator with a shop towel to prevent any internal damage.*

12. Remove the intake manifold bracket. Remove the exhaust manifold bracket and then the header pipe.

13. Remove and tag the ignition wires and then remove the distributor assembly. Be sure to scribe a line stating the position of the distributor assembly to the engine block for easy installation.

14. Remove the cylinder sensor. Remove the valve cover. Remove the timing belt middle cover.

15. Remove the crankshaft pulley and then remove the lower timing belt cover. Loosen the timing belt adjusting bolt and then remove the timing belt. Be sure to mark the rotation of the timing belt, if the belt is to be used again.

NOTE: *Do not crimp or bend the timing belt more than 90° or less than 25mm in diameter (width).*

16. Remove the camshaft holders, camshafts and rocker arms. Remove the cylinder head bolts (take notice of the bolt holes that the two longer bolts come out of) and remove the cylinder head.

17. Remove the exhaust manifold shroud and EGR pipe, then remove the exhaust manifold from the cylinder head. Remove the intake manifold from the cylinder head.

18. Thoroughly clean the mating surfaces to the head and block.

19. Always use a new gasket.

20. Install the head in reverse order of the removal procedure. Make sure the head dowel

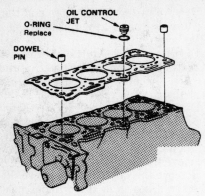

Cylinder head gasket installation—1955cc DOHC engine

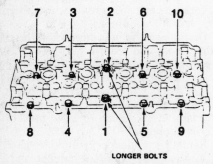

Cylinder head torque sequence—1955cc DOHC engine

pins and oil control jet are aligned. Make sure that the UP marks or cut-out on the timing belt pulleys is at the top. Torque the cylinder head bolts in two equal steps. Tighten all bolts to 22 ft. lbs. in sequence, then to 49 ft. lbs. in the final step.

21. Apply engine oil to all the cylinder head bolts and the washers. Place the two longer bolts in their proper position on the head.

22. Install the intake manifold and tighten the nuts in a criss cross pattern in two or three steps to 16 ft. lbs.

23. Install the exhaust manifold and bracket and tighten the nuts in a criss-cross pattern in two or three steps to 26 ft. lbs.

24. After the installation procedure is complete, check that all tubes, hoses and connectors are installed correctly. Adjust the valve timing.

CLEANING AND INSPECTION

1. Refer to the "Valves, Removal and Installation" in this section and remove the valve assemblies from the cylinder head.

2. Using a small wire power brush, clean the carbon from the combustion chambers and the valve ports.

3. Inspect the cylinder head for cracks in the

exhaust ports, combustion chambers or external cracks in the water chamber.

4. Throughly clean the valve guides using a suitable wire bore brush.

NOTE: *Excessive valve stem-to-bore clearance will cause excessive oil consumption and may cause valve breakage. Insufficient clearance will result in noisy and sticky functioning of the valve and disturb engine smoothness.*

5. Measure the valve stem clearance as follows:

a. Clamp a dial indicator on one side of the cylinder head rocker arm cover gasket rail.

b. Locate the indicator so movement of the valve stem from side-to-side (crosswise to the head) will cause a direct movement of the indicator stem. The indicator stem must contact the side of the valve stem just above the valve guide.

c. Prop the valve head about $1/16''$ off the valve seat.

d. Move the stem of the valve from side-to-side using light pressure to obtain a clearance reading. If the clearance exceeds specifica-

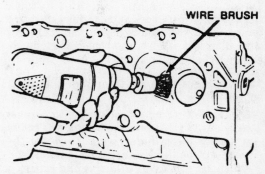

Remove the carbon from the cylinder head with a wire brush and electric drill

Using a dial indicator to measure the valve stem clearances

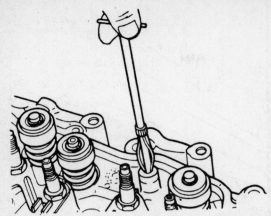

Using an expandable wire type cleaner to cleaner to clean the valve guides

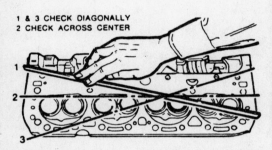

1 & 3 CHECK DIAGONALLY
2 CHECK ACROSS CENTER

Using a straight-edge to inspect the cylinder head for warpage

tions, it will be necessary to ream (for original valves) the valve guides.

6. Inspect the rocker arm studs for wear or damage.

7. Install a dial micrometer into the valve guide and check the valve seat for concentricity.

RESURFACING

1. Using a straightedge, check the cylinder for warpage.

2. If the warpage exceeds 0.076mm in a 152mm span or 0.152mm over the total length, the cylinder head must be resurfaced. Resurfacing can be performed at most machine shops.

Valves

REMOVAL AND INSTALLATION

1. Refer to the "Cylinder Head, Removal and Installation" and the "Camshaft, Removal and Installation" procedures in this section, then, remove the cylinder head from the engine and the camshaft from the cylinder head.

2. Using a plastic mallet, tap each valve stem to loosen the valve keepers.

3. Using a Valve Spring Compressor tool, compress the valve springs, then, remove the valve keepers, retainers and springs. Remove the valves from the opposite side of the cylinder head.

NOTE: *When removing the valves and components, keep them in order for reinstallation purposes.*

4. To replace the valve seals, simply pull the seal from the valve guide. If the valve seals are being reused, it is good idea to replace the springs around the seal's neck.

NOTE: *The exhaust valve seal uses a black spring, while the intake valve seal uses a white spring.*

5. Inspect the valves for wear, damage and/or cracks. If necessary, reface the valves on a valve grinding machine.

NOTE: *When replacing the valve springs, place the closely wound end toward the cylinder head.*

6. To assemble the cylinder head, use new valve seals, lubricate the valve parts with clean engine oil and reverse the disassembly procedures. After removing the valve spring compressor, tap the valve stems 2-3 times to make sure the valve keepers and valves are fully seated.

CAUTION: *When removing the valve spring compressor tool, remove it slowly and make sure the valve keepers are fully seated; otherwise, the springs may be launched like a missile.*

7. To complete the installation, use new gaskets and reverse the removal procedures.

INSPECTION

Inspect the valve faces and seats (in the head) for pits, burned spots and other evidence of poor seating. If a valve face is in such bad shape that the head of the valve must be ground, in order to true the face, discard the valve, because the sharp edge will run too hot. The correct angle for valve faces is 45°. We recommend the refacing be performed by a reputable machine shop.

Check the valve stem for scoring and burned spots. If not noticeably scored or damaged, clean the valve stem with solvent to remove all gum and varnish. Clean the valve guides using and an expanding wire-type valve guide cleaner. If you have access to a dial indicator for measuring valve stem-to-guide clearance, mount it so the stem of the indicator is at 90° to the valve stem and as closer to the valve guide as possible. Move the valve off its seat, then, measure the valve guide-to-stem clearance by rocking the stem back and for the actuate the dial indicator. Measure the valve stem diameter using a micrometer and compare it to specifications to determine whether the stem or guide wear is responsible for the excess clearance. If a dial indi-

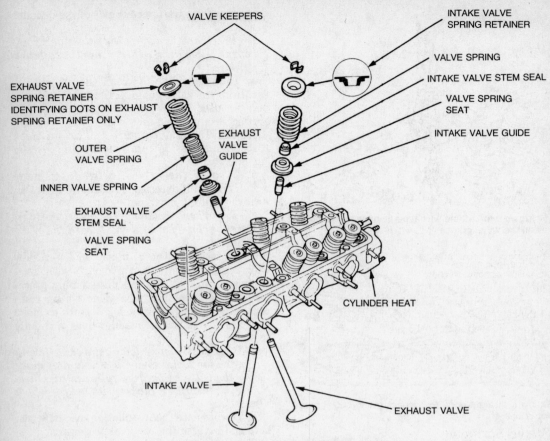

VALVE KEEPERS

INTAKE VALVE
SPRING RETAINER

EXHAUST VALVE
SPRING RETAINER
IDENTIFYING DOTS ON EXHAUST
SPRING RETAINER ONLY

VALVE SPRING

INTAKE VALVE STEM SEAL

VALVE SPRING
SEAT

OUTER
VALVE SPRING

EXHAUST
VALVE
GUIDE

INTAKE VALVE GUIDE

INNER VALVE SPRING

EXHAUST VALVE
STEM SEAL

VALVE SPRING
SEAT

CYLINDER HEAT

INTAKE VALVE

EXHAUST VALVE

Exploded view of the valve assemblies—typical

cator and micrometer are not available, take the cylinder head and valves to a reputable machine shop for inspection.

REFACING

NOTE: *All valve grinding operations should be performed by a qualified machine shop; ONLY the valve lapping operation is recommended to be performed by the inexperienced mechanic.*

Valve Lapping

When valve faces and seats have been refaced and/or recut, or if they are determined to be in good condition, the valves MUST BE lapped in to ensure efficient sealing when the valve closes against the seat.

1. Invert the cylinder head so the combustion chambers are facing upward.
2. Lightly lubricate the valve stems with clean engine oil and coat the valve seats with valve grinding compound. Install the valves in the cylinder head as numbered.
3. Using a valve lapping tool, attach the suction cup to a valve head. *You will probably have to*

moisten the suction cup to securely attach the tool to the valve.

4. Rotate the tool between the palms, changing position and lifting the tool often to prevent grooving. Lap the valve until a smooth polished seat is evident (you may have to add a bit more compound after some lapping is done).

5. Remove the valve and tool, then, remove

Lapping the valves by hand

Home made valve lapping tool

all traces of the grinding compound with a solvent-soaked rag or rinse the head with solvent.

NOTE: *Valve lapping can also be done by fastening a suction to a piece of drill rod in a hang egg-beater type drill. Proceed as above, using the drill as a lapping tool. Due to the higher speeds involved when using the hand drill, care must be exercised to avoid grooving the seat. Lift the tool and change direction of rotation often.*

Valve Springs

If the cylinder head is removed from the engine, refer to the "Valves, Removal and Installation" procedures in this section and remove the valve springs.

REMOVAL AND INSTALLATION

1. Refer to the "Rocker Arm, Removal and Installation" procedures in this section and remove the rocker arm assembly.

2. Using an old set of rocker arm shafts, install them in place of the rocker arm assembly; this will prevent bending or scratching the original set of shafts.

3. Remove the spark plug(s) from the cylinder head.

4. Rotate the crankshaft to position the cylinder (being worked on) to the TDC of its compression stroke.

5. Using a Spark Plug Air Hold tool, install it into the spark plug hold and inject compressed air into the cylinder to hold the valves in place.

6. Using the Spring Compressor tool, compress the spring(s) and remove the valve keepers. Relax the spring compressor tool, then, remove the valve retainer, the spring(s) and the

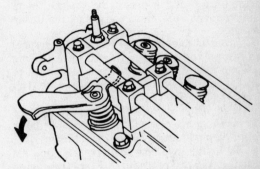

Using a spring compressor tool to remove the valve spring(s) from the cylinder head—typical

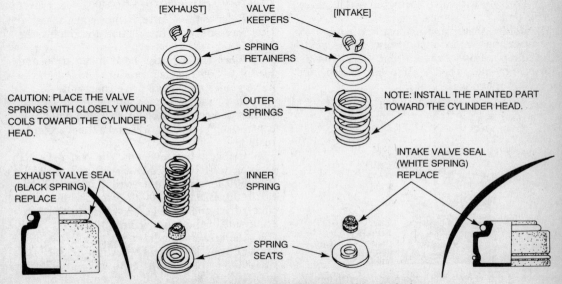

Exploded view of the valve spring assembly—typical

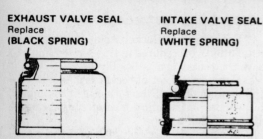

EXHAUST VALVE SEAL
Replace
(BLACK SPRING)

INTAKE VALVE SEAL
Replace
(WHITE SPRING)

Cross-sectional view of the valve seals—typical

valve seal; keep the parts in the order for reinstallation purposes.

NOTE: *If reusing the valve seals, it is recommended to replace the neck springs of the seal; the black spring is used on the exhaust valve seal and the white spring is used on the intake valve seal. The seals are not interchangeable between the intake and the exhaust valves.*

7. Inspect the springs for fatigue, cracks and/or uniformity; if necessary, replace them. Using a putty knife, clean the gasket mounting surfaces.

8. To assemble, use new seals (if necessary) and reverse the disassembly procedures. Using a plastic mallet, tap the valve a few times to make sure the valve keepers are seated correctly.

NOTE: *When installing the springs, be sure to position the closely wound coils ends or painted part toward the cylinder head.*

9. To install, use new gaskets, seals and reverse the removal procedures. Start the engine and check for leaks.

INSPECTION

1. Position the valve spring on a flat, clean surface next to a square.

2. Rotate the spring against the square to measure the distortion (out-of-roundness). If the spring height varies (between similar springs) by more than $\frac{1}{16}$", replace the spring.

NOT MORE THAN 5/64"

CLOSED COIL END DOWNWARD

Inspecting the valve spring distortion and height—typical

Using a dial indicator to inspect the valve seat—typical

Valve Seats

The valve seats can be machined during a valve job to provide optimum sealing between the valve and the seat.

The seating services should be performed by a professional machine shop which has the specialized knowledge and tools necessary to perform the service.

Valve Guides

If replacement valve guides are not available or you determine the replacement procedure is too involved, the guides can be reconditioned using a procedure known as knurling (machining the inner surface).

REMOVAL AND INSTALLATION

1. Refer to the "Valve, Removal and Installation" procedures in this section and remove the valves.

2. Place the cylinder head in an oven and heat it to 300°F; this procedure will loosen the valve guides enough to drive them out.

3. Place the new valve guides in the freezer section of a refrigerator for about an hour; this contraction procedure will make them easier to install.

4. Using a hammer and the Valve Guide Driver tool No. 07942-SA50000, 07942-8230000 or equivalent (exhaust) or 07942-6570100, 07942-6110000 or equivalent (intake), drive the valve guide(s) toward the camshaft side of the cylinder head.

5. Using a hammer and the Valve Guide Driver tool No. 07942-SA50000, 07942-8230000 or equivalent (exhaust) or 07942-6570100, 07942-6110000 or equivalent (intake), remove the new guide from the freezer

With the valve spring compressed, use a small magnet to remove the valve keepers

When the valve keepers are removed, lift off the valve springs

Compressing the valve spring using a valve spring compressor

and drive it into the cylinder head from the camshaft side until the guide projects 15.5mm above the cylinder head surface.

6. Using the Valve Guide Reamer tool No. 07984-SA50000, 07984-689010A or equivalent (exhaust) or 07984-6110000, 07984-657010A or equivalent, coat the reamer with cutting oil and ream the valve guides to the proper valve stem fit. Use the reamer with an in-out motion while rotating it. For the finished dimension of the valve guide, check the "Valve Specifications" chart.

NOTE: *Do not forget to install the valve guide seals.*

7. To assemble, reverse the disassembly procedures.

Auxiliary valve installation. Always use a new O-ring

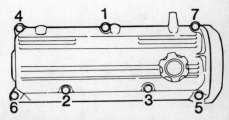

1342cc valve cover torque sequence

CVCC valve components, including auxiliary valve

Valve installation with head cleaned of all carbon

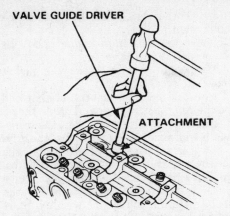

VALVE GUIDE DRIVER

ATTACHMENT

Installing the valve guide into the cylinder head

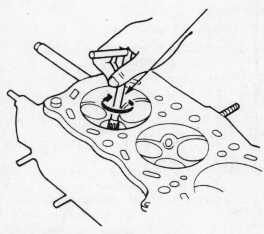

Reaming the valve guides

8. To complete the installation, use new gaskets and reverse the removal procedures. Refill the cooling system. Start the engine and check for leaks.

KNURLING

Knurling is a process in which the metal on the valve guide bore is displaced and raised, thereby reducing the clearance. It also provides excellent oil control. The option of knurling rather than reaming valve guides should be discussed with a reputable machinist or engine specialist.

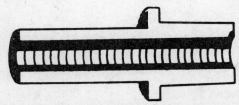

Cross-sectional view of a knurled valve guide

Oil Pan
REMOVAL AND INSTALLATION
All Engines Except 4WD Wagon

1. Firmly apply the parking brake and block the rear wheels.

2. Raise and support the front of the vehicle on jackstands.

NOTE: *On some vehicles, it may be necessary to attach a chain to the clutch cable bracket on the transaxle case and raise just enough to take the load off the center mount; do not remove the left engine mount.*

3. Position a clean drain pan under the engine, remove the drain plug and drain the engine oil.

CAUTION: *The EPA warns that prolonged contact with used engine oil may cause a number of skin disorders, including cancer! You should make every effort to minimize your exposure to used engine oil. Protective gloves should be worn when changing the oil. Wash your hands and any other exposed skin areas as soon as possible after exposure to used engine oil. Soap and water, or waterless hand cleaner should be used.*

4. If equipped, it may be necessary to remove the center beam and the engine lower mount.

5. If equipped with flywheel dust shield, it may be necessary to remove it.

6. Remove the oil pan-to-engine nuts/bolts (in a criss-cross pattern) and the oil pan; if necessary, use a mallet to tap the corners of the oil pan.

7. To install, use new gasket(s), sealant and reverse the removal procedures. Torque the oil pan-to-engine nuts/bolts to 9 ft. lbs. Refill the crankcase with clean engine oil.

4WD Wagon

1. Firmly apply the parking brake and block the rear wheels.

2. Raise and support the front of the vehicle on jackstands.

3. Remove the splash shields from under the engine and the transaxle.

4. Using an oil catch pan, position it under the engine, remove the drain plug and drain the engine oil.

CAUTION: *The EPA warns that prolonged contact with used engine oil may cause a number of skin disorders, including cancer! You should make every effort to minimize your exposure to used engine oil. Protective gloves should be worn when changing the oil. Wash your hands and any other exposed skin areas as soon as possible after exposure to used engine oil. Soap and water, or waterless hand cleaner should be used.*

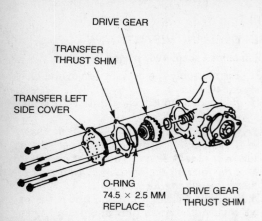

Exploded view of the transfer case left-side cover—4WD Civic wagon

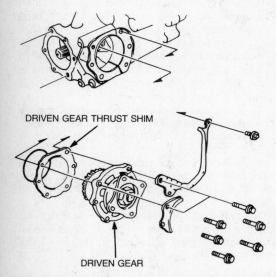

Exploded view of the driven gear assembly—4WD Civic wagon

5. Using an oil catch pan, position it under the transaxle, remove the drain plug and drain the transaxle oil.

6. Remove the exhaust header pipe to provide clearance under the engine.

7. Remove the driveshaft-to-transfer case flange bolts and separate the driveshaft from the transfer case.

8. Remove the left side cover-to-transfer case bolts, the side cover, the thrust shim, the O-ring, the driven gear and the drive gear thrust shim from the transfer case.

9. From the rear of the transfer case, remove the driven gear-to-transfer case bolts, the driven gear, the thrust shim and the O-ring.

10. Remove the transfer case-to-transaxle bolts and the transfer case.

11. Remove the clutch case cover-to-clutch case bolts and the cover.

12. Remove the oil pan-to-engine nuts/bolts and the oil pan from the engine.

13. Using a putty knife, clean the gasket mounting surfaces.

14. To install, use new gaskets, sealant and reverse the removal procedures. Torque the oil pan-to-engine nuts/bolts to 9 ft. lbs., the transfer case-to-transaxle bolts to 33 ft. lbs., the driven gear-to-transfer case bolts to 19 ft. lbs., the left side cover-to-transfer case bolts to 33 ft. lbs. and the driveshaft flange-to-driven gear flange bolts to 24 ft. lbs. After 30 minutes, to allow the sealant to set, refill the engine with oil. Start the engine and check for leaks.

Oil Pump

REMOVAL AND INSTALLATION

All Engines except 1342cc, 1488cc, 1493cc, 1590cc, 1829cc and 1955cc

1. Refer to the "Oil Pan, Removal and Installation" procedures in this section and remove the oil pan.

2. Remove the oil pump-to-engine bolts and the pump.

3. Using a putty knife, clean the gasket mounting surfaces.

NOTE: *If removing the oil pump screen, remove the screen-to-pump bolt and the screen.*

4. To install, use new gaskets, sealant and reverse the removal procedures. Torque the oil pump-to-engine bolts to 8 ft. lbs. Refill the crankcase with clean engine oil. Start the engine and check for leaks.

Removing the oil pump screen

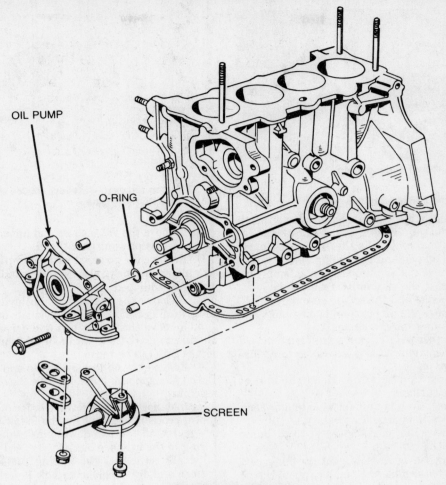

OIL PUMP

O-RING

SCREEN

1342 and 1488cc oil pump

Hidden oil pump retaining bolt (arrow)

Torquing the oil pump retaining bolts

Installing the oil pump screen

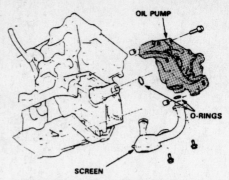

Oil pump removal— 1493cc, 1590cc and 1955cc DOHC engine

1342cc, and 1488cc Engines

1. Refer to the "Oil Pan, Removal and Installation" and the "Timing Belt, Removal and Installation" procedures in this section, then, remove the oil pan and the timing belt.

2. Remove the oil pump screen assembly-to-engine bolts, the oil pump screen assembly-to-oil pump bolts and the screen assembly.

3. Remove the oil pump-to-engine bolts and the oil pump from the engine.

NOTE: *When the oil pump has been removed from the engine, it is a good idea to replace the front oil seal.*

4. Using a putty knife, clean the gasket mounting surfaces.

5. Inspect the oil pump for wear and/or damage; replace the parts, if necessary.

6. Remove the oil pump cover-to-oil pump bolts and the cover.

7. Using petroleum jelly, pack the pump cavity, then, reassemble the pump cover to the oil pump. Torque the oil pump cover-to-oil pump bolts to 4 ft. lbs.

8. To install, use a new O-ring, new gasket(s), liquid gasket (oil pump) and reverse the removal procedures. Torque the oil pump-to-engine bolts to 9 ft. lbs. Check and/or adjust the timing. Refill the crankcase with clean engine oil.

1493cc, 1590cc and 1955cc DOHC Engines

1. Drain the engine oil. Turn the crankshaft and align the white groove on the crankshaft pulley with the pointer on the timing belt cover (align the **T** mark on the flywheel with the pointer on the crankcase on the Prelude).

CAUTION: *The EPA warns that prolonged contact with used engine oil may cause a number of skin disorders, including cancer! You should make every effort to minimize your exposure to used engine oil. Protective gloves should be worn when changing the oil. Wash your hands and any other exposed skin areas as soon as possible after exposure to used engine oil. Soap and water, or waterless hand cleaner should be used.*

2. Remove the valve cover and upper timing belt cover as previously outlined.

3. Remove the power steering pump belt and the alternator belt, also the air conditioning belt if so equipped.

4. Remove the crankshaft pulley and the lower timing belt cover as previously outlined.

5. Remove the timing belt and drive pulley. Be sure to mark the rotation of the timing belt if it is going to be reused.

6. Remove the oil pan, oil screen and remove the oil pump mount bolts. Remove the oil pump assembly.

7. Installation is the reverse order of the removal procedure, except for the following:

  a. Install the two dowel pins and new O-ring to the cylinder block.

  b. Be sure that the mating surfaces are clean and dry. Apply a suitable liquid gasket evenly, in a narrow bead centered on the mating surface.

  c. To prevent leakage of oil, apply a suitable thread sealer to the inner threads of the bolt holes.

  d. Do not allow the sealant to dry before assembling. But wait approximately 30 minutes after assembly before filling the engine with oil.

1829cc and 1955cc (except DOHC) Engines

1. Refer to the "Timing Belt, Removal and Installation" procedures in this section and remove the timing belt.

2. Remove the oil pump-to-engine bolts and the oil pump from the engine.

3. Using a putty knife, clean the gasket mounting surfaces.

NOTE: *If removing the oil pump pick-up screen, follow the procedure to remove the oil pan.*

4. Remove the pump cover-to-pump housing bolts and the cover.

5. Inspect the pump for wear and/or damage; replace the parts, if necessary.

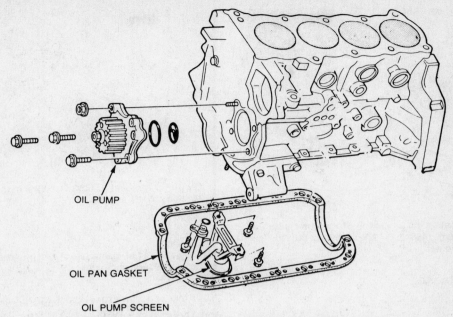

OIL PUMP

OIL PAN GASKET

OIL PUMP SCREEN

Exploded view of the oil pump—1829cc and 1955cc engines

6. Using petroleum jelly, pack the pump assembly. Reassemble the pump assembly and torque the pump cover-to-pump housing bolts to 5 ft. lbs.

7. To install, use a new O-rings and reverse the removal procedures. Torque the oil pump-to-engine nut/bolts to 9 ft. lbs. Check and/or adjust the timing. Start the engine and check for leaks.

OIL PUMP OVERHAUL

NOTE: *These procedures are performed with the oil pump removed from the engine.*

All Engines except 1342cc, 1488cc, 1493cc, 1590cc, 1829cc and 1955cc

1. Check the rotor radial clearance on both the inner and outer rotors. Clearance is 0.05-0.15mm.

2. Using a wire gauge, check body-to-rotor clearance of both rotors. Clearance is 0.10-0.18mm new, with 0.20mm as the service limit.

3. Using a feeler gauge and a straight edge, check the rotor end play between the rotor face and the gasket surface, gasket installed. End play should be 0.025-0.100mm new, with a service limit of 0.152mm.

4. If the rotors should require replacement, inner and outer rotors on both upper and lower halves are installed with the punch marks aligned adjacent to one another.

5. To install, reverse the removal procedures.

OUTER ROTOR

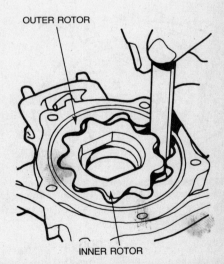

INNER ROTOR

Checking the radial clearance of the pump rotor—1342cc, 1488cc, 1493cc and 1590cc engines

1342cc, 1488cc, 1493cc, 1590cc 1829cc and 1955cc Engines

1. Check the rotor radial clearance on both the inner and outer rotors. Clearance is 0.152-0.203mm.

2. Using a feeler gauge, check body-to-rotor clearance of both rotors. Clearance is 0.10-0.18mm new, with 0.200mm as the service limit.

3. Using a feeler gauge and a straight edge,

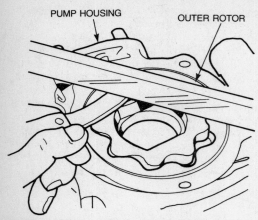

Checking the axial clearance of the outer pump rotor—1342cc, 1488cc, 1493cc, 1590cc, 1829cc and 1955cc engines

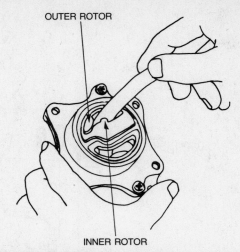

Checking the radial clearance of the pump rotor—1829cc and 1955cc engines

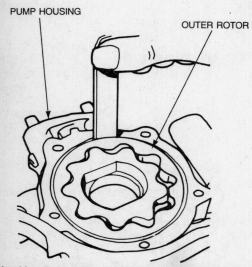

Checking the radial clearance between the housing and the outer rotor—1342cc, 1488cc, 1493cc and 1590cc engines

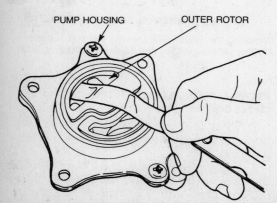

Checking the axial clearance of the outer pump rotor—1829cc and 1955cc engines

check the rotor end play between the rotor face and the gasket surface, gasket installed. End play should be 0.025-0.100mm new, with a service limit of 0.152mm.

4. If the rotors should require replacement, inner and outer rotors on both upper and lower halves are installed with the punch marks aligned adjacent to one another.

5. Using petroleum jelly, pack the pump cavity and reassemble it.

6. To install, reverse the removal procedures.

Timing Belt Cover and Seal
REMOVAL AND INSTALLATION

All except 1493cc, 1590cc and 1955cc DOHC engines

1. Rotate the crankshaft to align the crankshaft pulley (1170cc and 1237cc) or flywheel pointer (CVCC) to Top Dead Center (TDC) of the No. 1 cylinder's compression stroke.

2. Remove the upper timing belt cover bolts and the cover.

3. Loosen the alternator and air pump (if equipped), then, remove the pulley belt(s).

4. On all vehicles, except the Civic and CRX (1984-88), remove the water pump pulley-to-water pump bolts and the pulley.

5. Remove the crankshaft pulley-to-crankshaft bolt. Using a Wheel Puller tool, remove the crankshaft pulley.

6. Remove the timing gear cover retaining bolts and the timing gear cover.

7. To install, reverse the removal procedure. Make sure that the timing guide plates, pulleys and front oil seal are properly installed on the crankshaft end before replacing the cover.

Engine showing timing belt upper cover removed

The small washers can be removed from behind the tensioner and adjusting bolt to allow removal of the cover. Be sure to reinstall the washers

CAUTION: *Be sure not to upset the timing position already set (TDC).*

1493cc and 1590cc Engines

1. Remove the driver's side wheel well splash shield.

2. Remove the air conditioning compressor adjust pulley with bracket and the belt (if equipped with air conditioning).

3. Remove the side engine mount bracket.

Loosen the alternator adjust bolt and through bolt then remove the belt.

4. Remove the engine support bolts and nuts, then remove the side mount rubber.

5. Remove the valve cover. Remove the crankshaft pulley bolt and remove the crankshaft pulley.

6. Remove the timing belt upper cover and lower cover.

7. To install, reverse the removal procedure. Make sure that the timing guide plates, pulleys and the front oil seal are properly installed on the crankshaft before replacing the cover.

1955cc DOHC Engine

1. Remove the engine support bolts and nuts, then remove the side mount rubber and side mount brackets.

2. Remove the lower engine splash shield. Remove the power steering pump adjust pulley nut and the adjust bolt. Remove the adjust pulley, power steering pump and power steering belt.

3. Remove the alternator through bolt, mount bolt and the adjust nut. and remove the alternator and belt. On vehicles equipped with air conditioning, remove the air conditioning compressor mount bolts, compressor and belt.

4. Remove the ignition wire(s) from the valve cover. Remove the engine wire harness protector from the cylinder head cover. Remove the valve cover.

5. Remove the crankshaft pulley bolt and remove the crankshaft pulley.

6. Remove the timing belt middle and lower covers.

7. To install, reverse the removal procedure. Make sure that the timing guide plates, pulleys and the front oil seal are properly installed on the crankshaft before replacing the cover.

Timing Belt and Tensioner
REMOVAL AND INSTALLATION

All Except 1493cc, 1590cc and 1955cc DOHC Engines

1. Turn the crankshaft pulley until it is at Top Dead Center.

2. Remove the pulley belt, water pump pulley, crankshaft pulley, and timing gear cover. Mark the direction of timing belt rotation.

3. Loosen, but do not remove, the tensioner adjusting bolt and pivot bolt.

4. Slide the timing belt off of the camshaft timing gear and the crankshaft pulley gear and remove it from the engine.

5. To remove the camshaft timing gear pulley, first remove the center bolt and then remove the pulley with a pulley remover or a

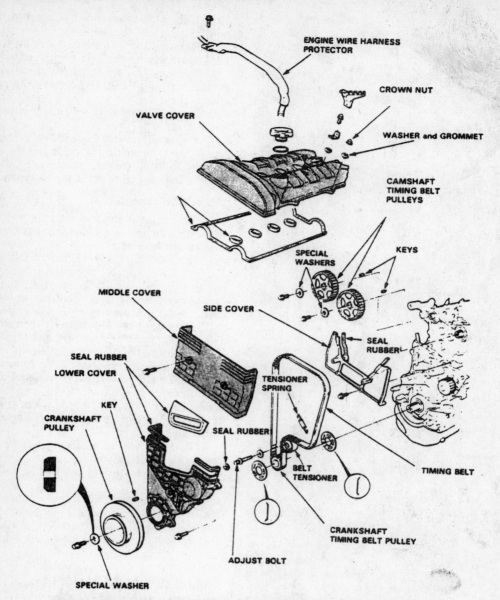

Timing belt covers removal & installation—1955cc DOHC engine

brass hammer. This can be accomplished by simply removing the timing belt upper cover, loosening the tensioner bolts, and sliding the timing belt off of the gear to expose the gear for removal.

NOTE: *If you remove the timing gear with the timing belt cover in place, be sure not to let the woodruff key fall inside the timing cover when removing the gear from the camshaft.*

Inspect the timing belt. Replace if over 10,000 miles old, if oil soaked (find source of oil leak also), or if worn on leading edges of belt teeth.

6. To install, reverse the removal procedure. Be sure to install the crankshaft pulley and the camshaft timing gear pulley in the top dead center position. (See "Cylinder Head Removal" for further details). On the non-CVCC engine, align the marks on the camshaft timing gear so they are parallel with the top of the cylinder head and the woodruff key is facing up. See the photograph for details on CVCC timing.

NOTE: *When installing the timing belt, do not allow oil to come in contact with the belt. Oil will cause the rubber to swell. Be careful not to bend or twist the belt unnecessarily,*

Inspecting the timing belt

Closeup of the adjustment and pivot bolts. The upper bolt is the pivot bolt, and the lower bolt is the adjustment bolt

On CVCC engines, when the camshaft pulley is in the correct position, the word "UP" will be facing up and the small mark on the camshaft pulley will be aligned with the arrow on the cylinder head. The marks are just slightly off in this photograph. On the opposite side of the cam gear, there is a small arrow pointing at a small line. This is used by Honda to indicate when the gear has been installed 180 degrees out of time. The marks are not really necessary since then the word "UP" would be pointing down

On non-CVCC engines, align the marks on the cam gear parallel with the top of the cylinder head

since it is made of fiberglass; nor should you use tools having sharp edges when installing or removing the belt. Be sure to install the belt with the arrow facing in the same direction it was facing during removal.

After installing the belt, adjust the belt tension by first rotating the crankshaft counterclockwise ¼ turn. Then, retighten the adjusting bolt and finally the tensioner pivot bolt.

WARNING: *Do not remove the adjusting or pivot bolts, only loosen them. When adjusting, do not use any force other than the adjuster spring. If the belt is too tight, it will result in a shortened belt life.*

1493cc and 1590cc Engines

1. Remove the driver's side wheel well splash shield.

2. Remove the air conditioning compressor adjust pulley with bracket and the belt (if equipped with air conditioning).

3. Remove the side engine mount bracket. Loosen the alternator adjust bolt and through bolt then remove the belt.

4. Remove the engine support bolts and nuts, then remove the side mount rubber.

5. Remove the valve cover. Remove the crankshaft pulley bolt and remove the crankshaft pulley.

6. Remove the timing belt upper cover and lower cover.

7. Mark the rotation of the timing belt (for easy installation). Loosen the adjusting bolt, remove the timing belt.

NOTE: *Inspect the timing belt. Replace it if it*

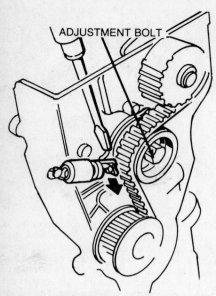

Timing belt tensioner adjustment bolt—1342 and 1488cc engines

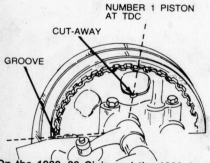

On the 1980–83 Civic and the 1983 Accord, when the No. 1 piston is set at TDC, the cut-away in the pulley is at the top and the groove on the pulley is aligned with the top of the cylinder head.

Frontal view of a non-CVCC engine showing the timing belt correctly installed. Note that the crankshaft key is pointing straight up and the marks on the cam gear are parallel with the top of the cylinder head

has been in service longer than 10,000 miles, if it is oil soaked (find source of oil leak also), or if it is worn on the leading edges of the belt teeth.

8. Installation is the reverse order of the removal procedure, be sure to adjust the timing belt as follows:

NOTE: *The tensioner is spring-loaded to apply proper tension to the timing belt automatically after making the following adjustment. Be sure to always adjust the timing belt tension with the engine cold.*

9. After installing the timing belt, adjust the belt tension by first rotating the crankshaft counterclockwise ¼ turn or 3 teeth on the camshaft pulley (this will put tension on the timing belt). Then, retighten the adjusting bolt and fi-

nally the tensioner pivot bolt. If the crankshaft pulley bolt broke loose while turning the crank, be sure to re-torque it to specifications.

CAUTION: *Do not remove the adjusting or pivot bolts, only loosen them. When adjusting, do not use any force other than the adjuster spring. If the belt is too tight, it will result in a shortened belt life.*

1955cc DOHC Engine

1. Remove the engine support bolts and nuts, then remove the side mount rubber and side mount brackets.

2. Remove the lower engine splash shield. Remove the power steering pump adjust pulley nut and the adjust bolt. Remove the adjust pulley, power steering pump and power steering belt.

3. Remove the alternator through bolt, mount bolt and the adjust nut. and remove the alternator and belt. On vehicles equipped with air conditioning, remove the air conditioning compressor mount bolts, compressor and belt.

4. Remove the ignition wire(s) from the valve cover. Remove the engine wire harness protector from the cylinder head cover. Remove the valve cover.

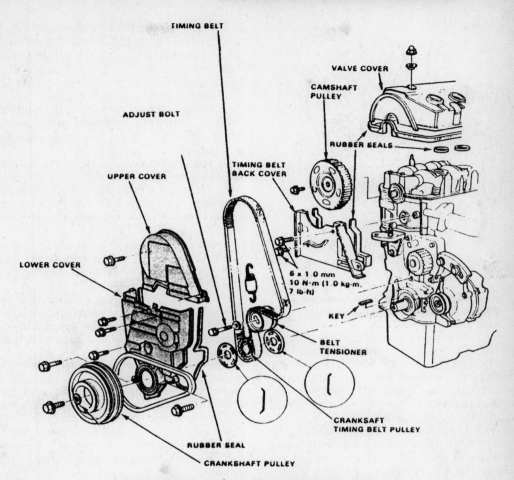

TIMING BELT

VALVE COVER

CAMSHAFT PULLEY

RUBBER SEALS

ADJUST BOLT

TIMING BELT BACK COVER

UPPER COVER

LOWER COVER

6 x 1.0 mm
10 N·m (1.0 kg-m,
7 lb-ft)

KEY

BELT TENSIONER

CRANKSAFT TIMING BELT PULLEY

RUBBER SEAL

CRANKSHAFT PULLEY

Timing belt removal—1493cc and 1590cc engines

5. Remove the crankshaft pulley bolt and remove the crankshaft pulley.

6. Remove the timing belt middle and lower covers. Mark the rotation of the timing belt, if it is to be reused.

7. Loosen the timing belt adjusting nut and remove the timing belt.

NOTE: *Inspect the timing belt. Replace it if it has been in service longer than 10,000 miles, if it is oil soaked (find source of oil leak also),*

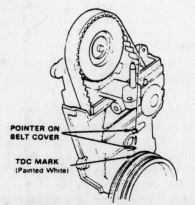

POINTER ON BELT COVER

TDC MARK (Painted White)

TDC locating marks—1493cc and 1590cc engines

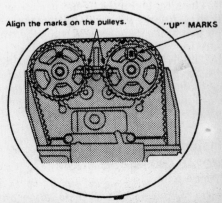

Align the marks on the pulleys.   "UP" MARKS

Aligning the timing marks on the camshaft pulleys—1955cc DOHC engine

ADJUST BOLT

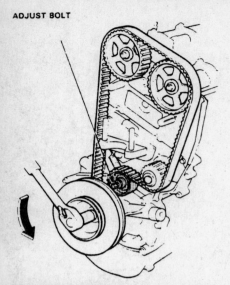

Adjusting the timing belt tensioner—
1955cc DOHC engine

or if it is worn on the leading edges of the belt teeth.

8. Be sure to install the timing belt with the number one piston at top dead center on the compression stroke. Installation is the reverse order of the removal procedure, be sure to adjust the timing belt as follows:

NOTE: *The tensioner is spring-loaded to apply proper tension to the timing belt automatically after making the following adjustment. Be sure to always adjust the timing belt tension with the engine cold. To set the number one cylinder at top dead center, align the hole on the camshaft with the hole in the number one camshaft holders and drive 5.0mm pin punches into the holes.*

9. After installing the timing belt, adjust the belt tension by first rotating the crankshaft counterclockwise ¼ turn or 3 teeth on the camshaft pulley (this will put tension on the timing belt). Then, retighten the adjusting bolt and finally the tensioner pivot bolt. If the crankshaft pulley bolt broke loose while turning the crank, be sure to re-torque it to specifications.

CAUTION: *Do not remove the adjusting or pivot bolts, only loosen them. When adjusting, do not use any force other than the adjuster spring. If the belt is too tight, it will result in a shortened belt life.*

Camshaft Sprockets
REMOVAL AND INSTALLATION

NOTE: *Be sure to use the timing cover and timing belt removal and installation procedures to aid in the success of the following procedure.*

1. Turn the crankshaft pulley until No. 1 is at Top Dead Center of the compression stroke. This can be determined by observing the valves (all closed) or by feeling for pressure in the spark plug hole (with your thumb or a compression gauge) as the engine is turned.

2. Remove the pulley belt, water pump pulley (if so equipped), crankshaft pulley, and timing gear cover. Mark the direction of timing belt rotation.

3. Loosen, but do not remove, the tensioner adjusting bolt and pivot bolt.

4. Slide the timing belt off the camshaft sprocket, crankshaft sprocket and the water pump sprocket (if so equipped), then remove it from the engine.

5. To remove the either camshaft or crankshaft timing sprocket, first remove the center bolt and then remove the sprocket with a pulley remover or a brass hammer.

6. To install, reverse the removal procedure. Be sure to position the crankshaft and camshaft timing sprockets in the Top Dead Center position. Torque the camshaft sprocket bolt to 30 ft. lbs.

When installing the timing belt, do not allow oil to come in contact with the belt. Oil will cause the rubber to swell. Be careful not to bend or twist the belt unnecessarily, since it is made of fiberglass; nor should you use tools having sharp edges when installing or removing the belt. Be sure to install the belt with the arrow facing in the same direction it was facing during removal.

After installing the timing belt, adjust the belt tension by first rotating the crankshaft counterclockwise ¼ turn or 3 teeth on the camshaft pulley. Then, retighten the adjusting bolt and finally the tensioner pivot bolt.

NOTE: *Do not remove the adjusting or pivot bolts, only loosen them. When adjusting, do not use any force other than the adjuster spring. If the belt is too tight, it will result in a shortened belt life.*

Camshaft

Most 1973-82 engines utilize an oil pump drive gear incorporated on the camshaft.

REMOVAL AND INSTALLATION
All Except 1955cc DOHC Engine

NOTE: *To facilitate the installation, make sure that No. 1 piston is at Top Dead Center before removing the camshaft.*

1. Follow the "Cylinder Head, Removal and Installation" procedures before attempting to remove the camshaft.

2. Loosen the camshaft and rocker arm shaft

Rocker arm assembly showing bolts partially removed

holder bolts in a criss-cross pattern, beginning on the outside holder.

3. For all, except the 1.3L and 1.5L (1984-88) engines, remove the rocker arms, shafts and holders as an assembly. For the 1.3L and 1.5L (1984-88) engines, remove the rocker arms/shafts as an assembly; the holders can remain on the cylinder.

4. Lift out the camshaft and right head seal.

5. Using a putty knife, clean the gasket mounting surfaces.

6. To install, reverse the removal procedures, being sure to install the holder bolts in the reverse order of removal.

NOTE: *Back off valve adjusting screws before installing rockers, then, adjust valves as outlined in Chapter 2.*

1955cc Dual Overhead Cam (DOHC) Engine

NOTE: *To facilitate installation, turn the camshaft pulleys until the UP marks are facing up and the front timing marks are*

Rocker arm assembly—CVCC engine

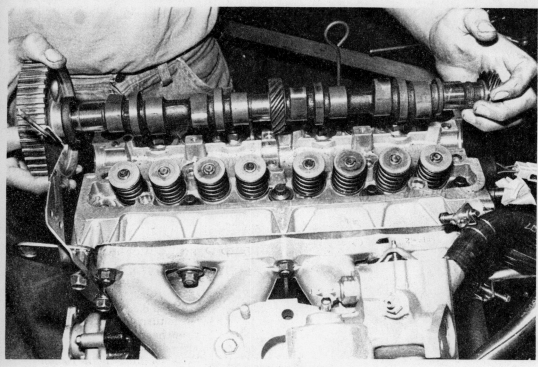

Removing the camshaft

aligned with both marks on the pulleys. This should put the No. 1 piston at Top Dead Center.

1. Follow the Cylinder Head removal procedure before attempting to remove the camshaft.

2. Remove the camshaft pulley retaining bolt and washer and remove the camshaft pulleys along with the woodruff keys, if so equipped.

3. Before removing the rocker arm assembly, check the camshaft end play as follows:

NOTE: *Do not rotate the camshaft during inspection loosen the adjusting screws before starting.*

a. Seat the camshaft by prying it toward the distributor end of the head.

b. Set a dial indicator on the end of the camshaft. Zero the dial indicator against the end of the distributor drive, then pry the camshaft back and forth, and read the end play (do this to both camshafts).

c. The standard camshaft end play for a new camshaft is 0.05-0.15mm.

d. The standard service limit for the camshaft end play is 0.5mm.

4. Loosen the camshaft and rocker arm shaft holder bolts in a crisscross pattern, beginning on the outside holder.

5. Remove the rocker arms, shafts, and holders as an assembly.

6. Lift out the camshafts.

7. Wipe the camshaft clean, then inspect the lift ramps. Replace the camshaft if the cam lobes are pitted, scored or excessively worn.

NOTE: *Be sure to Plastigage® the camshaft bearing journals. If the camshaft bearing radial clearance is out of tolerance and the camshaft has already been replaced, then the cylinder head must be replaced.*

8. After cleaning the camshaft and journal surfaces, lubricate both surfaces with the proper camshaft lubricant and install the camshaft.

9. Turn the camshaft until its keyway is facing up (number on cylinder at TDC). The valve locknuts should be loosened and the adjust screws backed off before installation.

10. Replace the rocker arms in their original positions. Place the rocker arms on the pivot bolts and the valve stems.

11. Install the camshafts and camshaft seals with the open side (spring) facing in. Take notice to the **I** or **E** marks that are stamped on the camshaft holders. Do not apply oil to the camshaft holder mating surface of the camshaft seals.

12. Apply liquid gasket to the head mating surfaces of the number one and number six camshaft holders, then install them along with the number two, three, our and five.

13. Make sure that the rocker arms are prop-

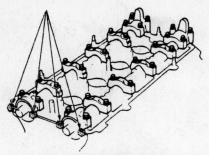

Non-hardening sealant application locations — 1955cc DOHC engine

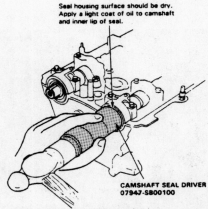

Seal housing surface should be dry. Apply a light coat of oil to camshaft and inner lip of seal.

CAMSHAFT SEAL DRIVER
07947-S800100

Installing the camshaft(s) oil seal — 1955cc DOHC engine

erly positioned on the valve stems and temporarily tighten the camshaft holders.

NOTE: *Apply a non-hardening sealant to the cylinder head surface on either side of the camshaft(s) seal surfaces.*

14. Using a suitable seal installer, install the new camshaft seals.

15. Tighten each rocker arm bolt two turns at a time in the proper sequence to ensure that the rockers do not bind on the valves.

16. Install the keys into the camshaft grooves. Push the camshaft pulleys onto the camshaft, then install a new washer with the retaining bolt. Torque the retaining bolt to 27 ft. lbs.

NOTE: *To set the number one cylinder at top dead center, align the hole on the camshaft with the hole in the number one camshaft holders and drive 5.0mm pin punches into the holes.*

17. Complete the installation procedure by reversing the removal procedure. Then adjust the valves.

INSPECTION

Degrease the camshaft using safe solvent, clean all oil grooves. Visually inspect the cam lobes and bearing journals for excessive wear. If a lobe is questionable, check all lobes and journals with a micrometer.

Measure the lobes from nose to base and again at 90°. The lift is determined by subtracting the second measurement from the first. If all exhaust lobes and all intake lobes are not identical, the camshaft must be reground or replaced. Measure the bearing journals and compare to specifications. If a journal is worn there is a good chance that the cam bearings are worn too, requiring replacement.

If the lobes and journals appear intact, place the front and rear cam journals in V-blocks and rest a dial indicator on the center journal. Rotate the camshaft to check for straightness, if deviation exceeds 0.025mm, replace the camshaft.

Pistons and Connecting Rods

REMOVAL AND INSTALLATION

For removal with the engine out of the vehicle, begin with Step 8.

1. Remove the turn signals (Civic 1973-77), grille and engine hood.

2. Drain the radiator.

CAUTION: *When draining the coolant, keep in mind that cats and dogs are attracted by the ethylene glycol antifreeze, and are quite likely to drink any that is left in an uncovered container or in puddles on the ground. This will prove fatal in sufficient quantity. Always drain the coolant into a sealable container. Coolant should be reused unless it is contaminated or several years old.*

3. Drain the engine oil.

CAUTION: *The EPA warns that prolonged contact with used engine oil may cause a number of skin disorders, including cancer! You should make every effort to minimize your exposure to used engine oil. Protective gloves should be worn when changing the oil. Wash your hands and any other exposed skin areas as soon as possible after exposure to used engine oil. Soap and water, or waterless hand cleaner should be used.*

4. Raise the front of the vehicle and support it with safety stands.

5. Attach a chain to the clutch cable bracket on the transaxle case and raise just enough to take the load off of the center mount.

NOTE: *Do not remove the left engine mount.*

6. Remove the center beam and engine lower mount.

7. Remove the cylinder head (see "Cylinder Head, Removal and Installation").

8. Loosen the oil pan bolts and remove the oil pan and flywheel dust shield. Loosen the oil pan bolts in a criss-cross pattern beginning with the outside bolt. To remove the oil pan, lightly tap

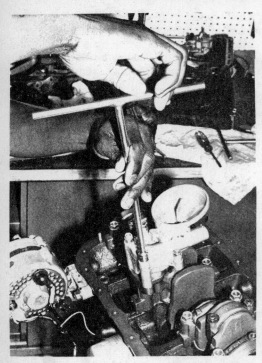

Mark the pistons for installation if they aren't already marked from the factory

Oil pump removal. There is a bolt hidden under the screen. See the photograph under "Oil Pump Removal"

the corners of the oil pan with a mallet. It is not necessary to remove the gasket unless it is damaged.

WARNING: *Do not pry the oil pan off with the tip of a screwdriver.*

9. Remove the oil passage block and the oil pump assembly.

WARNING: *As soon as the oil passage block bolts are loosened, the oil in the oil line may flow out.*

10. Working from the underside of the vehicle, remove the connecting rod bearing caps. Using the wooden handle of a hammer, push the pistons and connecting rods out of the cylinders.

NOTE: *Before removing the pistons, check the top of the cylinder bore for carbon build-up or a ridge. Remove the carbon or use a ridge reamer to remove the ridge before removing the pistons. Bearing caps, bearings, and pistons should be marked to indicate their location for reassembly.*

11. When removing the piston rings, be sure not to apply excessive force as the rings are made of cast iron and can be easily broken.

NOTE: *A hydraulic press is necessary for removing the piston pin. This is a job best left to the professional, if you need to go this far.*

12. Observe the following points when installing the piston rings:

The piston pins must be removed with a press

a. When installing the three-piece oil ring, first place the spacer and then the rails in position. The spacer and rail gaps must be staggered 20-30mm.

b. Install the second and top rings on the piston with their markings facing upward.

c. After installing all rings on the piston, rotate them to be sure they move smoothly without signs of binding.

Piston ring installation. Tools like this aren't really necessary, as rings can be easily installed by hand

Piston assembly

Make sure the recess in the cap and recess on the rod are on the same side (Arrows)

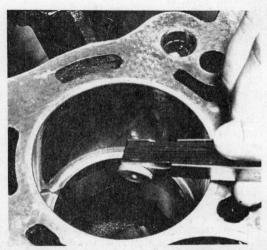

Check the ring end gap before installing the rings on the pistons

Torquing the connecting rod cap

d. The ring gaps must be staggered 120° and must NOT be in the direction of the piston pin boss or at right angles to the pin. The gap of the three-piece oil ring refers to that of the middle spacer.

NOTE: *Pistons and rings are also available in four oversizes, 0.25mm, 0.50mm, 0.75mm, and 1.00mm.*

13. Using a ring compressor, install the piston into the cylinder with the skirt protruding about ⅓ of the piston height below the ring compressor. Prior to installation, apply a thin coat of oil to the rings and to the cylinder wall.

NOTE: *When installing the piston, the connecting rod oil jet hole or the mark on the piston crown faces the intake manifold.*

14. Using the wooden handle of a hammer, slowly press the piston into the cylinder. Guide the connecting rod so it does not damage the crankshaft journals.

15. Reassemble the remaining components in the reverse order of removal. Install the connecting rod bearing caps so that the recess in the cap and the recess in the rod are on the same side. After tightening the cap bolts, move the rod back and forth on the journal to check for binding.

CLEANING AND INSPECTION

1. Use a piston ring expander and remove the rings from the piston.
2. Clean the ring grooves using an appropriate cleaning tool, exercise care to avoid cutting too deeply.
3. Clean all varnish and carbon from the piston with a safe solvent. Do not use a wire brush or caustic solution on the pistons.
4. Inspect the pistons for scuffing, scoring, cracks, pitting or excessive ring groove wear. If wear is evident, the piston must be replaced.
5. Have the piston and connecting rod assembly checked by a machine shop for correct alignment, piston pin wear and piston diameter. If the piston has collapsed it will have to be replace or knurled to restore original diameter. Connecting rod bushing replacement, piston pin fitting and piston changing can be handled by the machine shop.

CYLINDER BORE

Check the cylinder bore for wear using a telescope gauge and a micrometer, measure the cylinder bore diameter perpendicular to the piston pin at a point 63.5mm below the top of the engine block. Measure the piston skirt perpendicular to the piston pin. The difference between the two measurements is the piston clearance. If the clearance is within specifications, finish honing or glaze breaking is all that is required. If clearance is excessive a slightly oversize piston may be required. If greatly oversize, the engine will have to be bored and 0.25mm or larger oversized pistons installed.

FITTING AND POSITIONING PISTON RINGS

1. Take the new piston rings and compress them, one at a time into the cylinder that they will be used in. Press the ring about 25mm below the top of the cylinder block using an inverted piston.
2. Use a feeler gauge and measure the distance between the ends of the ring. This is called measuring the ring end gap. Compare the reading to the one called for in the specifications table. File the ends of the ring with a fine file to obtain necessary clearance.

NOTE: *If inadequate ring end gap is utilized, ring breakage will result.*

3. Inspect the ring grooves on the piston for excessive wear or taper. If necessary have the grooves recut for use with a standard ring and spacer. The machine shop can handle the job for you.
4. Check the ring grooves by rolling the new piston ring around the groove to check for burrs or carbon deposits. If any are found, remove with a fine file. Hold the ring in the groove and measure side clearance with a feeler gauge. If clearance is excessive, spacer(s) will have to be added.

NOTE: *Always add spacers above the piston ring.*

5. Install the ring on the piston, lower oil ring first. Use a ring installing tool on the compression rings. Consult the instruction sheet that comes with the rings to be sure they are installed with the correct side up. A mark on the ring usually faces upward.
6. When installing oil rings, first, install the expanding ring in the groove. Hold the ends of the ring butted together (they must not overlap) and install the bottom rail (scraper) with the end about 25mm away from the butted end of the control ring. Install the top rail about 25mm away from the butted end of the control but on the opposite side from the lower rail.
7. Install the two compression rings.
8. Consult the illustration for ring positioning, arrange the rings as shown, install a ring compressor and insert the piston and rod assembly into the engine.

Rear Main Seal

REMOVAL AND INSTALLATION

The rear oil seal on the Honda is installed in the rear main bearing cap. Replacement of the seal requires the removal of the transaxle, flywheel and clutch housing, as well as the oil pan. Refer to the appropriate sections for the remov-

Driving in the rear main seal using the Honda special tool

al and installation of the above components. Both the front and rear main seal are installed after the crankshaft has been torqued, in the event it was removed. Special drivers are used.

Crankshaft and Main Bearings

REMOVAL AND INSTALLATION

1. Remove the engine from the vehicle and place it on a work stand.

2. Remove the crankshaft pulley attaching bolts and washer.

3. Remove the front cover and the air conditioning idler pulley assembly, if so equipped. Remove cover assembly.

4. Check the timing belt deflection. Remove the timing belt and sprockets.

5. Invert the engine on work stand. Remove the flywheel and the rear seal cover. Remove the oil pan and gasket. Remove the oil pump inlet and the oil pump assembly.

6. Ensure all bearing caps (main and connecting rod) are marked so they can be installed in their original positions. Turn the crankshaft until the connecting rod from which cap is being removed is up. Remove the connecting rod cap. Push the connecting rod and piston assembly up in the cylinder. Repeat the procedure for the remaining connecting rod assemblies.

7. Remove the main bearing caps.

8. Carefully lift crankshaft out of block so upper thrust bearing surfaces are not damaged. WARNING: *Handle the crankshaft with care to avoid possible fracture or damage to the finished surfaces.*

To install:
NOTE: *If the bearings are to be reused they should be identified to ensure that they are installed in their original position.*

1. Remove the main bearing inserts from the block and bearing caps.

2. Remove the connecting rod bearing inserts from connecting rods and caps.

3. Install a new rear oil seal in rear seal cover.

4. Apply a thin coat of Polyethylene Grease to the rear crankshaft surface. Do not apply sealer to the area forward of oil sealer groove. Inspect all the machined surfaces on the crankshaft for nicks, scratches or scores which could cause premature bearing wear.

5. If the crankshaft main bearing journals have been refinished to a definite undersize, install the correct undersize bearings. Ensure the bearing inserts and bearing bores are clean. Foreign material under the inserts will distort the bearing and cause a failure.

6. Place the upper main bearing inserts in position in the bores with the tang fitted in the slot provided.

7. Install the lower main bearings inserts in the bearing caps.

8. Carefully lower the crankshaft into place.

9. Check the clearance of each main bearing. Select fit the bearings for proper clearance.

10. After the bearings have been fitted, apply a light coat of heavy engine oil, SAE 50 weight to journals and bearings. Install all the bearing caps.
NOTE: *The main bearing cap must be installed in their original positions.*

11. Align the upper thrust bearing.

12. Check the crankshaft end play.

13. If the end play exceeds specification, replace the upper thrust bearing. If the end play is less than the specification, inspect the thrust bearing faces for damage, dirt or improper alignment. Install the thrust bearing and align the faces. Check the end play.

14. Install the new bearing inserts in the connecting rods and caps. Check the clearance of each bearing.

15. If the bearing clearances are to specification, apply a light coat of heavy engine oil, SAE 50 weight to the journals and bearings.

16. Turn the crankshaft throw to the bottom of the stroke. Push the piston all the way down until the rod bearings seat on the crankshaft journal.

17. Install the connecting rod cap.

18. After the piston and connecting rod assemblies have been installed, check the connecting rod crankshaft journal.

19. Turn the engine on the work stand so the front end is up. Install the timing belt, sprock-

ets, front cover, oil seal and the crankshaft pulley.

20. Clean the oil pan, oil pump and the oil pump screen assembly.

21. Prime the oil pump by filling the inlet opening with oil and rotating the pump shaft until oil emerges from the outlet opening. Install the oil pump.

22. Position the flywheel on the crankshaft. Install the attaching bolts. Tighten to specification.

NOTE: *On the flywheel (manual transaxle only) locate clutch disc and install pressure plate.*

23. Turn the engine on the work stand so the engine is in the normal upright position. Install the oil level dipstick. Install the accessory drive pulley, if so equipped. Install and adjust the drive belt and the accessory belts to specification.

24. Install either the clutch assembly or the torque converter.

25. Install the oil pan.

26. Remove the engine from work stand. Install the engine in the vehicle.

CLEANING AND INSPECTION
BEARING OIL CLEARANCE

Remove cap from the bearing to be checked. Using a clean, dry rag, thoroughly clean all oil from crankshaft journal and bearing insert.

NOTE: *Plastigage® is soluble in oil, therefore, oil on the journal or bearing could result in erroneous readings.*

Place a pieced of Plastigage® along the full width of the bearing insert, reinstall cap, and torque to specifications.

NOTE: *Specifications are given in the engine specifications earlier in this chapter.*

Remove bearing cap, and determine bearing clearance by comparing width of Plastigage® to the scale on Plastigage® envelope. Journal taper is determined by comparing width of the bearing insert, reinstall cap, and torque to specifications.

NOTE: *Do not rotate crankshaft with*

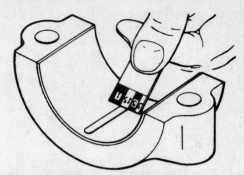

Measure Plastigage® to determine bearing clearance

Plastigage® installed. If bearing insert and journal appear intact, and are within tolerances, no further main bearing service is required. If bearing or journal appear defective, cause of failure should be determined before replacement.

CRANKSHAFT ENDPLAY/CONNECTING ROD SIDE PLAY

Place a pry bar between a main bearing cap and crankshaft casting taking care not to damage any journals. Pry backward and forward, measure the distance between the thrust bearing and crankshaft with a feeler gauge. Compare reading with specifications. If too great a

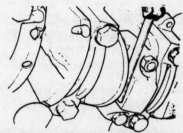

Check the connecting rod side clearance with a feeler gauge

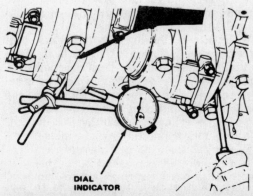

Check the crankshaft end-play with a dial indicator

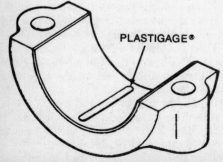

Plastigage® installed on the lower bearing shell

clearance is determined, a main bearing with a larger thrust surface or crank machining may be required. Check with an automotive machine shop for their advice.

Connecting rod clearance between the rod and crankthrow casting can be checked with a feeler gauge. Pry the rod carefully on one side as far as possible and measure the distance on the other side of the rod.

CRANKSHAFT REPAIRS

If a journal is damaged on the crankshaft, repair is possible by having the crankshaft machined to a standard undersize.

In most cases, however, since the engine must be removed from the car and disassembled, some thought should be given to replacing the damaged crankshaft with a reground shaft kit. A reground crankshaft kit contains the necessary main and rod bearings for installation. The shaft has been ground and polished to undersize specifications and will usually hold up well if installed correctly.

Flywheel/Flex Plate

REMOVAL AND INSTALLATION

1. Remove the transmission.
2. Remove the flywheel/flex plate attaching bolts and the flywheel.
3. The rear cover plate can be removed (manual transmission only).

To install:
All major rotating components including the flex plate/flywheel are individually balance to zero. Engine assembly balancing is not required. Balance weights should NOT be installed on new flywheels.

1. Install the rear cover plate, if removed.
2. Position the flywheel on the crankshaft and install the attaching bolts. Tighten the attaching bolts to specification shown in the Torque specification chart using the standard cross-tightening sequence.

EXHAUST SYSTEM

Inspect inlet pipes, outlet pipes and mufflers for cracked joints, broken welds and corrosion damage that would result in a leaking exhaust system. It is normal for a certain amount of moisture and staining to be present around the muffler seams. The presence of soot, light surface rust or moisture does not indicate a faulty muffler. Inspect the clamps, brackets and insulators for cracks and stripped or badly corroded bolt threads. When flat joints are loosened and/or disconnected to replace a shield

pipe or muffler, replace the bolts and flange nuts if there is reasonable doubt that its service life is limited.

The exhaust system, including brush shields, must be free of leaks, binding, grounding and excessive vibrations. These conditions are usually caused by loose or broken flange bolts, shields, brackets or pipes. If any of these conditions exist, check the exhaust system components and alignment. Align or replace as necessary. Brush shields are positioned on the underside of the catalytic converter and should be free from bends which would bring any part of the shield in contact with the catalytic converter or muffler. The shield should also be clear of any combustible material such as dried grass or leaves.

Muffler Assembly

REMOVAL AND INSTALLATION

1. Raise the vehicle and support on jackstands.
2. Remove the U-bolt assembly and the rubber insulators from the hanger brackets and remove the muffler assembly. Slide the muffler assembly toward the rear of the car to disconnect it from the converter.
3. Replace parts as needed.
4. Position the muffler assembly under the car and slide it forward onto the converter outlet pipe. Check that the slot in the muffler and the tab on the converter are fully engaged.
5. Install the rubber insulators on the hanger assemblies. Install the U-bolt and tighten
6. Check the system for leaks. Lower the vehicle.

Catalytic Converter and/or Pipe Assembly

REMOVAL AND INSTALLATION

1. Raise the vehicle and support on jackstands.
2. Remove the front catalytic converter flange fasteners at the flex joint and discard the flex joint gasket, remove the rear U-bolt connection.
3. Separate the catalytic converter inlet and outlet connections. Remove the converter.
4. Install the converter to the muffler. Install a new flex joint gasket.
5. Install the converter and muffler assembly to the inlet pipe/flex joint. Connect the air hoses and position the U-bolt.
6. Align the exhaust system into position and, starting at the front of the system, tighten all the nuts and bolts.
7. Check the system for leaks. Lower the vehicle.

Emission Controls

EMISSION CONTROLS

Emission controls on the Honda fall into one of three basic systems:
I. Crankcase Emission Control System.
II. Exhaust Emission Control System.
III. Evaporative Emission Control System.

Crankcase Emission Control System
OPERATION

The Honda's engine is equipped with a Dual Return System to prevent crankcase vapor emissions. Blow-by gas is returned to the combustion chamber through the intake manifold and carburetor air cleaner. When the throttle is partially opened, blow-by gas is returned to the intake manifold through breather tubes leading into the tee orifice located on the outside of the intake manifold. When the throttle is opened wide and vacuum in the air cleaner rises, blow-by gas is returned to the intake manifold through an additional passage in the air cleaner case.

SERVICE

1. Squeeze the lower end of the drain tube and drain any oil or water which may have collected.
2. Make sure that the intake manifold T-joint is clear by passing the shank end of a No. 65 (0.035″ diameter) drill through both ends (orifices) of the joint.
3. Check for any loose, disconnected or deteriorated tubes and replace (if necessary).

Exhaust Emission Control System
OPERATIONS
1973-74 Models

Control of exhaust emissions, hydrocarbon (HC), carbon monoxide (CO) and Oxides of nitrogen (NOx), is achieved by a combination of engine modifications and special control devices. Improvements to the combustion chamber, intake manifold, valve timing, carburetor and distributor comprise the engine modifications. These modifications, in conjunction with the special control devices, enable the engine to produce low emission with leaner air/fuel mixtures while maintaining good driveability. The special control devices consist of the following:
a. Intake air temperature control.
b. Throttle opener.
c. Ignition timing retard unit (1973 models only).
d. Transmission and temperature controlled spark advance (TCS) for the 4-speed transmission.
e. Temperature controlled spark advance for Hondamatic automatic transmission (1974 models only).

INTAKE AIR TEMPERATURE CONTROL

Intake air temperature control is designed to provide the most uniform carburetion possible under various ambient air temperature conditions by maintaining the intake air temperature within a narrow range. When the temperature in the air cleaner is below 100°F (38°C), the air bleed valve, which consists of a bimetallic strip and a rubber seal, remains closed. Intake manifold vacuum is then led to a vacuum motor, located on the snorkel of the air cleaner case, which moves the air control valve door, allowing only preheated air to enter the air cleaner.

When the temperature in the air cleaner becomes higher than approximatly 100°F (38°C), the air bleed valve opens and the air control valve door returns to the open position allowing only unheated air through the snorkel.

THROTTLE OPENER

When the throttle is closed suddenly at high engine speed, hydrocarbon (HC) emissions in-

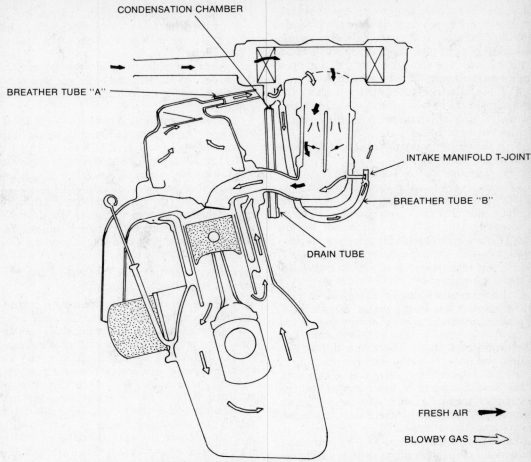

CONDENSATION CHAMBER

BREATHER TUBE "A"

INTAKE MANIFOLD T-JOINT

BREATHER TUBE "B"

DRAIN TUBE

FRESH AIR ➡

BLOWBY GAS ⇨

Crankcase ventilation system operation—1170, 1237 cc engines—CVCC similar

crease due to engine misfire caused by an incombustible mixture. The throttle opener is designed to prevent misfiring during deceleration by causing the throttle valve to remain slightly open, allowing better mixture control. The control valve is set to allow the passage of vacuum to the throttle opener diaphragm when the engine vacuum is equal to or greater than the control valve preset vacuum (20-23 in.Hg) during acceleration.

Under running conditions, other than fully closed throttle deceleration, the intake manifold vacuum is less than the control valve set vacuum; therefore the control valve is not actuated. The vacuum remaining in the throttle opener and control valve is returned to atmospheric pressure by the air passage at the valve center.

IGNITION TIMING RETARD UNIT

On 1973 models, when the engine is idling, the vacuum produced in the carburetor retarder port is communicated to the spark retard unit and the ignition timing, at idle, is retarded.

TCS SYSTEM

The transmission and temperature controlled spark advance for 4-speed transmissions is designed to reduce NOx emissions during normal vehicle operation.

On 1973 models, when the coolant temperature is approximately 120°F (49°C) or higher, and the transmission is in 1st, 2nd or 3rd gear, the solenoid valve cuts off the vacuum to the spark advance unit, resulting in lower NOx levels.

On 1974 models, the vacuum is cut off to the spark advance unit regardless of temperature when 1st, 2nd or 3rd gear is selected. Vacuum advance is restored when 4th gear is selected.

SERVICE

Intake Air Temperature Control System (Engine Cold)

1. Inspect for loose, disconnected, or deteriorated vacuum hoses and replace as necessary.
2. Remove the air cleaner cover and element.
3. With the transmission in Neutral and the

blue distributor disconnected, engage the starter motor for approximately two (2) seconds. Manifold vacuum to the vacuum motor should completely raise the air control valve door. Once opened, the valve door should stay open unless there is a leak in the system.

4. If the valve door does not open, check the intake manifold port by passing a No. 78 (0.016″ diameter) drill or compressed air through the orifice in the manifold.

5. If the valve door still does not open, proceed to the following steps:

a. Vacuum Motor Test: Disconnect the vacuum line from the vacuum motor inlet pipe. Fully open the air control valve door; block the vacuum motor inlet pipe, then release the door. If the door does not remain open, the vacuum motor is defective. Replace as necessary and repeat Steps 1-3.

b. Air Bleed Valve Test: Unblock the inlet pipe and make sure that the valve door fully closes without sticking or binding. Reconnect the vacuum line to the vacuum motor inlet pipe. Connect a vacuum source (e.g. hand vacuum pump) to the manifold vacuum line (disconnect at the intake manifold fixed orifice) and draw enough vacuum to fully open the valve door. If the valve door closes with the manifold vacuum line plugged (by the vacuum pump), then vacuum is leaking through the air bleed valve. Replace as necessary and repeat Steps 1-3.

WARNING: *Never force the air bleed valve (bi-metal strip) on or off its valve seat. The bi-metallic strip and the valve seat may be damaged.*

c. Check Valve Test: Again draw a vacuum (at the manifold vacuum line) until the valve door opens. Unplug the line by disconnecting the pump from the manifold vacuum line. If the valve door closes, vacuum is leaking past the check valve. Replace as necessary and repeat Steps 1-3.

6. After completing the above steps, replace the air cleaner element and cover and fit a vacuum gauge into the line leading to the vacuum motor.

7. Start the engine and raise the idle to 1500-2000 rpm. As the engine warms, the vacuum gauge reading should drop to zero.

NOTE: *Allow sufficient time for the engine to reach normal operating temperature — when the cooling fan cycles on and off.*

If the reading does not drop to zero before the engine reaches normal operating temperature, the air bleed valve is defective and must be replaced. Repeat Step 3 as a final check.

Temperature and Transaxle Controlled Spark Advance (Engine Cold) — All Models

1. Check for loose, disconnected or deteriorated vacuum hoses and replace (if necessary).

2. Check the coolant temperature sensor switch for proper operation with an ohmmeter or 12V light. The switch should normally be open (no continuity across the switch terminals) when the coolant temperature is below approximately 120°F (49°C). If the switch is closed (continuity across the terminals), replace the switch and repeat the check.

3. On manual transaxle models, check the transmission sensor switch. The switch should be open (no continuity across the connections) when Fourth gear is selected, and closed (continuity across the connections) in all other gear positions. Replace if necessary and repeat the check.

4. Remove the spark control vacuum tube, leading between the spark advance/retard unit and the solenoid valve, and connect a vacuum gauge to the now vacant hole in the solenoid valve, according to the diagram.

5. Start the engine and raise the idle to 2000 rpm. With a cold engine, the vacuum gauge

Start control solenoid valve

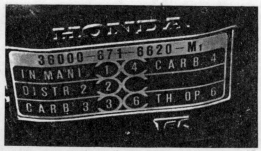

Emission control "black box" for electrical and vacuum hose connections

should read approximately 3 in.Hg or more. As the coolant temperature reaches 120°F (49°C), the vacuum reading should drop to 0. On manual transaxle models, vacuum should return when 4th gear is selected (transmission switch is opened). If this is not the case, proceed to the following steps:

NOTE: *If the engine is warm from the previous test, disconnect the coolant temperature switch wires when making the following tests.*

6. If vacuum is not initially available, disconnect the vacuum signal line from the charcoal canister and plug the open end, which will block a possible vacuum leak from the idle cut-off valve of the canister. With the line plugged, again check for vacuum at 2000 rpm. If vacuum is now available, reconnect the vacuum signal line and check the canister for vacuum leaks. (Refer to the Evaporative Emission Control System check.) If vacuum is still not available, stop the engine and disconnect the vacuum line from the solenoid valve (the line between the solenoid valve and the manifold T-joint) and insert a vacuum gauge in the line. If vacuum is not available, the vacuum port is blocked. Clear the port with compressed air and repeat the test sequence beginning with Step 3.

7. If vacuum is available in Step 5 after the engine is warm and in all ranges of the automatic transaxle and in 1st, 2nd and 3rd of the manual transaxle, stop the engine and check for electrical continuity between the terminals of the coolant temperature sensor:

NOTE: *After completing the following steps, repeat test procedure beginning with Step 4.*

a. If there is no continuity (engine is warm), replace the temperature sensor switch and recheck for continuity.

b. If there is continuity, check the battery voltage to the vacuum solenoid. If no voltage is available (ignition switch **ON**), check the wiring, fuses and connections.

c. If there is battery voltage and the temperature sensor is operating correctly, check connections and/or replace the solenoid valve.

Feedback Control System

NOTE: *These tests require the use of two hand held vacuum pumps. These must be designed to provide either air pressure or vacuum. Refer to the descriptive information and illustrations earlier in this chapter.*

1. Disconnect the air suction hose at the vacuum hose manifold. Tee in a vacuum pump as shown in the illustration. Hook up the pump so as to apply pressure. Then, use the vacuum pump to attempt to force air pressure into the

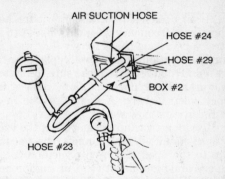

Tee in the vacuum pump to force air into the feedback control system as shown

system. If air does not flow, proceed to step 2. If it does, proceed to 2a.

2a. If air flows into the system, remove the air box cover and then pinch off the vacuum hose leading to frequency solenoid valve **A**. Then, blow air through the hose. If air flows, replace air control valve **B** and then recheck that air does not flow. If air does not flow, replace the frequency solenoid valve **A** and retest as in Step 1.

3. Disconnect vacuum hose #24 at surge tank **B**. Connect the vacuum pump to the end of this hose so as to apply pressure. Then, disconnect the hose leading from Air Control Valve **B** and frequency solenoid valve **A**. Connect the hand pump so as to apply pressure. Apply vacuum at hose #24 and blow air into the other hose (the B-valve side of the Air Control Valve). Air should flow. If it does, proceed to Step 4. If not, proceed to 3a.

3a. Replace air control valve **B** and then retest the system to make sure air does flow.

4. Jumper battery voltage (from the + terminal) to the green/white connector of connector box #2 (see illustration). Blow air into the vacuum hose going to frequency valve **A**. If air flows, the valve is okay and you should proceed to Step 5. If not, proceed to Step 4a.

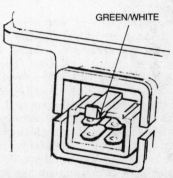

Jumper battery voltage to the green/white connector of connector box 2

4a. If air does not flow, disconnect the hose leading from frequency solenoid valve A to air control valve A and check for air flow with the pump in operation. If air flows, replace control valve A and then retest to make sure the system now works. If air does not flow, replace frequency solenoid valve A and re-test to make sure the system now works.

5. Disconnect vacuum hose #29 at the vacuum hose manifold and connect the vacuum pump to the open end. Apply vacuum to the open end and blow air into the air suction hose leading to Control Valve **A**. When there is vacuum applied via the pump, air should flow without resistance. When vacuum is released, air should flow into the system only with significant resistance; that is, pressure should build up on the gauge of the pump supplying pressure and then be released only gradually. If this occurs, reconnect the air suction hose and hose #29 and then go on to Step 6. If there is no such change in resistance, replace air control valve A and then repeat the test.

6. Jumper battery voltage from the battery (+) terminal to the frequency solenoid valve **B**. Disconnect the vacuum hose #23 from surge tank **B** and connect a vacuum pump to it. Then, apply vacuum. Vacuum should build up on the pressure gauge. If there is vacuum, go to Step 7. If not, pinch the hose leading from the frequency solenoid valve **B** to the constant vacuum valve. Then, repeat the test. If there is now vacuum, replace the constant vacuum valve and then retest to make sure the system is repaired. If there is still no vacuum, replace the frequency solenoid valve **B** and repeat the test to make sure the system is repaired.

7. Leaving the vacuum pump hooked up, disconnect the jumper wire leading to frequency solenoid valve **B**. Make sure there is still vacuum in the system. Vacuum should disappear when the wire is disconnected. If it does disappear, reconnect vacuum hose #23 and go on to Step 8. If it does not disappear, replace solenoid valve **B** and retest to make sure it now disappears.

8. Remove the cover of control box #2 and disconnect the hose connecting the constant vacuum valve and frequency solenoid valve **B** from its connection within the box. Then, connect a vacuum pump to the open end of the hose. Now, start the engine, allow it to idle, and measure the vacuum with a gauge. It should stabilize in the range 6-11 in.Hg (manual transaxle) vehicles and 2-7 in.Hg (automatic transaxle). If vacuum stabilizes in this range, the constant vacuum valve is okay, and you should reconnect the hose. If not, replace the constant vacuum valve, and then retest to make sure you have corrected the malfunction.

Testing the EGR Valve Used on Fuel Injection Engines

A very sophisticated electronic control system regulates the EGR valve. Testing this system requires a highly complex procedure. If, however, your vehicle exhibits problems that might be related to the EGR valve such as chronic detonation not due to poor fuel or advanced ignition timing, check the EGR valve as described here. You'll need a hand operated vacuum pump to perform the test.

1. Start the engine and allow it to idle (at normal operating temperature). Disconnect #16 vacuum hose at the EGR valve and connect the vacuum pump to the opening on the valve.

2. Apply 6 in.Hg vacuum. Watch the vacuum gauge on the pump and listen to the engine. If vacuum remains steady and the engine dies, the EGR valve is okay. If vacuum is lost and the engine does not stall, replace the EGR valve. If vacuum remains steady, but the engine does not stall, remove the EGR valve, check the valve and the manifold for blockages, clean and retest.

Testing the Cold Vacuum Advance System used with Fuel Injection

This system operates to improve cold driving performance only. Test it if your vehicle responds poorly when cold and runs fine after warm-up or if the engine knocks when hot, which might indicate that the system is working after the engine warms up.

1. Allow the engine to sit until it is overnight cold. Disconnect the vacuum advance line from the outer or cold advance diaphragm.

2. Connect a vacuum gauge to the open end of the hose and then start the engine, allowing it to idle. There should be vacuum. If so, go to Step 3. If not, check the line for leaks or blockages or poor connection at the other end. If you still do not get vacuum under these conditions, proceed to Step 5.

3. Wait for the engine to reach operating temperature. Then, check for vacuum. There should be no vacuum. If there is vacuum, proceed to Step 5. If not, proceed to Step 4.

4. Connect a tachometer. Then, accelerate the engine to 1500 rpm and recheck for vacuum. There should be vacuum under these conditions. If not, proceed to Step 5.

5. Remove the top from the vacuum control box. Disconnect the 6-prong electrical connector at the control box. Then, disconnect the lower vacuum hose running between the cold advance solenoid valve and the check valve at the check valve. Apply vacuum to the hose and then watch the gauge on the pump. The vacuum should remain steady. If it does not, replace the valve.

6. Connect the battery positive (+) terminal to the Black/Yellow terminal of the control box electrical connector. Connect the battery negative terminal to the Yellow/Green terminal. Again, apply vacuum to the hose and watch the gauge. Vacuum should be lost. If vacuum is maintained, replace the valve.

Temperature Controlled Spark Advance

OPERATION

Temperature controlled spark advance on 1973 vehicles equipped with Hondamatic transmission is designed to reduce NOx emissions by disconnecting the vacuum to the spark advance unit during normal vehicle operation. When the coolant temperature is approximately 120°F (49°C) or higher, the solenoid valve is energized, cutting off vacuum to the advance unit.

1975-79 1237cc Air Models

INTAKE AIR TEMPERATURE CONTROLS

Same as 1973-74 models.

THROTTLE OPENER

Same as 1973-74 models.

TRANSMISSION CONTROLLED SPARK ADVANCE

Same as 1974 models, with no coolant control override.

IGNITION TIMING RETARD UNIT

Same as 1973 models, but is used only on Hondamatic models and has no vacuum advance mechanism.

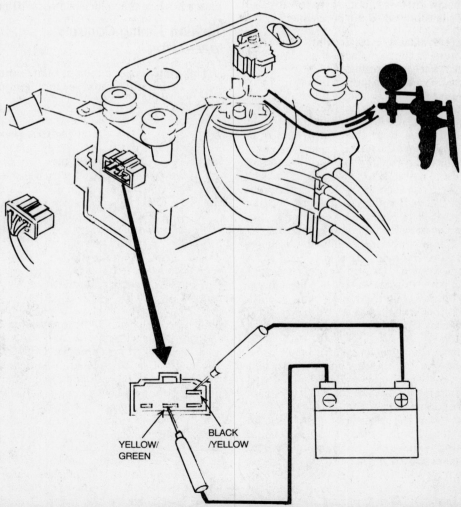

YELLOW/
GREEN

BLACK
/YELLOW

Making electrical connections to test the Cold Advance Solenoid valve used on late model fuel injection engines

Air Injection System
OPERATION

Beginning with the 1975 model year, an air injection system is used to control hydrocarbon and carbon monoxide emissions. With this system, a belt driven air pump delivers filtered air under pressure to injection nozzles located at each exhaust port. Here, the additional oxygen supplied by the vane type pump reacts with any uncombusted fuel mixture, promoting an afterburning effect in the hot exhaust manifold. To prevent a reverse flow in the air injection manifold when exhaust gas pressure exceeds air supply pressure, a non-return check valve is used. To prevent exhaust afterburning or backfiring during deceleration, an anti-afterburn valve delivers air to the intake manifold instead. When manifold vacuum rises above the preset vacuum of the air control valve and/or below that of the air bypass valve, air pump air is returned to the air cleaner.

1975-82 1487, 1600, 1751cc Models

INTAKE AIR TEMPERATURE CONTROL

Same as 1973-74 models.

Throttle Controls
OPERATION

This system controls the closing of the throttle during periods of gear shifting, deceleration, or any time the gas pedal is released. In preventing the sudden closing of the throttle during these conditions, an overly rich mixture is prevented which controls excessive emissions of hydrocarbons and carbon monoxide. This system has two main parts; a dashpot system and a throttle positioner system. The dashpot diaphragm and solenoid valve act to dampen or slow down the throttle return time to 1-4 seconds. The throttle positioner part consists of a speed sensor, a solenoid valve, a control valve and an opener diaphragm which will keep the throttle open and predetermined minimum amount any time the gas pedal is released when the vehicle is traveling 15 mph or faster, and closes it when the vehicle slows to 10 mph.

Ignition Timing Controls
OPERATION

This system uses a coolant temperature sensor to switch distributor vacuum ignition tim-

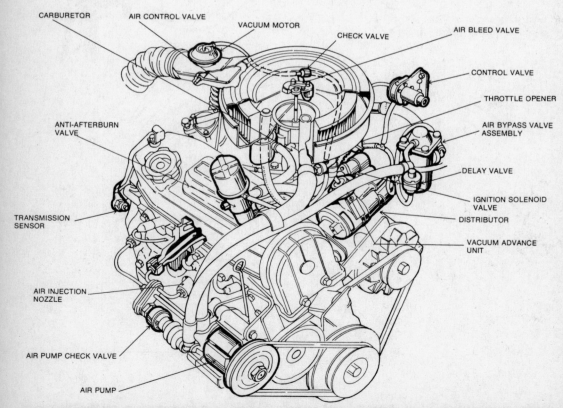

Location of emission control system components—1975 1237 cc AIR models with manual transmission; other years similar

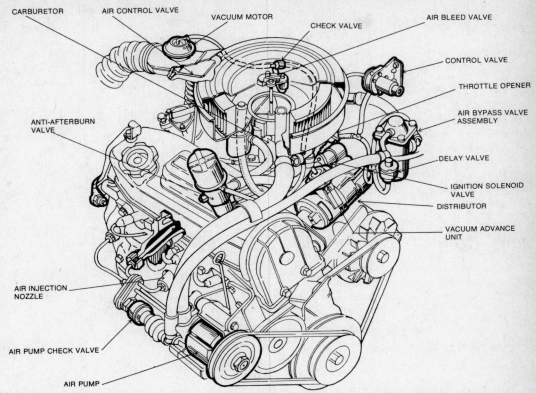

CARBURETOR

AIR CONTROL VALVE

VACUUM MOTOR

CHECK VALVE

AIR BLEED VALVE

CONTROL VALVE

THROTTLE OPENER

AIR BYPASS VALVE ASSEMBLY

ANTI-AFTERBURN VALVE

DELAY VALVE

IGNITION SOLENOID VALVE

DISTRIBUTOR

VACUUM ADVANCE UNIT

AIR INJECTION NOZZLE

AIR PUMP CHECK VALVE

AIR PUMP

Location of emission control system components—1975 1237 cc AIR models with Hondamatic—other years similar

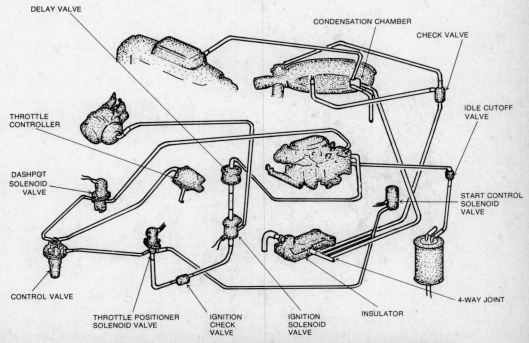

DELAY VALVE

CONDENSATION CHAMBER

CHECK VALVE

IDLE CUTOFF VALVE

THROTTLE CONTROLLER

DASHPOT SOLENOID VALVE

START CONTROL SOLENOID VALVE

CONTROL VALVE

THROTTLE POSITIONER SOLENOID VALVE

IGNITION CHECK VALVE

IGNITION SOLENOID VALVE

INSULATOR

4-WAY JOINT

Emission controls system schematic—Accord with manual transmission

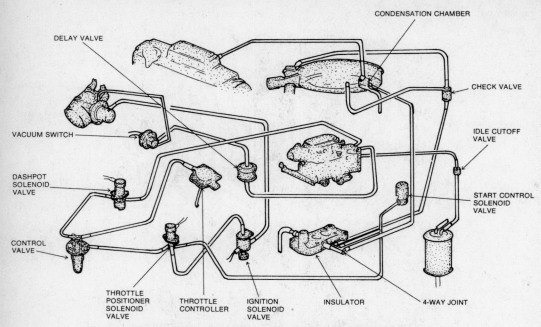

DELAY VALVE

VACUUM SWITCH

DASHPOT
SOLENOID
VALVE

CONTROL
VALVE

CONDENSATION CHAMBER

CHECK VALVE

IDLE CUTOFF
VALVE

START CONTROL
SOLENOID
VALVE

THROTTLE
POSITIONER
SOLENOID
VALVE

THROTTLE
CONTROLLER

IGNITION
SOLENOID
VALVE

INSULATOR

4-WAY JOINT

Emission controls system schematic—Accord with Hondamatic

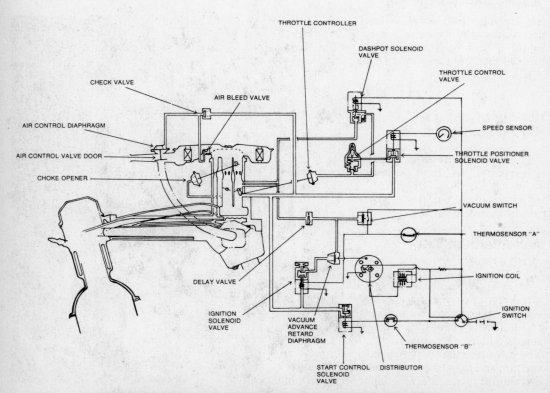

THROTTLE CONTROLLER

DASHPOT SOLENOID
VALVE

THROTTLE CONTROL
VALVE

CHECK VALVE

AIR BLEED VALVE

AIR CONTROL DIAPHRAGM

AIR CONTROL VALVE DOOR

CHOKE OPENER

SPEED SENSOR

THROTTLE POSITIONER
SOLENOID VALVE

VACUUM SWITCH

THERMOSENSOR "A"

IGNITION COIL

DELAY VALVE

IGNITION
SOLENOID
VALVE

VACUUM
ADVANCE
RETARD
DIAPHRAGM

START CONTROL
SOLENOID
VALVE

DISTRIBUTOR

THERMOSENSOR "B"

IGNITION
SWITCH

Emission control system schematic—Civic CVCC with Hondamatic

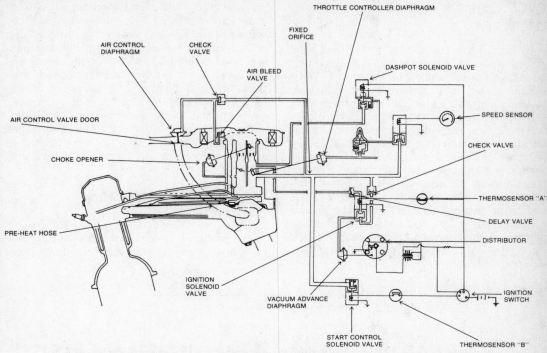

Emission control system schematic—Civic CVCC with manual transmission

ing controls on or off to reduce hydrocarbon and oxides of nitrogen emissions. The coolant switch is calibrated at 149°F (49°C) for 1487 and 1600cc engines, and 167°F (75°C) for 1751cc engines.

Hot Start Controls
OPERATION

This system is designed to prevent an overly rich mixture condition in the intake manifold due to vaporization of residual fuel when starting a hot engine. This reduces hydrocarbon and carbon monoxide emissions.

Anti-Afterburn Valve
OPERATION

1979-82 1751cc engines have an anti-afterburn valve. This unit is used only on models with manual transmission. The valve lets fresh air into the intake manifold when it senses sudden increases in manifold vacuum. The valve responds only to sudden increases in vacuum and the amount of time it stays open is determined by an internal diaphragm which is acted on by the vacuum level.

Vacuum delay valve mounted on air cleaner

CVCC Engine Modifications
OPERATION

By far, the most important part of the CVCC engine emission control system is the Compound Vortex Controlled Combustion (CVCC) cylinder head itself. Each cylinder has three valves: a conventional intake and conventional exhaust valve, and a smaller auxiliary intake valve. There are actually two combustion chambers per cylinder: a pre-combustion or auxiliary chamber, and the main chamber. During the intake stroke, an extremely lean mixture is drawn into the main combustion chamber. Simultaneously, a very rich mixture is drawn into the smaller precombustion chamber via the auxiliary intake valve. The spark plug, located in the precombustion chamber, easily ignites the rich pre-mixture, and this combustion spreads out into the main combustion chamber where the lean mixture is ignited. Due to the fact that the volume of the auxiliary chamber is much smaller than the main chamber, the overall mixture is very lean (about 18 parts air to one part fuel). The result is low hydrocarbon emissions due to the slow, stable combustion of the lean mixture in the main chamber; low carbon monoxide emissions due to the excess oxygen available; and low oxides of nitrogen emissions due to the lowered peak combustion temperatures. An added benefit of burning the lean mixture is the excellent gas mileage.

Feedback Control Systems
OPERATION

This system is used on most 1984-87 carbureted models and controls air fuel mixture pre-

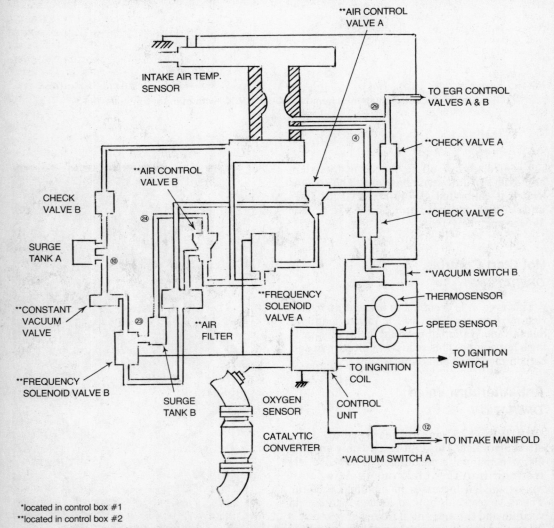

*located in control box #1
**located in control box #2

Diagram of the Feedback control system used on the 1984 Civic

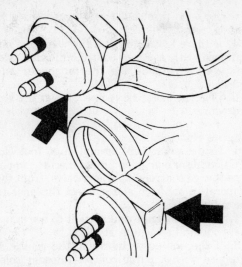

Thermosensors located on engine block. The upper thermosensor energizes a solenoid when the engine is cold, giving vacuum advance. The lower thermosensor is used when the engine is warm (1977 and earlier)

cisely. The reason for this is the used of a 3-way catalytic converter, which operates in two stages. Automotive emissions consist of two basic types: incompletely burned (or oxidized) fuel — hydrocarbons and carbon monoxide; and NOx nitrogen from the air that has combined with some oxygen. If the chemistry of burning can be kept at exactly the right mixture to burn up the fuel without any excess oxygen, the 3-way catalyst will actually reduce the nitrogen oxides to again become nitrogen as it combines that oxygen with the unburnt fuel.

This system is designed so the carburetor supplies a mixture that is just very slightly richer in fuel than is actually required. An oxygen sensor located in the exhaust system senses the presence of excess oxygen and fine-tunes the operation of two frequency solenoid valves to add precisely controlled amounts of air, via normal intake manifold vacuum.

The system employs an electronic control box to evaluate a number of signals, the most important of which is the oxygen sensor signal. It then very rapidly opens and closes two solenoid valves to supply precisely controlled amounts of air at a regular rate.

Emission Control Systems Used with Fuel Injection
OPERATION

A modern, high performance fuel injection system not only improves engine operating performance but simplifies emission control. En-

gines with fuel injection use a number of systems.

A PCV system of conventional type is used to recycle unburnt hydrocarbons from the crankcase back into the intake manifold. There is also a hose connecting the air inlet pipe to the valve cover to supply fresh air to the crankcase and effectively scavenge the unburnt gases.

There is a conventional charcoal canister with a two-way valve capable of interrupting flow from the fuel tank into the canister and a thermovalve capable of interruption flow from the canister into the intake manifold. The two-way valve opens only when pressure in the fuel tank is higher than in the canister. The thermovalve opens at 131°F (55°C) to allow the canister to be purged.

Ignition timing controls include a double vacuum advance diaphragm arrangement. The Primary diaphragm is operable at all times; the secondary diaphragm operates only when a cold advance solenoid valve is energized by low engine temperatures. Use of a check valve in the line leading to the cold advance line only ensures continuation of advance when the accelerator is opened and manifold vacuum drops.

The EGR control system is electronic and operates via the Electronic Control Unit. Vacuum is supplied to the system via a CVC controlling valve, with pulses that exist in the intake dampened via an air chamber. The EGR Control Solenoid valve then bleeds air under atmospheric pressure into the system in order to control actual EGR vacuum and therefore how far the valve opens. Parameters such as manifold absolute pressure, coolant temperature, etc. are fed to the ECU. The ECU actually compares valve position with ideal parameters programmed into it.

Air Jet Controller
OPERATION

Used on 1981 and later California and High Altitude models, this system senses atmospheric pressure and regulates carburetor air flow accordingly.

Oxygen Sensor
OPERATION

The oxygen sensor is mounted in the exhaust manifold. It is used to sense oxygen concentration in the exhaust gas. If the fuel/ratio is leaner than the stoichiometric ratio in the mixture (i.e. excessive amount of air), the exhaust gas contains more oxygen. On the other hand, if the fuel/ratio is richer than the stoichiometric ratio, the exhaust gas hardly contains any oxygen.

Evaporative Emission Control System

OPERATION

This system prevents gasoline vapors from escaping into the atmosphere from the fuel tank and carburetor and consists of the components listed in the illustration.

Fuel vapor is stored in the expansion chamber, in the fuel tank and in the vapor line. When the vapor pressure becomes higher than the set pressure of the one-way valve, the valve opens and allows vapor into the charcoal canister. While the engine is stopped or idling, the idle cut-off valve in the canister is closed and the vapor is absorbed by the charcoal.

At partially opened throttle, the idle cut-off valve is opened by manifold vacuum. The vapor that was stored in the charcoal canister and in the vapor line is purged into the intake manifold. Any excessive pressure or vacuum which might build up in the fuel tank is relieved by the two-way valve in the filler cap.

SERVICE

Purge Control/Unloader Solenoid Valve

CARBURETED

Engine Cold

NOTE: *The coolant temperature must be below the thermosensor(s) set temperature; the thermosensor(s) must have continuity.*

1. Using a Vacuum Pump/Gauge tool No. H/C 058369 or equivalent, disconnect the upper hose (purge control diaphragm valve) from the evaporative canister and connect the hose to the gauge.

2. Start the engine and allow it to idle; there should be no vacuum.

3. If there is vacuum and the vehicle is equipped with a purge control/unloader solenoid valve, perform the following procedures:

a. Disconnect the purge control/unloader solenoid valve electrical connector.

b. Using an ohmmeter, check for voltage at the connector.

c. If there is voltage, replace the purge control/unloader solenoid valve, then, retest.

d. If there is no voltage, for the 49ST/HI ALT models, inspect the wiring, the fuse and the Thermosensor A, then, retest. If there is no voltage, for the CAL models, inspect the

wiring, the fuse and the Thermosensor B, then, retest.

4. If there is vacuum and the vehicle is not equipped with a purge control/unloader solenoid valve, replace the thermosensor and retest.

5. To install, reverse the removal procedures.

Engine Hot

1. Using a Vacuum Pump/Gauge tool No. H/C 058369 or equivalent, disconnect the upper hose (purge control diaphragm valve) from the evaporative canister and connect the hose to the gauge.

2. Start the engine and allow it to warm up; there should be vacuum at idle.

3. If there is no vacuum and the vehicle is equipped with a purge control/unloader solenoid valve, perform the following procedures:

a. Disconnect the purge control/unloader solenoid valve electrical connector.

b. Using an ohmmeter, check for voltage at the connector.

c. If there is voltage, replace the thermosensor, then, retest.

d. If there is no voltage, replace the purge control/unloader solenoid valve, then, retest.

4. If there is no vacuum and the vehicle is not equipped with a purge control/unloader solenoid valve, perform the following procedures:

a. Pinch off the thermosensor-to-air filter hose; there should be vacuum.

b. If no vacuum is present, check the hoses for blockage or leaks.

5. To install, reverse the removal procedures.

Charcoal Canister

NOTE: *This procedure is to be performed with the engine Hot.*

1. Using a tachometer, connect it to the engine. Start the engine and allow it to reach normal operating temperatures; until the cooling fan turns On.

2. Remove the fuel filler cap.

3. Using a Vacuum Gauge tool No. H/C 081167 or equivalent, disconnect the charcoal

49ST/HI ALT

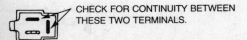

CHECK FOR CONTINUITY BETWEEN THESE TWO TERMINALS.

Purge control/unloader solenoid valve electrical connector

CAL

BLACK/YELLOW (+)

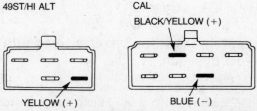

YELLOW (+)   BLUE (−)

Purge control/unloader solenoid valve electrical connector

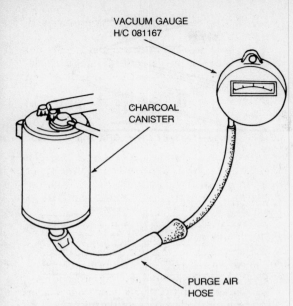

Testing charcoal canister with vacuum gauge tool

canister from the frame and connect the gauge to it.

4. Raise the engine speed to 3,500 rpm; vacuum should appear on the gauge in 1 minute. If vacuum appears, the canister is OK; end of test.

5. If no vacuum appears, perform the following procedures:

a. Disconnect the vacuum gauge and reinstall the fuel filler cap.

b. Remove the charcoal canister and check for signs of damage or defects.

c. If necessary, replace the canister.

6. Stop the engine and disconnect the PVC hose from the charcoal canister.

7. Using a Vacuum Gauge tool No. H/C058369 or equivalent, install it to purge control solenoid valve (on top of the canister) and perform the following procedures:

a. Hand pump the vacuum gauge to create vacuum.

b. If the vacuum remains steady, proceed with the next step; if the vacuum drops, replace the canister and retest.

8. Reconnect the PCV hose and start the engine; the Purge side vacuum should drop to zero. If the vacuum does not drop to zero, perform the following procedures:

a. Disconnect the hose from the PCV fitting and check for vacuum at the hose.

b. If vacuum exists, replace the canister and retest.

c. If no vacuum exists, recheck the thermosensor valve operation.

d. If the purge side vacuum drops to zero, connect the vacuum gauge to the purge hose and check for vacuum with the engine speed

at 3,500 rpm. If vacuum exists, replace the canister and retest; if no vacuum, inspect the hose and carburetor for blockage.

9. Connect the vacuum gauge to the fuel tank hose and check for vacuum. If no vacuum exists, replace the fuel filler cap — test complete. If vacuum exists, replace the canister and retest.

FUEL INJECTED
Engine Cold

Refer to the Carbureted, Cold Engine test procedures in this section; the test is identical.

Engine Hot

1. Using a Vacuum Pump/Gauge tool No. H/C 058369 or equivalent, disconnect the upper hose (purge control diaphragm valve) from the evaporative canister and connect the hose to the gauge.

2. Using a tachometer, connect it to the engine. Start the engine and allow it to reach normal operating temperatures; until the cooling fan turns On. There should be vacuum at idle with 5 seconds after starting.

3. If there is no vacuum and the vehicle is equipped with a purge control/unloader solenoid valve, check the valve operation.

4. Disconnect the vacuum gauge and reconnect the hose.

5. Remove the fuel filler cap.

6. Remove the canister purge air hose from the frame and connect the vacuum gauge to it.

7. Raise the engine speed to 3,500 rpm, vacuum should appear in 1 minute. If vacuum appears, remove the gauge, the test is complete; if no vacuum appears, disconnect the vacuum gauge and reinstall the fuel filler cap.

8. Remove the charcoal canister and check

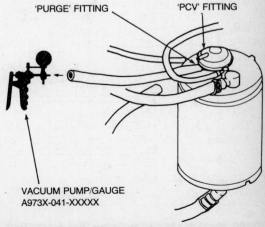

Attaching vacuum pump to charcoal canister

for damage or defects; if defective, replace the canister.

9. Stop the engine and disconnect the PCV hose from the canister. Using the vacuum gauge, connect it to the **purge** fitting (located under the canisters PCV fitting). Check for vacuum. If the vacuum remains steady, the canister is good; if the vacuum drops, replace the canister and retest.

10. Restart the engine and reconnect the PCV hose to the canister. The **purge** side vacuum should drop to zero; if not, replace the canister.

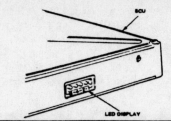

PGM-FI display—1985–87 Civic; CRX and 1985 Accord

PGM-FI and Feedback Carburetor — Self-Diagnostic System

OPERATION

Many Honda's are equipped with a self-diagnosis function. When an abnormality is detected, the LED display on the ECU comes on. The location of the emission device control systems trouble can be diagnosed from the LED display pattern. Some of the models have four LED displays (they are numbered 1, 2, 4 and 8 as counted from right to left), while the others have a single LED that flashes the trouble code. The

SELF-DIAGNOSIS INDICATOR BLINKS	SYSTEM INDICATED
0	ECU
1	OXYGEN CONTENT
3	MANIFOLD ABSOLUTE PRESSURE
5	
6	COOLANT TEMPERATURE
7	THROTTLE ANGLE
8	CRANK ANGLE (TDC)
9	CRANK ANGLE (CYL)
10	INTAKE AIR TEMPERATURE
12	EXHAUST GAS RECIRCULATION SYSTEM
13	ATMOSPHERIC PRESSURE

Trouble codes and related systems—1986–87 Accord Fuel Injected

LED Display	Possible Cause
○ ○ ○ ○ (Dash Warning Light ON only)	· Loose or poorly connected power line to ECU · Short circuit in combination meter or warning light wire · Faulty ECU
○ ○ ○ ✹ 1	· Disconnected oxygen sensor coupler · Spark plug mis-fire · Short or open circuit in oxygen sensor circuit · Faulty oxygen sensor
○ ○ ✹ ○ 2	· Faulty ECU
○ ○ ✹ ✹ 2 1	· Disconnected manifold air pressure sensor coupler · Short or open circuit in manifold air pressure sensor wire · Faulty manifold air pressure sensor
○ ✹ ○ ○ 4	· Faulty ECU
○ ✹ ○ ✹ 4 1	· Disconnected manifold air pressure sensor piping
○ ✹ ✹ ○ 4 2	· Disconnected coolant temperature sensor coupler · Open circuit in coolant temperature sensor wire · Faulty coolant temperature sensor (thermostat housing)
○ ✹ ✹ ✹ 4 2 1	· Disconnected throttle angle sensor coupler · Open or short circuit in throttle angle sensor wire · Faulty throttle angle sensor
✹ ○ ○ ○ 8	· Short or open circuit in crank angle sensor wire · Crank angle sensor wire interfering with high tension cord · Crank angle sensor at fault
✹ ○ ○ ✹ 8	Same as above
✹ ○ ✹ ○ 8 2	· Disconnected intake air temperature sensor · Open circuit in intake air temperature sensor wire · Faulty intake air temperature sensor
✹ ○ ✹ ✹ 8 2 1	· Disconnected idle mixture adjuster sensor coupler · Shorted or disconnected idle mixture adjuster sensor wire · Faulty idle mixture adjuster sensor
✹ ✹ ○ ○ 8 4	· Disconnected EGR control system coupler · Shorted or disconnected EGR control wire · Faulty EGR control system
✹ ✹ ○ ✹ 8 4 1	· Disconnected atmospheric pressure sensor coupler · Shorted or disconnected atmospheric pressure sensor wire · Faulty atmospheric pressure sensor
✹ ✹ ✹ ○ 8 4 2	· Faulty ECU
✹ ✹ ✹ ✹ 8 4 2 1	Same as above

Trouble codes and related systems—1985 Accord Fuel Injected

LED Display	Possible Cause
○ ○ ○ ○ (Dash warning light off)	· Loose or poorly connected power line to ECU · Disconnected control unit ground wire · Faulty ECU
○ ○ ○ ○ (Dash warning light on)	· Disconnected control unit ground wire · Short circuit in combination meter or warning light wire · Faulty ECU
○ ○ ○ ✹ 1	· Disconnected oxygen sensor connector · Spark plug mis-fire · Short or open circuit in oxygen sensor circuit · Faulty oxygen sensor
○ ○ ✹ ○ 2	· Faulty ECU
○ ○ ✹ ✹ 2 1	· Disconnected MAP sensor connector · Short or open circuit in MAP sensor wire · Faulty MAP sensor
○ ✹ ○ ○ 4	· Faulty ECU
○ ✹ ○ ✹ 4 1	· Disconnected MAP sensor piping
○ ✹ ✹ ✹ 4 2 1	· Disconnected TW sensor connector · Open circuit in TW sensor wire · Faulty TW sensor
○ ✹ ✹ ✹ 4 2 1	· Disconnected throttle angle sensor connector · Open or short circuit in throttle angle sensor wire · Faulty throttle angle sensor
✹ ○ ○ ✹ 8 1	· Short or open circuit in crank angle sensor wire · Crank angle sensor wire interfering with spark plug wires · Faulty crank angle sensor
✹ ○ ○ ✹ 8 1	Same as above
✹ ○ ✹ ○ 8 2	· Disconnected TA sensor connector · Open circuit in TA sensor wire · Faulty TA sensor
✹ ○ ✹ ✹ 8 2 1	· Disconnected IMA sensor connector · Open or short circuit in IMA sensor wire · Faulty IMA sensor
✹ ✹ ○ ○ 8 4	· Faulty ECU
✹ ✹ ○ ✹ 8 4 1	· Disconnected PA sensor connector · Open or short circuit in PA sensor wire · Faulty PA sensor
✹ ✹ ✹ ○ 8 4 2	· Faulty ECU
✹ ✹ ✹ ✹ 8 4 2 1	Same as above

Trouble codes and related systems—1985–87 Civic; CRX EFI

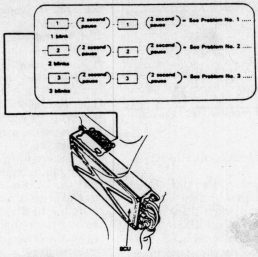

PGM-FI LED display—1986–87 Prelude shown, 1988
Prelude beneath right front carpent. 1986–88 Accord
ECU under driver's seat

No. of LED Blinks between 2 second pauses		Symptom	Possible cause
0	Warning light off	• Engine will not start	• Disconnected ECU ground wire • Faulty ECU
	Warning light on	• Engine will not start • No particular symptom shown	• Loose or poorly connected power line to ECU • Disconnected ECU ground wire • Short circuit in combination meter or warning light wire • Faulty ECU
1		• No particular symptom shown • Erratic idling (Erratic injector, connector and wiring Insufficient fuel)	• Disconnected O₂ sensor connector • Spark plug mis-fire • Short or open circuit in O₂ sensor cirucit • Faulty O₂ sensor • Faulty fuel system
2		• No particular symptom shown or system does not operate	• Faulty ECU
3		• Fuel fouled plug • Frequent engine stalling • Hesitation	• Disconnected MAP sensor connector • Short or open circuit in MAP sensor wire • Faulty MAP sensor
4		• No particular symptom shown or system does not operate	• Faulty ECU
5		• Hesitation • Fuel fouled plug • Frequent engine stalling	• Disconnected MAP sensor piping
6		• High idle speed during warm-up • High idle speed • Hard starting at low temp	• Disconnected TW sensor connector • Open or short circuit in TW sensor wire • Faulty TW sensor (thermostat housing)
7		• Poor engine response to opening throttle rapidly • High idle speed • Engine does not rev up when cold	• Disconnected throttle angle sensor connector • Open or short circuit in throttle angle sensor wire • Faulty throttle angle sensor
8		• Engine does not rev up • High idle speed • Erratic idling	• Short or open circuit in crank angle sensor wire • Crank angle sensor wire interfering with spark plug wires • Crank angle sensor at fault
9		• Same as above	• Same as above
10		• High idle speed • Erratic idling when very cold	• Disconnected TA sensor connector • Open or short circuit in TA sensor wire • Faulty TA sensor
11		• No particular symptom shown or system does not operate	• Faulty ECU
12		• Frequent engine stalling • Erratic or unstable running at low speed • No particular symptom shown	• Disconnected EGR control system connector • Shorted or disconnected EGR control wire • Faulty EGR control system
13		• Poor acceleration at high altitude • Hard starting at high altitude when cold	• Disconnected PA sensor connector • Shorted or disconnected PA sensor wire • Faulty PA sensor

Trouble codes and related systems—1986–87 Prelude Fuel Injected

SELF-DIAGNOSIS INDICATOR BLINKS	SYSTEM INDICATED
1	OXYGEN CONTENT
2	VEHICLE SPEED PULSER
3	MANIFOLD ABSOLUTE PRESSURE
4	VACUUM SWITCH SIGNAL
5	MANIFOLD ABSOLUTE PRESSURE
6	COOLANT TEMPERATURE
8	IGNITION COIL SIGNAL
10	INTAKE AIR TEMPERATURE
14	ELECTRONIC AIR CONTROL

Trouble codes and related systems—1988 Prelude Carbureted

LED(s) are part of the control unit, which is inside the vehicle.

If there is no voltage from the control unit when there should be voltage or if there is voltage from the control unit when there should not be voltage, first observe the LED display on the control unit. If the LED display lights, note the LED pattern and isolate the problem according to the table. If the LED does not light, check the input signal sources.

On 1985-87 Civic/CRX EFI, 1986-87 CRX carbureted and Accord 1985 EFI models, there are four LED displays. The LED's are part of the ECU, which is located under the passenger's seat in the Accord and Civic/CRX for the years stated previously. They are numbered 1, 2, 4 and 8, as counted from right to left.

On 1986-88 Accord, 1986-87 Prelude, and 1988 Civic/CRX EFI models, there is only one LED. The LED will blink consecutively to indicate the trouble code. The ECU is located under the driver's seat on the 1986-88 Accord and in the left side panel beside the rear seat on the 1986-87 Preludes. The 1988 Prelude's (carbu-reted and fuel injected) ECU is under the carpet of the passenger's floor. This also has only one LED indicator.

Sometimes the dash warning light and/or ECU LED(s) will come on, indicating a system problem, when, in fact, there is only a bad or intermittent electrical connection. To troubleshoot a bad connection, note the ECU LED code that is lit, refer to the diagnosis chart and check the connectors associated with the items mentioned in the "Possible Cause" column for that LED pattern (disconnect, clean or repair if necessary and reconnect those connections). Then, reset the ECU memory as described. Start the car and drive it for a few minutes and then re-check the LED(s). If the same code lights up, begin system troubleshooting; if it does not light up, the problem was only a bad connection.

To clear the ECU memory after making repairs, disconnect the negative battery cable from the battery negative terminal for at least 10 seconds. After reconnecting the cable, check that the LED display is turned off. Turn the ignition switch ON and all LED displays should come on for about 2 seconds and then go out.

VACUUM DIAGRAMS

NOTE: *It should be noted that because of the year coverage of this book and the page restrictions required while producing a product such as this, only "selected vacuum diagrams" have been included here.*

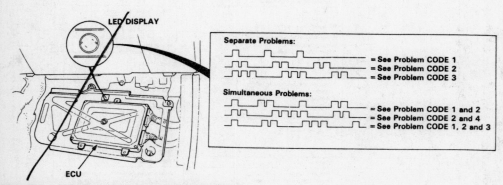

ECU location—1988 Prelude Carb and Fuel Injected

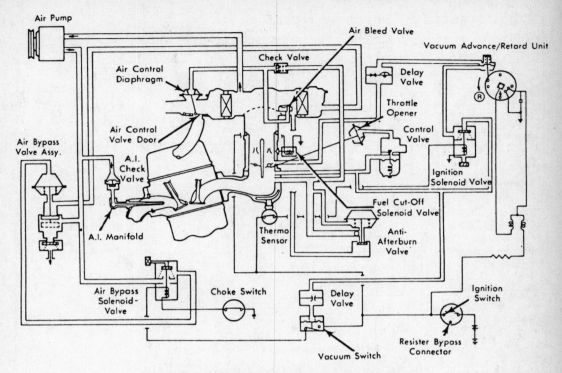

Civic 1200 with manual transmission—1979 model shown

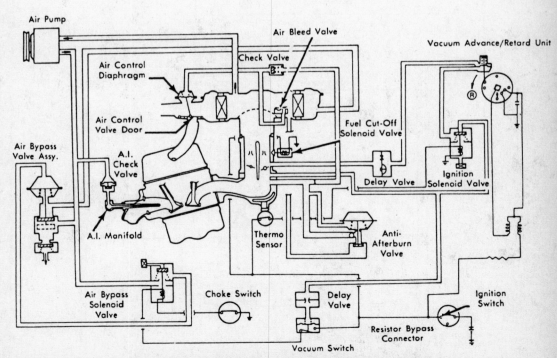

Civic 1200 with automatic transmission—1979 model shown

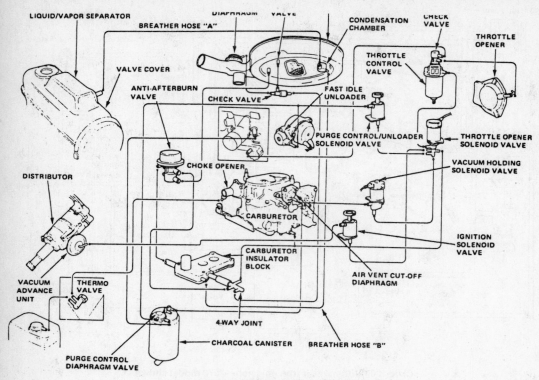

Civic 1300 CVCC 49 states—typical

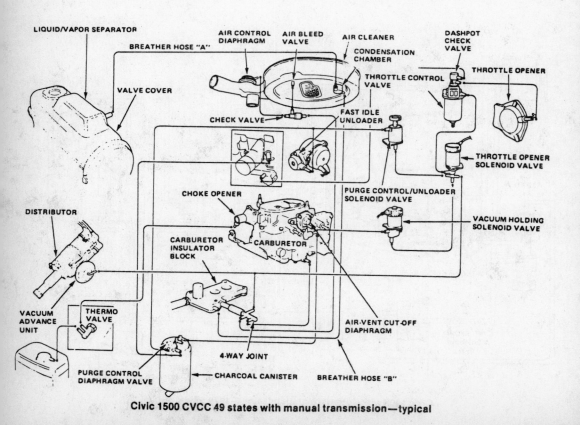

Civic 1500 CVCC 49 states with manual transmission—typical

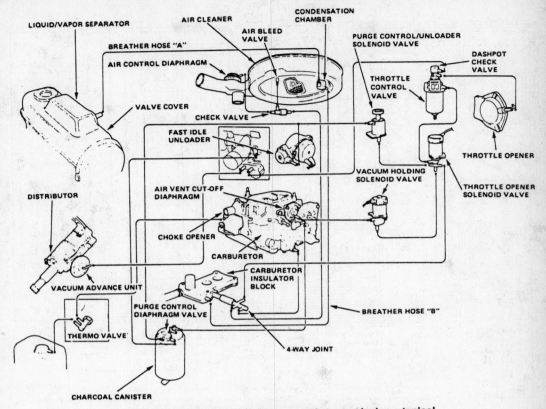

Civic 1500 CVCC 49 states with automatic transmission—typical

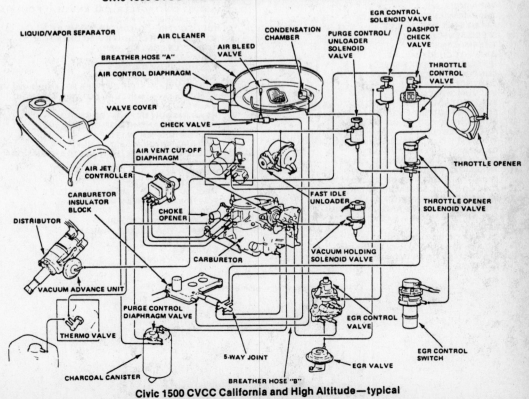

Civic 1500 CVCC California and High Altitude—typical

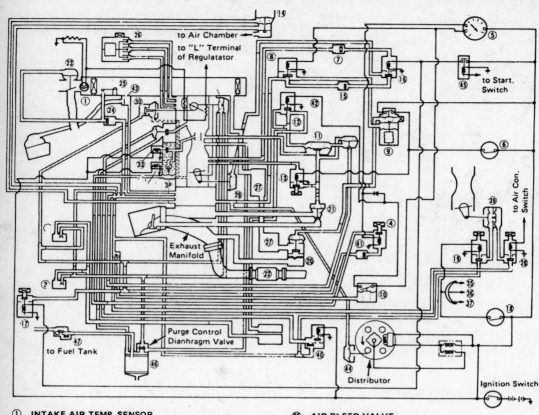

to Air Chamber →
to "L" Terminal of Regulatator
to Start. Switch
to Air Con. Switch
Exhaust Manifold
Purge Control Dianhragm Valve
to Fuel Tank
Distributor
Ignition Switch

① INTAKE AIR TEMP. SENSOR
② THERMOVALVE A
③ THERMOVALVE B
④ PJ CUT SOLENOID VALVE
⑤ SPEED SENSOR
⑥ THERMOSENSOR A
⑦ DASHPOT CHECK VALVE
  (EXCEPT 1300 49 ST 5-SPEED)
⑧ CONTROL SWITCH SOLENOID VALVE
⑨ CONTROL SWITCH
⑩ VACUUM SWITCH
⑪ EGR CONTROL VALVE A AND B
⑫ EGR CONTROL SOLENOID VALVE B
⑬ EGR CONTROL SOLENOID VALVE A
⑭ ANTI-AFTERBURN VALVE
⑮ THROTTLE CONTROLLER CHECK VALVE
⑯ CRANKING SOLENOID VALVE
⑰ CRANKING LEAK SOLENOID VALVE
⑱ THERMOSENSOR B
  (MANUAL TRANSMISSION ONLY)
⑲ IDLE CONTROL SOLENOID VALVE A
  (MANUAL TRANSMISSION ONLY)
⑳ AIR SUCTION VALVE AND AIR SUCTION
  CUT-OFF DIAPHRAGM VALVE
㉑ EGR VALVE
㉒ CATALYTIC CONVERTER
㉓ INTAKE AIR CONTROL DIAPHRAGM
㉔ CHECK VALVE FOR INTAKE AIR TEMPERATURE
  CONTROL

㉕ AIR BLEED VALVE
㉖ AIR JET CONTROLLER (CAL AND HI ALT ONLY)
㉗ AIR CHAMBERS A AND B
㉘ IDLE CONTROL SOLENOID VALVE B
  (CAR WITH AIR CONDITIONER ONLY)
㉙ THROTTLE CONTROLLER
㉚ CHOKE OPENER
㉛ FAST IDLE UNLOADER
㉜ AIR VENT CUT-OFF DIAPHRAGM
㉝ PRIMARY MAIN FUEL CUT-OFF SOLENOID VALVE
㉞ PRIMARY SLOW MIXTURE CUT-OFF SOLENOID
  VALVE
㉟ REAR WINDOW DEFROSTER SWITCH
  (MANUAL TRANSMISSION ONLY)
㊱ HEATER BLOWER SWITCH
  (MANUAL TRANSMISSION ONLY)
㊲ HEADLIGHT SWITCH (MANUAL TRANSMISSION
  ONLY)
㊳ POWER VALVE
㊴ IDLE CONTROLLER
㊵ VACUUM HOLDING SOLENOID VALVE
㊶ POWER VALVE CHECK VALVE
㊷ EGR AIR FILTER
㊸ CONDENSATION CHAMBER
㊹ DISTRIBUTOR VACUUM ADVANCE
㊺ STARTER RELAY
㊻ CANISTER
㊼ TWO-WAY VALVE

1982 Civic—all models

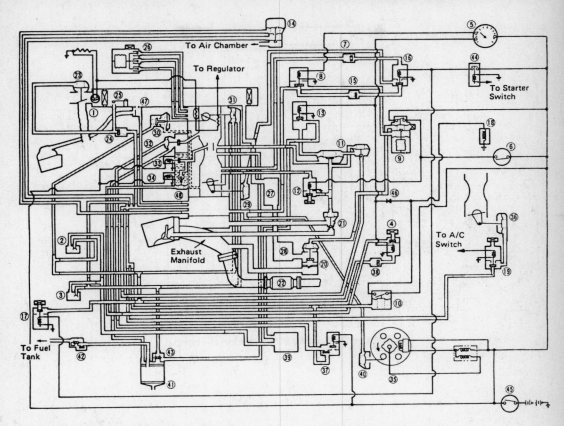

Exhaust Manifold

To Air Chamber →

To Regulator

To Starter Switch

To A/C Switch

To Fuel Tank

① INTAKE AIR TEMPERATURE SENSOR	㉕ AIR BLEED VALVE
② THERMOVALVE A	㉖ AIR JET CONTROLLER (CAL AND HI ALT ONLY)
③ THERMOVALVE B	㉗ AIR CHAMBERS A
④ POWER VALVE CONTROL SOLENOID VALVE	㉘ AIR CHAMBER B
⑤ SPEED SENSOR	㉙ THROTTLE CONTROLLER
⑥ THERMOSENSOR	㉚ CHOKE OPENER
⑦ DASHPOT CHECK VALVE	㉛ FAST IDLE UNLOADER
⑧ CONTROL SWITCH SOLENOID VALVE	㉜ AIR VENT CUT-OFF DIAPHRAGM
⑨ CONTROL SWITCH	㉝ PRIMARY MAIN FUEL CUT-OFF SOLENOID VALVE
⑩ VACUUM SWITCH	㉞ PRIMARY SLOW MIXTURE CUT-OFF SOLENOID
⑪ EGR CONTROL VALVE A AND B	VALVE
⑫ EGR CONTROL SOLENOID VALVE A	㉟ DISTRIBUTER
⑬ EGR CONTROL SOLENOID VALVE B	㊱ IDLE CONTROLLER (A/C)
⑭ ANTI-AFTERBURN VALVE	㊲ VACUUM HOLDING SOLENOID VALVE
⑮ THROTTLE CONTROLLER CHECK VALVE	㊳ POWER VALVE CHECK VALVE
⑯ CRANKING SOLENOID VALVE	㊴ AIR FILTER
⑰ CRANKING LEAK SOLENOID VALVE	㊵ DISTRIBUTOR VACUUM ADVANCE
⑱ AUXILIARY COIL	㊶ CANISTER
⑲ IDLE CONTROL SOLENOID VALVE (A/C)	㊷ TWO-WAY VALVE
⑳ AIR SUCTION VALVE AND AIR SUCTION	㊸ PURGE CONTROL DIAPHRAGM VALVE
CUT-OFF DIAPHRAGM VALVE	㊹ STARTER RELAY
㉑ EGR VALVE	㊺ IGNITION SWITCH
㉒ CATALYTIC CONVERTER	㊻ DIODE
㉓ INTAKE AIR CONTROL DIAPHRAGM	㊼ CONDENSATION CHAMBER
㉔ CHECK VALVE FOR INTAKE AIR TEMPERATURE	㊽ POWER VALVE
CONTROL	

1982 Accord and Prelude—typical

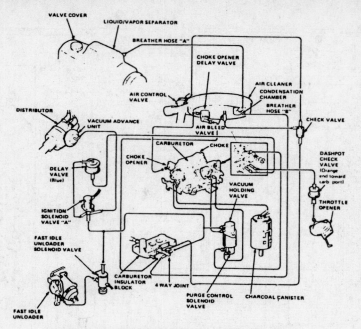

Accord and Prelude 49 state versions—typical

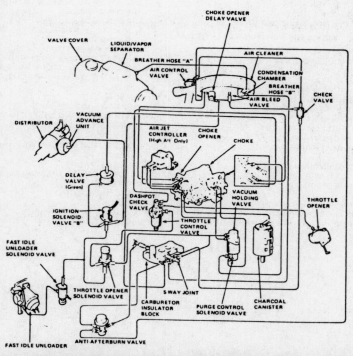

Accord and Prelude California and High Altitude versions with manual transmission—typical

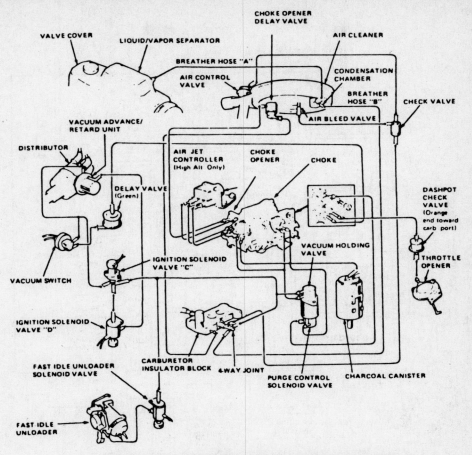

VALVE COVER

LIQUID/VAPOR SEPARATOR

CHOKE OPENER
DELAY VALVE

AIR CLEANER

BREATHER HOSE "A"

AIR CONTROL
VALVE

CONDENSATION
CHAMBER

BREATHER
HOSE "B"

CHECK VALVE

AIR BLEED VALVE

VACUUM ADVANCE/
RETARD UNIT

DISTRIBUTOR

AIR JET
CONTROLLER
(High Alt Only)

CHOKE
OPENER

CHOKE

DASHPOT
CHECK
VALVE
(Orange
end toward
carb port)

DELAY VALVE
(Green)

THROTTLE
OPENER

VACUUM HOLDING
VALVE

VACUUM SWITCH

IGNITION SOLENOID
VALVE "C"

IGNITION SOLENOID
VALVE "D"

FAST IDLE UNLOADER
SOLENOID VALVE

CARBURETOR
INSULATOR BLOCK

4-WAY JOINT

PURGE CONTROL
SOLENOID VALVE

CHARCOAL CANISTER

FAST IDLE
UNLOADER

**Accord and Prelude California and High Altitude versions with
automatic transmission—typical**

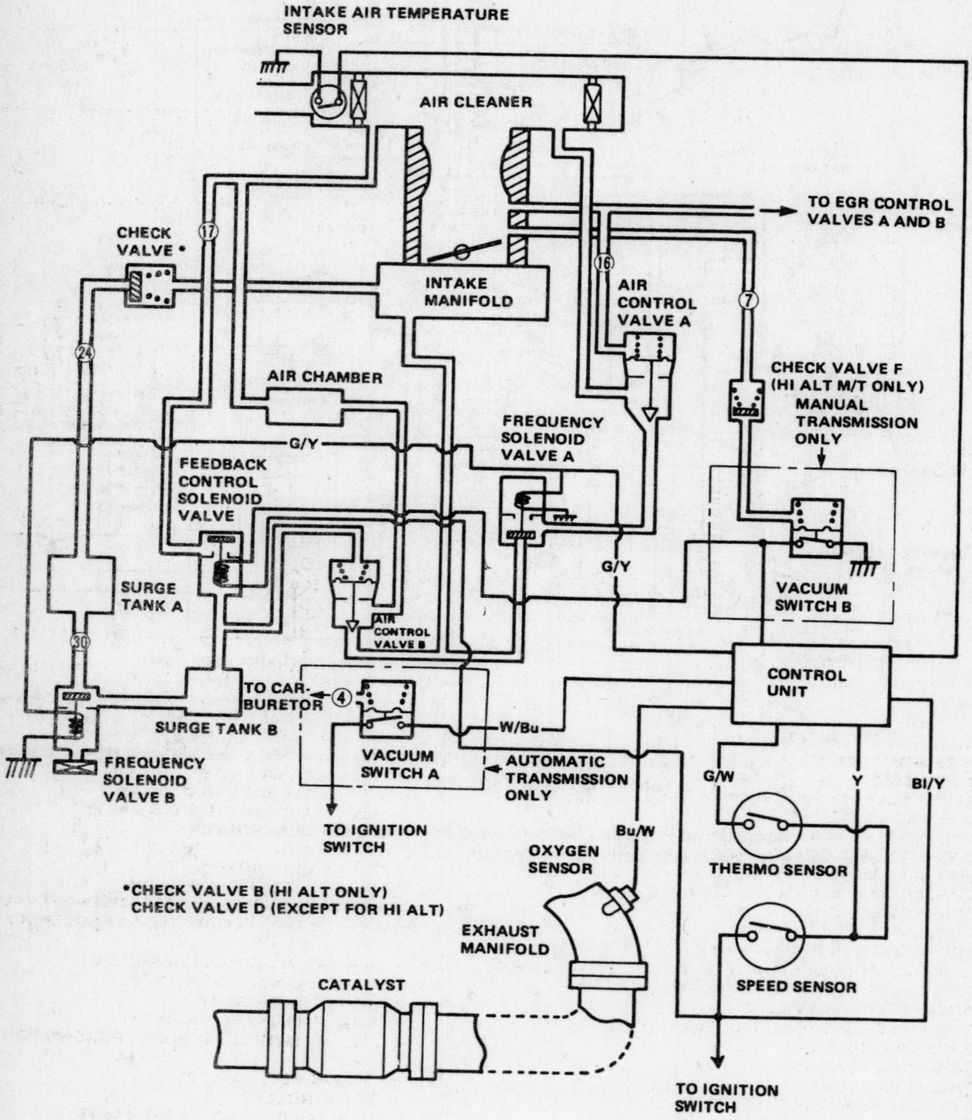

INTAKE AIR TEMPERATURE
SENSOR

AIR CLEANER

TO EGR CONTROL
VALVES A AND B

CHECK
VALVE *

17

24

AIR CHAMBER

INTAKE
MANIFOLD

16

AIR
CONTROL
VALVE A

7

CHECK VALVE F
(HI ALT M/T ONLY)
MANUAL
TRANSMISSION
ONLY

FEEDBACK
CONTROL
SOLENOID
VALVE

G/Y

FREQUENCY
SOLENOID
VALVE A

SURGE
TANK A

30

AIR
CONTROL
VALVE B

G/Y

VACUUM
SWITCH B

CONTROL
UNIT

TO CAR-
BURETOR

4

SURGE TANK B

FREQUENCY
SOLENOID
VALVE B

VACUUM
SWITCH A

W/Bu

AUTOMATIC
TRANSMISSION
ONLY

G/W

Y

Bl/Y

THERMO SENSOR

TO IGNITION
SWITCH

Bu/W

OXYGEN
SENSOR

*CHECK VALVE B (HI ALT ONLY)
CHECK VALVE D (EXCEPT FOR HI ALT)

EXHAUST
MANIFOLD

SPEED SENSOR

CATALYST

TO IGNITION
SWITCH

Feedback control system schematic

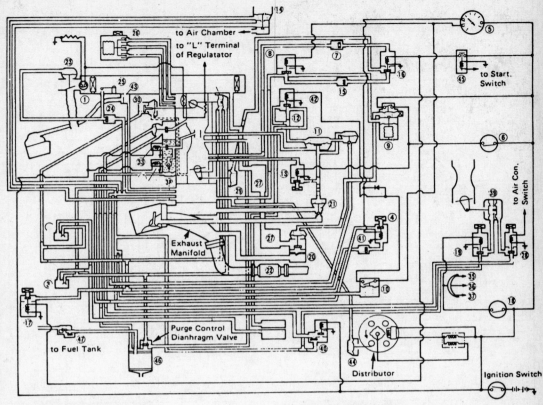

to Air Chamber

to "L" Terminal
of Regulatator

to Start.
Switch

to Air Con.
Switch

Exhaust
Manifold

Purge Control
Dianhragm Valve

to Fuel Tank

Distributor

Ignition Switch

① INTAKE AIR TEMP. SENSOR
② THERMOVALVE A
③ THERMOVALVE B
④ PJ CUT SOLENOID VALVE
⑤ SPEED SENSOR
⑥ THERMOSENSOR A
⑦ DASHPOT CHECK VALVE
　(EXCEPT 1300 49 ST 5-SPEED)
⑧ CONTROL SWITCH SOLENOID VALVE
⑨ CONTROL SWITCH
⑩ VACUUM SWITCH
⑪ EGR CONTROL VALVE A AND B
⑫ EGR CONTROL SOLENOID VALVE B
⑬ EGR CONTROL SOLENOID VALVE A
⑭ ANTI-AFTERBURN VALVE
⑮ THROTTLE CONTROLLER CHECK VALVE
⑯ CRANKING SOLENOID VALVE
⑰ CRANKING LEAK SOLENOID VALVE
⑱ THERMOSENSOR B
　(MANUAL TRANSMISSION ONLY)
⑲ IDLE CONTROL SOLENOID VALVE A
　(MANUAL TRANSMISSION ONLY)
⑳ AIR SUCTION VALVE AND AIR SUCTION
　CUT-OFF DIAPHRAGM VALVE
㉑ EGR VALVE
㉒ CATALYTIC CONVERTER
㉓ INTAKE AIR CONTROL DIAPHRAGM
㉔ CHECK VALVE FOR INTAKE AIR TEMPERATURE
　CONTROL

㉕ AIR BLEED VALVE
㉖ AIR JET CONTROLLER (CAL AND HI ALT ONLY)
㉗ AIR CHAMBERS A AND B
㉘ IDLE CONTROL SOLENOID VALVE B
　(CAR WITH AIR CONDITIONER ONLY)
㉙ THROTTLE CONTROLLER
㉚ CHOKE OPENER
㉛ FAST IDLE UNLOADER
㉜ AIR VENT CUT-OFF DIAPHRAGM
㉝ PRIMARY MAIN FUEL CUT-OFF SOLENOID VALVE
㉞ PRIMARY SLOW MIXTURE CUT-OFF SOLENOID
　VALVE
㉟ REAR WINDOW DEFROSTER SWITCH
　(MANUAL TRANSMISSION ONLY)
㊱ HEATER BLOWER SWITCH
　(MANUAL TRANSMISSION ONLY)
㊲ HEADLIGHT SWITCH (MANUAL TRANSMISSION
　ONLY)
㊳ POWER VALVE
㊴ IDLE CONTROLLER
㊵ VACUUM HOLDING SOLENOID VALVE
㊶ POWER VALVE CHECK VALVE
㊷ EGR AIR FILTER
㊸ CONDENSATION CHAMBER
㊹ DISTRIBUTOR VACUUM ADVANCE
㊺ STARTER RELAY
㊻ CANISTER
㊼ TWO-WAY VALVE

1982 HONDA CIVIC

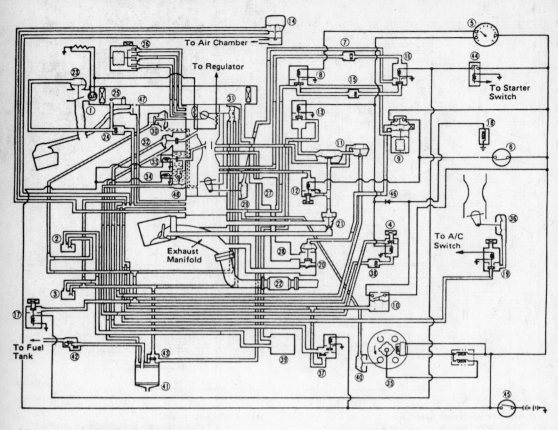

To Air Chamber
To Regulator
To Starter Switch
To A/C Switch
Exhaust Manifold
To Fuel Tank

① INTAKE AIR TEMPERATURE SENSOR	㉕	AIR BLEED VALVE
② THERMOVALVE A	㉖	AIR JET CONTROLLER (CAL AND HI ALT ONLY)
③ THERMOVALVE B	㉗	AIR CHAMBERS A
④ POWER VALVE CONTROL SOLENOID VALVE	㉘	AIR CHAMBER B
⑤ SPEED SENSOR	㉙	THROTTLE CONTROLLER
⑥ THERMOSENSOR	㉚	CHOKE OPENER
⑦ DASHPOT CHECK VALVE	㉛	FAST IDLE UNLOADER
⑧ CONTROL SWITCH SOLENOID VALVE	㉜	AIR VENT CUT-OFF DIAPHRAGM
⑨ CONTROL SWITCH	㉝	PRIMARY MAIN FUEL CUT-OFF SOLENOID VALVE
⑩ VACUUM SWITCH	㉞	PRIMARY SLOW MIXTURE CUT-OFF SOLENOID VALVE
⑪ EGR CONTROL VALVE A AND B	㉟	DISTRIBUTER
⑫ EGR CONTROL SOLENOID VALVE A	㊱	IDLE CONTROLLER (A/C)
⑬ EGR CONTROL SOLENOID VALVE B	㊲	VACUUM HOLDING SOLENOID VALVE
⑭ ANTI-AFTERBURN VALVE	㊳	POWER VALVE CHECK VALVE
⑮ THROTTLE CONTROLLER CHECK VALVE	㊴	AIR FILTER
⑯ CRANKING SOLENOID VALVE	㊵	DISTRIBUTOR VACUUM ADVANCE
⑰ CRANKING LEAK SOLENOID VALVE	㊶	CANISTER
⑱ AUXILIARY COIL	㊷	TWO-WAY VALVE
⑲ IDLE CONTROL SOLENOID VALVE (A/C)	㊸	PURGE CONTROL DIAPHRAGM VALVE
⑳ AIR SUCTION VALVE AND AIR SUCTION CUT-OFF DIAPHRAGM VALVE	㊹	STARTER RELAY
㉑ EGR VALVE	㊺	IGNITION SWITCH
㉒ CATALYTIC CONVERTER	㊻	DIODE
㉓ INTAKE AIR CONTROL DIAPHRAGM	㊼	CONDENSATION CHAMBER
㉔ CHECK VALVE FOR INTAKE AIR TEMPERATURE CONTROL	㊽	POWER VALVE

1983 HONDA ACCORD

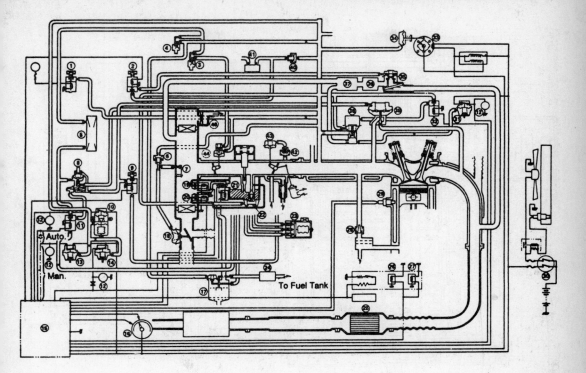

To Fuel Tank

1. Cranking Leak Solenoid Valve
2. Air Suction Control Solenoid Valve
3. Thermovalve A
4. Thermovalve B
5. Air Filter
6. Check Valve
   (Intake Air Control)
7. Air Bleed Valve
8. EGR Control Valves A & B
9. EGR Control Solenoid Valve A
10. Control Switch
11. EGR Control Solenoid Valve B
12. Auxiliary Coil
13. Vacuum Switch A
    (Manual: Main Air Jet)
    (Automatic: EGR)
14. Vacuum Switch B (Main Air Jet)
    (Federal & High Altitude)
15. Control Unit
16. Speed Sensor
17. Canister
18. Intake Air Control Diaphragm
19. Inner Vent Solenoid Valve
20. Main Air Jet Solenoid Valve
21. Air Vent Cut-Off Solenoid Valve
22. Power Valve
23. Air Jet Controller
    (Calif. & High Altitude)

24. 2-Way Valve
25. Catalytic Converter
26. Auxiliary Slow Mixture
    Cut-Off Solenoid Valve
27. Primary Slow Mixture
    Cut-Off Solenoid Valve
28. PCV Valve
29. Thermister
30. Ignition Switch
31. Vacuum Switch (Air Suction)
32. Anti-Afterburn Control
    Solenoid Valve
33. Distributor
34. Distributor Vacuum Advance
35. Air Suction Valve & Air
    Suction Cut-Off Diaphragm Valve
36. Air Chamber "A"
37. Air Chamber "B"
38. EGR Valve
39. Anti-Afterburn Valve
40. Check Valve
41. Vacuum Tank
42. Dashpot Check Valve
43. Throttle Opener
44. Choke Opener
45. Blow-By Filter

1983 HONDA PRELUDE

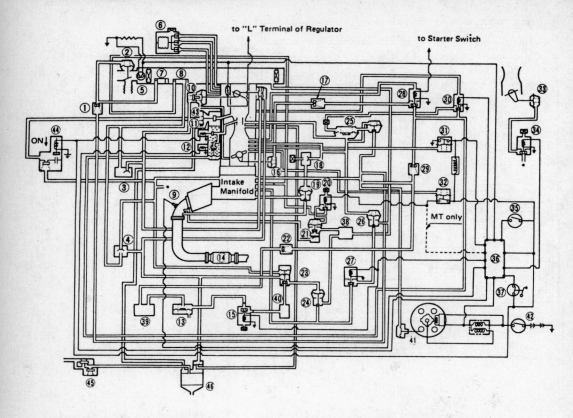

to "L" Terminal of Regulator

to Starter Switch

ON

MT only

Intake Manifold

①	CHECK VALVE (INTAKE AIR TEMP.)	㉔	AIR CONTROL VALVE B
②	AIR CONTROL DIAPHRAGM	㉕	EGR CONTROL VALVES A AND B
③	THERMOVALVE B	㉖	AIR CONTROL VALVE A
④	THERMOVALVE A	㉗	FREQUENCY SOLENOID VALVE A
⑤	INTAKE AIR TEMPERATURE SENSOR	㉘	CRANKING OPENER SOLENOID VALVE
⑥	AIR JET CONTROLLER (CAL AND HI ALT ONLY)	㉙	CHECK VALVE A
⑦	AIR BLEED VALVE	㉚	POWER VALVE CONTROL SOLENOID VALVE
⑧	AIR BLEED VALVE A	㉛	VACUUM SWITCH A
⑨	OXYGEN SENSOR	㉜	VACUUM SWITCH B
⑩	CHOKE OPENER	㉝	IDLE CONTROLLER
⑪	PRIMARY MAIN FUEL CUT-OFF SOLENOID VALVE	㉞	IDLE CONTROL SOLENOID VALVE
⑫	PRIMARY SLOW MIXTURE CUT-OFF SOLENOID VALVE	㉟	SPEED SENSOR
⑬	CONSTANT VACUUM VALVE	㊱	CONTROL UNIT
⑭	CATALYTIC CONVERTER	㊲	CLUTCH SWITCH FOR MANUAL
⑮	FREQUENCY SOLENOID VALVE B		NEUTRAL SWITCH FOR AUTOMATIC
⑯	THROTTLE CONTROLLER	㊳	AIR CHAMBER
⑰	DASHPOT CHECK VALVE	㊴	SURGE TANK A
⑱	THERMOVALVE C	㊵	SURGE TANK B
⑲	EGR VALVE	㊶	DISTRIBUTOR
⑳	AIR SUCTION CONTROL SOLENOID VALVE	㊷	IGNITION SWITCH
㉑	AIR SUCTION VALVE	㊸	AIR VENT CUT OFF DIAPHRAGM
㉒	CHECK VALVE B	㊹	VACUUM HOLDING SOLENOID VALVE
㉓	VACUUM CONTROL VALVE	㊺	TWO-WAY VALVE
		㊻	CHARCOAL CANISTER

1984 HONDA ACCORD

1300 4-SPEED

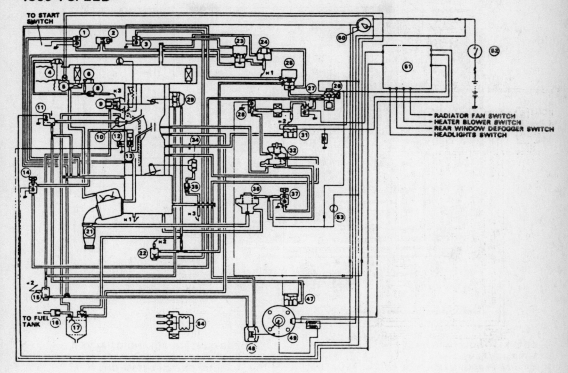

RADIATOR FAN SWITCH
HEATER BLOWER SWITCH
REAR WINDOW DEFOGGER SWITCH
HEADLIGHTS SWITCH

1300 5-SPEED

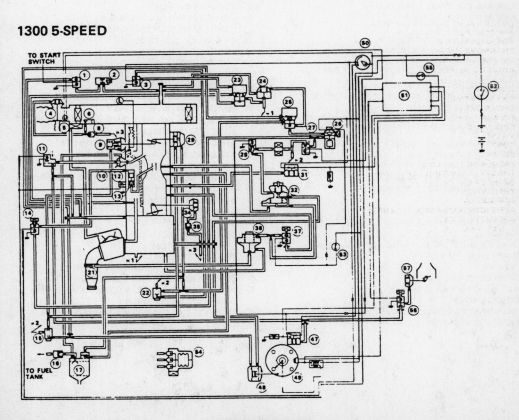

1984 HONDA CIVIC

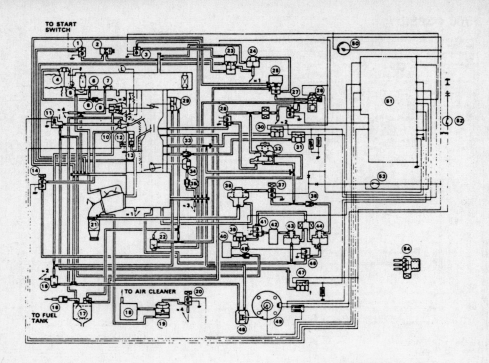

① CRANKING SOLENOID VALVE
② THERMOVALVE C
③ ANTI-AFTERBURN CONTROL SOLENOID VALVE
④ INTAKE AIR CONTROL DIAPHRAGM
⑤ INTAKE AIR TEMP. SENSOR
⑥ AIR BLEED VALVE A
⑦ AIR BLEED VALVE B (1500 ONLY)
⑧ CHECK VALVE (INTAKE AIR TEMP. CONTROL)
⑨ CHOKE OPENER
⑩ AIR CUT-OFF DIAPHRAGM
⑪ VACUUM HOLDING SOLENOID VALVE
⑫ PRIMARY SLOW MIXTURE CUT-OFF SOLENOID
⑬ POWER VALVE
⑭ POWER VALVE CONTROL SOLENOID VALVE
⑮ THERMOVALVE B
⑯ TWO—WAY VALVE
⑰ CANISTER
⑱ AIR CHAMBER (1500 ONLY)
⑲ AIR SUCTION VALVE (1500 ONLY)
⑳ AIR SUCTION CONTROL SOLENOID VALVE
   (1500 ONLY)
㉑ CATALYTIC CONVERTER
㉒ THERMOVALVE A (except for HIALT and CAL 1500
   automatic)
   THERMOVALVE D (HI ALT and CAL 1500 automatic)
㉓ ANTI-AFTERBURN VALVE
㉔ AIR VALVE
㉕ VACUUM CONTROL VALVE
   (HI ALT and CAL 1500 automatic)
㉖ CONTROL SWITCH
㉗ AIR CONTROL SOLENOID VALVE
   (MANUAL TRANSMISSION ONLY)

㉘ EGR CONTROL SOLENOID VALVE B
㉙ FAST IDLE UNLOADER
㉚ VACUUM SWITCH C (1500 ONLY)
㉛ VACUUM SWITCH B
㉜ EGR CONTROL VALVE A & B
㉝ CHECK VALVE C (1500 ONLY)
㉞ THROTTLE CONTROLLER
㉟ DASHPOT CHECK VALVE
㊱ EGR VALVE
㊲ EGR CONTROL SOLENOID VALVE A
㊳ CHECK VALVE A (1500 ONLY)
㊴ CONSTANT VACUUM VALVE (1500 ONLY)
㊵ SURGE TANK A (1500 ONLY)
㊶ FREQUENCY SOLENOID VALVE B (1500 ONLY)
㊷ SURGE TANK B (1500 ONLY)
㊸ AIR CONTROL VALVE B (1500 ONLY)
㊹ AIR CONTROL VALVE A (1500 ONLY)
㊺ CHECK VALVE B (1500 ONLY)
㊻ FREQUENCY SOLENOID VALVE A (1500 ONLY)
㊼ VACUUM SWITCH A
㊽ DISTRIBUTOR VACUUM ADVANCE
㊾ DISTRIBUTOR
㊿ SPEED SENSOR
51 CONTROL UNIT
52 IGNITION SWITCH
53 THERMO SENSOR
54 AIR JET CONTROLLER (CAL and HI ALT)
55 CLUTCH SWITCH (1300 5-SPEED ONLY)
56 THROTTLE CONTROL SOLENOID VALVE
   (1300 5-SPEED ONLY)
57 THROTTLE CLOSER (1300 5-SPEED ONLY)

1984 HONDA CIVIC

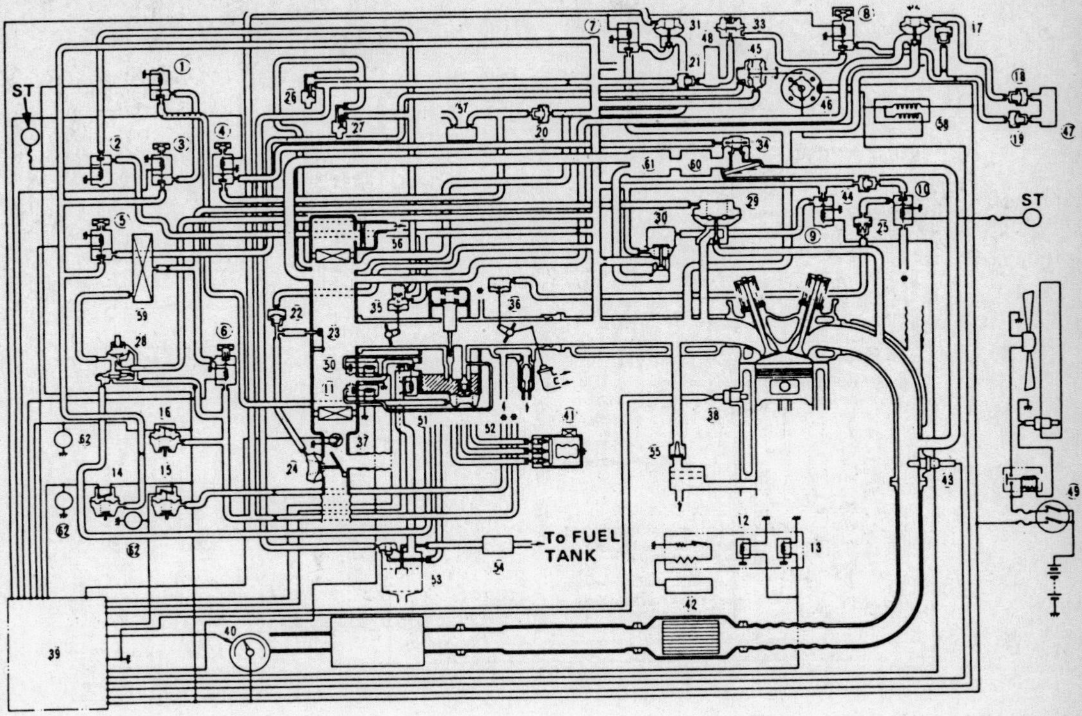

① POWER VALVE LOCK SOLENOID VALVE
② CRANKING LEAK SOLENOID VALVE
③ POWER VALVE CONTROL SOLENOID VALVE
④ AIR SUCTION CONTROL SOLENOID VALVE
⑤ VACUUM CONTROL SOLENOID VALVE
⑥ EGR CONTROL SOLENOID VALVE A
⑦ FREQUENCY SOLENOID VALVE A
⑧ FREQUENCY SOLENOID VALVE B
⑨ ANTI-AFTERBURN CONTROL SOLENOID VALVE
⑩ CRANKING OPENER SOLENOID VALVE
⑪ MAIN AIR JET CONTROL SOLENOID VALVE
⑫ RIGHT PRIMARY SLOW MIXTURE CUT-OFF SOLENOID VALVE
⑬ LEFT PRIMARY SLOW MIXTURE CUT-OFF SOLENOID VALVE
⑭ VACUUM SWITCH A
⑮ VACUUM SWITCH B
⑯ VACUUM SWITCH C
⑰ CHECK VALVE A
⑱ CHECK VALVE B
⑲ CHECK VALVE C
⑳ CHECK VALVE F
㉑ CHECK VALVE E
㉒ CHECK VALVE (INTAKE AIR TEMP.)
㉓ AIR BLEED VALVE
㉔ INTAKE AIR CONTROL DIAPHRAGM
㉕ DASHPOT CHECK VALVE
㉖ THERMOVALVE B
㉗ THERMOVALVE A
㉘ EGR CONTROL VALVES A & B
㉙ EGR VALVE
㉚ ANTI-AFTERBURN VALVE
㉛ AIR CONTROL VALVE A
㉜ AIR CONTROL VALVE B
㉝ CONSTANT VACUUM VALVE
㉞ AIR SUCTION VALVE
㉟ CHOKE OPENER
㊱ THROTTLE CONTROLLER
㊲ INTAKE AIR TEMPERATURE SWITCH
㊳ THERMOSENSOR
㊴ CONTROL UNIT
㊵ SPEED SENSOR
㊶ AIR JET CONTROLLER
㊷ CATALYTIC CONVERTER
㊸ OXYGEN SENSOR
㊹ CHECK VALVE D
㊺ DISTRIBUTOR VACUUM ADVANCE
㊻ DISTRIBUTOR
㊼ SURGE TANK A
㊽ SURGE TANK B
㊾ IGNITION SWITCH
㊿ INNER VENT SOLENOID VALVE
(51) AIR VENT CUT-OFF SOLENOID VALVE
(52) POWER VALVE
(53) CANISTER
(54) TWO-WAY VALVE
(55) PCV VALVE
(56) BLOW-BY FILTER
(57) VACUUM TANK
(58) IGNITION COIL
(59) AIR FILTER
(60) AIR CHAMBER A
(61) AIR CHAMBER B
(62) AUXILIARY COIL

1984 HONDA PRELUDE

1300

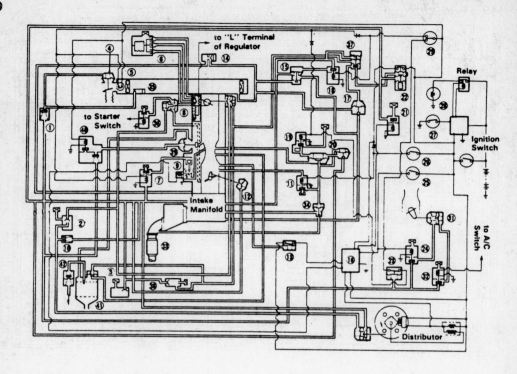

to "L" Terminal
of Regulator

to Starter
Switch

Relay

Ignition
Switch

to A/C
Switch

Intake
Manifold

Distributor

1500 except HF

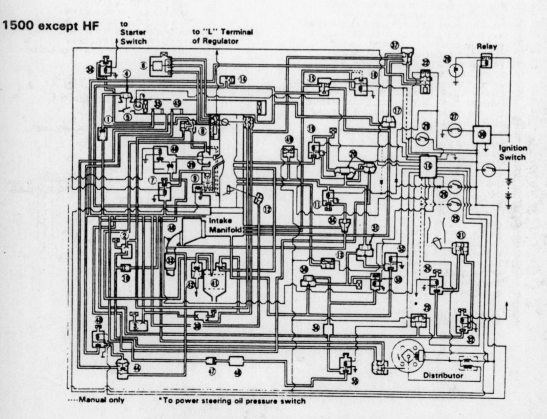

to
Starter
Switch

to "L" Terminal
of Regulator

Relay

Ignition
Switch

Intake
Manifold

Distributor

----Manual only   *To power steering oil pressure switch

Vacuum and electrical connections—1985 Civic

49 ST 1500HF

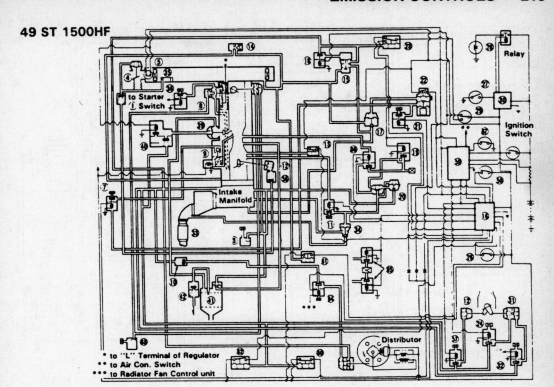

* to "L" Terminal of Regulator
* to Air Con. Switch
* to Radiator Fan Control unit

CAL 1500HF

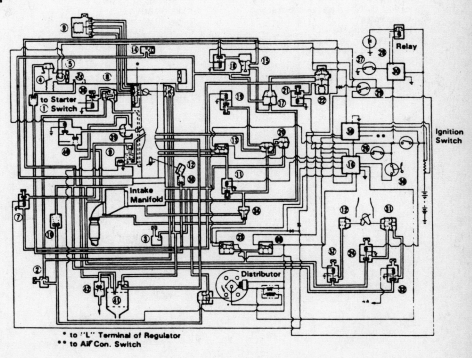

* to "L" Terminal of Regulator
* to Air Con. Switch

Vacuum and electrical connections – 1985 Civic

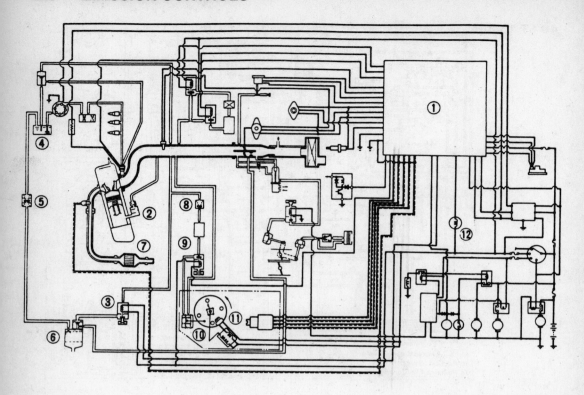

1. ELECTRONIC CONTROL UNIT
2. PCV VALVE
3. PURGE CUT-OFF SOLENOID VALVE
4. FUEL TANK
5. TWO-WAY VALVE
6. CHARCOAL CANISTER
7. CATALYTIC CONVERTER
8. CHECK VALVE
9. COLD ADVANCE SOLENOID VALVE
10. VACUUM CONTROLLER
11. DISTRIBUTOR
12. PGM-FI WARNING LIGHT

Vacuum and electrical connections — 1985 Civic CRX Si

HI ALT 1500HF

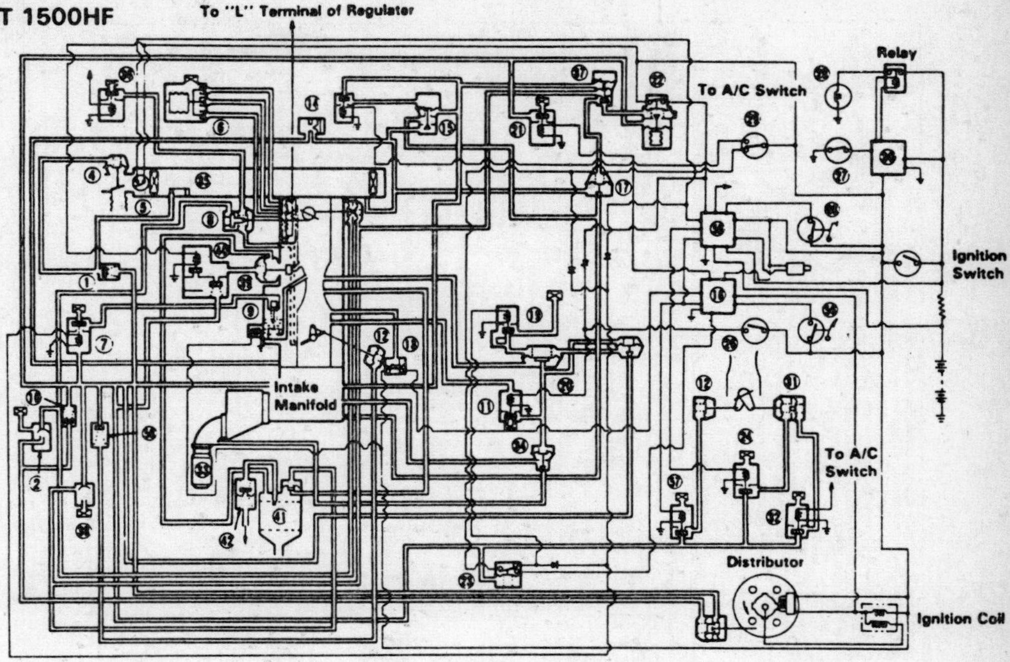
To "L" Terminal of Regulater
Relay
To A/C Switch
Ignition Switch
Intake Manifold
To A/C Switch
Distributor
Ignition Coil

① CHECK VALVE (INTAKE AIR TEMP. CONTROL)
② THERMOVALVE B (Except 49 ST 1500HF)
③ THERMOVALVE A (Except HI ALT 1300/1500HF and 49 ST/HI ALT 1500 Manual except HF)
④ AIR CONTROL DIAPHRAGM
⑤ INTAKE AIR TEMP. SENSOR
⑥ AIR JET CONTROLLER (Except 49 ST 1300/1500HF)
⑦ POWER VALVE CONTROL SOLENOID VALVE
⑧ CHOKE OPENER
⑨ PRIMARY SLOW MIXTURE CUT-OFF SOLENOID VALVE
⑩ CHECK VALVE E
⑪ EGR CONTROL SOLENOID VALVE A
⑫ THROTTLE CONTROLLER
⑬ VACUUM SWITCH A
⑭ THERMOVALVE C
⑮ ANTI-AFTERBURN VALVE
⑯ CONTROL UNIT
⑰ AIR VALVE
⑱ ANTI-AFTERBURN CONTROL SOLENOID VALVE
⑲ EGR CONTROL SOLENOID VALVE B (Except 1500 Manual except HF)
⑳ EGR CONTROL VALVES A & B
㉑ AIR CONTROL SOLENOID VALVE (1300 and 1500HF)
㉒ CONTROL SWITCH
㉓ VACUUM SWITCH B
㉔ IDLE BOOST SOLENOID VALVE (Except 1500 Automatic without power steering)
㉕ THERMOSENSOR A (Except 1500HF and Automatic)
㉖ THERMOSENSOR B
㉗ AIR TEMP. SENSOR
㉘ RADIATOR FAN
㉙ SPEED SENSOR
㉚ RADIATOR FAN TIMER
㉛ IDLE CONTROLLER
㉜ IDLE CONTROL SOLENOID VALVE
㉝ CATALYTIC CONVERTER
㉞ EGR VALVE
㉟ AIR BLEED VALVE A
㊱ CRANKING LEAK SOLENOID VALVE
㊲ VACUUM CONTROL VALVE (HT ALT 1300/1500HF and 49 ST/HI ALT 1500 Manual except HF)
㊳ THERMOVALVE D (HT ALT 1300/1500HF and 49 ST/ HI ALT 1500 Manual except HF)
㊴ AIR VENT CUT-OFF DIAPHRAGM
㊵ VACUUM HOLDING SOLENOID VALVE
㊶ CHARCOAL CANISTER
㊷ TWO-WAY VALVE
㊸ *AIR SUCTION CONTROL SOLENOID VALVE
㊹ *AIR CONTROL VALVE
㊺ *AIR BLEED VALVE B
㊻ *OXYGEN SENSOR
㊼ *CHECK VALVE B
㊽ *SURGE TANK A
㊾ *VACUUM SWITCH C
㊿ *AIR CONTROL VALVE B
(51) *AIR CONTROL VALVE A
(52) *FREQUENCY SOLENOID VALVE A
(53) *FEEDBACK CONTROL SOLENOID VALVE
(54) *SURGE TANK B
(55) *FREQUENCY SOLENOID VALVE B
(56) CLUTCH SWITCH (1500HF)
(57) THROTTLE CONTROL SOLENOID VALVE (1500HF)
(58) DASHPOT CHECK VALVE (1500HF)
(59) ALTERNATOR CONTROL UNIT (1500HF)
(60) VACUUM SWITCH D (49 ST/CAL 1500HF)
(61) VACUUM SWITCH E (49 ST 1500HF)
(62) VACUUM SWITCH F (49 ST 1500HF)
(63) THERMOVALVE E (49 ST 1500HF)
(64) COLD ADVANCE SOLENOID VALVE (49 ST 1500HF)
(65) PRIMARY AIR CUT-OFF SOLENOID VALVE (49 ST 1500HF)
(66) EGR CONTROL SOLENOID VALVE C (49 ST 1500HF)
(67) STEERING SWITCH (49 ST 1500HF)
(68) BRAKE SWITCH (HI ALT 1500HF)

*1500 except HF

Vacuum and electrical connections—1985 Civic

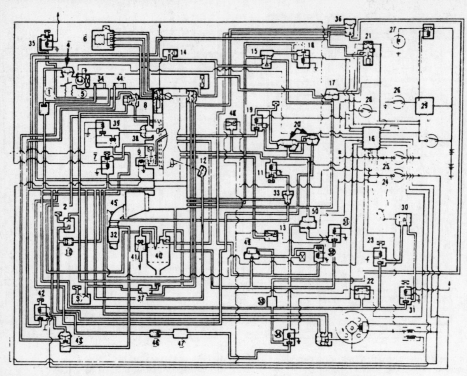

1. CHECK VALVE (INTAKE AIR TEMP. CONTROL)
2. THERMOVALVE B
3. THERMOVALVE A
4. AIR CONTROL DIAPHRAGM
5. INTAKE AIR TEMP. SENSOR
6. AIR JET CONTROLLER
7. POWER VALVE CONTROL SOLENOID VALVE
8. CHOKE OPENER
9. PRIMARY SLOW MIXTURE CUT-OFF SOLENOID VALVE
10. CHECK VALVE E
11. EGR CONTROL SOLENOID VALVE A
12. THROTTLE CONTROLLER
13. VACUUM SWITCH A
14. THERMOVALVE C
15. ANTI-AFTERBURN VALVE
16. CONTROL UNIT
17. AIR VALVE
18. ANTI-AFTERBURN CONTROL SOLENOID VALVE
19. EGR CONTROL SOLENOID VALVE C
20. EGR CONTROL VALVES A & B
21. CONTROL SWITCH
22. VACUUM SWITCH B
23. IDLE BOOST SOLENOID VALVE
24. THERMOSENSOR A
25. THERMOSENSOR B
26. AIR TEMP. SENSOR
27. RADIATOR FAN

28. SPEED SENSOR
29. RADIATOR FAN TIMER
30. IDLE CONTROLLER
31. IDLE CONTROL SOLENOID VALVE
32. CATALYTIC CONVERTER
33. EGR VALVE
34. AIR BLEED VALVE A
35. CRANKING LEAK SOLENOID VALVE
36. VACUUM CONTROL VALVE (49ST/HI ALT)
37. THERMOVALVE D (49ST/HI ALT)
38. AIR VENT CUT-OFF DIAPHRAGM
39. VACUUM HOLDING SOLENOID VALVE
40. CHARCOAL CANISTER
41. TWO-WAY VALVE
42. AIR SUCTION CONTROL SOLENOID VALVE
43. AIR CONTROL VALVE
44. AIR BLEED VALVE B
45. OXYGEN SENSOR
46. CHECK VALVE B
47. SURGE TANK A
48. VACUUM SWITCH C
49. AIR CONTROL VALVE B
50. AIR CONTROL VALVE A
51. FREQUENCY SOLENOID VALVE A
52. FEEDBACK CONTROL SOLENOID VALVE
53. SURGE TANK B
54. FREQUENCY SOLENOID VALVE B

Vacuum and electrical connections—1985 Civic Wagon 4WD

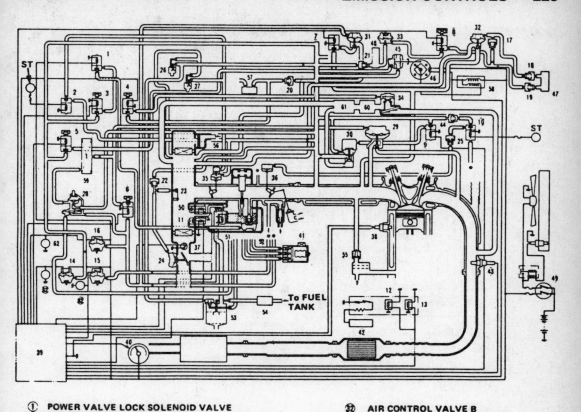

①	POWER VALVE LOCK SOLENOID VALVE	㉜	AIR CONTROL VALVE B
②	CRANKING LEAK SOLENOID VALVE	㉝	CONSTANT VACUUM VALVE
③	POWER VALVE CONTROL SOLENOID VALVE	㉞	AIR SUCTION VALVE
④	AIR SUCTION CONTROL SOLENOID VALVE	㉟	CHOKE OPENER
⑤	VACUUM CONTROL SOLENOID VALVE	㊱	THROTTLE CONTROLLER
⑥	EGR CONTROL SOLENOID VALVE A	㊲	INTAKE AIR TEMPERATURE SWITCH
⑦	FREQUENCY SOLENOID VALVE A	㊳	THERMOSENSOR
⑧	FREQUENCY SOLENOID VALVE B	㊴	CONTROL UNIT
⑨	ANTI-AFTERBURN CONTROL SOLENOID VALVE	㊵	SPEED SENSOR
⑩	CRANKING OPENER SOLENOID VALVE	㊶	AIR JET CONTROLLER
⑪	MAIN AIR JET CONTROL SOLENOID VALVE	㊷	CATALYTIC CONVERTER
⑫	RIGHT PRIMARY SLOW MIXTURE CUT-OFF SOLENOID VALVE	㊸	OXYGEN SENSOR
⑬	LEFT PRIMARY SLOW MIXTURE CUT-OFF SOLENOID VALVE	㊹	CHECK VALVE D
		㊺	DISTRIBUTOR VACUUM ADVANCE
⑭	VACUUM SWITCH A	㊻	DISTRIBUTOR
⑮	VACUUM SWITCH B	㊼	SURGE TANK A
⑯	VACUUM SWITCH C	㊽	SURGE TANK B
⑰	CHECK VALVE A	㊾	IGNITION SWITCH
⑱	CHECK VALVE B	㊿	INNER VENT SOLENOID VALVE
⑲	CHECK VALVE C	51	AIR VENT CUT-OFF SOLENOID VALVE
⑳	CHECK VALVE F	52	POWER VALVE
㉑	CHECK VALVE E	53	CANISTER
㉒	CHECK VALVE (INTAKE AIR TEMP.)	54	TWO-WAY VALVE
㉓	AIR BLEED VALVE	55	PCV VALVE
㉔	INTAKE AIR CONTROL DIAPHRAGM	56	BLOW-BY FILTER
㉕	DASHPOT CHECK VALVE	57	VACUUM TANK
㉖	THERMOVALVE B	58	IGNITION COIL
㉗	THERMOVALVE A	59	AIR FILTER
㉘	EGR CONTROL VALVES A & B	60	AIR CHAMBER A
㉙	EGR VALVE	61	AIR CHAMBER B
㉚	ANTI-AFTERBURN VALVE	62	AUXILIARY COIL
㉛	AIR CONTROL VALVE A		

Vacuum and electrical connections—1985 Prelude

1300 (49ST and CAL)

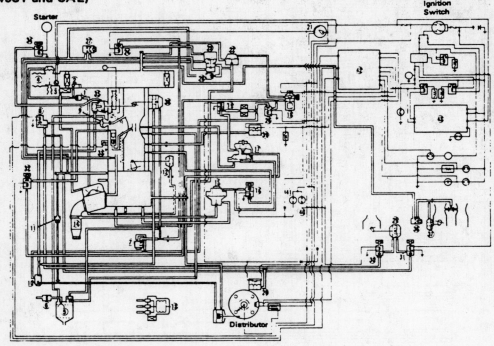

①	CHECK VALVE (INTAKE AIR TEMP.)	㉓	ANTI-AFTERBURN VALVE
②	AIR BLEED VALVE	㉔	ANTI-AFTERBURN CONTROL SOLENOID VALVE
③	INTAKE AIR TEMP. SENSOR	㉕	VACUUM CONTROL VALVE (HI ALT)
④	AIR CONTROL DIAPHRAGM	㉖	AIR CONTROL SOLENOID VALVE
⑤	CHARCOAL CANISTER	㉗	THERMOVALVE C
⑥	TWO-WAY VALVE	㉘	CHECK VALVE G
⑦	THERMOVALVE A	㉙	IDLE CONTROLLER
⑧	VACUUM HOLDING SOLENOID VALVE	㉚	IDLE BOOST SOLENOID VALVE
⑨	AIR VENT CUT-OFF DIAPRAGM	㉛	A/C IDLE BOOST SOLENOID VALVE
⑩	THERMOVALVE B	㉜	POWER VALVE CONTROL SOLENOID VALVE
⑪	CHECK VALVE E	㉝	PRIMARY SLOW MIXTURE CUT-OFF SOLENOID VALVE
⑫	THROTTLE CONTROLLER	㉞	CRANKING LEAK SOLENOID VALVE
⑬	AIR JET CONTROLLER (Except CAL)	㉟	CHOKE OPENER
⑭	CATALYTIC CONVERTER	㊱	THERMOVALVE D
⑮	EGR VALVE	㊲	SECONDARY DIAPHRAGM
⑯	EGR CONTROL SOLENOID VALVE A	㊳	FAST IDLE UNLOADER
⑰	EGR CONTROL VALVE A & B	㊴	VACUUM SWITCH A
⑱	CONTROL SWITCH	㊵	THERMOSENSOR A
⑲	EGR CONTROL SOLENOID VALVE B	㊶	THERMOSENSOR B
⑳	VACUUM SWITCH B	㊷	DEVICE CONTROL UNIT A
㉑	SPEED SENSOR	㊸	RADIATOR FAN TIMER
㉒	AIR VALVE		

Vacuum and electrical connections – 1986 Civic

1500 M/T (49 ST / HI ALT)

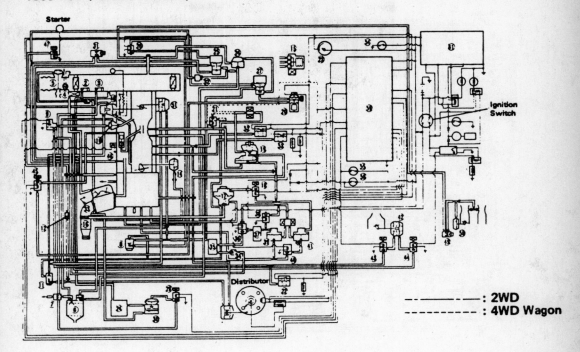

1500 M/T (CAL)

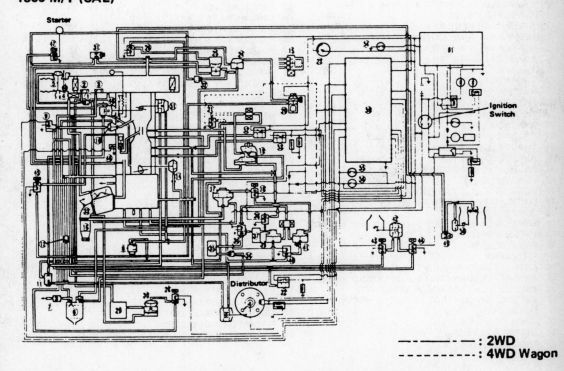

Vacuum and electrical connections—1986 Civic

1500 A/T

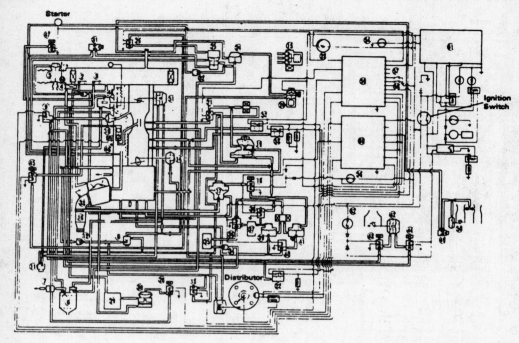

① CHECK VALVE (INTAKE AIR TEMP.)	㉝ OXYGEN SENSOR
② AIR BLEED VALVE A	㉞ CHECK VALVE A
③ AIR BLEED VALVE B	㉟ ACCUMULATOR
④ INTAKE AIR TEMP. SENSOR	㊱ FREQUENCY SOLENOID VALVE B
⑤ AIR CONTROL DIAPHRAGM	㊲ PULSE RECTIFIER
⑥ CHARCOAL CANISTER	㊳ FEEDBACK CONTROL SOLENOID VALVE
⑦ TWO-WAY VALVE	㊴ AIR CONTROL VALVE
⑧ THERMOVALVE A	㊵ FREQUENCY SOLENOID VALVE A
⑨ VACUUM HOLDING SOLENOID VALVE	㊶ AIR CONTROL VALVE A
⑩ AIR VENT CUT-OFF DIAPHRAGM	㊷ IDLE CONTROLLER
⑪ THERMOVALVE B	㊸ IDLE BOOST SOLENOID VALVE
⑫ CHECK VALVE E	(M/T and A/T with power steering)
⑬ COLD ADVANCE SOLENOID VALVE (A/T)	㊹ A/C IDLE BOOST SOLENOID VALVE
⑭ THROTTLE CONTROLLER	㊺ POWER VALVE CONTROL SOLENOID VALVE
⑮ AIR JET CONTROLLER	㊻ PRIMARY SLOW MIXTURE CUT-OFF SOLENOID VALVE
⑯ CATALYTIC CONVERTER	㊼ CRANKING LEAK SOLENOID VALVE
⑰ EGR VALVE	㊽ CHOKE OPENER
⑱ EGR CONTROL SOLENOID VALVE A	㊾ THERMOVALVE D
⑲ EGR CONTROL VALVE A & B	㊿ SECONDARY DIAPHRAGM
⑳ CONTROL SWITCH	�51 FAST IDLE UNLOADER
㉑ EGR CONTROL SOLENOID VALVE C (A/T & 4WD)	�52 VACUUM SWITCH C
㉒ VACUUM SWITCH B	�53 VACUUM SWITCH A
㉓ SPEED SENSOR	�54 AIR TEMP. SENSOR
㉔ AIR VALVE	�55 THERMOSNESOR A
㉕ ANTI-AFTERBURN VALVE	�56 THERMOSENSOR B
㉖ ANTI-AFTERBURN CONTROL SOLENOID VALVE	�57 NEUTRAL SWITCH (A/T)
㉗ VACUUM CONTROL VALVE (49 ST-M/T)	�58 PARKING SWITCH (A/T)
㉘ AIR SUCTION CONTROL SOLENOID VALVE	�59 DEVICE CONTROL UNIT A
㉙ SILENCER	�60 DEVICE CONTROL UNIT B (A/T)
㉚ AIR SUCTION VALVE	�61 RADIATOR FAN TIMER
㉛ THERMOVALVE C	�62 POWER STEERING OIL PRESSURE SWITCH
㉜ CHECK VALVE G	

Vacuum and electrical connections – 1986 Civic

HF (49 ST)

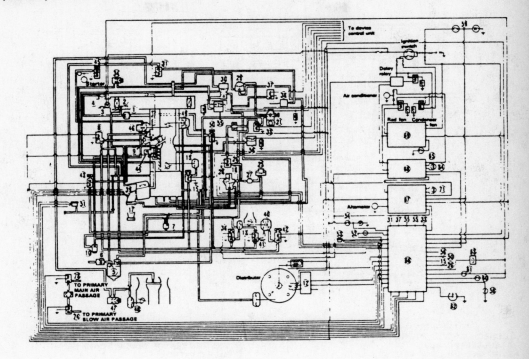

HF (CAL)

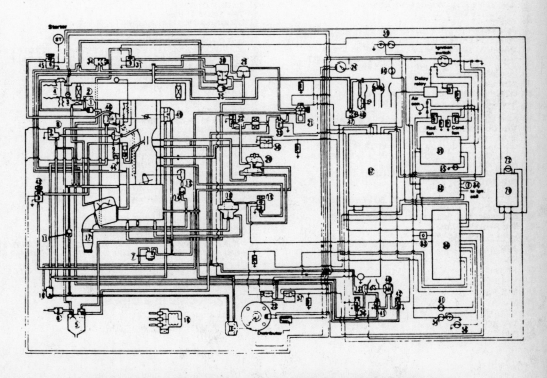

Vacuum and electrical connections—1986 Civic Si & CRX Si

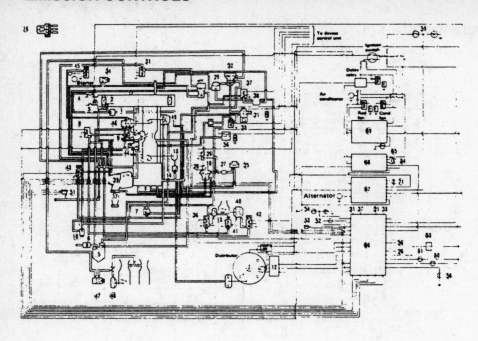

1. CHECK VALVE (INTAKE AIR TEMP.)
2. AIR BLEED VALVE
3. INTAKE AIR TEMP. SENSOR A
4. AIR CONTROL DIAPHRAGM
5. CHARCOAL CANISTER
6. TWO-WAY VALVE
7. THERMOVALVE A
8. VACUUM HOLDING SOLENOID VALVE
9. AIR VENT CUT-OFF DIAPHRAGM
10. THERMOVALVE B
11. CHECK VALVE E
12. IGNITION TIMING CONTROL UNIT (EXCEPT CAL)
13. THROTTLE CONTROLLER
14. DASHPOT CHECK VALVE (EXCEPT 49 ST)
15. DASHPOT CONTROL SOLENOID VALVE (49 ST)
16. AIR JET CONTROLLER (EXCEPT 49 ST)
17. CATALYTIC CONVERTER
18. EGR VALVE
19. EGR CONTROL SOLENOID VALVE A (CAL)
20. EGR CONTROL VALVES A & B (CAL)
21. CONTROL SWITCH
22. EGR CONTROL SOLENOID VALVE B (CAL)
23. VACUUM SWITCH F (CAL)
24. SPEED SENSOR (CAL)
25. CONSTANT VACUUM GENERATOR (EXCEPT CAL)
26. FREQUENCY SOLENOID VALVE B (EXCEPT CAL)
27. ACCUMULATOR (EXCEPT CAL)
28. EGR VALVE LIFT SENSOR (EXCEPT CAL)
29. AIR VALVE
30. ANTI-AFTERBURN VALVE
31. ANTI-AFTERBURN CONTROL SOLENOID VALVE
32. VACUUM CONTROL VALVE (HI ALT)
33. AIR CONTROL SOLENOID VALVE
34. THERMOVALVE C
35. CHECK VALVE G (CAL)
36. THROTTLE CONTROL SOLENOID VALVE
37. FREQUENCY SOLENOID VALVE A (EXCEPT CAL)
38. AIR CHAMBER (EXCEPT CAL)
39. OXYGEN SENSOR (EXCEPT CAL)
40. IDLE CONTROLLER
41. IDLE BOOST SOLENOID VALVE
42. A/C IDLE BOOST SOLENOID VALVE
43. POWER VALVE CONTROL SOLENOID VALVE
44. PRIMARY SLOW MIXTURE CUT-OFF SOLENOID VALVE
45. CRANKING LEAK SOLENOID VALVE
46. CHOKE OPENER
47. THERMOVALVE D
48. SECONDARY DIAPHRAGM
49. FAST IDLE UNLOADER
50. UNLOADER SOLENOID VALVE (49 ST)
51. MANIFOLD ABSOLUTE PRESSURE SENSOR (EXCEPT CAL)
52. COOLANT TEMPERATURE SENSOR A (EXCEPT CAL)
53. ATMOSPHERIC PRESSURE SENSOR (EXCEPT CAL)
54. BACK-UP LIGHT SWITCH
55. VACUUM SWITCH D (49 ST)
56. VACUUM SWITCH A
57. VACUUM SWITCH E (CAL)
58. SPEED PULSER
59. BRAKE LIGHT SWITCH
60. CLUTCH SWITCH
61. NEUTRAL SWITCH
62. STEERING SWITCH (49 ST)
63. SHIFT UP INDICATOR LIGHT
64. COOLANT TEMPERATURE SENSOR B
65. INTAKE AIR TEMP. SENSOR B
66. DEVICE CONTROL UNIT
67. ALTERNATOR CONTROL UNIT
68. RADIATOR FAN CONTROL UNIT
69. RADIATOR FAN TIMER
70. THERMO CONTROL UNIT (CAL)
71. RESISTOR
72. COOLANT TEMPERATURE SENSOR C (CAL)
73. PRIMARY MAIN AIR CUT-OFF SOLENOID VALVE (49 ST)
74. PRIMARY SLOW AIR CUT-OFF SOLENOID VALVE (49 ST)

Vacuum and electrical connections—1986 Civic SI & CRX SI

Std. M/T (49 ST/HI ALT)

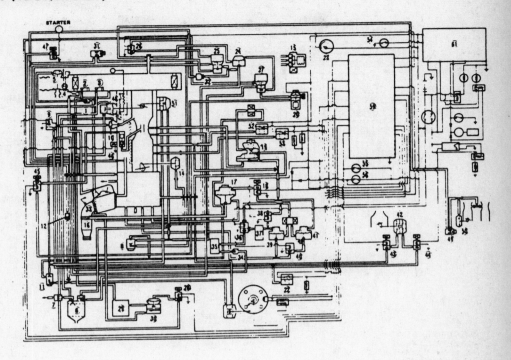

Std. M/T (CAL)

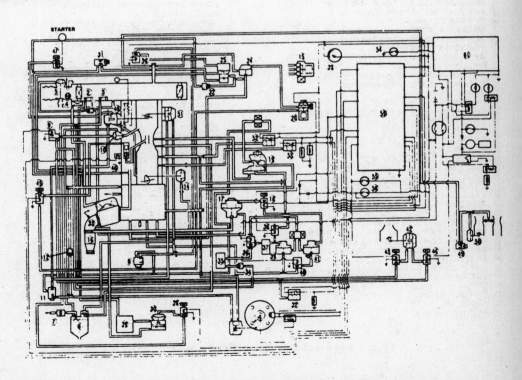

Vacuum and electrical connections — 1986 Civic Si & CRX Si

Std. A/T

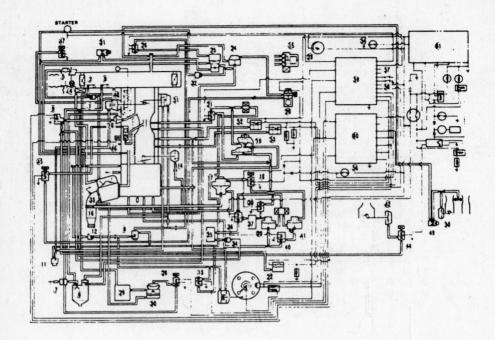

1. CHECK VALVE (INTAKE AIR TEMP.)
2. AIR BLEED VALVE A
3. AIR BLEED VALVE B
4. INTAKE AIR TEMP. SENSOR A
5. AIR CONTROL DIAPHRAGM
6. CHARCOAL CANISTER
7. TWO-WAY VALVE
8. THERMOVALVE A
9. VACUUM HOLDING SOLENOID VALVE
10. AIR VENT CUT-OFF DIAPHRAGM
11. THERMOVALVE B
12. CHECK VALVE E
13. COLD ADVANCE SOLENOID VALVE (A/T)
14. THROTTLE CONTROLLER
15. AIR JET CONTROLLER
16. CATALYTIC CONVERTER
17. EGR VALVE
18. EGR CONTROL SOLENOID VALVE A
19. EGR CONTROL VALVES A & B
20. CONTROL SWITCH
21. EGR CONTROL SOLENOID VALVE C (A/T)
22. VACUUM SWITCH B
23. SPEED SENSOR
24. AIR VALVE
25. ANTI-AFTERBURN VALVE
26. ANTI-AFTERBURN CONTROL SOLENOID VALVE
27. VACUUM CONTROL VALVE (M/T 49ST)
28. AIR SUCTION CONTROL SOLENOID VALVE
29. SILENCER
30. AIR SUCTION VALVE
31. THERMOVALVE C
32. CHECK VALVE G
33. OXYGEN SENSOR
34. CHECK VALVE A
35. ACCUMULATOR

36. FREQUENCY SOLENOID VALVE B
37. PULSE RECTIFIER
38. FEEDBACK CONTROL SOLENOID VALVE
39. AIR CONTROL VALVE B
40. FREQUENCY SOLENOID VALVE A
41. AIR CONTROL VALVE A
42. IDLE CONTROLLER
43. IDLE BOOST SOLENOID VALVE (M/T)
44. A/C IDLE BOOST SOLENOID VALVE
45. POWER VALVE CONTROL SOLENOID VALVE
46. PRIMARY SLOW MIXTURE CUT-OFF SOLENOID VALVE
47. CRANKING LEAK SOLENOID VALVE
48. CHOKE OPENER
49. THERMOVALVE D
50. SECONDARY DIAPHRAGM
51. FAST IDLE UNLOADER
52. VACUUM SWITCH C
53. VACUUM SWITCH A
54. INTAKE AIR TEMP. SENSOR B
55. THERMOSENSOR A
56. THERMOSENSOR B (M/T)
57. SHIFT POSITION SWITCH "N" (A/T)
58. SHIFT POSITION SWITCH "P" (A/T)
59. DEVICE CONTROL UNIT A
60. DEVICE CONTROL UNIT B (A/T)
61. RADIATOR FAN TIMER

Vacuum and electrical connections – 1986 Civic Si & CRX Si

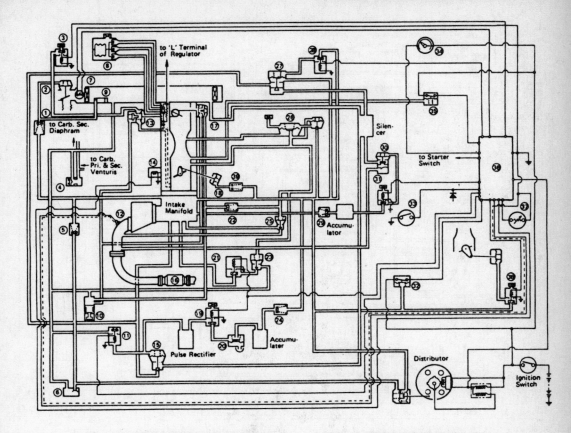

1. CHECK VALVE (INTAKE AIR TEMP. CONTROL)
2. AIR CONTROL DIAPHRAGM
3. CRANKING LEAK SOLENOID VALVE
4. THERMOVALVE C
5. CHECK VALVE E
6. THERMOVALVE B
7. INTAKE AIR TEMP. SENSOR
8. AIR JET CONTROLLER
9. AIR BLEED VALVE
10. THERMOVALVE A
11. FEEDBACK CONTROL SOLENOID VALVE
12. OXYGEN SENSOR
13. CHOKE OPENER
14. PRIMARY SLOW MIXTURE CUT-OFF
    SOLENOID VALVE
15. AIR CONTROL VALVE B
16. CONVERTER ASSY
17. FAST IDLE UNLOADER
18. THROTTLE CONTROLLER
19. FREQUENCY SOLENOID VALVE B
20. CV GENERATOR

21. FREQUENCY SOLENOID VALVE A
22. CHECK VALVE A
23. AIR CONTROL VALVE A
24. CHECK VALVE B
25. EGR VALVE
26. EGR CONTROL VALVE A&B
27. ANTI-AFTERBURN VALVE
28. ANTI-AFTERBURN CONTROL SOLENOID VALVE
29. CHECK VALVE C
30. AIR SUCTION VALVE
31. AIR SUCTION CONTROL SOLENOID VALVE
32. VACUUM SWITCH A
33. CLUTCH SWITCH
34. SPEED SENSOR
35. VACUUM SWITCH B
36. CONTROL UNIT
37. THERMOSENSOR
38. A/C IDLE BOOST SOLENOID VALVE
39. DASHPOT CHECK VALVE

Vacuum and electrical connections – 1986 Accord w/man. trans.

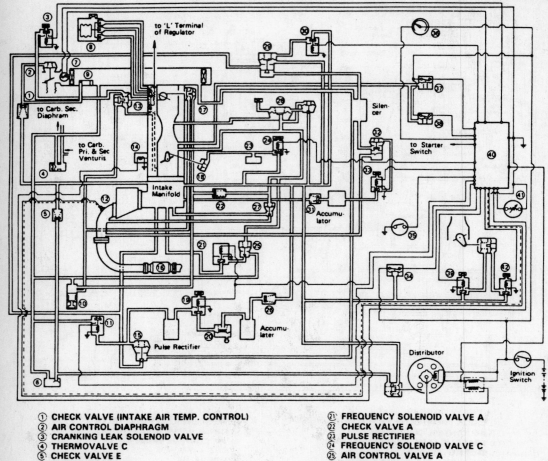

1. CHECK VALVE (INTAKE AIR TEMP. CONTROL)
2. AIR CONTROL DIAPHRAGM
3. CRANKING LEAK SOLENOID VALVE
4. THERMOVALVE C
5. CHECK VALVE E
6. THERMOVALVE B
7. INTAKE AIR TEMP. SENSOR
8. AIR JET CONTROLLER
9. AIR BLEED VALVE
10. THERMOVALVE A
11. FEEDBACK CONTROL SOLENOID VALVE
12. OXYGEN SENSOR
13. CHOKE OPENER
14. PRIMARY SLOW MIXTURE CUT-OFF
    SOLENOID VALVE
15. AIR CONTROL VALVE B
16. CONVERTER ASSY
17. FAST IDLE UNLOADER
18. THROTTLE CONTROLLER
19. FREQUENCY SOLENOID VALVE B
20. CV GENERATOR
21. FREQUENCY SOLENOID VALVE A
22. CHECK VALVE A
23. PULSE RECTIFIER
24. FREQUENCY SOLENOID VALVE C
25. AIR CONTROL VALVE A
26. CHECK VALVE B
27. EGR VALVE
28. EGR CONTROL VALVE A&B
29. ANTI-AFTERBURN VALVE
30. ANTI-AFTERBURN CONTROL SOLENOID VALVE
31. CHECK VALVE C
32. AIR SUCTION VALVE
33. AIR SUCTION CONTROL SOLENOID VALVE
34. VACUUM SWITCH A
35. SHIFT LEVER POSITION SWITCH
36. SPEED SENSOR
37. VACUUM SWITCH B
38. VACUUM SWITCH C (49 ST and HI ALT only)
39. IDLE BOOST SOLENOID VALVE
40. CONTROL UNIT
41. THERMOSENSOR
42. A/C IDLE BOOST SOLENOID VALVE

Vacuum and electrical connections — 1986 Accord w/auto. trans.

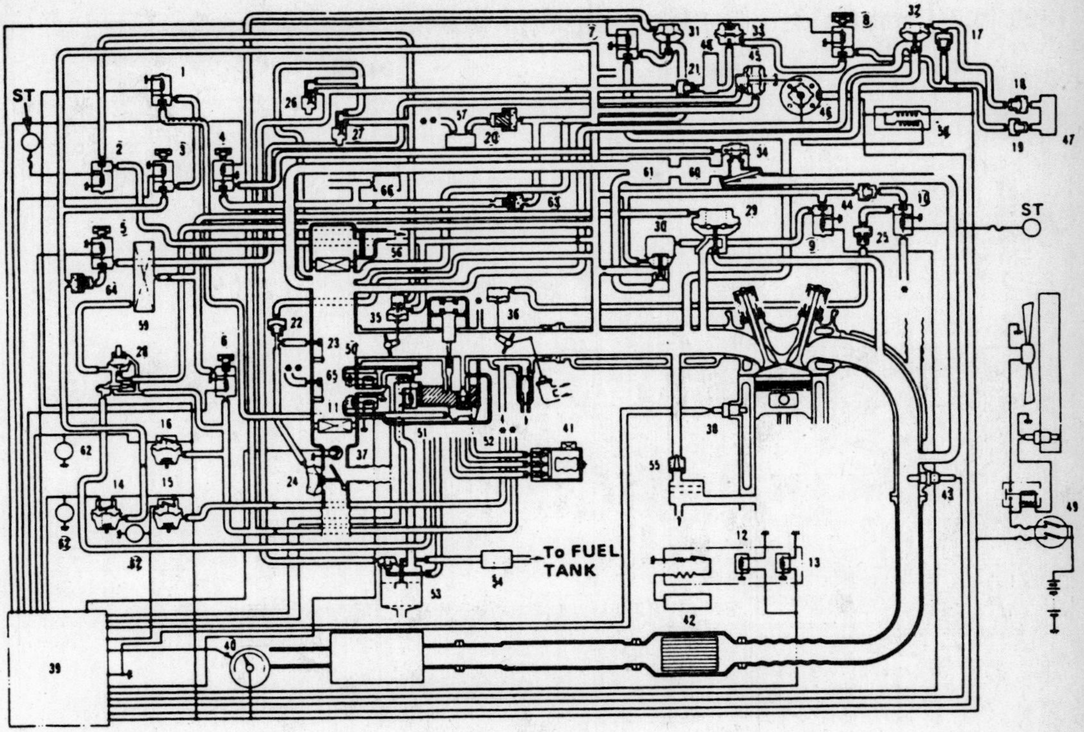

① POWER VALVE LOCK SOLENOID VALVE
② CRANKING LEAK SOLENOID VALVE
③ POWER VALVE CONTROL SOLENOID VALVE
④ AIR SUCTION CONTROL SOLENOID VALVE
⑤ VACUUM CONTROL SOLENOID VALVE
⑥ EGR CONTROL SOLENOID VALVE A
⑦ FREQUENCY SOLENOID VALVE A
⑧ FREQUENCY SOLENOID VALVE B
⑨ ANTI-AFTERBURN CONTROL SOLENOID VALVE
⑩ CRANKING OPENER SOLENOID VALVE
⑪ MAIN AIR JET CONTROL SOLENOID VALVE
⑫ RIGHT PRIMARY SLOW MIXTURE CUT-OFF SOLENOID VALVE
⑬ LEFT PRIMARY SLOW MIXTURE CUT-OFF SOLENOID VALVE
⑭ VACUUM SWITCH A
⑮ VACUUM SWITCH B
⑯ VACUUM SWITCH C
⑰ CHECK VALVE A
⑱ CHECK VALVE B
⑲ CHECK VALVE C
⑳ CHECK VALVE F
㉑ CHECK VALVE E
㉒ CHECK VALVE (INTAKE AIR TEMP.)
㉓ AIR BLEED VALVE A
㉔ INTAKE AIR CONTROL DIAPHRAGM
㉕ DASHPOT CHECK VALVE
㉖ THERMOVALVE B
㉗ THERMOVALVE A
㉘ EGR CONTROL VALVES A & B
㉙ EGR VALVE
㉚ ANTI-AFTERBURN VALVE
㉛ AIR CONTROL VALVE A
32 AIR CONTROL VALVE B
33 CONSTANT VACUUM VALVE
㉞ AIR SUCTION VALVE
㉟ CHOKE OPENER
㊱ THROTTLE CONTROLLER
㊲ INTAKE AIR TEMPERATURE SWITCH
㊳ THERMOSENSOR
㊴ CONTROL UNIT
㊵ SPEED SENSOR
㊶ AIR JET CONTROLLER
㊷ CATALYTIC CONVERTER
㊸ OXYGEN SENSOR
㊹ CHECK VALVE D
㊺ DISTRIBUTOR VACUUM ADVANCE
㊻ DISTRIBUTOR
㊼ SURGE TANK A
㊽ SURGE TANK B
㊾ IGNITION SWITCH
㊿ INNER VENT SOLENOID VALVE
(51) AIR VENT CUT-OFF SOLENOID VALVE
(52) POWER VALVE
(53) CANISTER
(54) TWO-WAY VALVE
(55) PCV VALVE
(56) BLOW-BY FILTER
(57) VACUUM TANK A
(58) IGNITION COIL
(59) AIR FILTER
(60) AIR CHAMBER A
61 AIR CHAMBER B
62 AUXILIARY COIL
(63) CHECK VALVE G
(64) CHECK VALVE H
(65) AIR BLEED VALVE B
(66) VACUUM TANK B

Vacuum and electrical connections—1986 Prelude

1300 (49ST and CAL)

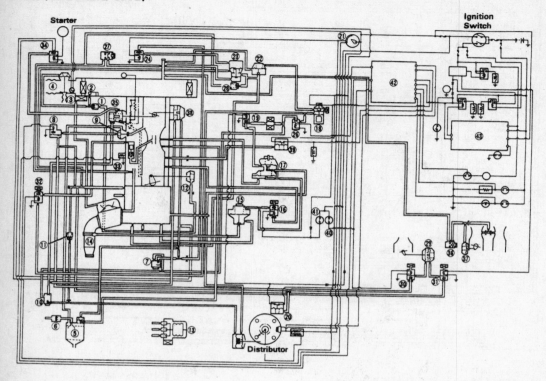

1300 (HI ALT)

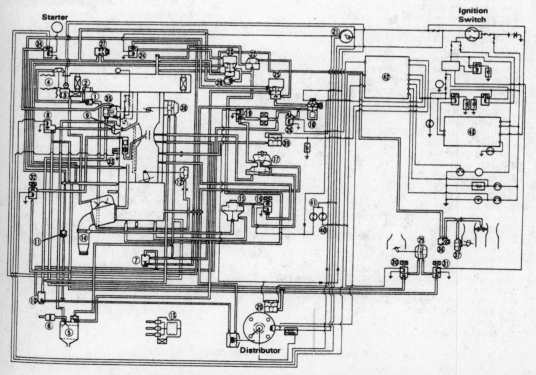

Vaccum and electrical connections—1987 Civic carbureted

① CHECK VALVE (INTAKE AIR TEMP.)
② AIR BLEED VALVE
③ INTAKE AIR TEMP. SENSOR
④ AIR CONTROL DIAPHRAGM
⑤ CHARCOAL CANISTER
⑥ TWO-WAY VALVE
⑦ THERMOVALVE A
⑧ VACUUM HOLDING SOLENOID VALVE
⑨ AIR VENT CUT-OFF DIAPHRAGM
⑩ THERMOVALVE B
⑪ CHECK VALVE E
⑫ THROTTLE CONTROLLER
⑬ AIR JET CONTROLLER (Except CAL)
⑭ CATALYTIC CONVERTER
⑮ EGR VALVE
⑯ EGR CONTROL SOLENOID VALVE A
⑰ EGR CONTROL VALVE A & B
⑱ CONTROL SWITCH
⑲ EGR CONTROL SOLENOID VALVE B
⑳ VACUUM SWITCH B
㉑ SPEED SENSOR
㉒ AIR VALVE
㉓ ANTI-AFTERBURN VALVE
㉔ ANTI-AFTERBURN CONTROL SOLENOID VALVE
㉕ VACUUM CONTROL VALVE (HI ALT)
㉖ AIR CONTROL SOLENOID VALVE
㉗ THERMOVALVE C
㉘ CHECK VALVE G
㉙ IDLE CONTROLLER
㉚ IDLE BOOST SOLENOID VALVE
㉛ A/C IDLE BOOST SOLENOID VALVE
㉜ POWER VALVE CONTROL SOLENOID VALVE
㉝ PRIMARY SLOW MIXTURE CUT-OFF SOLENOID VALVE
㉞ CRANKING LEAK SOLENOID VALVE
㉟ CHOKE OPENER
㊱ THERMOVALVE D
㊲ SECONDARY DIAPHRAGM
㊳ FAST IDLE UNLOADER
㊴ VACUUM SWITCH A
㊵ THERMOSENSOR A
㊶ THERMOSENSOR B
㊷ DEVICE CONTROL UNIT A
㊸ RADIATOR FAN TIMER

Vacuum and electrical connections—1987 Civic carbureted

1500 M/T (49 ST / HI ALT)

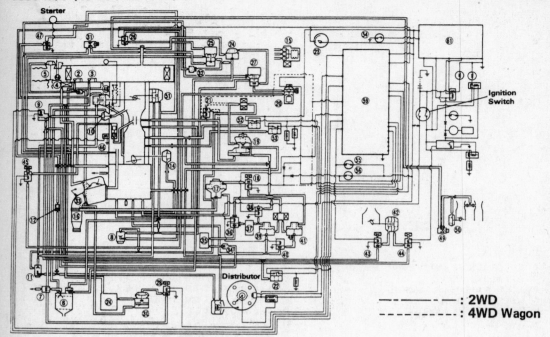

1500 M/T (CAL)

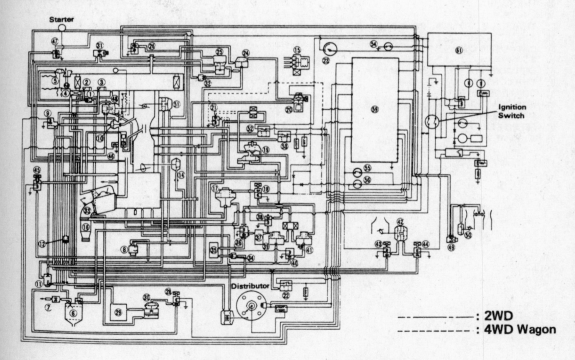

Vacuum and electrical connections—1987 Civic carbureted

1500 A/T

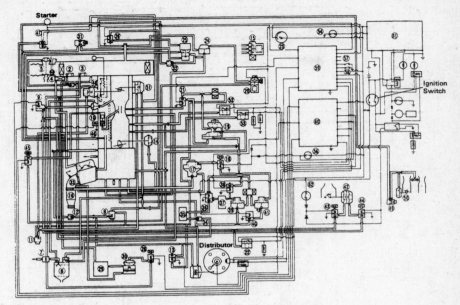

① CHECK VALVE (INTAKE AIR TEMP.)
② AIR BLEED VALVE A
③ AIR BLEED VALVE B
④ INTAKE AIR TEMP. SENSOR
⑤ AIR CONTROL DIAPHRAGM
⑥ CHARCOAL CANISTER
⑦ TWO-WAY VALVE
⑧ THERMOVALVE A
⑨ VACUUM HOLDING SOLENOID VALVE
⑩ AIR VENT CUT-OFF DIAPHRAGM
⑪ THERMOVALVE B
⑫ CHECK VALVE E
⑬ COLD ADVANCE SOLENOID VALVE (A/T)
⑭ THROTTLE CONTROLLER
⑮ AIR JET CONTROLLER
⑯ CATALYTIC CONVERTER
⑰ EGR VALVE
⑱ EGR CONTROL SOLENOID VALVE A
⑲ EGR CONTROL VALVE A & B
⑳ CONTROL SWITCH
㉑ EGR CONTROL SOLENOID VALVE C (A/T & 4WD)
㉒ VACUUM SWITCH B
㉓ SPEED SENSOR
㉔ AIR VALVE
㉕ ANTI-AFTERBURN VALVE
㉖ ANTI-AFTERBURN CONTROL SOLENOID VALVE
㉗ VACUUM CONTROL VALVE (49 ST-M/T)
㉘ AIR SUCTION CONTROL SOLENOID VALVE
㉙ SILENCER
㉚ AIR SUCTION VALVE
㉛ THERMOVALVE C
㉜ CHECK VALVE G

㉝ OXYGEN SENSOR
㉞ CHECK VALVE A
㉟ ACCUMULATOR
㊱ FREQUENCY SOLENOID VALVE B
㊲ PULSE RECTIFIER
㊳ FEEDBACK CONTROL SOLENOID VALVE
㊴ AIR CONTROL VALVE B
㊵ FREQUENCY SOLENOID VALVE A
㊶ AIR CONTROL VALVE A
㊷ IDLE CONTROLLER
㊸ IDLE BOOST SOLENOID VALVE
   (M/T and A/T with power steering)
㊹ A/C IDLE BOOST SOLENOID VALVE
㊺ POWER VALVE CONTROL SOLENOID VALVE
㊻ PRIMARY SLOW MIXTURE CUT-OFF SOLENOID VALVE
㊼ CRANKING LEAK SOLENOID VALVE
㊽ CHOKE OPENER
㊾ THERMOVALVE D
㊿ SECONDARY DIAPHRAGM
51 FAST IDLE UNLOADER
52 VACUUM SWITCH C
53 VACUUM SWITCH A
54 AIR TEMP. SENSOR
55 THERMOSNESOR A
56 THERMOSENSOR B
57 NEUTRAL SWITCH (A/T)
58 PARKING SWITCH (A/T)
59 DEVICE CONTROL UNIT A
60 DEVICE CONTROL UNIT B (A/T)
61 RADIATOR FAN TIMER
62 POWER STEERING OIL PRESSURE SWITCH

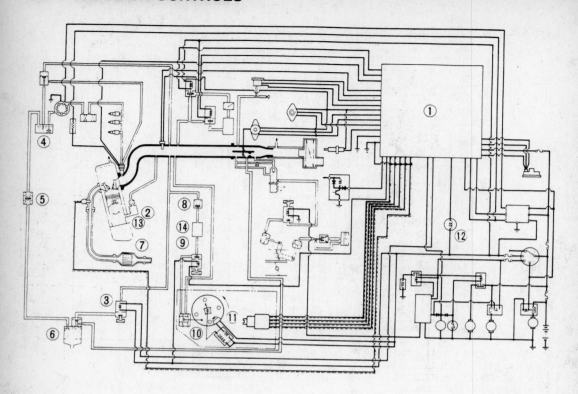

1 ECU (Electronic Control Unit)
2 PCV VALVE
3 PURGE CUT-OFF SOLENOID VALVE
4 FUEL TANK
5 TWO-WAY VALVE
6 CHARCOAL CANISTER
7 CATALYTIC CONVERTER
8 CHECK VALVE
9 IGNITION CONTROL SOLENOID VALVE
10 VACUUM ADVANCE DIAPHRAGM
11 DISTRIBUTOR
12 PGM-FI WARNING LIGHT
13 BREATHER CHAMBER
14 VACUUM TANK

Vacuum and electrical connections—1987 Civic w/PGM-FI

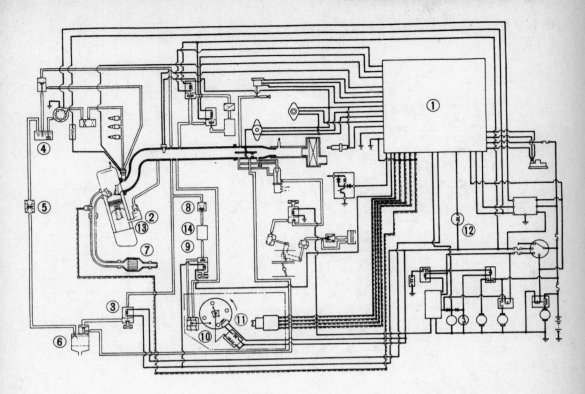

1 ECU (Electronic Control Unit)
2 PCV VALVE
3 PURGE CUT-OFF SOLENOID VALVE
4 FUEL TANK
5 TWO-WAY VALVE
6 CHARCOAL CANISTER
7 CATALYTIC CONVERTER
8 CHECK VALVE

9 IGNITION CONTROL SOLENOID VALVE
10 VACUUM ADVANCE DIAPHRAGM
11 DISTRIBUTOR
12 PGM-FI WARNING LIGHT
13 BREATHER CHAMBER
14 VACUUM TANK

Vacuum and electrical connections—1987 Civic CRX w/PGM-FI

HF (49 ST)

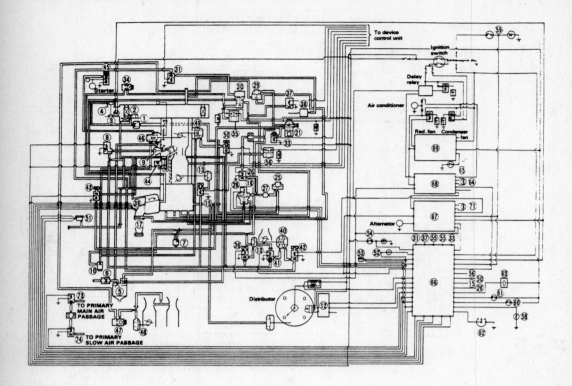

HF (CAL)

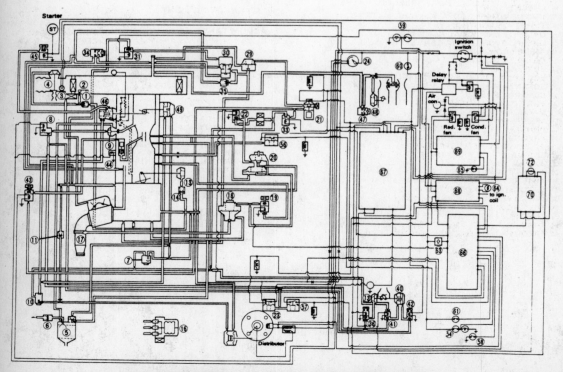

Vacuum and electrical connections—1987 Civic CRX carbureted

HF (HI ALT)

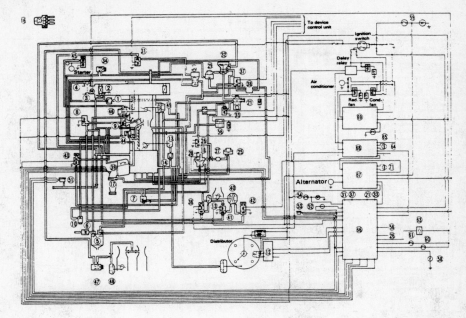

① CHECK VALVE (INTAKE AIR TEMP.)	㊳ AIR CHAMBER (EXCEPT CAL)
② AIR BLEED VALVE	㊴ OXYGEN SENSOR (EXCEPT CAL)
③ INTAKE AIR TEMP. SENSOR A	㊵ IDLE CONTROLLER
④ AIR CONTROL DIAPHRAGM	㊶ IDLE BOOST SOLENOID VALVE
⑤ CHARCOAL CANISTER	㊷ A/C IDLE BOOST SOLENOID VALVE
⑥ TWO-WAY VALVE	㊸ POWER VALVE CONTROL SOLENOID VALVE
⑦ THERMOVALVE A	㊹ PRIMARY SLOW MIXTURE CUT-OFF SOLENOID VALVE
⑧ VACUUM HOLDING SOLENOID VALVE	㊺ CRANKING LEAK SOLENOID VALVE
⑨ AIR VENT CUT-OFF DIAPHRAGM	㊻ CHOKE OPENER
⑩ THERMOVALVE B	㊼ THERMOVALVE D
⑪ CHECK VALVE E	㊽ SECONDARY DIAPHRAGM
⑫ IGNITION TIMING CONTROL UNIT (EXCEPT CAL)	㊾ FAST IDLE UNLOADER
⑬ THROTTLE CONTROLLER	㊿ UNLOADER SOLENOID VALVE (49 ST)
⑭ DASHPOT CHECK VALVE (EXCEPT 49 ST)	㉛ MANIFOLD ABSOLUTE PRESSURE SENSOR (EXCEPT CAL)
⑮ DASHPOT CONTROL SOLENOID VALVE (49 ST)	㉜ COOLANT TEMPERATURE SENSOR A (EXCEPT CAL)
⑯ AIR JET CONTROLLER (EXCEPT 49 ST)	㉝ ATMOSPHERIC PRESSURE SENSOR (EXCEPT CAL)
⑰ CATALYTIC CONVERTER	㉞ BACK-UP LIGHT SWITCH
⑱ EGR VALVE	㉟ VACUUM SWITCH D (49 ST)
⑲ EGR CONTROL SOLENOID VALVE A (CAL)	㊱ VACUUM SWITCH A
⑳ EGR CONTROL VALVES A & B (CAL)	㊲ VACUUM SWITCH E (CAL)
㉑ CONTROL SWITCH	㊳ SPEED PULSER
㉒ EGR CONTROL SOLENOID VALVE B (CAL)	㊴ BRAKE LIGHT SWITCH
㉓ VACUUM SWITCH F (CAL)	㊵ CLUTCH SWITCH
㉔ SPEED SENSOR (CAL)	㊶ NEUTRAL SWITCH
㉕ CONSTANT VACUUM GENERATOR (EXCEPT CAL)	㊷ STEERING SWITCH (49 ST)
㉖ FREQUENCY SOLENOID VALVE B (EXCEPT CAL)	㊸ SHIFT UP INDICATOR LIGHT
㉗ ACCUMULATOR (EXCEPT CAL)	㊹ COOLANT TEMPERATURE SENSOR B
㉘ EGR VALVE LIFT SENSOR (EXCEPT CAL)	㊺ INTAKE AIR TEMP. SENSOR B
㉙ AIR VALVE	㊻ DEVICE CONTROL UNIT
㉚ ANTI-AFTERBURN VALVE	㊼ ALTERNATOR CONTROL UNIT
㉛ ANTI-AFTERBURN CONTROL SOLENOID VALVE	㊽ RADIATOR FAN CONTROL UNIT
㉜ VACUUM CONTROL VALVE (HI ALT)	㊾ RADIATOR FAN TIMER
㉝ AIR CONTROL SOLENOID VALVE	㊿ THERMO CONTROL UNIT (CAL)
㉞ THERMOVALVE C	㉛ RESISTOR
㉟ CHECK VALVE G (CAL)	㉜ COOLANT TEMPERATURE SENSOR C (CAL)
㊱ THROTTLE CONTROL SOLENOID VALVE	㉝ PRIMARY MAIN AIR CUT-OFF SOLENOID VALVE (49 ST)
㊲ FREQUENCY SOLENOID VALVE A (EXCEPT CAL)	㉞ PRIMARY SLOW AIR CUT-OFF SOLENOID VALVE (49 ST)

Std. M/T (49 ST/HI ALT)

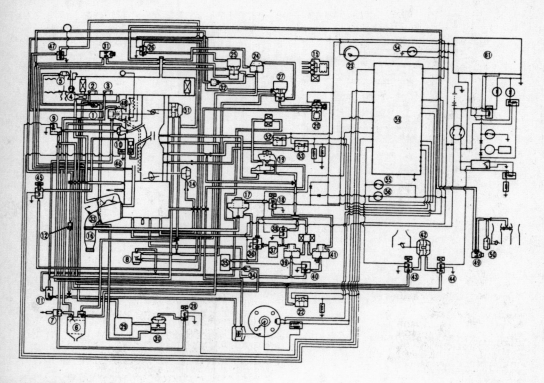

Std. M/T (CAL)

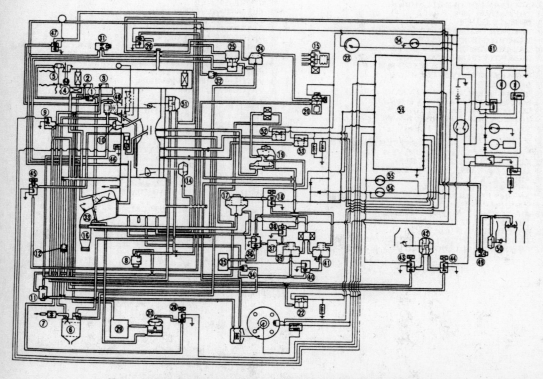

Vacuum and electrical connections—1987 Civic CRX carbureted

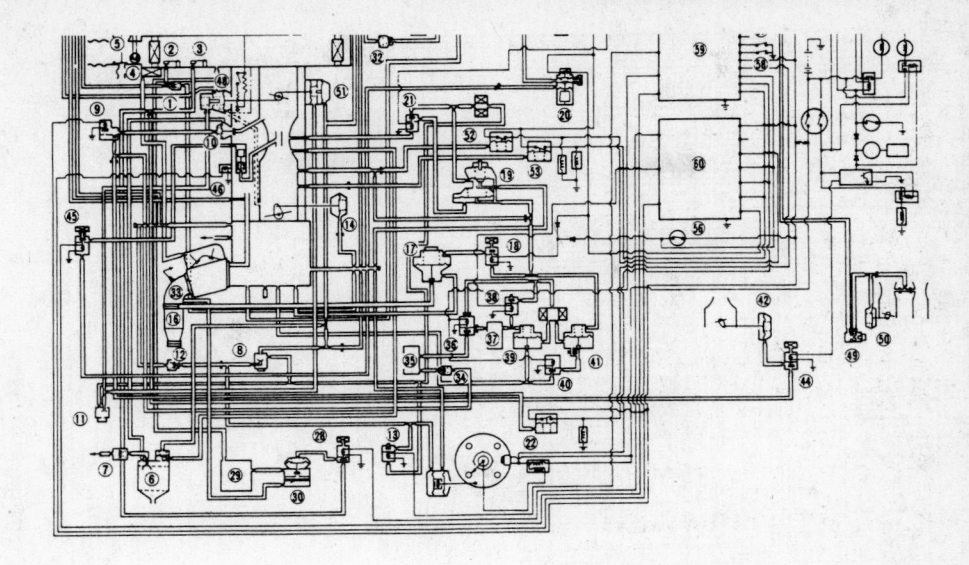

1. CHECK VALVE (INTAKE AIR TEMP.)
2. AIR BLEED VALVE A
3. AIR BLEED VALVE B
4. INTAKE AIR TEMP. SENSOR A
5. AIR CONTROL DIAPHRAGM
6. CHARCOAL CANISTER
7. TWO-WAY VALVE
8. THERMOVALVE A
9. VACUUM HOLDING SOLENOID VALVE
10. AIR VENT CUT-OFF DIAPHRAGM
11. THERMOVALVE B
12. CHECK VALVE E
13. COLD ADVANCE SOLENOID VALVE (A/T)
14. THROTTLE CONTROLLER
15. AIR JET CONTROLLER
16. CATALYTIC CONVERTER
17. EGR VALVE
18. EGR CONTROL SOLENOID VALVE A
19. EGR CONTROL VALVES A & B
20. CONTROL SWITCH
21. EGR CONTROL SOLENOID VALVE C (A/T)
22. VACUUM SWITCH B
23. SPEED SENSOR
24. AIR VALVE
25. ANTI-AFTERBURN VALVE
26. ANTI-AFTERBURN CONTROL SOLENOID VALVE
27. VACUUM CONTROL VALVE (M/T 49ST)
28. AIR SUCTION CONTROL SOLENOID VALVE
29. SILENCER
30. AIR SUCTION VALVE
31. THERMOVALVE C
32. CHECK VALVE G
33. OXYGEN SENSOR
34. CHECK VALVE A
35. ACCUMULATOR

36. FREQUENCY SOLENOID VALVE B
37. PULSE RECTIFIER
38. FEEDBACK CONTROL SOLENOID VALVE
39. AIR CONTROL VALVE B
40. FREQUENCY SOLENOID VALVE A
41. AIR CONTROL VALVE A
42. IDLE CONTROLLER
43. IDLE BOOST SOLENOID VALVE (M/T)
44. A/C IDLE BOOST SOLENOID VALVE
45. POWER VALVE CONTROL SOLENOID VALVE
46. PRIMARY SLOW MIXTURE CUT-OFF SOLENOID VALVE
47. CRANKING LEAK SOLENOID VALVE
48. CHOKE OPENER
49. THERMOVALVE D
50. SECONDARY DIAPHRAGM
51. FAST IDLE UNLOADER
52. VACUUM SWITCH C
53. VACUUM SWITCH A
54. INTAKE AIR TEMP. SENSOR B
55. THERMOSENSOR A
56. THERMOSENSOR B (M/T)
57. SHIFT POSITION SWITCH "N" (A/T)
58. SHIFT POSITION SWITCH "P" (A/T)
59. DEVICE CONTROL UNIT A
60. DEVICE CONTROL UNIT B (A/T)
61. RADIATOR FAN TIMER

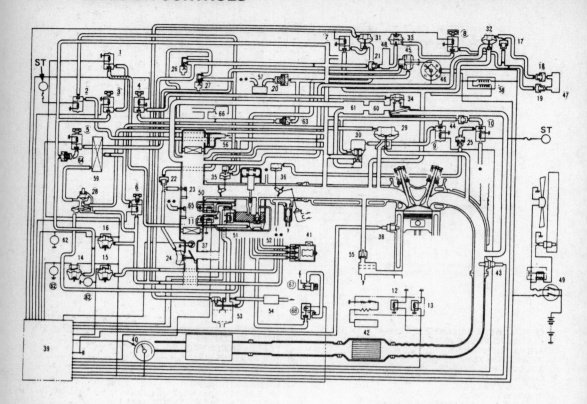

①	POWER VALVE LOCK SOLENOID VALVE	㉞	AIR SUCTION VALVE
②	CRANKING LEAK SOLENOID VALVE	㉟	CHOKE OPENER
③	POWER VALVE CONTROL SOLENOID VALVE	㊱	THROTTLE CONTROLLER
④	AIR SUCTION CONTROL SOLENOID VALVE	㊲	INTAKE AIR TEMPERATURE SWITCH
⑤	VACUUM CONTROL SOLENOID VALVE	㊳	THERMOSENSOR
⑥	EGR CONTROL SOLENOID VALVE A	㊴	CONTROL UNIT
⑦	FREQUENCY SOLENOID VALVE A	㊵	SPEED SENSOR
⑧	FREQUENCY SOLENOID VALVE B	㊶	AIR JET CONTROLLER
⑨	ANTI-AFTERBURN CONTROL SOLENOID VALVE	㊷	CATALYTIC CONVERTER
⑩	CRANKING OPENER SOLENOID VALVE	㊸	OXYGEN SENSOR
⑪	MAIN AIR JET CONTROL SOLENOID VALVE	㊹	CHECK VALVE D
⑫	RIGHT PRIMARY SLOW MIXTURE CUT-OFF SOLENOID VALVE	㊺	DISTRIBUTOR VACUUM ADVANCE
⑬	LEFT PRIMARY SLOW MIXTURE CUT-OFF SOLENOID VALVE	㊻	DISTRIBUTOR
		㊼	SURGE TANK A
⑭	VACUUM SWITCH A	㊽	SURGE TANK B
⑮	VACUUM SWITCH B	㊾	IGNITION SWITCH
⑯	VACUUM SWITCH C	㊿	INNER VENT SOLENOID VALVE
⑰	CHECK VALVE A	51	AIR VENT CUT-OFF SOLENOID VALVE
⑱	CHECK VALVE B	52	POWER VALVE
⑲	CHECK VALVE C	53	CANISTER
⑳	CHECK VALVE F	54	TWO-WAY VALVE
21	CHECK VALVE E	55	PCV VALVE
22	CHECK VALVE (INTAKE AIR TEMP.)	56	BLOW-BY FILTER
23	AIR BLEED VALVE A	57	VACUUM TANK A
24	INTAKE AIR CONTROL DIAPHRAGM	58	IGNITION COIL
25	DASHPOT CHECK VALVE	59	AIR FILTER
26	THERMOVALVE B	60	AIR CHAMBER A
27	THERMOVALVE A	61	AIR CHAMBER B
28	EGR CONTROL VALVES A & B	62	AUXILIARY COIL
29	EGR VALVE	63	CHECK VALVE G
30	ANTI-AFTERBURN VALVE	64	CHECK VALVE H
31	AIR CONTROL VALVE A	65	AIR BLEED VALVE B
32	AIR CONTROL VALVE B	66	VACUUM TANK B
33	CONSTANT VACUUM VALVE	67	THERMOVALVE C (in the air cleaner case)
		68	AIR LEAK SOLENOID VALVE

Vacuum and electrical connections—1987 Prelude carbureted

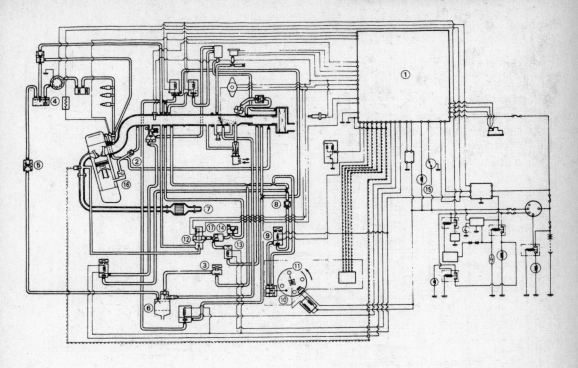

1 ECU (Electronic Control Unit)
2 PCV VALVE
3 THERMOVALVE
4 FUEL TANK
5 TWO-WAY VALVE
6 CHARCOAL CANISTER
7 CATALYTIC CONVERTER
8 CHECK VALVE
9 IGNITION CONTROL SOLENOID VALVE

9 IGNITION CONTROL SOLENOID VALVE
10 ADVANCE DIAPHRAGM
11 DISTRIBUTOR
12 EGR VALVE LIFT SENSOR
13 EGR CONTROL SOLENOID VALVE
14 CONSTANT VACUUM CONTROL (CVC) VALVE
15 PGM-FI WARNING LIGHT
16 BREATHER CHAMBER
17 AIR CHAMBER

Vacuum and electrical connections—1987 Prelude w/PGM-FI

Manual

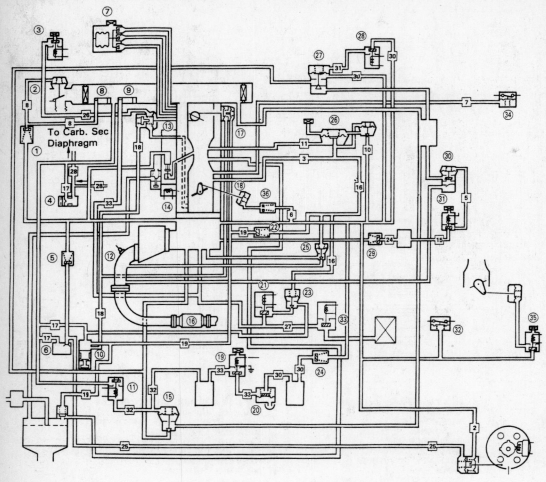

To Carb. Sec
Diaphragm

1. CHECK VALVE (INTAKE AIR TEMP. CONTROL)
2. INTAKE AIR CONTROL DIAPHRAGM
3. CRANKING LEAK SOLENOID VALVE
4. THERMOVALVE C
5. CHECK VALVE E
6. THERMOVALVE B
7. AIR JET CONTROLLER
8. AIR BLEED VALVE A
9. AIR BLEED VALVE B
10. THERMOVALVE A
11. FEEDBACK CONTROL SOLENOID VALVE
12. OXYGEN SENSOR
13. CHOKE OPENER
14. PRIMARY SLOW MIXTURE CUT-OFF
    SOLENOID VALVE
15. AIR CONTROL VALVE B
16. CATALYTIC CONVERTER
17. FAST IDLE UNLOADER
18. THROTTLE CONTROLLER

19. FREQUENCY SOLENOID VALVE B
20. CV GENERATOR
21. FREQUENCY SOLENOID VALVE A
22. CHECK VALVE A
23. AIR CONTROL VALVE A
24. CHECK VALVE B
25. EGR VALVE
26. EGR CONTROL VALVES A & B
27. ANTI-AFTERBURN VALVE
28. ANTI-AFTERBURN CONTROL SOLENOID VALVE
29. CHECK VALVE C
30. AIR SUCTION VALVE
31. AIR SUCTION CONTROL SOLENOID VALVE
32. VACUUM SWITCH A
33. AIR LEAK SOLENOID VALVE
34. VACUUM SWITCH B
35. A/C IDLE BOOST SOLENOID VALVE
36. DASHPOT CHECK VALVE

Vaccum connections—1987 Accord carbureted w/manual transmission

Automatic

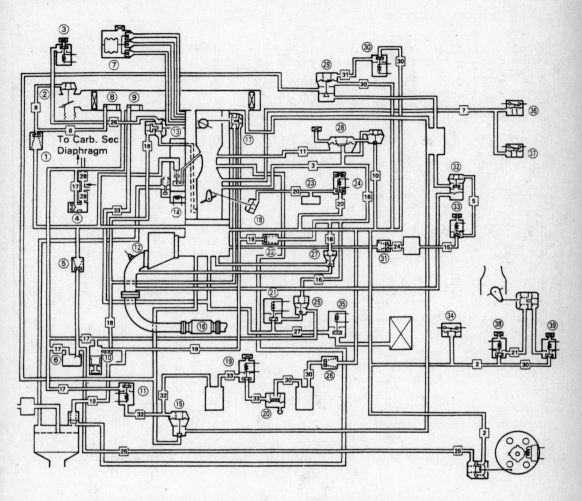

①	CHECK VALVE (INTAKE AIR TEMP. CONTROL)	
②	INTAKE AIR CONTROL DIAPHRAGM	
③	CRANKING LEAK SOLENOID VALVE	
④	THERMOVALVE C	
⑤	CHECK VALVE E	
⑥	THERMOVALVE B	
⑦	AIR JET CONTROLLER	
⑧	AIR BLEED VALVE A	
⑨	AIR BLEED VALVE B	
⑩	THERMOVALVE A	
⑪	FEEDBACK CONTROL SOLENOID VALVE	
⑫	OXYGEN SENSOR	
⑬	CHOKE OPENER	
⑭	PRIMARY SLOW MIXTURE CUT-OFF SOLENOID VALVE	
⑮	AIR CONTROL VALVE B	
⑯	CATALYTIC CONVERTER	
⑰	FAST IDLE UNLOADER	
⑱	THROTTLE CONTROLLER	
⑲	FREQUENCY SOLENOID VALVE B	
⑳	CV GENERATOR	
㉑	FREQUENCY SOLENOID VALVE A	
㉒	CHECK VALVE A	
㉓	PULSE RECTIFIER	
㉔	FREQUENCY SOLENOID VALVE C	
㉕	AIR CONTROL VALVE A	
㉖	CHECK VALVE B	
㉗	EGR VALVE	
㉘	EGR CONTROL VALVES A & B	
㉙	ANTI-AFTERBURN VALVE	
㉚	ANTI-AFTERBURN CONTROL SOLENOID VALVE	
㉛	CHECK VALVE C	
㉜	AIR SUCTION VALVE	
㉝	AIR SUCTION CONTROL SOLENOID VALVE	
㉞	VACUUM SWITCH A	
㉟	AIR LEAK SOLENOID VALVE	
㊱	VACUUM SWITCH B	
㊲	VACUUM SWITCH C (49 ST and HI ALT only)	
㊳	IDLE BOOST SOLENOID VALVE	
㊴	A/C IDLE BOOST SOLENOID VALVE	

Vacuum connections—1987 Accord carbureted w/automatic transmission

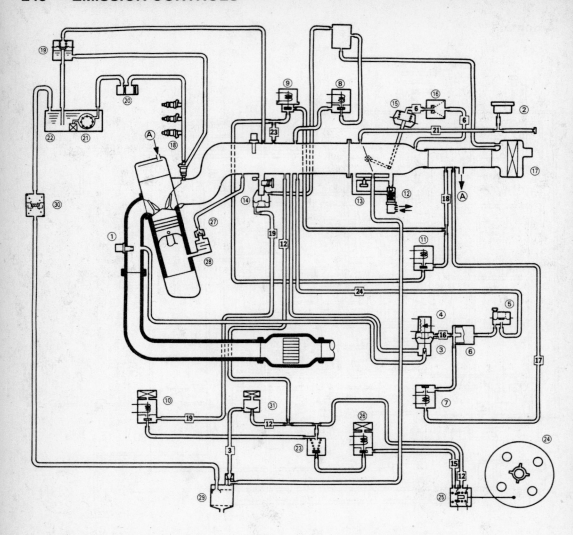

① OXYGEN (O₂) SENSOR	⑰ AIR CLEANER
② MANIFOLD ABSOLUTE PRESSURE (MAP) SENSOR	⑱ FUEL INJECTOR
③ EGR VALVE	⑲ PRESSURE REGULATOR
④ EGR VALVE LIFT SENSOR	⑳ FUEL FILTER
⑤ CONSTANT VACUUM CONTROL (CVC) VALVE	㉑ FUEL PUMP
⑥ AIR CHAMBER	㉒ FUEL TANK
⑦ EGR CONTROL SOLENOID VALVE	㉓ CHECK VALVE
⑧ IDLE CONTROL SOLENOID VALVE	㉔ DISTRIBUTOR
⑨ A/T IDLE CONTROL SOLENOID VALVE	㉕ VACUUM ADVANCE DIAPHRAGM
⑩ A/C IDLE BOOST SOLENOID VALVE	㉖ IGNITION CONTROL SOLENOID VALVE
⑪ FAST IDLE CONTROL SOLENOID VALVE	㉗ PCV VALVE
⑫ FAST IDLE VALVE	㉘ BREATHER CHAMBER
⑬ IDLE ADJUSTING SCREW	㉙ CHARCOAL CANISTER
⑭ A/C IDLE BOOST VALVE	㉚ TWO-WAY VALVE
⑮ DASHPOT DIAPHRAGM	㉛ THERMOVALVE
⑯ DASHPOT CHECK VALVE	

Vacuum connections—1987 Accord w/PGM-FI

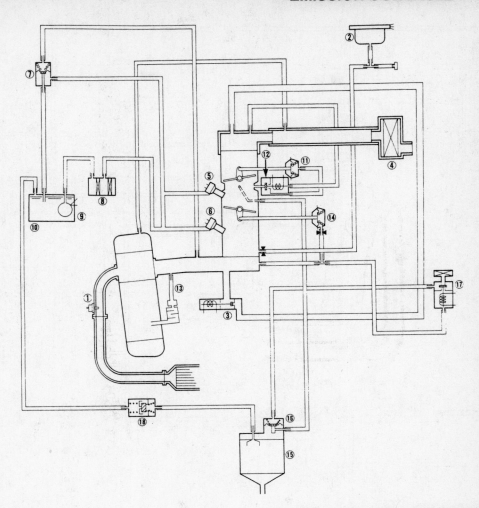

① OXYGEN (O₂) SENSOR
② MANIFOLD ABSOLUTE PRESSURE (MAP) SENSOR
③ ELECTRONIC AIR CONTROL VALVE (EACV)
④ AIR CLEANER
⑤ MAIN INJECTOR
⑥ AUX. INJECTOR
⑦ PRESSURE REGULATOR
⑧ FUEL FILTER
⑨ FUEL PUMP
⑩ FUEL TANK

⑪ TANDEM VALVE CONTROL DIAPHRAGM
⑫ TANDEM VALVE CONTROL SOLENOID VALVE
⑬ PCV VALVE
⑭ DASHPOT DIAPHRAGM
⑮ CHARCOAL CANISTER
⑯ PURGE CONTROL DIAPHRAGM VALVE
⑰ PURGE CUT-OFF SOLENOID VALVE
⑱ TWO-WAY VALVE

Vacuum connections—1988 Civic 1.5L

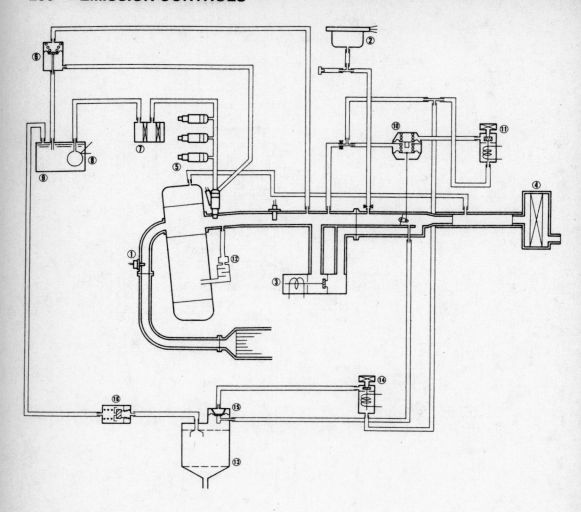

1 OXYGEN (O_2) SENSOR
2 MANIFOLD ABSOLUTE PRESSURE (MAP) SENSOR
3 ELECTRONIC AIR CONTROL VALVE (EACV)
4 AIR CLEANER
5 FUEL INJECTOR
6 PRESSURE REGULATOR
7 FUEL FILTER
8 FUEL PUMP
9 FUEL TANK
10 DASHPOT DIAPHRAGM

11 DASHPOT CONTROL SOLENOID VALVE
12 PCV VALVE
13 CHARCOAL CANISTER
14 PURGE CUT-OFF SOLENOID VALVE
15 PURGE CONTROL DIAPHRAGM VALVE
16 TWO-WAY VALVE

Vacuum connections—1988 Civic 1.6L

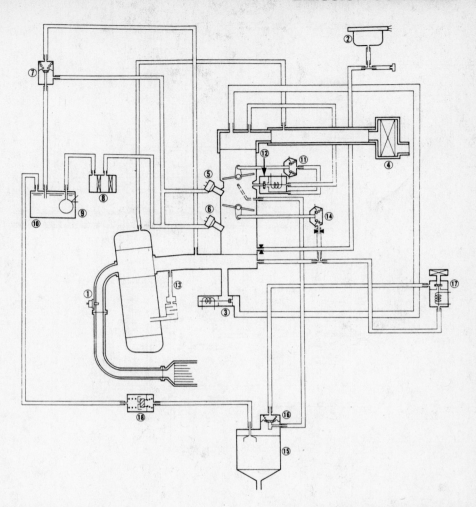

1. OXYGEN (O$_2$) SENSOR
2. MANIFOLD ABSOLUTE PRESSURE (MAP) SENSOR
3. ELECTRONIC AIR CONTROL VALVE (EACV)
4. AIR CLEANER
5. MAIN INJECTOR
6. AUX. INJECTOR
7. PRESSURE REGULATOR
8. FUEL FILTER
9. FUEL PUMP
10. FUEL TANK
11. TANDEM VALVE CONTROL DIAPHRAGM
12. TANDEM VALVE CONTROL SOLENOID VALVE
13. PCV VALVE
14. DASHPOT DIAPHRAGM
15. CHARCOAL CANISTER
16. PURGE CONTROL DIAPHRAGM VALVE
17. PURGE CUT-OFF SOLENOID VALVE
18. TWO-WAY VALVE

Vacuum connections—1988 Civic CRX Std.

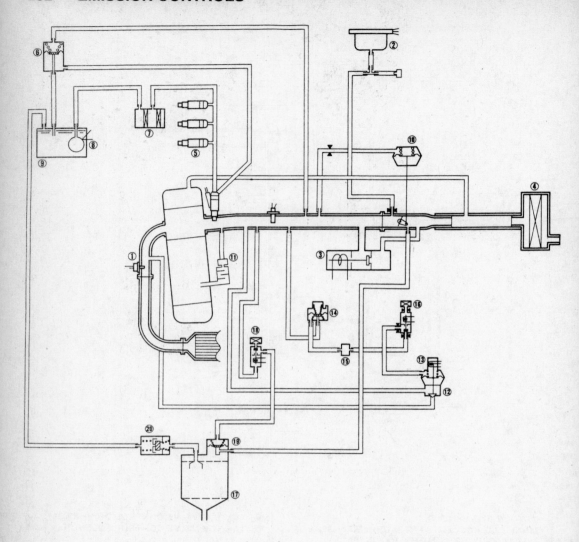

① OXYGEN (O₂) SENSOR
② MANIFOLD ABSOLUTE PRESSURE (MAP) SENSOR
③ ELECTRONIC AIR CONTROL VALVE (EACV)
④ AIR CLEANER
⑤ FUEL INJECTOR
⑥ PRESSURE REGULATOR
⑦ FUEL FILTER
⑧ FUEL PUMP
⑨ FUEL TANK
⑩ DASHPOT DIAPHRAGM

⑪ PCV VALVE
⑫ EGR VALVE
⑬ EGR VALVE LIFT SENSOR
⑭ CONSTANT VACUUM CONTROL (CVC) VALVE
⑮ AIR CHAMBER
⑯ EGR CONTROL SOLENOID VALVE
⑰ CHARCOAL CANISTER
⑱ PURGE CUT-OFF SOLENOID VALVE
⑲ PURGE CONTROL DIAPHRAGM VALVE
⑳ TWO-WAY VALVE

Vacuum connections—1988 Civic CRX HF

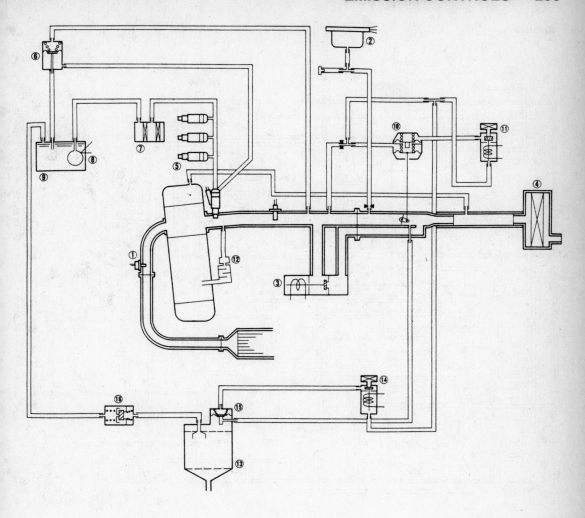

① OXYGEN (O₂) SENSOR
② MANIFOLD ABSOLUTE PRESSURE (MAP) SENSOR
③ ELECTRONIC AIR CONTROL VALVE (EACV)
④ AIR CLEANER
⑤ FUEL INJECTOR
⑥ PRESSURE REGULATOR
⑦ FUEL FILTER
⑧ FUEL PUMP
⑨ FUEL TANK
⑩ DASHPOT DIAPHRAGM

⑪ DASHPOT CONTROL SOLENOID VALVE
⑫ PCV VALVE
⑬ CHARCOAL CANISTER
⑭ PURGE CUT-OFF SOLENOID VALVE
⑮ PURGE CONTROL DIAPHRAGM VALVE
⑯ TWO-WAY VALVE

Vacuum connections—1988 Civic CRX Si

Manual

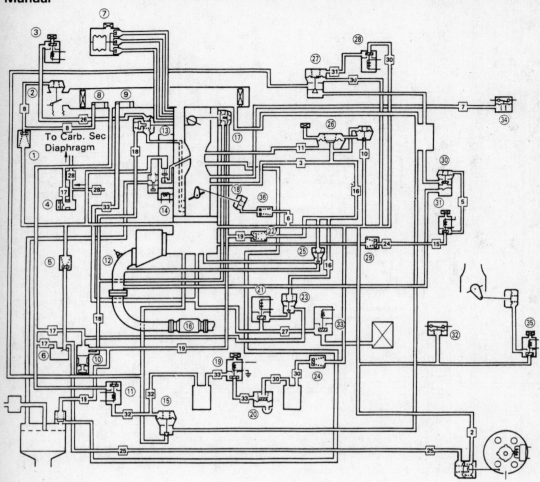

1. CHECK VALVE (INTAKE AIR TEMP. CONTROL)
2. INTAKE AIR CONTROL DIAPHRAGM
3. CRANKING LEAK SOLENOID VALVE
4. THERMOVALVE C
5. CHECK VALVE E
6. THERMOVALVE B
7. AIR JET CONTROLLER
8. AIR BLEED VALVE A
9. AIR BLEED VALVE B
10. THERMOVALVE A
11. FEEDBACK CONTROL SOLENOID VALVE
12. OXYGEN SENSOR
13. CHOKE OPENER
14. PRIMARY SLOW MIXTURE CUT-OFF SOLENOID VALVE
15. AIR CONTROL VALVE B
16. CATALYTIC CONVERTER
17. FAST IDLE UNLOADER
18. THROTTLE CONTROLLER

19. FREQUENCY SOLENOID VALVE B
20. CV GENERATOR
21. FREQUENCY SOLENOID VALVE A
22. CHECK VALVE A
23. AIR CONTROL VALVE A
24. CHECK VALVE B
25. EGR VALVE
26. EGR CONTROL VALVES A & B
27. ANTI-AFTERBURN VALVE
28. ANTI-AFTERBURN CONTROL SOLENOID VALVE
29. CHECK VALVE C (49S ONLY)
30. AIR SUCTION VALVE
31. AIR SUCTION CONTROL SOLENOID VALVE
32. VACUUM SWITCH A
33. AIR LEAK SOLENOID VALVE
34. VACUUM SWITCH B
35. A/C IDLE BOOST SOLENOID VALVE
36. DASHPOT CHECK VALVE

Vacuum connections—1988 Accord carbureted w/manual transmission

Automatic

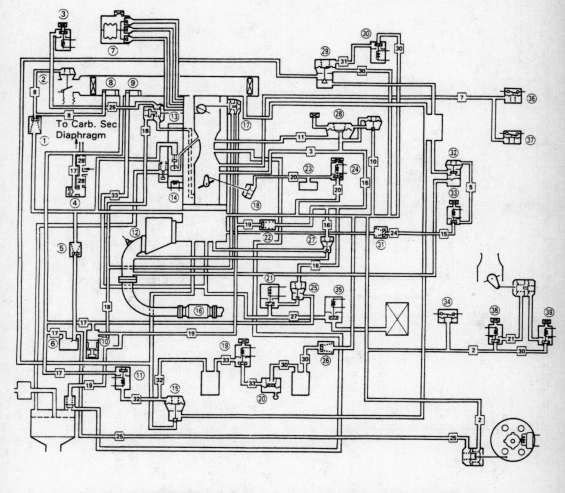

To Carb. Sec Diaphragm

(1) CHECK VALVE (INTAKE AIR TEMP. CONTROL)
(2) INTAKE AIR CONTROL DIAPHRAGM
(3) CRANKING LEAK SOLENOID VALVE
(4) THERMOVALVE C
(5) CHECK VALVE E
(6) THERMOVALVE B
(7) AIR JET CONTROLLER
(8) AIR BLEED VALVE A
(9) AIR BLEED VALVE B
(10) THERMOVALVE A
(11) FEEDBACK CONTROL SOLENOID VALVE
(12) OXYGEN SENSOR
(13) CHOKE OPENER
(14) PRIMARY SLOW MIXTURE CUT-OFF
     SOLENOID VALVE
(15) AIR CONTROL VALVE B
(16) CATALYTIC CONVERTER
(17) FAST IDLE UNLOADER
(18) THROTTLE CONTROLLER
(19) FREQUENCY SOLENOID VALVE B
(20) CV GENERATOR

(21) FREQUENCY SOLENOID VALVE A
(22) CHECK VALVE A
(23) PULSE RECTIFIER
(24) FREQUENCY SOLENOID VALVE C
(25) AIR CONTROL VALVE A
(26) CHECK VALVE B
(27) EGR VALVE
(28) EGR CONTROL VALVES A & B
(29) ANTI-AFTERBURN VALVE
(30) ANTI-AFTERBURN CONTROL SOLENOID VALVE
(31) CHECK VALVE C (49S ONLY)
(32) AIR SUCTION VALVE
(33) AIR SUCTION CONTROL SOLENOID VALVE
(34) VACUUM SWITCH A
(35) AIR LEAK SOLENOID VALVE
(36) VACUUM SWITCH B
(37) VACUUM SWITCH C (49 ST and HI ALT only)
(38) IDLE BOOST SOLENOID VALVE
(39) A/C IDLE BOOST SOLENOID VALVE

Vacuum connections—1988 Accord carbureted w/automatic transmission

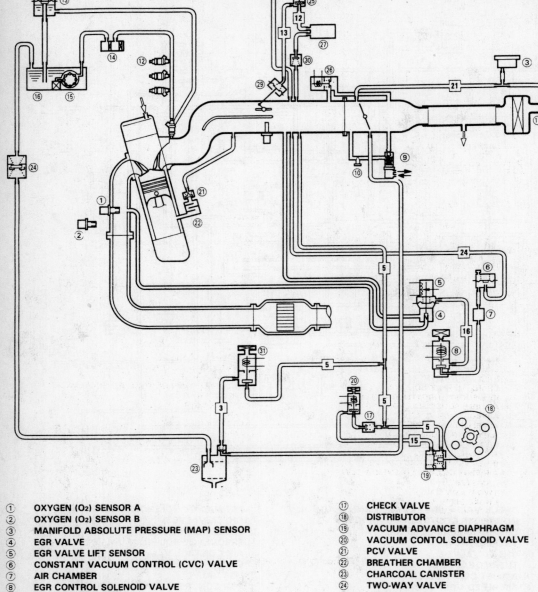

1. OXYGEN (O_2) SENSOR A
2. OXYGEN (O_2) SENSOR B
3. MANIFOLD ABSOLUTE PRESSURE (MAP) SENSOR
4. EGR VALVE
5. EGR VALVE LIFT SENSOR
6. CONSTANT VACUUM CONTROL (CVC) VALVE
7. AIR CHAMBER
8. EGR CONTROL SOLENOID VALVE
9. FAST IDLE VALVE
10. IDLE ADJUSTING SCREW
11. AIR CLEANER
12. FUEL INJECTOR
13. PRESSURE REGULATOR
14. FUEL FILTER
15. FUEL PUMP
16. FUEL TANK

17. CHECK VALVE
18. DISTRIBUTOR
19. VACUUM ADVANCE DIAPHRAGM
20. VACUUM CONTOL SOLENOID VALVE
21. PCV VALVE
22. BREATHER CHAMBER
23. CHARCOAL CANISTER
24. TWO-WAY VALVE
25. THERMOVALVE
26. EACV
27. SURGE TANK
28. BYPASS CONTROL SOLENOID VALVE
29. BYPASS CONTROL DIAPHRAGM
30. CHECK VALVE
31. PURGE CUT SOLENOID VALVE

Vacuum connections—1988 Accord w/PGM-FI

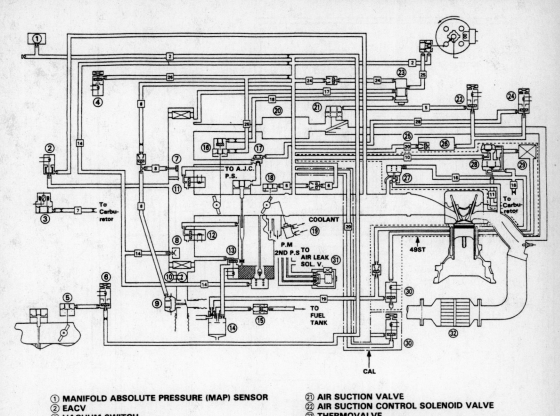

1. MANIFOLD ABSOLUTE PRESSURE (MAP) SENSOR
2. EACV
3. VACUUM SWITCH
4. CRANKING LEAK SOLENOID VALVE
5. IDLE BOOST THROTTLE CONTROLLER
6. A/C IDLE BOOST SOLENOID VALVE
7. AIR BLEED VALVE A
8. AIR BLEED VALVE B
9. AIR CONTROL DIAPHRAGM
10. INTAKE AIR TEMPERATURE (TA) SENSOR
11. AIR LEAK SOLENOID VALVE
12. INNER VENT SOLENOID VALVE
13. AIR VENT CUT-OFF SOLENOID VALVE
14. CANISTER
15. TWO-WAY VALVE
16. CHOKE OPENER
17. VACUUM PISTON CONTROL VALVE
18. THROTTLE CONTROLLER
19. THERMOWAX VALVE
20. SILENCER
21. AIR SUCTION VALVE
22. AIR SUCTION CONTROL SOLENOID VALVE
23. THERMOVALVE
24. VACUUM PISTON CONTROL SOLENOID VALVE
25. CHECK VALVE C
26. AIR CHAMBER
27. EGR VALVE
28. EGR CONTROL VALVE
29. AIR FILTER
30. PURGE CUT-OFF SOLENOID VALVE
31. AIR JET CONTROLLER
32. CATALYTIC CONVERTER

Vacuum and electrical connections—1988 Prelude carbureted

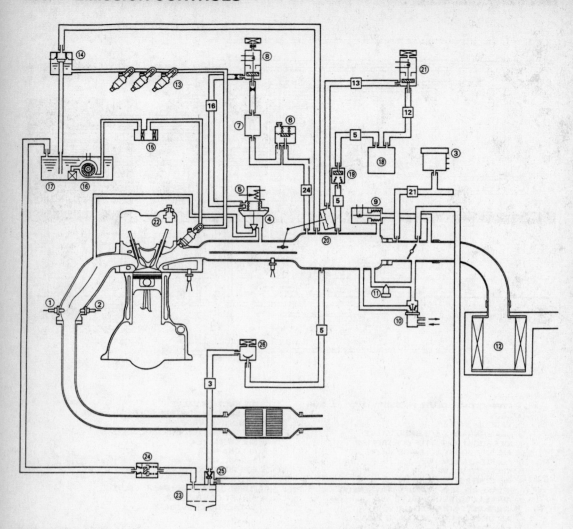

① OXYGEN (O₂) SENSOR A
② OXYGEN (O₂) SENSOR B
③ MANIFOLD ABSOLUTE PRESSURE (MAP) SENSOR
④ EGR VALVE
⑤ EGR VALVE LIFT SENSOR
⑥ CONSTANT VACUUM CONTROL (CVC) VALVE
⑦ AIR CHAMBER
⑧ EGR CONTROL SOLENOID VALVE*
⑨ ELECTRONIC AIR CONTROL VALVE (EACV)
⑩ FAST IDLE VALVE
⑪ IDLE ADJUSTING SCREW
⑫ AIR CLEANER
⑬ FUEL INJECTOR

⑭ PRESSURE REGULATOR
⑮ FUEL FILTER
⑯ FUEL PUMP
⑰ FUEL TANK
⑱ VACUUM TANK
⑲ CHECK VALVE
⑳ BYPASS CONTROL DIAPHRAGM
㉑ BYPASS CONTROL SOLENOID VALVE
㉒ PCV VALVE
㉓ CHARCOAL CANISTER
㉔ TWO-WAY VALVE
㉕ PURGE CONTROL DIAPHRAGM VALVE
㉖ THERMOVALVE

Vacuum and electrical connections—1988 Prelude w/PGM-FI

Fuel System

5

Troubleshooting Basic Fuel System Problems

Problem	Cause	Solution
Engine cranks, but won't start (or is hard to start) when cold	• Empty fuel tank • Incorrect starting procedure • Defective fuel pump • No fuel in carburetor • Clogged fuel filter • Engine flooded • Defective choke	• Check for fuel in tank • Follow correct procedure • Check pump output • Check for fuel in the carburetor • Replace fuel filter • Wait 15 minutes; try again • Check choke plate
Engine cranks, but is hard to start (or does not start) when hot— (presence of fuel is assumed)	• Defective choke	• Check choke plate
Rough idle or engine runs rough	• Dirt or moisture in fuel • Clogged air filter • Faulty fuel pump	• Replace fuel filter • Replace air filter • Check fuel pump output
Engine stalls or hesitates on acceleration	• Dirt or moisture in the fuel • Dirty carburetor • Defective fuel pump • Incorrect float level, defective accelerator pump	• Replace fuel filter • Clean the carburetor • Check fuel pump output • Check carburetor
Poor gas mileage	• Clogged air filter • Dirty carburetor • Defective choke, faulty carburetor adjustment	• Replace air filter • Clean carburetor • Check carburetor
Engine is flooded (won't start accompanied by smell of raw fuel)	• Improperly adjusted choke or carburetor	• Wait 15 minutes and try again, without pumping gas pedal • If it won't start, check carburetor

CARBURETED FUEL SYSTEM

On the 1170 and 1237cc models, a 2-bbl downdraft Hitachi carburetor is used. On the 1342cc, 1488cc, and 1955cc a 2-bbl Keihin carburetor is used. Fuel pressure is provided by a camshaft driven mechanical fuel pump. A replaceable fuel filter is located in the engine compartment inline between the fuel pump and carburetor.

On the 1335, 1487 and 1600cc Civic, Accord, 1751cc Accord and Prelude, a Keihin 3-bbl carburetor is used. On this carburetor, the primary and second venturi's deliver a lean air/fuel mixture to the main combustion chamber. Simultaneously, the third or auxiliary venturi which has a complete separate fuel metering circuit, delivers a small (in volume) but very rich air/fuel mixture to the precombustion chamber. Fuel pressure is provided by an electric fuel pump which is actuated when the ignition switch is turned to the ON position. The electric pump is located under the rear seat beneath a special access plate on sedan and hatchback models, and located under the rear of the vehicle adjacent to the fuel tank on station wagon and Accord models. A replaceable inline fuel filter located on the inlet side of the electric fuel pump is used on all later models.

On the 1829cc and 1955cc Prelude models twin Keihin 2-bbl sidedraft carburetors are used. Fuel pressure is supplied from an electric pump mounted near the left rear tire.

Mechanical Fuel Pump

REMOVAL AND INSTALLATION

1170 and 1237cc Engines

The fuel pump in the Civic is located in back of the engine, underneath the air cleaner snorkel.

1. Remove the air cleaner and cover assembly.
2. Remove the inlet and outlet fuel lines at the pump.
3. Loosen the pump nuts and remove the pump.

NOTE: *Do not disassemble the pump. Disassembly may cause fuel or oil leakage. If the pump is defective, replace it as an assembly.*

4. To install the fuel pump, reverse the removal procedure.

TESTING

1. Check the following items.
   a. Looseness of the pump connector.
   b. Looseness of the upper and lower body and cover screws.
   c. Looseness of the rocker arm pin.

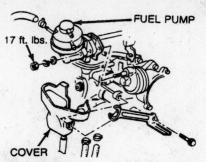

Mechanical fuel pump mounting—1342 and 1488cc carbureted engines

   d. Contamination or clogging of the air hole.
   e. Improper operation of the pump.
2. Check to see if there are signs of oil or fuel around the air hole. If so, the diaphragm is damaged and you must replace the pump.
3. To inspect the pump for operation, first disconnect the fuel line at the carburetor. Connect a fuel pressure gauge to the delivery side of the pump. Start the engine and measure the pump delivery pressure.
4. After measuring, stop the engine and check to see if the gauge drops suddenly. If the gauge drops suddenly and/or the delivery pressure is incorrect, check for a fuel or oil leak from the diaphragm or from the valves.
5. To test for volume, disconnect the fuel line from the carburetor and inset it into a one quart container. Crank the engine for 60 seconds at 600 rpm, or 40 seconds at 3,000 rpm. The bottle should be half full (1 pint).

Electric Fuel Pump

REMOVAL AND INSTALLATION

All except 1170cc, 1237cc, 1342cc and 1488cc Engines

1. Remove the gas filler cap to relieve any excess pressure in the system.

Mechanical fuel pump location. Arrow indicates air hole

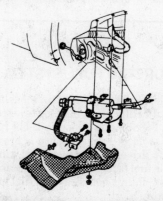

Electric fuel pump mounting—fuel injected models

2. Obtain a pair of suitable clamps to pinch shut the fuel lines to the pump.

3. Disconnect the negative battery cable.

4. Locate the fuel pump. On Civic sedan and hatchback models (1982 only), you will first have to remove the rear seat by removing the bolt at the rear center of the bottom cushion and pivoting the seat forward from the rear. The pump and filter are located on the driver's side of the rear seat floor section beneath an access plate retained by four Phillips head screws.

On station wagon and 1983 sedan & hatchback models and the Accord and Prelude, you will probably have to raise the rear of the car to obtain access to the pump. On Accord and Prelude models, remove the left rear wheel. In all cases, make sure, if you are crawling under the car, that the car is securely supported.

5. Pinch the inlet and outlet fuel lines shut. Loosen the hose clamps. On station wagon and Accord models, remove the filter mounting clip on the left hand side of the bracket.

6. Disconnect the positive lead wire and ground wire from the pump at their quick disconnect.

7. Remove the two fuel pump retaining bolts, taking care not to lose the two spacers and bolt collars.

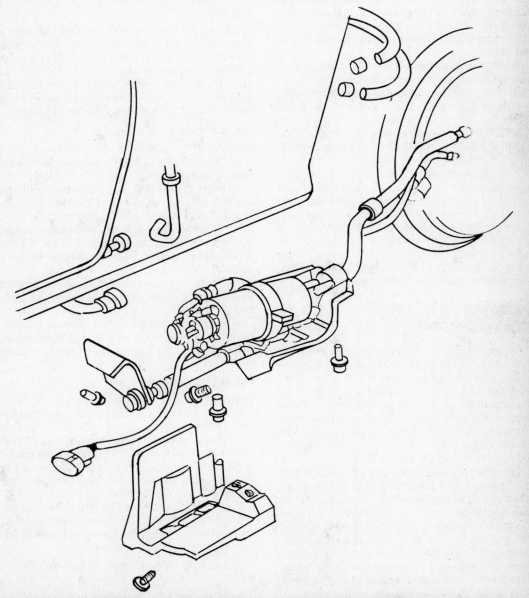

Injected engine electric fuel pump mounting on the Prelude and Accord (Civic models similar)

8. Remove the fuel lines and fuel pump.

9. Reverse the above procedure to install. The pump cannot be disassembled and must be replaced if defective. Operating fuel pump pressure is 2-3 psi.

PRESSURE TESTING

1. Relieve the fuel pressure from the system as previously outline in this section.

2. Remove the service bolt from the fuel filter and attach a pressure gauge. On carbureted models, disconnect the fuel line at the fuel filter and attach the pressure gauge to it.

3. On the carbureted models, remove the fuel cut off relay from the fuse box and connect a jumper wire in its place. Turn the ignition switch to **ON** until the pressure stabilizes and then turn it **OFF**. The pressure should be 2.6-3.3 psi.

4. On the fuel injected models, start the engine and measure the fuel pressure with the engine idling and the vacuum hose to the pressure regulator disconnected. The pressure should be 36-41 psi.

5. If the fuel pressure is not as specified, first check the fuel pump. If the fuel pump is good, check the following:

   a. If the pressure is higher than specified, inspect for a pinched or clogged fuel return hose or piping and faulty pressure regulator.

   b. If the pressure is lower than specified, inspect for a clogged fuel filter, pinched or clogged fuel hose from the fuel tank to the fuel pump, pressure regulator failure, leakage in the fuel line or pinched, broken or disconnected regulator vacuum hose.

Carburetor

TROUBLESHOOTING

Carburetor problems are among the most difficult internal combustion engine malfunctions to diagnose. If you have a carburetor problem, read the description of carburetor systems in the beginning of the carburetor section of this chapter. Consider which system or combination of systems are in operation when the problem occurs. Some troubleshooting tips are given in the system operation descriptions.

The most reliable way for a nonprofessional to diagnose a bad carburetor is to eliminate all other possible sources of the problem. If you suspect the carburetor is the problem, perform the adjustments given in this chapter. Check the ignition system to ensure that the spark plugs, contact points, and condenser are in good shape and adjusted properly. Check the emission control equipment following the instructions given in the first part of this chapter. Check the ignition timing adjustment. Check

all vacuum hoses on the engine for loose connections or splits or breaks. Make sure the carburetor and intake manifold attaching bolts are tightened to the proper torque.

If you do determine that the carburetor is malfunctioning, and the adjustments in this chapter don't help, you have three alternatives: you can take it to a professional mechanic and let him fix it, you can buy a new or rebuilt carburetor to replace the one now on your vehicle, or you can buy a carburetor rebuilding kit and overhaul your carburetor.

ADJUSTMENTS

Fast Idle

During cold engine starting and the engine warm-up period, a specially enriched fuel mixture is required. If the engine fails to run properly or if the engine over-revs with the choke knob pulled out in cold weather, the fast idle system should be checked and adjusted. This is accomplished with the carburetor installed.

1170 AND 1237cc MODELS

1973

1. Run the engine until it reaches normal operating temperature.

2. With the engine still running, pull the choke knob out to the first detent. The idle speed should rise to 1,500-2,000 rpm.

3. If the idle speed is not within this range, adjust by bending the choke rod. (See "Choke Adjustment" section below for further details.)

1974-79

1. Open the primary throttle plate and insert an 0.8mm diameter drill bit between the plate and the bore.

2. With the throttle plate opened 0.8mm, bend the reference tab so it is midway between the two scribed lines on the throttle control lever.

1487 AND 1600cc MODELS

1976-79

1. Run the engine until it reaches normal operating temperature.

2. Place the choke control knob in its second detent position (two clicks out from the dash). With the choke knob in this position, run the engine for 30 seconds and check that the fast idle speed is 2,500-3,500 rpm.

3. To adjust, bend the slot in the fast idle adjusting link. Narrow the slot to lower the fast idle, and widen the slot to increase. Make all adjustments in small increments.

1335, 1342, 1487 (1980-82) 1488, 1751 AND ACCORD 1829cc

1. Run the engine to normal operating temperature.

Fast idle adjusting location—CVCC models

2. Connect a tachometer according to the manufacturer's specifications.

3. Disconnect and plug the hose from the fast idle unloader.

4. Shut the engine off, hold the choke valve closed, and open and close the throttle to engage the fast idle cam.

5. Start the engine, run it for one minute. Fast idle speed should be 2,300-3,300 rpm (manual transaxle) or 2,200-3,200 rpm (automatic transaxle).

6. Adjust the idle by turning the fast idle screw.

1829cc PRELUDE

1. Start the engine and bring it to normal operating temperature. Turn the engine **OFF**.

2. Remove the E-clip and flat washer from the thermo-wax valve linkage, then, slide the linkage past the fast idle cam.

NOTE: *Be careful not to bend the linkage or the fast idle speed will be changed.*

3. While holding open the throttle, turn the fast idle cam counterclockwise until the fast idle lever is on the 3rd step.

4. Without touching the throttle, start the engine and check the idle speed. The idle speed should be 2,000 rpm. Adjustment of the idle speed can be made by turning the fast idle adjusting screw.

5. Stop the engine and reconnect the thermo-wax valve linkage.

6. Start the engine and check that as the engine warms up, the idle speed decreases.

NOTE: *If the idle speed doesn't drop, clean the linkage along with the carburetor. If the speed still doesn't drop, check for damaged or stuck linkage.*

Float and Fuel Level

Poor fuel combustion, black sooty exhaust, and fuel overflow are indications of improper float level. Lean running may also be a symptom, although you should also check for such causes as jets blocked by dirt and vacuum leaks.

1170 AND 1237cc MODELS

1. Check the float level by looking at the sight glass on the right of the carburetor. Fuel level should align with the dot on the sight glass. If the level is above or below the dot, the carburetor must be disassembled and the float level set.

NOTE: *Try to check float level with the dot at eye level.*

2. Remove the carburetor from the engine and disconnect the air horn assembly from the carburetor body.

3. Invert the air horn and raise the float.

4. Now lower the float carefully until the float tang just touches the needle valve stem. The valve stem is spring loaded, so do not allow the float to compress the spring during measurement. Measure the distance between the float and the air horn flange (without gasket). The distance should be 11mm. Adjust by bending the tang.

5. Raise the float until the float stop contacts the air horn body. Measure the distance between the float tang and the needle valve stem. The distance should be 1.3-1.77mm. Adjust by bending the float stop tang.

6. When the carburetor is installed, recheck the float level by looking into the carburetor float sight glass. Fuel level should be within the range oft he dot on the glass.

1335, 1342, 1487, 1488, 1600 AND 1751cc MODELS THROUGH 1981

Due to the rather unconventional manner in which the Keihin 3-bbl carburetor float level is checked and adjusted, this is one job best left to the dealer, or someone with Honda tool No. 07501-6570000 (1487 and 1600cc engines) or 07501-6950100 (1751cc engines); which is a special float level gauge/fuel catch tray/drain bottle assembly not generally available to the public. This carburetor is adjusted while mounted on a running engine. After the auxiliary and the primary/secondary main jet covers are removed, the special float gauge apparatus is installed over the jet apertures. With the engine running, the float level is checked against a red index line on the gauge. If adjustment proves necessary, there are adjusting screws provided for both the auxiliary and the primary/secondary circuits atop the carburetor.

1982 and later, except 1829cc Prelude

With the vehicle on level ground and at normal operating temperature, check the primary and secondary fuel level inspection windows. If

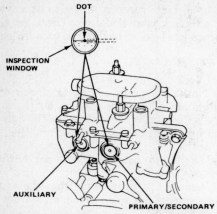

Inspection window showing the fuel level on the 1982 and later models, except 1829cc Prelude

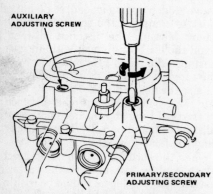

Float level adjustment screw—1982 and later models, except 1829cc Prelude

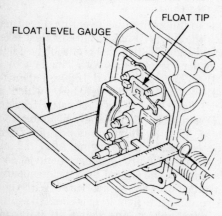

Float level measurement on the dual Keihin sidedraft carburetors—1829cc Prelude

the fuel level is not touching the dot, adjust it by turning the adjusting screws which are located in recessed bosses above the inspection windows.

NOTE: *Do not turn the adjusting screws more than 1 turn every 15 seconds.*

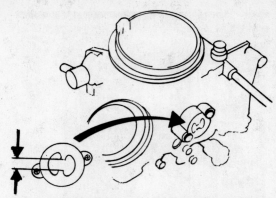

Reading fuel level at the inspection window on carbureted '86 Civics

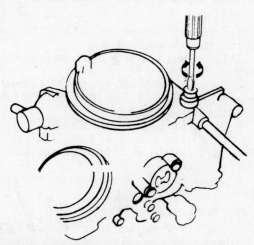

Adjusting fuel level on carbureted '86 Civics

1829cc PRELUDE

1. Remove the side draft carburetors from the engine and remove the float chambers from the carburetors.

2. Using a float level gauge, measure the float level with the float tip lightly touching the float valve and the float chamber surface tilted about 30° from vertical. The float level should be 16mm.

3. To adjust the float level on the sub carburetor, remove the float chamber. Using a float level gauge, measure the float level as described above.

NOTE: *The float level of the sub carburetor cannot be adjusted. If the float level is incorrect the float must be replaced.*

1986 CIVIC WITH 1488 AND 1342cc ENGINE

1. Make sure the vehicle is level. Start the engine and run it until it is warm. Remove the air cleaner and move it aside, leaving as many hoses connected as possible. Snap the throttle

open so the engine accelerates to 3,000 rpm several times, then allow the engine to idle.

2. Wait until the fuel level stabilizes, and then check its location in the inspection window. If it is not centered, use a small screwdriver to adjust the fuel level, turning the screw no more than ⅛ turn every 15 seconds (so the fuel level will stabilize). When fuel level is correct, it is a good idea to put a dab of white paint near the screw to indicate that fuel level has been properly set. Stop the engine and replace the air cleaner.

Throttle Linkage

1170 AND 1237cc MODELS

1. Check the gas pedal free-play (the amount of free movement before the throttle cable starts to pull the throttle valve). Adjust the free-play at the throttle cable adjusting nut (near the carburetor) so the pedal has 1.0-3.0mm freeplay.

2. Make sure that when the accelerator pedal is fully depressed, the primary and secondary throttle valves are opened fully (contact the stops). If the secondary valve does not open fully, adjust by bending the secondary throttle valve connecting rod.

1335, 1342, 1487, 1488, 1600 AND 1751cc MODELS

1. Remove the air cleaner assembly to provide access.

2. Check that the cable free-play (deflection) is 4.0-10.0mm (1335, 1487 and 1600cc engines) or 4.5-9.5mm (1751cc engines). This is measured right before the cable enters the throttle shaft bellcrank.

3. If deflection is not to specifications, rotate the cable adjusting nuts in the required direction.

4. As a final check, have a friend press the gas pedal all the way to the floor, while you look down inside the throttle bore checking that the

Throttle cable adjusting location—CVCC models

throttle plates reach the wide open throttle (WOT) vertical position.

5. Install the air cleaner.

Choke

1170 AND 1237cc MODELS

The choke valve should be **FULLY OPEN** when the choke knob is pushed **IN** and/or **FULLY CLOSED** with the choke knob pulled **OUT**. The choke valve is held in the fully closed position by spring action. Pull the choke knob to the fully closed position, then, open and close the choke valve by rotating the choke valve shaft. The movement should be free and unrestricted.

If adjustment is required, adjust the cable length by loosening the cable clamp bolt.

Precision Adjustment

1. Using a wire gauge, check the primary throttle valve opening, dimension **G1**, when the choke valve is fully closed. The opening should be 1.28-1.68mm.

2. If the opening is out of specification, adjust it by bending the choke rod. After installing make sure that the highest fast idle speed is 2,500-2,800 rpm while the engine is warm.

NOTE: *When adjusting the fast idle speed, be sure the throttle adjusting screw does not contact the stop.*

1487 AND 1600cc MODELS

1976-79

1. Push the choke actuator rod towards its diaphragm, so it does not contact the choke valve linkage.

2. Pull the choke knob out to the 1st detent (click) position from the dash. With the knob in this position, check the distance between the choke butterfly valve and the venturi opening with a ³⁄₁₆" drill (shank end).

3. Adjust as necessary by bending the relief lever adjusting tang with needle nose pliers.

4. Now, pull out the choke knob to its 2nd detent position from the dash. Again, make sure the choke actuator rod does not contact the choke valve linkage.

5. With the choke knob in this position, check that the clearance between the butterfly valve and venturi opening is ⅛" using the shank end of a ⅛" drill.

6. Adjust as necessary by bending the stop tab for the choke butterfly linkage.

1335, 1487 (1980-83) and 1751cc Models

1. With the engine **COLD**, remove the air cleaner.

2. Open and close the throttle all the way to engage the fast idle cam.

3. The choke plate should close to within ⅛" of the air horn wall.

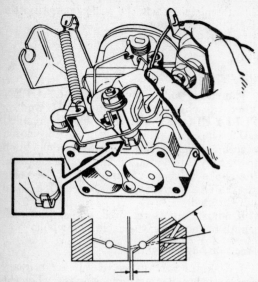

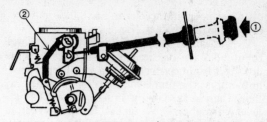

Choke cable adjustment—1974 and later 1237 cc models. Number one is the detent position, and number two is the link adjusting location

Precision choke adjustment—1170, 1237 cc models

1. Choke butterfly valve   2. Adjusting nut
3. Locknut

Choke cable adjustment—CVCC models

1. Make sure that the choke cable is correctly adjusted.

   a. With the choke knob in, the choke butterfly should be completely **OPEN**.

   b. Slowly pull out the choke knob and check for slack in the cable. Remove any excessive free-play and recheck for **FULL OPEN** when the knob is pushed **IN**.

2. Check the link rod adjustment by pulling the choke knob out to the 1st detent. The two scribed lines on the throttle control lever should align on either side of the reference tab. If not, adjust by bending the choke link rod.

1487 AND 1600cc MODELS

1. Remove the air cleaner assembly.

2. Push the choke knob all the way in at the dash. Check that the choke butterfly valve (choke plate) is **FULLY OPEN** (vertical).

3. Next, have a friend pull out the choke knob while you observe the action of the butterfly valve. When the choke knob is pulled out to the 2nd detent position, the butterfly valve should just close. Then, when the choke knob is pulled all the way out, the butterfly valve should remain in the **CLOSED** position.

4. To adjust, loosen the choke cable locknut

1. Stop tab
2. Relief lever adjusting tang
3. Actuator rod
4. Choke opener diaphragm

Choke adjusting components—CVCC models

4. If not, remove the choke cover and inspect the linkage for free movement. Repair or replace parts if necessary.

5. Install the cover and adjust so that the index marks align. Recheck the choke for proper closing clearance. If the clearance is not correct, replace the cap and retest.

Choke Cable

1974-79 1237cc MODELS

NOTE: *Perform the adjustment only after the throttle plate opening has been set and referenced, as in the preceding procedure.*

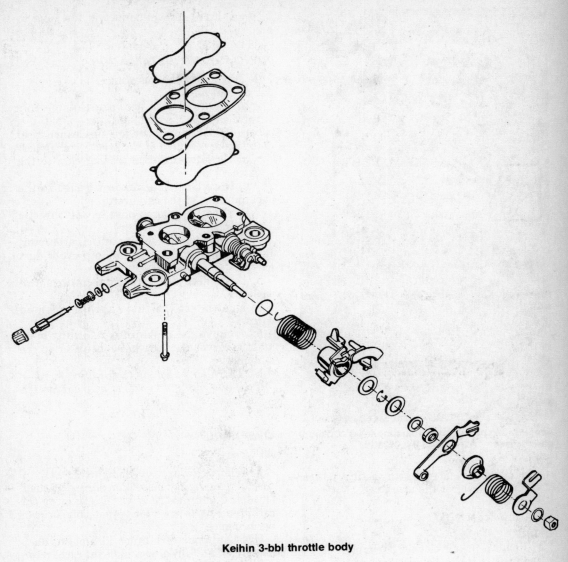

Keihin 3-bbl throttle body

and rotate the adjusting nut so that with the choke knob pushed flush against the dash (open position), the butterfly valve just rests against its positioning stop tab. Tighten the locknut.

5. If the choke butterfly valve is sticky in operation or if it does not close properly, check the butterfly valve and shaft for binding. Check also the operation of the return spring.

Throttle Valve Operation

1170 AND 1237cc MODELS

1. Check to see if the throttle valve opens fully when the throttle lever is moved to the fully open position. See if the valve closes fully when the lever is released.

2. Measure the clearance between the primary throttle valve and the chamber wall where the connecting rod begins to open the secondary throttle valve. The clearance should be 5.6-6.0mm.

3. If the clearance is out of specification, adjust by bending the connecting rod.

NOTE: *After adjusting, operate the throttle lever and check for any sign of binding.*

Accelerator Pump

1170 AND 1237cc MODELS

Check the pump for smooth operation. See if fuel squirts out of the pump nozzle by operating the pump lever or the throttle lever. When the pump is operated slowly, fuel must squirt out until the pump comes to the end of its travel. If the pump is defective, check for clogging or a defective piston. Adjust the pump by either

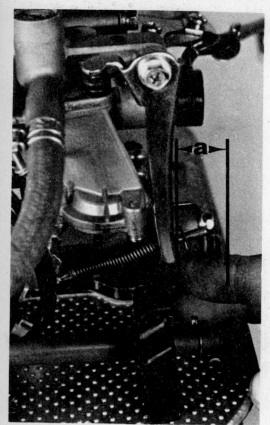

Accelerating pump travel adjustment—CVCC models. Distance "A" is 0.0311–0.0335 in.

repositioning the end of the connecting rod arm in the pump lever or the arm itself.

1487 AND 1600cc MODELS

1976-79

1. Remove the air cleaner assembly.
2. Check that the distance between the tang at the end of the accelerator pump lever and the lever stop at the edge of the throttle body (distance **A**) is 0.80-0.85mm (1975-77) or 14.5-15.0mm (1978-79). This corresponds to effective pump lever travel.
3. To adjust, bend the pump lever tang in the required direction.
4. Install the air cleaner.

1487 (1980-83) AND 1751cc MODELS

1. Remove the air cleaner.
2. Make sure that the pump shaft is moving freely throughout the pump stroke.
3. Check that the pump lever is in contact with the pump shaft.
4. Measure between the bottom end of the pump lever and the lever stop tang. The gap should be 14-15mm through 1980 or 11.5-

12.0mm (1981-82). If not, bend the tang to adjust.

REMOVAL AND INSTALLATION

1. Disconnect the following:
   a. Hot air tube.
   b. Vacuum hose between the one-way valve and the manifold at the manifold.
   c. Breather chamber (on air cleaner case) to intake manifold at the breather chamber.
   d. Hose from the air cleaner case to the valve cover.
   e. Hose from the carbon canister to the carburetor, at the carburetor.
   f. Throttle opener hose at the throttle opener.
2. Disconnect the fuel line at the carburetor. Plug the end of the fuel line to prevent dust entry.
3. Disconnect the choke and throttle control cables.
4. Disconnect the fuel shut-off solenoid wires.
5. Remove the carburetor retaining bolts and the carburetor. Leave the insulator on the manifold.
NOTE: *After removing the carburetor, cover the intake manifold parts to keep out foreign materials.*

OVERHAUL

All Types

Efficient carburetion depends greatly on careful cleaning and inspection during overhaul since dirt, gum, water or varnish in or on the carburetor parts are often responsible for poor performance.

Overhaul your carburetor in a clean, dust-free area. Carefully disassemble the carburetor, referring often to the exploded views. Keep all similar and look-alike parts segregated during disassembly and cleaning to avoid accidental interchange during assembly. Make a note of all jet sizes.

When the carburetor is disassembled, wash all parts (except diaphragms, electric choke units, pump plunger and any other plastic, leather, fiber or rubber parts) in clean carburetor solvent. Do not leave parts in the solvent any longer than is necessary to sufficiently loosen the deposits. Excessive cleaning may remove the special finish from the float bowl and choke valve bodies, leaving these parts unfit for service. Rinse all parts in clean solvent and blow them dry with compressed air or allow them to air dry. Wipe clean all cork, plastic, leather and fiber parts with a clean, lint-free cloth.

Blow out all passages and jets with compressed air and be sure that there are no restrictions or blockages. Never use wire or similar tools to clean jets, fuel passages or air bleeds. Clean all jets and valves separately to avoid accidental interchange.

Check all parts for wear or damage. If wear or damage is found, replace the defective parts. Especially check the following:

1. Check the float needle and seat for wear. If wear is found, replace the complete assembly.

2. Check the float hinge pin for wear and the float(s) for dents or distortion. Replace the float if fuel has leaked into it.

3. Check the throttle and choke shaft bores for wear or an out-of-round condition. Damage or wear to the throttle arm, shaft or shaft bore will often require replacement of the throttle body. These parts require a close tolerance of fit; wear may allow air leakage, which could affect starting and idling.

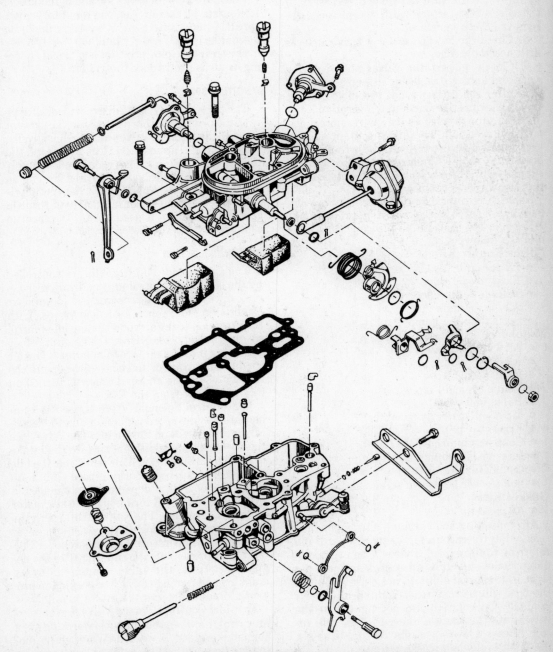

Exploded view of Keihin 3-bbl used on CVCC engines

NOTE: *Throttle shafts and bushings are not included in overhaul kits. They can be purchased separately.*

4. Inspect the idle mixture adjusting needles for burrs or grooves. Any such condition requires replacement of the needle, since you will not be able to obtain a satisfactory idle.

5. Test the accelerator pump check valves. They should pass air one way but not the other. Test for proper seating by blowing and sucking on the valve. Replace the valve if necessary. If the valve is satisfactory, wash the valve again to remove breath moisture.

6. Check the bowl cover for warped surfaces with a straightedge.

7. Closely inspect the valves and seats for wear and damage, replacing as necessary.

8. After the carburetor is assembled, check the choke valve for freedom of operation.

Carburetor overhaul kits are recommended for each overhaul. These kits contain all gaskets and new parts to replace those that deteriorate most rapidly. Failure to replace all parts supplied with the kit (especially gaskets) can result in poor performance later.

Some carburetor manufacturers supply overhaul kits of three basic types: minor repair; major repair; and gasket kits. Basically, they contain the following:

Minor Repair Kits:
- All gaskets
- Float needle valve
- Volume control screw
- All diaphragms
- Spring for the pump diaphragm

Major Repair Kits:
- All jets and gaskets
- All diaphragms
- Float needle valve
- Volume control screw
- Pump ball valve
- Main jet carrier
- Float
- Complete intermediate rod
- Intermediate pump lever
- Complete injector tube
- Some cover holddown screws and washers

Gasket Kits:
- All gaskets

After cleaning and checking all components, reassemble the carburetor, using new parts and referring to the exploded view. When reassembling, make sure that all screws and jets are tight in their seats, but do not overtighten, as the tips will be distorted. Tighten all screws gradually, in rotation. Do not tighten needle valves into their seats; uneven jetting will result. Always use new gaskets. Be sure to adjust the float level when reassembling.

PROGRAMMED FUEL INJECTION (PGM-FI) SYSTEM

General Description

Programmed Fuel Injection (PGM-FI) System consists of three sub-systems: Air intake, electronic control, and fuel.

Air Intake System

The system supplies air for all engine needs. It consists of the air cleaner, air intake pipe, throttle body, idle control system, fast idle mechanism, and intake manifold. A resonator in the air intake pipe provides additional silencing as air is drawn into the system.

THROTTLE BODY

The throttle body, is a 2-barrel sidedraft type with the primary air horn at the top. To prevent icing of the throttle valves and air horn walls, under certain atmospheric conditions of the throttle valves air air horn walls the lower portion of the throttle body is heated by engine coolant. A throttle sensor is attached to the primary throttle valve to sense changes in throttle opening. A dashpot is used to slow the throttle as it approaches the closed position.

IDLE CONTROL SYSTEM

The air/fuel ratio during idling is controlled by the electronic control unit and various solenoid valves such as idle control, fast idle and air conditioning idle control solenoid valves. With the exception of the air conditioning idle control solenoid valve, these change the amounts of air bypassing into the air intake manifold. The air conditioning control solenoid valve opens the throttle when the air conditioner is turned on by signals sent from the ECU.

Idle Control Solenoid Valve is used to compensate for idle speed reduction due to electrical, or other loads on the engine. The valve does this by bypassing additional air into the intake manifold. This additional air will allow the idle speed to increase to its normal speed (750 ± 50 rpm). The operation depends upon changes in the voltage at the **FR** terminal of the alternator for quick response. The valve also lowers the fast idle speed in steps during warm-up, after the coolant temperature has researched 131°F (55°C). To prevent erratic running after the engine first fires, the valve is opened during cranking and immediately after starting to provide additional air into the intake manifold.

Fast Idle Control Solenoid Valve prevents erratic running when the engine is warming up, a higher idle speed is needed. When the atmospheric pressure is 660mm Hg or less, the valve opens to bypass additional air into the intake manifold.

The air conditioning Idle Control Solenoid Valve maintains an idle speed of 750 ± 50 rpm when the air conditioner is turned on. The valve causes the air conditioning idle control diaphragm to open the throttle valve which raises the idle speed. The valve is also opened when coolant temperature is low (immediately after starting) thereby ensuring stable idling regardless of position of the air conditioning switch.

IDLE ADJUSTER (BYPASS CIRCUIT)

Fuel cut-off takes place at a set position or angle of the throttle valve. If the throttle valve is moved to adjust idle speed, this position or angle will be changed and the system may not cut off fuel supply. To solve this problem, the throttle body contains an adjustable bypass circuit. This circuit is designed to control the amount of air bypassing into the intake manifold without changing the position of throttle valve. The idle speed usually does not require system, while the idle control system is in operation, the idle screw has no effect on the idle speed.

Usually it does not require to adjust idle speed by idle adjust screw since idle speed is adjusted automatically by the operation of idle control system. Idle speed does not change by turning the idle adjust screw while idle control system is in operation.

FAST IDLE MECHANISM

To prevent erratic running when the engine is warming up, it is necessary to raise the idle speed. The air bypass valve is controlled by a thermowax plunger. When the thermowax is cold, the valve is open. When the thermowax is heated, the valve is closed. With the engine cold and the thermowax consequently cold, additional air is bypassed into the intake manifold so that the engine idles faster than normal. When the engine reaches operating temperature, the valve begins to close, reducing the amount of air bypassing into the manifold.

Electronic Control System

CONTROL SYSTEM

In order to get fuel into the cylinders at the correct instant and in correct amount, the control system must perform various separate functions. The ECU (Electronic Control Unit), the heart of the PGM-FI, uses an eight-bit microcomputer and consists of a CPU (Central Processing Unit), memories, and I/O (Input/Output) ports. Basic data stored in the memories are compensated by the signals sent

from the various sensors to provide the correct air/fuel mixture for all engine needs.

ELECTRONIC CONTROL UNIT (ECU)

The unit contains memories for the basic discharge duration at various engine speeds and manifold pressures. The basic discharge duration, after being read out from the memory, is further modified by signals sent from various sensors to obtain the final discharge duration. Other functions also include:

Starting Control: The fuel system must vary the air/fuel ratio to suit different operating requirements. For example, the mixture must be rich for starting. The memories also contain the basic discharge durations to be read out by signals from the starter switch, and engine speed and coolant temperature sensors, thereby providing extra fuel needed for starting.

Fuel Pump Control: When the speed of the engine falls below the prescribed limit, electric current to the fuel pump is cut off, preventing the injectors from discharging fuel.

Fuel Cut-Off Control: During deceleration with the throttle valve nearly closed, electric current to the injectors is cut off at speeds over 900 rpm, contributing to improved fuel economy. Fuel cut-off action also takes place when engine speed exceeds 7000 rpm regardless of the position of the throttle valve.

Safety: A fail-safe system monitors the sensors and detects any abnormality in the ECU, ensuring safe driving even if one or more sensors are faulty, or if the ECU malfunctions.

CRANK ANGLE SENSOR (TDC/CYL SENSORS)

The sensors and distributor are designed as an assembly to save space and weight. The entire unit consist of a pair of rotors, TDC and CYL, and a pickup for each rotor. Since the rotors are coupled to the camshaft, they turn together as a unit as the camshaft rotates. The CYL sensor detects the position of the No. 1 cylinder as the base for the Sequential Injection whereas the TDC sensor serves to determine the injection timing for each cylinder. The TDC sensor is also used to detect engine speed to read out the basic discharge duration for different operating conditions.

MANIFOLD AIR PRESSURE SENSOR (MAP SENSOR)

The sensor converts manifold air pressure readings into electrical voltage signals and sends them to the ECU. This information with signals from the crank angle sensor is then used to read out the basic discharge duration from the memory.

ATMOSPHERIC PRESSURE SENSOR (PA SENSOR)

Like the MAP sensor, the unit converts atmospheric pressures into voltage signals and sends them to the ECU. The signals then modify the basic discharge duration to compensate for changes in the atmospheric pressure.

COOLANT TEMPERATURE SENSOR (TW SENSOR)

The sensor uses a temperature dependent diode (thermistor) to measure differences in the coolant temperature. The basic discharge duration is read out by the signals sent from this sensor through the ECU. The resistance of the thermister decreases with a rise in coolant temperature.

INTAKE AIR TEMPERATURE SENSOR (TA SENSOR)

This device is also a thermistor and is placed in the intake manifold. It acts much like the water temperature sensor but with a reduced thermal capacity for for quicker response. The basic discharge duration read out from the memory is again compensated for different operating conditions by the signals sent from this sensor through the ECU.

THROTTLE ANGLE SENSOR

This sensor is essentially a variable resistor. In construction, the rotor shaft is connected to the throttle valve shaft such that, as the throttle valve is moved, the resistance varies, altering the output voltage to the control unit.

OXYGEN SENSOR

The oxygen sensor, by detecting the oxygen content in the exhaust gas, maintains the stoichiometric air/fuel ratio. In operation, the ECU receives the signals from the sensor and changes the duration during which fuel is injected. The oxygen sensor is located in the exhaust manifold.

The sensor is a hollow shaft of zirconia with a closed end. The inner and outer surfaces are plated with platinum, thus forming a platinum electrode. The inner surface or chamber is open to the atmosphere whereas the outer surface is exposed to the exhaust gas flow through the manifold.

Voltage is induced at the platinum electrode when there is any difference in oxygen concentration between the two layers of air over the surfaces. Operation of the device is dependent upon the fact that voltage induced changes sharply as the stoichiometric air/fuel ratio is exceeded when the electrode is heated above a certain temperature.

IDLE MIXTURE ADJUSTER SENSOR (IMA SENSOR)

The sensor is located in the control box. The primary objective of this unit is to maintain the correct air/fuel ratio at idling. No adjustment of the IMA sensor is necessary as the feedback control is performed by the oxygen sensor even during idling.

STARTER SWITCH

The air/fuel mixture must be rich for starting. During cranking, the ECU detects signal from the starter switch and increases the amount of fuel injected into the manifold according to the engine temperature. The amount of fuel injected is gradually reduced when the starter switch is turned off.

Fuel System

FUEL PUMP

The fuel pump is an inline, direct drive type. Fuel is drawn into the pump through a filter, flows around the armature through the one-way valve and is delivered to the engine compartment. A baffle is provided to prevent fuel pulsation. The fuel pump has a relief valve to prevent excessive pressure. It opens if there is a blockage in the discharge side. When the relief valve opens, fuel flows from the high pressure to the low pressure side. A check valve is provided to maintain fuel pressure in the line after the pump is stopped. This is to ease restarting.

The pump section is composed of a rotor, rollers and pump spacer. When the rotor turns, the rollers turn and travel along the inner surface of the pump spacer by centrifugal force. The volume of the cavity enclosed by these three parts changes, drawing and pressurizing the fuel.

PRESSURE REGULATOR

The fuel pressure regulator maintains a constant fuel pressure to the injectors. The spring chamber of the pressure regulator is connected to the intake manifold to constantly maintain the fuel pressure at 36 psi ($2.55 kg/cm_2$) higher than the pressure in the manifold. When the difference between the fuel pressure and manifold pressure exceeds 36 psi (2.55 kg/cm2), the diaphragm is pushed upward, and the excess fuel is fed back into the fuel tank through the return line.

INJECTOR

The injector is of the solenoid actuated constant stroke pintle type consisting of a solenoid, plunger, needle valve and housing. When current is applied to the solenoid coil, the valve lifts up and pressurized fuel fills the inside of the injector and is injected close to the intake valve. Because the needle valve lifts and the fuel pressure are constant, the injection quantity is determined by; the length of time that the valve is open, i.e., the duration the current is supplied to the solenoid coil. The injector is sealed by an

O-ring and seal ring at the top and bottom. These seals also reduce operating noise.

RESISTOR

The injector timing, which controls the opening and closing intervals, must be very accurate since it dictates the air/fuel mixture ratio. The injector must also be durable. For the best possible injector response, it is necessary to shorten the current rise time when voltage is applied to the injector coil. Therefore, the number of windings of the injector coil is reduced to reduce the inductance in the coil. This, however, makes low resistance in the coil, allowing a large amount of current to flow through the coil. As a result, the amount of heat generated is high, which compromises the durability of the coil. Flow of current in the coil is therefore restricted by a resistor installed in series between the electric power source and the injector coil.

MAIN RELAY

The main relay is a direct coupler type which contains the relays for the electronic control unit power supply and the fuel pump power supply. This relay is installed at the back of the fuse box.

SERVICE PRECAUTIONS

- Do not operate the fuel pump when the fuel lines are empty.
- Do not reuse fuel hose clamps.
- Make sure all ECU harness connectors are fastened securely. A poor connection can cause an extremely high surge voltage in the coil and condenser and result in damage to integrated circuits.
- Keep ECU all parts and harnesses dry during service.
- Before attempting to remove any parts, turn off the ignition switch and disconnect the battery ground cable.
- Always use a 12 volt battery as a power source.
- Do not attempt to disconnect the battery cables with the engine running.
- Do not depress the accelerator pedal when starting.
- Do not rev up the engine immediately after starting or just prior to shutdown.
- Do not apply battery power directly to injectors.

Diagnosis and Testing
SELF-DIAGNOSTIC SYSTEM

Self-Diagnosis Indicators

The quick reference chart covers the most common failure modes for the PGM-FI. The probable causes are listed in order of most easily checked first, then progressing to more difficult fixes. Run through all the causes listed. If problem is still unsolved, go on to the more detailed troubleshooting. Troubleshooting is divided into different LED displays. Find the correct light display and begin again.

For all the conditions listed, the PGM-FI warning light on the dashboard must be on (comes on and stays on). This indicates a problem in the electrical portion of the fuel injection system. At that time, check the LED display (self-diagnosis system) in the ECU.

On all Civic models and 1985 Accord models, there are four LED displays. They are part of the ECU, which is located under the passenger's seat in the Accord and Civic and in the left side panel beside the rear seat on Prelude. They are numbered 1, 2, 4 and 8, as counted from right to left.

On 1986-88 Accord and Prelude models, there is only one LED display. The LED will blink consecutively to indicate the trouble code. The ECU is located under the driver's seat on the Accord and in the left side panel beside the rear seat on the Prelude.

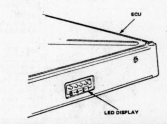

PGM-FI LED display—1985–88 Civic and 1985 Accord

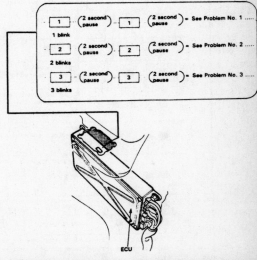

PGM-FI LED display—1986–88 Prelude shown, 1986–88 Accord ECU under driver's seat

Sometimes the dash warning light and/or ECU LED(s) will come on, indicating a system problem, when, in fact, there is only a bad or intermittent electrical connection. To troubleshoot a bad connection, note the ECU LED pattern that is lit, refer to the diagnosis chart and check the connectors associated with the items mentioned in the "Possible Cause" column for that LED pattern (disconnect, clean or repair if necessary and reconnect those connections).

Then, reset the ECU memory as described, restart the car and drive it for a few minutes and then recheck the car and drive it for a few minutes and then recheck the LED(s). If the same pattern lights up, begin system troubleshooting; if it does not light up, the problem was only a bad connection.

The memory for the PGM-FI warning light on the dashboard will be erased when the ignition switch is turned off; however, the memory

PGM-FI LED DISPLAY QUICK REFERENCE CHART
1985-88 CIVIC and 1985 ACCORD

LED Display	Symptom	Possible Cause
○ ○ ○ ○ (Dash warning light off)	· Engine will not start.	· Loose or poorly connected power line to ECU main relay resistor · Disconnected control unit ground wire · Faulty ECU
○ ○ ○ ○ (Dash warning light on)	· Engine will not start. · No particular symptom shown	· Disconnected control unit ground wire · Faulty ECU · Short circuit in combination meter or warning light wire
○ ○ ○ ● 1	· No particular symptom shown · Erratic idling (Erratic injector, coupler and wiring) · Insufficient fuel	· Disconnected oxygen sensor coupler · Spark plug mis-fire · Short or open circuit in oxygen sensor circuit · Faulty oxygen sensor
○ ○ ● ○ 2	· No particular symptom shown or system does not operate	· Faulty ECU
○ ○ ● ● 2 1	· Wet-plug · Frequent engine stalling · Engine fails to pick up speed	· Disconnected manifold air pressure sensor coupler · Short or open circuit in manifold air pressure sensor wire · Faulty manifold air pressure sensor
○ ● ○ ○ 4	· No particular symptom shown or system does not operate	· Faulty ECU
○ ● ○ ● 4 1	· Engine fails to pick up speed · Wet-plug · Frequent engine stalling	· Disconnected manifold air pressure sensor piping
○ ● ● ○ 4 2	· High idle speed during warm-up · High idle speed · Hard starting at low temp	· Disconnected coolant temperature sensor coupler · Open circuit in coolant temperature sensor wire · Faulty coolant temperature sensor (thermostat housing)
○ ● ● ● 4 2 1	· Poor engine response to opening throttle rapidly · High idle speed · Engine does not rev up when cold	· Disconnected throttle angle sensor coupler · Open or short circuit in throttle angle sensor wire · Faulty throttle angle sensor
● ○ ○ ○ 8	· Engine does not rev up · High idle speed · Erratic idling	· Short or open circuit in crank angle sensor wire · Crank angle sensor wire interfering with high tension cord · Crank angle sensor at fault
● ○ ○ ● 8 1	Same as above	Same as above
● ○ ● ○ 8 2	· High idle speed · Erratic idling when very cold	· Disconnected intake air temperature sensor · Open circuit in intake air temperature sensor wire · Faulty intake air temperature sensor
● ○ ● ● 8 2 1	· No particular symptom shown · High idle speed	· Disconnected idle mixture adjuster sensor coupler · Shorted or disconnected idle mixture adjuster sensor wire · Faulty idle mixture adjuster sensor
● ● ○ ○ 8 4	· No particular symptom shown or system does not operate at all.	· Faulty ECU
● ● ○ ● 8 4 1	· Poor acceleration at high altitude · Hard starting at high altitude when cold	· Disconnected atmospheric pressure sensor coupler · Shorted or disconnected atmospheric pressure sensor wire · Faulty atmospheric pressure sensor
● ● ● ○ 8 4 2	· No particular symptom shown or system does not operate at all	· Faulty ECU
● ● ● ● 8 4 2 1	Same as above	Same as above

NOTE: Some failure indications (such as when only the No. 1 indication is lit) require the full test procedures on the following pages to confirm that the failure has or has not been eliminated.

for the LED display(s) will not be canceled. Thus, the warning light will not come on when the ignition switch is again turned on unless the trouble is once more detected. Trouble-shooting should be done according to the LED display(s) even if the warning light is off.

Other ECU information:

• After making repairs, disconnect the battery negative cable from the battery negative terminal for at least 10 seconds and reset the ECU memory. After reconnecting the cable, check that the LED display is turned off.

• Turn the ignition switch on. The PGM-FI warning light should come on for about 2 seconds. If the warning light won't come on, check for:

   a. Blown warning light bulb

   b. Blown No. 3 fuse (causing faulty back up light, seat belt alarm, clock, memory function of the car radio)

PGM-FI LED DISPLAY QUICK REFERENCE CHART
1986-88 ACCORD AND PRELUDE

No. of LED Blinks between 2 second pauses		Symptom	Possible cause
0	Dash warning light off	• Engine will not start	• Disconnected control unit ground wire • Faulty ECU
	Dash warning light on	• Engine will not start • No particular symptom shown	• Loose or poorly connected power line to ECU • Disconnected control unit ground wire • Short circuit in combination meter or warning light wire • Faulty ECU
1		• No particular symptom shown • Erratic idling (Erratic injector, coupler and wiring Insufficient fuel)	• Disconnected oxygen sensor coupler • Spark plug mis-fire • Short or open circuit in oxygen sensor circuit • Faulty oxygen sensor • Faulty fuel system
2		• No particular symptom shown or system does not operate	• Faulty ECU
3		• Fuel fouled plug • Frequent engine stalling • Hesitation	• Disconnected manifold absolute pressure sensor coupler • Short or open circuit in manifold absolute pressure sensor wire • Faulty manifold absolute pressure sensor
4		• No particular symptom shown or system does not operate	• Faulty ECU
5		• Hesitation • Fuel fouled plug • Frequent engine stalling	• Disconnected manifold absolute pressure sensor piping
6		• High idle speed during warm-up • High idle speed • Hard starting at low temp	• Disconnected coolant temperature sensor coupler • Open or short circuit in coolant temperature sensor wire • Faulty coolant temperature sensor (thermostat housing)
7		• Poor engine response to opening throttle rapidly • High idle speed • Engine does not rev up when cold	• Disconnected throttle angle sensor coupler • Open or short circuit in throttle angle sensor wire • Faulty throttle angle sensor
8		• Engine does not rev up • High idle speed • Erratic idling	• Short or open circuit in crank angle sensor wire • Crank angle sensor wire interfering with spark plug wires • Crank angle sensor at fault
9		• Same as above	• Same as above
10		• High idle speed • Erratic idling when very cold	• Disconnected intake air temperature sensor • Open or short circuit in intake air temperature sensor wire • Faulty intake air temperature sensor
11		• No particular symptom shown or system does not operate	• Faulty ECU
12		• Frequent engine stalling • Erratic or unstable running at low speed • No particular symptom shown	• Disconnected EGR control system coupler • Shorted or disconnected EGR control wire • Faulty EGR control system
13		• Poor acceleration at high altitude • Hard starting at high altitude when cold	• Disconnected atmospheric pressure sensor coupler • Shorted or disconnected atmospheric pressure sensor wire • Faulty atmospheric pressure sensor

NOTE:
• If the number of blinks between 2 second pauses exceeds 13, or if the LED indicator stays on, the ECU is faulty.
• Some failure indications (such as, one blink) require the full test procedures on the following pages to confirm that the failure has or has not been eliminated.

c. Open circuit in Yellow wire between No. # 3 fuse and combination meter

d. Open circuit in Green/Orange wire between combination meter and control unit

• After the PGM-FI warning light and self-diagnosis indicators have been turned on, turn the ignition switch off. If the LED display fails to come on when the ignition switch is turned on again, check for:

a. Blown No. 10 fuse

b. Open circuit in White/Green wire between ECU A17 terminal and No. 10 fuse

• Replace the ECU only after making sure that all couplers and connectors are connected securely.

COMPONENT TEST PROCEDURES

Oxygen Sensor

1985-86 ACCORD, 1985-88 CIVIC AND 1986-88 PRELUDE

1. Disconnect connector of oxygen sensor.

2. Start engine and warm up for two minutes at 3000 rpm under no load. Raise engine speed to 4000 rpm and release throttle suddenly at least 5 times.

3. Within on minute after engine has been warmed up, measure voltage between connector terminal and body ground as described in in Steps 4 and 5.

NOTE: *If it takes more than one minute to complete checks, warm up engine as in Step 2 before continuing.*

4. Raise engine speed to 5,000 rpm, then lower to 2,000 rpm by operating accelerator pedal, immediately turn ignition switch off. Voltage should be below 0.4 volts.

5. Disconnect vacuum tube (between MAP sensor and throttle body on Civic models and hose #21 on Accord models) from throttle body; plug opening in throttle body. Connect a hand vacuum pump to open end of vacuum tube and apply 12 in. Hg (300mm Hg), and raise engine speed to 4,000 rpm. Voltage should be above 0.6 volts.

6. Replace oxygen sensor if voltages are out of ranges.

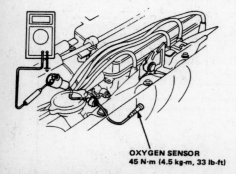

OXYGEN SENSOR
45 N·m (4.5 kg-m, 33 lb-ft)

Oxygen sensor test—typical

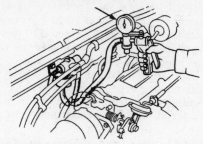

VACUUM PUMP/GAUGE

Manifold air pressure (MAP) sensor check—1985–86 Civic shown, 1985 Accord similar

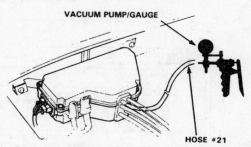

VACUUM PUMP/GAUGE

HOSE #21

Manifold air pressure (MAP) sensor check—1986 Accord and Prelude

Manifold Air Pressure (MAP) Sensor

1985-86 ACCORD AND CIVIC, AND 1986 PRELUDE

1. Disconnect vacuum hose (between MAP sensor and throttle body on Civic models and hose #21 on Accord models) from throttle body; plug opening in throttle body. Connect a vacuum hand pump to open end of vacuum tube.

2. Disconnect connector from control unit. Connect system checker harness (07999-PD6000A or equivalent) between control unit and wire harness connector.

3. Turn ignition switch on. Connect a digital voltmeter positive probe to **C11** terminal of system checker harness and negative probe to **C14** terminal. Measure voltage between two terminals. Voltmeter should indicate between 0.5 volts at 4 in. Hg (100mm Hg) of vacuum and 4.5 volts at 45 in. Hg (1200mm Hg).

4. If voltage is incorrect, check vacuum tube for leakage, and wires between control unit and sensor for open or short circuit. Replace sensor if wires are normal.

Atmospheric Pressure (PA) Sensor

1985-86 ACCORD AND CIVIC

1. Disconnect connector from control unit. Connect system checker harness (07999-PD6000A or equivalent) between control unit and wire harness connector.

2. Turn ignition switch on. Connect a digital voltmeter positive probe to **C9** terminal of sys-

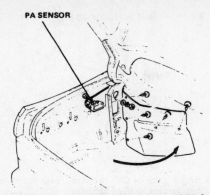

Atmospheric pressure sensor location—1985 Accord

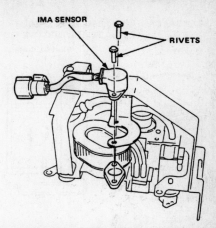

Idle mixture adjuster (IMA) sensor servicing—1985–88 Civic

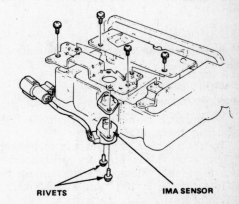

Idle mixture adjuster (IMA) sensor servicing—1985 Accord

tem checker harness and negative probe to **C12** terminal. Measure voltage between two terminals. Voltmeter should indicate 2.76-2.96 volts.

3. If voltage is outside ranges, check for open or short circuit between ECU and PA sensor. Replace PA sensor with a new one if wires are in good condition.

Idle Mixture Adjuster (IMA) Sensor

1985-88 CIVIC

1. Measure resistance between Green terminal and Yellow terminal (Yellow/White and Black terminal on 1987-88 models) of control box coupler. Resistance should be 0.25-6.2kΩ.

2. Replace IMA sensor if resistance are out of range.

1985 ACCORD

1. Open No. 1 control box lid and remove rivets attaching IMA sensor.

2. Disconnect IMA sensor 3P coupler.

3. Measure resistance between Brown terminal and Green terminal of IMA sensor while turning adjuster. Resistance should be 0.25-6.2kΩ.

4. Replace IMA sensor if resistance are out of range.

There should be: 0.25—6.2 kΩ

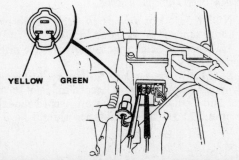

Idle mixture adjuster (IMA) sensor resistance check—1985 Civic

Intake Air Temperature (TA)/Coolant Temperature (TW) Sensor

1985 ACCORD AND 1985-88 CIVIC

1. Disconnect connector and remove TA/TW sensor from inlet manifold/cylinder head.

2. To test a sensor, suspend it in cold water and heat water slowly. Measure resistance between terminals. Measurements should be 0.98-1.34kΩ at 95°F (40°C) and 0.22-0.35kΩ at 176°F (80°C).

3. Replace sensor if resistance is outside of range.

Intake Air Temperature (TA) Sensor

1986 ACCORD AND 1986-88 PRELUDE

1. Disconnect connector and remove TA sensor from intake manifold.

2. To test a sensor, suspend it in cold water and heat water slowly. Measure resistance between terminals. Measurements should be 0.98-1.34kΩ at 104°F (40°C) and 0.22-0.35kΩ at 176°F (80°C).

STANDARDS: 0.98—1.34 kΩ at 40°C (95°F)
0.22—0.35 kΩ at 80°C (176°F)

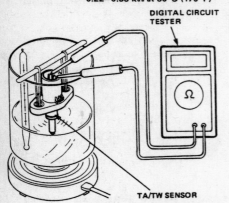

DIGITAL CIRCUIT TESTER

Ω

TA/TW SENSOR

Intake air temperature (TA)/coolant temperature (TW) sensor resistance test—1985-88 Civic and 1985 Accord

Resistance should be: 0.65—0.85 kΩ

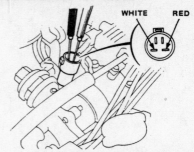

WHITE   RED

Crank angle sensor-CYL sensor resistance test— 1985 Civic shown, others similar

Resistance should be: 0.65—0.85 kΩ

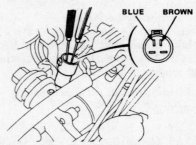

BLUE   BROWN

Crank angle sensor-TDC sensor resistance test— 1985 Civic shown, others similar

3. Replace sensor if resistance is outside of range.

Coolant Temperature (TW) Sensor

1986 ACCORD AND 1986-88 PRELUDE

1. Disconnect connector and remove TW sensor from thermostat housing.
2. To test a sensor, suspend it in cold water and heat water slowly. Measure resistance between terminals. Measurements should be 0.98-1.34kΩ at 95°F (40°C) and 0.22-0.35kΩ at 176°F (80°C).
3. Replace sensor if resistance is outside of range. On installing sensor, torque to 20 ft. lbs. (28 Nm).

Crank Angle Sensor (CYL Sensor)

1985-86 ACCORD, 1985-88 CIVIC AND 1986-88 PRELUDE

NOTE: *If either CYL or TDC sensor tests bad, replace as an assembly.*
1. Disconnect connector of crank angle sensor.
2. Measure resistance between (White and Red on 1985-88 Civic and 1985 Accord and White and Orange on 1986 Accord and 1986-88 Prelude) terminal at sensor. Resistance should be 0.65-0.85kΩ.
3. Measure insulation resistance between (White and Red on 1985-88 Civic and Accord and White and Orange on 1986 Accord and 1986-88 Prelude) terminal of sensor and crank angle sensor housing. Resistance should 100kΩ or more.

Crank Angle Sensor (TDC Sensor)

1985-86 ACCORD, 1985-88 CIVIC AND 1986-88 PRELUDE

NOTE: *If either CYL or TDC sensor tests bad, replace as an assembly.*

1. Disconnect connector of crank angle sensor.
2. Measure resistance between (Brown and Blue on 1985-88 Civic and Orange/Blue and White/Blue on 1986 Accord and 1986-88 Prelude) terminal at sensor. Resistance should be 0.65-0.85kΩ.
3. Measure insulation resistance between (Brown and Blue on 1985-88 Civic and Orange/Blue and White/Blue on 1986 Accord and 1986-88 Prelude) terminal of sensor and crank angle sensor housing. Resistance should be 100kΩ or more.

Throttle Angle Sensor

1985 ACCORD AND 1985-88 CIVIC

NOTE: *Do not adjust throttle valve stop screw since it is preset at factory.*
1. Disconnect connector of throttle angle sensor.
2. Measure full resistance between Brown/Black (Yellow on Accord models) terminal and Yellow/Red (Green on Accord models) terminal at sensor. Resistance should be 3.2-7.2kΩ.

1986 ACCORD AND 1986-88 PRELUDE

NOTE: *Do not adjust throttle valve stop screw since it is preset at factory.*

Resistance should be: 3.2—7.2 kΩ

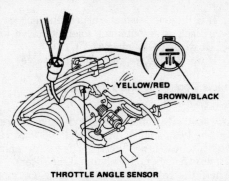

YELLOW/RED

BROWN/BLACK

THROTTLE ANGLE SENSOR

Throttle angle sensor resistance check—1985–86 Civic shown, others similar

1. Disconnect connector of throttle angle sensor.

2. Measure full resistance between Yellow/White terminal and Green/White terminal at sensor. Resistance should be 4-6kΩ.

Idle Control Solenoid Valve

1985-88 CIVIC

The idle control solenoid valve is activated by commands from the ECU. When the solenoid valve opens, this causes vacuum in the vacuum hose (between the air filter and the solenoid valve) and increases idle speed under the following conditions:

• For a short period after starting the engine.

• Whenever electrical loads are turned on (vacuum will disappear when engine rpm is raised over 1,700 rpm by operating the throttle).

While the solenoid valve is being activated, 9 volts or higher should be available between the Black (Black/Yellow on 1987-88 model) terminal (+) and Light Green (Green/White on 1987-88 models) terminal (−) of the valve leads.

1. Open control box lid and disconnect wire harness from control box.

2. Disconnect vacuum hose between idle control solenoid valve and the No. 10 vacuum hose (upper vacuum hose of idle control solenoid valve from 3-way joint on 1987-88 models) and connect vacuum pump to hose.

3. Apply vacuum to the hose. It should hold vacuum.

4. Connect battery positive terminal to Black terminal of control box and negative battery terminal to Light Green terminal.

5. Apply vacuum to hose. It should not hold vacuum. If vacuum holds, replace solenoid valve.

1985 ACCORD

The idle control solenoid valve is activated by commands from the ECU. When the solenoid valve opens, this causes vacuum in the vacuum hose (#26 on 1985 models and upper hose on 1986 models) and increases idle speed under the following conditions:

• For a short period after starting the engine.

• Whenever electrical loads are turned on (vacuum will disappear when engine rpm is raised over 1,500 rpm by operating the throttle).

While the solenoid valve is being activated, 9 volts or higher should be available between the Black/Yellow terminal (+) and Green/Black terminal (−) of the valve leads.

1. Disconnect wire harness from idle control solenoid valve.

2. Disconnect vacuum hose (**#26** from air flow tube on 1985 models and upper hose from intake manifold on 1986 models).

3. Pump air into hose **#26**. There should not be air flow.

4. Connect battery positive terminal to Black/Yellow terminal of solenoid valve and negative battery terminal to Green/Black terminal.

5. Disconnect vacuum hose **#28** from intake manifold.

6. Pump air into vacuum hose **#26**. There should be air flow.

1986 ACCORD AND 1986-88 PRELUDE

The idle control solenoid valve is activated by commands from the ECU. When the solenoid valve opens, this causes vacuum in the upper vacuum hose of the solenoid valve (from the intake manifold) and increases idle speed under the following conditions:

• For a short period after starting the engine.

• Whenever electrical loads are turned on (vacuum will disappear when engine rpm is raised over 1,500 rpm by operating the throttle).

While the solenoid valve is being activated, 9 volts or higher should be available between the Black/Yellow terminal (+) and Green/Black terminal (−) of the valve leads.

1. Disconnect wire harness from idle control solenoid valve.

2. Disconnect upper vacuum hose of solenoid valve from intake manifold.

3. Apply vacuum to hose. Vacuum should hold steady. If vacuum is not steady, replace valve.

4. Connect battery positive terminal to Black/Yellow terminal of solenoid valve and

negative battery terminal to Green/Black terminal.

5. Apply vacuum to hose. Vacuum should not hold. If valve holds vacuum, replace valve.

Idle Control Test

1987-88 ACCORD

1. Check vacuum line for proper connection, cracks, blockage or disconnected hoses.

2. Disconnect lower vacuum hose of idle control solenoid valve from air chamber and connect a vacuum gauge to vacuum hose.

3. Start engine and check for vacuum. Make check within 10 seconds. Vacuum should be present.

4. If no vacuum, go to IDLE CONTROL SOLENOID VALVE TEST I. If vacuum is present, raise engine speed above 1,500 rpm and check vacuum. Vacuum should not be present.

5. If vacuum is present, go to IDLE CONTROL SOLENOID VALVE TEST II.

Idle Control Solenoid Valve Test I

1987-88 ACCORD

1. Start engine and allow to idle.

2. Disconnect upper vacuum hose of idle control solenoid valve from intake manifold and check vacuum. Vacuum should be present.

3. If no vacuum, check vacuum port.

4. Stop engine.

5. Disconnect 2P connector on idle control solenoid valve.

6. Attach positive probe of voltmeter to Black/Yellow terminal and negative probe to Green/Black terminal.

7. Within 10 seconds after restarting engine, check voltage at idle.

8. If voltage is present, replace solenoid valve.

9. If no voltage, attach positive probe of voltmeter to Black/Yellow terminal of connector, and negative probe to body ground. Within 10 seconds after restarting engine, check voltage.

10. If no voltage, repair open in Black/Yellow wire between solenoid valve and fuse No. 1.

11. If voltage is present, inspect for an open in Green/Black wire between solenoid valve and ECU. If wire is OK, check ECU.

Idle Control Solenoid Valve Test II

1987-88 ACCORD

1. Start engine.

2. Disconnect 2P connector on idle control solenoid valve.

3. Attach positive probe of voltmeter to Black/Yellow terminal, and negative probe to Green/Black terminal.

4. Hold engine above 1,500 rpm and check voltage.

5. If voltage is present, inspect for a short in Green/Black wire between solenoid valve and ECU. If wire is OK, check ECU.

6. If no voltage, replace solenoid valve.

Fast Idle Control Solenoid Valve

1985-88 CIVIC

The fast idle control solenoid valve is open when the atmospheric pressure is 660mm Hg. or less. Vacuum is produced in the vacuum hose (between the solenoid valve and air filter).

When the valve is open, 9 volts or more should be available between the Black terminal (+) and Yellow terminal (−) (Black/Yellow terminal (+) and Green/Yellow terminal (−) on 1987-88 models) of the wire harness of the control box.

1. Open control box lid and disconnect wire harness from control box.

2. Disconnect vacuum hose between fast idle control solenoid valve and No. 10 vacuum hose (lower vacuum hose of fast idle control solenoid valve from 3-way joint on 1987-88 models) and connect vacuum pump.

3. Apply vacuum to hose. It should hold vacuum.

4. Connect battery positive terminal to Black terminal of control box coupler, and battery negative terminal to Yellow terminal.

5. Apply vacuum to hose. It should not hold vacuum. If vacuum hold, replace valve.

1985 ACCORD

The fast idle control solenoid valve is open when the coolant temperature is below 5°F (−15°C). If the coolant temperature is below 104°F (40°C), it is energized only when the atmospheric pressure is 660mm Hg or less. In either case, vacuum is produced in the vacuum hose **#18** between the solenoid valve and air flow tube.

When the valve is open, 9 volts or more should be available between the Black/Yellow terminal (+) and Blue/Black terminal (−) of the wire harness of the No. 1 control box.

1. Disconnect wire harness from No. 1 control box.

2. Disconnect vacuum hose **#18** from air flow tube.

3. Pump air into vacuum hose **#18**. There should be no air flow.

4. Connect battery positive terminal to Black terminal of No. 1 control box coupler, and battery negative terminal to Orange terminal.

5. Disconnect vacuum hose **#23** from intake manifold.

6. Pump air into vacuum hose **#18**. There should be air flow.

1986 ACCORD AND 1986-88 PRELUDE

The fast idle control solenoid valve is open when the coolant temperature is below 5°F (−15°C). If the coolant temperature is below 104°F (40°C), it is energized only when the atmospheric pressure is 660mm Hg or less. In either case, vacuum is produced in the vacuum hose **#18** between the solenoid valve and air flow tube. Also, the solenoid valve opens with the vehicle speed more than 10 mph and the engine speed more than 2,000 rpm. When the valve is open, 9 volts or more should be available between the Black/Yellow terminal (+) and Red/Green terminal (−) of the main harness at the control box.

1. Disconnect 6 cavity rectangle connector from control box.

2. Disconnect vacuum hose **#23** from vacuum hose manifold.

3. Apply vacuum to hose **#23**. Vacuum should hold. If valve does not hold vacuum, replace valve.

4. Connect battery positive terminal to Black/Yellow terminal of control box coupler, and battery negative terminal to Orange terminal.

5. Apply vacuum to hose **#23**. Valve should not hold vacuum. If valve holds vacuum, replace valve.

1987-88 ACCORD

1. Check vacuum line for proper connection, cracks, blockage or disconnected hoses.

2. Start engine and allow to idle.

3. Disconnect **#23** vacuum hose from; intake manifold and check vacuum.

4. If no vacuum, check vacuum port.

5. Turn ignition switch **OFF**.

6. Connect system checker harness (07999-PD6000A or equivalent) **B** connector to main wire harness only, not ECU.

7. Disconnect **#23** vacuum hose from vacuum hose manifold and connect a vacuum pump to hose.

8. Apply vacuum to hose. Vacuum should hold.

9. If vacuum does not hold, replace solenoid valve.

10. Turn ignition switch ON and apply vacuum to hose. Vacuum should hold.

11. If vacuum does not hold, repair short in Red/Green wire between solenoid valve and ECU.

NOTE: *On cars with automatic transmission, also inspect short in Green wire between automatic transmission idle control solenoid valve and ECU.*

12. Connect **B4** terminal to **A18** terminal and apply vacuum to hose. Vacuum should not hold.

13. If vacuum holds, turn ignition switch

OFF. Disconnect **6P** connector, then attach positive probe of voltmeter to Black/Yellow terminal, and negative probe to Red/Green terminal. Turn ignition switch **ON**.

14. If voltage is present, replace solenoid valve.

15. If no voltage, attach positive probe of volt-

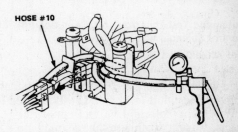

HOSE #10

Idle control solenoid valve vacuum check—1985–86 Civic shown

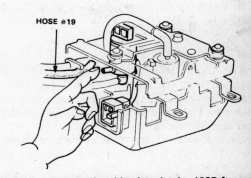

HOSE #26

Idle control solenoid valve vacuum check—1985 Accord

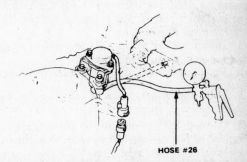

HOSE #19

A/C idle control solenoid valve check—1985 Accord

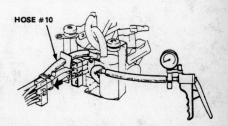

HOSE #10

Fast idle control solenoid valve—1985–86 Civic shown

meter to Black/Yellow terminal, and negative probe to body ground.

16. If no voltage, repair open in Black/Yellow wire between solenoid valve and No. 1 fuse.

17. If voltage is present, repair open in Red/Green wire between solenoid valve and ECU.

Automatic Transmission (Air Conditioning) Idle Control Solenoid Valve

1985 ACCORD

The automatic transmission idle control solenoid valve is energized when the automatic transmission shift lever is in **D4, D3, 2** and **R**.

When the solenoid valve is energized, it opens, causing vacuum in the vacuum hose #18 between the valve and air flow tube.

While the valve is energized, 9 volts or higher should be available between the Black/Yellow terminal (+) and Green terminal (−) of the No. 1 control box harness.

1. Disconnect wire harness from No.1 control box.

2. Disconnect vacuum hose **#18** from air flow tube.

3. Pump air into vacuum hose **#18**. There should be no air flow.

4. Connect battery positive terminal to Black terminal of No. 1 control box coupler and battery negative terminal to Yellow/Black terminal.

5. Disconnect vacuum hose **#23** from intake manifold.

6. Pump air into vacuum hose **#18**. There should be air flow.

1986 ACCORD AND 1986-88 PRELUDE

The automatic transmission idle control solenoid valve is energized when the automatic transmission shift lever is in gear, allowing air to bypass the throttle valve and maintain the specified idle speed.

While the valve is energized, 9 volts or higher

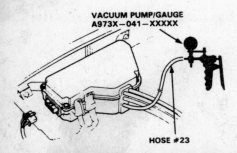

VACUUM PUMP/GAUGE
A973X−041−XXXXX

HOSE #23

Automatic transmission (A/T) idle control solenoid valve and fast idle control solenoid valve vacuum check — 1986 Accord and Prelude

should be available between the Black/Yellow terminal (+) and Green terminal (−) of the main harness at the control box.

1. Disconnect 6 cavity rectangle connector from control box.

2. Disconnect vacuum hose **#23** from vacuum hose manifold.

3. Apply vacuum to hose **#23**. Vacuum should hold. If valve does not hold vacuum, replace valve.

4. Connect battery positive terminal to Black/Yellow terminal of control box coupler, and battery negative terminal to Orange terminal.

5. Apply vacuum to hose **#23**. Valve should not hold vacuum. If valve holds vacuum, replace valve.

1987-88 ACCORD

1. Check vacuum line for proper connection, cracks, blockage or disconnected hoses.

2. Warm up engine normal operating temperature (cooling fan comes on).

NOTE: *Apply parking brake securely.*

3. Disconnect **#18** vacuum hose from air flow tube and connect a vacuum gauge to hose. Vacuum should not be present.

4. If vacuum is present, go to AUTOMATIC TRANSMISSION (automatic transmission) IDLE CONTROL SOLENOID VALVE TEST II.

5. Shift transmission into **D3** or **D4**. Vacuum should be present.

6. If no vacuum, go to AUTOMATIC TRANSMISSION (automatic transmission) IDLE CONTROL SOLENOID VALVE TEST I.

Automatic Transmission (Air Conditioning) Idle Control Solenoid Valve Test I

1987-88 ACCORD

1. With parking brake applied, start engine and allow to idle.

2. Disconnect **#23** vacuum hose from intake manifold and check for vacuum.

3. If no vacuum, check vacuum port.

4. Disconnect 6P connector.

5. Attach positive probe of voltmeter to Black/Yellow terminal, and negative probe to Green terminal.

6. Shift transmission into **D3** or **D4**.

7. If voltage is present, replace solenoid valve.

8. If no voltage, attach positive probe of voltmeter to Black/Yellow terminal, and negative probe to body ground. Check voltage.

9. If no voltage, repair open in Black/Yellow wire between solenoid valve and No. 1 fuse.

10. If voltage is present, inspect for an open in Green wire between solenoid valve and ECU. If wire is OK, check ECU.

Automatic Transmission (Air Conditioning) Idle Control Solenoid Valve Test II

1987-88 ACCORD

1. With parking brake applied, start engine.
2. Disconnect 6P connector.
3. Attach positive probe of voltmeter to Black/Yellow terminal, and negative probe to Green terminal.
4. If voltage is present, inspect for a short n Green wire between solenoid valve and ECU. If wire is OK, check ECU.
5. If no voltage, replace solenoid valve.

Air Conditioning (Automatic Transmission) Idle Control Solenoid Valve

1985 ACCORD

The air conditioning idle control solenoid valve is activated when the air conditioning switch is turned on. When the solenoid valve is activated, vacuum is generated in the vacuum hose #19 between the solenoid valve and idle diaphragm.

9 volts or high should be detected between the Black/Yellow terminal (+) and Blue/Yellow terminal (−) of the No.2 control box harness.

1. Disconnect wire harness from No. 2 control box.
2. Disconnect vacuum hose #19 from air flow tube.
3. Start engine and feel for vacuum at opening of solenoid valve. There should be no vacuum.
4. Connect battery positive terminal to Black/Yellow terminal of control box coupler and battery negative terminal to Blue/Yellow terminal.
5. Start engine and feel vacuum at opening of solenoid valve. There should be vacuum.

1986 ACCORD AND 1986-88 PRELUDE

When the solenoid valve is energized, vacuum is directed from vacuum hose #12 to the air conditioning idle boost valve through vacuum hose #19

9 volts or high should be detected between the Black/Yellow terminal (+) and Red termi-

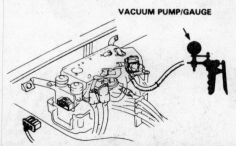

VACUUM PUMP/GAUGE

Air conditioning (A/C) idle boost solenoid valve vacuum check — 1986 Accord and Prelude shown, others similar

nal (−) of the main harness at the control box.

1. Open control box lid and disconnect 6 cavity rectangular connector form control box.
2. Disconnect lower vacuum hose of air conditioning idle boost solenoid valve (between valve and check valve) from check valve.
3. Apply vacuum to hose. Vacuum should hold. If no vacuum, check for check valve. If check valve is OK, replace solenoid valve.
4. Connect battery positive terminal to Black/Yellow terminal of control box coupler and battery negative terminal to Red terminal.
5. Apply vacuum to hose. Vacuum should not hold. If vacuum holds, check check valve. If check valve is OK, replace solenoid valve.

1987-88 ACCORD

1. Check vacuum line for improper connection, cracks, blockage or disconnected hoses.
2. Start engine and allow to idle.
3. Disconnect vacuum hose between air conditioning idle boost valve and air chamber from air conditioning idle boost valve and connect a vacuum gauge to valve. No vacuum should be present.
4. If vacuum is present, disconnect #19 vacuum hose from air conditioning idle boost valve and connect vacuum gauge to hose.
5. If no vacuum, replace air conditioning idle boost valve. If vacuum is present, go to AIR CONDITIONING IDLE BOOST SOLENOID VALVE TEST II.
6. Turn air conditioning switch and blower switch ON, then check that compressor and condenser cooling fan work. Vacuum should be present.
7. If no vacuum, disconnect #19 vacuum hose from air conditioning idle boost valve and connect vacuum gauge to hose.
8. If vacuum is present, replace air conditioning idle boost valve. If no vacuum, go to AIR CONDITIONING IDLE BOOST SOLENOID VALVE TEST I.

Air Conditioning Idle Boost Solenoid Valve Test I

1987-88 ACCORD

1. With parking brake applied, start engine and allow to idle.
2. Disconnect #12 vacuum hose from intake manifold and check for vacuum.
3. If no vacuum, check vacuum port.
4. Disconnect 6P connector.
5. Attach positive probe of voltmeter to Black/Yellow terminal, and negative probe to Red terminal.
6. Turn air conditioning switch and blower switch ON, then check that compressor and condenser cooling fan work.
7. If voltage is present, replace solenoid valve.

8. If no voltage, attach positive probe of voltmeter to Black/Yellow terminal, and negative probe to body ground. Check voltage.

9. If no voltage, repair open in Black/Yellow wire between solenoid valve and No. 1 fuse.

10. If voltage is present, inspect for an open in Red wire between solenoid valve and ECU. If wire is OK, check ECU.

Air Conditioning Idle Boost Solenoid Valve Test II
1987-88 ACCORD

1. Start engine.
2. Disconnect 6P connector.
3. Attach positive probe of voltmeter to Black/Yellow terminal, and negative probe to Red terminal.
4. If voltage is present, inspect for a short in Red wire between solenoid valve an ECU. If wire is OK, check ECU.
5. If no voltage, replace solenoid valve.

Fast Idle Valve
(Idle Speed Too High After Warm Up)
1985-88 ACCORD AND CIVIC
1986-88 PRELUDE

NOTE: *Fast idle valve is factory adjusted, it should not be disassembled. Check PCV (engine breather) circuit tubing for breakage, disconnection, clogging, etc. Check that throttle valve are fully closed.*

1. Confirm that engine is adequately warmed up.
2. Check whether idling control function is normal.
3. Remove cover of fast idle valve.
4. Check that valve is completely closed. If not, air is being sucked from valve seat area. It can be detected by putting your finger on valve seat area.
5. If any suction sound is heard, valve is leaking. Replace fast idle valve and adjust idle speed.

Fast Idle Valve
(Idle Speed Too Low After Warm Up)
1985-88 ACCORD AND CIVIC
1986-88 PRELUDE

NOTE: *Fast idle valve is factory adjusted, it should not be disassembled. Check PCV*

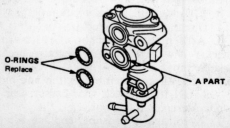

Fast idle valve assembly—typical

O-RINGS
Replace

A PART

(engine breather) circuit tubing for breakage, disconnection, clogging, etc. Check that throttle valve are fully closed.

1. Remove idle adjusting screw.
2. Wash idle adjusting screw and air bypass channel with carburetor cleaner.
3. Readjust idle speed after cleaning.

Fast Idle Valve
(Fast Idle Speed Is Low When Engine Is Cold)
1985-88 ACCORD AND CIVIC
1986-88 PRELUDE

NOTE: *Fast idle valve is factory adjusted, it should not be disassembled. Fast idle speed should be 1,250-2,250 rpm for Civic models and 1,000-1,800 rpm for Accord models.*

1. Remove fast idle valve assembly from throttle body.
2. Apply cold water and cool down wax part of fast idle valve to 41-86°F (5-30°C).
3. Blow through part A of fast valve, and check that a fairly large amount of air flows without resistance.
4. If air does not flow or resistance is large, replace fast idle valve and adjust idle speed.

Dashpot
1985-86 ACCORD
1987-88 CIVIC
1986-88 PRELUDE

1. With engine off, slowly open throttle arm until dashpot rod is raised up as far as it will go.
2. Release throttle arm and measure time until throttle arm contacts stop screw. Time should be less than 2 seconds.
3. If time is over 2 seconds, replace dashpot check valve.
4. If rod does not operate, check for bound linkage, or for clogged check valve or vacuum line. If OK, replace dashpot.

1987-88 ACCORD

1. Check vacuum line for leaks, blockage or disconnected hose.

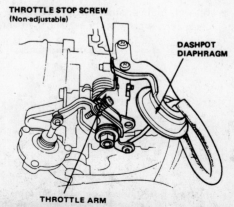

THROTTLE STOP SCREW
(Non-adjustable)

DASHPOT
DIAPHRAGM

THROTTLE ARM

Dashpot system—typical

CHILTON'S
FUEL ECONOMY
& TUNE-UP TIPS

55 WAYS TO IMPROVE FUEL ECONOMY

Tune-up • Spark Plug Diagnosis • Emission Controls

Fuel System • Cooling System • Tires and Wheels

General Maintenance

CHILTON'S FUEL ECONOMY & TUNE-UP TIPS

Fuel economy is important to everyone, no matter what kind of vehicle you drive. The maintenance-minded motorist can save both money and fuel using these tips and the periodic maintenance and tune-up procedures in this Repair and Tune-Up Guide.

There are more than 130,000,000 cars and trucks registered for private use in the United States. Each travels an average of 10-12,000 miles per year, and, and in total they consume close to 70 billion gallons of fuel each year. This represents nearly ⅔ of the oil imported by the United States each year. The Federal government's goal is to reduce consumption 10% by 1985. A variety of methods are either already in use or under serious consideration, and they all affect you driving and the cars you will drive. In addition to "down-sizing", the auto industry is using or investigating the use of electronic fuel delivery, electronic engine controls and alternative engines for use in smaller and lighter vehicles, among other alternatives to meet the federally mandated Corporate Average Fuel Economy (CAFE) of 27.5 mpg by 1985. The government, for its part, is considering rationing, mandatory driving curtailments and tax increases on motor vehicle fuel in an effort to reduce consumption. The government's goal of a 10% reduction could be realized — and further government regulation avoided — if every private vehicle could use just 1 less gallon of fuel per week.

How Much Can You Save?

Tests have proven that almost anyone can make at least a 10% reduction in fuel consumption through regular maintenance and tune-ups. When a major manufacturer of spark plugs sur-

TUNE-UP

1. Check the cylinder compression to be sure the engine will really benefit from a tune-up and that it is capable of producing good fuel economy. A tune-up will be wasted on an engine in poor mechanical condition.

2. Replace spark plugs regularly. New spark plugs alone can increase fuel economy 3%.

3. Be sure the spark plugs are the correct type (heat range) for your vehicle. See the Tune-Up Specifications.

Heat range refers to the spark plug's ability to conduct heat away from the firing end. It must conduct the heat away in an even pattern to avoid becoming a source of pre-ignition, yet it must also operate hot enough to burn off conductive deposits that could cause misfiring.

The heat range is usually indicated by a number on the spark plug, part of the manufacturer's designation for each individual spark plug. The numbers in bold-face indicate the heat range in each manufacturer's identification system.

Periodically, check the spark plugs to be sure they are firing efficiently. They are excellent indicators of the internal condition of your engine.

Manufacturer	Typical Designation
AC	R **45** TS
Bosch (old)	WA **145** T30
Bosch (new)	HR **8** Y
Champion	RBL **15** Y
Fram/Autolite	4**15**
Mopar	P-**62** PR
Motorcraft	BRF-**42**
NGK	BP **5** ES-15
Nippondenso	W **16** EP
Prestolite	14GR **5** 2A

On AC, Bosch (new), Champion, Fram/Autolite, Mopar, Motorcraft and Prestolite, a higher number indicates a hotter plug. On Bosch (old), NGK and Nippondenso, a higher number indicates a colder plug.

4. Make sure the spark plugs are properly gapped. See the Tune-Up Specifications in this book.

5. Be sure the spark plugs are firing efficiently. The illustrations on the next 2 pages show you how to "read" the firing end of the spark plug.

6. Check the ignition timing and set it to specifications. Tests show that almost all cars have incorrect ignition timing by more than 2°.

veyed over 6,000 cars nationwide, they found that a tune-up, on cars that needed one, increased fuel economy over 11%. Replacing worn plugs alone, accounted for a 3% increase. The same test also revealed that 8 out of every 10 vehicles will have some maintenance deficiency that will directly affect fuel economy, emissions or performance. Most of this mileage-robbing neglect could be prevented with regular maintenance.

Modern engines require that all of the functioning systems operate properly for maximum efficiency. A malfunction anywhere wastes fuel. You can keep your vehicle running as efficiently and economically as possible, by being aware of your vehicle's operating and performance characteristics. If your vehicle suddenly develops performance or fuel economy problems it could be due to one or more of the following:

PROBLEM	POSSIBLE CAUSE
Engine Idles Rough	Ignition timing, idle mixture, vacuum leak or something amiss in the emission control system.
Hesitates on Acceleration	Dirty carburetor or fuel filter, improper accelerator pump setting, ignition timing or fouled spark plugs.
Starts Hard or Fails to Start	Worn spark plugs, improperly set automatic choke, ice (or water) in fuel system.
Stalls Frequently	Automatic choke improperly adjusted and possible dirty air filter or fuel filter.
Performs Sluggishly	Worn spark plugs, dirty fuel or air filter, ignition timing or automatic choke out of adjustment.

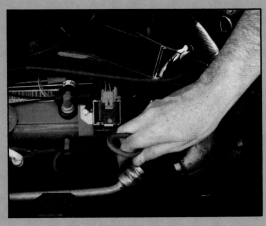

Check spark plug wires on conventional point type ignition for cracks by bending them in a loop around your finger.

Be sure that spark plug wires leading to adjacent cylinders do not run too close together. (Photo courtesy Champion Spark Plug Co.)

7. If your vehicle does not have electronic ignition, check the points, rotor and cap as specified.

8. Check the spark plug wires (used with conventional point-type ignitions) for cracks and burned or broken insulation by bending them in a loop around your finger. Cracked wires decrease fuel efficiency by failing to deliver full voltage to the spark plugs. One misfiring spark plug can cost you as much as 2 mpg.

9. Check the routing of the plug wires. Misfiring can be the result of spark plug leads to adjacent cylinders running parallel to each other and too close together. One wire tends to pick up voltage from the other causing it to fire "out of time".

10. Check all electrical and ignition circuits for voltage drop and resistance.

11. Check the distributor mechanical and/or vacuum advance mechanisms for proper functioning. The vacuum advance can be checked by twisting the distributor plate in the opposite direction of rotation. It should spring back when released.

12. Check and adjust the valve clearance on engines with mechanical lifters. The clearance should be slightly loose rather than too tight.

SPARK PLUG DIAGNOSIS

Normal

APPEARANCE: This plug is typical of one operating normally. The insulator nose varies from a light tan to grayish color with slight electrode wear. The presence of slight deposits is normal on used plugs and will have no adverse effect on engine performance. The spark plug heat range is correct for the engine and the engine is running normally.

CAUSE: Properly running engine.

RECOMMENDATION: Before reinstalling this plug, the electrodes should be cleaned and filed square. Set the gap to specifications. If the plug has been in service for more than 10-12,000 miles, the entire set should probably be replaced with a fresh set of the same heat range.

Oil Deposits

APPEARANCE: The firing end of the plug is covered with a wet, oily coating.

CAUSE: The problem is poor oil control. On high mileage engines, oil is leaking past the rings or valve guides into the combustion chamber. A common cause is also a plugged PCV valve, and a ruptured fuel pump diaphragm can also cause this condition. Oil fouled plugs such as these are often found in new or recently overhauled engines, before normal oil control is achieved, and can be cleaned and reinstalled.

RECOMMENDATION: A hotter spark plug may temporarily relieve the problem, but the engine is probably in need of work.

Incorrect Heat Range

APPEARANCE: The effects of high temperature on a spark plug are indicated by clean white, often blistered insulator. This can also be accompanied by excessive wear of the electrode, and the absence of deposits.

CAUSE: Check for the correct spark plug heat range. A plug which is too hot for the engine can result in overheating. A car operated mostly at high speeds can require a colder plug. Also check ignition timing, cooling system level, fuel mixture and leaking intake manifold.

RECOMMENDATION: If all ignition and engine adjustments are known to be correct, and no other malfunction exists, install spark plugs one heat range colder.

Carbon Deposits

APPEARANCE: Carbon fouling is easily identified by the presence of dry, soft, black, sooty deposits.

CAUSE: Changing the heat range can often lead to carbon fouling, as can prolonged slow, stop-and-start driving. If the heat range is correct, carbon fouling can be attributed to a rich fuel mixture, sticking choke, clogged air cleaner, worn breaker points, retarded timing or low compression. If only one or two plugs are carbon fouled, check for corroded or cracked wires on the affected plugs. Also look for cracks in the distributor cap between the towers of affected cylinders.

RECOMMENDATION: After the problem is corrected, these plugs can be cleaned and reinstalled if not worn severely.

MMT Fouled

APPEARANCE: Spark plugs fouled by MMT (Methycyclopentadienyl Maganese Tricarbonyl) have reddish, rusty appearance on the insulator and side electrode.

CAUSE: MMT is an anti-knock additive in gasoline used to replace lead. During the combustion process, the MMT leaves a reddish deposit on the insulator and side electrode.

RECOMMENDATION: No engine malfunction is indicated and the deposits will not affect plug performance any more than lead deposits (see Ash Deposits). MMT fouled plugs can be cleaned, regapped and reinstalled.

High Speed Glazing

APPEARANCE: Glazing appears as shiny coating on the plug, either yellow or tan in color.

CAUSE: During hard, fast acceleration, plug temperatures rise suddenly. Deposits from normal combustion have no chance to fluff-off; instead, they melt on the insulator forming an electrically conductive coating which causes misfiring.

RECOMMENDATION: Glazed plugs are not easily cleaned. They should be replaced with a fresh set of plugs of the correct heat range. If the condition recurs, using plugs with a heat range one step colder may cure the problem.

Ash (Lead) Deposits

APPEARANCE: Ash deposits are characterized by light brown or white colored deposits crusted on the side or center electrodes. In some cases it may give the plug a rusty appearance.

CAUSE: Ash deposits are normally derived from oil or fuel additives burned during normal combustion. Normally they are harmless, though excessive amounts can cause misfiring. If deposits are excessive in short mileage, the valve guides may be worn.

RECOMMENDATION: Ash-fouled plugs can be cleaned, gapped and reinstalled.

Detonation

APPEARANCE: Detonation is usually characterized by a broken plug insulator.

CAUSE: A portion of the fuel charge will begin to burn spontaneously, from the increased heat following ignition. The explosion that results applies extreme pressure to engine components, frequently damaging spark plugs and pistons.

Detonation can result by over-advanced ignition timing, inferior gasoline (low octane) lean air/fuel mixture, poor carburetion, engine lugging or an increase in compression ratio due to combustion chamber deposits or engine modification.

RECOMMENDATION: Replace the plugs after correcting the problem.

Photos Courtesy Champion Spark Plug Co.

EMISSION CONTROLS

13. Be aware of the general condition of the emission control system. It contributes to reduced pollution and should be serviced regularly to maintain efficient engine operation.

14. Check all vacuum lines for dried, cracked or brittle conditions. Something as simple as a leaking vacuum hose can cause poor performance and loss of economy.

15. Avoid tampering with the emission control system. Attempting to improve fuel econ-

---

FUEL SYSTEM

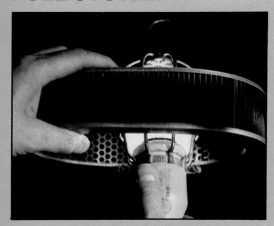

Check the air filter with a light behind it. If you can see light through the filter it can be reused.

Extremely clogged filters should be discarded and replaced with a new one.

18. Replace the air filter regularly. A dirty air filter richens the air/fuel mixture and can increase fuel consumption as much as 10%. Tests show that 1/3 of all vehicles have air filters in need of replacement.

19. Replace the fuel filter at least as often as recommended.

20. Set the idle speed and carburetor mixture to specifications.

21. Check the automatic choke. A sticking or malfunctioning choke wastes gas.

22. During the summer months, adjust the automatic choke for a leaner mixture which will produce faster engine warm-ups.

COOLING SYSTEM

29. Be sure all accessory drive belts are in good condition. Check for cracks or wear.

30. Adjust all accessory drive belts to proper tension.

31. Check all hoses for swollen areas, worn spots, or loose clamps.

32. Check coolant level in the radiator or ex- pansion tank.

33. Be sure the thermostat is operating properly. A stuck thermostat delays engine warm-up and a cold engine uses nearly twice as much fuel as a warm engine.

34. Drain and replace the engine coolant at least as often as recommended. Rust and scale

---

TIRES & WHEELS

38. Check the tire pressure often with a pencil type gauge. Tests by a major tire manufacturer show that 90% of all vehicles have at least 1 tire improperly inflated. Better mileage can be achieved by over-inflating tires, but never exceed the maximum inflation pressure on the side of the tire.

39. If possible, install radial tires. Radial tires deliver as much as 1/2 mpg more than bias belted tires.

40. Avoid installing super-wide tires. They only create extra rolling resistance and decrease fuel mileage. Stick to the manufacturer's recommendations.

41. Have the wheels properly balanced.

omy by tampering with emission controls is more likely to worsen fuel economy than improve it. Emission control changes on modern engines are not readily reversible.

16. Clean (or replace) the EGR valve and lines as recommended.

17. Be sure that all vacuum lines and hoses are reconnected properly after working under the hood. An unconnected or misrouted vacuum line can wreak havoc with engine performance.

23. Check for fuel leaks at the carburetor, fuel pump, fuel lines and fuel tank. Be sure all lines and connections are tight.

24. Periodically check the tightness of the carburetor and intake manifold attaching nuts and bolts. These are a common place for vacuum leaks to occur.

25. Clean the carburetor periodically and lubricate the linkage.

26. The condition of the tailpipe can be an excellent indicator of proper engine combustion. After a long drive at highway speeds, the inside of the tailpipe should be a light grey in color. Black or soot on the insides indicates an overly rich mixture.

27. Check the fuel pump pressure. The fuel pump may be supplying more fuel than the engine needs.

28. Use the proper grade of gasoline for your engine. Don't try to compensate for knocking or "pinging" by advancing the ignition timing. This practice will only increase plug temperature and the chances of detonation or pre-ignition with relatively little performance gain.

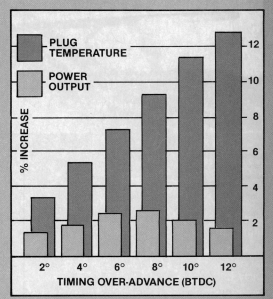

Increasing ignition timing past the specified setting results in a drastic increase in spark plug temperature with increased chance of detonation or preignition. Performance increase is considerably less. (Photo courtesy Champion Spark Plug Co.)

that form in the engine should be flushed out to allow the engine to operate at peak efficiency.

35. Clean the radiator of debris that can decrease cooling efficiency.

36. Install a flex-type or electric cooling fan, if you don't have a clutch type fan. Flex fans use curved plastic blades to push more air at low speeds when more cooling is needed; at high speeds the blades flatten out for less resistance. Electric fans only run when the engine temperature reaches a predetermined level.

37. Check the radiator cap for a worn or cracked gasket. If the cap does not seal properly, the cooling system will not function properly.

42. Be sure the front end is correctly aligned. A misaligned front end actually has wheels going in differed directions. The increased drag can reduce fuel economy by .3 mpg.

43. Correctly adjust the wheel bearings. Wheel bearings that are adjusted too tight increase rolling resistance.

Check tire pressures regularly with a reliable pocket type gauge. Be sure to check the pressure on a cold tire.

GENERAL MAINTENANCE

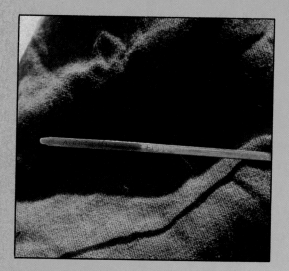

Check the fluid levels (particularly engine oil) on a regular basis. Be sure to check the oil for grit, water or other contamination.

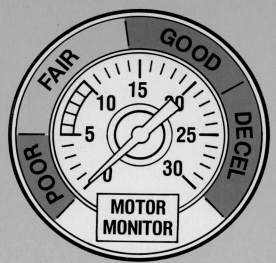

A vacuum gauge is another excellent indicator of internal engine condition and can also be installed in the dash as a mileage indicator.

44. Periodically check the fluid levels in the engine, power steering pump, master cylinder, automatic transmission and drive axle.

45. Change the oil at the recommended interval and change the filter at every oil change. Dirty oil is thick and causes extra friction between moving parts, cutting efficiency and increasing wear. A worn engine requires more frequent tune-ups and gets progressively worse fuel economy. In general, use the lightest viscosity oil for the driving conditions you will encounter.

46. Use the recommended viscosity fluids in the transmission and axle.

47. Be sure the battery is fully charged for fast starts. A slow starting engine wastes fuel.

48. Be sure battery terminals are clean and tight.

49. Check the battery electrolyte level and add distilled water if necessary.

50. Check the exhaust system for crushed pipes, blockages and leaks.

51. Adjust the brakes. Dragging brakes or brakes that are not releasing create increased drag on the engine.

52. Install a vacuum gauge or miles-per-gallon gauge. These gauges visually indicate engine vacuum in the intake manifold. High vacuum = good mileage and low vacuum = poorer mileage. The gauge can also be an excellent indicator of internal engine conditions.

53. Be sure the clutch is properly adjusted. A slipping clutch wastes fuel.

54. Check and periodically lubricate the heat control valve in the exhaust manifold. A sticking or inoperative valve prevents engine warm-up and wastes gas.

55. Keep accurate records to check fuel economy over a period of time. A sudden drop in fuel economy may signal a need for tune-up or other maintenance.

2. Disconnect #6 vacuum hose from dashpot diaphragm, and connect a vacuum pump/gauge to hose.

3. Start engine.

4. Raise engine speed to 3,500 rpm. Vacuum should appear on gauge.

5. If no vacuum, check that vacuum port on throttle body.

6. Release throttle. Vacuum should go out slowly.

6f If vacuum holds or goes out quickly, replace dashpot check valve.

8. Connect a vacuum pump to dashpot diaphragm.

9. Apply vacuum and check that rod pulls in and vacuum holds. Rod should pull in and vacuum should hold.

10. If vacuum does not hold or rod does not move, replace dashpot diaphragm.

Injector Test

1985-88 ACCORD AND CIVIC
1986-88 PRELUDE

NOTE: *Check following items before testing idle speed, ignition timing, valve clearance and idle CO%.*

1. If engine will run, disconnect injector couplers with engine idling, and inspect change in idling speed. Idle should drop the same for each cylinder.

2. Check clicking sound of each injector by means of a stethoscope when engine is idling.

3. If any injector fails to make typical clicking sound, check wiring between ECU and injector. Voltage at injector coupler should fluctuate between 0-2 volts. If voltage is OK, replace injector.

4. If engine can not be started, remove coupler of injector, and measure resistance between terminals of injector. Resistance should be 1.5-2.5Ω.

5. If resistance is not as specified, replace injector. If resistance is normal, check wiring between resistor and injector, wiring between resistors and control unit, and resistors.

Fuel System Resistor

1985-88 ACCORD AND CIVIC
1986-88 PRELUDE

1. Disconnect resistor coupler.

2. Check for resistance between each of resistor terminals **E, D, C and B** and power terminal **A**. Resistance should be 5-7Ω.

3. Replace resistor with a new one if any of resistances are outside of specification.

Fuel Pressure Testing

1985-88 ACCORD AND CIVIC
1986-88 PRELUDE

1. Relieve fuel pressure.

2. Remove service bolt and attach fuel pressure gauge.

3. Start engine. Measure fuel pressure with engine idling and vacuum hose of pressure regulator disconnected. Pressure should be 36 ± 3 psi (255 ± 20 kPa).

4. If fuel pressure is not as specified, first check fuel pump. If pump is OK, check following:

   a. If pressure is higher than specified, inspect for pinched or clogged fuel return hose or piping, and faulty pressure regulator.

   b. If pressure is lower than specified, inspect for clogged fuel filter, pinched or clogged fuel hose from fuel tank to fuel pump, pressure regulator failure, leakage in fuel line, or pinched, broken or disconnected regulator vacuum hose.

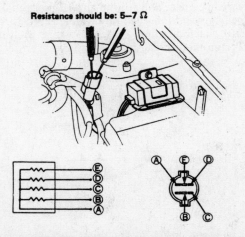

Resistance should be: 5—7 Ω

Fuel system resistor testing — 1985 Civic shown, others similar

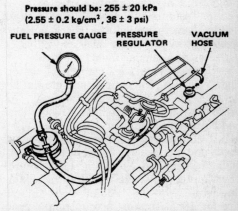

Pressure should be: 255 ± 20 kPa
(2.55 ± 0.2 kg/cm², 36 ± 3 psi)

FUEL PRESSURE GAUGE   PRESSURE REGULATOR   VACUUM HOSE

Pressure regulator testing — Civic shown, Prelude and Accord similar

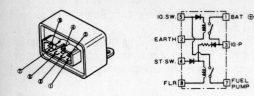

Main relay pin identification—typical

Main Relay Testing

1985-88 ACCORD AND CIVIC
1986-88 PRELUDE

1. Remove main relay, near under-dash fuse box.

2. Connect battery positive terminal to No. 4 terminal and battery negative terminal to No. 8 terminal of main relay.

3. Check for continuity between No. 5 terminal and No. 7 terminal of main relay. If no continuity, replace main relay.

4. Connect battery positive terminal to No. 5 terminal and battery negative terminal to No. 2 terminal of main relay.

5. Check that there is continuity between No. 1 terminal and No. 3 terminal of main relay. If there is no continuity, replace main relay.

6. Connect battery positive terminal to No. 3 terminal and battery negative terminal to No. 8 terminal of main relay.

7. Check that there is continuity between No. 5 terminal and No. 7 terminal of main relay. If there is no continuity, replace main relay.

Harness Testing

1985 ACCORD AND 1985-88 CIVIC

1. Keep ignition switch in off position.

2. Disconnect main relay connector.

3. Connect positive probe of circuit tester to Yellow/White wire for 1985-86 Civic (Yellow/Blue wire for 1985 Accord) in coupler and ground negative probe of tester to body ground. Tester should read battery voltage.

4. If there is no voltage, check wiring between battery and main relay as well as ECU fuse in engine compartment.

5. Connect positive terminal of tester to Black/Yellow wire of coupler and ground negative terminal of tester to body ground.

6. Turn ignition switch on. Tester should read battery voltage.

7. If no voltage, check wiring from ignition switch and main relay as well as fuse No. 4 for 1985-86 Civic (fuse No. 11 for 1985 Accord).

8. Connect positive terminal of tester to Blue/White wire for 1985-86 Civic (Blue/Red wire for 1985 Accord) in coupler and ground negative terminal to body.

9. Turn ignition switch to start position. Tester should read battery voltage.

10. If no voltage, check wiring between ignition switch and main relay as well as starter fuse No. 1 for 1985-86 Civic (fuse No. 21 for 1985 Accord).

11. Connect a jumper wire between Yellow/White wire and Yellow wire for 1985-86 Civic (Black/Yellow wire and Yellow wire on 1987-88 Civic) (Yellow/Blue and Black/Yellow wire for 1985 Accord) in coupler. Fuel pump should work.

12. If pump does not work, check wiring between battery and fuel pump and wiring from fuel pump to ground (Black wire).

1986-88 ACCORD AND PRELUDE

1. Keep ignition switch in off position.

2. Disconnect main relay coupler.

3. On 1987-88 models, check continuity between Black wire in connector and body ground.

4. Connect positive probe of circuit tester to Yellow/Blue wire in coupler and ground negative probe of tester to body ground (on 1987-88 models, Black wire). Tester should read battery voltage.

5. If there is no voltage, check wiring between battery and main relay as well as No.1 fuse in engine compartment.

6. Connect positive terminal of tester to Black/Yellow wire of coupler and ground negative terminal of tester to body ground (on 1987-88 models, Black wire).

7. Turn ignition switch on. Tester should read battery voltage.

8. If no voltage, check wiring from ignition switch and main relay as well as fuse No. 1 for Accord (regulator fuse for Prelude).

9. Connect positive terminal of tester to Blue/Red for Accord (Black/White for Prelude) wire in coupler and ground negative terminal to body ground (on 1987-88 models, Black wire).

10. Turn ignition switch to start position. Tester should read battery voltage.

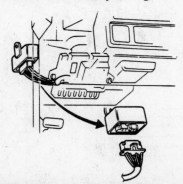

Harness and main relay location—typical

11. If no voltage, check wiring between ignition switch and main relay as well as fuse No. 10 for Accord (starter signal fuse for Prelude).

12. Connect a jumper wire between Yellow/Blue (Black/Yellow on 1987-88) and Yellow wire for Accord (Yellow/Blue and Yellow/Black wire for 1986 Prelude and Black/Yellow and Yellow/Black for 1987-88 Prelude) in connector. Fuel pump should work.

13. If pump does not work, check wiring between battery and fuel pump and wiring from fuel pump to ground (Black wire).

Fuel System Pressure Relieving

1985-88 ACCORD AND CIVIC
1986-88 PRELUDE

CAUTION: *Keep open flames or sparks from work area. Do not smoke while working on fuel system. Be sure to relieve fuel pressure while engine is off.*

NOTE: *Before disconnecting fuel pipes or hoses, release pressure from system by loosen 6mm service bolt at top of fuel filter.*

1. Disconnect battery negative cable from battery negative terminal.

2. Use a box end wrench on 6mm service bolt at top of fuel filter, while holding special banjo bolt with another wrench.

3. Place a rag or a shop towel over 6mm service bolt.

4. Slowly loosen 6mm service bolt one complete turn.

NOTE: *A fuel pressure gauge can be attached at 6mm service bolt hole. Always replace washer between service bolt and Special Banjo Bolt, whenever service bolt is loosened to relieve fuel pressure. Replace all washers whenever bolts are removed to disassemble parts.*

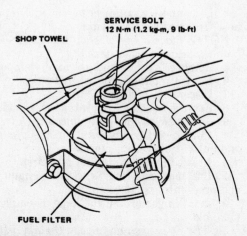

SHOP TOWEL

SERVICE BOLT
12 N·m (1.2 kg-m, 9 lb-ft)

FUEL FILTER

Relieving fuel pressure—typical

Fuel Injector

REMOVAL AND INSTALLATION

1985-86 Civic

1. Disconnect battery negative cable from battery negative.

2. Relieve fuel pressure.

3. Disconnect coupler of injector.

4. Disconnect vacuum hose and fuel return hose from pressure regulator.

NOTE: *Place a rag or shop towel over hose and tube before disconnecting.*

5. Loosen retainer nuts.

6. Disconnect fuel pipe.

7. Remove injector from intake manifold.

8. Slide new cushion onto injector.

9. Coat new O-rings with clean engine oil and put O-rings on injectors.

10. Insert injectors into fuel pipe.

NOTE: *To prevent damage to O-ring, insert injector into fuel pipe squarely and carefully.*

11. Coat new seal rings with clean engine oil and press into intake manifold.

12. Install injector and fuel pipe assembly in manifold.

NOTE: *To prevent damage to O-ring, install injectors in fuel pipe first, then install in intake manifold.*

13. Tighten retainer nuts.

14. Connect vacuum hose ad fuel return hose to pressure regulator.

15. Install couplers of injectors.

16. Turn ignition switch on but do not operate starter. After fuel pump runs for approximately two seconds, fuel pressure in fuel line rises. Repeat this two or three times, then check whether there is any fuel leakage.

1985 Accord

1. Disconnect battery negative cable from battery negative.

2. Relieve fuel pressure.

3. Remove air cleaner case.

4. Disconnect coupler of injector.

5. Disconnect vacuum hose and fuel return hose from pressure regulator.

NOTE: *Place a rag or shop towel over hose and tube before disconnecting.*

6. Disconnect two ground cables from intake manifold.

7. Disconnect fuel lines.

8. Remove injector from intake manifold.

NOTE: *Use new O-rings, seal rings and cushion rings whenever disassembled. When installing injector, check O-ring and seal ring are installed properly. Coat new O-rings and seal rings with clean engine oil before assembly. Install injector with center line of* coupler aligned with index mark on intake manifold.

9. Slide new cushion onto injector.

10. Put O-ring onto injector.

11. Press seal ring into intake manifold, and install injector and fuel pipe assembly on manifold. Tighten retainer nuts securely.

12. Connect two ground cables.

13. Connect vacuum hose and fuel return hose to pressure regulator.

14. Install couplers of injectors.

15. Turn ignition switch on but do not operate starter. After fuel pump runs for approximately two seconds, fuel pressure in fuel line rises. Repeat this two or three times, then check whether there is any fuel leakage.

1986-88 Accord and Prelude

1. Disconnect battery negative cable from battery negative.

2. Relieve fuel pressure.

3. Disconnect coupler of injector.

4. Disconnect vacuum hose and fuel return hose from pressure regulator.

NOTE: *Place a rag or shop towel over hose and tube before disconnecting.*

5. Loosen retainer nuts on fuel pipe.

6. Disconnect fuel pipe.

7. Remove injector from intake manifold.

8. Slide new cushion onto injector.

9. Coat new O-rings with clean engine oil and put O-rings on injectors.

10. Insert injectors into fuel pipe first.

NOTE: *To prevent damage to O-ring, insert injector into fuel pipe squarely and carefully, then install them in intake manifold.*

11. Coat new seal rings with clean engine oil and press into intake manifold.

12. Install injector and fuel pipe assembly in manifold.

NOTE: *To prevent damage to O-ring, install injectors in fuel pipe first, then install in intake manifold.*

13. Align center line on coupler with mark on fuel pipe.

14. Install and tighten retainer nuts.

15. Connect vacuum hose ad fuel return hose to pressure regulator.

16. Install couplers of injectors.

17. Turn ignition switch on but do not operate starter. After fuel pump runs for approximately two seconds, fuel pressure in fuel line rises. Repeat this two or three times, then check whether there is any fuel leakage.

1987-88 Civic

1. Disconnect battery negative cable from battery negative.

2. Relieve fuel pressure.

3. Disconnect connector of injectors.

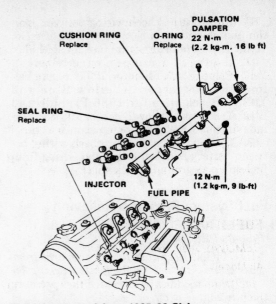

Fuel injector servicing—1985–88 Civic

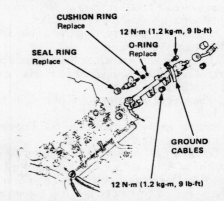

Fuel injector servicing—1985 Accord shown, 1986–88 Accord and Prelude similar

4. Disconnect vacuum hose and fuel return hose from pressure regulator.

NOTE: *Place a rag or shop towel over hose and tube before disconnecting.*

5. Remove fuel line and pulsation damper.

6. Loosen retainer nuts on fuel pipe.

7. Disconnect fuel pipe.

8. Remove injector from intake manifold.

9. Slide new cushion onto injector.

10. Coat new O-rings with clean engine oil and put O-rings on injectors.

11. Insert injectors into fuel pipe first.

12. Coat new seal rings with clean engine oil and press into intake manifold.

13. Install injector and fuel pipe assembly in manifold.

NOTE: *To prevent damage to O-ring, install injectors in fuel pipe first, then install in intake manifold.*

14. Align center line on connector with mark on fuel pipe.

15. Install and tighten retainer nuts.

16. Install fuel line and pulsation damper.

17. Connect vacuum hose ad fuel return hose to pressure regulator.

18. Install couplers of injectors.

19. Turn ignition switch on but do not operate starter. After fuel pump runs for approximately two seconds, fuel pressure in fuel line rises. Repeat this two or three times, then check whether there is any fuel leakage.

FUEL TANK

REMOVAL AND INSTALLATION

All Models

1. Drain the tank by loosening the tank drain bolt.

NOTE: *Catch the fuel in a clean, safe container.*

Filler tube location

2. Disconnect the fuel tubes, filler neck connecting tube and the clear vinyl tube.

NOTE: *Disconnect the fuel tubes by removing the clips, taking care not to damage the tubes.*

3. Disconnect the fuel meter unit wire at its connection.

4. Remove the fuel tank by removing its attaching bolts.

5. To install, reverse the removal procedures. Be sure that all tubes and fuel lines are securely fastened by the clips.

Chassis Electrical

6

UNDERSTANDING AND TROUBLESHOOTING ELECTRICAL SYSTEMS

At the rate which both import and domestic manufacturers are incorporating electronic control systems into their production lines, it won't be long before every new vehicle is equipped with one or more on-board computer. These electronic components (with no moving parts) should theoretically last the life of the vehicle, provided nothing external happens to damage the circuits or memory chips.

While it is true that electronic components should never wear out, in the real world malfunctions do occur. It is also true that any computer-based system is extremely sensitive to electrical voltages and cannot tolerate careless or haphazard testing or service procedures. An inexperienced individual can literally do major damage looking for a minor problem by using the wrong kind of test equipment or connecting test leads or connectors with the ignition switch ON. When selecting test equipment, make sure the manufacturers instructions state that the tester is compatible with whatever type of electronic control system is being serviced. Read all instructions carefully and double check all test points before installing probes or making any test connections.

The following section outlines basic diagnosis techniques for dealing with computerized automotive control systems. Along with a general explanation of the various types of test equipment available to aid in servicing modern electronic automotive systems, basic repair techniques for wiring harnesses and connectors is given. Read the basic information before attempting any repairs or testing on any computerized system, to provide the background of information necessary to avoid the most common and obvious mistakes that can cost both time and money. Although the replacement and test-ing procedures are simple in themselves, the systems are not, and unless one has a thorough understanding of all components and their function within a particular computerized control system, the logical test sequence these systems demand cannot be followed. Minor malfunctions can make a big difference, so it is important to know how each component affects the operation of the overall electronic system to find the ultimate cause of a problem without replacing good components unnecessarily. It is not enough to use the correct test equipment; the test equipment must be used correctly.

Safety Precautions

CAUTION: *Whenever working on or around any computer based microprocessor control system, always observe these general precautions to prevent the possibility of personal injury or damage to electronic components.*

- Never install or remove battery cables with the key ON or the engine running. Jumper cables should be connected with the key OFF to avoid power surges that can damage electronic control units. Engines equipped with computer controlled systems should avoid both giving and getting jump starts due to the possibility of serious damage to components from arcing in the engine compartment when connections are made with the ignition ON.

- Always remove the battery cables before charging the battery. Never use a high output charger on an installed battery or attempt to use any type of "hot shot" (24 volt) starting aid.

- Exercise care when inserting test probes into connectors to insure good connections without damaging the connector or spreading the pins. Always probe connectors from the rear (wire) side, NOT the pin side, to avoid accidental shorting of terminals during test procedures.

- Never remove or attach wiring harness

connectors with the ignition switch ON, especially to an electronic control unit.

• Do not drop any components during service procedures and never apply 12 volts directly to any component (like a solenoid or relay) unless instructed specifically to do so. Some component electrical windings are designed to safely handle only 4 or 5 volts and can be destroyed in seconds if 12 volts are applied directly to the connector.

• Remove the electronic control unit if the vehicle is to be placed in an environment where temperatures exceed approximately 176°F (80°C), such as a paint spray booth or when arc or gas welding near the control unit location in the car.

ORGANIZED TROUBLESHOOTING

When diagnosing a specific problem, organized troubleshooting is a must. The complexity of a modern automobile demands that you approach any problem in a logical, organized manner. There are certain troubleshooting techniques that are standard:

1. Establish when the problem occurs. Does the problem appear only under certain conditions? Were there any noises, odors, or other unusual symptoms?

2. Isolate the problem area. To do this, make some simple tests and observations; then eliminate the systems that are working properly. Check for obvious problems such as broken wires, dirty connections or split or disconnected vacuum hoses. Always check the obvious before assuming something complicated is the cause.

3. Test for problems systematically to determine the cause once the problem area is isolated. Are all the components functioning properly? Is there power going to electrical switches and motors? Is there vacuum at vacuum switches and/or actuators? Is there a mechanical problem such as bent linkage or loose mounting screws? Doing careful, systematic checks will often turn up most causes on the first inspection without wasting time checking components that have little or no relationship to the problem.

4. Test all repairs after the work is done to make sure that the problem is fixed. Some causes can be traced to more than one component, so a careful verification of repair work is important to pick up additional malfunctions that may cause a problem to reappear or a different problem to arise. A blown fuse, for example, is a simple problem that may require more than another fuse to repair. If you don't look for a problem that caused a fuse to blow, for example, a shorted wire may go undetected.

Experience has shown that most problems tend to be the result of a fairly simple and obvious cause, such as loose or corroded connectors or air leaks in the intake system; making careful inspection of components during testing essential to quick and accurate troubleshooting. Special, hand held computerized testers designed specifically for diagnosing the EEC-IV system are available from a variety of aftermarket sources, as well as from the vehicle manufacturer, but care should be taken that any test equipment being used is designed to diagnose that particular computer controlled system accurately without damaging the control unit (ECU) or components being tested.

NOTE: *Pinpointing the exact cause of trouble in an electrical system can sometimes only be accomplished by the use of special test equipment. The following describes commonly used test equipment and explains how to put it to best use in diagnosis. In addition to the information covered below, the manufacturer's instructions booklet provided with the tester should be read and clearly understood before attempting any test procedures.*

TEST EQUIPMENT

Jumper Wires

Jumper wires are simple, yet extremely valuable, pieces of test equipment. Jumper wires are merely wires that are used to bypass sections of a circuit. The simplest type of jumper wire is merely a length of multistrand wire with an alligator clip at each end. Jumper wires are usually fabricated from lengths of standard automotive wire and whatever type of connector (alligator clip, spade connector or pin connector) that is required for the particular vehicle being tested. The well equipped tool box will have several different styles of jumper wires in several different lengths. Some jumper wires are made with three or more terminals coming from a common splice for special purpose testing. In cramped, hard-to-reach areas it is advisable to have insulated boots over the jumper wire terminals in order to prevent accidental grounding, sparks, and possible fire, especially when testing fuel system components.

Jumper wires are used primarily to locate open electrical circuits, on either the ground (−) side of the circuit or on the hot (+) side. If an electrical component fails to operate, connect the jumper wire between the component and a good ground. If the component operates only with the jumper installed, the ground circuit is open. If the ground circuit is good, but the component does not operate, the circuit between the power feed and component is open. You can sometimes connect the jumper wire directly from the battery to the hot terminal of the component, but first make sure the compo-

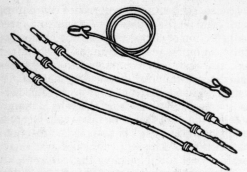

Typical jumper wires with various terminal ends

nent uses 12 volts in operation. Some electrical components, such as fuel injectors, are designed to operate on about 4 volts and running 12 volts directly to the injector terminals can burn out the wiring. By inserting an inline fuseholder between a set of test leads, a fused jumper wire can be used for bypassing open circuits. Use a 5 amp fuse to provide protection against voltage spikes. When in doubt, use a voltmeter to check the voltage input to the component and measure how much voltage is being applied normally. By moving the jumper wire successively back from the lamp toward the power source, you can isolate the area of the circuit where the open is located. When the component stops functioning, or the power is cut off, the open is in the segment of wire between the jumper and the point previously tested.

CAUTION: *Never use jumpers made from wire that is of lighter gauge than used in the circuit under test. If the jumper wire is of too small gauge, it may overheat and possibly melt. Never use jumpers to bypass high resistance loads (such as motors) in a circuit. Bypassing resistances, in effect, creates a short circuit which may, in turn, cause damage and fire. Never use a jumper for anything other than temporary bypassing of components in a circuit.*

12 Volt Test Light

The 12 volt test light is used to check circuits and components while electrical current is flowing through them. It is used for voltage and ground tests. Twelve volt test lights come in different styles but all have three main parts; a ground clip, a probe, and a light. The most commonly used 12 volt test lights have pick-type probes. To use a 12 volt test light, connect the ground clip to a good ground and probe wherever necessary with the pick. The pick should be sharp so that it can penetrate wire insulation to make contact with the wire, without making a large hole in the insulation. The wrap-around light is handy in hard to reach areas or where it is difficult to support a wire to push a probe pick into it. To use the wrap around light, hook the wire to probed with the hook and pull the trigger. A small pick will be forced through the wire insulation into the wire core.

CAUTION: *Do not use a test light to probe electronic ignition spark plug or coil wires. Never use a pick-type test light to probe wiring on computer controlled systems unless specifically instructed to do so. Any wire insulation that is pierced by the test light probe should be taped and sealed with silicone after testing.*

Like the jumper wire, the 12 volt test light is used to isolate opens in circuits. But, whereas the jumper wire is used to bypass the open to operate the load, the 12 volt test light is used to locate the presence of voltage in a circuit. If the test light glows, you know that there is power up to that point; if the 12 volt test light does not glow when its probe is inserted into the wire or connector, you know that there is an open circuit (no power). Move the test light in successive steps back toward the power source until the light in the handle does glow. When it does glow, the open is between the probe and point previously probed.

NOTE: *The test light does not detect that 12*

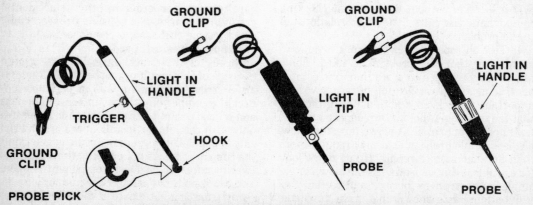

Examples of various types of 12 volt test lights

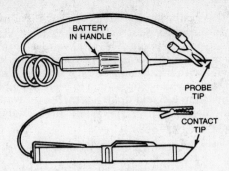

BATTERY
IN HANDLE

PROBE
TIP

CONTACT
TIP

Two types of self-powered test lights

volts (or any particular amount of voltage) is present; it only detects that some voltage is present. It is advisable before using the test light to touch its terminals across the battery posts to make sure the light is operating properly.

Self-Powered Test Light

The self-powered test light usually contains a 1.5 volt penlight battery. One type of self-powered test light is similar in design to the 12 volt test light. This type has both the battery and the light in the handle and pick-type probe tip. The second type has the light toward the open tip, so that the light illuminates the contact point. The self-powered test light is dual purpose piece of test equipment. It can be used to test for either open or short circuits when power is isolated from the circuit (continuity test). A powered test light should not be used on any computer controlled system or component unless specifically instructed to do so. Many engine sensors can be destroyed by even this small amount of voltage applied directly to the terminals.

Open Circuit Testing

To use the self-powered test light to check for open circuits, first isolate the circuit from the vehicle's 12 volt power source by disconnecting the battery or wiring harness connector. Connect the test light ground clip to a good ground and probe sections of the circuit sequentially with the test light. (start from either end of the circuit). If the light is out, the open is between the probe and the circuit ground. If the light is on, the open is between the probe and end of the circuit toward the power source.

Short Circuit Testing

By isolating the circuit both from power and from ground, and using a self-powered test light, you can check for shorts to ground in the circuit. Isolate the circuit from power and ground. Connect the test light ground clip to a

good ground and probe any easy-to-reach test point in the circuit. If the light comes on, there is a short somewhere in the circuit. To isolate the short, probe a test point at either end of the isolated circuit (the light should be on). Leave the test light probe connected and open connectors, switches, remove parts, etc., sequentially, until the light goes out. When the light goes out, the short is between the last circuit component opened and the previous circuit opened.

NOTE: *The 1.5 volt battery in the test light does not provide much current. A weak battery may not provide enough power to illuminate the test light even when a complete circuit is made (especially if there are high resistances in the circuit). Always make sure that the test battery is strong. To check the battery, briefly touch the ground clip to the probe; if the light glows brightly the battery is strong enough for testing. Never use a self-powered test light to perform checks for opens or shorts when power is applied to the electrical system under test. The 12 volt vehicle power will quickly burn out the 1.5 volt light bulb in the test light.*

Voltmeter

A voltmeter is used to measure voltage at any point in a circuit, or to measure the voltage drop across any part of a circuit. It can also be used to check continuity in a wire or circuit by indicating current flow from one end to the other. Voltmeters usually have various scales on the meter dial and a selector switch to allow the selection of different voltages. The voltmeter has a positive and a negative lead. To avoid damage to the meter, always connect the negative lead to the negative ($-$) side of circuit (to ground or nearest the ground side of the circuit) and connect the positive lead to the positive ($+$) side of the circuit (to the power source or the nearest power source). Note that the negative voltmeter lead will always be black and that the positive voltmeter will always be some color other than black (usually red). Depending on how the voltmeter is connected into the circuit, it has several uses.

A voltmeter can be connected either in parallel or in series with a circuit and it has a very high resistance to current flow. When connected in parallel, only a small amount of current will flow through the voltmeter current path; the rest will flow through the normal circuit current path and the circuit will work normally. When the voltmeter is connected in series with a circuit, only a small amount of current can flow through the circuit. The circuit will not work properly, but the voltmeter reading will show if the circuit is complete or not.

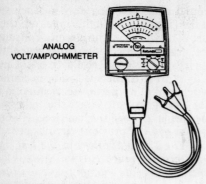

ANALOG
VOLT/AMP/OHMMETER

Typical analog type voltmeter

Available Voltage Measurement

Set the voltmeter selector switch to the 20V position and connect the meter negative lead to the negative post of the battery. Connect the positive meter lead to the positive post of the battery and turn the ignition switch ON to provide a load. Read the voltage on the meter or digital display. A well charged battery should register over 12 volts. If the meter reads below 11.5 volts, the battery power may be insufficient to operate the electrical system properly. This test determines voltage available from the battery and should be the first step in any electrical trouble diagnosis procedure. Many electrical problems, especially on computer controlled systems, can be caused by a low state of charge in the battery. Excessive corrosion at the battery cable terminals can cause a poor contact that will prevent proper charging and full battery current flow.

Normal battery voltage is 12 volts when fully charged. When the battery is supplying current to one or more circuits it is said to be "under load". When everything is off the electrical system is under a "no-load" condition. A fully charged battery may show about 12.5 volts at no load; will drop to 12 volts under medium load; and will drop even lower under heavy load. If the battery is partially discharged the voltage decrease under heavy load may be excessive, even though the battery shows 12 volts or more at no load. When allowed to discharge further, the battery's available voltage under load will decrease more severely. For this reason, it is important that the battery be fully charged during all testing procedures to avoid errors in diagnosis and incorrect test results.

Voltage Drop

When current flows through a resistance, the voltage beyond the resistance is reduced (the larger the current, the greater the reduction in voltage). When no current is flowing, there is no voltage drop because there is no current flow. All points in the circuit which are connected to the power source are at the same voltage as the power source. The total voltage drop always equals the total source voltage. In a long circuit with many connectors, a series of small, unwanted voltage drops due to corrosion at the connectors can add up to a total loss of voltage which impairs the operation of the normal loads in the circuit.

INDIRECT COMPUTATION OF VOLTAGE DROPS

1. Set the voltmeter selector switch to the 20 volt position.
2. Connect the meter negative lead to a good ground.
3. Probe all resistances in the circuit with the positive meter lead.
4. Operate the circuit in all modes and observe the voltage readings.

DIRECT MEASUREMENT OF VOLTAGE DROPS

1. Set the voltmeter switch to the 20 volt position.
2. Connect the voltmeter negative lead to the ground side of the resistance load to be measured.
3. Connect the positive lead to the positive side of the resistance or load to be measured.
4. Read the voltage drop directly on the 20 volt scale.

Too high a voltage indicates too high a resistance. If, for example, a blower motor runs too slowly, you can determine if there is too high a resistance in the resistor pack. By taking voltage drop readings in all parts of the circuit, you can isolate the problem. Too low a voltage drop indicates too low a resistance. If, for example, a blower motor runs too fast in the MED and/or LOW position, the problem can be isolated in the resistor pack by taking voltage drop readings in all parts of the circuit to locate a possibly shorted resistor. The maximum allowable voltage drop under load is critical, especially if there is more than one high resistance problem in a circuit because all voltage drops are cumu-

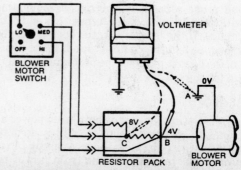

VOLTMETER

LO   MED
OFF   HI

BLOWER
MOTOR
SWITCH

0V

8V

C   4V

B

RESISTOR PACK

BLOWER
MOTOR

Measuring available voltage in a blower circuit

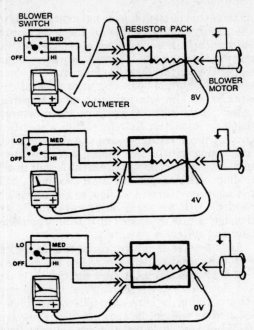

Direct measurement of voltage drops in a circuit

lative. A small drop is normal due to the resistance of the conductors.

HIGH RESISTANCE TESTING

1. Set the voltmeter selector switch to the 4 volt position.
2. Connect the voltmeter positive lead to the positive post of the battery.
3. Turn on the headlights and heater blower to provide a load.
4. Probe various points in the circuit with the negative voltmeter lead.
5. Read the voltage drop on the 4 volt scale. Some average maximum allowable voltage drops are:

FUSE PANEL — 7 volts
IGNITION SWITCH — 5 volts
HEADLIGHT SWITCH — 7 volts
IGNITION COIL (+) — 5 volts
ANY OTHER LOAD — 1.3 volts

NOTE: *Voltage drops are all measured while a load is operating; without current flow, there will be no voltage drop.*

Ohmmeter

The ohmmeter is designed to read resistance (ohms) in a circuit or component. Although there are several different styles of ohmmeters, all will usually have a selector switch which permits the measurement of different ranges of resistance (usually the selector switch allows the multiplication of the meter reading by 10, 100, 1,000, and 10,000). A calibration knob allows the meter to be set at zero for accurate mea-

surement. Since all ohmmeters are powered by an internal battery (usually 9 volts), the ohmmeter can be used as a self-powered test light. When the ohmmeter is connected, current from the ohmmeter flows through the circuit or component being tested. Since the ohmmeter's internal resistance and voltage are known values, the amount of current flow through the meter depends on the resistance of the circuit or component being tested.

The ohmmeter can be used to perform continuity test for opens or shorts (either by observation of the meter needle or as a self-powered test light), and to read actual resistance in a circuit. It should be noted that the ohmmeter is used to check the resistance of a component or wire while there is no voltage applied to the circuit. Current flow from an outside voltage source (such as the vehicle battery) can damage the ohmmeter, so the circuit or component should be isolated from the vehicle electrical system before any testing is done. Since the ohmmeter uses its own voltage source, either lead can be connected to any test point.

NOTE: *When checking diodes or other solid state components, the ohmmeter leads can only be connected one way in order to measure current flow in a single direction. Make sure the positive (+) and negative (−) terminal connections are as described in the test procedures to verify the one-way diode operation.*

In using the meter for making continuity checks, do not be concerned with the actual resistance readings. Zero resistance, or any resistance readings, indicate continuity in the circuit. Infinite resistance indicates an open in the circuit. A high resistance reading where there should be none indicates a problem in the circuit. Checks for short circuits are made in the same manner as checks for open circuits except that the circuit must be isolated from both power and normal ground. Infinite resistance indicates no continuity to ground, while zero resistance indicates a dead short to ground.

RESISTANCE MEASUREMENT

The batteries in an ohmmeter will weaken with age and temperature, so the ohmmeter must be calibrated or "zeroed" before taking measurements. To zero the meter, place the selector switch in its lowest range and touch the two ohmmeter leads together. Turn the calibration knob until the meter needle is exactly on zero.

NOTE: *All analog (needle) type ohmmeters must be zeroed before use, but some digital ohmmeter models are automatically calibrated when the switch is turned on. Self-calibrating digital ohmmeters do not have an ad-*

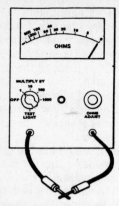

Analog voltmeters must be calibrated before use by touching the probes together and turning the adjustment knobs

justing knob, but its a good idea to check for a zero readout before use by touching the leads together. All computer controlled systems require the use of a digital ohmmeter with at least 10 megohms impedance for testing. Before any test procedures are attempted, make sure the ohmmeter used is compatible with the electrical system or damage to the on-board computer could result.

To measure resistance, first isolate the circuit from the vehicle power source by disconnecting the battery cables or the harness connector. Make sure the key is OFF when disconnecting any components or the battery. Where necessary, also isolate at least one side of the circuit to be checked to avoid reading parallel resistances. Parallel circuit resistances will always give a lower reading than the actual resistance of either of the branches. When measuring the resistance of parallel circuits, the total resistance will always be lower than the smallest resistance in the circuit. Connect the meter leads to both sides of the circuit (wire or component) and read the actual measured ohms on the meter scale. Make sure the selector switch is set to the proper ohm scale for the circuit being tested to avoid misreading the ohmmeter test value.

WARNING: *Never use an ohmmeter with power applied to the circuit. Like the self-powered test light, the ohmmeter is designed to operate on its own power supply. The normal 12 volt automotive electrical system current could damage the meter!*

Ammeters

An ammeter measures the amount of current flowing through a circuit in units called amperes or amps. Amperes are units of electron flow which indicate how fast the electrons are flowing through the circuit. Since Ohms Law

dictates that current flow in a circuit is equal to the circuit voltage divided by the total circuit resistance, increasing voltage also increases the current level (amps). Likewise, any decrease in resistance will increase the amount of amps in a circuit. At normal operating voltage, most circuits have a characteristic amount of amperes, called "current draw" which can be measured using an ammeter. By referring to a specified current draw rating, measuring the amperes, and comparing the two values, one can determine what is happening within the circuit to aid in diagnosis. An open circuit, for example, will not allow any current to flow so the ammeter reading will be zero. More current flows through a heavily loaded circuit or when the charging system is operating.

An ammeter is always connected in series with the circuit being tested. All of the current that normally flows through the circuit must also flow through the ammeter; if there is any other path for the current to follow, the ammeter reading will not be accurate. The ammeter itself has very little resistance to current flow and therefore will not affect the circuit, but it will measure current draw only when the circuit is closed and electricity is flowing. Exces-

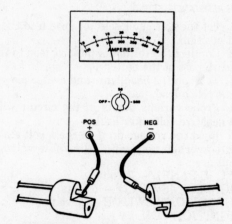

An ammeter must be connected in series with the circuit being tested

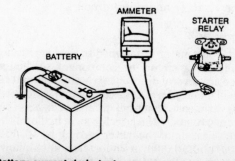

Battery current drain test

sive current draw can blow fuses and drain the battery, while a reduced current draw can cause motors to run slowly, lights to dim and other components to not operate properly. The ammeter can help diagnose these conditions by locating the cause of the high or low reading.

Multimeters

Different combinations of test meters can be built into a single unit designed for specific tests. Some of the more common combination test devices are known as Volt/Amp testers, Tach/Dwell meters, or Digital Multimeters. The Volt/Amp tester is used for charging system, starting system or battery tests and consists of a voltmeter, an ammeter and a variable resistance carbon pile. The voltmeter will usually have at least two ranges for use with 6, 12 and 24 volt systems. The ammeter also has more than one range for testing various levels of battery loads and starter current draw and the carbon pile can be adjusted to offer different amounts of resistance. The Volt/Amp tester has heavy leads to carry large amounts of current and many later models have an inductive ammeter pickup that clamps around the wire to simplify test connections. On some models, the ammeter also has a zero-center scale to allow testing of charging and starting systems without switching leads or polarity. A digital multimeter is a voltmeter, ammeter and ohmmeter combined in an instrument which gives a digital readout. These are often used when testing solid state circuits because of their high input impedance (usually 10 megohms or more).

The tach/dwell meter combines a tachometer and a dwell (cam angle) meter and is a specialized kind of voltmeter. The tachometer scale is marked to show engine speed in rpm and the dwell scale is marked to show degrees of distributor shaft rotation. In most electronic ignition systems, dwell is determined by the control unit, but the dwell meter can also be used to check the duty cycle (operation) of some electronic engine control systems. Some tach/dwell meters are powered by an internal battery, while others take their power from the car battery in use. The battery powered testers usually require calibration much like an ohmmeter before testing.

Special Test Equipment

A variety of diagnostic tools are available to help troubleshoot and repair computerized engine control systems. The most sophisticated of these devices are the console type engine analyzers that usually occupy a garage service bay, but there are several types of aftermarket electronic testers available that will allow quick circuit tests of the engine control system by plugging directly into a special connector located in the engine compartment or under the dashboard. Several tool and equipment manufacturers offer simple, hand held testers that measure various circuit voltage levels on command to check all system components for proper operation. Although these testers usually cost about $300-500, consider that the average computer control unit (or ECM) can cost just as much and the money saved by not replacing perfectly good

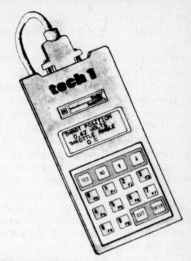

General Motors TECH–1 tester

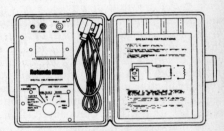

DIGITAL VOLT/OHMMETER

Digital volt-ohmmeter used to test Ford systems

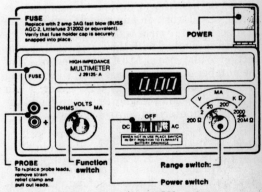

Typical multimeter used to test GM systems

sensors or components in an attempt to correct a problem could justify the purchase price of a special diagnostic tester the first time it's used.

These computerized testers can allow quick and easy test measurements while the engine is operating or while the car is being driven. In addition, the on-board computer memory can be read to access any stored trouble codes; in effect allowing the computer to tell you where it hurts and aid trouble diagnosis by pinpointing exactly which circuit or component is malfunctioning. In the same manner, repairs can be tested to make sure the problem has been corrected. The biggest advantage these special testers have is their relatively easy hookups that minimize or eliminate the chances of making the wrong connections and getting false voltage readings or damaging the computer accidentally.

NOTE: *It should be remembered that these testers check voltage levels in circuits; they don't detect mechanical problems or failed components if the circuit voltage falls within the preprogrammed limits stored in the tester PROM unit. Also, most of the hand held testes are designed to work only on one or two systems made by a specific manufacturer.*

A variety of aftermarket testers are available to help diagnose different computerized control systems. Owatonna Tool Company (OTC), for example, markets a device called the OTC Monitor which plugs directly into the assembly line diagnostic link (ALDL). The OTC tester makes diagnosis a simple matter of pressing the correct buttons and, by changing the internal PROM or inserting a different diagnosis cartridge, it will work on any model from full size to subcompact, over a wide range of years. An adapter is supplied with the tester to allow connection to all types of ALDL links, regardless of the number of pin terminals used. By inserting an updated PROM into the OTC tester, it can be easily updated to diagnose any new modifications of computerized control systems.

Wiring Harnesses

The average automobile contains about ½ mile of wiring, with hundreds of individual connections. To protect the many wires from damage and to keep them from becoming a confusing tangle, they are organized into bundles, enclosed in plastic or taped together and called wire harnesses. Different wiring harnesses serve different parts of the vehicle. Individual wires are color coded to help trace them through a harness where sections are hidden from view.

A loose or corroded connection or a replacement wire that is too small for the circuit will add extra resistance and an additional voltage drop to the circuit. A ten percent voltage drop

can result in slow or erratic motor operation, for example, even though the circuit is complete. Automotive wiring or circuit conductors can be in any one of three forms:

1. Single strand wire
2. Multistrand wire
3. Printed circuitry

Single strand wire has a solid metal core and is usually used inside such components as alternators, motors, relays and other devices. Multistrand wire has a core made of many small strands of wire twisted together into a single conductor. Most of the wiring in an automotive electrical system is made up of multistrand wire, either as a single conductor or grouped together in a harness. All wiring is color coded on the insulator, either as a solid color or as a colored wire with an identification stripe. A printed circuit is a thin film of copper or other conductor that is printed on an insulator backing. Occasionally, a printed circuit is sandwiched between two sheets of plastic for more protection and flexibility. A complete printed circuit, consisting of conductors, insulating material and connectors for lamps or other components is called a printed circuit board. Printed circuitry is used in place of individual wires or harnesses in places where space is limited, such as behind instrument panels.

Wire Gauge

Since computer controlled automotive electrical systems are very sensitive to changes in resistance, the selection of properly sized wires is critical when systems are repaired. The wire gauge number is an expression of the cross section area of the conductor. The most common system for expressing wire size is the American Wire Gauge (AWG) system.

Wire cross section area is measured in circular mils. A mil is 1/1000" (0.001"); a circular mil is the area of a circle one mil in diameter. For example, a conductor ¼" in diameter is 0.250" or 250 mils. The circular mil cross section area of the wire is 250 squared (250")or 62,500 circular mils. Imported car models usually use metric wire gauge designations, which is simply the cross section area of the conductor in square millimeters (mm").

Gauge numbers are assigned to conductors of various cross section areas. As gauge number increases, area decreases and the conductor becomes smaller. A 5 gauge conductor is smaller than a 1 gauge conductor and a 10 gauge is smaller than a 5 gauge. As the cross section area of a conductor decreases, resistance increases and so does the gauge number. A conductor with a higher gauge number will carry less current than a conductor with a lower gauge number.

NOTE: *Gauge wire size refers to the size of*

the conductor, not the size of the complete wire. It is possible to have two wires of the same gauge with different diameters because one may have thicker insulation than the other.

12 volt automotive electrical systems generally use 10, 12, 14, 16 and 18 gauge wire. Main power distribution circuits and larger accessories usually use 10 and 12 gauge wire. Battery cables are usually 4 or 6 gauge, although 1 and 2 gauge wires are occasionally used. Wire length must also be considered when making repairs to a circuit. As conductor length increases, so does resistance. An 18 gauge wire, for example, can carry a 10 amp load for 10 feet without excessive voltage drop; however if a 15 foot wire is required for the same 10 amp load, it must be a 16 gauge wire.

An electrical schematic shows the electrical current paths when a circuit is operating properly. It is essential to understand how a circuit works before trying to figure out why it doesn't. Schematics break the entire electrical system down into individual circuits and show only one particular circuit. In a schematic, no attempt is made to represent wiring and components as they physically appear on the vehicle; switches and other components are shown as simply as possible. Face views of harness connectors show the cavity or terminal locations in all multi-pin connectors to help locate test points.

If you need to backprobe a connector while it is on the component, the order of the terminals must be mentally reversed. The wire color code can help in this situation, as well as a keyway, lock tab or other reference mark.

COMMON SYMBOLS FOR AUTOMOTIVE COMPONENTS USED IN SCHEMATIC DIAGRAMS

Automotive service manuals use schematic diagrams to show how electrical and other types of components work, and how such components are connected to make circuits. Components that are shown whole are represented in full lines in a rectangular shape, and are identified by name; where only a part of a component is shown in a schematic diagram, the rectangular shape is outlined with a dashed line.

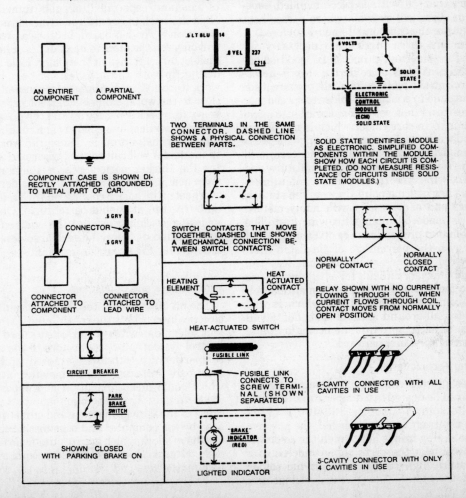

NOTE: *Wiring diagrams are not included in this book. As cars have become more complex and available with longer option lists, wiring diagrams have grown in size and complexity. It has become almost impossible to provide a readable reproduction of a wiring diagram in a book this size. Information on ordering wiring diagrams from the vehicle manufacturer can be found in the owner's manual.*

WIRING REPAIR

Soldering is a quick, efficient method of joining metals permanently. Everyone who has the occasion to make wiring repairs should know how to solder. Electrical connections that are soldered are far less likely to come apart and will conduct electricity much better than connections that are only "pig-tailed" together. The most popular (and preferred) method of soldering is with an electrical soldering gun. Soldering irons are available in many sizes and wattage ratings. Irons with higher wattage ratings deliver higher temperatures and recover lost heat faster. A small soldering iron rated for no more than 50 watts is recommended, especially on electrical systems where excess heat can damage the components being soldered.

There are three ingredients necessary for successful soldering; proper flux, good solder and sufficient heat. A soldering flux is necessary to clean the metal of tarnish, prepare it for soldering and to enable the solder to spread into tiny crevices. When soldering, always use a resin flux or resin core solder which is non-corrosive and will not attract moisture once the job is finished. Other types of flux (acid core) will leave a residue that will attract moisture and cause the wires to corrode. Tin is a unique metal with a low melting point. In a molten state, it dissolves and alloys easily with many metals. Solder is made by mixing tin with lead. The most common proportions are 40/60, 50/50 and 60/40, with the percentage of tin listed first. Low priced solders usually contain less tin, making them very difficult for a beginner to use because more heat is required to melt the solder. A common solder is 40/60 which is well suited for all-around general use, but 60/40 melts easier, has more tin for a better joint and is preferred for electrical work.

Soldering Techniques

Successful soldering requires that the metals to be joined be heated to a temperature that will melt the solder — usually 360-460°F (182-238°C). Contrary to popular belief, the purpose of the soldering iron is not to melt the solder itself, but to heat the parts being soldered to a temperature high enough to melt the solder when it is touched to the work. Melting flux-cored solder on the soldering iron will usually destroy the effectiveness of the flux.

NOTE: *Soldering tips are made of copper for good heat conductivity, but must be "tinned" regularly for quick transference of heat to the project and to prevent the solder from sticking to the iron. To "tin" the iron, simply heat it and touch the flux-cored solder to the tip; the solder will flow over the hot tip. Wipe the excess off with a clean rag, but be careful as the iron will be hot.*

After some use, the tip may become pitted. If so, simply dress the tip smooth with a smooth file and "tin" the tip again. An old saying holds that "metals well cleaned are half soldered." Flux-cored solder will remove oxides but rust, bits of insulation and oil or grease must be removed with a wire brush or emery cloth. For maximum strength in soldered parts, the joint must start off clean and tight. Weak joints will result in gaps too wide for the solder to bridge.

If a separate soldering flux is used, it should be brushed or swabbed on only those areas that are to be soldered. Most solders contain a core of flux and separate fluxing is unnecessary. Hold the work to be soldered firmly. It is best to solder on a wooden board, because a metal vise will only rob the piece to be soldered of heat and make it difficult to melt the solder. Hold the soldering tip with the broadest face against the work to be soldered. Apply solder under the tip close to the work, using enough solder to give a heavy film between the iron and the piece being soldered, while moving slowly and making sure the solder melts properly. Keep the work level or the solder will run to the lowest part and favor the thicker parts, because these require more heat to melt the solder. If the soldering tip overheats (the solder coating on the face of the tip burns up), it should be retinned. Once the soldering is completed, let the soldered joint stand until cool. Tape and seal all soldered wire splices after the repair has cooled.

Wire Harness and Connectors

The on-board computer (ECM) wire harness electrically connects the control unit to the various solenoids, switches and sensors used by the control system. Most connectors in the engine compartment or otherwise exposed to the elements are protected against moisture and dirt which could create oxidation and deposits on the terminals. This protection is important because of the very low voltage and current levels used by the computer and sensors. All connectors have a lock which secures the male and female terminals together, with a secondary lock holding the seal and terminal into the connec-

WIRE HARNESS REPAIR PROCEDURES

Condition	Location	Correction
Non-continuity	Using the electric wiring diagram and the wiring harness diagram as a guideline, check the continuity of the circuit in question by using a tester, and check for breaks, loose connector couplings, or loose terminal crimp contacts.	**Breaks**—Reconnect the point of the break by using solder. If the wire is too short and the connection is impossible, extend it by using a wire of the same or larger size.

Solder

Be careful concerning the size of wire used for the extension

Loose couplings—Hold the connector securely, and insert it until there is a definite joining of the coupling. If the connector is equipped with a locking mechanism, insert the connector until it is locked securely.

Crimp by using pliers

Solder

← **Loose terminal crimp contacts**—Remove approximately 2 in. (5mm) of the insulation covering from the end of the wire, crimp the terminal contact by using a pair of pliers, and then, in addition, complete the repair by soldering.

Condition	Location	Correction
Short-circuit	Using the electric wiring diagram and the wiring harness diagram as a guideline, check the entire circuit for pinched wires.	Remove the pinched portion, and then repair any breaks in the insulation covering with tape. Repair breaks of the wire by soldering.
Loose terminal	Pull the wiring lightly from the connector. A special terminal removal tool may be necessary for complete removal.	Raise the terminal catch pin, and then insert it until a definite clicking sound is heard.

Catch pin

Note: There is the chance of short circuits being caused by insulation damage at soldered points. To avoid this possibility, wrap all splices with electrical tape and use a layer of silicone to seal the connection against moisture. Incorrect repairs can cause malfunctions by creating excessive resistance in a circuit.

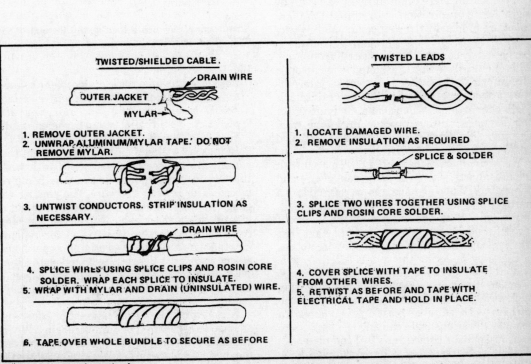

TWISTED/SHIELDED CABLE.

DRAIN WIRE
OUTER JACKET
MYLAR→

1. REMOVE OUTER JACKET.
2. UNWRAP ALUMINUM/MYLAR TAPE. DO NOT REMOVE MYLAR.

3. UNTWIST CONDUCTORS. STRIP INSULATION AS NECESSARY.

DRAIN WIRE

4. SPLICE WIRES USING SPLICE CLIPS AND ROSIN CORE SOLDER. WRAP EACH SPLICE TO INSULATE.
5. WRAP WITH MYLAR AND DRAIN (UNINSULATED) WIRE.

6. TAPE OVER WHOLE BUNDLE TO SECURE AS BEFORE

TWISTED LEADS

1. LOCATE DAMAGED WIRE.
2. REMOVE INSULATION AS REQUIRED

SPLICE & SOLDER

3. SPLICE TWO WIRES TOGETHER USING SPLICE CLIPS AND ROSIN CORE SOLDER.

4. COVER SPLICE WITH TAPE TO INSULATE FROM OTHER WIRES.
5. RETWIST AS BEFORE AND TAPE WITH ELECTRICAL TAPE AND HOLD IN PLACE.

Typical wire repair methods

tor. Both terminal locks must be released when disconnecting ECM connectors.

These special connectors are weather-proof and all repairs require the use of a special terminal and the tool required to service it. This tool is used to remove the pin and sleeve terminals. If removal is attempted with an ordinary pick, there is a good chance that the terminal will be bent or deformed. Unlike standard blade type terminals, these terminals cannot be straightened once they are bent. Make certain that the connectors are properly seated and all of the sealing rings in place when connecting leads. On some models, a hinge-type flap provides a backup or secondary locking feature for the terminals. Most secondary locks are used to improve the connector reliability by retaining the terminals if the small terminal lock tangs are not positioned properly.

Molded-on connectors require complete replacement of the connection. This means splicing a new connector assembly into the harness. All splices in on-board computer systems should be soldered to insure proper contact. Use care when probing the connections or replacing terminals in them as it is possible to short between opposite terminals. If this happens to the wrong terminal pair, it is possible to damage certain components. Always use jumper wires between connectors for circuit checking and never probe through weatherproof seals.

Open circuits are often difficult to locate by sight because corrosion or terminal misalignment are hidden by the connectors. Merely wiggling a connector on a sensor or in the wiring harness may correct the open circuit condition. This should always be considered when an open circuit or a failed sensor is indicated. Intermittent problems may also be caused by oxidized or loose connections. When using a circuit tester for diagnosis, always probe connections from the wire side. Be careful not to damage sealed connectors with test probes.

All wiring harnesses should be replaced with identical parts, using the same gauge wire and connectors. When signal wires are spliced into a harness, use wire with high temperature insulation only. With the low voltage and current levels found in the system, it is important that the best possible connection at all wire splices be made by soldering the splices together. It is seldom necessary to replace a complete harness. If replacement is necessary, pay close attention to insure proper harness routing. Secure the harness with suitable plastic wire clamps to prevent vibrations from causing the harness to wear in spots or contact any hot components.

NOTE: *Weatherproof connectors cannot be replaced with standard connectors. Instruc-*

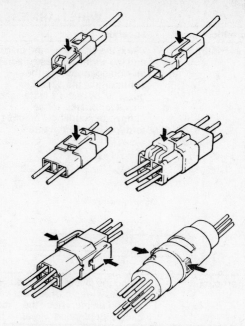

Various types of locking harness connectors. Depress locks at the arrows to separate connectors

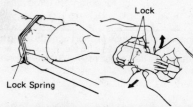

Some connectors use a lock spring instead of the molded locking tabs

tions are provided with replacement connector and terminal packages. Some wire harnesses have mounting indicators (usually pieces of colored tape) to mark where the harness is to be secured.

In making wiring repairs, it's important that you always replace damaged wires with wires that are the same gauge as the wire being replaced. The heavier the wire, the smaller the gauge number. Wires are color-coded to aid in identification and whenever possible the same color coded wire should be used for replacement. A wire stripping and crimping tool is necessary to install solderless terminal connectors. Test all crimps by pulling on the wires; it should not be possible to pull the wires out of a good crimp.

Wires which are open, exposed or otherwise damaged are repaired by simple splicing. Where possible, if the wiring harness is accessible and the damaged place in the wire can be located, it is best to open the harness and check for all possible damage. In an inaccessible harness, the wire must be bypassed with a new insert, usually taped to the outside of the old harness.

When replacing fusible links, be sure to use fusible link wire, NOT ordinary automotive wire. Make sure the fusible segment is of the same gauge and construction as the one being replaced and double the stripped end when crimping the terminal connector for a good contact. The melted (open) fusible link segment of the wiring harness should be cut off as close to the harness as possible, then a new segment spliced in as described. In the case of a damaged fusible link that feeds two harness wires, the harness connections should be replaced with two fusible link wires so that each circuit will have its own separate protection.

NOTE: *Most of the problems caused in the wiring harness are due to bad ground connections. Always check all vehicle ground connections for corrosion or looseness before performing any power feed checks to eliminate the chance of a bad ground affecting the circuit.*

Repairing Hard Shell Connectors

Unlike molded connectors, the terminal contacts in hard shell connectors can be replaced. Weatherproof hard-shell connectors with the leads molded into the shell have non-replaceable terminal ends. Replacement usually involves the use of a special terminal removal tool that depress the locking tangs (barbs) on the connector terminal and allow the connector to be removed from the rear of the shell. The connector shell should be replaced if it shows any evidence of burning, melting, cracks, or breaks. Replace individual terminals that are burnt, corroded, distorted or loose.

NOTE: *The insulation crimp must be tight to prevent the insulation from sliding back on the wire when the wire is pulled. The insulation must be visibly compressed under the crimp tabs, and the ends of the crimp should be turned in for a firm grip on the insulation.*

The wire crimp must be made with all wire strands inside the crimp. The terminal must be fully compressed on the wire strands with the ends of the crimp tabs turned in to make a firm grip on the wire. Check all connections with an ohmmeter to insure a good contact. There should be no measurable resistance between the wire and the terminal when connected.

Mechanical Test Equipment

Vacuum Gauge

Most gauges are graduated in inches of mercury (in.Hg), although a device called a manometer reads vacuum in inches of water (in. H2O).

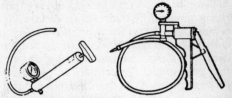

Typical hand vacuum pumps

The normal vacuum reading usually varies between 18 and 22 in.Hg at sea level. To test engine vacuum, the vacuum gauge must be connected to a source of manifold vacuum. Many engines have a plug in the intake manifold which can be removed and replaced with an adapter fitting. Connect the vacuum gauge to the fitting with a suitable rubber hose or, if no manifold plug is available, connect the vacuum gauge to any device using manifold vacuum, such as EGR valves, etc. The vacuum gauge can be used to determine if enough vacuum is reaching a component to allow its actuation.

Hand Vacuum Pump

Small, hand-held vacuum pumps come in a variety of designs. Most have a built-in vacuum gauge and allow the component to be tested without removing it from the vehicle. Operate the pump lever or plunger to apply the correct amount of vacuum required for the test specified in the diagnosis routines. The level of vacuum in inches of Mercury (in.Hg) is indicated on the pump gauge. For some testing, an additional vacuum gauge may be necessary.

Intake manifold vacuum is used to operate various systems and devices on late model vehicles. To correctly diagnose and solve problems in vacuum control systems, a vacuum source is necessary for testing. In some cases, vacuum can be taken from the intake manifold when the engine is running, but vacuum is normally provided by a hand vacuum pump. These hand vacuum pumps have a built-in vacuum gauge that allow testing while the device is still attached to the component. For some tests, an additional vacuum gauge may be necessary.

HEATING AND AIR CONDITIONING

Heater or Heater/Air Conditioning Blower Motor

NOTE: *For discharging and charging procedures for the air conditioning system, please refer to Chapter 1.*

REMOVAL AND INSTALLATION

Civic (1973-79)

NOTE: *These procedures do not apply to vehicles equipped with air conditioning. On ve-*

hicles equipped with air conditioning, heater removal may differ from the procedures listed below. Only a trained air conditioning specialist should disassemble air conditioning equipped units. Air conditioning units contain pressurized Freon which can be extremely dangerous (e.g. frostbite burns and/or blindness) to the untrained.

1. Drain the radiator.

CAUTION: *When draining the coolant, keep in mind that cats and dogs are attracted by the ethylene glycol antifreeze, and are quite likely to drink any that is left in an uncovered container or in puddles on the ground. This will prove fatal in sufficient quantity. Always drain the coolant into a sealable container. Coolant should be reused unless it is contaminated or several years old.*

2. Disconnect the right and left defroster hoses.

3. Disconnect the inlet and outlet water hoses at the heater assembly.

NOTE: *There will be a coolant leakage when disconnecting the hoses. Catch the coolant in a container to prevent damage to the interior.*

4. Disconnect the following items:
   a. Fre/Rec control cable.
   b. Temperature control rod.
   c. Room/Def. control cable.
   d. Fan motor switch connector.
   e. Upper attaching bolts.
   f. Lower attaching bolts.
   g. Lower bracket.

5. Remove the heater assembly through the passenger side.

6. To install the heater assembly, reverse the removal procedure. Pay attention to the following points:
   a. When installing the heater assembly, do not forget to connect the motor ground wire to the right side of the upper bracket.
   b. Connect the inlet and outlet water hoses SECURELY.

NOTE: *The inlet hose is a straight type, and the outlet hose is an L-type.*

   c. Install the defroster nozzles in the correct position.
   d. Connect the control cables securely. Operate the control valve and lever to check for proper operation.
   e. Be sure to bleed the cooling system (see Chapter 1).

Civic and CRX 1980 and Later

1. Drain the radiator.

CAUTION: *When draining the coolant, keep in mind that cats and dogs are attracted by the ethylene glycol antifreeze, and are quite likely to drink any that is left in an uncovered container or in puddles on the ground. This will prove fatal in sufficient quantity. Always drain the coolant into a sealable container. Coolant should be reused unless it is contaminated or several years old.*

2. Remove the dashboard on models through 1983.

3. Disconnect both heater hoses at the firewall and drain the coolant into a container.

4. Remove the heater lower mounting nut on the firewall. On 1984-86 models, remove the dashboard at this point.

5. Remove the two heater duct retaining clips on models through 1983.

6. Disconnect the control cables from the heater.

7. Remove the heater valve cable cover on models through 1983. On 1984-86 models, remove the two mounting bolts at the top. Remove the heater assembly.

8. To install, reverse the removal procedures. Bleed cooling system and make sure cables are properly adjusted. On 1984-88 models, apply a sealant to the grommets and make sure inlet and outlet hoses are connected to the right connections and are secure.

Accord 1976-83

1. The heater blower assembly can be removed by removing the glove box, the fresh air control cable, and the three bolts that hold the blower.

2. To remove the heater core, first drain the radiator.

CAUTION: *When draining the coolant, keep in mind that cats and dogs are attracted by the ethylene glycol antifreeze, and are quite likely to drink any that is left in an uncovered container or in puddles on the ground. This will prove fatal in sufficient quantity. Always drain the coolant into a sealable container. Coolant should be reused unless it is contaminated or several years old.*

3. Remove the instrument panel (see the instrument panel removal section later in this chapter).

4. Once the instrument panel is removed, remove the hoses from the core.

5. Remove the control cables from their clips.

6. Remove the left and right upper bolts.

7. Remove the lower bolts and remove the heater core.

8. To install, reverse the removal procedures. Keep the following points in mind:
   a. Don't interchange the inlet and outlet water hoses.
   b. Make sure all the cables operate correctly.
   c. Bleed the air from the cooling system (see chapter one).

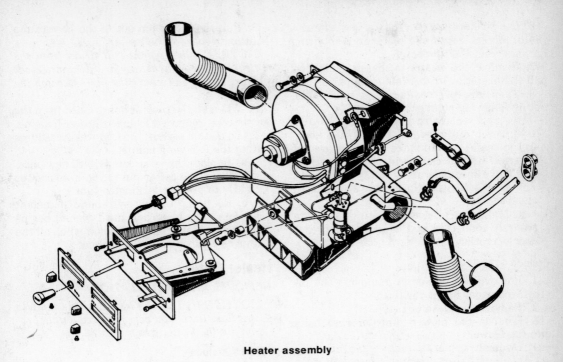

Heater assembly

Accord 1984-85

1. Drain coolant from the bottom of the radiator and collect it for re-use. Put a drain pan underneath the hose connections at the firewall, carefully note hose locations, and then disconnect those two connections.

CAUTION: *When draining the coolant, keep in mind that cats and dogs are attracted by the ethylene glycol antifreeze, and are quite likely to drink any that is left in an uncovered container or in puddles on the ground. This will prove fatal in sufficient quantity. Always drain the coolant into a sealable container. Coolant should be reused unless it is contaminated or several years old.*

2. Disconnect the heater valve cable from the heater water valve. Remove the heater lower mounting nut.

3. See the procedure below and remove the dashboard.

4. Remove the heater duct.

5. Disconnect the heater function cable and the air mix door cable at the heater unit.

6. Pry out retainer clips and then remove the floor ducts from both sides of the vehicle. Disconnect the vacuum hose at the 5-way connector.

7. Remove the two heater mounting bolts (at top) and the heater from under the dash.

8. To install, reverse the removal procedures and note the following points:

 a. Apply sealant to all grommets.

 b. Check routing of inlet and outlet hoses to the heater core to make sure they are not reversed. Install clamps in proper positions and make sure they are securely tightened.

 c. Refill and bleed the cooling system using the bleed bolt.

 d. Make sure all door operating cables are securely connected and adjusted for proper door operation.

Accord 1986-88

1. Drain coolant from the bottom of the radiator and collect it for reuse. Put a drain pan underneath the hose connections at the firewall, carefully note hose locations and then disconnect the two connections.

CAUTION: *When draining the coolant, keep in mind that cats and dogs are attracted by the ethylene glycol antifreeze, and are quite likely to drink any that is left in an uncovered container or in puddles on the ground. This will prove fatal in sufficient quantity. Always drain the coolant into a sealable container. Coolant should be reused unless it is contaminated or several years old.*

2. Disconnect the heater valve cable from the heater valve. Remove the two lower heater mounting nuts.

3. On push button type heaters, disconnect the cool vent cable at the heater. On lever type heaters, disconnect the function cable and the air mix cable from the heater.

4. Remove the dashboard.

5. Remove the heater ducts.

6. On pushbutton type heaters, disconnect the air mix cable from the heater and the wiring harness from the connector.

7. Remove the heater-to-chassis bolts and pull the heater away from its mounts.

8. To install, reverse the reverse procedures, noting following points:

a. Apply sealant to all grommets.

b. Check routing of inlet and outlet hoses to the heater core to make sure they are not reversed. Install clamps in proper positions and make sure they are securely tightened.

c. Refill and bleed the cooling system with the bleed bolt.

d. Make sure all door operating cables are securely connected and adjusted for proper door operation.

Prelude 1979-82

1. Remove the blower by removing the instrument panel side cover.

2. Remove the glove box.

3. Remove the blower-to-heater case bolts and the blower.

4. Drain the coolant.

CAUTION: *When draining the coolant, keep in mind that cats and dogs are attracted by the ethylene glycol antifreeze, and are quite likely to drink any that is left in an uncovered container or in puddles on the ground. This will prove fatal in sufficient quantity. Always drain the coolant into a sealable container. Coolant should be reused unless it is contaminated or several years old.*

5. Remove the lower dash panel.

6. Place a drain pan under the case and disconnect both heater hoses from the core tubes.

7. Remove the lower heater-to-firewall nut.

8. Disconnect the cable at the water valve.

9. Remove the control cables from the heater case.

10. Remove the upper heater mount bolts and the heater.

NOTE: *Only the Prelude (1983-88) models may have the heater core replaced without removing the heater assembly.*

Prelude (1983-88)

1. Drain the cooling system. Remove the heater pipe cover and heater pipe clamps.

CAUTION: *When draining the coolant, keep in mind that cats and dogs are attracted by the ethylene glycol antifreeze, and are quite likely to drink any that is left in an uncovered container or in puddles on the ground. This will prove fatal in sufficient quantity. Always drain the coolant into a sealable container. Coolant should be reused unless it is contaminated or several years old.*

2. Remove the heater core retaining plate.

3. Pull the cotter pin out of the hose clamp joint and separate the heater pipes.

NOTE: *Engine coolant will drain from the heater pipes when they are disconnected. Place a drip pan under the pipes to catch the coolant.*

4. When all the coolant has drained from heater core, remove it from the heater housing.

5. To install, reverse the removal procedures noting the following points:

a. Replace the hose clamps with new ones.

b. Turn the cotter pin in the hose clamps tightly to prevent leaking coolant.

c. Refill the cooling system with coolant and open the bleed bolt until coolant begins to flow from it. Tighten the bolt when all the air has escaped from the system.

Heater Core

REMOVAL AND INSTALLATION

NOTE: *Only the 1983-89 Prelude models may have the heater core replaced without removing the heater assembly.*

1983-89 Prelude

1. Drain the cooling system. Remove the heater pipe cover and heater pipe clamps.

CAUTION: *When draining the coolant, keep in mind that cats and dogs are attracted by the ethylene glycol antifreeze, and are quite likely to drink any that is left in an uncovered container or in puddles on the ground. This will prove fatal in sufficient quantity. Always drain the coolant into a sealable container. Coolant should be reused unless it is contaminated or several years old.*

2. Remove the heater core retaining plate.

3. Pull the cotter pin out of the hose clamp joint and separate the heater pipes.

NOTE: *Engine coolant will drain from the heater pipes when they are disconnected. Place a drip pan under the pipes to catch the coolant.*

4. When all the coolant has drained from heater core, remove it from the heater housing.

5. Installation is the reverse of the removal procedure, please note the following:

a. Replace the hose clamps with new ones.

b. Turn the cotter pin in the hose clamps tightly to prevent leaking coolant.

c. Fill the cooling system with coolant and open the bleed bolt until coolant begins to flow from it. Tighten the bolt when all the air has escaped from the system.

RADIO

WARNING: *Never operate the radio without a speaker; severe damage to the output tran-*

*sistors will result. If the speaker must be re-
placed, use a speaker of the correct impedance
(ohms) or else the output transistors will be
damaged and require replacement.*

REMOVAL AND INSTALLATION

Civic

1. From under the dash, remove the rear radio bracket-to-back tray screw. Remove the ra-
dio-to-bracket wing nut and the bracket.

2. Remove the control knobs, hex nuts and
trim plate from the radio control shafts.

3. Disconnect the antenna and speaker leads,
the bullet type radio fuse and the white lead
connected directly over the radio opening.

4. Drop the radio out, bottom first, through
the package tray.

5. To install, reverse the removal
procedures.

NOTE: *When inserting the radio through
the package tray, be sure the bottom side is up
and the control shafts are facing toward the
engine. Otherwise, you will not be able to position the radio properly through its opening
in the dash.*

Accord and Prelude

1. Remove the center lower lid screws and
the lid.

2. From under the lid, remove the radio
mounting screws.

3. Remove the radio knobs and the faceplate.

4. Remove the heater fan switch knob and
the heater lever knobs.

5. Remove the heater control bezel and the
center panel. To do this, remove the three center panel screws and the ash tray. Slide the panel to the left to remove it. Disconnect the ciga-
rette lighter leads.

6. Remove the radio electrical leads and the
radio.

7. To install, reverse the removal
procedures.

WINDSHIELD WIPERS

Windshield Wiper Motor

REMOVAL AND INSTALLATION

All Models (1973-83)

The wiper motor is connected to the engine
compartment wall, below the front windshield.

1. Remove the negative (−) terminal from
the battery.

2. Disconnect the motor leads from the
connector.

3. Remove the motor water seal cover clamp
and the seal from the motor.

Wiper motor location

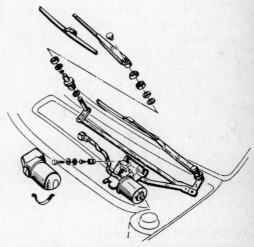

Windshield wiper motor and linkage schematic

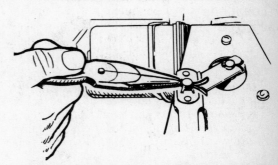

Removing the cotter pin from the motor arm linkage

4. Remove the wiper arm-to-pivot shaft nuts
and the arms.

5. Remove the pivot nuts from both sides
and push the pivots downward.

6. Remove the wiper motor mounting bolts
and the wiper/linkage assembly from the engine
compartment.

7. Pull out the motor arm cotter pin and separate the linkage from the motor.

8. Remove the motor bracket bolts and the motor.

9. To install, reverse the removal procedures. Be sure to inspect the linkage and pivots for wear and looseness. When installing the motor, be sure it is in the **automatic stop** position.

All Models 1984-88

1. Note the installation angles of the wiper arms, then, remove the cap nuts.

2. Remove the air inlet grille and hood seal. NOTE: *On the Civic and CRX, pry out the clips. On the Accord and Prelude, unscrew the Phillips screws and remove the clips.*

3. Using a small prybar, carefully pry the wiper linkage connection from the wiper motor. Then remove the linkage by pushing the wiper pivots through the cowl. On the Civic and CRX, pull off the clip and remove the motor cover.

4. Disconnect the electrical connector. Remove the mounting bolts from the cowl. Remove the motor, being careful not to lose the mounting bolts, which slide into slots on the motor assembly via grommets.

5. To install, grease the linkage joints and reverse the removal procedures. Make sure the linkage operates smoothly and that wipers are installed at the correct angle.

COMPONENT LOCATION

Relay, Sensors And Computer Locations

NOTE: *When using this section, some of the components may not be used on a particular vehicle. This is because the particular component in question may be used on an earlier model or a later model. If a component is not listed, it may have been do to the lack of information from the manufacturer. This section is being published from the latest information available at the time of this publication.*

ACCORD

• **Air Conditioning Compressor Clutch Relay** is located on the front left corner of the engine compartment.

• **Air Conditioning Delay Control Unit** is located under the right side of the instrument panel, on the left side of the blower motor housing.

• **Air Conditioning Diode** is located on the front left corner of the engine compartment.

• **Air Conditioning Heater Blower Mo-**tor is located behind the glove box, on the bottom of the blower motor housing.

• **Air Conditioning Idle Boost Solenoid Valve** is located on the carburetor.

• **Air Conditioning Idle-Up Solenoid Valve (EFI)** is located on the rear center of the engine compartment.

• **Air Conditioning Low Pressure Switch** is located on the front left side of the engine compartment.

• **Air Conditioning Thermostat** is located behind the center console, on the evaporator core housing.

• **Air Suction Control Solenoid Valve** is located in the carburetor emission control box.

• **Anti-Afterburn Control Solenoid Valve** is located on the carburetor.

• **Automatic Transaxle Idle Control Solenoid Valve** is located in the EFI emission control box.

• **Atmospheric Pressure Sensor (EFI)** is located under the right side of the instrument panel.

• **Back-Up Light Switch (manual transaxle)** is located on the clutch housing, toward the front of the car.

• **Brake Fluid Level Sensor** is located in the brake master cylinder reservoir cap.

• **Brake Light Failure Sensor** is attached to the tail light assembly.

• **Brake Light Switch** is located on the bracket above the brake pedal.

• **Check Valve** is located in the emission control box.

• **Cold Advance Solenoid Valve** is located in the EFI emission control box.

• **Condenser Fan Motor** is located on the front left side of engine compartment, behind radiator.

• **Condenser Fan Relay** is located in the relay box.

• **Constant Vacuum Control Valve** is located In EFI emission control box.

• **Coolant Temperature Sending Unit** is located in the thermostat housing.

• **Coolant Temperature Sensor** is located on top of the engine.

• **Cooling Fan Diode** is located on the left front corner of the engine compartment.

• **Cooling Fan Motor** is located on the front right side of the engine compartment, behind the radiator.

• **Cooling Fan Relay** is located in the relay box.

• **Cooling Fan Thermoswitch** is located on the bottom right corner of radiator, below the cooling fan.

• **Cooling Fan Temperature Switch** is located on the bottom right corner of radiator, below the cooling fan.

- **Cooling Fan Temperature Switch B** is located on the center of the engine.
- **Cooling Fan Timer Control Unit** is located under the front right seat.
- **Crank Angle Sensor** is located on the distributor end of the engine.
- **Cranking Leak Solenoid Valve** is located in the carburetor emission control box.
- **Cruise Control Actuator** is located on the left side of the engine compartment.
- **Cruise Control Clutch Switch (manual transaxle)** is located on the bracket above the clutch pedal.
- **Cruise Control Unit** is located under the left side of instrument panel above the fuse box.
- **Dash light Brightness Control Unit** is attached to the instrument panel lower panel.
- **EFE Heater (Carbureted Only)** is located inside of the carburetor.
- **EFE Heater Control Unit (Carbureted)** is located under the driver's seat.
- **EFE Heater Relay** is located on the rear right side of engine compartment.
- **EFI Resistor** is located on the left fender apron.
- **EGR Control Solenoid Valve** is located in the emission control box.
- **Emission Control Box** is located on the right side of the firewall.
- **Fast Idle Control Solenoid Valve** is located in the EFI emission control box.
- **Feedback Control Solenoid Valve** is located on the carburetor.
- **Fuel Cut-Off Relay (Carbureted Only)** is located on the back side of the fuse box.
- **Fuel Gauge Sending Unit** is located in the fuel tank under the right access cover.
- **Fuel Pump Motor** is located in the fuel tank under the left access cover.
- **Fuse Box** is located behind the left side of instrument panel.
- **Headlight Retractor Motor** is located behind the headlight.
- **Headlight Retractor Relays (2)** are located on the front left side of the engine compartment.
- **Idle Boost Solenoid Valve** is located in the carburetor emission box.
- **Idle Control Solenoid Valve (EFI)** is located on the rear left corner of the engine compartment.
- **Intake Air Temperature Sensor** is located in the air cleaner housing, near the snorkel.
- **Integrated Control Unit** is located in the center console under the heater.
- **Intermittent Windshield Wiper Relay** is located on the back side of fuse box.
- **Lights-On Chime** is located on the instrument panel lower panel.

- **Main Relay** is located on the left kick panel near the fuse box.
- **MAP Sensor** is located in the EFI emission control box.
- **Neutral Start Switch (automatic transaxle)** is located at the base of the shift lever.
- **Oxygen Sensor (Carbureted)** is located on the left center of the engine compartment, on the exhaust manifold.
- **Oxygen Sensor (EFI)** is located on the center of the engine compartment, on the exhaust manifold.
- **Oil Pressure Sending Unit** is located on the cylinder block, above the oil filter.
- **Oil Pressure Switch** is located on the top of engine above the oil filter.
- **Parking Brake Switch** is located at the base of the parking brake lever.
- **PGM-FI ECU** is located under the driver's seat.
- **Power Antenna Motor** is located under the left side of instrument panel, above the fuse box.
- **Power Door Lock Control Unit** is located under the front right seat.
- **Power Window Control Unit** is located within the driver's door.
- **Power Window Relay** is located in the relay box.
- **Radiator Fan Relay** is located in the relay box.
- **Rear Window Defogger Relay** is located on the back side of fuse box.
- **Rear Window Wiper Motor** is located on the center of liftgate.
- **Relay Box** is located on the right side of engine compartment, near battery.
- **Retractor Headlight Control Unit** is located on the left kick panel, left of the fuse box.
- **Seat Belt Switch** is located at the base of the driver's seat belt buckle.
- **Shift Lever Position Switch** is located attached to the shift lever.
- **Slow Mixture Cut-Off Solenoid Valve** is located on the carburetor.
- **Solenoid Valve Control Unit (Carbureted)** is located under the driver's seat.
- **Sunroof Motor** is located on the rear center of the roof.
- **Sunroof Relays (2)** is located under the front right seat.
- **Thermosensor** is located in the cylinder head, near the thermostat housing.
- **Throttle Angle Sensor** is located on the rear center of the engine compartment.
- **Turn Signal/Hazard Relay** is located on the back side of the fuse box.
- **Vacuum Holding Solenoid Valve** is lo-

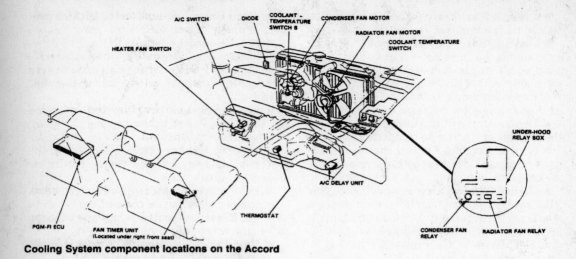

Cooling System component locations on the Accord

cated in the carburetor emission control box.
- **Vacuum Switches (3)** are located in the carburetor emission control box.
- **Washer Pumps (2)** are located behind the left side of the bumper, under washer reservoir.
- **Windshield Wiper Motor** is located on the left rear corner of the engine compartment, on firewall.

CIVIC/CRX
- **Air Conditioning Clutch Relay** is located on the right front corner of the engine compartment.
- **Air Conditioning Condenser Fan Relay** is located on the right front corner of the engine compartment.
- **Air Conditioning Diode** is located on the right front corner of the engine compartment.
- **Air Conditioning-Heater Blower Motor** is located under the right side of the instrument panel.
- **Air Conditioning Heater Blower Motor Resistor** is located on the blower motor housing.
- **Air Conditioning Idle Boost Solenoid (Si Models)** is located on the firewall near the hood latch.
- **Air Conditioning Thermostat** is located on the bottom side of the orator core housing.
- **Air Intake Temperature Sensor** is located in the air intake duct.
- **Air Control Solenoid Valve (Except 4WD & 1.5L)** is located on the in the number one emission control box.
- **Air Control Valves A & B** (4WD & 1.5L w/manual transaxle) are located in the number two emission control box.

- **Air Suction Control Solenoid** is located on in the number one emission control box.
- **Anti-Afterburn Control Solenoid** is located in the number one emission control box.
- **Alternator Control Unit (Except CRX Models)** is located under the left side of instrument panel.
- **Alternator Control Unit (High Altitude CRX HF Models)** is located under the left side of the instrument panel.
- **Atmospheric Pressure Sensor** is located behind the left side of instrument cluster.
- **Back-Up Light Switch** is located on the transaxle housing near the speedometer holder.
- **Block Thermosensor** is located on the side of engine block, near oil the filter.
- **Brake Check Relay (Except CRX Si Models)** is located under the left side of the instrument panel.
- **Brake Check Relay (CRX Si Models)** is located under the left side of the instrument panel.
- **Brake Fluid Level Sensor** is located on the brake master cylinder.
- **Brake Fluid Level Switch** is located in the brake fluid reservoir cap.
- **Brake/Stoplight Switch** is located above the brake pedal on bracket.
- **Clutch Switch** is located on the clutch pedal bracket.
- **Cold Advance Solenoid (CRX Si Models)** is located on the left front inner fender panel.
- **Cold Advance Solenoid Valve (Federal 1.5L HF Only)** is located on the In emission control box No.1.
- **Control Solenoid Valves A & B** (4WD) is located in the transmission control box.
- **Coolant Temperature Switch** is located on the left center of the engine.

- **Cooling Fan Control Unit** is located below the right side of the instrument cluster.
- **Cooling Fan Relay** is located on the right front corner of the engine compartment, if so equipped.
- **Cooling Fan Relay** is located on the right front inner fender panel, if so equipped.
- **Cooling Fan Thermosensor** is located in the lower right side of the radiator.
- **Crank Angle Sensor** is located in the distributor assembly.
- **Cranking Leak Solenoid Valve** is located in the number one emission control box.
- **Dashlight Brightness Controller** is located in the left hand side of the instrument panel.
- **EGR Control Solenoid Valve A** is located in the number one emission control box.
- **EGR Control Solenoid Valve B** is located in the number one emission control box.
- **EGR Control Solenoid Valve C (Federal 1.5L HF Only)** is located in the number one emission control box.
- **EGR Control Valve A & B** is located in the number one emission control.
- **Electric Load Detect Unit** is located in the main fuse block.
- **Electronic Control Unit** is located under the passenger seat.
- **Emission Control Box Number One #1** is located on the left side of the engine compartment.
- **Emission Control Box Number Two #2** is located on the right side of the engine compartment.
- **Emission Control Switch** is located in the number one emission control box.
- **Fast Idle Control Solenoid (CRX Si Models)** is located on the left front inner fender panel.
- **Feedback Control Solenoid Valve** is located in the number two emission control box.
- **Frequency Solenoid Valves A & B** are located in the number two emission control box.
- **Front Washer Motor** is located on the right side of the engine compartment near the battery.
- **Front Wiper Motor** is located under the left side of the air scoop.
- **Fuel Cut-Off Solenoid Valve** is located on the fuel inlet side of carburetor.
- **Fuel Pump** is located at the left side of fuel tank (right rear on wagon).
- **Function Control Motor** is located on the side of the blower housing.
- **Fuse/Relay Block** is located under the left side of the instrument panel.
- **Idle Boost Solenoid Valve** is located in the number one emission control box.

- **Idle Control Solenoid (CRX Si Models)** is located on the left front inner fender panel.
- **Idle Mixture Adjusting Sensor** is located on the left front inner fender panel.
- **Ignitor Unit** is located on the side of the ignition distributor.
- **Intake Air Temperature Sensor** is located in the air cleaner housing.
- **Integrated Control Unit** is located in the fuse/relay block.
- **Intermittent Wiper Relay** is located in the fuse/relay block.
- **Main Fuse Block** is located right hand rear corner of the engine compartment.
- **Main Relay** is located under the left side of instrument panel.
- **Manifold Air Pressure Sensor** is located at the rear of the engine compartment.
- **Neutral/Back-Up Light Switch** is located under the selector lever console.
- **Oil Pressure Sending Unit** is located on the side of the cylinder block, near the oil filter.
- **Opener Solenoid Valve (4WD)** is located in the transmission control box.
- **Oxygen Sensor** is located in the exhaust manifold.
- **Parking Brake Switch** is located under the rear of parking brake lever.
- **PGM-FI Electronic Control Unit** is located under the passenger seat, or behind the right hand side of the instrument panel, near the kick panel.
- **PGM-FI Relay** is located on the left hand side kick panel, near the hood opener.
- **Primary Main Air Cut Solenoid Valve (Federal 1.5L HF)** is located in the number two emission control box.
- **Primary Slow Mixture Solenoid Valve (Federal 1.5L HF)** is located in the number two emission control box.
- **Purge Cut-Off Solenoid** is located on the left front inner fender panel.
- **Power Door Lock Control Unit** is located in the middle of the driver's side door.
- **Power Valve Control Solenoid** is located in the number one emission control box.
- **Power Window Relay** is located in the fuse/relay block.
- **Radiator Fan Relay** is located on the right front corner of the engine compartment.
- **Rear Defogger Relay** is located in the fuse/relay block, under the left side of the instrument panel.
- **Rear Wiper Motor** is located behind the trim panel in the liftgate.
- **Recirculation Control Motor** is located on the side of the blower housing.
- **RPM Sensor** is incorporated into the tachometer.
- **Seat Belt Buzzer/Timer** is located under

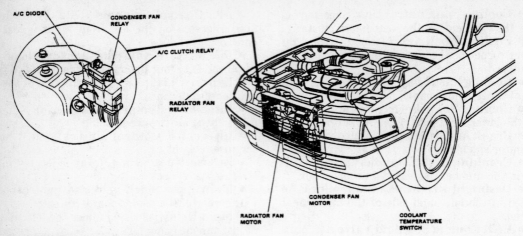

Cooling System component locations on the Civic

the instrument panel, near the steering column.

- **Shift Indicator Control Unit** is located under the left side of the instrument panel.
- **Side Mark Control Unit (Except CRX Models)** is located under the left side of the instrument panel.
- **Side Mark Control Unit (CRX Models)** is located under the left side of the instrument panel.
- **Speed Sensor** is located incorporated into the speedometer.
- **Sunroof Relay (CRX Models)** is located under the left side of the instrument panel.
- **Sunroof Relay (CRX Si Models)** is located under the left side of the instrument panel.
- **System Resistor** is located on the left front inner fender panel.
- **Temperature Gauge Sending Unit** is located in the thermostat housing.

- **Throttle Angle Sensor** is located on the throttle body.
- **Throttle Control Solenoid Valve** is located in the number one emission control box.
- **Turn Signal/Hazard Flasher** is located in the fuse/relay block.
- **Vacuum Brake Switch**
- **Vacuum Brake Switch A** is located in the number one emission control box.
- **Vacuum Brake Switch A** is located in the number two emission control box.
- **Vacuum Brake Switch B** is located in the number one emission control box.
- **Vacuum Brake Switch B** is located in the number two emission control box.
- **Vacuum Brake Switch C** is located in the number one emission control box.
- **Vacuum Brake Switch D** is located in the number one emission control box.
- **Vacuum Brake Switch E** is located in the number one emission control box.

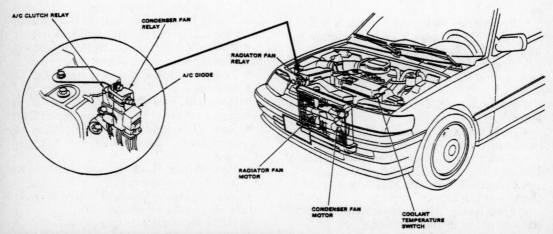

Cooling System component locations on the Civic/CRX

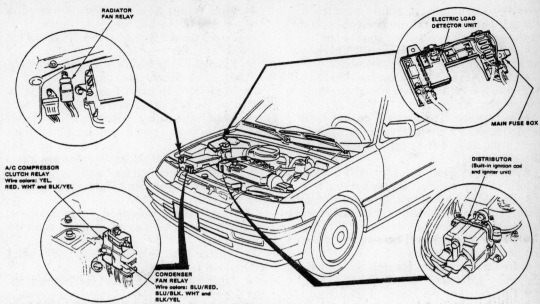

Engine compartment component locations for all Civic models

- **Vacuum Brake Switch F** is located in the number one emission control box.
- **Vacuum Holding Solenoid Valve** is located in the number one emission control box.

PRELUDE

- **Air Conditioning Compressor Clutch Relays** are located on the right front corner of the engine compartment, near the battery.
- **Air Conditioning Compressor Control Unit** is located under the right hand side of the instrument panel, near the kick panel.

- **Air Conditioning Heater Blower Motor** is located under the right side of instrument panel.
- **Air Conditioning Heater Blower Motor Relay** is located below the right side of the instrument panel.
- **Air Conditioning Low Pressure Switch** is located in the high pressure line near the air conditioning receiver/drier.
- **Air Conditioning Thermostatic Switch** is located on the evaporator housing.
- **Air Suction Control Solenoid Valve** is

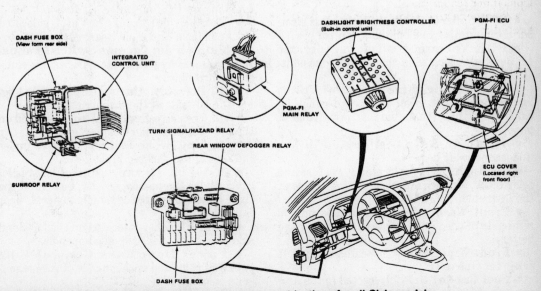

Instrument panel and passenger compartment component loctions for all Civic models

located in the number on emission control box.

- **Air Suction Vacuum Switch** is located in the number two emission control box.
- **Air Vent Cut-Off Solenoid Valve** is located under the air cleaner assembly.
- **Anti-Afterburn Control Solenoid Valve** is located in the number two emission control box.
- **Automatic Transaxle Control Unit** is located under the passenger seat, or behind the right hand side of the instrument panel, near the kick panel.
- **Auxiliary Slow Fuel Cut-Off Solenoid** is located on the side of the carburetor.
- **Back-Up Light Switch (manual transaxle)** is located on the side of transaxle near the speedometer holder.
- **Brake Fluid Level Sensor** is located in the brake master cylinder.
- **Brake/Stoplight Switch** is located on the brake pedal bracket.
- **Condenser Fan Motor** is located on the back left side of the radiator.
- **Condenser Fan Relay** is located in the underhood relay box, on the later models.
- **Condenser Fan Relay** is located in the left front corner of the engine compartment.
- **Control Switch Solenoid Valve** is located in the number one emission control box.
- **Coolant Temperature Sending Unit** is located on the front of the intake manifold.
- **Coolant Thermosensor** is located on the side of engine block, above the oil filter.
- **Cooling Fan Thermosensor** is located on the bottom right corner of the radiator.
- **Cranking Leak Solenoid Valve** is located in the number one emission control box.
- **EGR Control Solenoid Valve A** is located in the number one emission control.
- **EGR Control Solenoid Valve B** is located in the number one emission control box.
- **EGR Vacuum Switch (automatic transaxle)** is located in the number one emission control box.
- **Dashlight Brightness Control Unit** is located behind the lower dashboard panel, located under the left hand side of the instrument panel.
- **Dimmer Relay** is located in the underhood relay box.
- **Fog Light Relay** is located in the fuse and relay block, located under the left hand side of the instrument panel.
- **Front Washer Motor** is located on the right side of the engine compartment near the battery.
- **Front Wiper Motor** is located on the left side of engine cowl.
- **Fuel Cut-Off Relay** is located in the fuse and relay block under the left side of the instrument panel.

- **Fuel Gauge Sending Unit** is located in the top rear of the fuel tank.
- **Fuel Pump** is located at the left side of the fuel tank.
- **Fuse & Relay Block** is located under the left side of the instrument panel.
- **Headlight Retract Control Unit** is located on the left kick panel.
- **Headlight Retract Relays (2)** are located in the left front corner of engine compartment.
- **Headlight Retractor Motors** are located behind each headlight assembly.
- **Headlight Warning Chime** is located on the left kick panel.
- **Idle Control Solenoid Valve** is located on the bracket near the number two emission control box.
- **Igniter Unit** is located on the right hand front strut tower.
- **Inhibitor Switch (automatic transaxle)** is located under the selector level console.
- **Inner Vent Solenoid Valve** is located under the air cleaner assembly.
- **Intake Air Temperature Sensor** is located in the air cleaner housing.
- **Interior Light Timer** is located behind the left side of the instrument panel.
- **Integrated Control Unit** is located under the center of the instrument panel, under the heater unit.
- **Intermittent Wiper Relay** is located behind the instrument cluster.
- **Left Headlight Retractor Relay** is located behind the left headlight.
- **Lighting Relay** is located in the underhood relay box.
- **Low Fuel Thermistor** is located in the fuel tank on the fuel gauge sending unit.
- **Main Air Jet Solenoid Valve** is located on the bottom of the air cleaner housing.
- **Main Air Jet Vacuum Switch (manual transaxle)** is located in the number one emission control box.
- **Oil Pressure Alarm Unit** is located below the left side of the instrument panel.
- **Oil Pressure Sending Unit** is located on the top of the oil filter adapter.
- **Parking Brake Switch** is located under the rear of the parking brake lever.
- **PGM-FI Electronic Control Unit** is located under the passenger seat, or behind the right hand side of the instrument panel, near the kick panel.
- **PGM-FI Relay** is located on the left hand side kick panel, near the hood opener.
- **Power Door Lock Control Unit (w/4WS)** is located in the middle of the passenger's side door.
- **Power Window Control Unit** is located in the middle of the driver's side door.

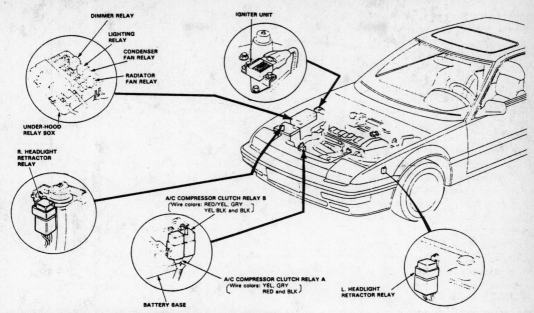

Engine compartment component locations on the Prelude

- **Power Window Relay** is located in the fuse and relay block under left side of the instrument panel.
- **Primary Slow Fuel Cut-Off Solenoid** is located on the fuel inlet side of the carburetor.
- **Radiator Cooling Fan Motor** is located on the back of the radiator.
- **Radiator Cooling Fan Relay** is located in the underhood relay box.
- **Rear Window Defogger Relay** is located in the fuse and relay block under left side of the instrument panel.

- **Recirculation Solenoids** is located under the right side of the instrument panel.
- **Right Headlight Retractor Relay** is located behind the right headlight.
- **Seat Belt/Key Timer** is located near the fuse and relay block under the left side of instrument panel.
- **Side Marker Relay** is located under the left side of the instrument panel.
- **Solenoid Control Valve Unit** is located under the right side of the instrument panel.
- **Speed Sensor** is located in the speedometer gear housing.

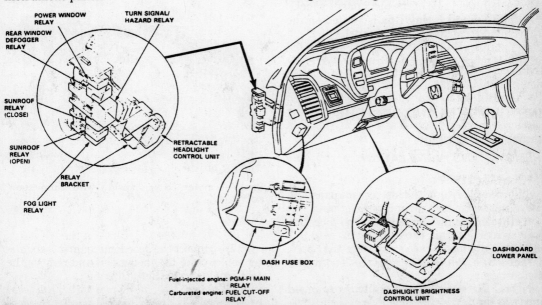

Instrument panel component loctions on the Prelude

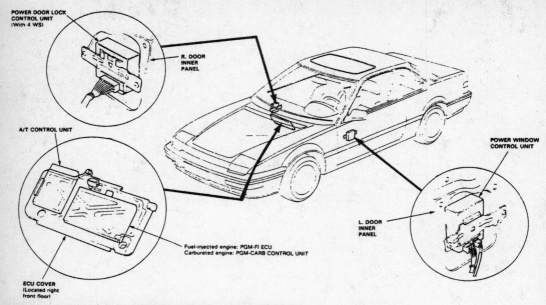

Passenger's compartment component loctions on the Prelude

- **Speed Sensor Amplifier** is located on the back of the speedometer.
- **Sunroof Motor** is located at the front of the sunroof under headliner.
- **Sunroof Close Relay** is located in the fuse and relay block, located under the left hand side of the instrument panel.
- **Sunroof Open Relay** is located in the fuse and relay block, located under the left hand side of the instrument panel.
- **Turn Signal/Hazard Flasher Relay** is located in the fuse and relay block, located under the left hand side of the instrument panel.
- **Underhood Relay Box** is located on the right hand front inner fender panel.
- **Vacuum Switches A, B & C** are located in the number one emission control box.

Meter case removed from car

INSTRUMENTS AND SWITCHES

Instrument Cluster

REMOVAL AND INSTALLATION

Meter Case Assembly

1. From the rear of the instrument panel, remove the meter case mounting wing nuts.
2. Disconnect the speedometer and tachometer drive cables from the engine.
3. Pull the meter case away from the panel. Disconnect the meter wires from the connectors.
   NOTE: *Be sure to label the wires to avoid confusion during reassembly.*

Back of meter case showing wire connection points

4. Disconnect the speedometer and tachometer cables from the meter case and remove the case from the vehicle.
5. To install, reverse the removal procedures.

Switch Panel

1. Loosen the steering wheel column cover screws, then, remove the upper and lower covers.

2. Remove the steering column bolts (remove the upper bolts 1st) and rest the steering assembly on the floor.

3. From the rear of the instrument panel, remove the switch panel screws.

4. To release the switch panel, remove the switches in the following manner:

    a. Remove the light switch by prying the cover off the front of the knob. Pinch the retaining tabs and pull off the knob.

    b. Remove the wiper switch by pushing the knob in and turning counterclockwise, then, remove the retaining nut.

    c. Remove the choke knob by loosening the set screw, then, remove the retaining nut.

5. To install, reverse the removal procedures.

Civic 1973-79

1. Loosen the steering wheel column cover screws, then, remove the upper and lower covers.

2. Remove the steering column bolts (remove the upper two bolts 1st) and rest the steering assembly on the floor.

3. Remove the screw on the outside edge of each fresh air vent and pry off the vents with a prybar.

4. Disconnect the instrument panel wiring harness from their cabin harnesses by removing the connectors and couplers.

5. Disconnect the speedometer and tachometer cables from the engine.

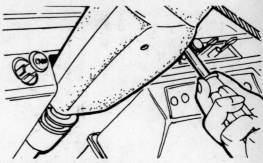

Removing steering column cover

6. Disconnect the choke cable from the panel.

7. Remove the following switches:

    a. Remove the light switch by prying the cover off the front of the knob. Pinch the retaining tabs together and pull off the knob.

    b. Remove the wiper switch by pushing the knob in and turning counterclockwise, then, remove the retaining nut.

    c. Loosen the choke knob set screw and remove the retaining nut.

8. Disconnect the three heater control cables.

9. Remove the heater fan motor wire connector.

10. Remove the six panel bolts.

11. Pull the instrument panel out slightly, then, disconnect the speedometer and tachometer cables from the instruments. Remove the instrument panel.

12. To install, reverse the removal procedures and pay attention to the following points:

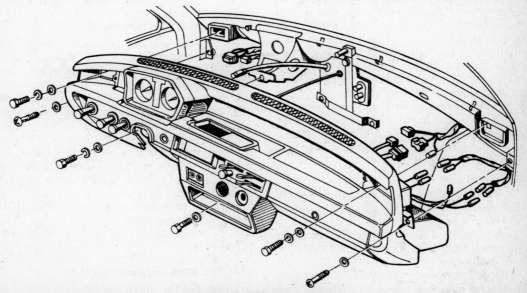

Instrument panel removal

a. Connect the speedometer and tachometer cables to the instruments, then, install the panel in place with the center pin in the panel locating hole.

b. Temporarily tighten the bolts which secure the upper, right and left sides of the instrument panel. Make sure that the wiring harnesses are properly routed.

Civic (1980-82)

1. On 1980-81 models, remove the steering column.
2. On 1982 models, lower the steering column.
3. On 1980-81 models, remove the bulb access panel and the two upper mounting screws through the access panel, then, the lower mounting bolt and screws.
4. On 1982 models, remove the four screws and trim cover.
5. Disconnect the speedometer cable and tachometer cable (if equipped).
6. Disconnect any remaining mount screws and wire connectors, then, remove the instrument panel.
7. To install, reverse the removal procedures.

Accord (1975-85) and Prelude (1979-82)

1. Remove the instrument cluster.
2. Remove the speaker grille, the the clock panel and the clock.
3. Remove the control knobs and the heater control panel from the instrument panel.
4. Remove the inner instrument panel screws. The center panel and the heater control assembly are tightened together.
5. Remove the both-side instrument panel covers and the two bolts on either side.
6. Remove the two bolts from the center of the instrument panel.
7. Remove the bolt behind the clock panel and the instrument panel.
8. To install, reverse the removal procedures and remember the following points:

a. Avoid bending the heater lever when installing the dashboard. Make sure the heater levers move freely without binding.

b. Make sure the instrument wiring harnesses aren't pinched.

Prelude (1983-88)

NOTE: *Be careful not to disturb the wiring connections while removing the lower dashboard panel.*

1. Remove the fuse box cover and the lower trim panel. Remove the mounting bolts and the lower dash panel.
2. Open the glove box and reach in to remove the ashtray. Remove the mounting bolts and the glovebox trim panel. Disconnect the glove box light, ashtray light, radio and antenna wiring.
3. Remove the mounting screws and the heater control panel. Remove the heater cable mounting screws and the cable, then, disconnect the wiring harness.
4. Remove the steering column bolts and lower the column. Remove the instrument cluster screws and pull the cluster out far enough to reach the wiring connectors. Disconnect the wiring connectors and remove the instrument cluster panel.
5. Remove the mounting screws for the gauges and lift the gauge assembly, then, disconnect the wiring connectors by pulling on the connectors. Disconnect the speedometer cable.
6. Remove the gauge assembly and the clock.
7. Disconnect the wiring harness from the following points:

a. The fuse box.
b. Side wiring harness.
c. Instrument sub-harness.
d. Heater wire harness.
e. Interior light timer unit.
f. Chime.

8. Remove the dashboard bolts, then, lift up slightly on the dashboard as you pull it straight out off the guide pin (located near the middle of the dash).
9. To install, reverse the removal procedures.

NOTE: *Make sure the dash fits squarely onto the guide pin when sliding it in place when you slide it into position. Before tightening the mounting bolts, make sure there is no spot where the wiring harness is pinched between the dash and vehicle body.*

Accord (1986-88)
Civic Coupe (CRX) (1984-88)

1. Remove the lower dash panel screws, clips and the panel.
2. Remove the lower heater control knob and the lower panel.
3. Remove the heater control mount screws and the upper screws from the instrument panel.
4. Pull the panel out and disconnect the wire connectors. Remove the instrument panel.
5. Remove the 4 screws, then, lift out the gauge assembly and disconnect the wire connectors.
6. Disconnect the speedometer cable, then, remove the gauge assembly.
7. To install, reverse the removal procedures.

Civic Hatchback and Sedan (1984-88)

1. Remove the upper instrument panel caps, screws and the panel.

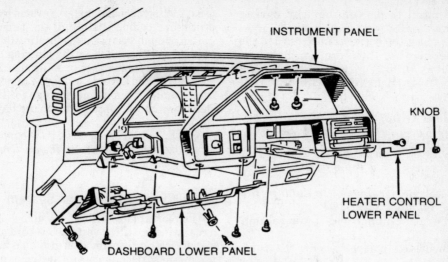

1984 and later CRX instrument panel

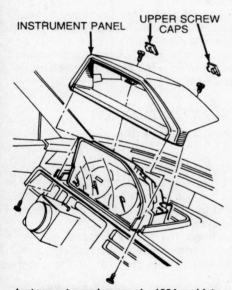

Instrument panel removal—1984 and later Civic Hatchback & Sedan

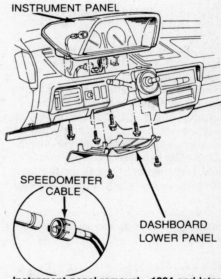

Instrument panel removal—1984 and later Civic Wagon

2. Remove the gauge assembly screws and lift out the assembly to disconnect the wire connectors.

3. Disconnect the speedometer cable and remove the gauge assembly.

4. To install, reverse the removal procedures.

Civic Wagon (1984-88)

1. Remove the dashboard lower panel screws and the panel; this allows access to the instrument panel retaining bolts.

2. Remove the instrument panel bolts, raise the panel, then, disconnect the wiring connec-

tors and the speedometer cable. Remove the instrument panel with the gauge assembly.

3. Remove the gauge assembly screws and the assembly from the instrument panel.

4. To install, reverse the removal procedures.

Accord (1982-85)

1. Lower the steering column.

2. Remove the top instrument panel screws.

3. Pull the instrument panel outward, then, disconnect the wiring connectors and remove the panel.

4. Remove the gauge assembly screws, then,

lift the panel to disconnect the wiring connectors.

5. Disconnect the wiring connectors and the speedometer cable, then, remove the gauge assembly.

6. To install, reverse the removal procedures.

Windshield Wiper Switch

REMOVAL AND INSTALLATION

1. Remove the steering wheel.

2. Disconnect the column wiring harness and coupler.

CAUTION: *Be careful not to damage the steering column or shaft.*

3. Remove the upper and lower column covers.

4. On models so equipped, remove the cruise control slip ring.

5. Remove the turn signal canceling sleeve.

6. On later models, remove the switch retaining screws, then remove the switch.

7. Loosen the screw on the turn signal switch cam nut and lightly tap its head to permit the cam nut to loosen. Then remove the turn signal switch assembly and the steering shaft upper bushing.

8. To assemble and install, reverse the above procedure. When installing the turn signal switch assembly, engage the locating tab on the switch with the notch in the steering column. The steering shaft upper bushing should be installed with the flat side facing the upper side of the column. The alignment notch for the turn signal switch will be centered on the flat side of the bushing.

NOTE: *On earlier models, if the cam nut has been removed, be sure to install it with the small end up.*

Headlight Switch

REMOVAL AND INSTALLATION

1. Remove the steering wheel.

2. Disconnect the column wiring harness and coupler.

CAUTION: *Be careful not to damage the steering column or shaft.*

3. Remove the upper and lower column covers.

4. On models so equipped, remove the cruise control slip ring.

5. Remove the turn signal canceling sleeve.

6. On later models, remove the switch retaining screws, then remove the switch.

7. Loosen the screw on the turn signal switch cam nut and lightly tap its head to permit the cam nut to loosen. Then remove the turn signal switch assembly and the steering shaft upper bushing.

8. To assemble and install, reverse the above procedure. When installing the turn signal switch assembly, engage the locating tab on the switch with the notch in the steering column. The steering shaft upper bushing should be installed with the flat side facing the upper side of the column. The alignment notch for the turn signal switch will be centered on the flat side of the bushing.

NOTE: *On earlier models, if the cam nut has been removed, be sure to install it with the small end up.*

Rear Window Defogger System

The rear window defogger system consists of a rear window with 2 vertical bus bars and a series of electrically connected grid lines baked on the inside surface. A control switch and a relay are also used in this system.

NOTE: *Since the grid lines can be damaged or scraped off with sharp instruments, caution should be used when cleaning the glass or removing foreign materials, decals or stickers. Normal glass cleaning solvents or hot water used with rags or toweling is recommended.*

REMOVAL AND INSTALLATION

Rear Window Defogger Switch

ACCORD

1. Disconnect the negative battery cable. Remove the combination meter housing.

2. Pull out the combination meter housing far enough to gain access to the rear defroster switch retaining screws.

3. Disconnect the switch electrical connector. Remove the switch retaining screws and remove the switch from the rear of the meter housing.

4. Installation is the reverse order of the removal procedure.

CIVIC

1. Disconnect the negative battery cable and remove the lower dashboard panel (except for the wagon models).

2. Disconnect the wire harness from behind the console. Depress the switch locking pawls and remove the switch from the front of the dash panel.

3. Installation is the reverse order of the removal procedure.

PRELUDE

1. Disconnect the negative battery cable. Lower the steering column and remove the lower dashboard panel.

2. Remove the 4 instrument panel retaining

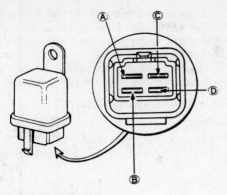

Testing the defrost relay

screws. Pull the instrument panel out and disconnect the wire connectors.

3. Remove the instrument panel. Remove the rear defroster switch retaining screws and pull the switch out of the instrument panel.

4. Installation is the reverse order of the removal procedure.

COMPONENT TESTING

Rear Defroster Relay

1. Check for continuity between top left **A** terminal and the bottom left B terminal, when applying battery voltage to upper right C terminal and grounding the lower right D terminals.

2. Once the voltage is removed from the C and D terminals, there should be no continuity

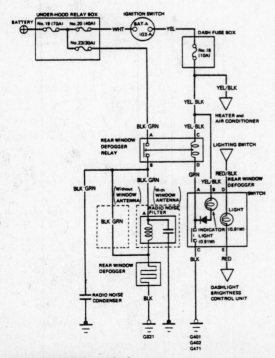

Defogger circuit—typical

in the relay. If the relay fails this test, replace it. The relays are located under the dash on the left side.

Rear Window Defogger Grid

1. Turn **ON** the rear window defroster switch. Connect the positive lead of a voltmeter to the center of each filament and connect the negative lead to the body of the vehicle.

2. The standard voltage at the center of the filament is 6 volts. If the meter is higher than 6 volts, the problem exists in the ground side of the filament.

3. If the meter indication is low or 0, the problem is between the center and the power side. Isolate the problem grid line and mark the break in the grid wire.

HONDA CRUISE CONTROL SYSTEM

The cruise control system maintains the vehicle speed at a setting selected by the driver by mean of mechanical, electrical, and vacuum operated devices.

The cruise control unit receives command signals from the cruise control main switch and the cruise control set/resume switch. The control unit also receives information about operating conditions from the brake switch, the distributor, speed sensor, the clutch switch (with manual tranaxle), or the shift lever position switch (with automatic tranaxle). The cruise control unit, in turn, sends operational signals to the devices that regulate the throttle position. The throttle position maintains the selected vehicle speed. The cruise control compares the actual speed of the vehicle to the selected speed. Then, the control unit uses the result of that comparison to open or close the throttle.

The control unit will disengage the instant the driver depresses the brake pedal. The brake switch sends an electronic signal to the control unit when the brake pedal is depressed; the control unit responds by allowing the throttle to close. The shift lever position switch (automatic transaxle) or the clutch switch (manual tranaxle) sends a disengage signal input to the control unit that also allows the throttle to close.

NOTE: *The use of the speed control is not recommended when driving conditions do not permit maintaining a constant speed, such as in heavy traffic or on roads that are winding, icy, snow covered or slippery.*

SYSTEM OPERATION

The cruise control system will set and automatically maintain any speed above 30 mph (45 kph). To set the system, make sure that the main switch is in the **ON** position. After reaching the desired speed, press the set switch. The cruise control unit will receive a set signal input and, in turn, will actuate the cruise control actuator. When the set switch is depressed and the cruise control system is on, the cruise control on indicator on the warning display will light up.

To cancel the cruise control system, press the main switch to **OFF**. This removes power to the control unit and erases the set speed from memory. If the system is disengaged temporarily by the brake switch, clutch switch, or gear selector switch and vehicle speed is still above 30 mph, press the resume switch. With the resume switch depressed and the set memory retained, the vehicle automatically returns to the previous set speed.

For a gradual acceleration without depressing the accelerator pedal, push the resume switch down and hold it there until the desired speed is reached. This will send an acceleration signal input to the control unit. When the switch is released, the system will be reprogrammed for the new speed. To slow the vehicle down, depress the set switch. This will send a deceleration signal input to the control unit causing the vehicle to coast until the desired speed is reached. When the desired speed is reached, release the set switch. This will reprogram the system for the new speed.

ADJUSTMENT

Actuator Cable

1. Check that actuator cable operates smoothly with no binding or sticking.
2. Start engine.
3. Measure amount of movement of actuator rod until cable pulls on accelerator lever (engine speed starts to increase). Free-play should be 11mm ± 1.5mm.
4. If free play is not within specifications, loosen locknut and turn adjusting nut as required.

5. Retighten locknut and recheck free-play.
6. Test car under drive to make sure that overshoot and undershoot are held within ± 2 mph of set speed.

NOTE: *If necessary, check throttle cable free-play, then recheck actuator rod free-play.*

REMOVAL AND REPLACEMENT

Main Switch

1. Remove fuse panel door.
2. Push out switch from behind dashboard panel.
3. Disconnect electrical connector from switch.
4. To install, reverse removal procedure.

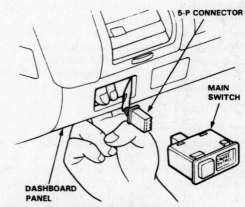

Cruise control main switch servicing

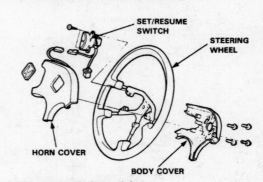

Set/resume switch servicing

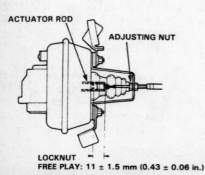

Actuator cable adjustment—typical

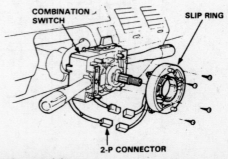

Slip ring servicing

Set/Resume Switch

1. Remove steering wheel.
2. Separate horn cover and body cover by removing 4 screws.
3. Remove 3 screws and set/resume switch from steering wheel.
4. To install, reverse removal procedure.

Slip Ring

1. Remove steering wheel.
2. Remove upper and lower steering column covers.
3. Remove 4 screws and remove slip ring assembly.
4. To install, reverse removal procedure.

Actuator/Cable

1. Pull back boot and loosen locknut, then disconnect cable from bracket.
2. Disconnect cable end from actuator rod.
3. Disconnect 4 pin connector.
4. Pull ventilation hose from grommet.
5. Disconnect vacuum hose from check valve.
6. Remove 2 mount bolts and actuator with bracket.
7. If necessary, disconnect cable end from linkage over accelerator pedal.
8. To install, reverse removal procedure and

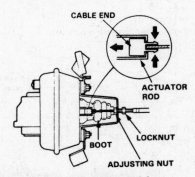

Cruise control actuator cable servicing

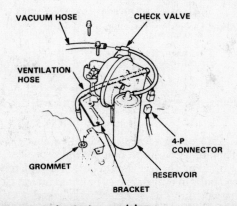

Cruise control actuator servicing

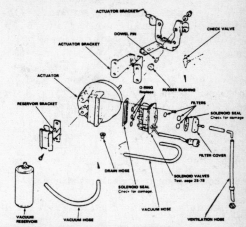

Cruise control actuator exploded view

adjust free-play at actuator rod after connecting cable.

Diagnosis and Testing

COMPONENT TESTING

Slip Ring

1. Remove column cover, then disconnect 3 pin connector.
2. Check continuity between connector terminal with blue/red wire and terminal **A**.
3. Check continuity between connector terminal with light green/red and terminal **B**.
4. Check continuity between connector terminal with light green/black and terminal **C**.
5. Replace slip ring assembly if 1 or more do not have continuity.

Actuator Solenoid

1. Disconnect 4 pin connector from actuator solenoid.
2. Connect ohmmeter between connector terminal with brown/white wire and brown/black wire (vacuum solenoid) and measure resistance. Resistance should be 30-50Ω.

NOTE: *Resistance will vary slightly with*

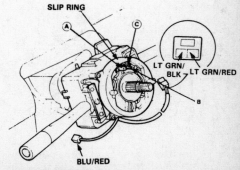

Slip ring continuity test

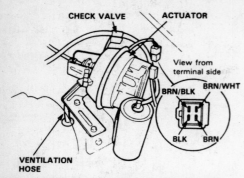

Cruise control actuator solenoid resistance test

temperature. Resistance values given are at 70°F (21°C).

3. Connect ohmmeter between connector terminal with brown/white wire and brown wire (vent solenoid) and measure resistance. Resistance should be 40-60Ω.

4. Connect ohmmeter between connector terminal with brown/white wire and black wire (safety solenoid) and measure resistance. Resistance should be 40-60Ω.

5. If any resistance values are not as specified, check/replace actuator solenoid.

Actuator

1. Disconnect actuator cable from actuator rod.

2. Disconnect 4 pin connector.

3. Connect battery positive wire to brown/white terminal and negative to brown/black, brown and black terminals.

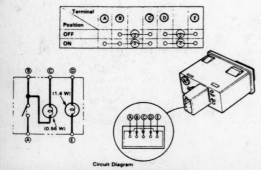

Cruise control actuator vacuum hold test

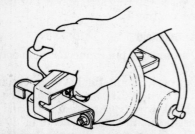

Cruise control main switch continuity test

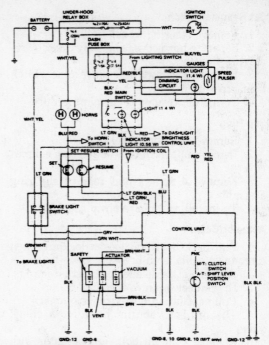

Cruise control wiring schematic

Terminal Position	GROUND WIRE	PNK
2	o———o	o———o
D₃	o———o	o———o
D₄	o———o	o———o
N		
R		
P		

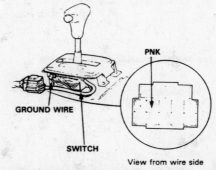

Shift Lever Position switch continuity test

4. Connect a vacuum pump to check valve. Then apply vacuum to actuator.

5. Actuator rod should pull in completely. If rod pulls in only part way or not at all for a leaking vacuum line or defective solenoid.

6. With voltage and vacuum still applied, try

to pull actuator rod out by hand. Actuator rod should not pull out. If it does, replace actuator.

7. Disconnect battery negative wire from brown terminal. Actuator rod should return. If it does not return and ventilation hose and filter are free, replace actuator.

8. Repeat Steps 3-7, but disconnect battery negative wire from black terminal. Actuator rod should return. If not and ventilation hose and filter are free, replace solenoid valve assembly.

NOTE: *If solenoid valve assembly is replaced, be sure to use new O-rings at each solenoid.*

Cruise control circuit check chart

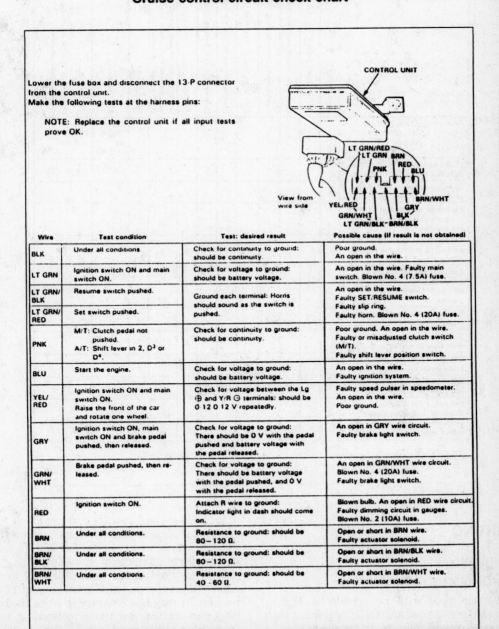

Lower the fuse box and disconnect the 13-P connector from the control unit.
Make the following tests at the harness pins:

NOTE: Replace the control unit if all input tests prove OK.

Wire	Test condition	Test: desired result	Possible cause (if result is not obtained)
BLK	Under all conditions	Check for continuity to ground: should be continuity.	Poor ground. An open in the wire.
LT GRN	Ignition switch ON and main switch ON.	Check for voltage to ground: should be battery voltage.	An open in the wire. Faulty main switch. Blown No. 4 (7.5A) fuse.
LT GRN/ BLK	Resume switch pushed.	Ground each terminal: Horns should sound as the switch is pushed.	An open in the wire. Faulty SET/RESUME switch. Faulty slip ring. Faulty horn. Blown No. 4 (20A) fuse.
LT GRN/ RED	Set switch pushed.		
PNK	M/T: Clutch pedal not pushed. A/T: Shift lever in 2, D³ or D⁴.	Check for continuity to ground: should be continuity.	Poor ground. An open in the wire. Faulty or misadjusted clutch switch (M/T). Faulty shift lever position switch.
BLU	Start the engine.	Check for voltage to ground: should be battery voltage.	An open in the wire. Faulty ignition system.
YEL/ RED	Ignition switch ON and main switch ON. Raise the front of the car and rotate one wheel	Check for voltage between the Lg ⊕ and Y/R ⊖ terminals: should be 0-12 0 12 V repeatedly.	Faulty speed pulser in speedometer. An open in the wire. Poor ground.
GRY	Ignition switch ON, main switch ON and brake pedal pushed, then released.	Check for voltage to ground: There should be 0 V with the pedal pushed and battery voltage with the pedal released.	An open in GRY wire circuit. Faulty brake light switch.
GRN/ WHT	Brake pedal pushed, then released.	Check for voltage to ground: There should be battery voltage with the pedal pushed, and 0 V with the pedal released.	An open in GRN/WHT wire circuit. Blown No. 4 (20A) fuse. Faulty brake light switch.
RED	Ignition switch ON.	Attach R wire to ground: Indicator light in dash should come on.	Blown bulb. An open in RED wire circuit. Faulty dimming circuit in gauges. Blown No. 2 (10A) fuse.
BRN	Under all conditions.	Resistance to ground: should be 80-120 Ω.	Open or short in BRN wire. Faulty actuator solenoid.
BRN/ BLK	Under all conditions.	Resistance to ground: should be 80-120 Ω.	Open or short in BRN/BLK wire. Faulty actuator solenoid.
BRN/ WHT	Under all conditions.	Resistance to ground: should be 40-60 Ω.	Open or short in BRN/WHT wire. Faulty actuator solenoid.

Cruise control diagnostic chart

NOTE:
- The numbers in the table show the troubleshooting sequence.
- Before troubleshooting:
  - Check the No.2 (10A) and No.4 (7.5A) fuses in the fuse box, and the No.4 (20A) fuse in the relay box.
  - Check that the horns sound.
  - Check the tachometer for proper operation.

Symptom / Item to be inspected	Main switch	SET/RESUME switch	Brake light switch and mounting	Clutch switch and mounting (M/T)	Shift lever position switch (A/T)	Speedometer pulser or cable (page 25-83)	Dimming circuit in gauges (page 25-83)	Actuator	Disconnected, clogged or restricted vacuum lines/stuck check valve/leaky vacuum reservoir	Control unit	Poor ground	Open circuit in wires or loose or disconnected terminals
Cruise control can't be set.	2	3	4	5					6	1	GND-6 GND-8, 10 GND-12	LT GRN, BLK/RED
Cruise control can be set, but indicator light does not go on.							2			1	GND-12	YEL or RED
Cruise speed noticeably higher or lower than what was set.						1		2		3		
Excessive overshooting and/or undershooting when trying to set speed.						2		1		3		
Steady speed not held even on a flat road with cruise control set.						1		2	3	4		
Car does not decelerate or accelerate accordingly when SET or RESUME button is pushed.		1								2		LT GRN/BLK
Set speed not cancelled when clutch pedal is pushed (M/T).				1						2		
Set speed not cancelled when shift lever is moved to N (A/T).					1					2		
Set speed not cancelled when brake pedal is pushed.			1							2		
Set speed not cancelled when main switch is pushed OFF.	1									2		
Set speed not resumed when RESUME button is pushed (with main switch on, but set speed temporarily cancelled).		1								2		LT GRN/BLK

LIGHTING

Headlights

REMOVAL AND INSTALLATION

1. If equipped with retractable headlights, turn the retractor switch **ON**. If equipped with a garnish panel, remove it by removing the screws and slide it upward. Remove the retaining ring screws and the ring. DO NMOT touch the headlight adjustment screws.

2. While holding the connector plug by the rear of the bulb, pull the headlight out of the housing; it may be necessary to work the bulb back and forth a few times to break it loose from the connector.

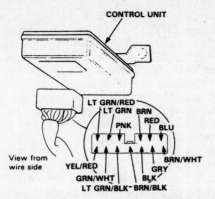

Cruise control unit connector wiring identification

Terminal	A	B	C	D
Brake Pedal				
RELEASED	o—o			
PUSHED			o—o	

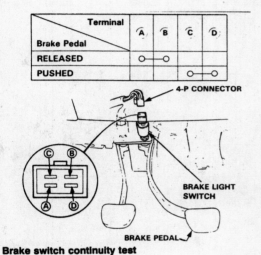

Brake switch continuity test

Terminal	LT GRN/ BLK	BLU/ RED	LT GRN/ RED
Position			
OFF			
SET (ON)	o—o		
RESUME (ON)		o—o	

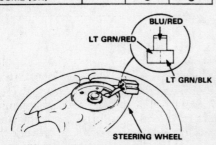

Set/resume switch continuity test

Retaining screw location

Removing the lower retaining screw

Removing the headlight connector

3. Insert the replacement bulb into the connector, then, install the retaining ring and screws.

TRAILER WIRING

Wiring the car for towing is fairly easy. There are a number of good wiring kits available and these should be used, rather than trying to design your own. All trailers will need brake lights and turn signals as well as tail lights and side marker lights. Most states require extra marker lights for overly wide trailers. Also, most states have recently required back-up lights for trailers, and most trailer manufacturers have been building trailers with back-up lights for several years.

Additionally, some Class I, most Class II and just about all Class III trailers will have electric brakes.

Add to this number an accessories wire, to operate trailer internal equipment or to charge the trailer's battery, and you can have as many as seven wires in the harness.

Determine the equipment on your trailer and buy the wiring kit necessary. The kit will contain all the wires needed, plus a plug adapter set which included the female plug, mounted on the bumper or hitch, and the male plug, wired into, or plugged into the trailer harness.

When installing the kit, follow the manufacturer's instructions. The color coding of the wires is standard throughout the industry.

One point to note: some domestic vehicles, and most imported vehicles, have separate turn signals. On most domestic vehicles, the brake lights and rear turn signals operate with the same bulb. For those vehicles with separate turn signals, you can purchase an isolation unit so that the brake lights won't blink whenever the turn signals are operated, or, you can go to your local electronics supply house and buy four diodes to wire in series with the brake and turn signal bulbs. Diodes will isolate the brake and turn signals. The choice is yours. The isolation units are simple and quick to install, but far more expensive than the diodes. The diodes, however, require more work to install properly, since they require the cutting of each bulb's wire and soldering in place of the diode.

One final point, the best kits are those with a spring loaded cover on the vehicle mounted socket. This cover prevents dirt and moisture from corroding the terminals. Never let the vehicle socket hang loosely; always mount it securely to the bumper or hitch.

Main circuit fusible link location

Accord and Prelude fuse box

Light Bulb Specifications

Measurements given in watts except as noted

Headlights	50/40
Front Turn Signal/Parking Lights	32/3 cp
Side Marker Lights—front and rear	4 cp
Gauge Indicator Lights	1
Interior Light	5
Rear Turn/Stop/Taillight	32/32/3 cp
Back-up Lights	32 cp
License Plate Lights	4 cp

cp candle-power

CIRCUIT PROTECTION

Fuses

LOCATIONS

The fuse box is located below the glove compartment, on the right bulkhead on Civic models. The Accord is equipped with a fuse tray which swings down from the instrument panel. It contains 8 fuses, some of which are rated at 10 amps and others at 15 amps. The rating and function of each fuse is posted inside the fuse box cap for quick reference.

Civic fuse box location

Fuses can be replaced or removed simply by pulling them out of their retaining clips. Since each fuse protects more than one circuit, detection of a fuse blowout is an easy task of elimination.

Troubleshooting Basic Windshield Wiper Problems

Problem	Cause	Solution
Electric Wipers		
Wipers do not operate— Wiper motor heats up or hums	• Internal motor defect • Bent or damaged linkage • Arms improperly installed on linking pivots	• Replace motor • Repair or replace linkage • Position linkage in park and reinstall wiper arms
Wipers do not operate— No current to motor	• Fuse or circuit breaker blown • Loose, open or broken wiring • Defective switch • Defective or corroded terminals • No ground circuit for motor or switch	• Replace fuse or circuit breaker • Repair wiring and connections • Replace switch • Replace or clean terminals • Repair ground circuits
Wipers do not operate— Motor runs	• Linkage disconnected or broken	• Connect wiper linkage or replace broken linkage
Vacuum Wipers		
Wipers do not operate	• Control switch or cable inoperative • Loss of engine vacuum to wiper motor (broken hoses, low engine vacuum, defective vacuum/fuel pump) • Linkage broken or disconnected • Defective wiper motor	• Repair or replace switch or cable • Check vacuum lines, engine vacuum and fuel pump • Repair linkage • Replace wiper motor
Wipers stop on engine acceleration	• Leaking vacuum hoses • Dry windshield • Oversize wiper blades • Defective vacuum/fuel pump	• Repair or replace hoses • Wet windshield with washers • Replace with proper size wiper blades • Replace pump

Troubleshooting Basic Turn Signal and Flasher Problems

Most problems in the turn signals or flasher system, can be reduced to defective flashers or bulbs, which are easily replaced. Occasionally, problems in the turn signals are traced to the switch in the steering column, which will require professional service.

F = Front   R = Rear   ● = Lights off   ○ = Lights on

Problem		Solution
Turn signals light, but do not flash		• Replace the flasher
No turn signals light on either side		• Check the fuse. Replace if defective. • Check the flasher by substitution • Check for open circuit, short circuit or poor ground
Both turn signals on one side don't work		• Check for bad bulbs • Check for bad ground in both housings
One turn signal light on one side doesn't work		• Check and/or replace bulb • Check for corrosion in socket. Clean contacts. • Check for poor ground at socket
Turn signal flashes too fast or too slow		• Check any bulb on the side flashing too fast. A heavy-duty bulb is probably installed in place of a regular bulb. • Check the bulb flashing too slow. A standard bulb was probably installed in place of a heavy-duty bulb. • Check for loose connections or corrosion at the bulb socket
Indicator lights don't work in either direction		• Check if the turn signals are working • Check the dash indicator lights • Check the flasher by substitution
One indicator light doesn't light		• On systems with 1 dash indicator: See if the lights work on the same side. Often the filaments have been reversed in systems combining stoplights with taillights and turn signals. Check the flasher by substitution • On systems with 2 indicators: Check the bulbs on the same side Check the indicator light bulb Check the flasher by substitution

Troubleshooting Basic Dash Gauge Problems

Problem	Cause	Solution
Coolant Temperature Gauge		
Gauge reads erratically or not at all	• Loose or dirty connections • Defective sending unit	• Clean/tighten connections • Bi-metal gauge: remove the wire from the sending unit. Ground the wire for an instant. If the gauge registers, replace the sending unit.
	• Defective gauge	• Magnetic gauge: disconnect the wire at the sending unit. With ignition ON gauge should register COLD. Ground the wire; gauge should register HOT.
Ammeter Gauge—Turn Headlights ON (do not start engine). Note reaction		
Ammeter shows charge Ammeter shows discharge Ammeter does not move	• Connections reversed on gauge • Ammeter is OK • Loose connections or faulty wiring • Defective gauge	• Reinstall connections • Nothing • Check/correct wiring • Replace gauge
Oil Pressure Gauge		
Gauge does not register or is inaccurate	• On mechanical gauge, Bourdon tube may be bent or kinked	• Check tube for kinks or bends preventing oil from reaching the gauge
	• Low oil pressure	• Remove sending unit. Idle the engine briefly. If no oil flows from sending unit hole, problem is in engine.
	• Defective gauge	• Remove the wire from the sending unit and ground it for an instant with the ignition ON. A good gauge will go to the top of the scale.
	• Defective wiring	• Check the wiring to the gauge. If it's OK and the gauge doesn't register when grounded, replace the gauge.
	• Defective sending unit	• If the wiring is OK and the gauge functions when grounded, replace the sending unit
All Gauges		
All gauges do not operate	• Blown fuse • Defective instrument regulator	• Replace fuse • Replace instrument voltage regulator
All gauges read low or erratically	• Defective or dirty instrument voltage regulator	• Clean contacts or replace
All gauges pegged	• Loss of ground between instrument voltage regulator and car • Defective instrument regulator	• Check ground • Replace regulator
Warning Lights		
Light(s) do not come on when ignition is ON, but engine is not started	• Defective bulb • Defective wire • Defective sending unit	• Replace bulb • Check wire from light to sending unit • Disconnect the wire from the sending unit and ground it. Replace the sending unit if the light comes on with the ignition ON.
Light comes on with engine running	• Problem in individual system • Defective sending unit	• Check system • Check sending unit (see above)

Troubleshooting Basic Lighting Problems

Problem	Cause	Solution
Lights		
One or more lights don't work, but others do	· Defective bulb(s) · Blown fuse(s) · Dirty fuse clips or light sockets · Poor ground circuit	· Replace bulb(s) · Replace fuse(s) · Clean connections · Run ground wire from light socket housing to car frame
Lights burn out quickly	· Incorrect voltage regulator setting or defective regulator · Poor battery/alternator connections	· Replace voltage regulator · Check battery/alternator connections
Lights go dim	· Low/discharged battery · Alternator not charging · Corroded sockets or connections · Low voltage output	· Check battery · Check drive belt tension; repair or replace alternator · Clean bulb and socket contacts and connections · Replace voltage regulator
Lights flicker	· Loose connection · Poor ground · Circuit breaker operating (short circuit)	· Tighten all connections · Run ground wire from light housing to car frame · Check connections and look for bare wires
Lights "flare"—Some flare is normal on acceleration—if excessive, see "Lights Burn Out Quickly"	· High voltage setting	· Replace voltage regulator
Lights glare—approaching drivers are blinded	· Lights adjusted too high · Rear springs or shocks sagging · Rear tires soft	· Have headlights aimed · Check rear springs/shocks · Check/correct rear tire pressure
Turn Signals		
Turn signals don't work in either direction	· Blown fuse · Defective flasher · Loose connection	· Replace fuse · Replace flasher · Check/tighten all connections
Right (or left) turn signal only won't work	· Bulb burned out · Right (or left) indicator bulb burned out · Short circuit	· Replace bulb · Check/replace indicator bulb · Check/repair wiring
Flasher rate too slow or too fast	· Incorrect wattage bulb · Incorrect flasher	· Flasher bulb · Replace flasher (use a variable load flasher if you pull a trailer)
Indicator lights do not flash (burn steadily)	· Burned out bulb · Defective flasher	· Replace bulb · Replace flasher
Indicator lights do not light at all	· Burned out indicator bulb · Defective flasher	· Replace indicator bulb · Replace flasher

Troubleshooting the Heater

Problem	Cause	Solution
Blower motor will not turn at any speed	· Blown fuse · Loose connection · Defective ground · Faulty switch · Faulty motor · Faulty resistor	· Replace fuse · Inspect and tighten · Clean and tighten · Replace switch · Replace motor · Replace resistor

Troubleshooting the Heater (cont.)

Problem	Cause	Solution
Blower motor turns at one speed only	· Faulty switch · Faulty resistor	· Replace switch · Replace resistor
Blower motor turns but does not circulate air	· Intake blocked · Fan not secured to the motor shaft	· Clean intake · Tighten security
Heater will not heat	· Coolant does not reach proper temperature · Heater core blocked internally · Heater core air-bound · Blend-air door not in proper position	· Check and replace thermostat if necessary · Flush or replace core if necessary · Purge air from core · Adjust cable
Heater will not defrost	· Control cable adjustment incorrect · Defroster hose damaged	· Adjust control cable · Replace defroster hose

Drive Train

7

UNDERSTANDING THE MANUAL TRANSAXLE

Because of the way an internal combustion engine breathes, it can produce torque, or twisting force, only within a narrow speed range. Most modern, overhead valve engines must turn at about 2,500 rpm to produce their peak torque. By 4,500 rpm they are producing so little torque that continued increases in engine speed produce no power increases.

The torque peak on overhead camshaft engines is, generally, much higher, but much narrower.

The manual transmission and clutch are employed to vary the relationship between engine speed and the speed of the wheels so that adequate engine power can be produced under all circumstances. The clutch allows engine torque to be applied to the transmission input shaft gradually, due to mechanical slippage. The car can, consequently, be started smoothly from a full stop.

The transmission changes the ratio between the rotating speeds of the engine and the wheels by the use of gears. 4-speed or 5-speed transmissions are most common. The lower gears allow full engine power to be applied to the wheels during acceleration at low speeds.

The clutch drive plate is a thin disc, the center of which is splined to the transmission input shaft. Both sides of the disc are covered with a layer of material which is similar to brake lining and which is capable of allowing slippage without roughness or excessive noise.

The clutch cover is bolted to the engine flywheel and incorporates a diaphragm spring which provides the pressure to engage the clutch. The cover also houses the pressure plate. The driven disc is sandwiched between the pressure plate and the smooth surface of the flywheel when the clutch pedal is released, thus forcing it to turn at the same speed as the engine crankshaft.

The transmission contains a mainshaft which passes all the way through the transmission, from the clutch to the halfshafts. This shaft is separated at one point, so that front and rear portions can turn at different speeds.

Power is transmitted by a countershaft in the lower gears and reverse. The gears of the countershaft mesh with gears on the mainshaft, allowing power to be carried from one to the other. All the countershaft gears are integral with that shaft, while several of the mainshaft gears can either rotate independently of the shaft or be locked to it. Shifting from one gear to the next causes one of the gears to be freed from rotating with the shaft and locks another to it. Gears are locked and unlocked by internal dog clutches which slide between the center of the gear and the shaft. The forward gears usually employ synchronizers; friction members which smoothly bring gear and shaft to the same speed before the toothed dog clutches are engaged.

The clutch is operating properly if:

1. It will stall the engine when released with the vehicle held stationary.

2. The shift lever can be moved freely between 1st and reverse gears when the vehicle is stationary and the clutch disengaged.

A clutch pedal free-play adjustment is incorporated in the linkage. If there is about 25-50mm of motion before the pedal begins to release the clutch, it is adjusted properly. Inadequate free-play wears all parts of the clutch releasing mechanisms and may cause slippage. Excessive free-play may cause inadequate release and hard shifting of gears.

Some clutches use a hydraulic system in place of mechanical linkage. If the clutch fails to release, fill the clutch master cylinder with fluid to the proper level and pump the clutch pedal to fill the system with fluid. Bleed the system in the same way as a brake system. If leaks are located, tighten loose connections or overhaul the master or slave cylinder as necessary.

Front wheel drive cars do not have conventional rear axles or drive shafts. Instead, power is transmitted from the engine to a transaxle, or a combination of transmission and drive axle, in one unit. Both the transmission and drive axle accomplish the same function as their counterparts in a front engine/rear drive axle design. The difference is in the location of the components.

In place of a conventional driveshaft, a front wheel drive design uses two driveshafts, sometimes called halfshafts, which couple the drive axle portion of the transaxle to the wheels. Universal joints or constant velocity joints are used just as they would in a rear wheel drive design.

Manual Transaxle

The Honda utilizes a transaxle arrangement where the transmission and the differential are contained within the same housing. Power is transmitted from the engine to the transmission and in turn, to the differential. The front drive axle halfshafts transfer the power from the differential to the front wheels.

The Civic without the CVCC engine, 1973-80, utilizes a standard design 4-speed, fully synchronized transmission. The transmission is located on the right side of the engine, along with the differential. A similar 5-speed is used on Civic and Accord CVCC models in these years. The 5-speed becomes available on all models in 1981-88.

A simple 2-speed, semi-automatic transmission, Hondamatic, is available on models built 1973-80. As in all automatic transmissions, power is transmitted from the engine to the transmission through a fluid coupling known as a torque converter. Forward gears are selected simply by moving the shift lever to the proper position — D1 (low speed range) or D2 (high speed range). The gears are engaged through the use of a complex clutch system in each gear range.

In 1981, the Hondamatic was replaced with a more conventional type of automatic transmission with 3, self-shifting forward ranges. The major difference between this transaxle and the one that preceded it is that it not only shifts by itself but determines, through hydraulic pressures, when shifts are to occur.

In 1983, this transaxle received a 4th gear ratio to improve the cruise fuel economy while maintaining performance at low speeds. This transaxle also locks up the torque converter to eliminate its slip under steady cruise conditions.

Adjustments

SHIFT LINKAGE ADJUSTMENT

All Except Civic 4WD Model

The Honda shift linkage on those models is non-adjustable. However, if the linkage is binding, or if there is excessive play, check the linkage bushings and pivot points. Lubricate with light oil, or replace worn bushings as necessary.

Civic 4WD Models

SELECTOR CABLE ADJUSTMENT

1. Remove the console.
2. With the transmission in neutral, check that the groove in the lever bracket is aligned with the index mark on the selector cable.
3. If the index mark is not aligned with the groove in the cable, loosen the lock nuts and turn the adjuster as necessary.

NOTE: *After adjustment, check the operation of the gearshift lever. Also check that the threads of the cables do not extend out of the cable adjuster by more than 10mm.*

GEARSHIFT CABLE ADJUSTMENT

1. Remove the console.
2. Place the transmission in 4th gear.
3. Measure the clearance between the gearshift lever bracket and the stopper while pushing the lever forward.
4. If the clearance is outside the specifica-

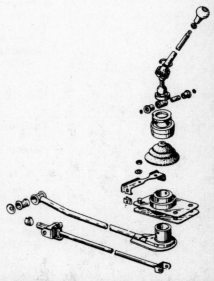

Exploded view of the gearshift mechanism

Troubleshooting the Manual Transmission and Transfer Case

Problem	Cause	Solution
Transmission shifts hard	• Clutch adjustment incorrect • Clutch linkage or cable binding • Shift rail binding	• Adjust clutch • Lubricate or repair as necessary • Check for mispositioned selector arm roll pin, loose cover bolts, worn shift rail bores, worn shift rail, distorted oil seal, or extension housing not aligned with case. Repair as necessary.
	• Internal bind in transmission caused by shift forks, selector plates, or synchronizer assemblies • Clutch housing misalignment • Incorrect lubricant • Block rings and/or cone seats worn	• Remove, dissemble and inspect transmission. Replace worn or damaged components as necessary. • Check runout at rear face of clutch housing • Drain and refill transmission • Blocking ring to gear clutch tooth face clearance must be 0.030 inch or greater. If clearance is correct it may still be necessary to inspect blocking rings and cone seats for excessive wear. Repair as necessary.
Gear clash when shifting from one gear to another	• Clutch adjustment incorrect • Clutch linkage or cable binding • Clutch housing misalignment • Lubricant level low or incorrect lubricant • Gearshift components, or synchronizer assemblies worn or damaged	• Adjust clutch • Lubricate or repair as necessary • Check runout at rear of clutch housing • Drain and refill transmission and check for lubricant leaks if level was low. Repair as necessary. • Remove, disassemble and inspect transmission. Replace worn or damaged components as necessary.
Transmission noisy	• Lubricant level low or incorrect lubricant • Clutch housing-to-engine, or transmission-to-clutch housing bolts loose • Dirt, chips, foreign material in transmission • Gearshift mechanism, transmission gears, or bearing components worn or damaged • Clutch housing misalignment	• Drain and refill transmission. If lubricant level was low, check for leaks and repair as necessary. • Check and correct bolt torque as necessary • Drain, flush, and refill transmission • Remove, disassemble and inspect transmission. Replace worn or damaged components as necessary. • Check runout at rear face of clutch housing
Jumps out of gear	• Clutch housing misalignment • Gearshift lever loose • Offset lever nylon insert worn or lever attaching nut loose • Gearshift mechanism, shift forks, selector plates, interlock plate, selector arm, shift rail, detent plugs, springs or shift cover worn or damaged • Clutch shaft or roller bearings worn or damaged	• Check runout at rear face of clutch housing • Check lever for worn fork. Tighten loose attaching bolts. • Remove gearshift lever and check for loose offset lever nut or worn insert. Repair or replace as necessary. • Remove, disassemble and inspect transmission cover assembly. Replace worn or damaged components as necessary. • Replace clutch shaft or roller bearings as necessary

Troubleshooting the Manual Transmission and Transfer Case (cont.)

Problem	Cause	Solution
Jumps out of gear (cont.)	· Gear teeth worn or tapered, synchronizer assemblies worn or damaged, excessive end play caused by worn thrust washers or output shaft gears	· Remove, disassemble, and inspect transmission. Replace worn or damaged components as necessary.
	· Pilot bushing worn	· Replace pilot bushing
Will not shift into one gear	· Gearshift selector plates, interlock plate, or selector arm, worn, damaged, or incorrectly assembled	· Remove, disassemble, and inspect transmission cover assembly. Repair or replace components as necessary.
	· Shift rail detent plunger worn, spring broken, or plug loose	· Tighten plug or replace worn or damaged components as necessary
	· Gearshift lever worn or damaged	· Replace gearshift lever
	· Synchronizer sleeves or hubs, damaged or worn	· Remove, disassemble and inspect transmission. Replace worn or damaged components.
Locked in one gear—cannot be shifted out	· Shift rail(s) worn or broken, shifter fork bent, setscrew loose, center detent plug missing or worn	· Inspect and replace worn or damaged parts
	· Broken gear teeth on countershaft gear, clutch shaft, or reverse idler gear	· Inspect and replace damaged part
	Gearshift lever broken or worn, shift mechanism in cover incorrectly assembled or broken, worn damaged gear train components	· Disassemble transmission. Replace damaged parts or assemble correctly.
Transfer case difficult to shift or will not shift into desired range	· Vehicle speed too great to permit shifting	· Stop vehicle and shift into desired range. Or reduce speed to 3–4 km/h (2–3 mph) before attempting to shift.
	· If vehicle was operated for extended period in 4H mode on dry paved surface, driveline torque load may cause difficult shifting	· Stop vehicle, shift transmission to neutral, shift transfer case to 2H mode and operate vehicle in 2H on dry paved surfaces
	· Transfer case external shift linkage binding	· Lubricate or repair or replace linkage, or tighten loose components as necessary
	· Insufficient or incorrect lubricant	· Drain and refill to edge of fill hole with SAE 85W-90 gear lubricant only
	· Internal components binding, worn, or damaged	· Disassemble unit and replace worn or damaged components as necessary
Transfer case noisy in all drive modes	· Insufficient or incorrect lubricant	· Drain and refill to edge of fill hole with SAE 85W-90 gear lubricant only. Check for leaks and repair if necessary. Note: If unit is still noisy after drain and refill, disassembly and inspection may be required to locate source of noise.
Noisy in—or jumps out of four wheel drive low range	· Transfer case not completely engaged in 4L position	· Stop vehicle, shift transfer case in Neutral, then shift back into 4L position
	· Shift linkage loose or binding	· Tighten, lubricate, or repair linkage as necessary
	· Shift fork cracked, inserts worn, or fork is binding on shift rail	· Disassemble unit and repair as necessary
Lubricant leaking from output shaft seals or from vent	· Transfer case overfilled	· Drain to correct level
	· Vent closed or restricted	· Clear or replace vent if necessary

Troubleshooting the Manual Transmission and Transfer Case (cont.)

Problem	Cause	Solution
Lubricant leaking from output shaft seals or from vent (cont.)	• Output shaft seals damaged or installed incorrectly	• Replace seals. Be sure seal lip faces interior of case when installed. Also be sure yoke seal surfaces are not scored or nicked. Remove scores, nicks with fine sandpaper or replace yoke(s) if necessary.
Abnormal tire wear	• Extended operation on dry hard surface (paved) roads in 4H range	• Operate in 2H on hard surface (paved) roads

tions 4.3mm, loosen the lock nuts and turn the adjuster in or out until the correct clearance is obtained.

NOTE: *After adjustment, check the operation of the gearshift lever. Also check that the threads of the cables do not extend out of the cable adjuster by more than 10mm.*

Transaxle
REMOVAL AND INSTALLATION
Civic 1973-79

1. Drain the transaxle.
2. Raise and support the front of the vehicle on jackstands.

3. Remove the front wheels.
4. Disconnect the negative battery terminals from the battery and the transaxle case.
5. Disconnect the positive battery terminal from the starter and the wire from the solenoid. Remove the starter.
6. Disconnect the following cables and wires:
   a. Clutch cable at the release arm.
   b. Back-up light switch wires.
   c. Transmission Controlled Spark (TCS) switch wires.
   d. Speedometer cable.

WARNING: *When removing the speedometer cable from the transaxle, it is not necessary to remove the entire cable holder. Remove the end boot (gear holder seal) and the cable retaining clip, then, pull the cable out of the holder. In no way should you disturb the holder, unless it is absolutely necessary. For further details, see "Engine Removal" section in Chapter 3.*

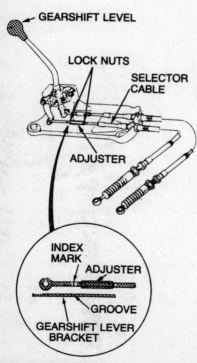

Selector cable adjustment

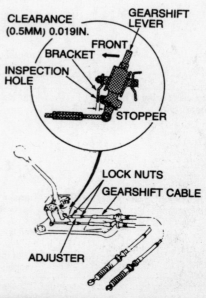

Gearshift cable adjustment

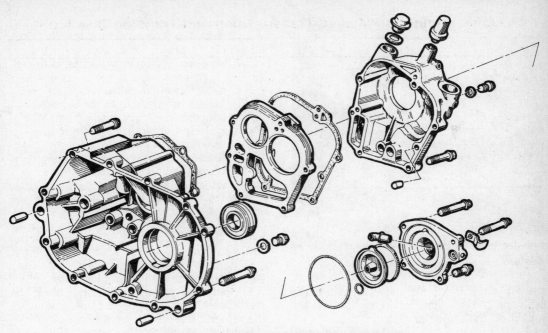

Five speed transmission housing and related parts

7. Using a Ball Joint Remover tool, disconnect the left and right lower ball joints from the steering knuckle.

8. Pull on both wheel hubs to disconnect the driveshafts from the differential case.

9. Using a drift punch, drive out the gearshift rod pin (8mm) and disconnect the rod at the transaxle case.

10. Disconnect the gearshift extension from the clutch housing.

11 Screw in the engine hanger bolts to the engine torque rod bolt hole and to the hole just to

Driving out the gearshift rod pin

Center engine mount nuts (arrows)

the left of the distributor. Hook a chain to the bolts and lift the engine just enough to take the weight off the engine mounts.

12. After making sure that the engine is properly supported, remove the two center beam-to-lower engine mount nuts. Remove the center beam and the lower engine mount.

13. Reinstall the center beam (without mount) and lower the engine until it rests on the beam.

14. Place a floor jack under the transaxle and loosen the attaching bolts. Using the jack to support the transaxle, slide it away from the engine and lower the jack until the transaxle clears the vehicle.

15. To install, reverse the removal procedures. Be sure to pay attention to the following points:

 a. Tighten all mounting nuts and bolts to their specified torque (see the "Engine Removal" section in Chapter 3).

 b. Use a new shift rod pin.

 c. After installing the driveshafts, attempt to move the inner joint housing in and out of the differential housing. If it moves easily, the driveshaft end clips should be replaced.

 d. Make sure that the control cables and wires are properly connected.

 e. Be sure the transmission is refilled to the proper level.

Civic 1980-87

NOTE: *The Civic 4WD Wagon transaxle must be removed with the engine. For removal procedures please refer to Engine Removal & Installation in Chapter 3. Once the engine/transaxle assembly is removed from the vehicle, then the transaxle can be separated with the transfer case from the engine.*

1. Disconnect the battery ground.

2. Unlock the steering and place the transmission in neutral.

3. Disconnect the following wires in the engine compartment:

 a. battery positive cable.

 b. black/white wire from the solenoid.

 c. temperature gauge sending unit wire.

 d. ignition timing thermo-sensor wire.

 e. back-up light switch.

 f. distributor wiring.

 g. transmission ground cable.

4. Unclip and remove the speedometer cable at the transmission. Do not disassemble the speedometer gear holder!

5. Remove the clutch save cylinder with the hydraulic line attached, or disconnect the clutch cable at the release arm.

6. Remove the side and top starter mounting bolts. Loosen the front wheel lug nuts.

7. Apply the parking brake and block the rear wheels. Raise and support the front end of the vehicle. Remove the front wheels.

8. Attach a suitable chain hoist to the rear of the engine then raise the engine slightly to take the weight off of the mounts. Drain the transmission, then reinstall the drain plug and washer.

9. Remove the splash shields from the underside.

10. Remove the stabilizer bar.

11. Disconnect the left and right lower ball joints and tie end rods, using a ball joint remover.

CAUTION: *In 1984-87 Civics use caution when removing the ball joints. Place a floor jack under the lower control arm securely at the ball joint. Otherwise, the lower control arm may jump suddenly away from the steering knuckle as the ball joint is removed!*

12. Turn the right steering knuckle out as far as it will go. Place a prybar against the inboard CV-joint, pry the right axle out of the transmission about ½". This will force the spring clip out of the groove inside the differential gear splines. Pull it out the rest of the way. Repeat this procedure on the other side.

13. Disconnect the shift lever torque rod from the clutch housing.

14. Slide the pin retainer back, drive out the spring pin using a pin punch, then disconnect the shift rod. Remove the bolt from the shift rod clevis, if so equipped.

15. Place a transmission jack under the transaxle and raise the transmission jack securely against the transaxle to take up the weight.

16. Remove the engine torque rods and brackets. Remove the bolts from the front transaxle mount. Remove the transaxle housing bolts from the engine torque bracket.

17. Remove the remaining starter mounting bolts and take out the starter.

18. Remove the remaining transmission mounting bolts and the upper bolt from the engine damper bracket. Remove the clutch housing bolts from the rear transaxle mounting bracket. Remove the one remaining bolt from the engine.

19. Start backing the transmission away from the engine and remove the two lower damper bolts.

20. Pull the transmission clear of the engine and lower the jack.

21. To ease installation, fabricate two 14mm diameter dowel pins and install them in the clutch housing.

22. Raise the transmission and slide it onto the dowels. Slide the transmission onto position aligning the mainshaft splines with the clutch plate.

23. Attach the damper lower bolts when the positioning allows. Tighten both bolts until the clutch housing is seated against the block.

24. Install two lower mounting bolts and torque them to 33 ft. lbs.

25. Install the front and rear torque rod brackets. Torque the front torque rod bolts to 54 ft. lbs., the front bracket bolts to 33 ft. lbs., the rear torque rod bolts to 54 ft. lbs., and the rear bracket bolts to 47 ft. lbs.

26. Remove the transmission jack.

27. Install the starter and torque the mounting bolts to 33 ft. lbs.

28. Turn the right steering knuckle out far enough to fit the end into the transmission. Use new 26mm spring clips on both axles. Repeat procedure for the other side.

CAUTION: *Make sure that the axles bottom fully so that you feel the spring clip engage the differential.*

29. Install the lower ball joints. Torque the nuts to 32 ft. lbs.

30. Install the tie rods. Torque the nuts to 32 ft. lbs.

31. Connect the shift linkage.

32. Connect the shift lever torque rod to the clutch housing and torque the bolt to 7 ft. lbs. (84 inch lbs.).

33. Install the stabilizer bar.

34. Install the lower shields.

35. Install the front wheels and torque the lugs to specifications.

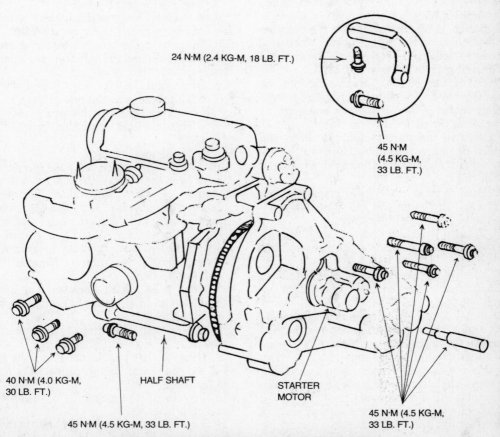

24 N·M (2.4 KG-M, 18 LB. FT.)

45 N·M (4.5 KG-M, 33 LB. FT.)

40 N·M (4.0 KG-M, 30 LB. FT.)

HALF SHAFT

STARTER MOTOR

45 N·M (4.5 KG-M, 33 LB. FT.)

45 N·M (4.5 KG-M, 33 LB. FT.)

Separating the engine and transmission on 4WD Civics

36. Install the remaining starter bolts and torque to 33 ft. lbs.

37. Install the clutch slave cylinder and or install the clutch cable at the release arm.

38. Install the speedometer cable using a new O-ring coated with clean engine oil.

39. Connect all engine compartment wiring.

40. Fill the transmission with SAE 10W-40 engine oil.

Civic 1988

1. Disconnect the battery cables from the battery.

2. Remove the three mount bolts and loosen the one bolt located at the side of the battery base. Remove the intake hose band of the throttle body.

3. Remove the air cleaner case complete with the intake hose. Disconnect the starter and transaxle ground cables.

4. Disconnect the speedometer, but be sure not to disassemble the speedometer gear holder.

5. Disconnect the back-up light switch connector and the clutch cable release arm.

6. Drain the transmission fluid into a suitable drain pan. Disconnect the connectors and remove the mount bolts.

7. Scribe an alignment line on the distributor assembly and the cylinder head (to be used for easy installation), then remove the distributor assembly from the cylinder head.

NOTE: *It may be easier at installation, if the number one engine piston is brought up to top dead center of its compression stroke before removing the distributor assembly.*

8. Remove the starter mounting bolts and remove the starter assembly. Remove the engine splash shield and the right wheelwell splash shield.

9. Remove the header pipe. Remove the cotter pin and the lower arm ball joint nut, separate the ball joint and lower arm.

10. Remove the bolts and nut, then remove the right radius rod. Remove the right and left driveshafts.

11. Remove the header pipe bracket. Remove the shift lever torque rod and shift rod from the clutch housing.

12. Install a bolt at the cylinder head and attach suitable chain hoist to the bolt and the other end to the engine hanger plate. Lift the engine slightly to unload the mounts.

13. Place a suitable transmission jack under the transaxle and raise it just enough to take the weights off of the mounts.

14. Remove the front transaxle mounting bolts. Remove the rear transaxle mounting bolts. Remove the side transaxle mount, remove the five remaining transaxle mounting

bolts and pull the transaxle assembly far enough away from the engine to clear the 14mm dowel pins.

15. Separate the mainshaft from the clutch pressure plate and remove the transaxle by lowering the jack.

16. To install, reverse the removal procedure. Be sure to pay attention to the following points:

a. Tighten all mounting nuts and bolts.

b. Use a new shift rod pin.

c. After installing the driveshafts, attempt to move the inner joint housing in and out of the differential housing. If it moves easily, the driveshaft end clips should be replaced.

d. Make sure that the control cables and wires are properly connected.

e. Be sure the transmission is refilled to the proper level.

f. Be sure to recheck the ignition timing since the distributor assembly was removed during this procedure.

Accord 1976-79

1. Drain the transaxle.

2. Raise and support the front of the vehicle on jackstands.

3. Remove the front wheels.

4. Disconnect the negative battery terminals from the battery and the transaxle case.

5. Disconnect the positive battery terminal from the starter and the wire from the solenoid. Remove the starter.

6. Disconnect the following cables and wires:

a. Clutch cable at the release arm.

b. Back-up light switch wires.

c. Transmission Controlled Spark (TCS) switch wires.

d. Speedometer cable.

WARNING: *When removing the speedometer cable from the transaxle, it is not necessary to remove the entire cable holder. Remove the end boot (gear holder seal) and the cable retaining clip, then, pull the cable out of the holder. In no way should you disturb the holder, unless it is absolutely necessary. For further details, see "Engine Removal" section in Chapter 3.*

7. Using a Ball Joint Remover tool, disconnect the left and right lower ball joints from the steering knuckle.

8. Pull on both wheel hubs to disconnect the driveshafts from the differential case.

9. Using a drift punch, drive out the gearshift rod pin (8mm) and disconnect the rod at the transaxle case.

10. Disconnect the gearshift extension from the clutch housing.

11 Screw in the engine hanger bolts to the engine torque rod bolt hole and to the hole just to the left of the distributor. Hook a chain to the

bolts and lift the engine just enough to take the weight off the engine mounts.

12. After making sure that the engine is properly supported, remove the two center beam-to-lower engine mount nuts. Remove the center beam and the lower engine mount.

13. Reinstall the center beam (without mount) and lower the engine until it rests on the beam.

14. Place a floor jack under the transaxle and loosen the attaching bolts. Using the jack to support the transaxle, slide it away from the engine and lower the jack until the transaxle clears the vehicle.

15. To install, reverse the removal procedures. Be sure to pay attention to the following points:

a. Tighten all mounting nuts and bolts to their specified torque (see the "Engine Removal" section in Chapter 3).

b. Use a new shift rod pin.

c. After installing the driveshafts, attempt to move the inner joint housing in and out of the differential housing. If it moves easily, the driveshaft end clips should be replaced.

d. Make sure that the control cables and wires are properly connected.

e. Be sure the transmission is refilled to the proper level.

Accord 1980-83

1. Disconnect the battery ground cable at the battery and the transmission case. Unlock the steering column; place the transmission in neutral.

2. Disconnect the following cables and wires:

a. Clutch cable at the release arm.

b. Back-up light switch wires.

c. TCS (Transmission Controlled Spark) switch wires.

d. Black/white wire from the starter solenoid.

3. Release the engine sub wiring harness from the clamp at the clutch housing. Remove the upper two transaxle mounting bolts.

4. Raise the front of the car and support it with safety stands. Drain the transmission.

5. Remove the front wheels. Disconnect the speedometer cable.

NOTE: *When removing the speedometer cable from the transmission, it is not necessary to remove the entire cable holder. Remove the end boot (gear holder seal), the cable retaining clip and then pull the cable out of the holder. In no way should you disturb the holder, unless it is absolutely necessary. For further details, see the Engine Removal section.*

6. Disconnect the shift lever torque rod from

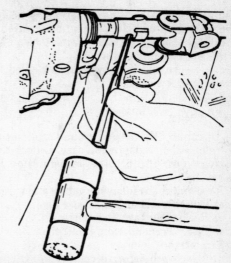

Driving out the gearshift rod pin

the clutch housing. Remove the bolt from the shift rod clevis.

7. Disconnect the tie rod ball joints and remove them using a suitable ball joint remover.

8. Remove the lower arm ball joint bolt from the right side lower control arm, then using a puller to disconnect the ball joint from the knuckle. Remove the damper fork bolt.

9. Drive out the gearshift rod pin (8mm) with a drift and disconnect the rod at the transmission case.

10. Disconnect the gearshift extension at the clutch housing.

11. Screw in the engine hanger bolts (see the Engine Removal section) to the engine torque rod bolt hole and to the hole just to the left of the distributor. Hook a chain onto the bolts and lift the engine just enough to take the load off the engine mounts.

12. After making sure that the engine is properly supported, remove the two center beam-to-lower engine mount nuts. Next, remove the center beam, followed by the lower engine mount.

13. Reinstall the center beam (without mount) and lower the engine until it rests on the beam.

14. Place a jack under the transmission and loosen the 4 attaching bolts. Using the jack to support the transmission, slide it away from the engine and lower the jack until the transmission clears the car.

15. To install, reverse the removal procedure. Be sure to pay attention to the following points:

a. Tighten all mounting nuts and bolts.

b. Use a new shift rod pin.

c. After installing the driveshafts, attempt to move the inner joint housing in and out of the differential housing. If it moves easily, the driveshaft end clips should be replaced.

d. Make sure that the control cables and wires are properly connected.

e. Be sure the transmission is refilled to the proper level.

Accord 1984-88

1. Disconnect the battery ground cable at the battery and the transmission case. Unlock the steering column; place the transmission in neutral.

2. Disconnect the following cables and wires:

a. Clutch cable at the release arm.

b. Back-up light switch wires.

c. TCS (Transmission Controlled Spark) switch wires.

d. Black/white wire from the starter solenoid.

3. Release the engine sub wiring harness from the clamp at the clutch housing. Remove the upper two transaxle mounting bolts.

4. Raise the front of the car and support it with safety stands. Drain the transmission.

5. Remove the front wheels. Place a suitable transaxle jack into position under the transaxle.

6. Disconnect the speedometer cable.

NOTE: *When removing the speedometer cable from the transmission, it is not necessary to remove the entire cable holder. Remove the end boot (gear holder seal), the cable retaining clip and then pull the cable out of the holder. In no way should you disturb the holder, unless it is absolutely necessary. For further details, see the Engine Removal section.*

7. Disconnect the shift lever torque rod from the clutch housing. Remove the bolt from the shift rod clevis.

8. Disconnect the tie rod ball joints and remove them using a suitable ball joint remover.

9. Remove the lower arm ball joint bolt from the right side lower control arm, then using a puller to disconnect the ball joint from the knuckle. Remove the damper fork bolt.

10. Turn each steering knuckle to its most outboard position. Using a suitable tool, pry the right side CV-joint out approximately ½", then pull the sub axle out of the transaxle housing. Repeat this procedure for the opposite side. Remove the right side radius rod.

11. Remove the damper bracket from the transaxle. Remove the clutch housing bolts from the front transaxle mount.

12. Remove the clutch housing bolts from the rear transaxle mounting bracket. Remove the clutch cover.

13. Remove the starter mounting bolts and remove the starter assembly through the chassis. Remove the transaxle mounting bolt.

14. Pull the transaxle away from the engine block to clear the two 14mm dowel pins and lower the transaxle jack.

15. To install, reverse the removal procedure. Be sure to pay attention to the following points:

a. Tighten all mounting nuts and bolts.

b. Use a new shift rod pin.

c. After installing the driveshafts, attempt to move the inner joint housing in and out of the differential housing. If it moves easily, the driveshaft end clips should be replaced.

d. Make sure that the control cables and wires are properly connected.

e. Be sure the transmission is refilled to the proper level.

Prelude 1979-83

1. Disconnect the battery ground cable at the battery and the transmission case. Unlock the steering column; place the transmission in neutral.

2. Disconnect the following cables and wires:

a. Clutch cable at the release arm.

b. Back-up light switch wires.

c. TCS (Transmission Controlled Spark) switch wires.

d. Black/white wire from the starter solenoid.

3. Release the engine sub wiring harness from the clamp at the clutch housing. Remove the upper two transaxle mounting bolts.

4. Raise the front of the car and support it with safety stands. Drain the transmission.

5. Remove the front wheels. Disconnect the speedometer cable.

NOTE: *When removing the speedometer cable from the transmission, it is not necessary to remove the entire cable holder. Remove the end boot (gear holder seal), the cable retaining clip and then pull the cable out of the holder. In no way should you disturb the holder, unless it is absolutely necessary. For further details, see the Engine Removal section.*

6. Disconnect the shift lever torque rod from the clutch housing. Remove the bolt from the shift rod clevis.

7. Disconnect the tie rod ball joints and remove them using a suitable ball joint remover.

8. Remove the lower arm ball joint bolt from the right side lower control arm, then using a puller to disconnect the ball joint from the knuckle. Remove the damper fork bolt.

9. Drive out the gearshift rod pin (8mm) with a drift and disconnect the rod at the transmission case.

10. Disconnect the gearshift extension at the clutch housing.

11. Screw in the engine hanger bolts (see the Engine Removal section) to the engine torque rod bolt hole and to the hole just to the left of the distributor. Hook a chain onto the bolts and lift the engine just enough to take the load off the engine mounts.

12. After making sure that the engine is properly supported, remove the two center beam-to-lower engine mount nuts. Next, remove the center beam, followed by the lower engine mount.

13. Reinstall the center beam (without mount) and lower the engine until it rests on the beam.

14. Place a jack under the transmission and loosen the 4 attaching bolts. Using the jack to support the transmission, slide it away from the engine and lower the jack until the transmission clears the car.

15. To install, reverse the removal procedure. Be sure to pay attention to the following points:

   a. Tighten all mounting nuts and bolts.

   b. Use a new shift rod pin.

   c. After installing the driveshafts, attempt to move the inner joint housing in and out of the differential housing. If it moves easily, the driveshaft end clips should be replaced.

   d. Make sure that the control cables and wires are properly connected.

   e. Be sure the transmission is refilled to the proper level.

Prelude 1984-87

1. Disconnect the battery ground cable at the battery and the transmission case. Unlock the steering column; place the transmission in neutral.

2. Disconnect the following cables and wires:

   a. Clutch cable at the release arm.

   b. Back-up light switch wires.

   c. TCS (Transmission Controlled Spark) switch wires.

   d. Black/white wire from the starter solenoid.

3. Release the engine sub wiring harness from the clamp at the clutch housing. Remove the upper two transaxle mounting bolts.

4. Raise the front of the car and support it with safety stands. Drain the transmission.

5. Remove the front wheels. Place a suitable transaxle jack into position under the transaxle.

6. Disconnect the speedometer cable.

NOTE: *When removing the speedometer cable from the transmission, it is not necessary to remove the entire cable holder. Remove the end boot (gear holder seal), the cable retaining clip and then pull the cable out of the holder. In no way should you disturb the holder, unless it is absolutely necessary. For*

further details, see the Engine Removal section.

7. Disconnect the shit lever torque rod from the clutch housing. Remove the bolt from the shift rod clevis.

8. Disconnect the tie rod ball joints and remove them using a suitable ball joint remover.

9. Remove the lower arm ball joint bolt from the right side lower control arm, then using a puller to disconnect the ball joint from the knuckle. Remove the damper fork bolt.

10. Turn each steering knuckle to its most outboard position. Using a suitable tool, pry the right side CV-joint out approximately ½", then pull the sub axle out of the transaxle housing. Repeat this procedure for the opposite side. Remove the right side radius rod.

11. Remove the damper bracket from the transaxle. Remove the clutch housing bolts from the front transaxle mount.

12. Remove the clutch housing bolts from the rear transaxle mounting bracket. Remove the clutch cover.

13. Remove the starter mounting bolts and remove the starter assembly through the chassis. Remove the transaxle mounting bolt.

14. Pull the transaxle away from the engine block to clear the two 14mm dowel pins and lower the transaxle jack.

15. To install, reverse the removal procedure. Be sure to pay attention to the following points:

   a. Tighten all mounting nuts and bolts.

   b. Use a new shift rod pin.

   c. After installing the driveshafts, attempt to move the inner joint housing in and out of the differential housing. If it moves easily, the driveshaft end clips should be replaced.

   d. Make sure that the control cables and wires are properly connected.

   e. Be sure the transmission is refilled to the proper level.

Prelude 1988

1. Disconnect the battery ground cable at the battery and the transmission case. Unlock the steering column; place the transmission in neutral.

2. Disconnect the following wires:

   a. Back-up light switch wires.

   b. Black/white wire from the starter solenoid.

3. On the fuel injected models, remove the air cleaner assembly.

4. Remove the power steering speed sensor from the transaxle without removing the power steering hose.

5. Remove the shift cable and the select cable from the top cover of the transaxle. Remove the mounting bolt from the cable stay. Be sue not to

bend or kink the cable more than necessary. Remove both cables and the stay together.

6. Remove the upper transaxle mounting bracket. Remove the four transaxle to block attachment bolts that must be removed from the engine compartment.

7. Raise and support the vehicle safely. Remove both front wheels and remove the undercarriage splash shield.

8. Drain the transmission oil into a suitable drain pan. Remove the clutch slave cylinder.

9. Remove the center beam. Remove the right radius rod completely. Remove the right and left drive shafts.

10. Remove the engine stiffener. Remove the clutch cover. Support the transaxle with a suitable transmission jack.

11. Remove the three lower bolts from the rear engine mounting bracket. Loosen but do not remove the top bolt. This bolt will support the weight of the engine.

12. Remove the two remaining engine to transaxle mounting bolts.

13. With the transaxle on a suitable transmission jack, disengage the input shaft from the clutch disc and lower the transaxle out of the vehicle.

14. To install, reverse the removal procedure. Be sure to pay attention to the following points:

   a. Tighten all mounting nuts and bolts.

   b. Use a new shift rod pin.

   c. After installing the driveshafts, attempt to move the inner joint housing in and out of the differential housing. If it moves easily, the driveshaft end clips should be replaced.

   d. Make sure that the control cables and wires are properly connected.

   e. Be sure the transmission is refilled to the proper level.

OVERHAUL

4- and 5-Speed Transaxle

DISASSEMBLY

1. Remove the transmission end cover. Check the transmission mainshaft and countershaft end-play. End-play should be between 0.0508-0.0762mm. If the clearance is excessive, inspect the ball bearings after transmission disassembly.

2. Remove the locking tab from the mainshaft locknut. The mainshaft locknut has left hand threads. Place the transmission in gear and place the proper size wrench on the

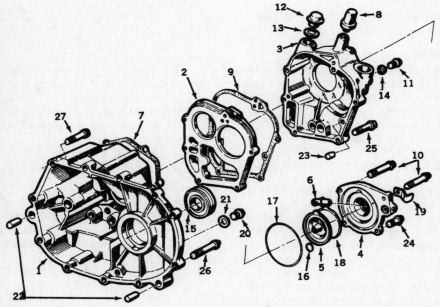

1 Housing, transmission	10 Bolt, flanged, 6 x 85 mm	19 Bracket, wire harness
2 Spacer, transmission housing	11 Bolt, oil check	20 Bolt, drain plug, 14 mm
3 Cover, transmission	12 Bolt, plug 25 mm	21 Washer, drain plug, 14 mm
4 Cover, right side	13 Washer, sealing, 25 mm	22 Pin, dowel, 14 x 20 mm
5 Plate, oil barrier	14 Washer, 8 mm	23 Pin, dowel, 8 x 14 mm
6 Tube, breather	15 Oil seal, 35 x 56 x 9 mm	24 Bolt, flanged, 6 x 20 mm
7 Gasket, transmission housing	16 O-ring, 9.4 x 2.4	25 Bolt, flanged, 6 x 45 mm
8 Cap, breather	17 O-ring, 64.5 x 3	26 Bolt, flanged, 8 x 40 mm
9 Gasket, transmission case	18 O-ring, 42 x 2.4	27 Bolt, flanged, 8 x 45 mm

Exploded view of housing and cover assemblies

countershaft to keep it from moving. Remove the mainshaft locknut.

3. Remove the mainshaft bearing and the large snapring.

4. Loosen the 3 shift detent lock ball screws. Remove the screws, springs and balls.

5. Remove the transmission case bolts. Lightly tap the case with a hammer and drift and separate the case. Do not pry the case apart.

6. Remove the reverse idler gear and shaft. Remove the reverse shift fork.

7. Remove the shift selector assembly. If repair to the shift selector is necessary, disassemble as follows:

    a. Remove the two screws and retaining plate. Stake the screws when reinstalling.

    b. Push the shift arm into the reverse position (towards the large spring). Then release it.

    c. The pivot shaft holds a spring loaded detent. Do not lose the detent ball and spring when removing. Remove the pivot shaft.

    d. Remove the interlock bar and shift arms.

    e. During reassembly, insert a small prybar into the reverse side (large spring end) of the arm assembly to hold down the detent ball, while inserting the pivot shaft.

8. Remove the shift fork retaining bolts and pull the shift shafts up until they clear the case. Remove the forks and shafts.

NOTE: *When reinstalling the fork retaining bolts, turn the shaft so the threaded portion of the hole is facing away from the bolt.*

9. Remove the mainshaft and countershaft and at the same time by holding the 2 shafts and lightly taping the flywheel end of the mainshaft.

10. Remove the shift rod boot, shift rim, lock washer and bolt. Remove the shift rod and shift arm.

NOTE: *During installation of the shift arm retaining bolt, turn the shaft so that the threaded portion of the hole is facing away from the bolt.*

11. Measure the side clearance of the low gear with a feeler gauge, if the clearance is excessive, replace the thrust plate. Perform the same measurement on the remaining gears, if the clearance is beyond the service limit, replace the bearing race (spacer). See chart for specifications.

12. If the countershaft must be disassembled to adjust the clearances, or replace gears, remove the locknut by installing the shaft in case and holding the differential securely.

NOTE: *Place the end lugs of the holder in the case and center the lug in the hole of the differential carrier.*

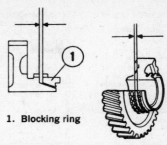

1. Blocking ring

Measuring the clearance between the synchronizer ring and gear hub

13. Remove the two screws and retaining plate which hold the countershaft bearing. Remove the countershaft bearing with a bearing puller.

14. Clean all component parts thoroughly in the proper solvent.

15. Inspect the surfaces of each gear and blocking ring for roughness or damage. Apply a thin coat of oil to the tapered surfaces of each gear and push them together with a rotating motion. Measure the distance between the ring and gear. Replace all necessary parts. Clearance should be between 3.0-3.5mm.

16. Measure the clearance between the shift forks and synchronizer sleeves. The clearance should be between 1.0-4.5mm. If clearances are excessive, replace the shift forks, synchronizers or both.

17. Ensure that there are no restrictions in the oil holes on the countershaft. Check the splines for wear.

18. Inspect the condition of the mainshaft and countershaft bearing surfaces. Check runout, gear tooth and spline condition.

19. Check the condition of all the gears. Check the condition of all bearing surfaces.

20. Inspect the bearing race (spacer) of each gear.

21. Replace all questionable parts.

ASSEMBLY

1. Transmission should be assembled in the reverse order of disassembly. During assembly, note the following points:

2. Check the differential bearing clearance.

3. Apply a thin coat of oil to all parts before they are installed.

4. Be certain that hub and synchronizer teeth match when they are assembled.

5. The mainshaft and countershaft must be installed at the same time. Next, install the 3rd/4th shift fork and shaft, 1st/2nd shift fork and shaft and then the reverse lever.

6. When the shift selector assembly is installed, there are two special bolts which must be inserted 1st. These bolts locate the assembly.

1. Needle roller bearing set
   plate
2. Needle roller bearing
3. Clutch case
4. Reverse gear shaft
5. Reverse idle gear
6. Reverse shift fork
7. Shift selector assembly
8. Countershaft gear assembly
9. Main shaft
10. First/second fork shaft
11. Reverse fork shaft
12. Third/fourth fork shaft
13. Steel ball
14. Ball set spring
15. Drain plug washer
16. Set ball spring screw
17. Ball bearing
18. Needle roller bearing
19. 48 mm snap ring
20. Ball bearing
21. 62 mm snap ring
22. 23 mm lock nut
23. 20 mm lock nut
24. Transmission rear cover
25. Speedometer gear

Exploded view of typical Honda manual transmission

7. Lock the mainshaft and countershaft lock-nuts with a punch.

8. Make sure that the mainshaft and countershaft turn smoothly and that all gears engage freely. Check and be certain that all bolts are properly torqued.

5-Speed Transaxle w/Super Low (6-Speed) Transfer Driven Gear

DISASSEMBLY

1. Slide the driven gear assembly into the clutch housing and secure with retaining bolts, if the unit had previously been removed.

2. Hold the companion flange with a flange holding tool and remove the locking nut with the proper socket.

3. Remove the tool and the companion flange. Remove the driven gear from the housing by tapping on the driven gear shaft.

4. Remove the inner driven gear bearing from the driven gear shaft, using a bearing puller tool.

5. Pry the oil seal from the transfer rear cover. Remove the bearing races from the transfer rear cover as required.

6. To reassemble, press the inner and outer bearing races into the housing.

7. To check the gear preload, special tools are needed. However, the following procedure can be used.

a. Assemble the following components in the transfer rear cover, the new transfer spacer, the drive gear, companion flange the lockwasher and the locknut.

NOTE: *Install the lockwasher with the dished side towards the companion flange.*

b. Temporarily install the driven gear assembly and the retaining bolts in the transfer case.

c. To measure the preload, tighten the locknut to the specified torque of 87 ft. lbs. (120 Nm), using the flange holder tool and the proper socket and wrench combination.

d. Remove the driven gear assembly from the transfer case and position the assembly in a vise with protective jaws. Measure the preload.

e. Measure the preload by first turning the companion flange several times to assure normal bearing to race contact. Rotate the shaft assembly with the appropriate torque wrench.

f. The preload should be 7.0-9.5 inch lbs. (0.8-1.1 Nm). Replace the transfer spacer with a new spacer and readjust. Do not attempt to adjust the preload by loosening the locknut.

g. If the preload is less than 7.0 inch lbs. (0.8 Nm), adjust by tightening the locknut a little at a time until the proper preload is achieved.

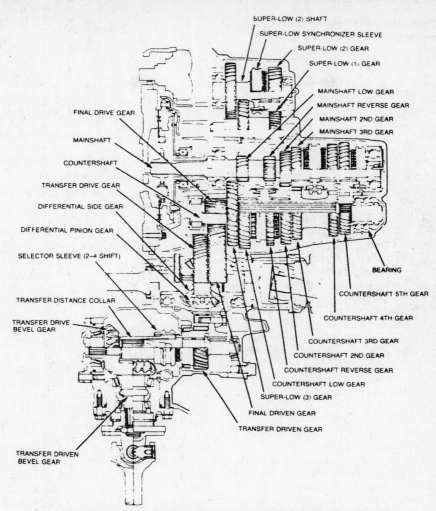

SUPER-LOW (2) SHAFT
SUPER-LOW SYNCHRONIZER SLEEVE
SUPER-LOW (2) GEAR
SUPER-LOW (1) GEAR

MAINSHAFT LOW GEAR
MAINSHAFT REVERSE GEAR
MAINSHAFT 2ND GEAR
MAINSHAFT 3RD GEAR

FINAL DRIVE GEAR

MAINSHAFT

COUNTERSHAFT

TRANSFER DRIVE GEAR

DIFFERENTIAL SIDE GEAR

DIFFERENTIAL PINION GEAR

SELECTOR SLEEVE (2–4 SHIFT)

BEARING

COUNTERSHAFT 5TH GEAR

TRANSFER DISTANCE COLLAR

COUNTERSHAFT 4TH GEAR

TRANSFER DRIVE
BEVEL GEAR

COUNTERSHAFT 3RD GEAR

COUNTERSHAFT 2ND GEAR

COUNTERSHAFT REVERSE GEAR

COUNTERSHAFT LOW GEAR

SUPER-LOW (3) GEAR

FINAL DRIVEN GEAR

TRANSFER DRIVEN GEAR

TRANSFER DRIVEN
BEVEL GEAR

Cross section of Honda 5 speed manual transaxle with Super-Low

h. Replace the transfer spacer with a new 1 if the preload is still outside the specified limits when the locknut is tightened to 166 ft. lbs. (230 Nm).

ASSEMBLY

1. Apply sealant to the clutch case mating surfaces of the transfer case.

NOTE: *The transaxle uses no gaskets between the major housing, depending upon sealant to prevent fluid leakages.*

2. Install the transfer case.

3. Install the following parts, the transfer thrust shim, the drive gear, the drive gear thrust shim and the left side cover.

4. Assemble the following parts: the driven gear thrust shim, the driven gear assembly and the driven gear assembly bolts.

5. Measure the total bearing preload by rotating the companion flange several times to assure normal bearing to race contact. Place the selector lever in the 2WD position and measure the preload with an appropriate torque wrench.

6. The total bearing preload should be 6.1-8.75 inch lbs. (0.7-1.0 Nm). This preload is greater than the preload on the driven gear assembly when tested alone. Example: If the preload of the driven assembly alone was 7.9 inch lbs. (0.9 Nm), the total bearing preload should be between 14-16 inch lbs. (1.6-1.9 Nm).

7. If the preload is outside of the specifications, adjust it by replacing the transfer thrust shim.

a. If the total bearing preload is less than specifications, reduce the size of the transfer thrust shim.

b. If the total bearing preload is more than specifications, increase the size of the transfer thrust shim.

Transfer Driven Gear Assembly

BACKLASH INSPECTION

1. Shift the selector lever to the 2WD position.

2. With the drive shaft disconnected, check the backlash at the companion flange with the use of a dial indicator mounted to the transaxle case.

3. Measure the backlash, turn the companion flange 180° and remeasure. The standard measurement is 0.10-0.15mm.

4. If the backlash is out of specifications, the driven gear thrust washer must be changed. Proper tooth contact must be retained after the backlash adjustment has been completed.

5. To check for proper tooth contact, remove the driven gear assembly from the transfer case and paint the driven gear teeth evenly with Prussian Blue or equivalent.

6. Reinstall the driven gear assembly back into the transfer case and tighten the bolts evenly to 20 ft. lbs. (26 Nm).

7. With the selector lever in 2WD, rotate the companion flange 1 full turn in both directions.

8. Remove the driven gear assembly from the transfer case and note the gear impressions on the gear. The correct tooth contact should be in the center of the tooth face and even between the top of the tooth and the bottom of the tooth.

9. The checking and adjustment of the driven gear assembly must be continued until the proper tooth contact is obtained.

a. If the tooth pattern shows toe contact, use a thicker drive gear thrust shim and increase the thickness of the transfer thrust shim and increase the thickness of the transfer thrust shim and equal amount.

b. If the pattern of the teeth shows heel contact, too much back lash is indicated. To correct this condition, reduce the thickness of the drive gear thrust shim. The thickness of the transfer thrust shim must also be reduced by the amount by which the drive gear thrust washer shim is reduced.

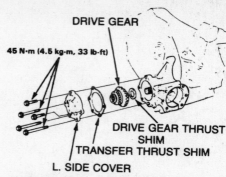

Exploded view of drive gear of transfer case assembly

(Labels in figure: DRIVE GEAR; 45 N·m (4.5 kg-m, 33 lb-ft); DRIVE GEAR THRUST SHIM; TRANSFER THRUST SHIM; L. SIDE COVER)

c. The driven gear thrust shim will have to be changed also to compensate for the change in backlash.

d. To correct face contact (contact too near the tooth edge), use a thicker driven gear thrust shim to move the drive gear away from the drive gear. The backlash should remain within limits.

e. To correct flank contact (contact too near the bottom of the tooth), move the driven gear in towards the drive gear by using a thinner shim for the driven gear, while retaining the correct backlash.

10. When the tooth contact and backlash is correct, apply a coating of sealant to the mating surfaces of the clutch and transfer cases. No gaskets are used.

11. Install the thrust shim and the O-ring on the driven gear assembly and install the assembly into the transfer case opening. Torque the bolts to 20 ft. lbs. (26 Nm). Slide the drive gear thrust shim and drive gear onto the transfer shaft.

12. Place the transfer thrust shim and O-ring on the left side cover and install the cover on the transfer case. Torque the bolts to 33 ft. lbs. (45 Nm). Remeasure the total bearing preload after the assembly, which should be 6.1-7.9 inch lbs. (0.7-1.0 Nm).

DISASSEMBLY OF TRANSAXLE

1. Remove the Reverse idle shaft bolt, the super low shift lever bolt and the super low shift set ball screw.

2. Remove the bolts attaching the clutch case to the transaxle housing.

3. Remove the sealing bolt and the circlip holding the countershaft ball bearings.

4. Separate the clutch housing from the transaxle housing.

5. Remove the thrust shim, the dish spring and oil guide plate from the transmission housing.

6. With the cover removed, a clearance in-

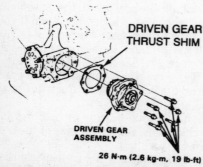

Exploded view of driven gear of transfer case assembly

(Labels in figure: DRIVEN GEAR THRUST SHIM; DRIVEN GEAR ASSEMBLY; 26 N·m (2.6 kg-m, 19 lb-ft))

spection must be made before any further disassembly is done to the unit.

a. Measure the clearance between the reverse shift fork and the 5th/Reverse shift
piece pin.

b. The service limit is 0.5mm. If the clearance is outside the limits, measure the width
of the L-groove in the reverse shift fork. This
clearance should be 7.00-7.25mm. Replace
the shift fork if the measurement exceeds the
maximum.

c. Measure the clearance between the reverse idler gear and the reverse shift fork.
The service limit is 1.8mm.

d. If the clearance exceeds the service limit, measure the width of the reverse shift fork

pawl groove opening. The opening measurement should be 13.0-13.3mm. If the measurement is outside the limits, replace the
shift fork with a new 1.

Mainshaft/Countershaft

REMOVAL

1. Remove the revere idler shaft and reverse
idler gear from the clutch housing.

2. Remove the following parts from the reverse shift holder assembly:

a. 1st/2nd shift fork shaft.
b. Super-low shift piece bar.
c. Super-low shift lever.
d. Super-low shift piece.
e. 1st/2nd shift fork.

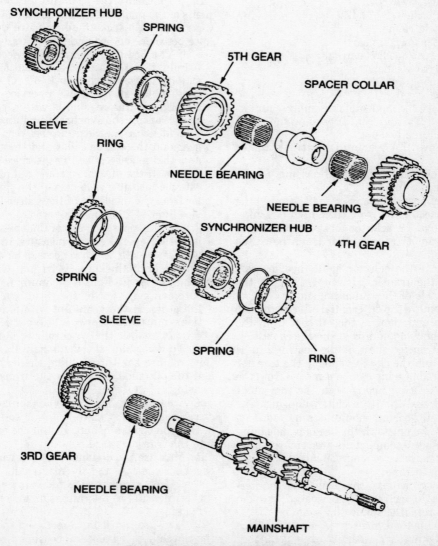

Exploded view of mainshaft assembly

3. Remove the following parts from the clutch housing:

    a. Special bolt (6mm).

    b. Lock plate.

    c. 5th/reverse shift fork shaft.

    d. 3rd/4th shift fork.

    e. Reverse shift fork.

4. Remove the reverse shift holder assembly from the clutch housing.

5. Remove the following parts from the clutch housing and the Super-low/2nd shaft assembly

    a. Ball bearing.

    b. Spacer collar with flanges.

    c. Super-low/2nd gear.

    d. Synchronizer ring.

    e. Super-low shift fork shaft assembly.

    f. Needle bearing.

    g. Thrust washer.

    h. Super-low/1st shaft.

    i. Spacer collar.

    j. Super-low/1st gear.

    k. Thrust needle bearing.

    l. Thrust washer.

    m. Spring washer.

    n. Space collar.

6. Remove the mainshaft assembly, countershaft assembly and the Super-low/2nd shaft form the clutch housing.

7. Remove the bearing from the transfer shaft.

8. Remove the differential assembly from the clutch housing.

9. To remove the transfer shaft, remove the 2nd/4th selector rod from the clutch housing.

10. Remove the selector fork, selector sleeve and the transfer spacer collar from the clutch housing.

11. Remove the selector shaft, needle bearings and the transfer driven gear from the transaxle side of the clutch housing.

12. To remove the differential oil seal, remove the circlip and remove the oil seal from the transaxle housing and from the clutch case.

13. The transfer shaft needle bearing can be removed from the clutch housing, the transfer shaft tapered bearing can be removed from the transaxle housing, along with the mainshaft bearing/oil seal from the clutch housing. The countershaft bearing should be removed from the clutch housing with the use of a slide hammer tool. As the components are removed from the major units, new components can be installed at that time.

14. Inspect the mainshaft and the countershaft for damage, excessive wear or broken teeth. Examine the splines for wear.

15. Examine the synchronizer units for worn teeth, roughness or wear, scoring galling or cracks.

16. To measure the clearance between the ring and the gear, hold the ring against the gear evenly while measuring the clearance with a feeler gauge. The service limit is 0.4mm. If necessary, replace the unit.

17. To assemble the mainshaft, install the components in the following order on the mainshaft:

    a. Needle bearing

    b. 3rd gear

    c. Synchronizer assembly

    d. 4th gear

    e. Needle bearings

    f. Spacer collar

    g. Needle bearing

    h. 5th gear

    i. Synchronizer assembly

    j. Ball bearing

18. To measure the clearance of the components of the mainshaft, push down on the bearing race with a socket and measure the clearance between the 3rd and 2nd gears.

    a. The 3rd gear clearance service limit is 0.3mm. If the measurement is out of specifications, measure the thickness of the 3rd gear, which should have a service limit of 32.3mm. If this reading is within specifications, replace the synchronizer hub.

    b. Measure the clearance between the 4th gear and the spacer collar and the 5th gear and the spacer collar. The service limit is 0.3mm. If the measurement is out of specifications, measure each side of the spacer collar from the inside lip of the spacer lug. Service limit of 26.0mm is allowed.

    c. If the measurement of the spacer collar is within specifications measure the thickness of the 4th and 5th gears. The 4th gear service limit thickness is 31mm, while the 5th gear service limit is 30.3mm. if the measurements are out of specifications, replace the gears. If the gears are within specifications, but the clearance is still out of specifications, replace the synchronizer hub.

19. To determine the mainshaft shim selection, remove the thrust shim, the dish spring and the oil guide plate from the transmission housing.

20. Install the 3rd/4th synchronizer hub, spacer collar, 5th synchronizer hub and the ball bearing on the mainshaft. Install the assembly into the transaxle case.

21. Measure the distance between the end of the transaxle case and the mainshaft.

    a. Use a straight edge and vernier caliper.

    b. Measure at 3 locations and average the readings.

22. Measure the distance between the end of the clutch housing and the bearing inner race. Again, average the readings.

23. Calculate the thickness of the shim to be added, as follows

a. Add the measurement recorded in Step 21 and Step 22.

b. Subtract 1.0mm, representing the height of the dish spring after installation and the remainder is the thickness of the shim needed.

Shim needed would be 1.60mm.

c. When making this measurement, if the inner race protrudes above the clutch housing, measure the height it protrudes and subtract this amount from the measurement. Then subtract the 1.0mm dish spring to compute the shim needed.

Shim needed would be 1.60mm.

d. Thickness of the shims vary from 1.10mm to 2.15mm, available in thickness of 0.05mm increments, for a total of 22 different sizes.

24. Check the thrust clearance as outlined in the following steps:

a. Install the dish spring and shim selected in the transaxle housing.

b. Install the mainshaft into the clutch housing.

c. Place the transaxle cover housing over the mainshaft and onto the clutch housing.

d. Tighten the clutch and transaxle retaining bolts.

e. Reach through the 18mm sealing bolt hole and measure the clearance between the dish spring and the thrush shim at its opening.

f. The scale 0.3mm side should fit while the scale side 0.49mm side should not of the special measuring tool, 07998SD9000A or its equivalent.

g. If the clearance is incorrect, the adjusting shims must be changed to correct the specifications.

Countershaft

CLEARANCE INSPECTION

1. Assemble the gears, spacer collars, thrust washers, synchronizer hub and rings to the countershaft, in the following manner:

a. Super-low gear

b. Selective thrust washer

c. Needle bearing

d. Low gear

e. Reverse gear and synchronizer assembly

f. 2nd gear

g. Spacer collar

h. Needle bearing

i. 3rd gear

j. 4th gear

k. 5th gear

l. Ball bearing

m. Lockwasher and locknut

2. Tighten the countershaft locknut to a torque of 80 ft. lbs. (110 Nm).

NOTE: *Place the countershaft assembly in a soft jawed vise before tightening the locknut.*

3. Measure and record the clearance between the Super-low gear and thrust washer. The service limit is 0.18mm.

4. If the clearance is out of specifications, select the appropriate thrust washer or spacer collar for the correct clearance.

5. Measure the clearance between the 2nd gear and 3rd gears. The service limit is 0.18mm.

6. If the clearance is out of specifications, select the appropriate thrust washer or collar for the correct clearance.

ASSEMBLY OF TRANSAXLE

1. Install the guide plate, dish spring and mainshaft thrust shim in the transaxle housing.

NOTE: *Use the correct thrust shim for the mainshaft for the proper thrust clearance.*

2. Install the oil gutter and collect plates in the transaxle housing.

3. Install the transfer shaft assembly and the 2nd/4th selector rod.

4. Install the differential assembly in the clutch housing.

5. Install the bearing on the transfer shaft.

6. Install the super-low/2nd shaft, countershaft assembly and the mainshaft assembly in the clutch housing.

7. Install the super-low shift piece and the shift fork on the super-low shift fork shaft.

8. Assemble the super-low shift fork shaft assembly with the following components:

a. Ball bearing

b. Flanged spacer collar

c. Super-low/2nd gear

d. Synchronizer hub assembly

e. Needle bearing

9. Install the following components into the clutch housing:

a. Spacer collar

b. Lock washer

c. Thrust washer

d. Thrust needle bearing

e. Super-low/1st gear

f. Needle bearing

g. Spacer collar

h. Super-low/1st shaft

i. Thrust washer

NOTE: *Align the lug on the end of the super-low/1st shaft with the groove in the clutch case. Install the lock washer with the dished end facing upward.*

10. Install the reverse shift holder assembly into the clutch housing.

11. Install the reverse shift fork, the 3rd/4th

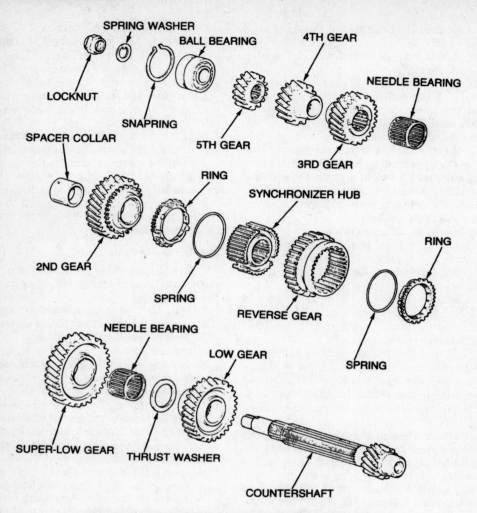

SPRING WASHER

BALL BEARING

4TH GEAR

NEEDLE BEARING

LOCKNUT

SNAPRING

SPACER COLLAR

5TH GEAR

3RD GEAR

RING

SYNCHRONIZER HUB

RING

2ND GEAR

SPRING

REVERSE GEAR

NEEDLE BEARING

LOW GEAR

SPRING

SUPER-LOW GEAR

THRUST WASHER

COUNTERSHAFT

Exploded view of countershaft assembly with Super-Low

shift fork and the 5th shift fork onto the mainshaft.

12. Slide the 5th/Reverse shift fork shaft down through each shift fork.

CAUTION: *Install the fork shaft with the detent hole facing the countershaft.*

13. Install the 1st/2nd shift fork, the super-low shift piece and the super-low shift lever.

14. Slide the 1st/2nd shift fork shaft through the shift pieces and the shift lever.

15. Install the super-low shift piece bar in the reverse shift holder assembly.

16. Install the reverse idler gear and idler gear shaft in the clutch housing.

NOTE: *Install the reverse idler shaft with the threads facing towards the outside.*

17. Apply sealant to the transaxle mating surfaces and install the dowel pins.

18. Install the transaxle housing over the clutch housing and carefully line-up the shafts.

19. Torque the retaining bolts to 19 ft. lbs. (26 Nm).

20. Install the reverse idler shaft retaining bolt and washer. Install the detent ball, spring, washer and super-low shift detent ball screw. Install the super-low shift lever bolt.

21. Install the circlip in the bore of the transaxle housing.

22. Install the oil seal into the transaxle housing and the oil seal in the clutch housing.

23. Fill with oil and install in the vehicle.

Halfshafts

REMOVAL AND INSTALLATION

All Except Left Side 4WD Models

The front driveshaft assembly consists of a sub-axle shaft and a driveshaft with two universal joints.

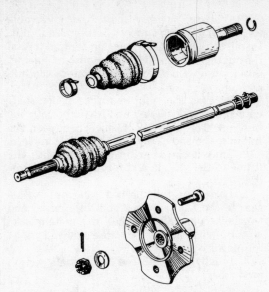

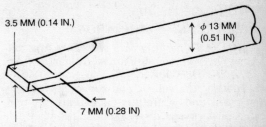

Procure or fabricate a tool similar to that shown to disassemble the left side driveshaft on four wheel drive vehicles

Exploded view of driveshaft and related parts

A constant velocity ball joint is used for both universal joints, which are factory packed with special grease and enclosed in sealed rubber boots. The outer joint cannot be disassembled except for removal of the boot.

1. Remove the hubcap from the front wheel and then remove the center cap.

2. Pull out the 4mm cotter pin and loosen but do not remove the spindle nut.

3. Raise and support the front of the vehicle on jackstands.

4. Remove the wheel lug nuts and the wheel.

5. Remove the spindle nut.

6. Drain the transaxle.

7. Using a Ball Joint Remover tool, remove the lower arm ball joints from the knuckle.

WARNING: *On Civic models (1984-88), make sure that a floor jack is positioned securely under the lower control arm, at the ball joint. Otherwise, the lower control arm may "jump" suddenly away from the steering knuckle as the ball joint is removed.*

On Prelude models (1983-88), remove the damper fork bolt, damper locking bolt and the damper fork.

8. To remove the driveshaft, hold the knuckle and pull it toward you. Then slide the driveshaft out of the knuckle. Pry the CV joint out about ½". Pull the inboard joint side of the driveshaft out of the differential case.

9. To install, reverse the removal procedures. If either the inboard or outboard joint boot bands have been removed for inspection or disassembly of the joint (only the inboard joint can be disassembled), be sure to repack the joint with a sufficient amount of bearing grease.

WARNING: *Make sure the CV-joint sub-axle bottoms so that the spring clip may hold the sub-axle securely in the transaxle.*

Left Side 4WD Models

NOTE: *To perform this procedure, make sure you have a tool similar to an ordinary, flat blade screwdriver with dimensions close to those shown. This tool is necessary to pry parts apart in disassembly.*

1. Remove the spindle nut. Raise and support the front of the vehicle on jackstands. Remove the wheel.

WARNING: *Position a floor jack securely under the lower control arm. If the support is not secure, the tension from the torsion bar could cause the control arm to be forced violently away from the steering knuckle when the ball joint separates.*

2. Remove the cotter pin and ball joint retaining nut, then, press off the ball joint.

3. Pull the front hub outward until it is free of the driveshaft.

WARNING: *Make sure that, in the following step, you hold the inboard joint horizontal until the driveshaft clears the intermediate shaft. Failure to do this could cause damage to the intermediate shaft seal.*

4. Using the special tool pictured above, gently pry the inboard joint away from the intermediate shaft, holding the shaft horizontal. As you pry, the spring clip will be forced out of the groove in the differential. Once the clip has been freed, pull the driveshaft out of the intermediate shaft.

5. Replace the (28mm) spring clip by gently working it into the groove in the splined area of the inboard joint. Then, insert the inboard joint into the intermediate shaft until the clip locks in the shaft groove. MAKE SURE that the CV-joint subaxle bottoms in the differential and that the spring clip actually locks in the groove in the differential side gear.

6. To complete the installation, reverse of the removal procedures.

4WD Propeller Shaft
REMOVAL AND INSTALLATION

NOTE: *To perform this procedure, you will need a Companion Flange Holder tool No. 07926-SD90000.*

1. Raise the vehicle and support it securely on axle stands. Carefully matchmark the relationship between driveshaft flanges, transaxle and rear axle companion flanges so the driveshaft can be reinstalled in the same position. This is necessary for balance.

2. Remove the protective band for the No. 1 (front) section of the propeller shaft.

3. Remove the 3rd section of the propeller shaft by disconnecting the U-joints.

4. Remove the rear bearing support bolts and the 2nd propshaft section.

5. Remove the front bearing support bolts, then, disconnect the U-joint and remove the No. 1 (front) propeller shaft section.

6. Install a tool to hold the companion flange and remove the propshaft hub nut.

7. Remove the center bearing support bolt and lower the support. Hold the support in one hand as you lightly tap on the end of the shaft with a soft hammer. Make sure you continue tapping on the shaft until it clears the bearing support.

NOTE: *If you can't remove the shaft with gentle tapping, USE A PULLER. If it's necessary to use a puller, REPLACE THE BEARING SUPPORT WHEN REINSTALLING THE DRIVESHAFT. DON'T RE-USE THE OLD ONE.*

PROPELLER SHAFT HUB

PROPELLER SHAFT HUB NUT
22 × 1.5 MM
60 N·M (6.0 KG-M, 43 LB. FT.)

COMPANION
FLANGE HOLDER
07926-SD90000

To remove the propshaft on 4 WD vehicles, you'll need a means of holding the companion flange stationary, such as Honda part No. 07926-SD90000. You may be able to fabricate a device which will function similarly.

8. To install the driveshaft, first reassemble the center bearing support, hub and nub nut. Install the companion flange holder and torque the nut to 94 ft. lbs. to force the bearing support into its proper position; then, remove the hub and nut.

9. Position the hub on the propeller shaft with the marks aligned and install it with the hub nut. Torque to 43 ft. lbs. Then, peen the nut over the end of the shaft to lock it in place.

10. Install the bearing supports onto the frame of the vehicle and torque bolts to 29 ft. lbs.

11. Loosely install the bolts and nuts to assemble the shaft flanges and differential and transaxle companion flanges with matchmarks aligned. When all the nuts are installed loosely, torque each to 24 ft. lbs.

12. Finally, reinstall the No. 1 shaft section protector.

CLUTCH

CAUTION: *The clutch driven disc contains asbestos, which has been determined to be a cancer causing agent. Never clean clutch surfaces with compressed air! Avoid inhaling any dust from any clutch surface! When cleaning clutch surfaces, use a commercially available brake cleaning fluid.*

Understanding the Clutch

The purpose of the clutch is to disconnect and connect engine power from the transmission. A car at rest requires a lot of engine torque to get all that weight moving. An internal combustion engine does not develop a high starting torque (unlike steam engines), so it must be allowed to operate without any load until it builds up enough torque to move the car. Torque increases with engine rpm. The clutch allows the engine to build up torque by physically disconnecting the engine from the transmission, relieving the engine of any load or resistance. The transfer of engine power to the transmission (the load) must be smooth and gradual; if it weren't, drive line components would wear out or break quickly. This gradual power transfer is made possible by gradually releasing the clutch pedal. The clutch disc and pressure plate are the connecting link between the engine and transmission. When the clutch pedal is released, the disc and plate contact each other (clutch engagement), physically joining the engine and transmission. When the pedal is pushed in, the disc and plate separate (the clutch is disengaged), disconnecting the engine from the transmission.

The clutch assembly consists of the flywheel, the clutch disc, the clutch pressure plate, the throwout bearing and fork, the actuating linkage and the pedal. The flywheel and clutch pressure plate (driving members) are connected to the engine crankshaft and rotate with it. The clutch disc is located between the flywheel and pressure plate, and splined to the transmission shaft. A driving member is one that is attached to the engine and transfers engine power to a driven member (clutch disc) on the transmission shaft. A driving member (pressure plate) rotates (drives) a driven member (clutch disc) on contact and, in so doing, turns the transmission shaft. There is a circular diaphragm spring within the pressure plate cover (transmission side). In a relaxed state (when the clutch pedal is fully released), this spring is convex; that is, it is dished outward toward the transmission. Pushing in the clutch pedal actuates an attached linkage rod. Connected to the other end of this rod is the throwout bearing fork. The throwout bearing is attached to the fork. When the clutch pedal is depressed, the clutch linkage pushes the fork and bearing forward to contact the diaphragm spring of the pressure plate. The outer edges of the spring are secured to the pressure plate and are pivoted on rings so that when the center of the spring is compressed by the throwout bearing, the outer edges bow outward and, by so doing, pull the pressure plate in the same direction - away from the clutch disc. This action separates the disc from the plate, disengaging the clutch and allowing the transmission to be shifted into another gear. A coil type clutch return spring attached to the clutch pedal arm permits full release of the pedal. Releasing the pedal pulls the throwout bearing away from the diaphragm spring resulting in a reversal of spring position. As bearing pressure is gradually released from the spring center, the outer edges of the spring bow outward, pushing the pressure plate into closer contact with the clutch disc. As the disc and plate move closer together, friction between the two increases and slippage is reduced until, when full spring pressure is applied (by fully releasing the pedal), The speed of the disc and plate are the same. This stops all slipping, creating a direct connection between the plate and disc which results in

Troubleshooting Basic Clutch Problems

Problem	Cause
Excessive clutch noise	Throwout bearing noises are more audible at the lower end of pedal travel. The usual causes are: • Riding the clutch • Too little pedal free-play • Lack of bearing lubrication A bad clutch shaft pilot bearing will make a high pitched squeal, when the clutch is disengaged and the transmission is in gear or within the first 2″ of pedal travel. The bearing must be replaced. Noise from the clutch linkage is a clicking or snapping that can be heard or felt as the pedal is moved completely up or down. This usually requires lubrication. Transmitted engine noises are amplified by the clutch housing and heard in the passenger compartment. They are usually the result of insufficient pedal free-play and can be changed by manipulating the clutch pedal.
Clutch slips (the car does not move as it should when the clutch is engaged)	This is usually most noticeable when pulling away from a standing start. A severe test is to start the engine, apply the brakes, shift into high gear and SLOWLY release the clutch pedal. A healthy clutch will stall the engine. If it slips it may be due to: • A worn pressure plate or clutch plate • Oil soaked clutch plate • Insufficient pedal free-play
Clutch drags or fails to release	The clutch disc and some transmission gears spin briefly after clutch disengagement. Under normal conditions in average temperatures, 3 seconds is maximum spin-time. Failure to release properly can be caused by: • Too light transmission lubricant or low lubricant level • Improperly adjusted clutch linkage
Low clutch life	Low clutch life is usually a result of poor driving habits or heavy duty use. Riding the clutch, pulling heavy loads, holding the car on a grade with the clutch instead of the brakes and rapid clutch engagement all contribute to low clutch life.

the transfer of power from the engine to the transmission. The clutch disc is now rotating with the pressure plate at engine speed and, because it is splined to the transmission shaft, the shaft now turns at the same engine speed. Understanding clutch operation can be rather difficult at first; if you're still confused after reading this, consider the following analogy. The action of the diaphragm spring can be compared to that of an oil can bottom. The bottom of an oil can is shaped very much like the clutch diaphragm spring and pushing in on the can bottom and then releasing it produces a similar effect. As mentioned earlier, the clutch pedal return spring permits full release of the pedal and reduces linkage slack due to wear. As the linkage wears, clutch free-pedal travel will increase and free-travel will decrease as the clutch wears. Free-travel is actually throwout bearing lash.

The diaphragm spring type clutches used are available in two different designs: flat diaphragm springs or bent spring. The bent fingers are bent back to create a centrifugal boost ensuring quick re-engagement at higher engine speeds. This design enables pressure plate load to increase as the clutch disc wears and makes low pedal effort possible even with a heavy duty clutch. The throwout bearing used with the bent finger design is 32mm long and is shorter than the bearing used with the flat finger design. These bearings are not interchangeable. If the longer bearing is used with the bent finger clutch, free-pedal travel will not exist. This results in clutch slippage and rapid wear.

The transmission varies the gear ratio between the engine and drive wheels. It can be shifted to change engine speed as driving conditions and loads change. The transmission allows disengaging and reversing power from the engine to the wheels.

Adjustments
PEDAL HEIGHT
Civic

1976-79

Check the clutch pedal height and if necessary, adjust the upper stop, so that the clutch and brake pedals rest at approximately the same height from the floor. First, be sure that the brake pedal free-play is properly adjusted.

1980-84

The pedal height should be 20mm minimum from the floor.

1984-86

Pedal height should be: 1984 models — 175mm; 1985 — 179mm (except coupe),

175mm (coupe); 1986 — 179mm. Pedal height is not adjustable and improper dimension would indicate worn pedal mounting parts.

Accord and Prelude

1. Pedal height should be 184mm measured from the front of the pedal to the floorboard (mat removed).
2. Adjust by turning the pedal stop bolt in or out until height is correct. Tighten the locknut after adjustment.

FREE PLAY
Civic 1973-88

Adjust the clutch release lever so that it has 3-4mm 1973-80 or 4.4-5.4mm 1981-88 of play when you move the clutch release lever at the transaxle with your hand. This adjustment is made at the outer cable housing adjuster, near the release lever on non-CVCC models. Less than 3mm of free-play may lead to clutch slippage, while more than 3mm clearance may cause difficult shifting.

WARNING: *Make sure that the upper and lower adjusting nuts are tightened after adjustment.*

On CVCC models, the free-play adjustment is made on the cable at the firewall. Remove the C-clip and then rotate the threaded control cable housing until there is 3-4mm free-play at the release lever. On Accord and Prelude models (1976-81), adjustment is made at the slave cylinder. Simply loosen the lock nut and turn the adjusting nut until the correct free play is obtained. Free play should be 2.0-3.5mm at the release lever. On the 1982-88 Accord and Prelude, adjustment is made on the cable at the firewall. Remove the C-clip and rotate the threaded control cable until 5.0-6.5mm exists at the clutch release lever.

Civic Models

1984

1. Measure the clutch pedal free play — the distance the pedal moves before spring pressure abruptly increases (the clutch begins to disengage). It should be 16.0-21.0mm.
2. If necessary, adjust the free play by turning the adjusting nut, located just below the release arm. When pedal play meets specification, check the play at the release arm. It should be 4.0-5.0mm.

1985-87

1. Measure the clutch pedal free play — the distance the pedal moves before spring pressure abruptly increases (the clutch begins to disengage). For all vehicles, except the 1985 Coupe, it

should be 16-21mm. On the 1985 Coupe, it should be 16-21mm.

2. If necessary, adjust the free play by turning the adjusting nut, located just below the release arm. When pedal play meets specification, check the play at the release arm; it should be 4-5mm.

Driven Disc and Pressure Plate
REMOVAL AND INSTALLATION

CAUTION: *The clutch driven disc contains asbestos, which has been determined to be a cancer causing agent. Never clean clutch surfaces with compressed air! Avoid inhaling any dust from any clutch surface! When cleaning clutch surfaces, use a commercially available brake cleaning fluid.*

1. Refer to the "Manual Transaxle, Removal and Installation" procedures in this chapter and remove the transaxle. Matchmark the flywheel and clutch for reassembly.

2. Using a large pry bar or other fabricated tool (see illustration), lock the flywheel ring gear. Remove the pressure plate-to-flywheel bolts, the pressure plate and the clutch disc.

NOTE: *Loosen the retaining bolts two turns at a time in a circular pattern. Removing one bolt while the rest are tight may warp the diaphragm spring.*

3. The flywheel can now be removed, if it needs repairing or replacing.

4. To separate the pressure plate from the diaphragm spring, remove the 4 retracting clips.

5. To remove the release, or throw-out, bearing, first straighten the locking tab and remove the 8mm bolt, followed by the release shaft and release arm with the bearing attached.

NOTE: *It is recommended that the release bearing be removed after the release arm has been removed from the casing. Trying to remove or install the bearing with the release arm in the case, will damage the retaining clip.*

6. If a new release bearing is to be installed, separate the bearing from the holder, using a bearing drift.

7. To assemble and install the clutch, reverse the removal procedures. Be sure to pay attention to the following points:

　a. Make sure that the flywheel and the end of the crankshaft are clean before assembling.

　b. When installing the pressure plate, align the mark on the outer edge of the flywheel with the alignment mark on the pressure plate. Failure to align these marks will result in imbalance.

　c. When tightening the pressure plate bolts, use a pilot shaft to center the friction

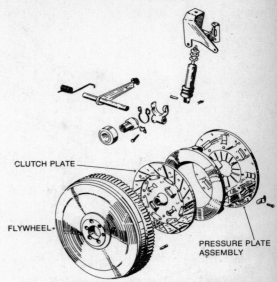

CLUTCH PLATE

FLYWHEEL

PRESSURE PLATE ASSEMBLY

Civic CVCC clutch, flywheel, and related parts

Clutch disc

Pressure plate

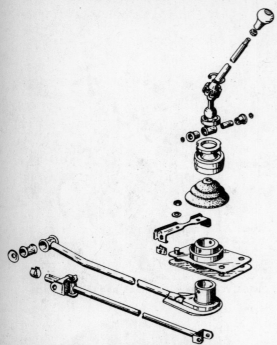

Exploded view of gearshift mechanism and related parts

disc; the pilot shaft can be bought at any large auto supply store or fabricated from a wooden dowel. After centering the disc, tighten the bolts two turns at a time, in a circular pattern to avoid warping the diaphragm spring.

d. When installing the release shaft and arm, place a lock tab washer under the retaining bolt.

e. When installing the transaxle, make sure that the mainshaft is properly aligned with the disc spline and the alignment pins are in place, before tightening the case bolts.

Master Cylinder
REMOVAL AND INSTALLATION

1. The clutch master cylinder is located on the firewall.

2. Disconnect and plug the hydraulic line at the clutch master cylinder.

3. From under the instrument panel, remove the clutch master cylinder rod-to-clutch pedal arm pin.

4. Remove the clutch master cylinder-to-firewall bolts and the master cylinder.

5. To install, reverse the removal procedures. Refill the master cylinder reservoir and bleed the system.

OVERHAUL

1. Remove the stopper plate snapring.

2. Once the snapring is removed, use com-

pressed air to remove the piston assembly; note the order of all components. The piston assembly is in two parts — the piston and the spring assembly.

3. Inspect the inside of the cylinder bore for rust, pitting or scratching. Light scores or scratches can be removed with a brake cylinder hone. If the bore won't clean up with a few passes of the hone, the entire cylinder will have to be replaced.

4. Replace the interior components with new ones. Overhaul kits will simply be two pieces — a new piston and a new spring assembly. Reassemble them in the correct order. Coat the inside of the cylinder with brake fluid before installing the parts.

5. Install the master cylinder and bleed the system.

Slave Cylinder
REMOVAL AND INSTALLATION

The slave cylinder is retained by two bolts. To remove the cylinder, simply disconnect the hydraulic line, remove the return spring and the bolts. To install, reverse the removal procedures. Refill the master cylinder and bleed the system.

OVERHAUL

1. There is little you can do to the slave cylinder other than replace the piston and seal inside the cylinder.

2. Using compressed air, blow the piston out of the cylinder; the seal will probably come out with it.

3. Once the piston and seal are removed, check the inside of the cylinder bore for pitting, rust or scratching. The bore can be honed but

Accord slave cylinder (arrow)

Closeup of Accord and Prelude slave cylinder showing locknut and adjusting nut

it's probably not worth the effort. A new slave cylinder would make more sense.

AUTOMATIC TRANSAXLE

Understanding Automatic Transmissions

The automatic transmission allows engine torque and power to be transmitted to the drive wheels within a narrow range of engine operating speeds. The transmission will allow the engine to turn fast enough to produce plenty of power and torque at very low speeds, while keeping it at a sensible rpm at high vehicle speeds. The transmission performs this job entirely without driver assistance. The transmission uses a light fluid as the medium for the transmission of power. This fluid also works in the operation of various hydraulic control circuits and as a lubricant. Because the transmission fluid performs all of these three functions, trouble within the unit can easily travel from one part to another. For this reason, and because of the complexity and unusual operating principles of the transmission, a very sound understanding of the basic principles of operation will simplify troubleshooting.

THE TORQUE CONVERTER

The torque converter replaces the conventional clutch. It has three functions:

1. It allows the engine to idle with the vehicle at a standstill, even with the transmission in gear.

2. It allows the transmission to shift from range to range smoothly, without requiring that the driver close the throttle during the shift.

3. It multiplies engine torque to an increasing extent as vehicle speed drops and throttle opening is increased. This has the effect of making the transmission more responsive and reduces the amount of shifting required.

The torque converter is a metal case which is shaped like a sphere that has been flattened on opposite sides. It is bolted to the rear end of the engine's crankshaft. Generally, the entire metal case rotates at engine speed and serves as the engine's flywheel.

The case contains three sets of blades. One set is attached directly to the case. This set forms the torus or pump. Another set is directly connected to the output shaft, and forms the turbine. The third set is mounted on a hub which, in turn, is mounted on a stationary shaft through a one-way clutch. This third set is known as the stator.

A pump, which is driven by the converter hub at engine speed, keeps the torque converter full of transmission fluid at all times. Fluid flows continuously through the unit to provide cooling.

Under low speed acceleration, the torque converter functions as follows:

The torus is turning faster than the turbine. It picks up fluid at the center of the converter and, through centrifugal force, slings it outward. Since the outer edge of the converter moves faster than the portions at the center, the fluid picks up speed.

The fluid then enters the outer edge of the turbine blades. It then travels back toward the center of the converter case along the turbine blades. In impinging upon the turbine blades, the fluid loses the energy picked up in the torus.

If the fluid were now to immediately be returned directly into the torus, both halves of the converter would have to turn at approximately the same speed at all times, and torque input and output would both be the same.

In flowing through the torus and turbine, the fluid picks up two types of flow, or flow in two separate directions. It flows through the turbine blades, and it spins with the engine. The stator, whose blades are stationary when the vehicle is being accelerated at low speeds, converts one type of flow into another. Instead of allowing the fluid to flow straight back into the torus, the stator's curved blades turn the fluid almost 90° toward the direction of rotation of the engine. Thus the fluid does not flow as fast toward the torus, but is already spinning when the torus picks it up. This has the effect of allowing the torus to turn much faster than the turbine. This difference in speed may be compared to the difference in speed between the smaller and larger gears in any gear train. The result is that engine power output is higher, and engine torque is multiplied.

As the speed of the turbine increases, the fluid spins faster and faster in the direction of engine rotation. As a result, the ability of the stator to redirect the fluid flow is reduced. Under cruising conditions, the stator is eventually forced to rotate on its one-way clutch in the direction of engine rotation. Under these conditions, the torque converter begins to behave almost like a solid shaft, with the torus and turbine speeds being almost equal.

THE PLANETARY GEARBOX

The ability of the torque converter to multiply engine torque is limited. Also, the unit tends to be more efficient when the turbine is rotating at relatively high speeds. Therefore, a planetary gearbox is used to carry the power output of the turbine to the halfshafts.

Planetary gears function very similarly to conventional transmission gears. However, their construction is different in that three elements make up one gear system, and, in that all three elements are different from one another. The three elements are: an outer gear that is shaped like a hoop, with teeth cut into the inner surface; a sun gear, mounted on a shaft and located at the very center of the outer gear; and a set of three planet gears, held by pins in a ring-like planet carrier, meshing with both the sun gear and the outer gear. Either the outer gear or the sun gear may be held stationary, providing more than one possible torque multiplication factor for each set of gears. Also, if all three gears are forced to rotate at the same speed, the gearset forms, in effect, a solid shaft.

Most modern automatics use the planetary gears to provide either a single reduction ratio of about 1.8:1, or two reduction gears: a low of about 2.5:1, and an intermediate of about 1.5:1. Bands and clutches are used to hold various portions of the gearsets to the transmission case or to the shaft on which they are mounted. Shifting is accomplished, then, by changing the portion of each planetary gearset which is held to the transmission case or to the shaft.

THE SERVOS AND ACCUMULATORS

The servos are hydraulic pistons and cylinders. They resemble the hydraulic actuators used on many familiar machines, such as bulldozers. Hydraulic fluid enters the cylinder, under pressure, and forces the piston to move to engage the band or clutches.

The accumulators are used to cushion the engagement of the servos. The transmission fluid must pass through the accumulator on the way to the servo. The accumulator housing contains a thin piston which is sprung away from the discharge passage of the accumulator. When fluid passes through the accumulator on the way to the servo, it must move the piston against spring pressure, and this action smooths out the action of the servo.

THE HYDRAULIC CONTROL SYSTEM

The hydraulic pressure used to operate the servos comes from the main transmission oil pump. This fluid is channeled to the various servos through the shift valves. There is generally a manual shift valve which is operated by the transmission selector lever and an automatic shift valve for each automatic upshift the transmission provides: i.e., 2-speed automatics have a low/high shift valve, while 3-speeds have a 1-2 valve, and a 2-3 valve.

There are two pressures which effect the operation of these valves. One is the governor pressure which is affected by vehicle speed. The other is the modulator pressure which is affected by intake manifold vacuum or throttle position. Governor pressure rises with an increase in vehicle speed, and modulator pressure rises as the throttle is opened wider. By responding to these two pressures, the shift valves cause the upshift points to be delayed with increased throttle opening to make the best use of the engine's power output.

Most transmissions also make use of an auxiliary circuit for downshifting. This circuit may be actuated by the throttle linkage or the vacuum line which actuates the modulator, or by a cable or solenoid. It applies pressure to a special downshift surface on the shift valve or valves.

The transmission modulator also governs the line pressure, used to actuate the servos. In this way, the clutches and bands will be actuated with a force matching the torque output of the engine.

Adjustments
SHIFT LINKAGE
Inspection

1. Set the parking brake lever and run the engine at idle speed, while depressing the brake pedal.

2. By moving the shift selector lever slowly forward and backward from the **N** position, make sure that the distance between the **N** and the points where the **D** clutch is engaged for the **2** and **R** positions are the same. The **D** clutch engaging point is just before the slight response is felt. The reverse gears will make a noise when the clutch engages. If the distances are not the same, adjustment is necessary.

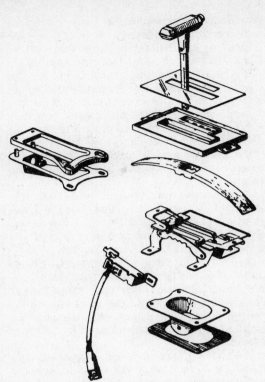

Exploded view of automatic transmission shift lever control

Adjustment — 2-Speed

1. Remove the center console screws and it pull away to expose the shift control cable and turnbuckle.

2. Adjust the length of the control cable by turning the turnbuckle, located at the front bottom of the shift lever assembly.

After adjustment, the cable and turnbuckle should twist toward the left (driver's) side of the vehicle when shifted toward the **2** position and toward the right side when shifted into the **R** position.

Adjustment — 3-Speed and 4-Speed

1. Remove the shift console.

2. Shift into **REVERSE** and remove the lock-pin from the cable adjuster.

3. With the lock-pin removed, the hole in the adjuster, from which the lock-pin was removed, should be perfectly aligned with the corresponding hole in the shift cable.

4. If they are not perfectly aligned, turn the adjusting nuts as required.

5. Install the lock-pin.

NOTE: *If there is any binding on the lock-pin as it is installed, there is some misalignment. Check and/or adjust as required.*

THROTTLE CABLE ADJUSTMENT
Carbureted Models

1. Attach a weight of approximately 3 lbs. to the accelerator pedal. Raise the pedal, then release it, this will allow the weight to remove the normal free play from the throttle cable.

2. Secure the throttle control cable with clamps. Remove the air intake duct.

3. Lay the end of the throttle control cable over the the shock tower. Adjust the distance between the throttle cable end and the first locknut to 85.0-85.5mm on all models except the 1988-89 Prelude which is 158.0mm.

4. Insert the end of the throttle control cable into the groove of the throttle control lever. Insert the throttle control cable in the bracket and secure it with the last locknut. Be sure the cable is not kinked or twisted.

5. Check the cable moves freely by depressing the accelerator. Start the engine and check the synchronization between the carburetor and the throttle control cable.

6. The throttle control lever should start to move as the engine speed is increased.

7. If the throttle control lever moves before the engine speed increases, turn the cable top locknut counterclockwise and tighten the bottom locknut.

8. If the throttle control lever moves after the engine speed increases, turn the cable top locknut clockwise and tighten the bottom locknut.

Fuel Injected Models

1. Loosen both locknuts on the throttle control cable. Press down on the throttle control cable until it stops.

2. While pressing down on the throttle control lever, pull on the throttle link to check the amount of throttle control cable free play.

3. Remove all the throttle control cable free play by gradually turning the top locknut.

4. Keep turning the top locknut until no movement can be felt in the throttle link, while continuing to press down on the throttle control lever, pull open the throttle link. The control lever should start to move at precisely the same time as the link. When you get to this point, tighten up the bottom locknut.

NOTE: *The correct (FINE TUNE) adjustment of the throttle control cable is critical for proper operation of the transaxle and lockup torque converter.*

5. Depress the accelerator to the floor. While depressed, check that there is play in the throttle control lever (more than 2mm). Check that the cable moves freely by depressing the accelerator pedal.

Transaxle
REMOVAL AND INSTALLATION

The automatic transaxle is removed in the same basic manner as the manual transaxle (refer to for Manual Transaxle, Removal and Installation). The following exceptions should be noted during automatic transaxle removal and installation.

1. Remove the center console and control rod pin.

2. Remove the front floor center mat and control cable bracket nuts.

3. Raise and support the front of the vehicle on jackstands.

4. Remove the two selector lever bracket nuts from the front side.

5. Loosen the bolts securing the control cable holder and support beam and disconnect the control cable.

6. Disconnect the transaxle cooler lines from the transaxle.

7. Remove the transaxle together with the engine. Remove the engine mounts and torque converter case cover.

8. Remove the starter motor and separate the transaxle from the engine.

9. To install, reverse the removal procedures. Pay close attention to the following points:

   a. Be sure that the stator hub is correctly located and moves smoothly. The stator shaft can be used for this purpose.

   b. Align the stator, stator shaft, main shaft and torque converter turbine serrations.

   c. After installation of the engine/transaxle unit in vehicle, make all required adjustments.

Halfshafts
REMOVAL AND INSTALLATION

The front driveshaft assembly consists of a sub-axle shaft and a driveshaft with two universal joints.

A constant velocity ball joint is used for both universal joints, which are factory packed with special grease and enclosed in sealed rubber boots. The outer joint cannot be disassembled except for removal of the boot.

1. Remove the hubcap from the front wheel and then remove the center cap.

2. Pull out the 4mm cotter pin and loosen but do not remove the spindle nut.

3. Raise and support the front of the vehicle on jackstands.

4. Remove the wheel lug nuts and the wheel.

5. Remove the spindle nut.

6. Drain the transaxle.

7. Using a Ball Joint Remover tool, remove the lower arm ball joints from the knuckle.

WARNING: *On Civic models (1984-88), make sure that a floor jack is positioned securely under the lower control arm, at the ball joint. Otherwise, the lower control arm may "jump" suddenly away from the steering knuckle as the ball joint is removed.*

On Prelude models (1983-88), remove the damper fork bolt, damper locking bolt and the damper fork.

8. To remove the driveshaft, hold the knuckle and pull it toward you. Then slide the driveshaft out of the knuckle. Pry the CV joint out about ½". Pull the inboard joint side of the driveshaft out of the differential case.

9. To install, reverse the removal procedures. If either the inboard or outboard joint boot bands have been removed for inspection or disassembly of the joint (only the inboard joint can be disassembled), be sure to repack the joint with a sufficient amount of bearing grease.

WARNING: *Make sure the CV-joint sub-axle bottoms so that the spring clip may hold the sub-axle securely in the transaxle.*

TRANSFER CASE
REMOVAL AND INSTALLATION
Civic Wagon 4WD

1. Raise the car and support on jackstands.

2. Remove the splash shield from beneath the engine.

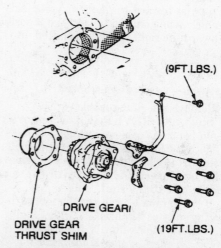

(9FT.LBS.)

DRIVE GEAR

DRIVE GEAR
THRUST SHIM

(19FT.LBS.)

Transfer case drive gear side assembly

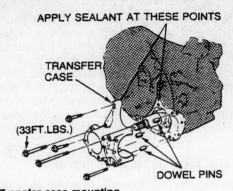

APPLY SEALANT AT THESE POINTS

TRANSFER CASE

(33FT.LBS.)

DOWEL PINS

Transfer case mounting

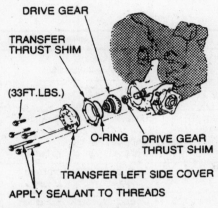

DRIVE GEAR

TRANSFER THRUST SHIM

(33FT.LBS.)

O-RING   DRIVE GEAR THRUST SHIM

TRANSFER LEFT SIDE COVER

APPLY SEALANT TO THREADS

Transfer case left side assembly

3. Drain the oil from both the engine and the transmission.

4. Remove the head pipe from the engine.

5. Disconnect the driveshaft from the transmission.

6. Remove the splash pan from beneath the transmission.

7. Remove the left side cover from the transfer case.

8. Remove the driven gear from the transfer case.

9. Remove the transfer case from the clutch housing.

10. To install, replace the components beneath the transfer left side cover in the following order:

   a. Drive gear thrust shim

   b. Drive gear (coat with oil)

   c. O-ring

   d. Transfer thrust shim

   e. Transfer left side cover

11. Install the following components on the drive output side of the transfer case:

   a. O-ring

   b. Drive gear thrust shim

   c. Drive gear (coat with oil)

DRIVELINE

Front Intermediate Shaft

REMOVAL AND INSTALLATION

Civic Wagon 4WD and Prelude 4WS

1. Raise the car and support on jackstands.

2. Drain the oil from the transmission.

3. Remove the three 10mm bolts from the bearing support.

4. Lower the bearing support close to the steering gearbox and remove the intermediate shaft from the differential.

NOTE: *To avoid damage to the differential oil seal, keep the intermediate shaft in the horizontal position until it is clear of the differential.*

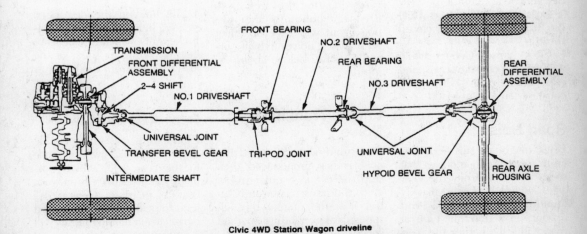

FRONT BEARING

TRANSMISSION

FRONT DIFFERENTIAL ASSEMBLY

2–4 SHIFT

NO.1 DRIVESHAFT

NO.2 DRIVESHAFT

REAR BEARING

NO.3 DRIVESHAFT

REAR DIFFERENTIAL ASSEMBLY

UNIVERSAL JOINT

TRANSFER BEVEL GEAR

TRI-POD JOINT

UNIVERSAL JOINT

INTERMEDIATE SHAFT

HYPOID BEVEL GEAR

REAR AXLE HOUSING

Civic 4WD Station Wagon driveline

REAR AXLE

Understanding Drive Axles

The drive axle is a special type of transmission that reduces the speed of the drive from the engine and transmission and divides the power to the wheels. Power enters the axle from the driveshaft via the companion flange. The flange is mounted on the drive pinion shaft. The drive pinion shaft and gear which carry the power into the differential turn at engine speed. The gear on the end of the pinion shaft drives a large ring gear the axis of rotation of which is 90° away from the of the pinion. The pinion and gear reduce the gear ratio of the axle, and change the direction of rotation to turn the axle shafts which drive both wheels. The axle gear ratio is found by dividing the

Troubleshooting Basic Driveshaft and Rear Axle Problems

When abnormal vibrations or noises are detected in the driveshaft area, this chart can be used to help diagnose possible causes. Remember that other components such as wheels, tires, rear axle and suspension can also produce similar conditions.

BASIC DRIVESHAFT PROBLEMS

Problem	Cause	Solution
Shudder as car accelerates from stop or low speed	• Loose U-joint • Defective center bearing	• Replace U-joint • Replace center bearing
Loud clunk in driveshaft when shifting gears	• Worn U-joints	• Replace U-joints
Roughness or vibration at any speed	• Out-of-balance, bent or dented driveshaft • Worn U-joints • U-joint clamp bolts loose	• Balance or replace driveshaft • Replace U-joints • Tighten U-joint clamp bolts
Squeaking noise at low speeds	• Lack of U-joint lubrication	• Lubricate U-joint; if problem persists, replace U-joint
Knock or clicking noise	• U-joint or driveshaft hitting frame tunnel • Worn CV joint	• Correct overloaded condition • Replace CV joint

BASIC REAR AXLE PROBLEMS

First, determine when the noise is most noticeable.

Drive Noise: Produced under vehicle acceleration.

Coast Noise: Produced while the car coasts with a closed throttle.

Float Noise: Occurs while maintaining constant car speed (just enough to keep speed constant) on a level road.

Road Noise

Brick or rough surfaced concrete roads produce noises that seem to come from the rear axle. Road noise is usually identical in Drive or Coast and driving on a different type of road will tell whether the road is the problem.

Tire Noise

Tire noises are often mistaken for rear axle problems. Snow treads or unevenly worn tires produce vibrations seeming to originate elsewhere. **Temporarily** inflating the tires to 40 lbs will significantly alter tire noise, but will have no effect on rear axle noises (which normally cease below about 30 mph).

Engine/Transmission Noise

Determine at what speed the noise is most pronounced, then stop the car in a quiet place. With the transmission in Neutral, run the engine through speeds corresponding to road speeds where the noise was noticed. Noises produced with the car standing still are coming from the engine or transmission.

Front Wheel Bearings

While holding the car speed steady, lightly apply the footbrake; this will often decease bearing noise, as some of the load is taken from the bearing.

Rear Axle Noises

Eliminating other possible sources can narrow the cause to the rear axle, which normally produces noise from worn gears or bearings. Gear noises tend to peak in a narrow speed range, while bearing noises will usually vary in pitch with engine speeds.

NOISE DIAGNOSIS

The Noise Is	Most Probably Produced By
· Identical under Drive or Coast	· Road surface, tires or front wheel bearings
· Different depending on road surface	· Road surface or tires
· Lower as the car speed is lowered	· Tires
· Similar with car standing or moving	· Engine or transmission
· A vibration	· Unbalanced tires, rear wheel bearing, unbalanced driveshaft or worn U-joint
· A knock or click about every 2 tire revolutions	· Rear wheel bearing
· Most pronounced on turns	· Damaged differential gears
· A steady low-pitched whirring or scraping, starting at low speeds	· Damaged or worn pinion bearing
· A chattering vibration on turns	· Wrong differential lubricant or worn clutch plates (limited slip rear axle)
· Noticed only in Drive, Coast or Float conditions	· Worn ring gear and/or pinion gear

number of pinion gear teeth into the number of ring gear teeth.

The ring gear drives the differential case. The case provides the two mounting points for the ends of a pinion shaft on which are mounted two pinion gears. The pinion gears drive the two side gears, one of which is located on the inner end of each axle shaft.

By driving the axle shafts through the arrangement, the differential allows the outer drive wheel to turn faster than the inner drive wheel in a turn.

The main drive pinion and the side bearings, which bear the weight of the differential case, are shimmed to provide proper bearing preload, and to position the pinion and ring gears properly.

WARNING: *The proper adjustment of the relationship of the ring and pinion gears is critical. It should be attempted only by those with extensive equipment and/or experience.*

Limited slip differentials include clutches which tend to link each axle shaft to the differential case. Clutches may be engaged either by spring action or by pressure produced by the torque on the axles during a turn. During turning on a dry pavement, the effects of the clutches are overcome, and each wheel turns at the required speed. When slippage occurs at either wheel, however, the clutches will transmit some of the power to the wheel which has the greater amount of traction. Because of the presence of clutches, limited slip units require a special lubricant.

Determining Axle Ratio

The drive axle is said to have a certain axle ratio. This number (usually a whole number and a decimal fraction) is actually a comparison of the number of gear teeth on the ring gear and the pinion gear. For example, a 4.11 rear means that theoretically, there are 4.11 teeth on the ring gear and one tooth on the pinion gear or, put another way, the driveshaft must turn 4.11 times to turn the wheels once. Actually, on a 4.11 rear, there might be 37 teeth on the ring gear and 9 teeth on the pinion gear. By dividing the number of teeth on the pinion gear into the number of teeth on the ring gear, the numerical axle ratio (4.11) is obtained. This also provides a good method of ascertaining exactly what axle ratio one is dealing with.

Another method of determining gear ratio is to jack up and support the car so that both rear wheels are off the ground. Make a chalk mark on the rear wheel and the driveshaft. Put the transmission in neutral. Turn the rear wheel one complete turn and count the number of turns that the driveshaft makes. The number of turns that the driveshaft makes in one complete revolution of the rear wheel is an approximation of the rear axle ratio.

Differential Overhaul

A differential overhaul is a complex, highly technical, and time-consuming operation, which requires a great many tools, extensive knowledge of the unit and the way it works, and a high degree of mechanical experience and ability. It is highly advisable that the amateur mechanic not attempt any work on the differential unit.

Rear Driveshafts

REMOVAL AND INSTALLATION

Civic Wagon 4WD

1. Raise the car and support it on jackstands.
2. Mark the position of the driveshafts on both of the flanges for reassembly.
3. Remove the No. 1 driveshaft protector.
4. Remove the No. 3 driveshaft by disconnecting the U-joints.

5. Remove the bolts holding the rear bearing support, then remove the No. 2 driveshaft.

6. Remove the bolts holding the front bearing support, then remove the No. 1 driveshaft by disconnecting the U-joint.

7. To install, reverse the removal procedures.

Rear Halfshafts
REMOVAL AND INSTALLATION
Prelude 4WS

1. Loosen the rear wheels lug nuts. Raise and support the rear of the vehicle safely. Remove the rear wheels. Drain the oil from rear gear box (if necessary.

2. Turn the rear wheel being worked on to its full outward position. Using a suitable tie rod separator, remove the tie rod from the rear steering knuckle.

3. Slide the rear steering joint guard (boot) towards the front. Remove the steering yoke bolt.

4. Remove the rear halfshaft from the rear steering box. Repeat this procedure to the opposite side.

5. Installation is the reverse order of the removal procedure.

Rear Axle Shafts and Bearings
REMOVAL
Civic Wagon 4WD

1. Raise the rear of the car and support it securely on jackstands.

2. Remove the rear wheel and tire assembly, then remove the brake drum.

3. Disconnect and plug the brake line from the brake cylinder.

4. Remove the brake shoes and the parking brake cable.

5. Remove the axle shaft retainer 10mm self-locking nuts.

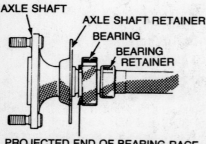

PROJECTED END OF BEARING RACE

Rear axle and bearing assembly

6. Using a slide hammer, pull the axle shaft from the axle housing.

7. Remove the axle seal from the axle housing.

8. Grind the bearing retainer on the axle down until it's about 0.5mm thick.

NOTE: *Be careful not to damage the axle during these procedures.*

9. Place the axle in a vice, and split the bearing retainer using a chisel and hammer.

10. Place the axle and bearing in a hydraulic press with the appropriate adapters and press the bearing off the axle.

INSTALLATION
Civic Wagon 4WD

1. Drive a new seal into the rear axle housing.

2. Coat the sealing lip of the oil seal with grease.

3. Thoroughly clean the axle shaft; install the axle retainer, the bearing and the bearing retainer on the axle.

NOTE: *DO NOT oil or grease the contact surfaces of the axle, bearing or the bearing retainer. The projected end of the bearing race must face outward.*

4. Using the appropriate adapters and a hydraulic press, press the new bearing onto the axle shaft.

5. Measure the following dimensions:
   a. The width of the axle bearing outer race.
   b. The thickness of the backing plate.
   c. The depth from the edge of the axle housing to the bearing seating surface.

X	Shims required
−0.16−0.10 mm (−0.0063−0.0039 in.)	None
0.10−0.25 mm (0.0039−0.0098 in.)	Use one 0.1 mm shim
0.25−0.40 mm (0.0098−0.0157 in.)	Use one 0.25 mm shim

Part Numbers:
0.1 mm shim: 42150−SC2−000
0.25 mm shim: 42154−SC2−000

Rear axle shim chart

Using the above measurements calculate the correct shim thickness using the following formula:
$$a - (b + c) = X.$$

6. Apply a thin coat of sealant to the backing plate face of the shim.

7. Apply a thin coat of sealant to the axle retainer contacting the face of the shim.

8. Push the axle into the axle housing aligning its splines with the differential side gear splines.

NOTE: *Before installing the axle, coat the inner corner of the bearing housing seat with sealant.*

9. Using a slide hammer with the appropriate adapters install the axle into the axle housing.

10. Install and tighten the bolts on the axle retainer.

11. Install the brake shoes and the parking brake cable.

12. Reconnect the brake line to the wheel cylinder.

13. Install the brake drum and bleed the brakes.

14. Install the wheel and lower the car to the ground.

Suspension and Steering

FRONT SUSPENSION

All models, except Prelude 1983-88 and Civic 1984-88, use a MacPherson strut type front suspension. Each steering knuckle is suspended by a lower control arm at the bottom and a combined coil spring/shock absorber unit at the top. A front stabilizer bar, mounted between each lower control arm and the body, doubles as a locating rod for the suspension. Caster and camber are not adjustable and are fixed by the location of the strut assemblies in their respective sheet metal towers.

The Prelude 1983-88 uses a completely redesigned front suspension. A double wishbone system, the lower wishbone consists of a forged transverse link with a locating stabilizer bar. The lower end of the shock absorber has a fork shape to allow the driveshaft to pass through it. The upper arm is located in the wheel well and is twist mounted, angled forward from its inner mount, to clear the shock absorber.

The Civic 1984-88 models also use a redesigned front suspension. This change was made to lower the hood line, thus making the vehicle more aerodynamic. The new suspension consists of two independent torsion bars and front shock absorbers similar to a front strut assembly but without a spring. Both lower forged radius arms are connected with a stabilizer bar.

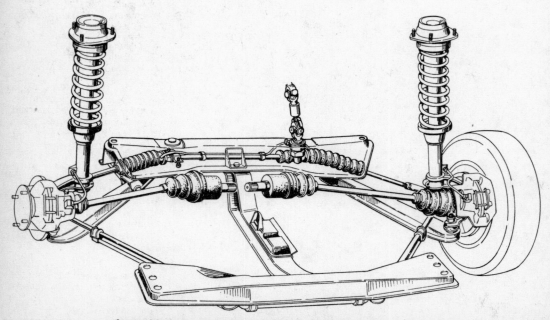

Assembled view of front suspension and steering assemblies

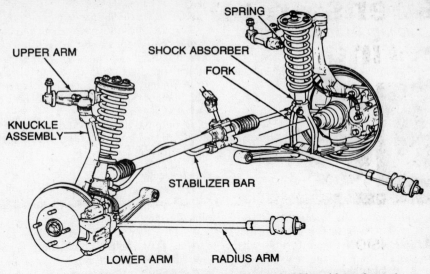

SPRING

UPPER ARM

SHOCK ABSORBER

FORK

KNUCKLE
ASSEMBLY

STABILIZER BAR

LOWER ARM   RADIUS ARM

Front suspension—1983 and later Prelude, and 1986 and later Accord

Troubleshooting Basic Steering and Suspension Problems

Problem	Cause	Solution
Hard steering (steering wheel is hard to turn)	• Low or uneven tire pressure • Loose power steering pump drive belt • Low or incorrect power steering fluid • Incorrect front end alignment • Defective power steering pump • Bent or poorly lubricated front end parts	• Inflate tires to correct pressure • Adjust belt • Add fluid as necessary • Have front end alignment checked/adjusted • Check pump • Lubricate and/or replace defective parts
Loose steering (too much play in the steering wheel)	• Loose wheel bearings • Loose or worn steering linkage • Faulty shocks • Worn ball joints	• Adjust wheel bearings • Replace worn parts • Replace shocks • Replace ball joints
Car veers or wanders (car pulls to one side with hands off the steering wheel)	• Incorrect tire pressure • Improper front end alignment • Loose wheel bearings • Loose or bent front end components • Faulty shocks	• Inflate tires to correct pressure • Have front end alignment checked/adjusted • Adjust wheel bearings • Replace worn components • Replace shocks
Wheel oscillation or vibration transmitted through steering wheel	• Improper tire pressures • Tires out of balance • Loose wheel bearings • Improper front end alignment • Worn or bent front end components	• Inflate tires to correct pressure • Have tires balanced • Adjust wheel bearings • Have front end alignment checked/adjusted • Replace worn parts
Uneven tire wear	• Incorrect tire pressure • Front end out of alignment • Tires out of balance	• Inflate tires to correct pressure • Have front end alignment checked/adjusted • Have tires balanced

Torsion Bars

REMOVAL AND INSTALLATION

Civic 1984-88

1. Raise and support the front of the vehicle on jackstands.

2. Remove the height adjusting nut and the torque tube holder.

3. Remove the 33mm circlip.

4. Remove the torsion bar cap, then, the torsion bar clip by tapping the bar out of the torque tube.

NOTE: *The torsion bar will slide easier if you move the lower arm up and down.*

5. Tap the torsion bar backward, out of the torque tube and remove the torque tube.

6. Install a new seal onto the torque tube. Coat the torque tube seal and torque with grease, then, install them on the rear beams.

7. Grease the ends of the torsion bar and insert into the torque tube from the back.

8. Align the projection on the torque tube splines with the cutout in the torsion bar splines and insert the torsion bar approximately 10mm.

NOTE: *The torsion bar will slide easier if the lower arm is moved up and down.*

9. Install the torsion bar clip and cap, then, install the 30mm circlip and the torque tube cap.

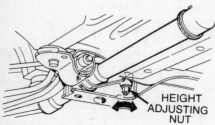

Torsion bar adjustment—1984 and later Civic

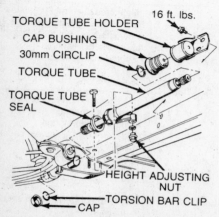

Torsion bar assembly—1984 and later Civic

NOTE: *Push the torsion bar to the front so there is no clearance between the torque tube and the 30mm circlip.*

10. Coat the cap bushing with grease and install it on the torque tube. Install the torque tube holder.

11. Temporarily tighten the height adjusting nut.

12. Remove the jackstands and lower the vehicle to the ground. Adjust the torsion bar spring height.

ADJUSTMENT

1. Measure the torsion bar spring height between the ground and the highest point of the wheel arch.
- COUPE (CRX) 639-649mm.
- HATCHBACK 641-651mm.
- SEDAN 646-656mm.
- WAGON 644-654mm.

2. If the spring height does not meet the specifications above, make the following adjustment.

    a. Raise and support the front of the vehicle on jackstands with the wheels off the ground.

    b. Adjust the spring height by turning the height adjusting nut. Tightening the nut raises the height and loosening the nut lowers the height.

NOTE: *The height varies 5mm per revolution of the adjusting nut.*

Lower the front wheels to the ground, then, bounce the vehicle up and down several times and recheck the spring height to see if it is within specifications.

Shock Absorbers

REMOVAL AND INSTALLATION

Civic 1984-88

1. Raise and support the front of the vehicle on jackstands. Remove the front wheels.

2. Remove the brake hose clamp bolt.

3. Using a floor jack, place it beneath the lower control arm to support it.

4. Remove the lower shock retaining bolt from the steering knuckle, then, slowly lower the jack.

WARNING: *Be sure the jack is positioned securely beneath the lower control arm at the ball joint. Otherwise, the tension from the torsion bar may cause the lower control arm to suddenly "jump" away from the shock absorber as the pinch bolt is removed.*

5. Compress the shock absorber by hand, then, remove the two upper lock nuts and shock absorber.

6. To install, reverse the removal procedures, taking note of the following:

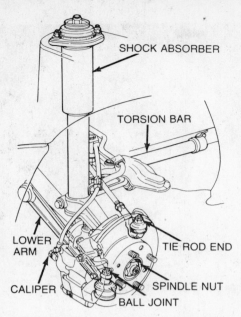

Front suspension—1984 and later Civic

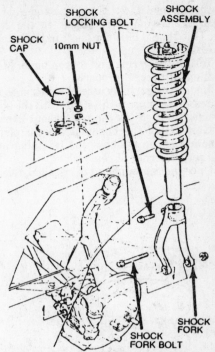

Front shock mounting—1983 and later
Prelude, and 1986 and later Accord

a. Use new self locking nuts on the top of the shock assembly and torque to 28 ft. lbs.

b. Tighten the lower pinch bolt to 47 ft. lbs.

c. Install and tighten the brake hose clamp to 16 ft. lbs.

Accord 1986-88 and Prelude 1983-88

1. Raise and support the front of the vehicle on jackstands. Remove the front wheels.

2. Remove the shock absorber locking bolt.

3. Remove the shock fork bolt and the shock fork.

4. Remove the shock absorber assembly.

5. To install, reverse the removal procedures, taking note of the following:

a. Align the shock absorber aligning tab with the slot in the shock absorber fork.

b. The mounting base bolt should be tightened with the weight of the vehicle placed on the shock.

c. Torque the upper mounting bolts to 29 ft. lbs., the shock locking bolt to 32 ft. lbs. and the shock fork bolt to 47 ft. lbs.

INSPECTION

1. Check for wear or damage to bushings.

2. Check for oil leaks from the shocks.

3. Check all rubber parts for wear or damage.

4. Bounce the vehicle to check shock absorbing effectiveness. The vehicle should continue to bounce for no more than two cycles.

MacPherson Struts

REMOVAL AND INSTALLATION

1. Raise and support the front of the vehicle on jackstands. Remove the front wheels.

2. Disconnect the brake pipe at the strut and remove the brake hose retaining clip.

3. Remove the strut-to-steering knuckle bolt, then, push down firmly while tapping it with a hammer until the knuckle is free of the strut.

4. Remove the strut-to-body nuts and the strut from the vehicle.

5. To install, reverse the removal procedures. Be sure to properly match the mating surface of the strut and the knuckle notch.

OVERHAUL

1. Disassemble the strut according to the procedure given in the rear strut disassembly section.

2. Remove the rubber cover and the center retaining nuts.

3. Slowly release the compressor and remove the spring.

4. Remove the upper mounting cap, washers, thrust plates, bearings and bushing.

NOTE: *Before discarding any parts, check a parts list to determine which parts are available as replacements.*

5. To reassemble, 1st: pull the strut shaft all

the way out, hold it in this position and slide the rubber bumper down the shaft to the strut body. This should hold the shaft in the extended position.

6. Install the spring and its top plate. Make sure the spring seats properly.

7. Install the partially assembled strut in the compressor. Compress the strut until the shaft protrudes through the top plate about 25mm.

8. Now install the bushings, thrust plates, top mounting cap washers and retaining nuts in the reverse order of removal.

9. Once the retaining nut is installed, release

Upper strut removal points

Front strut

Lower strut retaining bolt (arrow)

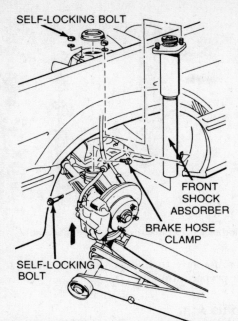

SELF-LOCKING BOLT

FRONT SHOCK ABSORBER

BRAKE HOSE CLAMP

SELF-LOCKING BOLT

Front shock mounting—1984 and later Civic

the tension on the compressor and loosen the thumbscrew on the bottom plate. Separate the bottom plates and remove the compressor.

INSPECTION

1. Check for wear or damage to bushings and needle bearings.
2. Check for oil leaks from the struts.
3. Check all rubber parts for wear or damage.
4. Bounce the vehicle to check shock absorbing effectiveness. The vehicle should continue to bounce for no more than two cycles.

Lower Ball Joint
INSPECTION

Check ball joint play as follows:
   a. Raise and support the front of the vehicle on jackstands.
   b. Using a dial indicator clamp it onto the lower control arm and place the indicator tip on the steering knuckle, near the ball joint.
   c. Using a pry bar, place it between the lower control arm and the steering knuckle.
   d. Work the ball joint to check for looseness; if the play exceeds 0.5mm, replace the ball joint.

LUBRICATION

1. Remove the screw plug from the bottom of the ball joint and install a grease nipple.
2. Lubricate the ball joint with NLGI No. 2 multipurpose type grease.

3. Remove the nipple and reinstall the screw plug.
4. Repeat for the other ball joint.

REMOVAL AND INSTALLATION

All Except Accord 1986-88 and Prelude 1983-88

1. Raise and support the front of the vehicle on jackstands.
2. Remove the front wheel.
3. Remove the cotter pin and ball joint castle nut.
4. Using a Ball Joint Remover tool, separate the ball joint from the steering knuckle.
5. To install, reverse the removal procedures. Torque the ball joint nut to 29-35 ft. lbs.. Be sure to grease the ball joint.

Accord 1986-88 and Prelude 1983-88

NOTE: *This procedure is performed after the removal of the steering knuckle and requires the use of the following special tools or their equivalent: Ball Joint Remover/Installation tool No. 07965-SB00100, Ball Joint Removal Base tool No. 07965-SB00200, Ball Joint Installation tool No. 07965-SB00300 and Clip Guide tool No. 07974-SA50700.*

1. Pry the snapring off and remove the boot.
2. Pry the snapring out of the groove in the ball joint.
3. Using the Ball Joint Removal tool No. 07965-SB00100 with the large end facing out, tighten the ball joint nut.
4. Position the Ball Joint Removal Base tool No. 07965-SB00200 on the ball joint and set the assembly in a large vise. Press the ball joint out of the steering knuckle.
5. Position the new ball joint into the hole of the steering knuckle.
6. Install the Ball Joint Installer tool No. 07965-SB00300 with the small end facing out.
7. Position the Ball Joint Installation Base tool No. 07965-SB00100 on the ball joint and set the assembly in a large vise. Press the ball joint into the steering knuckle.
8. Seat the snapring in the groove of the ball joint.
9. Using the Clip Guide tool No. 07974-SA50700, install the boot and snapring.

Upper Control Arm and Bushing
REMOVAL AND INSTALLATION

1988-89 Civic

1. Raise and support the front of the vehicle safely.
2. Remove the front wheels. Rock the upper ball joint back and forth, replace the upper control arm bushings as follows if there is any play.
3. Remove the self locking nuts, upper con-

trol arm bolts and upper control anchor bolts. Separate the upper ball joint using a suitable ball joint separator.

4. Place the upper control arm assembly into a suitable holding fixture and drive out the upper arm bushing.

5. Drive the new upper arm bushing into the the upper arm anchor bolts. Be sure to center the bushing so that 9mm protrudes from each side of the anchor bolt.

6. Install the upper control arm assembly and install the upper arm bolts, then tighten the self locking nuts. Be sure to align the upper arm anchor bolt with the mark on the upper arm.

1983-89 Prelude and 1986-89 Accord

1. Raise and support the front of the vehicle safely.

2. Remove the front wheels. Rock the upper ball joint back and forth, replace the upper control arm bushings as follows if there is any play.

3. Remove the self locking nuts, upper control arm bolts and upper control anchor bolts. Separate the upper ball joint using a suitable ball joint separator.

4. Place the upper control arm assembly into a suitable holding fixture and remove the self locking nut, upper arm bolt, upper arm anchor bolts and housing seals.

5. Remove the upper arm collar. Drive out the upper arm bushing, using a suitable drift.

6. Replace the upper control arm bushings, bushing seals and upper control arm collar with new ones. Be sure to coat the ends and the insides of the upper control arm bushings, and the sealing lips of the upper control arm bushing with grease.

7. After Step 6 is completed, apply sealant to the threads and underside of the upper arm bolt heads and self locking nut. Install the upper arm bolt and tighten the self locking nut.

8. To complete installation reverse the removal procedure.

Lower Control Arm and Stabilizer Bar

REMOVAL AND INSTALLATION

1. Raise and support the front of the vehicle on jackstands. Remove the front wheels.

2. Disconnect the lower arm ball joint. Be careful not to damage the seal.

3. Remove the stabilizer bar retaining brackets, starting with the center brackets.

4. Remove the lower arm pivot bolt.

5. Disconnect the radius rod and remove the lower arm.

6. To install, reverse the removal proce-

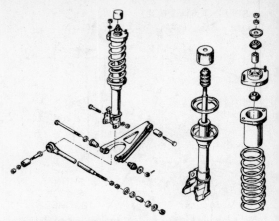

Exploded view of lower control arm assembly

dures. Be sure to tighten the components to their proper torque.

Radius Arm

REMOVAL AND INSTALLATION

Civic 1984-88

1. Raise and support the front of the vehicle on jackstands. Remove the front wheels.

2. Place a floor jack beneath the lower control arm, then, remove the ball joint cotter pin and nut.

WARNING: *Be sure to place the jack securely beneath the lower control arm at the ball joint. Otherwise, the tension from the torsion bar may cause the arm to suddenly "jump" away from the steering knuckle as the ball joint is removed.*

3. Using a Ball Joint Remover tool No.

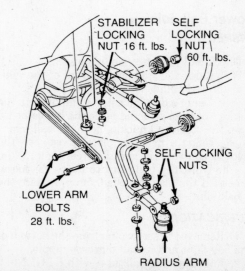

STABILIZER LOCKING NUT 16 ft. lbs.

SELF LOCKING NUT 60 ft. lbs.

SELF LOCKING NUTS

LOWER ARM BOLTS 28 ft. lbs.

RADIUS ARM

Radius arm—1984 and later Civic

Torque Specifications

Part(s)	Torque (ft. lbs.)
Lower ball joint retaining nut	
Civic	22–29
Accord and Prelude	33
Lower control arm-to-body mount bolts	
Civic	25–36
Accord and Prelude	40
Front radius rod-to-knuckle bolt	40
Rear radius rod-to-carrier bolt	40–54
Rear radius rod-to-body bolt	40
Front stabilizer mount bolts	5–9
Strut center nut (front and rear)	40–50
Strut to body retaining bolts (front and rear)	16
Front strut-to-knuckle retaining bolt	36–43
Rear strut-to-carrier mount bolts	26–35
Rear strut-to-control arm bolt	36–47

07965-SB00100, remove the ball joint from the steering knuckle.

4. Remove the radius arm locking nuts and the stabilizer locking nut, then, separate the radius arm from the stabilizer bar.

5. Remove the lower arm bolts and the radius arm by pulling it down and forward.

6. To install, reverse the removal procedures. Tighten all the rubber bushings and dampened parts only after the vehicle is placed back on the ground.

Knuckle and Spindle

REMOVAL AND INSTALLATION

1. Raise and support the front of the vehicle on jackstands. Remove the front wheel.

2. Remove the spindle nut cotter pin and the spindle nut.

3. Remove the brake caliper bolts and the caliper from the steering knuckle. DO NOT allow the caliper hang by the brake hose, support it with a length of wire.

NOTE: *In case it is necessary to remove the disc, hub, bearings and/or outer dust seal, use Steps 4 and 5 given below. You will need a hydraulic press for this.*

4. Install a hub puller attachment against the hub with the lug nuts.

5. Attach a slide hammer in the center hole of the attachment and press the hub, with the disc attached, from the steering knuckle.

6. Using the Ball Joint Remover tool, remove the tie rod from the steering knuckle; use care not to damage the ball joint seals.

7. Using the Ball Joint Remover tool, remove the lower arm from the steering knuckle.

8. Loosen the strut-to-steering knuckle lockbolt. Using a hammer, tap the top of the steering knuckle and slide it off the shock.

9. Remove the steering knuckle and hub, if still attached, by sliding the driveshaft out of the hub.

10. To install, reverse the removal procedures. If the hub was removed, visually check the steering knuckle for visible signs of wear and/or damage and the condition of the inner bearing dust seals.

Front Hub and Bearings

CAUTION: *Brake shoes contain asbestos, which has been determined to be a cancer causing agent. Never clean the brake surfaces with compressed air! Avoid inhaling any dust from any brake surface! When cleaning brake surfaces, use a commercially available brake cleaning fluid.*

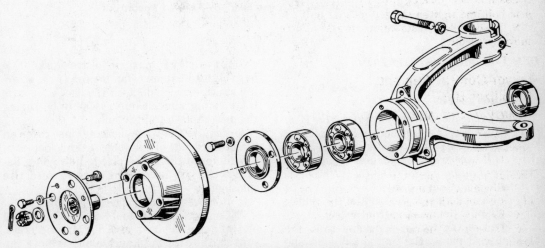

Exploded view of front wheel bearings, rotor, and related parts

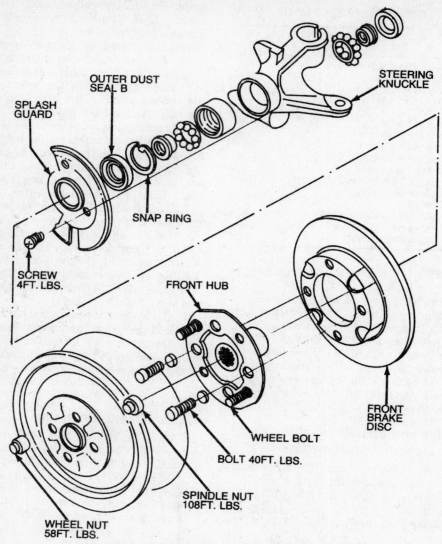

SPLASH GUARD

OUTER DUST SEAL B

STEERING KNUCKLE

SNAP RING

SCREW 4FT. LBS.

FRONT HUB

FRONT BRAKE DISC

WHEEL BOLT

BOLT 40FT. LBS.

SPINDLE NUT 108FT. LBS.

WHEEL NUT 58FT. LBS.

Front steering knuckle, hub and bearing—1980–81 Accord

REMOVAL AND INSTALLATION

All Models Except Civic 1982-88, Accord 1983-88 and Prelude 1982-88

NOTE: *The following procedure for the Honda wheel bearing removal and installation necessitates the use of an hydraulic press. You will have to go to a machine or auto shop equipped with a press. DO NOT attempt this procedure without a press.*

1. Raise and support the front of the vehicle on jackstands. Remove the front wheel.
2. Remove the caliper assembly from the brake disc. Separate the tie rod ball joint and lower ball joint from the knuckle.

3. Loosen the front strut-to-steering knuckle bolt. Using a hammer, tap the top of the steering knuckle and slide it off the shock. Remove the steering knuckle/hub assembly by sliding the driveshaft out of the hub.
4. Remove the wheel bearing dust cover on the inboard side of the steering knuckle.
5. Remove the brake disc-to-hub bolts. Remove the splashguard screws and the splashguard.
6. Remove the outer bearing retainer.
7. Using the Special tool No. 07965-6340300 or two support plates and a hydraulic press, support the steering knuckle and remove the wheel bearings. Make sure that the plates do

not overlap the outer bearing race. Using the Driver tool No. 07947-6340400 and Handle tool No. 07949-6110000, remove the bearings.

NOTE: *Whenever the wheel bearings are removed, always replace with a new set of bearings and outer dust seal.*

8. Using wheel bearing grease, pack each bearing before installing.

9. Using the Driver tool No. 07947-6340400, the Handle tool No. 07949-6110000 and the Installation Base tool No. 07965-634040, press the bearings into the steering knuckle.

NOTE: *The front wheel bearings are the angular contact type. It is important that they be installed with the manufacturer's markings facing inward.*

10. Press to the hub into the steering knuckle.

11. To complete the installation, reverse the removal procedures.

CLEANING AND REPACKING

1. Clean all old grease from the driveshafts spindles on the vehicle.

2. Remove all old grease from the hub/steering knuckle, then, thoroughly dry and wipe clean all components.

3. When fitting new bearings, you must pack them with wheel bearing grease. To do this, place a glob of grease in your palm, then, holding one of the bearings in your other hand, drag the face of the bearing heavily through the grease. This must be done to work as much grease as possible through the ball bearings and the cage. Turn the bearing and continue to pull it through the grease, until the grease is thoroughly packed between the bearing balls and the cage, all around the bearing. Repeat this operation until all of the bearings are packed with grease.

4. Pack the inside of the rotor and knuckle hub with a moderate amount of grease. DO NOT overload the hub with grease.

5. Apply a small amount of grease to the spindle and to the lip of the inner seal before installing.

6. To install the bearings, check the above procedures. Adjust the spindle nut torque.

1982-83 Civic
1983-85 Accord
1982 Prelude

1. Pry the lock tab away from the spindle, then loosen the nut. Slightly loosen the lug nuts.

2. Raise the front of the car and support it with safety stands. Remove the front wheel and spindle nut.

3. Remove the bolts retaining the brake cali-

per and remove the caliper from the knuckle. Do not let the caliper hang by the brake hose, support it with a length of wire.

4. Remove the disc brake rotor retaining screws (if so equipped). Screw two 8 x 1.25 x 12mm bolts into the disc brake removal holes, and turn the bolts to push the rotor away from the hub.

NOTE: *Turn each bolt only two turns at a time to prevent cocking the disc excessively.*

5. Remove the tie rod from the knuckle using a tie rod end removal tool. Use care not to damage the ball joint seals.

6. Remove the cotter pin from the lower arm ball joint and remove the castle nut.

7. Remove the lower arm from the knuckle using the ball joint remover.

8. Loosen the lockbolt which retains the strut in the knuckle. Tap the top of the knuckle with a hammer and slide it off the shock.

9. Remove the knuckle and hub, if still attached, by sliding the assembly off the driveshaft.

10. Remove the hub from the knuckle using special tools and a hydraulic press. Bearing Removal:

11. Remove the splash guard and the snapring, then remove the outer bearing.

12. Turn the knuckle over and remove the inboard dust seal, bearing and inner race.

13. Press the bearing outer race out of the knuckle using special tools and a hydraulic press.

14. Remove the outboard bearing inner race from the hub using special tools and a bearing puller.

15. Remove the outboard dust seal from the hub.

NOTE: *Whenever the wheel bearings are removed, always replace them with a new set of bearings and outer dust seal.*

16. Clean all old grease from the driveshafts and spindles on the car.

17. Remove all old grease from the hub and knuckle and thoroughly dry and wipe clean all components.

18. When fitting new bearings, you must pack them with wheel bearing grease. To do this, place a glob of grease in your left palm, then, holding one of the bearings in your right hand, drag the face of the bearing heavily through the grease. This must be done to work as much grease as possible through the ball bearings and the cage. Turn the bearing and continue to pull it through the grease, until the grease is thoroughly packed between the bearing balls and the cage, all around the bearing. Repeat this operation until all of the bearings are packed with grease.

19. Pack the inside of the rotor and knuckle

hub with a moderate amount of grease. Do not overload the hub with grease.

20. Apply a small amount of grease to the spindle and to the lip of the inner seal before installing.

21. To install the bearings, press the bearing outer race into the knuckle using the special tools used as above, plus the installing base tool.

22. Install the outboard ball bearing and its inner race in the knuckle.

23. Install the snapring. Pack grease in the groove around the sealing lip of the outboard grease dust seal.

24. Drive the outboard grease seal into the knuckle, using a seal driver and hammer, until it is flush with the knuckle surface.

25. Install the splash guard, then turn the knuckle upside down and install the inboard ball bearing and its inner race.

26. Place the hub in the special tool fixture, then set the knuckle in position on the press and apply downward pressure.

27. Pack grease in the groove around the sealing lip of the inboard dust seal.

28. Drive the dust seal into the knuckle using a seal driver.

29. The remaining step are the reverse of the removal procedure. Use a new spindle nut, and stake after torquing.

1984-88 Civic

1. Pry the lock tab away from the spindle, then loosen the nut. Slightly loosen the lug nuts.

2. Raise the front of the car and support it with safety stands. Remove the front wheel and spindle nut.

3. Remove the bolts retaining the brake caliper and remove the caliper from the knuckle. Do not let the caliper hang by the brake hose, support it with a length of wire.

4. Remove the disc brake rotor retaining screws (if so equipped). Screw two 8 x 1.25 x 12mm bolts into the disc brake removal holes, and turn the bolts to push the rotor away from the hub.

NOTE: *Turn each bolt only two turns at a time to prevent cocking the disc excessively.*

5. Remove the tie rod from the knuckle using a tie rod end removal tool. Use care not to damage the ball joint seals.

6. Use a floor jack to support the lower control arm, then remove the cotter pin from the lower arm ball joint and remove the castle nut.

CAUTION: *Be sure to place the jack securely beneath the lower control arm at the ball joint. Otherwise, the tension from the torsion bar may cause the arm to suddenly jump*

away from the steering knuckle as the ball joint is removed.

7. Remove the cotter pin and loosen the lower arm ball joint nut half the length of the joint threads. Separate the ball joint and lower the arm using a suitable puller.

8. Remove the knuckle protector. Remove the cotter pin and remove the upper ball pin nut. Separate the upper ball joint and knuckle using ball joint remover 07941-6920-2 or equivalent.

9. Loosen the pinchbolt which retains the shock in the knuckle. Tap the top of the knuckle with a hammer and slide it off the shock.

10. Remove the knuckle and hub, if still attached, by sliding the assembly off of the driveshaft.

11. Remove the hub from the knuckle using special tools and a hydraulic press. Bearing Removal:

12. Remove the splash guard and the snapring.

13. Press the bearing outer race of the knuckle using special tools and a hydraulic press.

14. Remove the outboard bearing inner race from the hub using special tools and a bearing puller.

NOTE: *Whenever the wheel bearings are removed, always replace with a new set of bearings and outer dust seal.*

15. Clean all old grease from the driveshafts and spindles on the car. Remove the old grease from the hub and knuckle and thoroughly dry and wipe clean all components.

16. To install the bearings, press the bearing outer race into the knuckle using the special tools as used above, plus the installing base tool.

17. Install the snapring, then install the splash guard.

18. Place the hub in the special tool fixture, then set the knuckle in position on the press and apply downward pressure.

19. The remaining steps are the reverse of the removal procedure. Use a new spindle nut, and stake after torquing.

1983-88 Prelude and 1986-88 Accord

1. Pry the lock tab away from the spindle, then loosen the nut. Slightly loosen the lug nuts.

2. Raise the front of the car and support it with safety stands. Remove the front wheel and spindle nut.

3. Remove the bolts retaining the brake caliper and remove the caliper from the knuckle. Do not let the caliper hang by the brake hose, support it with a length of wire.

4. Remove the disc brake rotor retaining screws (if so equipped). Screw two 8 x 1.25 x

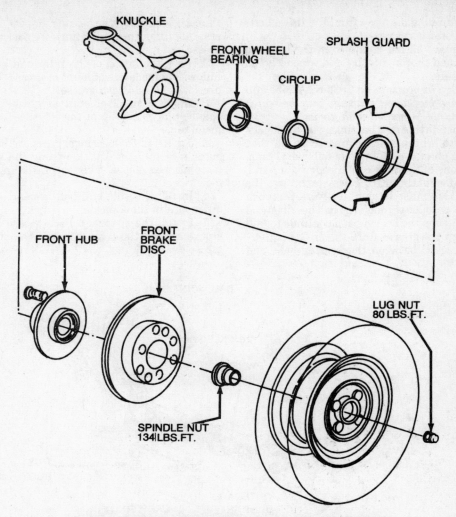

KNUCKLE

FRONT WHEEL
BEARING

SPLASH GUARD

CIRCLIP

FRONT HUB

FRONT
BRAKE
DISC

LUG NUT
80 LBS.FT.

SPINDLE NUT
134 LBS.FT.

Front steering knuckle, hub and bearing—1984 and later Civic

12mm bolts into the disc brake removal holes, and turn the bolts to push the rotor away from the hub.

NOTE: *Turn each bolt only two turns at a time to prevent cocking the disc excessively.*

5. Remove the tie rod from the knuckle using a tie rod end removal tool. Use care not to damage the ball joint seals.

6. Remove the cotter pin from the lower arm ball joint and remove the castle nut.

7. Remove the lower arm from the knuckle using the ball joint remover.

8. Remove the cotter pin from the upper arm ball joint and remove the castle nut.

9. Remove the upper arm from the knuckle using the ball joint remover.

10. Remove the knuckle and hub by sliding the assembly off of the driveshaft.

11. Remove the two back splash guard screws from the knuckle.

12. Remove the hub from the knuckle using special tools and a hydraulic press.

Bearing Removal:

13. Remove the splash guard, dust seal and the snapring, then remove the outer bearing race.

14. Turn the knuckle over and remove the inboard dust seal, bearing and inner race and bearing.

15. Press the bearing outer race out of the knuckle using special tools and a hydraulic press.

16. Remove the outboard bearing inner race from the hub using special tools and a bearing puller.

17. Remove the outboard dust seal from the hub.

NOTE: *Whenever the wheel bearings are removed, always replace with a new set of bearings and outer dust seal.*

18. Clean all old grease from the driveshafts spindles on the car.

19. Remove all old grease from the hub and knuckle and thoroughly dry and wipe clean all components.

NOTE: *The bearings on 1986-89 Accord and certain replacement bearings may be sealed and cannot be packed with grease.*

20. When fitting new bearings, you must pack them with wheel bearing grease. To do this, place a glob of grease in your left palm, then, holding one of the bearings in your right hand, drag the face of the bearing heavily through the grease. This must be done to work as much grease as possible through the ball bearings and the cage. Turn the bearing and continue to pull it through the grease, until the grease is thoroughly packed between the bearing balls and

the cage, all around the bearing. Repeat this operation until all of the bearings are packed with grease.

21. Pack the inside of the rotor and knuckle hub with a moderate amount of grease. Do not overload the hub with grease.

22. Apply a small amount of grease to the spindle and to the lip of the inner seal before installing.

23. To install the bearings, press the bearing outer race into the knuckle using the special tools used as above, plus the installing base tool.

24. Install the outboard ball bearing and its inner race in the knuckle.

25. Install the snapring. Pack grease in the groove around the sealing lip of the outboard grease dust seal.

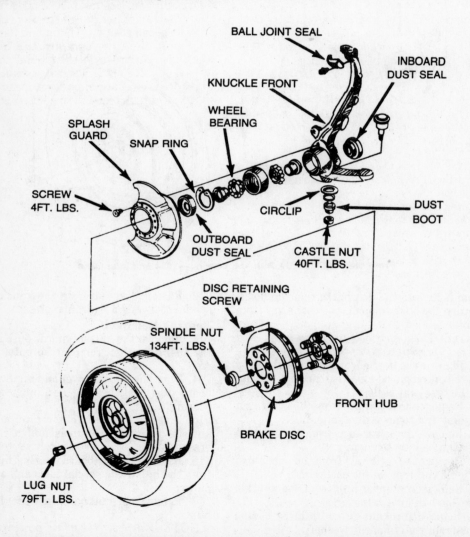

Front steering knuckle, hub and bearing—1983 and later Prelude, 1986 and later Accord similar

26. Drive the outboard grease seal into the knuckle, using a seal driver and hammer, until it is flush with the knuckle surface.

27. Install the splash guard, then turn the knuckle upside down and install the inboard ball bearing and its inner race.

28. Place the hub in the special tool fixture, then set the knuckle in position on the press and apply downward pressure.

29. Pack grease in the groove around the sealing lip of the inboard dust seal.

30. Drive the dust seal into the knuckle using a seal driver.

31. The remaining steps are the reverse of the removal procedure. Use a new spindle nut, and stake after torquing.

Front End Alignment

Front wheel alignment (also known as front end geometry) is the position of the front wheels relative to each other and to the vehicle. Correct alignment must be maintained to provide safe, accurate steering, vehicle stability and minimum tire wear. The factors which determine wheel alignment are interdependent. Therefore, when one of the factors is adjusted, the others must be adjusted to compensate.

CASTER

Caster angle is the number of degrees that a line, drawn through the center of the upper and lower ball joints and viewed from the side, can be tilted forward or backward. Positive caster means that the top of the upper ball joint is tilted toward the rear of the vehicle and negative caster means that it is tilted toward the front. A vehicle with a slightly positive caster setting will have its lower ball joint pivot slightly ahead of the tire's center. This will assist the directional stability of the vehicle by causing a drag at the bottom center of the wheel when it turns, thereby, resisting the turn and tending to hold the wheel steady in whatever direction the vehicle is pointed. Therefore, the vehicle is less susceptible to crosswinds and road surface deviations. A vehicle with too much (positive) caster will be hard to steer and shimmy at low speeds. A vehicle with insufficient (negative) caster may tend to be unstable at high speeds and may respond erratically when the brakes are applied.

CAMBER

Camber angle is the number of degrees that the wheel itself is tilted from a vertical line when viewed from the front. Positive camber means that the top of the wheel is slanted away from the vehicle, while negative camber means that it is tilted toward the vehicle. Ordinarily, a vehicle will have a slight positive camber when unloaded. Then, when the vehicle is loaded and rolling down the road, the wheels will just about be vertical. If you started with no camber at all, then, loading the vehicle would produce a negative camber. Excessive camber (either positive or negative) will produce rapid tire wear, since one side of the tire will be more heavily loaded than the other side.

STEERING AXIS INCLINATION

Steering axis inclination is the number of degrees that a line drawn through the upper and lower ball joints and viewed from the front, is tilted to the left or the right. This, in combination with caster, is responsible for the directional stability and self-centering of the steering. As the steering knuckle swings from lock-to-lock, the spindle generates an arc, causing the vehicle to be raised when its turned from the straight-ahead position. The reason the vehicle body must rise is straight-forward: since the wheel is in contact with the ground, it cannot move down. However, when it is swung away from the straight-ahead position, it must move either up or down (due to the arc generated by

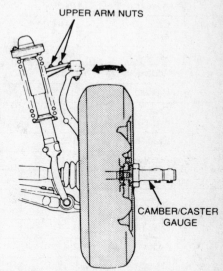

Camber adjustment—1983 and later Prelude

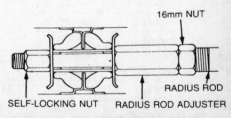

Caster adjustment—1983 and later Prelude

Wheel Alignment

Year	Model	Caster Range (deg.)	Caster Preferred Setting (deg.)	Camber Range (deg.)	Camber Preferred Setting (deg.)	Toe-in (in.)	Steering Axis Inclination (deg.)
1973	Civic	0–1P	1/2P	0–1P	1/2P	1/32	9 5/16
1974	Civic exc. SW	0–1P	1/2P	0–1P	1/2P	1/32	9 5/16
1975	Civic exc. SW	0–1P	1/2P	0–1P	1/2P	1/32	9 5/16
	Civic SW	0–1P	1/2P	0–1P	1/2P	1/32	9 5/16
1976	Civic exc. SW	0–1P	1/2P	0–1P	1/2P	1/32	9 5/16
	Civic SW	0–1P	1/2P	0–1P	1/2P	1/32	9 5/16
	Accord	1P–3P	2P	1/4N–1 3/4P	3/4P	3/64	12 3/16
1977	Civic exc. SW	0–1P	1/2P	0–1P	1/2P	1/32	9 5/16
	Civic SW	0–1P	1/2P	0–1P	1/2P	1/32	9 5/16
	Accord	1P–3P	2P	1/4N–1 3/4P	3/4P	3/64	12 3/16
1978	Civic exc. SW	0–1P	1/2P	0–1P	1/2P	1/32	9 5/16
	Civic SW	0–1P	1/2P	0–1P	1/2P	1/32	9 5/16
	Accord	1P–3P	2P	1/4N–1 3/4P	3/4P	3/64	12 3/16
1979	Civic exc. SW	1/4P–1 1/4P	3/4P	0–1P	1/2P	3/64	9 5/16
	Civic SW	0–1P	1/2P	0–1P	1/2P	3/64	9 5/16
	Accord	3/4P–1 3/4P	1 1/4P	0–1P	1/2P	1/32	12 3/16
	Prelude	1/2P–2 1/2P	1 1/2P	1N–1P	0	0	12 13/16
1980	Civic exc. SW	3/4P–2 3/4P	1 3/4P	1N–1P	0	0	12 15/16
	Civic SW	0–2P	1P	1N–1P	0	0	12 15/16
	Accord	3/4P–1 3/4P	1 1/4P	0–1P	1/2P	1/32	12 3/16
	Prelude	1/2P–2 1/2P	1 1/2P	1N–1P	0	0	12 13/16
1981	Civic exc. SW	3/4P–2 3/4P	1 3/4P	1N–1P	0	0	12 5/16
	Civic SW	0–2P	1P	1N–1P	0	0	12 5/16
	Accord	1 1/16P–2 11/16P	1 11/16	11/16N–1 5/16P	5/16	3/64	12 1/2
	Prelude	1/2P–2 1/2P	1 1/2P	1N–1P	0	0	12 13/16
1982	Civic exc. SW	1 1/2P–3 1/2P	2 1/2P	1N–1P	0	0	12 11/32
	Civic SW	5/16P–2 5/16P	1 5/16P	1N–1P	0	0	12 11/32
	Accord	7/16P–2 7/16P	1 7/16	1N–1P	0	0	12 1/2
	Prelude	1/2P–2 1/2P	1 1/2P	1N–1P	0	0	12 13/16
1983	Civic exc. SW	1 1/2P–3 1/2P	2 1/2P	1N–1P	0	0	12 11/32
	Civic SW	5/16P–2 5/16P	1 5/16P	1N–1P	0	0	12 11/32
	Accord	7/16P–2 7/16P	1 7/16	1N–1P	0	0	12 1/2
	Prelude	1N–1P	0	1N–1P	0	0	6 13/16

Wheel Alignment (cont.)

Year	Model	Caster Range (deg.)	Caster Preferred Setting (deg.)	Camber Range (deg.)	Camber Preferred Setting (deg.)	Toe-in (in.)	Steering Axis Inclination (deg.)
1984	Civic exc. SW	1 5/16P–3 5/16P	2 5/16P	1N–1P	0	0	12 13/16
	Civic SW	1 1/8P–3 1/8P	2 1/8P	1N–1P	0	0	12
	Accord	7/16P–2 7/16P	1 7/16	1N–1P	0	0	12 1/2
	Prelude	1N–1P	0	1N–1P	0	0	6 13/16
1985	Civic exc. SW	1 1/2P–3 1/2P ①	2 1/2P ②	1N–1P	0	0	13
	Civic SW	1P–3P	2P	1N–1P	0	0	12
	Accord	1/2P–2 1/2P	1 1/2P	1N–1P	0	0	12 1/2
	Prelude	1N–1P	0	1N–1P	0	0	6 13/16
1986	Civic exc. SW	1 1/2P–3 1/2P ①	2 1/2P ②	1N–1P	0	0	13
	Civic SW	1P–3P	2P	1N–1P	0	0	12
	Accord	1/2N–1 1/2P	1/2P	1N–1P	0	0	6 13/16
	Prelude	1N–1P	0	1N–1P	0	0	6 13/16
1987	Civic exc. SW	1 1/2P–3 1/2P ①	2 1/2P ②	1N–1P	0	0	13
	Civic SW	1P–3P	2P	1N–1P	0	0	12
	Accord	1/2N–1 1/2P	1/2P	1N–1P	0	0	6 13/16
	Prelude	1N–1P	0	1N–1P	0	0	6 13/16
1988	Civic exc. SW	2P–4P	3P	1N–1P	0	0	7 5/16
	Civic SW	1 15/16P–3 15/16P	2 15/16P	11/16N–1 5/16P	5/16P	0	7 1/4
	Civic 4wd	1 15/16P–3 15/16P	2 15/16P	7/16N–1 9/16P	9/16P	0	6 15/16
	Accord	1/2N–1 1/2P	1/2P	1N–1P	0	0	6 13/16
	Prelude	1 13/16P–2 13/16P	2 3/8P	1N–1P	0	0	6 13/16

SW Station Wagon
P Positive
N Negative
① With power steering 2P–4P
② With power steering 3P

the steering knuckle). Not being able to move down, it must move up. Then, the weight of the vehicle acts against this lift and attempts to return the spindle to the straight-ahead position when the steering wheel is released.

TOE-IN

Toe-in is the difference (in inches) between the front and the rear of the front tires. On a vehicle with toe-in, the distance between the front wheels is less at the front than at the rear. Toe-in is normally only a few fractions of an inch, it is necessary to ensure parallel rolling of the front wheels and to prevent excessive tire wear. As the vehicle is driven at increasingly faster speeds, the steering linkage has a tendency to expand slightly, thereby, allowing the front wheels to turn out and away from each other. Therefore, initially setting the front wheels so that they are pointing slightly inward (toe-in), allows them to turn straight ahead when the vehicle is underway.

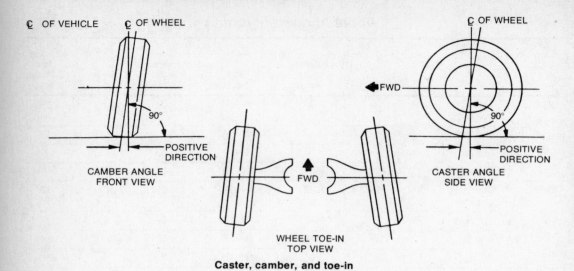

Caster, camber, and toe-in

REAR SUSPENSION

All Civic sedan and hatchback models utilize an independent MacPherson strut arrangement for each rear wheel. Each suspension unit consists of a combined coil spring/shock absorber strut, a lower control arm and a radius rod.

Station wagon models use a more conventional leaf spring rear suspension with a solid rear axle. The springs are three-leaf, semi-elliptic types located longitudinally with a pair of telescopic shock absorbers to control rebound. The solid axle and leaf springs allow for a greater load carrying capacity for the wagon over the sedan.

The 4WD wagon uses a live (or solid) rear axle located by upper and lower fore and aft control arms and a Panhard rod. The fore and aft arms keep the axle located fore and aft and vertically. The Panhard rod runs from the right side of the axle up to a bushed mounting point on the wagon's body and stabilizes the axle in

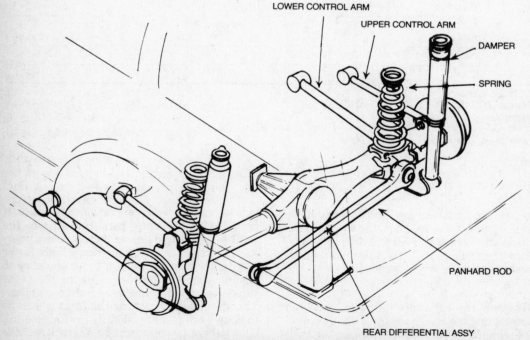

The 4 wheel drive rear suspension system

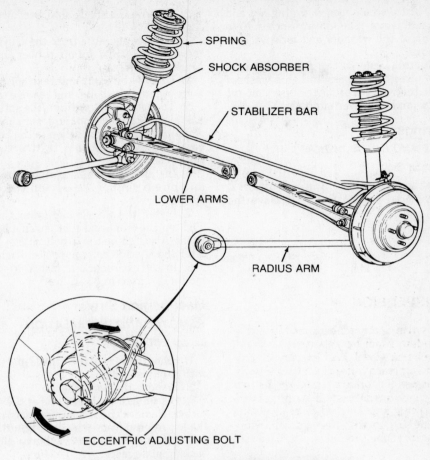

SPRING

SHOCK ABSORBER

STABILIZER BAR

LOWER ARMS

RADIUS ARM

ECCENTRIC ADJUSTING BOLT

1983 and later Accord and Prelude rear suspension

terms of side-to-side motion. Coil springs which are separate from conventional shock absorbers complete the rear suspension system.

Coil Springs and Shock Absorber 4WD Station Wagon

REMOVAL AND INSTALLATION

1. Support the rear of the vehicle securely and remove the rear wheels. Support the rear axle housing securely with a floor jack.

2. Remove the damper access covers from inside. Remove the cap and unscrew the two nuts on each side.

3. If you are removing the shocks only, lower the axle just enough for the rod to clear the body. Otherwise, lower the axle until the shock and spring parts are all free. Remove the springs and upper and lower seats (if necessary) and then unbolt the shocks at the axle and remove them too.

4. If springs have been removed, install the upper spring seats into the body. Place the lower spring seats on the axle and position the springs on the seats.

5. Install the shocks upright in the axle housing and bolt them loosely at the bottom. Then, gradually raise the axle with a floor jack until the piston rods of the shocks can be guided through the holes in the vehicle body. As you do this, also check that the springs are in the proper positions.

6. When the piston rods are well through the body holes, install the two locknuts on either side. Use an Allen wrench to hold the nuts, and torque the lower nuts to 14 ft. lbs. and the upper to 16 ft. lbs. Install the cap and access cover. Install the wheels and lower the vehicle to the floor. Final torque the lower shock mounting bolts to 60 ft. lbs.

Shock Absorbers 2WD Station Wagon

REMOVAL AND INSTALLATION

1. It is not necessary to raise the vehicle or remove the wheels unless you require working

clearance. Unbolt the upper mounting nut and lower bolt and remove the shock absorber. Note the position of the washers and lock washers upon removal.

2. To install, reverse the removal procedures. Be sure the washers and lock washers are installed correctly. Torque the upper mount to 44 ft. lbs. and the lower mount to 33 ft. lbs.

Leaf Springs
REMOVAL AND INSTALLATION
Station Wagon Only

1. Raise the rear of the vehicle and support it on stands placed on the frame. Remove the wheels.

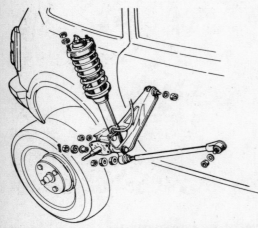

Rear suspension—sedan and hatchback models

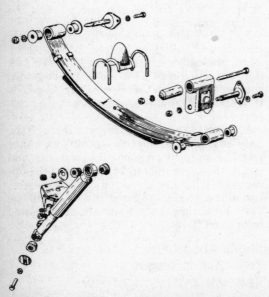

Exploded view of rear suspension—station wagon models

2. Remove the shock absorber lower mounting bolt.

3. Remove the nuts from the U-bolt and remove the U-bolts, bump rubber, and clamp bracket.

4. Unbolt the front and rear spring shackle bolts, remove the bolts, and remove the spring.

5. To install, first position the spring on the axle and install the front and rear shackle bolts. Apply a soapy water solution to the bushings to ease installation. Do not tighten the shackle nuts yet.

6. Install the U-bolts, spring clamp bracket and bump rubber loosely on the axle and spring.

7. Install the wheels and lower the vehicle. Tighten the front and rear shackle bolts to 33 ft. lbs. Also tighten the U-bolt nuts to 33 ft. lbs., after the shackle bolts have been tightened.

8. Install the shock absorber to the lower mount. Tighten to 33 ft. lbs.

MacPherson Struts
REMOVAL AND INSTALLATION
Except 2WD Wagon

1. Raise the rear of the vehicle and support it with safety stands.

2. Remove the rear wheel.

3. Disconnect the brake line at the shock absorber. Remove the retaining clip and separate the brake hose from the shock absorber.

4. Disconnect the parking brake cable at the backing plate lever.

5. Remove the lower strut retaining bolt and hub carrier pivot bolt. To remove the pivot bolt, you first have to remove the castle nut and its cotter pin.

6. Remove the two upper strut retaining nuts and remove the strut from the vehicle.

7. To install, reverse the removal procedure. Be sure to install the top of the strut in the body first. After installation, bleed the brake lines (see Chapter 9).

2WD Wagon

1. Raise the rear of the vehicle and support is securely on stands. Remove the rear wheels.

2. Support the rear axle securely on a floor jack. On each side, remove the damper cover from inside the vehicle; then remove the self-locking nut. To remove the self-locking nut, use an Allen wrench to hold the shock absorber rod.

3. Lower the axle carefully until all spring pressure is released. Remove the self locking bolt from the lower end of the damper. Remove the damper assembly and the spring and upper spring seat above it.

4. To install the struts, first fit the upper spring seat into the frame. Install the spring

and then the bolt fastening the lower strut to the axle. Just tighten the bolt slightly. Perform this step on both sides.

5. Fit the damper upper rubber mount into the body (on both sides). Then, carefully jack up the axle, making sure the damper shaft fits into the hole in the body far enough that you can install the self-locking retaining nut just far enough so that all threads are engaged. Carefully lower the vehicle.

6. Final tighten the self-locking bolts at the lower ends of the struts to 40 ft. lbs. and the self locking nuts on top to 16 ft. lbs. Install the damper covers.

OVERHAUL

1. Use a coil spring compressor to disassemble the strut. When assembling the compressor onto the strut, the long studs should be installed so that they are flush with the bottom plate and also flush with the retaining nut on the top end. The adjustable plate in the center cup should be screwed all the way in.

2. Insert the strut in the compressor and compress the strut about 2″. Then remove the center retaining nut.

3. Loosen the compressor and remove the strut.

4. Remove the top plate, rubber protector, spring and rubber bumper.

5. To assemble, reverse the removal procedure after checking the shock for oil leaks and all rubber parts for damage, wear or deterioration.

Control Arms
REMOVAL AND INSTALLATION
All Except Wagon

1. Remove the control arm outboard and inboard pivot bolts.

2. Pull the inboard side of the arm down until it clears the body.

3. Slide the arm towards the center of the vehicle until it is free of the hub carrier.

4. To install, reverse the removal procedure. Be sure to check the bushings at each end of the control arm and the control arm for damage and wear.

Rear Wheel Bearings
REPLACEMENT
1973-83 Civic
1979-83 Prelude
1976-85 Accord

1. Slightly loosen the rear lug nuts. Raise the car and support safely on jackstands.

2. Release the parking brake. Remove the rear wheels.

Rear control arm

3. Remove the rear bearing hub cap and cotter pin and pin holder.

4. Remove the spindle nut, then pull the hub and drum off the spindle.

5. Drive the outboard inboard bearing races out of the hub. Punch in a criss-cross pattern to avoid cocking the bearing race in the bore.

6. Clean the bearing seats thoroughly before going on to the next step.

7. Using a bearing driver, drive the inboard bearing race into the hub.

8. Turn the hub over and drive the outboard bearing race in the same way.

9. Check to see that the bearing races are seated properly.

10. When fitting new bearings, you must pack them with wheel bearing grease. To do this, place a glob of grease in your left palm, then, holding one of the bearings in your right hand, drag the face of the bearing heavily through the grease. This must be done to work as much grease as possible through the ball bearings and the cage. Turn the bearing and continue to pull it through the grease, until the grease is thoroughly packed between the bearing balls and

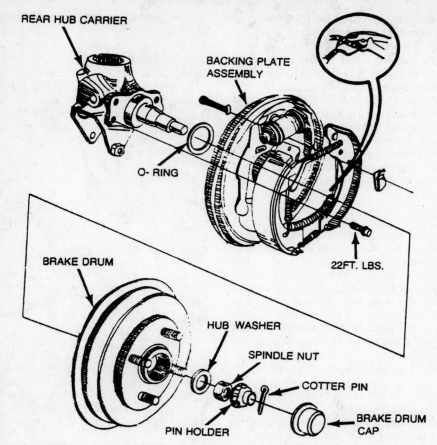

Rear hub and bearing—all except 1984 and later Civic and Prelude, and 1986 and later Accord

the cage, all around the bearing. Repeat this operation until all of the bearings are packed with grease.

11. Pack the inside of the hub with a moderate amount of grease. Do not overload the hub with grease.

12. Apply a small amount of grease to the spindle and to the lip of the inner seal before installing.

13. Place the inboard bearings into the hub.

14. Apply grease to the hub seal, and carefully tap into place. Tap in a criss-cross pattern to avoid cocking the seal in the bore.

15. Slip the hub and drum over the spindle, then insert the outboard bearing, hub, washer, and spindle nut.

16. Follow the procedures below under, Adjustment.

1984-89 Prelude Except 4WD

1. Slightly loosen the rear lug nuts. Raise the car and support safely on jackstands.

2. Release the parking brake. Remove the rear wheels.

3. Remove the bolts retaining the brake caliper and remove the caliper from the knuckle. Do not let the caliper hang by the brake hose, support it with a length of wire.

4. Remove the rear bearing hub cap and cotter pin and pin holder. Remove the spindle nut, then pull the hub and disc off of the spindle.

5. Drive the outboard and inboard bearing races out of the disc. Punch in a criss-cross pat-

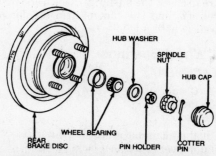

Rear hub and bearing–Prelude 1984 and later

tern to avoid cocking the bearing race in the bore.

6. Clean the bearing seats thoroughly before going on to the next step.

7. Using a bearing driver, drive the inboard bearing race into the disc.

8. Turn the disc over and drive the outboard bearing race in the same way.

9. Check to see that the bearing races are seated properly.

10. When fitting new bearings, you must pack them with wheel bearing grease. To do this, place a glob of grease in your left palm, then, holding one of the bearings in your right hand, drag the face of the bearing heavily through the grease. This must be done to work as much grease as possible through the ball bearings and the cage. Turn the bearing and continue to pull it through the grease, until the grease is thoroughly packed between the bearing balls and the cage, all around the bearing. Repeat this operation until all of the bearings are packed with grease.

11. Pack the inside of the hub with a moderate amount of grease. Do not overload the hub with grease.

12. Apply a small amount of grease to the spindle and to the lip of the inner seal before installing.

13. Place the inboard bearing into the hub.

14. Apply grease to the hub seal, and carefully tap into place. Tap in a criss-cross pattern to avoid cocking the seal in the bore.

15. Slip the hub and disc over the spindle, then insert the outboard bearing, hub washer, and spindle nut.

16. Follow the procedures below for adjustment.

1988 Prelude 4WD

1. Slightly loosen the rear lug nuts. Raise the car and support safely on jackstands.

2. Release the parking brake. Remove the rear wheels.

3. Remove the bolts retaining the brake caliper and remove the caliper from the knuckle. Do not let the caliper hang by the brake hose, support it with a length of wire.

4. Remove the two 6mm screws from the brake disc. Tighten the 8 x 12mm bolts into the holes of the brake disc, then remove the brake disc from the rear hub.

5. Remove the cotter pin of the lower arm tie rod and remove the castle nut.

6. Separate the tie rod ball joint using a suitable ball joint removal tool.

7. Remove the cotter pin and loosen the lower arm ball joint nut half the length of the joint threads.

8. Separate the ball joint and lower arm using a suitable puller. Remove the cotter pin and castle nut, and separate the tie rod ball joint using a ball joint removal tool.

9. Tap the outboard joint of the driveshaft to extract it from the knuckle, then remove the knuckle.

10. Remove the rear hub nut from the rear hub. Remove the splash guard mounting bolts. Using a hydraulic press, separate the hub from the knuckle.

NOTE: *Set the rear hub at the hub/disc assembly base firmly so that the knuckle will not tilt the assembly in the press. Take care not to distort the splash guard. Hold onto the hub to keep it from falling after it is pressed out.*

11. Remove the splash guard and 68mm circlip from the knuckle.

12. Using a hydraulic press and special press tools, press the wheel bearing out of the knuckle.

13. Remove the bearing inner race using a suitable bearing remover.

14. When fitting new bearings, you must pack them with wheel bearing grease. If a bearing packer is not available or can not be used on this type of bearing, grease the bearing as follows, place a glob of grease in your left palm, then, holding one of the bearings in your right hand, drag the face of the bearing heavily through the grease. This must be done to work as much grease as possible through the ball bearings and the cage. Turn the bearing and continue to pull it through the grease, until the grease is thoroughly packed between the bearing balls and the cage, all around the bearing. Repeat this operation until all of the bearings are packed with grease.

15. Place the rear wheel bearing in a special tool fixture (07GAf-SE00101 or equivalent) then set the knuckle into position and apply downward pressure with a hydraulic press. Fit the 68mm circlip into the groove of the knuckle.

16. Install the splash guard. Place the hub in a special tool fixture, then set the knuckle into position and apply downward pressure with a hydraulic press. Place the rear hub nut and tighten it.

17. The remaining steps are the reverse of the removal procedure. Use a new spindle nut, and stake after torquing.

1984-88 Civic
1986-88 Accord

1. Slightly loosen the rear lug nuts. Raise the car and support safely on jackstands.

2. Release the parking brake. Remove the rear wheel and the brake drum.

3. Remove the rear bearing hub cap and nut.

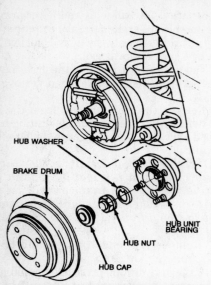

HUB WASHER

BRAKE DRUM

HUB UNIT BEARING

HUB NUT

HUB CAP

Rear hub and bearing—Civic 1984 and later, and Accord 1986 and later

Civic rear suspension showing toe-in adjustment point (arrow)

4. Pull the hub unit off of the spindle.

5. Installation is the reverse order of removal. Tighten the new spindle nut to 134 ft. lbs., then stake the nut.

ADJUSTMENT

1. Apply grease or oil on the spindle nut and spindle threads.

2. Install and tighten the spindle nut to 18 ft. lbs. and rotate the drum/disc 2-3 turns by hand, then retighten the spindle nut to 18 ft. lbs.

3. Repeat the above step until the spindle nut hold that torque.

4. Loosen the spindle nut to 0 ft. lbs. NOTE: *Loosen the nut until it just breaks free, but doesn't turn.*

5. Retorque the spindle nut to 4 ft. lbs.

6. Set the pin holder so the slots will be as close as possible to the hole in the spindle.

7. Tighten the spindle nut just enough to align the slot and hole, then secure it with a new cotter pin.

Rear End Alignment

Toe-in is adjustable on the rear wheels of all models except the station wagon. On the Civic, the toe-in is adjusted by means of a threaded radius rod. On the Accord and Prelude, a cam-type adjuster is used.

STEERING

All Honda's are equipped with rack and pinion steering. Movement of the steering wheel is transmitted through the linkage to the input

Rear toe-in adjustment point on Accord (arrow)

shaft, which in turn is connected to the pinion gear. The pinion gear engages the rack and rotation of the pinion, transmitted from the input shaft, causes the rack to move laterally.

Steering Wheel

REMOVAL AND INSTALLATION

1. Using a small pry bar, lift the pad from the steering wheel.

2. Remove the steering wheel retaining nut. Gently hit the backside of each of the steering wheel spokes with equal force from the palms of your hands.

WARNING: *Avoid hitting the wheel or the shaft with excessive force. Damage to the shaft could result.*

3. To install, reverse the removal procedures. Torque the steering wheel nut to 26-36 ft. lbs.

Troubleshooting the Steering Column

Problem	Cause	Solution
Will not lock	• Lockbolt spring broken or defective	• Replace lock bolt spring
High effort (required to turn ignition key and lock cylinder)	• Lock cylinder defective • Ignition switch defective • Rack preload spring broken or deformed • Burr on lock sector, lock rack, housing, support or remote rod coupling • Bent sector shaft • Defective lock rack • Remote rod bent, deformed • Ignition switch mounting bracket bent • Distorted coupling slot in lock rack (tilt column)	• Replace lock cylinder • Replace ignition switch • Replace preload spring • Remove burr • Replace shaft • Replace lock rack • Replace rod • Straighten or replace • Replace lock rack
Will stick in "start"	• Remote rod deformed • Ignition switch mounting bracket bent	• Straighten or replace • Straighten or replace
Key cannot be removed in "off-lock"	• Ignition switch is not adjusted correctly • Defective lock cylinder	• Adjust switch • Replace lock cylinder
Lock cylinder can be removed without depressing retainer	• Lock cylinder with defective retainer • Burr over retainer slot in housing cover or on cylinder retainer	• Replace lock cylinder • Remove burr
High effort on lock cylinder between "off" and "off-lock"	• Distorted lock rack • Burr on tang of shift gate (automatic column) • Gearshift linkage not adjusted	• Replace lock rack • Remove burr • Adjust linkage
Noise in column	• One click when in "off-lock" position and the steering wheel is moved (all except automatic column) • Coupling bolts not tightened • Lack of grease on bearings or bearing surfaces • Upper shaft bearing worn or broken • Lower shaft bearing worn or broken • Column not correctly aligned • Coupling pulled apart • Broken coupling lower joint • Steering shaft snap ring not seated • Shroud loose on shift bowl. Housing loose on jacket—will be noticed with ignition in "off-lock" and when torque is applied to steering wheel.	• Normal—lock bolt is seating • Tighten pinch bolts • Lubricate with chassis grease • Replace bearing assembly • Replace bearing. Check shaft and replace if scored. • Align column • Replace coupling • Repair or replace joint and align column • Replace ring. Check for proper seating in groove. • Position shroud over lugs on shift bowl. Tighten mounting screws.
High steering shaft effort	• Column misaligned • Defective upper or lower bearing • Tight steering shaft universal joint • Flash on I.D. of shift tube at plastic joint (tilt column only) • Upper or lower bearing seized	• Align column • Replace as required • Repair or replace • Replace shift tube • Replace bearings
Lash in mounted column assembly	• Column mounting bracket bolts loose • Broken weld nuts on column jacket • Column capsule bracket sheared	• Tighten bolts • Replace column jacket • Replace bracket assembly

Troubleshooting the Steering Column (cont.)

Problem	Cause	Solution
Lash in mounted column assembly (cont.)	· Column bracket to column jacket mounting bolts loose	· Tighten to specified torque
	· Loose lock shoes in housing (tilt column only)	· Replace shoes
	· Loose pivot pins (tilt column only)	· Replace pivot pins and support
	· Loose lock shoe pin (tilt column only)	· Replace pin and housing
	· Loose support screws (tilt column only)	· Tighten screws
Housing loose (tilt column only)	· Excessive clearance between holes in support or housing and pivot pin diameters	· Replace pivot pins and support
	· Housing support-screws loose	· Tighten screws
Steering wheel loose—every other tilt position (tilt column only)	· Loose fit between lock shoe and lock shoe pivot pin	· Replace lock shoes and pivot pin
Steering column not locking in any tilt position (tilt column only)	· Lock shoe seized on pivot pin	· Replace lock shoes and pin
	· Lock shoe grooves have burrs or are filled with foreign material	· Clean or replace lock shoes
	· Lock shoe springs weak or broken	· Replace springs
Noise when tilting column (tilt column only)	· Upper tilt bumpers worn	· Replace tilt bumper
	· Tilt spring rubbing in housing	· Lubricate with chassis grease
One click when in "off-lock" position and the steering wheel is moved	· Seating of lock bolt	· None. Click is normal characteristic sound produced by lock bolt as it seats.
High shift effort (automatic and tilt column only)	· Column not correctly aligned	· Align column
	· Lower bearing not aligned correctly	· Assemble correctly
	· Lack of grease on seal or lower bearing areas	· Lubricate with chassis grease
Improper transmission shifting— automatic and tilt column only	· Sheared shift tube joint	· Replace shift tube
	· Improper transmission gearshift linkage adjustment	· Adjust linkage
	· Loose lower shift lever	· Replace shift tube

Troubleshooting the Ignition Switch

Problem	Cause	Solution
Ignition switch electrically inoperative	· Loose or defective switch connector	· Tighten or replace connector
	· Feed wire open (fusible link)	· Repair or replace
	· Defective ignition switch	· Replace ignition switch
Engine will not crank	· Ignition switch not adjusted properly	· Adjust switch
Ignition switch wil not actuate mechanically	· Defective ignition switch	· Replace switch
	· Defective lock sector	· Replace lock sector
	· Defective remote rod	· Replace remote rod
Ignition switch cannot be adjusted correctly	· Remote rod deformed	· Repair, straighten or replace

Combination Switch

REMOVAL AND INSTALLATION

1. Refer to the "Steering Wheel, Removal and Installation" procedures in this section and remove the steering wheel.

2. Disconnect the column wiring harness and coupler.

WARNING: *Be careful not to damage the steering column or shaft.*

3. Remove the upper and lower column covers.

Troubleshooting the Turn Signal Switch

Problem	Cause	Solution
Turn signal will not cancel	• Loose switch mounting screws • Switch or anchor bosses broken • Broken, missing or out of position detent, or cancelling spring	• Tighten screws • Replace switch • Reposition springs or replace switch as required
Turn signal difficult to operate	• Turn signal lever loose • Switch yoke broken or distorted • Loose or misplaced springs • Foreign parts and/or materials in switch • Switch mounted loosely	• Tighten mounting screws • Replace switch • Reposition springs or replace switch • Remove foreign parts and/or material • Tighten mounting screws
Turn signal will not indicate lane change	• Broken lane change pressure pad or spring hanger • Broken, missing or misplaced lane change spring • Jammed wires	• Replace switch • Replace or reposition as required • Loosen mounting screws, reposition wires and retighten screws
Turn signal will not stay in turn position	• Foreign material or loose parts impeding movement of switch yoke • Defective switch	• Remove material and/or parts • Replace switch
Hazard switch cannot be pulled out	• Foreign material between hazard support cancelling leg and yoke	• Remove foreign material. No foreign material impeding function of hazard switch—replace turn signal switch.
No turn signal lights	• Inoperative turn signal flasher • Defective or blown fuse • Loose chassis to column harness connector • Disconnect column to chassis connector. Connect new switch to chassis and operate switch by hand. If vehicle lights now operate normally, signal switch is inoperative • If vehicle lights do not operate, check chassis wiring for opens, grounds, etc.	• Replace turn signal flasher • Replace fuse • Connect securely • Replace signal switch • Repair chassis wiring as required
Instrument panel turn indicator lights on but not flashing	• Burned out or damaged front or rear turn signal bulb • If vehicle lights do not operate, check light sockets for high resistance connections, the chassis wiring for opens, grounds, etc. • Inoperative flasher • Loose chassis to column harness connection • Inoperative turn signal switch • To determine if turn signal switch is defective, substitute new switch into circuit and operate switch by hand. If the vehicle's lights operate normally, signal switch is inoperative.	• Replace bulb • Repair chassis wiring as required • Replace flasher • Connect securely • Replace turn signal switch • Replace turn signal switch
Stop light not on when turn indicated	• Loose column to chassis connection • Disconnect column to chassis connector. Connect new switch into system without removing old.	• Connect securely • Replace signal switch

Troubleshooting the Turn Signal Switch (cont.)

Problem	Cause	Solution
Stop light not on when turn indicated (cont.)	Operate switch by hand. If brake lights work with switch in the turn position, signal switch is defective.	
	• If brake lights do not work, check connector to stop light sockets for grounds, opens, etc.	• Repair connector to stop light circuits using service manual as guide
Turn indicator panel lights not flashing	• Burned out bulbs • High resistance to ground at bulb socket • Opens, ground in wiring harness from front turn signal bulb socket to indicator lights	• Replace bulbs • Replace socket • Locate and repair as required
Turn signal lights flash very slowly	• High resistance ground at light sockets • Incorrect capacity turn signal flasher or bulb • If flashing rate is still extremely slow, check chassis wiring harness from the connector to light sockets for high resistance • Loose chassis to column harness connection • Disconnect column to chassis connector. Connect new switch into system without removing old. Operate switch by hand. If flashing occurs at normal rate, the signal switch is defective.	• Repair high resistance grounds at light sockets • Replace turn signal flasher or bulb • Locate and repair as required • Connect securely • Replace turn signal switch
Hazard signal lights will not flash— turn signal functions normally	• Blow fuse • Inoperative hazard warning flasher • Loose chassis-to-column harness connection • Disconnect column to chassis connector. Connect new switch into system without removing old. Depress the hazard warning lights. If they now work normally, turn signal switch is defective. • If lights do not flash, check wiring harness "K" lead for open between hazard flasher and connector. If open, fuse block is defective	• Replace fuse • Replace hazard warning flasher in fuse panel • Conect securely • Replace turn signal switch • Repair or replace brown wire or connector as required

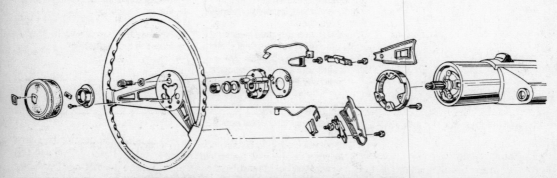

Exploded view of steering wheel and related parts

Troubleshooting the Manual Steering Gear

Problem	Cause	Solution
Hard or erratic steering	· Incorrect tire pressure	· Inflate tires to recommended pressures
	· Insufficient or incorrect lubrication	· Lubricate as required (refer to Maintenance Section)
	· Suspension, or steering linkage parts damaged or misaligned	· Repair or replace parts as necessary
	· Improper front wheel alignment	· Adjust incorrect wheel alignment angles
	· Incorrect steering gear adjustment	· Adjust steering gear
	· Sagging springs	· Replace springs
Play or looseness in steering	· Steering wheel loose	· Inspect shaft spines and repair as necessary. Tighten attaching nut and stake in place.
	· Steering linkage or attaching parts loose or worn	· Tighten, adjust, or replace faulty components
	· Pitman arm loose	· Inspect shaft splines and repair as necessary. Tighten attaching nut and stake in place
	· Steering gear attaching bolts loose	· Tighten bolts
	· Loose or worn wheel bearings	· Adjust or replace bearings
	· Steering gear adjustment incorrect or parts badly worn	· Adjust gear or replace defective parts
Wheel shimmy or tramp	· Improper tire pressure	· Inflate tires to recommended pressures
	· Wheels, tires, or brake rotors out-of-balance or out-of-round	· Inspect and replace or balance parts
	· Inoperative, worn, or loose shock absorbers or mounting parts	· Repair or replace shocks or mountings
	· Loose or worn steering or suspension parts	· Tighten or replace as necessary
	· Loose or worn wheel bearings	· Adjust or replace bearings
	· Incorrect steering gear adjustments	· Adjust steering gear
	· Incorrect front wheel alignment	· Correct front wheel alignment
Tire wear	· Improper tire pressure	· Inflate tires to recommended pressures
	· Failure to rotate tires	· Rotate tires
	· Brakes grabbing	· Adjust or repair brakes
	· Incorrect front wheel alignment	· Align incorrect angles
	· Broken or damaged steering and suspension parts	· Repair or replace defective parts
	· Wheel runout	· Replace faulty wheel
	· Excessive speed on turns	· Make driver aware of conditions
Vehicle leads to one side	· Improper tire pressures	· Inflate tires to recommended pressures
	· Front tires with uneven tread depth, wear pattern, or different cord design (i.e., one bias ply and one belted or radial tire on front wheels)	· Install tires of same cord construction and reasonably even tread depth, design, and wear pattern
	· Incorrect front wheel alignment	· Align incorrect angles
	· Brakes dragging	· Adjust or repair brakes
	· Pulling due to uneven tire construction	· Replace faulty tire

4. If equipped cruise control, remove the slip ring.

5. Remove the turn signal canceling sleeve.

6. On later models, remove the switch retaining screws, then, remove the switch.

7. Loosen the turn signal switch cam nut screw and lightly tap its head to permit the cam nut to loosen. Remove the turn signal switch assembly and the steering shaft upper bushing.

8. To install, reverse the removal proce-

Troubleshooting the Power Steering Gear

Problem	Cause	Solution
Hissing noise in steering gear	• There is some noise in all power steering systems. One of the most common is a hissing sound most evident at standstill parking. There is no relationship between this noise and performance of the steering. Hiss may be expected when steering wheel is at end of travel or when slowly turning at standstill.	• Slight hiss is normal and in no way affects steering. Do not replace valve unless hiss is extremely objectionable. A replacement valve will also exhibit slight noise and is not always a cure. Investigate clearance around flexible coupling rivets. Be sure steering shaft and gear are aligned so flexible coupling rotates in a flat plane and is not distorted as shaft rotates. Any metal-to-metal contacts through flexible coupling will transmit valve hiss into passenger compartment through the steering column.
Rattle or chuckle noise in steering gear	• Gear loose on frame	• Check gear-to-frame mounting screws. Tighten screws to 88 N·m (65 foot pounds) torque.
	• Steering linkage looseness	• Check linkage pivot points for wear. Replace if necessary.
	• Pressure hose touching other parts of car	• Adjust hose position. Do not bend tubing by hand.
	• Loose pitman shaft over center adjustment	• Adjust to specifications
	NOTE: A slight rattle may occur on turns because of increased clearance off the "high point." This is normal and clearance must not be reduced below specified limits to eliminate this slight rattle.	
	• Loose pitman arm	• Tighten pitman arm nut to specifications
Squawk noise in steering gear when turning or recovering from a turn	• Damper O-ring on valve spool cut	• Replace damper O-ring
Poor return of steering wheel to center	• Tires not properly inflated	• Inflate to specified pressure
	• Lack of lubrication in linkage and ball joints	• Lube linkage and ball joints
	• Lower coupling flange rubbing against steering gear adjuster plug	• Loosen pinch bolt and assemble properly
	• Steering gear to column misalignment	• Align steering column
	• Improper front wheel alignment	• Check and adjust as necessary
	• Steering linkage binding	• Replace pivots
	• Ball joints binding	• Replace ball joints
	• Steering wheel rubbing against housing	• Align housing
	• Tight or frozen steering shaft bearings	• Replace bearings
	• Sticking or plugged valve spool	• Remove and clean or replace valve
	• Steering gear adjustments over specifications	• Check adjustment with gear out of car. Adjust as required.
	• Kink in return hose	• Replace hose
Car leads to one side or the other (keep in mind road condition and wind. Test car in both directions on flat road)	• Front end misaligned	• Adjust to specifications
	• Unbalanced steering gear valve	• Replace valve
	NOTE: If this is cause, steering effort will be very light in direction of lead and normal or heavier in opposite direction	

Troubleshooting the Power Steering Gear (cont.)

Problem	Cause	Solution
Momentary increase in effort when turning wheel fast to right or left	• Low oil level • Pump belt slipping • High internal leakage	• Add power steering fluid as required • Tighten or replace belt • Check pump pressure. (See pressure test)
Steering wheel surges or jerks when turning with engine running especially during parking	• Low oil level • Loose pump belt • Steering linkage hitting engine oil pan at full turn • Insufficient pump pressure • Pump flow control valve sticking	• Fill as required • Adjust tension to specification • Correct clearance • Check pump pressure. (See pressure test). Replace relief valve if defective. • Inspect for varnish or damage, replace if necessary
Excessive wheel kickback or loose steering	• Air in system • Steering gear loose on frame • Steering linkage joints worn enough to be loose • Worn poppet valve • Loose thrust bearing preload adjustment • Excessive overcenter lash	• Add oil to pump reservoir and bleed by operating steering. Check hose connectors for proper torque and adjust as required. • Tighten attaching screws to specified torque • Replace loose pivots • Replace poppet valve • Adjust to specification with gear out of vehicle • Adjust to specification with gear out of car
Hard steering or lack of assist	• Loose pump belt • Low oil level **NOTE:** Low oil level will also result in excessive pump noise • Steering gear to column misalignment • Lower coupling flange rubbing against steering gear adjuster plug • Tires not properly inflated	• Adjust belt tension to specification • Fill to proper level. If excessively low, check all lines and joints for evidence of external leakage. Tighten loose connectors. • Align steering column • Loosen pinch bolt and assemble properly • Inflate to recommended pressure
Foamy milky power steering fluid, low fluid level and possible low pressure	• Air in the fluid, and loss of fluid due to internal pump leakage causing overflow	• Check for leak and correct. Bleed system. Extremely cold temperatures will cause system aeriation should the oil level be low. If oil level is correct and pump still foams, remove pump from vehicle and separate reservoir from housing. Check welsh plug and housing for cracks. If plug is loose or housing is cracked, replace housing.
Low pressure due to steering pump	• Flow control valve stuck or inoperative • Pressure plate not flat against cam ring	• Remove burrs or dirt or replace. Flush system. • Correct
Low pressure due to steering gear	• Pressure loss in cylinder due to worn piston ring or badly worn housing bore • Leakage at valve rings, valve body-to-worm seal	• Remove gear from car for disassembly and inspection of ring and housing bore • Remove gear from car for disassembly and replace seals

Troubleshooting the Power Steering Pump

Problem	Cause	Solution
Chirp noise in steering pump	• Loose belt	• Adjust belt tension to specification
Belt squeal (particularly noticeable at full wheel travel and stand still parking)	• Loose belt	• Adjust belt tension to specification
Growl noise in steering pump	• Excessive back pressure in hoses or steering gear caused by restriction	• Locate restriction and correct. Replace part if necessary.
Growl noise in steering pump (particularly noticeable at stand still parking)	• Scored pressure plates, thrust plate or rotor • Extreme wear of cam ring	• Replace parts and flush system • Replace parts
Groan noise in steering pump	• Low oil level • Air in the oil. Poor pressure hose connection.	• Fill reservoir to proper level • Tighten connector to specified torque. Bleed system by operating steering from right to left—full turn.
Rattle noise in steering pump	• Vanes not installed properly • Vanes sticking in rotor slots	• Install properly • Free up by removing burrs, varnish, or dirt
Swish noise in steering pump	• Defective flow control valve	• Replace part
Whine noise in steering pump	• Pump shaft bearing scored	• Replace housing and shaft. Flush system.
Hard steering or lack of assist	• Loose pump belt • Low oil level in reservoir **NOTE:** Low oil level will also result in excessive pump noise • Steering gear to column misalignment • Lower coupling flange rubbing against steering gear adjuster plug • Tires not properly inflated	• Adjust belt tension to specification • Fill to proper level. If excessively low, check all lines and joints for evidence of external leakage. Tighten loose connectors. • Align steering column • Loosen pinch bolt and assemble properly • Inflate to recommended pressure
Foaming milky power steering fluid, low fluid level and possible low pressure	• Air in the fluid, and loss of fluid due to internal pump leakage causing overflow	• Check for leaks and correct. Bleed system. Extremely cold temperatures will cause system aeriation should the oil level be low. If oil level is correct and pump still foams, remove pump from vehicle and separate reservoir from body. Check welsh plug and body for cracks. If plug is loose or body is cracked, replace body.
Low pump pressure	• Flow control valve stuck or inoperative • Pressure plate not flat against cam ring	• Remove burrs or dirt or replace. Flush system. • Correct
Momentary increase in effort when turning wheel fast to right or left	• Low oil level in pump • Pump belt slipping • High internal leakage	• Add power steering fluid as required • Tighten or replace belt • Check pump pressure. (See pressure test)
Steering wheel surges or jerks when turning with engine running especially during parking	• Low oil level • Loose pump belt • Steering linkage hitting engine oil pan at full turn • Insufficient pump pressure	• Fill as required • Adjust tension to specification • Correct clearance • Check pump pressure. (See pressure test). Replace flow control valve if defective.

Troubleshooting the Power Steering Pump (cont.)

Problem	Cause	Solution
Steering wheel surges or jerks when turning with engine running especially during parking (cont.)	• Sticking flow control valve	• Inspect for varnish or damage, replace if necessary
Excessive wheel kickback or loose steering	• Air in system	• Add oil to pump reservoir and bleed by operating steering. Check hose connectors for proper torque and adjust as required.
Low pump pressure	• Extreme wear of cam ring • Scored pressure plate, thrust plate, or rotor • Vanes not installed properly • Vanes sticking in rotor slots • Cracked or broken thrust or pressure plate	• Replace parts. Flush system. • Replace parts. Flush system. • Install properly • Freeup by removing burrs, varnish, or dirt • Replace part

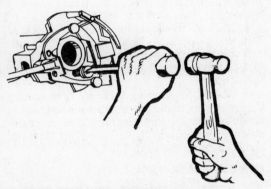

Loosening the turn signal cam nut screw

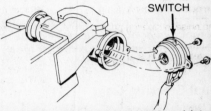

Ignition switch removal—1982 and later Accord, 1984 and later Civic and 1983 and later Prelude.

dures. When installing the turn signal switch assembly, engage the locating tab on the switch with the notch in the steering column. The steering shaft upper bushing should be installed with the flat side facing the upper side of the column. The alignment notch for the turn signal switch will be centered on the flat side of the bushing.

NOTE: *If the cam nut has been removed on the earlier models, be sure to install it with the small end up.*

Ignition Switch

REMOVAL AND INSTALLATION

1. Remove the steering column bolts and lower the column from the instrument panel to expose the ignition switch.

2. Remove the steering column housing upper and lower covers.

3. Disconnect the ignition switch wiring at the couplers.

4. The ignition switch assembly is held onto the column by two shear bolts. Using a drill, remove the screws and the ignition switch.

5. To install, reverse the removal procedures. You will have to replace the shear bolts with new ones.

On Accords 1982-88, Preludes 1983-88 and Civics 1984-88, the mechanical part of the switch does not have to be removed to replace the electrical part.

To remove the electrical part or base of the switch, proceed as follows:

1. Remove the steering column lower cover.

2. Disconnect the electrical connector from the switch.

3. Insert the key and turn it to **LOCK** position.

4. Remove the two switch retaining screws and the switch (base) from the rest of the switch.

Steering Linkage

REMOVAL AND INSTALLATION

Tie Rod Ends

1. Raise and support the front of the vehicle on jackstands. Remove the front wheels.

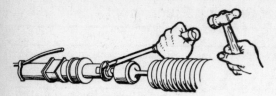

Tie-rod lockwasher removal

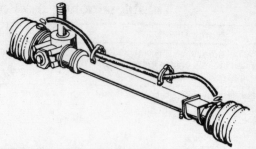

Separate the air tube from the dust seal bellows

2. For the Civic, use a Ball Joint Remover tool, press the tie rod end from the steering knuckle.

3. Remove the tie rod dust seal bellows clamps and move the rubber bellows on the tie rod and rack joints. On the Civic, disconnect the air tube at the dust seal joint.

4. Straighten the tie rod lockwasher tabs at the tie rod-to-rack joint and remove the tie rod by turning it with a wrench.

5. To install, reverse the removal procedures. Always use a new tie rod lockwasher during reassembly.

NOTE: *Fit the locating lugs into the slots on the rack and bend the outer edge of the washer over the flat part of the rod, after the tie rod nut has been properly tightened.*

Manual Steering Gear

TESTING

1. Remove the dust seal bellows retaining bands and slide the dust seals off the both sides of the gearbox housing.

2. Turn the front wheels full left and, using your hand, attempt to move the steering rack in an up-down direction.

3. Repeat with the wheel turned full right.

4. If any movement is felt, adjust the steering gearbox.

ADJUSTMENTS

1. Make sure that the rack is well lubricated.

2. Loosen the rack guide adjusting locknut.

3. Tighten the adjusting screw just to the point where the front wheels cannot be turned by hand.

4. Back off the adjusting screw 45° and hold it in that position while adjusting the locknut.

5. Recheck the play, then, move the wheels lock-to-lock, to make sure that the rack moves freely.

6. Check the steering force by first raising the front wheels and placing them in a straight-ahead position. Using a spring scale, turn the steering wheel, check the steering force; it should be no more than 3.3 lbs.

REMOVAL AND INSTALLATION

1. Raise and support the front end on jackstands.

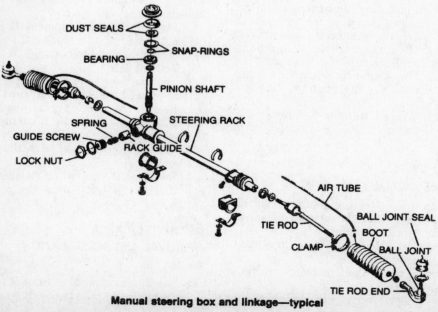

Manual steering box and linkage—typical

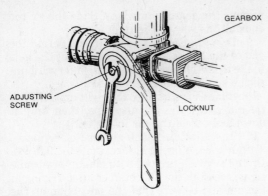

Steering gearbox adjustment

2. Remove the cover panel and steering joint cover. Unbolt and separate the steering shaft at the coupling.

3. Remove the front wheels.

4. Remove the cotter pins and unscrew the castle nuts on the tie rod ends. Using a ball joint tool disconnect the tie rod ends. Lift the tie rod ends out out the steering knuckles.

5. On cars with manual transmissions:

● Disconnect the shift lever torque rod from the clutch housing.

● Slide the pin retainer out of the way, drive out the spring pin and disconnect the shift rod.

6. On cars with automatic transmissions, remove the shift cable guide from the floor and pull the shift cable down by hand.

7. Remove the two nut connecting the exhaust header pipe to the exhaust pipe and move the exhaust pipe out of the way.

8. Push the rack all the way to the right and remove the gearbox brackets. Slide the tie rod ends all the way to the right.

9. Drop the gearbox far enough to permit the end of the pinion shaft to come out of the hole in the frame channel, then rotate it forward until the shaft is pointing rearward.

10. Slide the gearbox to the right until the left tie rod clears the exhaust pipe, then drop it down and out of the car to the left.

11. Installation is the reverse of removal. Torque the mounting bracket bolts to 29 ft. lbs. On the models equipped with manual transmissions, reinstall the pin retainer after driving in the pin and be sure that the projection on the pin retainer is in the hole.

Steering Torque Specifications
(ft. lbs.)

Tie-rod end locknut	29.0–35.0
Tie-rod ball joint nut	29.0–25.0
Bask guide locknut	29.0–36.0
Steering wheel retaining nut(s)	22.0–33.0

Power Steering Gear
ADJUSTMENT
Accord & Civic

1. Make sure that the rack is well lubricated.

2. Loosen the rack guide adjusting locknut.

3. Tighten the adjusting screw until it compresses the spring and seats against the guide, then loosen it. Retorque it to 35 inch lbs. then back it off 25°.

4. Hold it in that position while adjusting the locknut to 18 ft. lbs.

5. Recheck the play, and then move the wheels lock-to-lock, to make sure that the rack moves freely.

6. Check the steering force by first raising the front wheels and then placing them in a straight ahead position. Turn the steering wheel with a spring scale to check the steering force. Steering force should be no more than 4 lbs.

Prelude

1. Make sure that the rack is well lubricated.

2. Loosen the rack guide adjusting locknut.

3. Tighten the adjusting screw until it compresses the spring and seats against the guide, then loosen it. Retorque it to 24 inch lbs. then back it off 25° (3 ft. lbs. and 30-40° 4WD models).

4. Hold it in that position while adjusting the locknut to 18 ft. lbs.

5. Recheck the play, and then move the wheels lock-to-lock, to make sure that the rack moves freely.

6. Check the steering force by first raising the front wheels and then placing them in a straight ahead position. Turn the steering wheel with a spring scale to check the steering force. Steering force should be no more than 4 lbs.

REMOVAL AND INSTALLATION
Accord and Prelude

1. Raise and support the front end on jackstands.

2. Remove the steering shaft joint cover and disconnect the steering shaft at the coupling.

3. Drain the power steering fluid by disconnecting the return hose at the box and running the engine while turning the steering wheel lock to lock until fluid stops draining.

4. Remove the gearbox shield.

5. Remove the front wheels.

6. Using a ball joint tool, disconnect the tie rods from the knuckles.

7. On cars with manual transmissions:

Remove the shift extension from the transmission case.

Disconnect the gear shift rod from the

transmission case by removing the 8mm bolt.

8. On cars with automatic transmissions, remove the control cable clamp.

9. Remove the center beam.

10. On the 4WD models only, separate the joint guard cap and the joint guard. Remove the joint bolt from the driven pinion side. Remove the joint bolt from the center steering shaft side, then slide the joint back to disconnect it from the driven pinion.

11. Disconnect the exhaust header pipe at the manifold.

12. Remove the exhaust header pipe joint nuts.

13. Disconnect the hydraulic lines at the steering control until.

14. Shift the tie rods all the way right.

15. Remove the gearbox mounting bolts.

16. Slide the gearbox right so that the left tie rod clears the bottom of the rear beam. Remove the gearbox.

17. Installation is the reverse of removal. Torque the gearbox clamp bolts to 16 ft. lbs.

NOTE: *Some 1984-85 Accord and 1984-86 Prelude models may experience a power steering moan noise. This noise comes from the power steering rack and is usually heard on hard left turns. The corrective action to be taken in this case is to remove and replace the old power steering control valve with the new improved control valve available from the manufacturer.*

Civic

1. Raise and support the front end on jackstands.

2. Remove the cover panel and steering joint cover. Unbolt and separate the steering shaft at the coupling.

3. Drain the power steering fluid by disconnecting the return hose at the box and running the engine while turning the steering wheel lock to lock until fluid stops draining. Remove the gearbox shield. Remove the front wheels.

4. Remove the cotter pins and unscrew the castle nuts on the tie rod ends. Using a ball joint tool disconnect the tie rod ends. Lift the tie rod ends out out the steering knuckles.

5. On cars with manual transmissions:

Disconnect the shift lever torque rod from the clutch housing.

Slide the pin retainer out of the way, drive out the spring pin and disconnect the shift rod.

6. On cars with automatic transmissions, remove the shift cable guide from the floor and pull the shift cable down by hand.

7. Remove the two nut connecting the exhaust header pipe to the exhaust pipe and move the exhaust pipe out of the way. Disconnect the three hydraulic lines from the control unit.

8. Push the rack all the way to the right and

remove the gearbox brackets. Slide the tie rod ends all the way to the right.

9. Drop the gearbox far enough to permit the end of the pinion shaft to come out of the hole in the frame channel, then rotate it forward until the shaft is pointing rearward.

10. Slide the gearbox to the right until the left tie rod clears the exhaust pipe, then drop it down and out of the car to the left.

11. Installation is the reverse of removal. Torque the mounting bracket bolts to 29 ft. lbs. On the models equipped with manual transmissions, reinstall the pin retainer after driving in the pin and be sure that the projection on the pin retainer is in the hole.

Power Steering Pump
REMOVAL AND INSTALLATION

1. Using a drain pan, disconnect the cooler return hose from the reservoir and drain the fluid. Start the engine and allow it to run at fast idle. Turn the steering wheel from lock-to-lock several times, until the fluid stops running from the hose. Turn **OFF** the engine and discard the fluid. Reattach the hose.

2. Disconnect the inlet and outlet hoses from the pump.

3. Remove the drive belt.

4. Remove the bolts and the pump.

5. To install, reverse the removal procedures. Adjust the drive belt tension.

6. Refill the reservoir with fresh fluid, to the Full mark. Use only genuine Honda power steering fluid; ATF or other brands of fluid will damage the system. Bleed the power steering system.

BELT ADJUSTMENT

1. Loosen the adjuster arm bolt.

2. Move the pump, until the belt can be depressed approximately 15mm at the midpoint between the two pulleys under moderate thumb pressure. If the tension adjustment is being made on a new belt, the deflection should only be about 11mm, to allow for the initial stretching of the belt.

There is a raised bump on the top of the adjusting arm. If the belt has stretched to the point where the adjustment bolt is at or beyond the bump, the belt should be replaced.

BLEEDING

1. Check and/or refill the power steering reservoir.

2. Start the engine and operate it at fast idle.

3. Turn the steering wheel from side-to-side several times, lightly contacting the stops; this will bleed the system of air.

4. Check the reservoir level and add fluid if necessary.

BRAKE SYSTEM

Understanding the Brakes

HYDRAULIC SYSTEM

The brake pedal operates a hydraulic system that is used for 2 reasons. First, fluid under pressure can be carried to all parts of the vehicle by small hoses or metal lines without taking up a lot of room or causing routing problems. Second, the hydraulic fluid offers a great mechanical advantage—little foot pressure is required on the pedal, but a great deal of pressure is generated at the wheels.

The brake pedal is linked to a piston in the brake master cylinder, which is filled with hydraulic brake fluid. The master cylinder consists of a cylinder, containing a small piston and a fluid reservoir.

Modern master cylinders are actually 2 separate cylinders. These systems are called a dual circuit, because the front cylinder is connected to the front brakes and the rear cylinder to the rear brakes; some vehicles are connected diagonally. The 2 cylinders are actually separated, allowing for emergency stopping power should one part of the system fail.

The entire hydraulic system from the master cylinder to the wheels is full of hydraulic brake fluid. When the brake pedal is depressed, the pistons in the master cylinder are forced to move, exerting tremendous force on the fluid in the lines. The fluid has nowhere to go and forces the wheel cylinder piston (drum brakes) or caliper pistons (disc brakes) to exert pressure on the brake shoes or pads. The resulting friction between the brake shoe and wheel drum or the brake pad and disc slows the vehicle and eventually stops it.

Also attached to the brake pedal is a switch which lights the brake lights as the pedal is depressed. The lights stay **ON** until the brake pedal is released and returns to its normal position.

Each wheel cylinder in a drum brake system contains 2 pistons, one at either end, which push outward in opposite directions. In disc brake systems, the wheel cylinders are part of the caliper; there can be as many as 4 or as few as 1. Whether disc or drum type, all pistons use some type of rubber seal to prevent leakage around the piston and a rubber dust boot seals the outer ends of the wheel cylinders against dirt and moisture.

When the brake pedal is released, a spring pushes the master cylinder pistons back to their normal position. Check valves in the master cylinder piston allow fluid to flow toward the wheel cylinders or calipers as the piston returns. As the brake shoe return springs pull the brake shoes back to the released position, excess fluid returns to the master cylinder through compensating ports, which have been uncovered as the pistons move back. Any fluid that has leaked from the system will also be replaced through the compensating ports.

All dual circuit brake systems use a switch to activate a light, warning of brake failure. The switch is located in a valve mounted near the

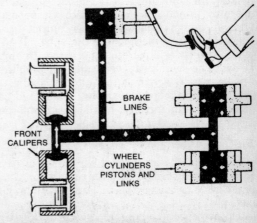

BRAKE LINES

FRONT CALIPERS

WHEEL CYLINDERS PISTONS AND LINKS

Hydraulic system schematic

master cylinder. A piston in the valve receives pressure on each end from the front and rear brake circuits. When the pressures are balanced, the piston remains stationary but when one circuit has a leak, greater pressure during the application of the brakes will force the piston to one side or the other, closing the switch and activating the warning light.

Disc brake systems also have a metering valve to prevent the front disc brakes from engaging before the rear brakes have contacted the drums. This ensures that the front brakes will not normally be used alone to stop the vehicle. A proportioning valve is also used to limit pressure to the rear brakes to prevent rear wheel lock-up during hard braking.

DRUM BRAKES

Drum brakes use two brake shoes mounted on a stationary backing plate. These shoes are positioned inside a circular cast iron drum which rotates with the wheel assembly. The shoes are held in place by springs; this allows them to slide toward the drums (when they are applied) while keeping the linings and drums in alignment. The shoes are actuated by a wheel cylinder which is usually mounted at the top of the backing plate. When the brakes are applied, hydraulic pressure forces the wheel cylinder's two actuating links outward. Since these links bear directly against the top of the brake shoes, the tops of the shoes are forced outward against the inner side of the drum. This action forces the bottoms of the two shoes to contact the brake drum by rotating the entire assembly slightly (known as servo action). When pressure within the wheel cylinder is relieved, return springs pull the shoes back away from the drum.

Most modern drum brakes are designed to self-adjust during application when the vehicle is moving in reverse. This motion causes both shoes to rotate very slightly with the drum, rocking an adjusting lever. The self-adjusters are only intended to compensate for normal wear. Although the adjustment is "automatic", there is a definite method to actuate the self-adjuster, which is done during normal driving. Driving the vehicle in reverse and applying the brakes usually activates the automatic adjusters. If the brake pedal was low, you should be able to feel an increase in the height of the brake pedal.

DISC BRAKES

Instead of the traditional expanding brakes that press outward against a circular drum, disc brake systems utilize a cast iron disc with brake pads positioned on either side of it. Braking effect is achieved in a manner similar to the way you would squeeze a spinning disc between your fingers. The disc (rotor) is a one-piece casting with cooling fins between the two braking surfaces. This enables air to circulate between the braking surfaces making them less sensitive to heat buildup and more resistant to fade. Dirt and water do not affect braking action since contaminants are thrown off by the centrifugal action of the rotor or scraped off by the pads. Also, the equal clamping action of the two brake pads tends to ensure uniform, straight-line stops. All disc brakes are inherently self-adjusting.

There are three general types of disc brake:
1. A fixed caliper, 4-piston type.
2. A floating caliper, single piston type.
3. A sliding caliper, single piston type.

The fixed caliper design uses two pistons mounted on either side of the rotor (in each side of the caliper). The caliper is mounted rigidly and does not move.

The sliding and floating designs are quite similar and often considered as one. The pad on the inside of the rotor is moved into contact with the rotor by hydraulic force. The caliper, which is not held in a fixed position, moves slightly, bringing the outside pad into contact with the rotor. There are various methods of attaching floating calipers; some pivot at the bottom or top and some slide on mounting bolts.

POWER BRAKE BOOSTERS

Power brakes operate just as standard brake systems except in the actuation of the master cylinder pistons. A vacuum diaphragm is located behind the master cylinder and assists the driver in applying the brakes, reducing both the effort and travel he must put into moving the brake pedal.

The vacuum diaphragm housing is connected to the intake manifold by a vacuum hose. A check valve at the point where the hose enters the diaphragm housing ensures that during periods of low manifold vacuum brake assist vacuum will not be lost.

Depressing the brake pedal closes off the vacuum source and allows atmospheric pressure to enter on one side of the diaphragm. This causes the master cylinder pistons to move and apply the brakes. When the brake pedal is released, vacuum is applied to both sides of the diaphragm and return springs return the diaphragm and master cylinder pistons to the released position. If the vacuum fails, the brake pedal rod will butt against the end of the master cylinder actuating rod and direct mechanical application will occur as the pedal is depressed.

The hydraulic and mechanical problems that apply to conventional brake systems also apply to power brakes.

Honda uses a dual hydraulic system, with the brakes connected diagonally. In other words, the right front and left rear brakes are on the same hydraulic line and the left front and right rear are on the other line. This has the added advantage of front disc emergency braking, should either of the hydraulic systems fail. The diagonal rear brake serves to counteract the sway from single front disc braking.

A leading/trailing drum brake is used for the rear brakes, with disc brakes for the front. All Honda's are equipped with a brake warning light, which is activated when a defect in the brake system occurs.

Adjustments

REAR DRUM BRAKE ADJUSTMENT

1. Block the front wheels and release the parking brake. Raise and support the rear of the vehicle on jackstands.
2. Depress the brake pedal 2-3 times and release.
3. The adjuster is located on the inboard side, underneath the control arm. Turn the adjuster clockwise until the wheel no longer turns.
4. Back off the adjuster two (2) clicks and turn the wheel to see if the brake shoes are dragging. If they are dragging, back off the adjuster one more click.

BRAKE PEDAL FREE-PLAY

Free-play is the distance the pedal travels from the stop (brake light switch) until the pushrod actuates the master cylinder.

To check free-play, first measure the distance (with the carpet removed) from the floor to the brake pedal. Then disconnect the return spring

Drum brake adjustment

and again measure the distance from the floor to the brake pedal. The difference between the two measurements is the pedal free-play. The specified free-play is 1.0-5.0mm. Free-play adjustment is made by loosening the locknut on the brake light switch and rotating the switch body until the specified clearance is obtained.

WARNING: *If there is no free-play, the master cylinder pistons will not return to their stops. This can block the compensating ports, which will prevent the brake pads and linings from returning fully when the pedal is released. This will result in rapid brake burn-up. Free-play provides a safety factor against normal rubber swell and expansion or deflection of body parts and pedal linkage.*

HYDRAULIC SYSTEM

The hydraulic system is composed of the master cylinder and brake booster, the brake lines, the brake pressure differential valve(s), the wheel cylinders (drum brakes) and calipers (disc brakes).

The master cylinder serves as a brake fluid reservoir and (along with the booster) as a hydraulic pump. Brake fluid is stored in the two sections of the master cylinder. Each section corresponds to each part of the dual braking system. This tandem master cylinder is required by Federal law as a safety device.

When the brake pedal is depressed, it moves a piston mounted in the bottom of the master cylinder. The movement of this piston creates hydraulic pressure in the master cylinder. This pressure is carried to the wheel cylinders or the calipers by brake lines, passing through the pressure differential or proportioning valve.

When the hydraulic pressure reaches the wheels, after the pedal has been depressed, it enters the wheel cylinders or calipers. Here it comes into contact with a piston(s). The hydraulic pressure causes the piston(s) to move, which moves the brake shoes or pads (disc brakes), causing them to contact the drums or rotors (disc brakes). Friction between the brake shoes and the drums causes the vehicle to slow. There is a relationship between the amount of pressure that is applied to the brake peal and the amount of force which moves the brake shoes against the drums. Therefore, the harder the brake pedal is depressed, the quicker the vehicle will stop.

Since the hydraulic system is one which operates on fluids, air is a natural enemy of the brake system. Air in the hydraulic system retards the passage of hydraulic pressure from the master cylinder to the wheels. Anytime a hydraulic component below the master cylinder is opened or removed, the system must be bled of air to ensure proper operation. Air trapped in the hydraulic system can also cause the brake warning light to turn **ON**, even though the system has not failed. This is especially true after repairs have been performed on the system.

Master Cylinder
REMOVAL AND INSTALLATION

Before removing the master cylinder, cover the body surfaces with fender covers and rags to prevent damage to painted surfaces by brake fluid.

1. Disconnect the brake lines from the master cylinder.
2. Remove the master cylinder-to-vacuum booster attaching bolts and the master cylinder from the vehicle.
3. To install, reverse the removal procedures. Bleed the brake system.

OVERHAUL

1. Remove the fluid reservoir caps and floats, then, drain the reservoirs.
2. Loosen the retaining clamps and remove the reservoirs.
3. Remove the primary piston stop bolt.
4. Remove the piston retaining clip, washer and the primary piston.
5. Wrap a rag around the end of the master cylinder, so that it blocks the bore. Hold your finger over the stop bolt hole and direct a small amount of compressed air into the primary outlet. This should slide the primary piston to the end of the master cylinder bore, so it can be removed.
6. Remove the two union caps, washers, check valves and springs.
7. For overhaul procedures, check the following:
   a. Clogged orifices in the pistons and cylinder.

Closeup of master cylinder stop bolt

Removing retaining clip

Piston removal

Disassembled master cylinder

   b. Damage to the reservoir attaching surface.
   c. Damage to the check valves.
   d. Wear or damage to the piston cups.
   e. The clearance between the master cylin-

der bore and the pistons. The clearance should be 0.020-0.127mm.

8. To assemble of the master cylinder, reverse the disassembly procedures. Be sure to check the following:

a. The check valves and piston cups should be replaced when the master cylinder is assembled, regardless of their condition.

b. Apply a thin coat of brake fluid to the pistons before installing. When installing the pistons, push in while rotating to prevent damage to the piston cups.

c. Tighten the union cap and stop bolts securely.

Power Brake Booster

INSPECTION

A preliminary check of the vacuum booster can be made as follows:

a. Depress the brake pedal several times using normal pressure. Make sure that the pedal height does not vary.

b. Hold the pedal in the depressed position and start the engine. The pedal should drop slightly.

c. Hold the pedal in the above position and stop the engine. The pedal should stay in the depressed position for approximately 30 seconds.

d. If the pedal does not drop when the engine is started or rises after the engine is stopped, the booster is not functioning properly.

REMOVAL AND INSTALLATION

1. Disconnect the vacuum hose from the booster.

2. Disconnect the brake lines from the master cylinder.

3. Remove the brake pedal-to-booster link pin and the booster-to-firewall nuts. The pushrod and nuts are located inside the vehicle on the passenger side, under the dash.

4. Remove the booster with the master cylinder attached.

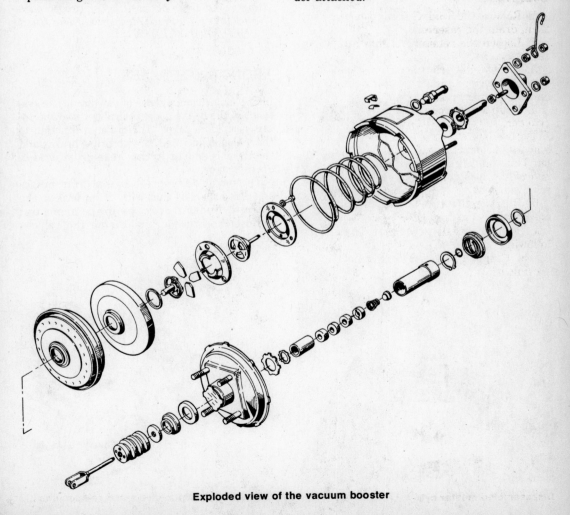

Exploded view of the vacuum booster

5. To install, reverse the removal procedures. Bleed the brake system.

Bleeding

When it is necessary to flush the brake hydraulic system because of parts replacement or fluid contamination, the following procedure should be observed:

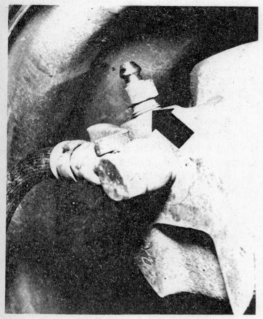

Closeup of front bleeder

Bleeding the rear brakes

1. Loosen the wheel cylinder bleeder screw. Drain the brake fluid by pumping the brake pedal. Pump the pedal until all of the old fluid has been pumped out and replaced by new fluid.

2. The flushing procedure should be performed in the following sequence:

    a. Bleed the left front brake.
    b. Bleed the right rear brake.
    c. Bleed the right front brake.
    d. Bleed the left rear brake.

3. Bleed the back of the master cylinder before the front, through the two bleed valves. Fasten one end of a plastic tube onto the bleed valve and immerse the other end in a clear jar filled with brake fluid. When air bubbles cease to emerge from the end of the tubing, the bleeding is completed. Be sure to keep the fluid reservoir filled at all times during the bleeding process so air does not enter the system.

WARNING: *Brake fluid is adversely affected by contamination from dirt, automotive petroleum products and water. Contaminants can plug parts of the hydraulic system, causing rapid wear or swelling of rubber parts and lower the boiling point of the fluid. KEEP FLUID CLEAN.*

FRONT DISC BRAKES

The major components of the disc brake system are the brake pads, the caliper and the rotor (disc). The caliper is similar in function to the wheel cylinder used with drum brakes and the rotor is similar to the brake drum used in drum brakes.

The major difference between drum brakes and disc brakes is that with drum brakes, the wheel cylinder forces the brake shoes out against the brake drum to stop the vehicle,

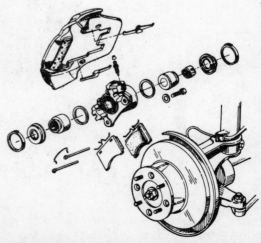

Exploded view of the disc brake components

while with disc brakes, the caliper forces the brake pads inward to squeeze the rotor and stop the vehicle. The biggest advantage of disc brakes over drum brakes is that the caliper and brake pads enclose only a small portion of the rotor, leaving the rest of it exposed to outside air. This aids in rapid heat dissipation, reducing brake fade and throws off water fast.

CAUTION: *Brake shoes contain asbestos, which has been determined to be a cancer causing agent. Never clean the brake surfaces with compressed air! Avoid inhaling any dust from any brake surface! When cleaning brake surfaces, use a commercially available brake cleaning fluid.*

Brake Pads
REMOVAL AND INSTALLATION
1973-78 Models

1. Raise and support the vehicle on jackstands. Remove the wheels.
2. After removing the wheel, remove the pad retaining clip which is fitted in the holes of the pad retaining pins.
3. Using a pair of pliers, remove the two retaining pins and fitting springs. When removing them, care must be taken to prevent the springs from flying apart.
4. The front brake pad can be removed, together with the shim, after removing the springs and pins. If the pads are difficult to remove, open the bleeder valve and move the caliper in the direction of the piston. The pads will become loose and can be easily removed.
NOTE: *After the pads are removed, the brake pedal must not be touched.*
The disc pads should be replaced when approximately 2mm lining thickness remains (thickness of lining material only).
To provide space for installing the pad, loosen the bleed valve and push the inner piston back into the cylinder. Also push back the outer piston by applying pressure to the caliper. After providing space for the pads, close the bleed valve and insert the pad. Insert a shim behind each pad with the arrow on the shim pointing up. Incorrect installation of the shims can cause squealing brakes.

1979-88 Models

1. Raise and support the vehicle on jackstands. Remove the wheels.
2. Remove the lower caliper support pin and pivot the caliper up, away from the rotor.
3. Remove the pads, shim and anti-rattle spring. Clean all points where the shoes and shim touch the caliper and mount. Apply a thin film of silicone grease to the cleaned areas.

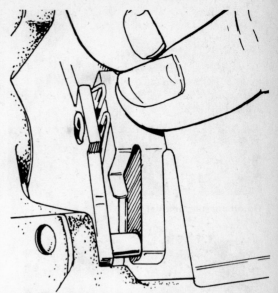
Removing the pad retaining clip

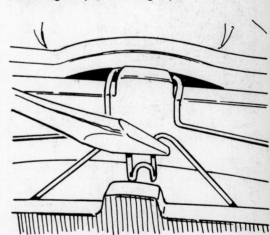
Removing the retaining pin springs

4. Place the anti-rattle springs in position.
5. Install the pads with the shim against the outside shoe.
6. Loosen the bleed screw slightly and push in the caliper piston to allow mounting of the caliper over the rotor. Tighten the bleed screw.
7. Pivot the caliper down over the rotor and install the lower support pin. Tighten the pin to 13 ft. lbs.

Brake Caliper
REMOVAL AND INSTALLATION

1. Raise and support the front of the vehicle on jackstands. Remove the front wheels.
2. Loosen the brake line from the wheel cylinder.
3. The caliper housing is mounted to the

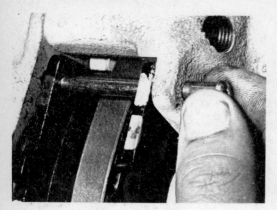

Retaining pin removal

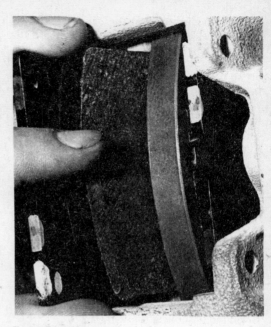

Removing the pads

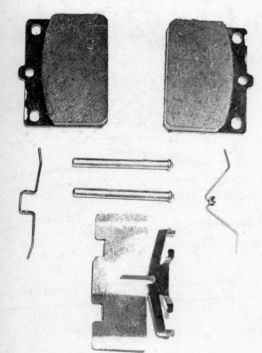

Disc brake pads, springs and pins

Closeup showing retaining pins

steering knuckle with two bolts located behind the cylinder. Remove these bolts and the caliper.

To install, reverse the removal procedures. Be sure to inspect all parts before installing and bleed the brake system before operating the vehicle.

OVERHAUL

NOTE: *Wash all parts in brake fluid. DO NOT use cleaning solvent or gasoline.*

1. Remove the inner and outer pad springs and pin clips, then, the pins and pads.

NOTE: *The springs are different, so note the*

Caliper housing removal

Retaining ring removal

location and method of installation before removing.

2. Push the yoke toward the rear (inboard side) of the cylinder, until it is free to separate the yoke from the cylinder. You may have to tap lightly with a plastic hammer (where the mounting bolts are located) to remove the cylinder. Exercise extreme care to avoid damaging the cylinder body. If only the cylinder body moves, without the outer piston, a gentle tap on the piston should loosen it.

3. To dismantle the cylinder, first remove the retaining rings at both ends of the cylinder with a screwdriver, being careful not to damage the rubber boot.

4. Both pistons can be removed from the cylinder body either by pushing through one end with a wooden rod or by blowing compressed air into the cylinder inlet port.

NOTE: *If the wheel cylinder pistons are removed for any reason, the piston seals must be replaced.*

5. Using a small pry bar, remove the piston seals, installed on the inside of the cylinder at both ends.

6. Inspect the caliper operation. If the lining wear differs greatly between the inner and outer pads, the caliper may be unable to move properly due to rust an dirt on the sliding surfaces. Clean the sliding part of the caliper and apply brake grease.

NOTE: *All brake parts are critical items. If there is any question as to the serviceability of any brake part—replace it.*

7. Check the piston-to-cylinder clearance. The specified clearance is 0.020-0.127mm. Also check the pistons and cylinder bore for scuffing and scratching.

8. Check the dust covers, retaining rings, nylon retainers and all other parts for wear or damage.

9. To reassemble the caliper, reverse the removal procedures. Bleed the brake system.

Piston removal

Piston seal

Note the discoloration in the caliper. If it cannot be cleaned up easily, it will have to be replaced

Installing piston in caliper

Brake Disc (Rotor)

REMOVAL AND INSTALLATION

1973-79 Civic and 1979-81 Accord Models

NOTE: *The following procedure for the brake disc removal necessitates the use of a hydraulic press. You will have to go to a machine or auto shop equipped with a press; DO NOT attempt this procedure without a press.*

1. Raise and support the front of the vehicle on jackstands. Remove the front wheels.
2. Remove the center spindle nuts.
3. Remove the caliper assembly; DO NOT let the caliper assembly hang by the brake hose.
4. Use a slide hammer with a hub puller attachment or a conventional hub puller, to extract the hub with the disc attached.
5. Remove the four bolts and separate the hub from the disc.

6. Remove the steering knuckle from the vehicle.
7. Remove the wheel bearings from the knuckle.

NOTE: *If, for any reason, the hub is removed, the front wheel bearings must be replaced.*

8. To install the disc, you have to use a hydraulic press for both the bearings and the hub. After installing the bearings (see below), install the front hub using the Special Base tool No. 07965-6340300 and Drift tools No. 07965-6340100 and 07965-6340200. Position the hub with the steering knuckle under the base and press it through the base.

1980-88 Civic, 1982-88 Accord and 1979-88 Prelude Models

1. Raise and support the front of the vehicle on jackstands. Remove the front wheels.
2. Remove the caliper assembly; DO NOT let the caliper assembly hang by the brake hose.
3. Remove the retaining screw from the brake rotor and remove the rotor from the hub.
4. To install the disc, reverse the removal procedure.

INSPECTION

1. The brake disc develops circular scores after long or even short usage when there is frequent braking. Excessive scoring not only causes a squealing brake, but also shortens the service life of the brake pads. However, light scoring of the disc surface, not exceeding 0.38mm in depth, will result from normal use and is not detrimental to brake operation.

NOTE: *Differences in the left and right disc surfaces can result in uneven braking.*

2. Disc runout is the movement of the disc from side-to-side. Position a dial indicator in the middle of the pad wear area and turn the disc, while checking the indicator. If disc runout exceeds 0.15mm, replace the disc.

3. Disc parallelism is the measurement of variations in disc thickness at several locations on the disc circumference. To measure parallelism, place a mark on the disc and measure the disc thickness with a micrometer. Repeat this measurement at eight (8) equal increments on the circumference of the disc. If the measurements vary more than 0.07mm, replace the disc.

NOTE: *Only the outer portion of the disc can be checked while installed on the vehicle. If the installed parallelism check is within specifications but you have reason to suspect that parallelism is the problem, remove the disc and repeat the check using the center of pad wear for a checking point.*

Checking disc runout

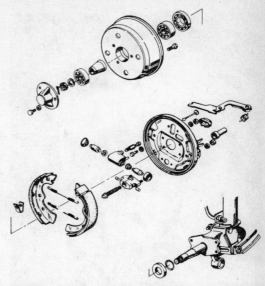

Exploded view of rear drum brake assembly—Civic sedan and hatchback

REAR DRUM BRAKES

CAUTION: *Brake shoes contain asbestos, which has been determined to be a cancer causing agent. Never clean the brake surfaces with compressed air! Avoid inhaling any dust from any brake surface! When cleaning brake surfaces, use a commercially available brake cleaning fluid.*

All Honda's employ a leading/trailing type of drum brake, in which there are two curved brake shoes supported by an anchor plate and wheel cylinder. When the brake pedal is depressed and hydraulic pressure is delivered to the wheel cylinder, the wheel cylinder expands to force the shoes against the drum.

Friction between the brake shoes and the drum causes the vehicle to slow and stop. When the brake pedal is released, the brake shoe return springs move the brakes away from the drum. If the lining on the brakes becomes contaminated or the lining/drum becomes grooved, the engagement of the brakes and drum will become very harsh, causing the brakes to lock up and/or squeal. If the brake shoes on one wheel contact the drum before the same action occurs in the other wheels, the brakes will pull to one side when applied.

Brake Drums

REMOVAL AND INSTALLATION

1. Raise and support the rear of the vehicle on jackstands. Remove the rear wheels. Make sure that the parking brake is **OFF**.

2. Remove the bearing cap and the castle nut.

3. Pull off the rear brake drum. If the drum is difficult to remove, use a brake drum puller or a front hub puller and slide hammer.

4. To install, reverse the removal procedures. Torque the rear hub nut to 83 ft. lbs. (Civic 1973-79).

Bearing cap removal on the Civic

Cotter pin removal

Bearing cap removal on the Accord and Prelude

Castle nut removal

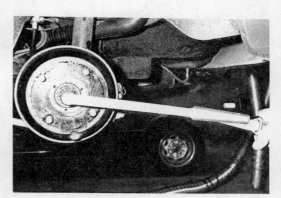

Torquing the rear hub nut on the Civic

INSPECTION

Check the drum for cracks and the inner surface of the shoe for excessive wear and damage. The inner diameter (I.D.) of the drum should be no more than specifications, nor should the drum be more than 0.10mm out-of-round.

Brake Shoes

REMOVAL AND INSTALLATION

1. Refer to the "Brake Drum, Removal and Installation" procedures in this section and remove the brake drum.

2. Remove the tension pin clips, the two brake return springs and the shoes. If you are installing new shoes, back off the adjusters.

WARNING: *The upper and lower brake shoe return springs on the sedan are different and*

5. On the Accord, Prelude and Civic (1980-88), which have tapered roller bearings, use the following procedure:

   a. Torque the hub nut to 18 ft. lbs.

   b. Rotate the drum by hand several times and loosen the nut.

   c. Torque the nut to 3.6 ft. lbs.

   d. If the spindle nut is not aligned with the hole in spindle, tighten the nut just enough to align the nut and the hole.

   e. Insert the cotter pin holder and a new cotter pin.

Rear brake shoes

Closeup of brake shoe retaining clip

Disassembled wheel cylinder

OVERHAUL

Remove the wheel cylinder dust seals from the grooves to permit the removal of the cylinder pistons.

Wash all parts in fresh brake fluid and check the cylinder bore and pistons for scratches and other damage, replacing where necessary. Check the clearance between the piston and the cylinder bore, by taking the difference between the piston diameter and the bore diameter. The specified clearance is 0.020-0.100mm.

When assembling the wheel cylinder, apply a coat of brake fluid to the pistons, piston cups and cylinder walls.

should not be interchanged. The upper spring is designed so that the spring coils are located on the outboard side of the shoe, while the lower spring is designed so that its coils are located on the inboard side of the shoe with the crossbar facing downward.

3. To install, reverse the removal procedure. Be sure to check the brake lining thickness before assembly. If the thickness is less than 2mm, replace the lining.

Wheel Cylinders

REMOVAL AND INSTALLATION

1. Refer to the "Brake Shoes, Removal and Installation" procedures in this section and remove the brake shoes.

2. Disconnect the parking brake cable and brake lines from the backing plate; be sure to have a drip pan to catch the brake fluid.

3. Remove the two wheel cylinder-to-backing plate nuts and the wheel cylinder.

4. To install, reverse the removal procedures. When assembling, apply a thin coat of grease to the grooves of the wheel cylinder piston and the sliding surfaces of the backing plate.

REAR DISC BRAKES

The major components of the disc brake system are the brake pads, the caliper and the rotor (disc). The caliper is similar in function to the wheel cylinder used with drum brakes and the rotor is similar to the brake drum used in drum brakes.

The major difference between drum brakes and disc brakes is that with drum brakes, the wheel cylinder forces the brake shoes out against the brake drum to stop the vehicle, while with disc brakes, the caliper forces the brake pads inward to squeeze the rotor and stop the vehicle. The biggest advantage of disc brakes over drum brakes is that the caliper and brake pads enclose only a small portion of the rotor, leaving the rest of it exposed to outside air. This aids in rapid heat dissipation, reducing brake fade and throws off water fast.

CAUTION: *Brake shoes contain asbestos, which has been determined to be a cancer causing agent. Never clean the brake surfaces with compressed air! Avoid inhaling any dust from any brake surface! When cleaning brake surfaces, use a commercially available brake cleaning fluid.*

Brake Pads

REMOVAL AND INSTALLATION

Prelude Si Models

1. Raise and support the vehicle on jackstands. Remove the wheels.

2. Remove the caliper shield.

3. Remove the parking brake cable from the caliper.

4. Remove the caliper bolts, then remove the caliper assembly.

5. Remove the pads, shim and anti-rattle spring. Clean all points where the shoes and shim touch the caliper and mount. Apply a thin film of silicone grease to the cleaned areas.

6. Place the anti-rattle springs in position.

7. Install the pads with the shim against the outside shoe.

8. Rotate the caliper piston clockwise into place in the cylinder, then align the cutout in the piston with the tab on the inner pad by turning back the piston.

9. Pivot the caliper down over the rotor and install the caliper bolts. Tighten the bolts to 17 ft. lbs.

10. Install the parking brake cable and the caliper shield.

Brake Caliper

REMOVAL AND INSTALLATION

1. Raise and support the front of the vehicle on jackstands. Remove the front wheels.

2. Remove the parking brake cable.

3. The caliper housing is mounted to the knuckle with two bolts located behind the cylinder. Remove these bolts and the caliper.

4. To install, position the caliper on the knuckle and tighten the caliper bolts to 17 ft. lbs. Be sure to inspect all parts before installing and bleed the brake system before operating the vehicle.

Brake Disc

REMOVAL AND INSTALLATION

Prelude Si

1. Raise and support the front of the vehicle on jackstands. Remove the front wheels.

2. Remove the caliper assembly; DO NOT let the caliper assembly hang by the brake hose.

3. Remove the retaining screw from the brake rotor and remove the rotor from the hub.

4. To install the disc, position it on the hub and install the retaining screw.

INSPECTION

1. The brake disc develops circular scores after long or even short usage when there is frequent braking. Excessive scoring not only causes a squealing brake, but also shortens the service life of the brake pads. However, light scoring of the disc surface, not exceeding 0.38mm in depth, will result from normal use and is not detrimental to brake operation.

NOTE: *Differences in the left and right disc surfaces can result in uneven braking.*

2. Disc runout is the movement of the disc from side-to-side. Position a dial indicator in the middle of the pad wear area and turn the disc, while checking the indicator. If disc runout exceeds 0.15mm, replace the disc.

3. Disc parallelism is the measurement of variations in disc thickness at several locations on the disc circumference. To measure parallel-

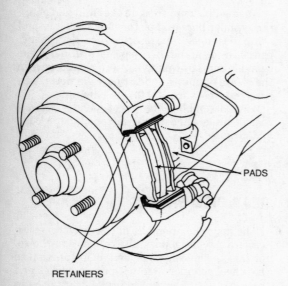

PADS

RETAINERS

Rear disc brake retainer locations

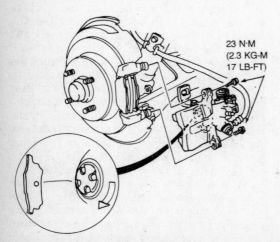

23 N·M
(2.3 KG-M
17 LB-FT)

Caliper piston and pad alignment

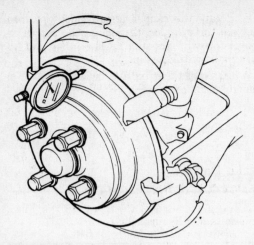

Checking brake disc run-out

ism, place a mark on the disc and measure the disc thickness with a micrometer. Repeat this measurement at eight (8) equal increments on the circumference of the disc. If the measurements vary more than 0.015mm, replace the disc.

> NOTE: *Only the outer portion of the disc can be checked while installed on the vehicle. If the installed parallelism check is within specifications but you have reason to suspect that parallelism is the problem, remove the disc and repeat the check using the center of pad wear for a checking point.*

PARKING BRAKE
Cable

The parking brake is a mechanical type which applies braking force to the rear wheels, through the rear brake shoes. The cable, which is attached to the tail end of the parking brake lever, extends to the equalizer and to the both rear brakes. When the lever is pulled, the cable becomes taut, pulling both the both parking brake arms fitted to the brake shoes.

REMOVAL AND INSTALLATION

1. Remove the adjusting nut from the equalizer mounted on the rear axle or in the console (Accord 1982-88, Prelude 1983-88 and Civic 1984-88) and separate the cable from the equalizer.

2. Set the parking brake to a fully released position and remove the cotter pin from the side of the brake lever.

3. After removing the cotter pin, pull out the pin which connects the cable and the lever.

4. Detach the cable from the guides at the front and right side of the fuel tank, then, remove the cable.

5. To install, grease the cable/guides and reverse the removal procedures.

ADJUSTMENT
Inspect the following items:

   a. Check the ratchet for wear.
   b. Check the cables for wear or damage

Exploded view of parking brake components

and the cable guide and equalizer for looseness.

c. Check the equalizer cable where it contacts the equalizer and apply grease (if necessary).

d. Check the rear brake adjustment.

The rear wheels should be locked when the handbrake lever is pulled 1-5 notches (1973-78) or 3-7 notches (1979-88). Adjustment is made by lifting the lever one notch and turning the nut located at the equalizer, between the lower control arms or console.

Brake Specifications

Year	Model	Lug Nut Torque (ft. lbs.)	Brake Disc		Standard Brake Drum Diameter	Minimum Lining Thickness	
			Minimum Thickness	Maximum Runout		Front	Rear
1973	Civic	51–65	0.354	0.006	7.066	0.063	0.079
	Civic Wagon	51–65	0.449	0.006	7.087	0.300	0.079
1974	Civic	51–65	0.354	0.006	7.066	0.063	0.079
	Civic Wagon	51–65	0.449	0.006	7.087	0.300	0.079
1975	Civic	51–65	0.354	0.006	7.066	0.063	0.079
	Civic Wagon	51–65	0.449	0.006	7.087	0.300	0.079
1976	Civic	51–65	0.354	0.006	7.066	0.063	0.079
	Civic Wagon	51–65	0.449	0.006	7.087	0.300	0.079
	Accord	51–65	0.433	0.006	7.080	0.063	0.079
1977	Civic	51–65	0.354	0.006	7.066	0.063	0.079
	Civic Wagon	51–65	0.449	0.006	7.087	0.300	0.079
	Accord	51–65	0.433	0.006	7.080	0.063	0.079
1978	Civic	51–65	0.354	0.006	7.066	0.063	0.079
	Civic Wagon	51–65	0.449	0.006	7.087	0.300	0.079
	Accord	51–65	0.433	0.006	7.080	0.063	0.079
1979	Civic	51–65	0.354	0.006	7.066	0.063	0.079
	Civic Wagon	51–65	0.449	0.006	7.087	0.300	0.079
	Accord	51–65	0.413	0.006	7.080	0.063	0.079
	Prelude	80	0.413	0.006	7.087	0.063	0.079
1980	Civic	51–65	①	0.006	7.066	0.063	0.079
	Civic Wagon	51–65	①	0.006	7.87	0.063	0.079
	Accord	51–65	0.413	0.006	7.080	0.063	0.079
	Prelude	80	0.413	0.006	7.080	0.063	0.079
1981	Civic	51–65	①	0.006	7.066	0.063	0.079
	Civic Wagon	51–65	①	0.006	7.870	0.063	0.079
	Accord	51–65	0.413	0.006	7.080	0.063	0.079
	Prelude	80	0.413	0.006	7.080	0.063	0.079
1982	Civic	51–65	①	0.006	7.066	0.063	0.079
	Civic Wagon	51–65	①	0.006	7.87	0.063	0.079
	Accord	51–65	0.600	0.006	7.870	0.063	0.079
	Prelude	80	0.413	0.006	7.080	0.063	0.079

Brake Specifications (cont.)

Year	Model	Lug Nut Torque (ft. lbs.)	Brake Disc		Standard Brake Drum Diameter	Minimum Lining Thickness	
			Minimum Thickness	Maximum Runout		Front	Rear
1983	Civic	51–65	①	0.006	7.066	0.063	0.079
	Civic Wagon	51–65	①	0.006	7.870	0.063	0.079
	Accord	80	0.60	0.006	7.870	0.063	0.079
	Prelude	80	0.67	0.006	7.870	0.120	0.080
1984	Civic	80	②	0.004	7.090	0.120	0.080
	Civic Wagon	80	0.59	0.004	7.870	0.120	0.080
	Civic CRX	80	③	0.004	7.090	0.120	0.080
	Accord	80	0.67	0.006	7.870	0.059	0.080
	Prelude	80	0.67 ④	0.004	—	0.120	0.060
1985	Civic	80	②	0.004	7.090	0.120	0.080
	Civic Wagon	80	0.59	0.004	7.870	0.120	0.080
	Civic CRX	80	③	0.004	7.090	0.120	0.080
	Accord	80	0.67	0.004	7.870	0.059	0.080
	Prelude	80	0.67 ④	0.004	—	0.120	0.060
1986	Civic	80	②	0.004	7.090	0.120	0.080
	Civic Wagon	80	0.59	0.004	7.870	0.120	0.080
	Civic CRX	80	③	0.004	7.090	0.120	0.080
	Accord	80	0.67	0.004	7.870	0.120	0.080
	Prelude	80	0.67 ④	0.004	—	0.120	0.060
1987	Civic	80	②	0.004	7.090	0.120	0.080
	Civic Wagon	80	0.59	0.004	7.870	0.120	0.080
	Civic CRX	80	③	0.004	7.090	0.120	0.080
	Accord	80	0.67	0.004	7.870	0.120	0.080
	Prelude	80	0.67 ④	0.004	—	0.120	0.060
1988	Civic	80	0.67	0.004	7.090	0.120	0.080
	Civic Wagon	80	0.67	0.004	7.870	⑧	0.080
	Civic CRX	80	0.67 ⑤	0.004	7.090	0.120	0.080
	Accord	80	④ ⑥	0.006	7.870	⑦	0.080
	Prelude	80	④ ⑥	0.004	—	0.120	0.080

① 1980–83 1300 4 spd: 0.350
  1980–83 1300 5 spd: 0.390
  1980–82 1500: 0.394
  1983 1500: 0.590
② Civic 1300: 0.39
  Civic 1500: 0.59
③ CRX 1300 & HF: 0.35
  CRX 1500: 0.59
④ Rear disc: 0.31

⑤ CRX exc. HF: 0.67
  CRX HF: 0.59
⑥ DX/LX and S models: 0.67
  LX-i and Si models: 0.75
⑦ DX/LX models: 0.120
  LX-i models: 0.060
⑧ 4x2 models: 0.080
  4x4 models: 0.120

Body

10

EXTERIOR

Doors

REMOVAL AND INSTALLATION

Front and Rear

1. Place a jack or stand beneath the door to support its weight.

NOTE: *Place a rag at lower edge of the door and jack or stand to prevent damage to painted surface.*

2. Remove door without hinge.
3. Remove the door hinge.
4. Installation is in the reverse order of removal.

NOTE: *When installing hinge, coat the hinge link with recommended multipurpose grease.*

ADJUSTMENT

Front and Rear

Proper door alignment can be obtained by adjusting the door hinge and door lock striker. The door hinge and striker can be moved up

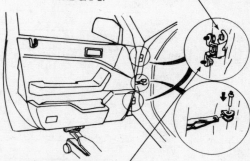

HINGE MOUNTING BOLTS
LOOSEN THE BOLTS, AND MOVE THE DOOR BACKWARD OR FORWARD, UP OR DOWN AS NECESSARY TO EQUALIZE THE GAPS.

DOOR MOUNTING BOLTS
LOOSEN THE BOLTS SLIGHTLY TO MOVE THE DOOR IN OR OUT UNTIL FLUSH WITH THE BODY. IF NECESSARY, YOU CAN INSTALL A SHIM BEHIND ONE HINGE TO MAKE THE DOOR EDGES PARALLEL WITH THE BODY.

Door hinge adjustment—typical

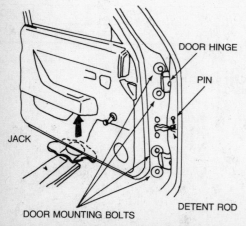

DOOR HINGE

PIN

JACK

DOOR MOUNTING BOLTS

DETENT ROD

Front and/or rear door mounting—typical

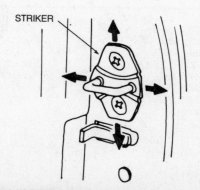

STRIKER

Striker plate adjustment—typical

and down fore and aft in enlarged holes by loosening the attaching bolts.

NOTE: *The door should be adjusted for an even and parallel fit for the door opening and surrounding body panels.*

Hood

REMOVAL AND INSTALLATION

1. Open the hood and protect the body with covers to protect the painted surfaces.

2. Mark the hood hinge locations on the hood for proper reinstallation.

3. Holding both sides of the hood, unscrew the bolts securing the hinge to the hood. This operation requires a helper.

4. Installation is the reverse of removal.

ALIGNMENT

The hood can be adjusted with bolts attaching the hood to the hood hinges, hood lock mechanism and hood bumpers. Adjust the hood for an even fit between the front fenders.

1. Adjust the hood fore and aft by loosening the bolts attaching the hood to the hinge and repositioning hood.

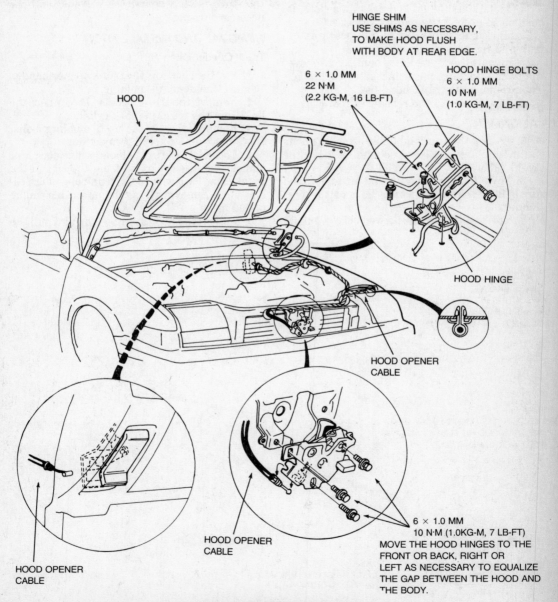

HINGE SHIM
USE SHIMS AS NECESSARY,
TO MAKE HOOD FLUSH
WITH BODY AT REAR EDGE.

6 × 1.0 MM
22 N·M
(2.2 KG-M, 16 LB-FT)

HOOD HINGE BOLTS
6 × 1.0 MM
10 N·M
(1.0 KG-M, 7 LB-FT)

HOOD

HOOD HINGE

HOOD OPENER CABLE

HOOD OPENER CABLE

HOOD OPENER CABLE

HOOD OPENER CABLE

6 × 1.0 MM
10 N·M (1.0KG-M, 7 LB-FT)
MOVE THE HOOD HINGES TO THE
FRONT OR BACK, RIGHT OR
LEFT AS NECESSARY TO EQUALIZE
THE GAP BETWEEN THE HOOD AND
THE BODY.

Hood replacement—typical

2. Loosen the hood bumper lock nuts and lower bumpers until they do not contact the front of the hood when the hood is closed.

3. Set the striker at the center of the hood lock, and tighten the hood lock securing bolts temporarily.

4. Raise the two hood bumpers until the hood is flush with the fenders.

5. Tighten the hood lock securing bolts after the proper adjustment has been obtained.

Trunk Lid

REMOVAL AND INSTALLATION

1. Open the trunk lid and position a cloth or cushion to protect the painted areas.

2. Mark the trunk lid hinge locations or trunk lid for proper reinstallation.

3. Support the trunk lid by hand and remove the bolts attaching the trunk lid to the hinge. Then remove the trunk lid.

4. Installation is the reverse of removal.

ALIGNMENT

1. Loosen the trunk lid hinge attaching bolts until they are just loose enough to move the trunk lid.

2. Move the trunk lid for and aft to obtain a flush fit between the trunk lid and the rear fender.

3. To obtain a snug fit between the trunk lid and weatherstrip, loosen the trunk lid lock striker attaching bolts enough to move the lid, working the striker up and down and from side to side as required.

4. After the adjustment is made tighten the striker bolts securely.

Power Trunk and Liftgate System

The power liftgate release system consists of a release switch (usually found on the dash panel), a wiring harness, lock solenoid and linkage rods. The power trunk system consists of a push button release switch (usually found in the glove box), a door latch solenoid and the necessary wiring.

REMOVAL AND INSTALLATION

Trunk Opener Latch

1. Pry the cover off the trunk opener handle. Remove the door sill molding.

2. Remove the trunk opener. Disconnect the link from the trunk lid lock cylinder.

3. Remove the trunk latch molding bolts. Disconnect all electrical connections.

4. Loosen the trunk opener cable lock nut and remove the cable end from the slot in the trunk lock. Tie a wire to the trunk end of the cable before removing it, so the new cable can be pulled in.

5. Pull off the door opening trim and pull the

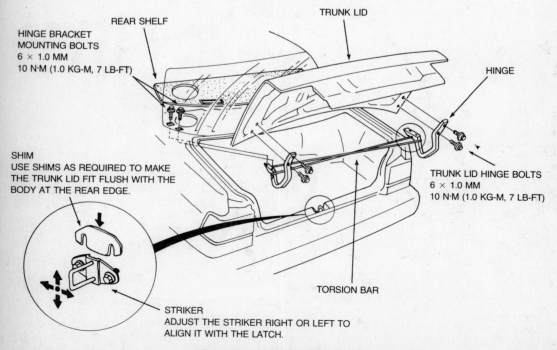

REAR SHELF

TRUNK LID

HINGE BRACKET
MOUNTING BOLTS
6 × 1.0 MM
10 N·M (1.0 KG-M, 7 LB-FT)

HINGE

SHIM
USE SHIMS AS REQUIRED TO MAKE
THE TRUNK LID FIT FLUSH WITH THE
BODY AT THE REAR EDGE.

TRUNK LID HINGE BOLTS
6 × 1.0 MM
10 N·M (1.0 KG-M, 7 LB-FT)

STRIKER
ADJUST THE STRIKER RIGHT OR LEFT TO
ALIGN IT WITH THE LATCH.

TORSION BAR

Trunk lid replacement—typical

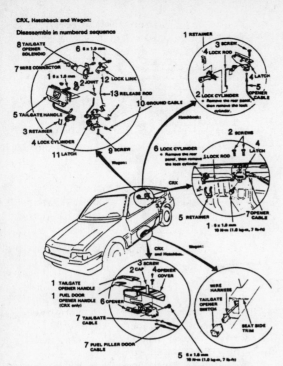

CRX, Hatchback and Wagon:
Disassemble in numbered sequence

Power tailgate and latch removal and installation

cable out between the quarter panel and body.

6. Install a new cable and installation is the reverse order of the removal procedure.

COMPONENT TESTING

Power Trunk Latch Test

There should be continuity between the G/BI lead and the ground when the trunk lid is open and no continuity when the trunk lid is closed.

Power Tailgate Switch Test

There should be continuity between the switch terminals when the switch is in the **ON** position and no continuity when the switch is in the **OFF** position.

Power Tailgate Solenoid Test

Using a suitable ohmmeter, check for continuity between the terminal and the solenoid body ground. There should be continuity. If there is no continuity, replace the solenoid.

Manual Hatchback or Tailgate Lid

REMOVAL AND INSTALLATION

1. Open the lid and disconnect the rear defogger harness if so equipped.
2. Mark the hinge locations on the lid for proper relocation.

3. Position rags between the roof and the upper end of the lid to prevent scratching the paint.
4. Support the lid and remove the support bolts the the hinge retaining bolts and remove the lid.
5. Installation is the reverse of removal.
NOTE: *Be careful not to scratch the lift support rods. A scratched rod may cause oil or gas leakage*

ALIGNMENT

1. Open the hatchback lid.
2. Loosen the lid hinge to body attaching bolts until they are just loose enough to move the lid.
3. Move the lid up and down to obtain a flush fit between the lid and the roof.
4. After adjustment is completed tighten the hinge attaching bolts securely.

Electric Sunroofs

The sunroof is operated by a switch, which is usually located on the left side of the instrument panel. The system is consists of the sunroof switch, motor drive cables and relay(s), which are located in a fuse/relay junction block in the engine compartment.

Several fuses, located in a fuse/relay junction block in the engine compartment and dash fuse box, are used to power/protect the system. The sunroof can be closed manually, (should it be necessary) by removing the headliner plug, insert the handle and turn the gear to close the sunroof.

NOTE: *The sunroof assembly is equipped with water drain tubes. It is important to keep these drain tubes open. So it is recommended to blow compressed air through the drain tubes at regular intervals, in order to keep the drain tubes clear.*

ADJUSTMENTS

Sunroof Glass

The roof molding should be even with the glass weather strip, to within 1.0mm ± 1.5mm all the way around. If it is not, slide the sunshade back and follow this procedure.

1. Pry the plug out of the glass mount bracket cover, remove the screw, then slide the cover off to the rear.
2. Loosen the mount bracket nuts and install shims between the glass frame and bracket. Repeat this on the other side if necessary.

Side Clearance

If the glass weather strip fits too tightly against the roof molding on either side when

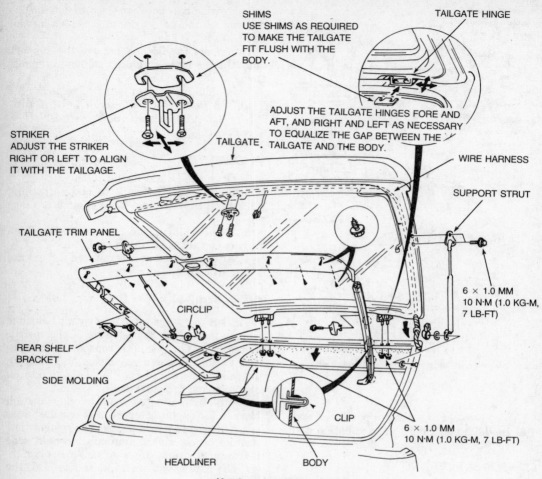

SHIMS
USE SHIMS AS REQUIRED
TO MAKE THE TAILGATE
FIT FLUSH WITH THE
BODY.

TAILGATE HINGE

ADJUST THE TAILGATE HINGES FORE AND
AFT, AND RIGHT AND LEFT AS NECESSARY
TO EQUALIZE THE GAP BETWEEN THE
TAILGATE AND THE BODY.

STRIKER
ADJUST THE STRIKER
RIGHT OR LEFT TO ALIGN
IT WITH THE TAILGAGE.

TAILGATE.

WIRE HARNESS

SUPPORT STRUT

TAILGATE TRIM PANEL

6 × 1.0 MM
10 N·M (1.0 KG-M,
7 LB-FT)

CIRCLIP

REAR SHELF
BRACKET

SIDE MOLDING

CLIP

6 × 1.0 MM
10 N·M (1.0 KG-M, 7 LB-FT)

HEADLINER   BODY

Hatch replacement—typical

closed, slide the sunshade back and follow this procedure.

1. Pry the plug out of each mount bracket cover, remove the screw, then slide the cover off to the rear.

2. Loosen all 8 mount bracket nuts. Move the glass right or left as necessary and tighten the mount bracket nuts.

Rear Edge Closing

Open the glass approximately 1 ft., then close it to check where the rear edge begins to rise. If it rises too soon and seat too tightly against the roof molding or too late and does not seat tightly enough, adjust as follows:

1. Open the glass fully. Remove the rail covers from both sides and loosen the lift-up guide screws.

2. Move the guide forward or backward, then tighten the screws and recheck the roof closing. The guides have notches 1.5mm each and can be adjusted 2 notches forward or backward.

REMOVAL AND INSTALLATION

Sunroof Glass and Sunshade

1. Slide the sunshade all the way back. Pry the plug out of each mount bracket cover, remove the screw, then slide the cover off to the rear.

2. Close the glass fully. Remove the nuts from the front and
rear mounts on both sides.

3. Remove the glass by lifting it up and pulling it towards the front of the vehicle. Once the glass is removed, pull the sunshade out. When removing the sunshade, it is correct to bend the sunshade slightly to aid in the removal.

4. Installation is the reverse order of the removal procedure.

Sunroof Motor, Drain Tube and Frame

1. Remove the headliner from inside of the vehicle.

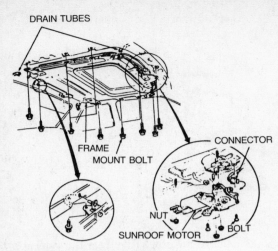

DRAIN TUBES

FRAME
MOUNT BOLT

CONNECTOR

NUT
SUNROOF MOTOR
BOLT

Sunroof motor and frame assembly

2. Remove the sunroof motor by removing 2 bolts and 3 nuts from the bottom of the motor mount plate. Disconnect the motor wire harness at the connector and remove the motor.

3. Slide back the drain tube clamps and remove the drain tubes. Remove the 11 mounting bolts from the sunroof frame and remove the frame from the vehicle.

4. To install, insert the frame's rear pins into the body holes, then install the rest of the assembly in the reverse order of the removal procedure.

NOTE: *Before installing the sunroof motor, measure the effort required to close the sliding panel using a suitable spring scale. If the load is over 22 lbs., check the side clearance and the glass height adjustment. Be sure when using the spring scale to protect the leading edge of the sunroof with a shop rag.*

Sunroof Cable Replacement

With the sun roof out of the vehicle, remove the guide rail mounting nuts, lift off the guide rails and remove the cables with the rear mounts attached. Be sure to fill the groove in each grommet with a suitable sealant and apply a suitable grease to the inner cable.

Wind Deflector

A gap between the deflector seal and roof molding will cause wind noise when driving at high speed with the roof opening.

1. Open the sunroof and pry the rail covers off of both sides. Loosen the deflector mounting nuts. The wind deflector can be adjusted 2.0mm forward or backward.

2. Adjust the deflector forward or backward so that the edge of its seal touches the roof molding evenly.

3. The height of the deflector when opened can not be adjusted. If it is damaged or deformed, replace it.

Sunroof Rear Mount Bracket Disassembly

1. Remove the side guides from the rear mount brackets. It is advisable to replace the guides with new ones whenever they are disassembled.

2. Pry the E-clip off of the pin and remove the rear mount bracket from the cable.

3. Assembly is the reverse order of the disassembly procedure.

COMPONENT TESTING

Sunroof Relay

5-PIN RELAY

1. Remove relay from dash relay holder.

2. Check for continuity between terminals **B** and **C**.

3. Apply battery voltage to terminal **E** and ground terminal **F**.

4. Check for continuity between terminals **A** and **C**.

5. If either test fails, replace relay.

4-PIN RELAY

1. Remove relay from dash relay holder.

2. There should be no continuity between terminals **A** and **B**.

3. Apply battery voltage to terminal **C** and ground terminal **D**.

4. There should be continuity between terminals **A** and **B**.

5. If either test fails, replace relay.

Sunroof Closing Force Check (With The Motor Installed)

1. After installing all removed parts, using a second person, have them hold the switch to close the sunroof while measuring the force required to stop the sunroof with a suitable spring scale.

2. Read the force on the scale as soon as the glass stops moving, then immediately release the switch and spring scale. The closing force should be 44-56 lbs.

3. If the force required to stop the sunroof is not within specifications, adjust it, by turning the sunroof motor clutch adjusting nut. Turn clockwise to increase the force and counterclockwise to decrease the force.

4. After the proper adjustment has been made, install a new lockwasher and bend it against the flat on the adjusting nut.

Bumpers

REMOVAL AND INSTALLATION

Front and Rear

1. Disconnect all electrical connectors at bumper assembly if so equipped.
2. Remove bumper mounting bolts and bumper assembly.
3. Remove shock absorbers from bumper (if so equipped).

CAUTION: *The shock absorber is filled with a high pressure gas and should not be disassembled, drilled or exposed to an open flame.*

4. Install shock absorbers (if so equipped) and bumper in reverse order of removal.

Grille

REMOVAL AND INSTALLATION

1. Remove radiator grille bracket bolts.
NOTE: *Early models use clips to hold the radiator grille assembly to the vehicle.*

2. Remove radiator grille from the vehicle.
3. To install reverse the removal procedures.
NOTE: *The radiator grille assembly is made of plastic, thus never use excessive force to remove it.*

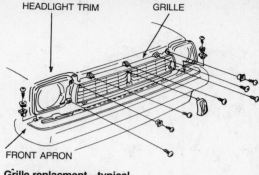

Grille replacment—typical

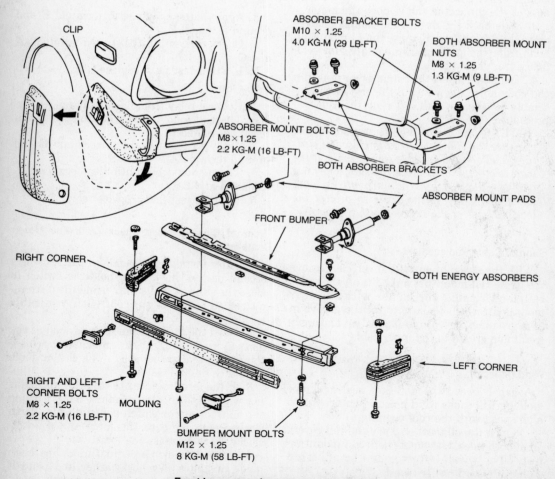

Front bumper replacement—early models

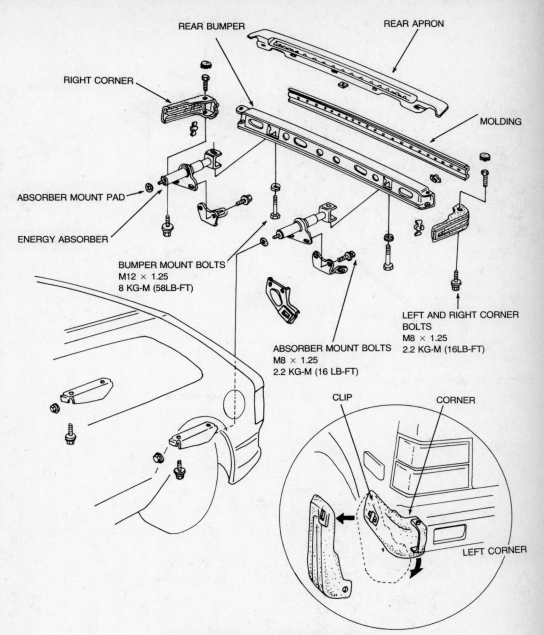

REAR BUMPER

REAR APRON

RIGHT CORNER

MOLDING

ABSORBER MOUNT PAD

ENERGY ABSORBER

BUMPER MOUNT BOLTS
M12 × 1.25
8 KG-M (58LB-FT)

ABSORBER MOUNT BOLTS
M8 × 1.25
2.2 KG-M (16 LB-FT)

LEFT AND RIGHT CORNER
BOLTS
M8 × 1.25
2.2 KG-M (16LB-FT)

CLIP

CORNER

LEFT CORNER

Rear bumper replacement—early models

Outside Mirrors
REMOVAL AND INSTALLATION
Manual
1. Remove control knob handle.
2. Remove door corner finisher panel.
3. Remove mirror body attaching screws, and then remove mirror body
4. Installation is in the reverse order of removal.

NOTE: *Apply sealer to the rear surface of door corner finisher panel during installation to prevent water leak.*

Power
1. Remove door corner finisher panel.
2. Remove mirror body attaching screws, and then remove mirror body
3. Disconnect the electrical connection.
NOTE: *It may be necessary to remove the*

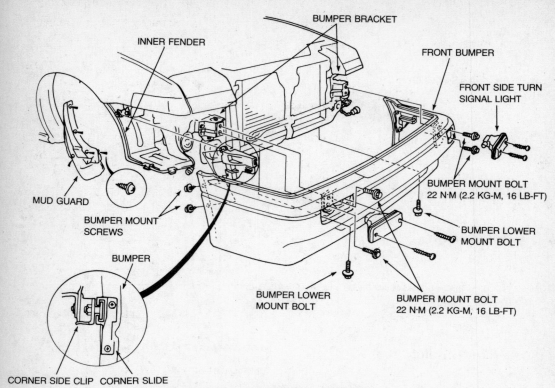

BUMPER BRACKET

INNER FENDER

FRONT BUMPER

FRONT SIDE TURN
SIGNAL LIGHT

BUMPER MOUNT BOLT
22 N·M (2.2 KG-M, 16 LB-FT)

BUMPER LOWER
MOUNT BOLT

MUD GUARD

BUMPER MOUNT
SCREWS

BUMPER

BUMPER LOWER
MOUNT BOLT

BUMPER MOUNT BOLT
22 N·M (2.2 KG-M, 16 LB-FT)

CORNER SIDE CLIP   CORNER SLIDE

Front bumper replacement—late models

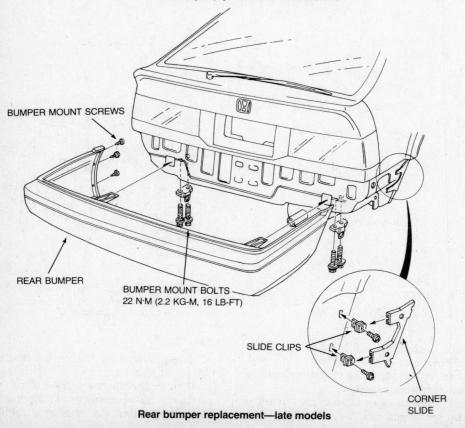

BUMPER MOUNT SCREWS

REAR BUMPER

BUMPER MOUNT BOLTS
22 N·M (2.2 KG-M, 16 LB-FT)

SLIDE CLIPS

CORNER
SLIDE

Rear bumper replacement—late models

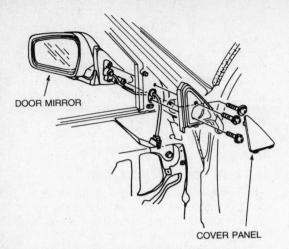

Power rear view mirror replacement—typical

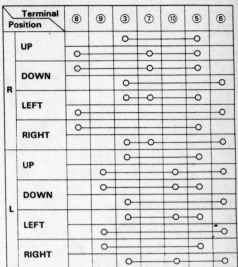

Position	Terminal	⑧	⑨	③	⑦	⑩	⑤	⑥
R	UP			O			O	
		O			O		O	
	DOWN	O			O		O	
				O				O
	LEFT			O				O
		O						O
	RIGHT	O						O
L	UP			O			O	
			O			O		O
	DOWN		O			O		O
				O			O	
	LEFT			O			O	
			O					O
	RIGHT		O					O

door trim panel to gain access to the electrical connection.

4. Installation is in the reverse order of removal.

Power Mirror Switch

The power mirrors are controlled by a single switch assembly, located on the instrument panel. The motors that operate the mirrors are part of the mirror assembly and cannot be replaced separately.

The mirror switch consists of a left-right change over select knob and control knobs. The switch is ready to function only when the ignition switch is in the **ACC** or **ON** position. Movement of the mirror is accomplished by the motors, located in the mirror housing.

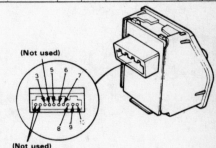

Honda power mirror switch test

REMOVAL AND INSTALLATION

1. Disconnect the negative battery cable.
2. Remove the lower instrument panel trim cover.
3. Remove the screw retaining the switch and, using a small pry bar, remove the switch from the instrument panel.
4. Disconnect the electrical lead and remove the switch from the vehicle.
5. To install, connect the electrical lead to the switch and push it into the instrument panel.
6. Install the retaining screw and install the lower trim panel.
7. Connect the battery cable.

Mirror Assembly

1. Disconnect the negative battery cable.
2. Remove the door panel.
3. Disconnect the electrical leads from the mirror harness connector.

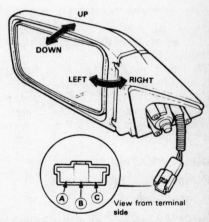

Honda power mirror connector terminal locations—used for continuity checks

4. Using a small pry bar, remove the mirror cover panel lid.
5. Remove the 2 screws retaining the mirror cover panel and remove the cover panel.
6. While holding the mirror assembly, re-

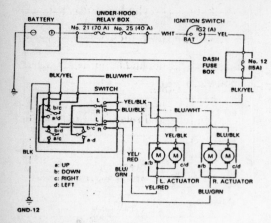

Honda power mirror circuit

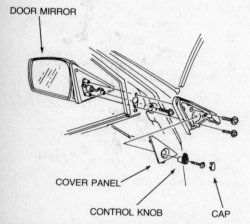

COVER PANEL

CONTROL KNOB   CAP

Manual rear view mirror replacement—typical

move the mounting screws and remove the mirror assembly.

7. To install, position the mirror assembly and install the mounting screws.

8. Install the cover panel and the cover panel lid. Attach the wiring harness connector.

9. Install the door panel. Connect the negative battery cable.

Diagnosis and Testing

COMPONENT TESTING

Power Mirror Switch

Remove the switch from the instrument panel. Check for continuity between the terminals in each switch position.

Mirror Assembly

1. Remove the door trim panel and disconnect the electrical lead to the mirror.

2. Test the mirror operation using the following procedures:

  a. Tilt up: connect 12V power source to the **C** terminal and ground the **B** terminal.

  b. Tilt down: connect 12V power source to the **B** terminal and ground the **C** terminal.

  c. Swing right: connect 12V power source to the **A** terminal and ground the **B** terminal.

  d. Swing left: connect 12V power source to the **B** terminal and ground the **A** terminal.

3. If the mirror does not operate properly in any of these tests, replace the assembly.

Antenna

REMOVAL AND INSTALLATION

1. Remove antenna mounting nut or screws.

2. Disconnect the antenna lead at the radio.

3. Tie a cord to the end on the antenna lead.

4. Remove antenna from vehicle while fishing out the cord.

5. Installation is in the reverse order of removal. Use the cord to pull the new antenna lead through the body.

INTERIOR

Door Panel, Glass and Regulator

REMOVAL AND INSTALLATION

Front and Rear

1. Remove the regulator handle by pushing the set pin spring.

2. Remove the arm rest, door inside handle escutcheon and door lock.

3. Remove the door finisher and sealing screen.

4. On some models it may be necessary to remove the outer door molding.

5. Lower the door glass with the regulator handle until the regulator-to-glass attaching bolts appear at the access holes in the door inside panel.

6. Raise the door glass and draw it upwards.

7. Remove the regulator attaching bolts and remove the regulator assembly through the large access hole in the door panel.

8. Install the window regulator assembly in the door.

9. Connect all mounting bolts and check for proper operation.

10. Adjust the window if necessary and install the door trim panel.

11. Install all the attaching components to the door panel.

12. Install the window regulator handle.

Manual Door Locks

REMOVAL AND INSTALLATION

1. Remove the door panel and sealing screen.

2. Remove the lock cylinder from the rod by turning the resin clip.

3. Loosen the nuts attaching the outside door handle and remove the outside door handle.

4. Remove the screws retaining the inside door handle and door lock, and remove the door lock assembly from the hole in the inside of the door.

5. Remove the lock cylinder by removing the retaining clip.

6. Install the lock cylinder and clip to the door.

7. Install the door lock assembly and handles.

8. Install door panel and all attaching parts.

Power Door Locks

The power door locking system consists of switches, actuators and relays. Control switch-

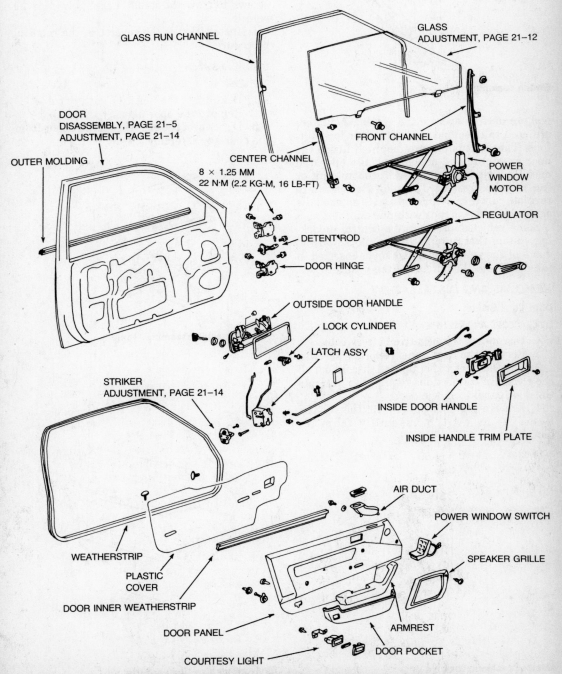

Exploded view of door, regulator and lock assembly—typical

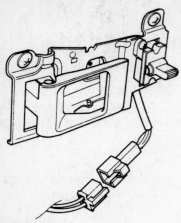

Switch assembly

(es) are used to operate the system. Actuators are used to raise and lower the door lock buttons. These actuators are mounted inside the door assembly and are electrically operated once the switch is depressed. A control unit or functional relay is used to allow the system to regulate current, to function and to align all the actuators and switches with one another.

Some vehicles incorporate a central unlocking system that automatically unlocks all the doors of the vehicle once the key is inserted in the door from the outside of the vehicle.

REMOVAL AND INSTALLATION

Door Lock Switch

CIVIC, ACCORD AND PRELUDE

1. Disconnect the negative battery cable.
2. Remove the door panel retaining screws.
3. Lift the door panel up and disconnect all the electrical connections required to separate the door panel from the door.
4. Remove the door panel from the vehicle. Remove the switch assembly from its mounting.

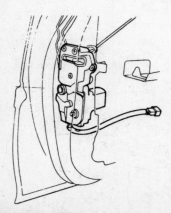

Actuator assembly location

5. Installation is the reverse of the removal procedure.

Door Lock Actuator

CIVIC, ACCORD AND PRELUDE

1. Disconnect the negative battery cable.
2. Remove the door panel.
3. Disconnect the actuator electrical connector. Disconnect the required linkage rods.
4. Remove the actuator assembly retaining screws. Remove the actuator assembly from the vehicle.
5. Installation is the reverse of the removal procedure.

Door Key Switch

PRELUDE

1. Disconnect the negative battery cable.
2. Remove the door panel.
3. Disconnect the electrical connections from the door key assembly.

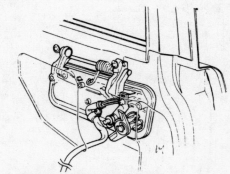

Door key switch assembly—Prelude

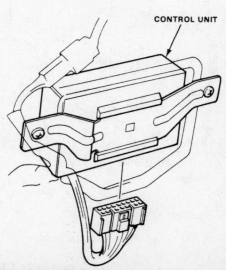

Relay assembly—Civic and Prelude

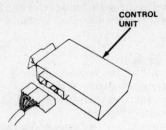

Relay assembly—Accord

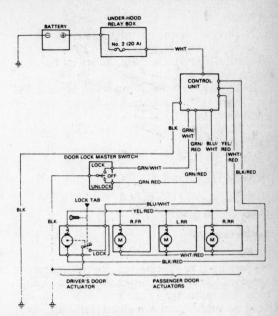

4. Remove the door key assembly retaining clip. Remove the
switch from its mounting.

5. Installation is the reverse of the removal procedure.

Door Lock Relay

CIVIC AND PRELUDE

1. Disconnect the negative battery cable.
2. Remove the left side door panel on Civic. Remove the right side door panel on Prelude.
3. Disconnect the relay electrical connectors.
4. Remove the relay retaining screws. Remove the relay from its mounting.
5. Installation is the reverse of the removal procedure.

Electrical schematic—Accord

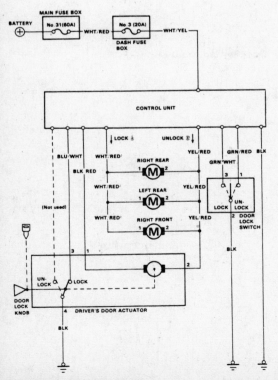

Electrical schematic—Civic

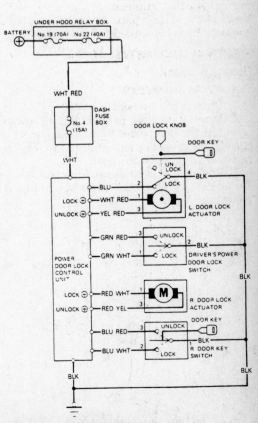

Electrical schematic—Prelude

ACCORD

1. Disconnect the negative battery cable.
2. Remove the right side front seat retaining bolts. Lift the seat and disconnect all the electrical connectors.
3. Remove the relay retaining screws. Remove the relay from its mounting under the right seat.
4. Installation is the reverse of the removal procedure.

Power Windows
REMOVAL AND INSTALLATION
Motor and Regulator
ACCORD
CIVIC
PRELUDE

1. Remove the trim plate and the speaker.
2. Remove the screws attaching the armrest.

3. Remove the door trim panel by removing the attaching screws and the clips then pull it upward.
4. Lower the door glass until the mounting bolts can be seen.
5. Disconnect the power window harnesses, remove the screws then the armrest.
6. Support the glass and remove the glass to regulator attaching bolts.
7. Remove the regulator mounting bolts, then take out the regulator through the lower hole in the door.
8. With the regulator removed from the door panel, remove the attaching bolts and the motor from the regulator.
CAUTION: *The regulator gear will move suddenly when the motor is removed, because the regulator spring is tensioned against the gear.*
9. For installation, reverse the removal procedure.

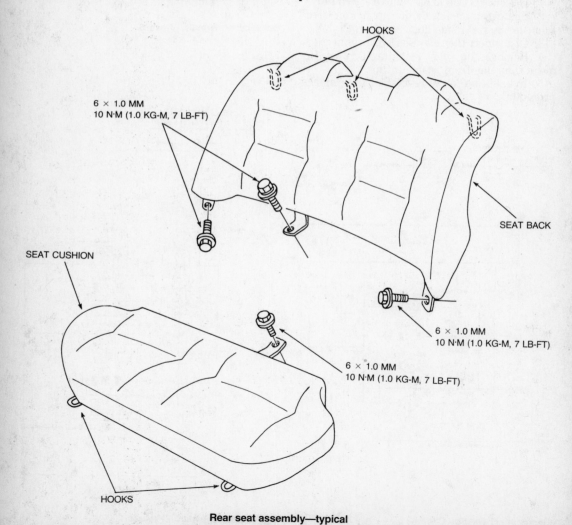

HOOKS

6 × 1.0 MM
10 N·M (1.0 KG-M, 7 LB-FT)

SEAT BACK

SEAT CUSHION

6 × 1.0 MM
10 N·M (1.0 KG-M, 7 LB-FT)

6 × 1.0 MM
10 N·M (1.0 KG-M, 7 LB-FT)

HOOKS

Rear seat assembly—typical

Inside Rear View Mirror
REMOVAL AND INSTALLATION

1. Remove rear view mirror mounting bolt cover.
2. Remove rear view mirror mounting bolts.
3. Remove mirror.
4. Installation is in the reverse order of removal.

Seats
REMOVAL AND INSTALLATION
Front

1. Remove front seat mounting bolts
2. Remove front seat assembly.
3. Installation is in the reverse order of removal.

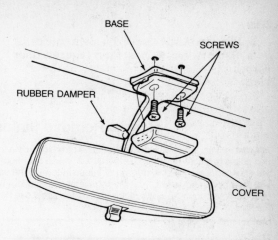

Interior rear view mirror assembly—typical

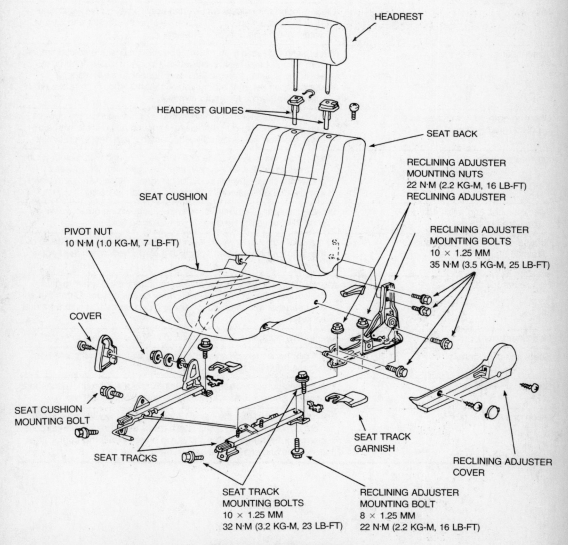

Front seat assembly—typical

Rear

1. Remove rear seat cushion mounting bolts.
2. Remove screw attaching luggage floor carpet.

3. Remove rear seat back by tilting forward and pulling straight up.

NOTE: *On hatchback models the rear seat back is remove similar as above.*

How to Remove Stains from Fabric Interior

For rest results, spots and stains should be removed as soon as possible. Never use gasoline, lacquer thinner, acetone, nail polish remover or bleach. Use a 3' x 3" piece of cheesecloth. Squeeze most of the liquid from the fabric and wipe the stained fabric from the outside of the stain toward the center with a lifting motion. Turn the cheesecloth as soon as one side becomes soiled. When using water to remove a stain, be sure to wash the entire section after the spot has been removed to avoid water stains. Encrusted spots can be broken up with a dull knife and vacuumed before removing the stain.

Type of Stain	How to Remove It
Surface spots	Brush the spots out with a small hand brush or use a commercial preparation such as K2R to lift the stain.
Mildew	Clean around the mildew with warm suds. Rinse in cold water and soak the mildew area in a solution of 1 part table salt and 2 parts water. Wash with upholstery cleaner.
Water stains	Water stains in fabric materials can be removed with a solution made from 1 cup of table salt dissolved in 1 quart of water. Vigorously scrub the solution into the stain and rinse with clear water. Water stains in nylon or other synthetic fabrics should be removed with a commercial type spot remover.
Chewing gum, tar, crayons, shoe polish (greasy stains)	Do not use a cleaner that will soften gum or tar. Harden the deposit with an ice cube and scrape away as much as possible with a dull knife. Moisten the remainder with cleaning fluid and scrub clean.
Ice cream, candy	Most candy has a sugar base and can be removed with a cloth wrung out in warm water. Oily candy, after cleaning with warm water, should be cleaned with upholstery cleaner. Rinse with warm water and clean the remainder with cleaning fluid.
Wine, alcohol, egg, milk, soft drink (non-greasy stains)	Do not use soap. Scrub the stain with a cloth wrung out in warm water. Remove the remainder with cleaning fluid.
Grease, oil, lipstick, butter and related stains	Use a spot remover to avoid leaving a ring. Work from the outisde of the stain to the center and dry with a clean cloth when the spot is gone.
Headliners (cloth)	Mix a solution of warm water and foam upholstery cleaner to give thick suds. Use only foam—liquid may streak or spot. Clean the entire headliner in one operation using a circular motion with a natural sponge.
Headliner (vinyl)	Use a vinyl cleaner with a sponge and wipe clean with a dry cloth.
Seats and door panels	Mix 1 pint upholstery cleaner in 1 gallon of water. Do not soak the fabric around the buttons.
Leather or vinyl fabric	Use a multi-purpose cleaner full strength and a stiff brush. Let stand 2 minutes and scrub thoroughly. Wipe with a clean, soft rag.
Nylon or synthetic fabrics	For normal stains, use the same procedures you would for washing cloth upholstery. If the fabric is extremely dirty, use a multi-purpose cleaner full strength with a stiff scrub brush. Scrub thoroughly in all directions and wipe with a cotton towel or soft rag.

Mechanic's Data

11

TAX
1":254mm
10.16mm
Liter
Parts
Overhaul

General Conversion Table

Multiply By	To Convert	To	
		LENGTH	
2.54	Inches	Centimeters	.3937
25.4	Inches	Millimeters	.03937
30.48	Feet	Centimeters	.0328
.304	Feet	Meters	3.28
.914	Yards	Meters	1.094
1.609	Miles	Kilometers	.621
		VOLUME	
.473	Pints	Liters	2.11
.946	Quarts	Liters	1.06
3.785	Gallons	Liters	.264
.016	Cubic inches	Liters	61.02
16.39	Cubic inches	Cubic cms.	.061
28.3	Cubic feet	Liters	.0353
		MASS (Weight)	
28.35	Ounces	Grams	.035
.4536	Pounds	Kilograms	2.20
—	To obtain	From	Multiply by

Multiply By	To Convert	To	
		AREA	
.645	Square inches	Square cms.	.155
.836	Square yds.	Square meters	1.196
		FORCE	
4.448	Pounds	Newtons	.225
.138	Ft./lbs.	Kilogram/meters	7.23
1.36	Ft./lbs.	Newton-meters	.737
.112	In./lbs.	Newton-meters	8.844
		PRESSURE	
.068	Psi	Atmospheres	14.7
6.89	Psi	Kilopascals	.145
		OTHER	
1.104	Horsepower (DIN)	Horsepower (SAE)	.9861
.746	Horsepower (SAE)	Kilowatts (KW)	1.34
1.60	Mph	Km/h	.625
.425	Mpg	Km/1	2.35
	To obtain	From	Multiply by

Tap Drill Sizes

National Coarse or U.S.S.

Screw & Tap Size	Threads Per Inch	Use Drill Number
No. 5	40	39
No. 6	32	36
No. 8	32	29
No. 10	24	25
No. 12	24	17
1/4	20	8
5/16	18	F
3/8	16	5/16
7/16	14	U
1/2	13	27/64
9/16	12	31/64
5/8	11	17/32
3/4	10	21/32
7/8	9	49/64

National Coarse or U.S.S.

Screw & Tap Size	Threads Per Inch	Use Drill Number
1	8	7/8
1 1/8	7	63/64
1 1/4	7	1 7/64
1 1/2	6	1 11/32

National Fine or S.A.E.

Screw & Tap Size	Threads Per Inch	Use Drill Number
No. 5	44	37
No. 6	40	33
No. 8	36	29
No. 10	32	21

National Fine or S.A.E.

Screw & Tap Size	Threads Per Inch	Use Drill Number
No. 12	28	15
1/4	28	3
6/16	24	1
3/8	24	Q
7/16	20	W
1/2	20	29/64
9/16	18	33/64
5/8	18	37/64
3/4	16	11/16
7/8	14	13/16
1 1/8	12	1 3/64
1 1/4	12	1 11/64
1 1/2	12	1 27/64

Drill Sizes In Decimal Equivalents

Inch	Decimal	Wire	mm
1/64	.0156		.39
	.0157		.4
	.0160	78	
	.0165		.42
	.0173		.44
	.0177		.45
	.0180	77	
	.0181		.46
	.0189		.48
	.0197		.5
	.0200	76	
	.0210	75	
	.0217		.55
	.0225	74	
	.0236		.6
	.0240	73	
	.0250	72	
	.0256		.65
	.0260	71	
	.0276		.7
	.0280	70	
	.0292	69	
	.0295		.75
	.0310	68	
1/32	.0312		.79
	.0315		.8
	.0320	67	
	.0330	66	
	.0335		.85
	.0350	65	
	.0354		.9
	.0360	64	
	.0370	63	
	.0374		.95
	.0380	62	
	.0390	61	
	.0394		1.0
	.0400	60	
	.0410	59	
	.0413		1.05
	.0420	58	
	.0430	57	
	.0433		1.1
	.0453		1.15
	.0465	56	
3/64	.0469		1.19
	.0472		1.2
	.0492		1.25
	.0512		1.3
	.0520	55	
	.0531		1.35
	.0550	54	
	.0551		1.4
	.0571		1.45
	.0591		1.5
	.0595	53	
	.0610		1.55
1/16	.0625		1.59
	.0630		1.6
	.0635	52	
	.0650		1.65
	.0669		1.7
	.0670	51	
	.0689		1.75
	.0700	50	
	.0709		1.8
	.0728		1.85

Inch	Decimal	Wire	mm
	.0730	49	
	.0748		1.9
	.0760	48	
	.0768		1.95
5/64	.0781		1.98
	.0785	47	
	.0787		2.0
	.0807		2.05
	.0810	46	
	.0820	45	
	.0827		2.1
	.0846		2.15
	.0860	44	
	.0866		2.2
	.0886		2.25
	.0890	43	
	.0906		2.3
	.0925		2.35
	.0935	42	
3/32	.0938		2.38
	.0945		2.4
	.0960	41	
	.0965		2.45
	.0980	40	
	.0981		2.5
	.0995	39	
	.1015	38	
	.1024		2.6
	.1040	37	
	.1063		2.7
	.1065	36	
	.1083		2.75
7/64	.1094		2.77
	.1100	35	
	.1102		2.8
	.1110	34	
	.1130	33	
	.1142		2.9
	.1160	32	
	.1181		3.0
	.1200	31	
	.1220		3.1
1/8	.1250		3.17
	.1260		3.2
	.1280		3.25
	.1285	30	
	.1299		3.3
	.1339		3.4
	.1360	29	
	.1378		3.5
	.1405	28	
9/64	.1406		3.57
	.1417		3.6
	.1440	27	
	.1457		3.7
	.1470	26	
	.1476		3.75
	.1495	25	
	.1496		3.8
	.1520	24	
	.1535		3.9
	.1540	23	
5/32	.1562		3.96
	.1570	22	
	.1575		4.0
	.1590	21	
	.1610	20	

Inch	Decimal	Wire & Letter	mm
	.1614		4.1
	.1654		4.2
	.1660	19	
	.1673		4.25
	.1693		4.3
	.1695	18	
11/64	.1719		4.36
	.1730	17	
	.1732		4.4
	.1770	16	
	.1772		4.5
	.1800	15	
	.1811		4.6
	.1820	14	
	.1850	13	
	.1850		4.7
	.1870		4.75
3/16	.1875		4.76
	.1890	12	
	.1890		4.8
	.1910	11	
	.1929		4.9
	.1935	10	
	.1960	9	
	.1969		5.0
	.1990	8	
	.2008		5.1
	.2010	7	
13/64	.2031		5.16
	.2040	6	
	.2047		5.2
	.2055	5	
	.2067		5.25
	.2087		5.3
	.2090	4	
	.2126		5.4
	.2130	3	
	.2165		5.5
7/32	2188		5.55
	.2205		5.6
	.2210	2	
	.2244		5.7
	.2264		5.75
	.2280	1	
	.2283		5.8
	.2323		5.9
	.2340	A	
15/64	.2344		5.95
	.2362		6.0
	.2380	B	
	.2402		6.1
	.2420	C	
	.2441		6.2
	.2460	D	
	.2461		6.25
	.2480		6.3
1/4	.2500	E	
	.2520		6.
	.2559		6.5
	.2570	F	
	.2598		6.6
	.2610	G	
	.2638		6.7
17/64	.2656		6.74
	.2657		6.75
	.2660	H	
	.2677		6.8

Inch	Decimal	Letter	mm
	.2717		6.9
	.2720	I	
	.2756		7.0
	.2770	J	
	.2795		7.1
	.2810	K	
9/32	.2812		7.14
	.2835		7.2
	.2854		7.25
	.2874		7.3
	.2900	L	
	.2913		7.4
	.2950	M	
	.2953		7.5
19/64	.2969		7.54
	.2992		7.6
	.3020	N	
	.3031		7.7
	.3051		7.75
	.3071		7.8
	.3110		7.9
5/16	.3125		7.93
	.3150		8.0
	.3160	O	
	.3189		8.1
	.3228		8.2
	.3230	P	
	.3248		8.25
	.3268		8.3
21/64	.3281		8.33
	.3307		8.4
	.3320	Q	
	.3346		8.5
	.3386		8.6
	.3390	R	
	.3425		8.7
11/32	.3438		8.73
	.3445		8.75
	.3465		8.8
	.3480	S	
	.3504		8.9
	.3543		9.0
	.3580	T	
	.3583		9.1
23/64	.3594		9.12
	.3622		9.2
	.3642		9.25
	.3661		9.3
	.3680	U	
	.3701		9.4
	.3740		9.5
3/8	.3750		9.52
	.3770	V	
	.3780		9.6
	.3819		9.7
	.3839		9.75
	.3858		9.8
	.3860	W	
	.3898		9.9
25/64	.3906		9.92
	.3937		10.0
	.3970	X	
	.4040	Y	
13/32	.4062		10.31
	.4130	Z	
	.4134		10.5
27/64	.4219		10.71

Inch	Decimal	mm
	.4331	11.0
7/16	.4375	11.11
	.4528	11.5
29/64	.4531	11.51
15/32	.4688	11.90
	.4724	12.0
31/64	.4844	12.30
	.4921	12.5
1/2	.5000	12.70
	.5118	13.0
33/64	.5156	13.09
17/32	.5312	13.49
	.5315	13.5
35/64	.5469	13.89
	.5512	14.0
9/16	.5625	14.28
	.5709	14.5
37/64	.5781	14.68
	.5906	15.0
19/32	.5938	15.08
39/64	.6094	15.47
	.6102	15.5
5/8	.6250	15.87
	.6299	16.0
41/64	.6406	16.27
	.6496	16.5
21/32	.6562	16.66
	.6693	17.0
43/64	.6719	17.06
11/16	.6875	17.46
	.6890	17.5
45/64	.7031	17.85
	.7087	18.0
23/32	.7188	18.25
	.7283	18.5
47/64	.7344	18.65
	.7480	19.0
3/4	.7500	19.05
49/64	.7656	19.44
	.7677	19.5
25/32	.7812	19.84
	.7874	20.0
51/64	.7969	20.24
	.8071	20.5
13/16	.8125	20.63
	.8268	21.0
53/64	.8281	21.03
27/32	.8438	21.43
	.8465	21.5
55/64	.8594	21.82
	.8661	22.0
7/8	.8750	22.22
	.6858	22.5
57/64	.8906	22.62
	.9055	23.0
29/32	.9062	23.01
59/64	.9219	23.41
	.9252	23.5
15/16	.9375	23.81
	.9449	24.0
61/64	.9531	24.2
	.9646	24.5
31/32	.9688	24.6
	.9843	25.0
63/64	.9844	25.0
1	1.0000	25.4

AIR/FUEL RATIO: The ratio of air to gasoline by weight in the fuel mixture drawn into the engine.

AIR INJECTION: One method of reducing harmful exhaust emissions by injecting air into each of the exhaust ports of an engine. The fresh air entering the hot exhaust manifold causes any remaining fuel to be burned before it can exit the tailpipe.

ALTERNATOR: A device used for converting mechanical energy into electrical energy.

AMMETER: An instrument, calibrated in amperes, used to measure the flow of an electrical current in a circuit. Ammeters are always connected in series with the circuit being tested.

AMPERE: The rate of flow of electrical current present when one volt of electrical pressure is applied against one ohm of electrical resistance.

ANALOG COMPUTER: Any microprocessor that uses similar (analogous) electrical signals to make its calculations.

ARMATURE: A laminated, soft iron core wrapped by a wire that converts electrical energy to mechanical energy as in a motor or relay. When rotated in a magnetic field, it changes mechanical energy into electrical energy as in a generator.

ATMOSPHERIC PRESSURE: The pressure on the Earth's surface caused by the weight of the air in the atmosphere. At sea level, this pressure is 14.7 psi at 32°F (101 kPa at 0°C).

ATOMIZATION: The breaking down of a liquid into a fine mist that can be suspended in air.

AXIAL PLAY: Movement parallel to a shaft or bearing bore.

BACKFIRE: The sudden combustion of gases in the intake or exhaust system that results in a loud explosion.

BACKLASH: The clearance or play between two parts, such as meshed gears.

BACKPRESSURE: Restrictions in the exhaust system that slow the exit of exhaust gases from the combustion chamber.

BAKELITE: A heat resistant, plastic insulator material commonly used in printed circuit boards and transistorized components.

BALL BEARING: A bearing made up of hardened inner and outer races between which hardened steel ball roll.

BALLAST RESISTOR: A resistor in the primary ignition circuit that lowers voltage after the engine is started to reduce wear on ignition components.

BEARING: A friction reducing, supportive device usually located between a stationary part and a moving part.

BIMETAL TEMPERATURE SENSOR: Any sensor or switch made of two dissimilar types of metal that bend when heated or cooled due to the different expansion rates of the alloys. These types of sensors usually function as an on/off switch.

BLOWBY: Combustion gases, composed of water vapor and unburned fuel, that leak past the piston rings into the crankcase during normal engine operation. These gases are removed by the PCV system to prevent the build-up of harmful acids in the crankcase.

BRAKE PAD: A brake shoe and lining assembly used with disc brakes.

BRAKE SHOE: The backing for the brake lining. The term is, however, usually applied to the assembly of the brake backing and lining.

BUSHING: A liner, usually removable, for a bearing; an anti-friction liner used in place of a bearing.

BYPASS: System used to bypass ballast resistor during engine cranking to increase voltage supplied to the coil.

CALIPER: A hydraulically activated device in a disc brake system, which is mounted straddling the brake rotor (disc). The caliper contains at least one piston and two brake pads. Hydraulic pressure on the piston(s) forces the pads against the rotor.

CAMSHAFT: A shaft in the engine on which are the lobes (cams) which operate the valves. The camshaft is driven by the crankshaft, via a belt, chain or gears, at one half the crankshaft speed.

CAPACITOR: A device which stores an electrical charge.

CARBON MONOXIDE (CO): a colorless, odorless gas given off as a normal byproduct of combustion. It is poisonous and extremely dangerous in confined areas, building up slowly to toxic levels without warning if adequate ventilation is not available.

CARBURETOR: A device, usually mounted on the intake manifold of an engine, which mixes the air and fuel in the proper proportion to allow even combustion.

CATALYTIC CONVERTER: A device installed in the exhaust system, like a muffler, that converts harmful byproducts of combustion into carbon dioxide and water vapor by means of a heat-producing chemical reaction.

CENTRIFUGAL ADVANCE: A mechanical method of advancing the spark timing by using flyweights in the distributor that react to centrifugal force generated by the distributor shaft rotation.

CHECK VALVE: Any one-way valve installed to permit the flow of air, fuel or vacuum in one direction only.

CHOKE: A device, usually a moveable valve, placed in the intake path of a carburetor to restrict the flow of air.

CIRCUIT: Any unbroken path through which an electrical current can flow. Also used to describe fuel flow in some instances.

CIRCUIT BREAKER: A switch which protects an electrical circuit from overload by opening the circuit when the current flow exceeds a predetermined level. Some circuit breakers must be reset manually, while other reset automatically

COIL (IGNITION): A transformer in the ignition circuit which steps of the voltage provided to the spark plugs.

COMBINATION MANIFOLD: An assembly which includes both the intake and exhaust manifolds in one casting.

COMBINATION VALVE: A device used in some fuel systems that routes fuel vapors to a charcoal storage canister instead of venting them into the atmosphere. The valve relieves fuel tank pressure and allows fresh air into the tank as fuel level drops to prevent a vapor lock situation.

COMPRESSION RATIO: The comparison of the total volume of the cylinder and combustion chamber with the piston at BDC and the piston at TDC.

CONDENSER: 1. An electrical device which acts to store an electrical charge, preventing voltage surges.
2. A radiator-like device in the air conditioning system in which refrigerant gas condenses into a liquid, giving off heat.

CONDUCTOR: Any material through which an electrical current can be transmitted easily.

CONTINUITY: Continuous or complete circuit. Can be checked with an ohmmeter.

COUNTERSHAFT: An intermediate shaft which is rotated by a mainshaft and transmits, in turn, that rotation to a working part.

CRANKCASE: The lower part of an engine in which the crankshaft and related parts operate.

CRANKSHAFT: The main driving shaft of an engine which receives reciprocating motion from the pistons and converts it to rotary motion.

CYLINDER: In an engine, the round hole in the engine block in which the piston(s) ride.

CYLINDER BLOCK: The main structural member of an engine in which is found the cylinders, crankshaft and other principal parts.

CYLINDER HEAD: The detachable portion of the engine, fastened, usually, to the top of the cylinder block, containing all or most of the combustion chambers. On overhead valve engines, it contains the valves and their operating parts. On overhead cam engines, it contains the camshaft as well.

DEAD CENTER: The extreme top or bottom of the piston stroke.

DETONATION: An unwanted explosion of the air fuel mixture in the combustion chamber caused by excess heat and compression, advanced timing, or an overly lean mixture. Also referred to as "ping".

DIAPHRAGM: A thin, flexible wall separating two cavities, such as in a vacuum advance unit.

DIESELING: A condition in which hot spots in the combustion chamber cause the engine to run on after the key is turned off.

DIFFERENTIAL: A geared assembly which allows the transmission of motion between drive axles, giving one axle the ability to turn faster than the other.

DIODE: An electrical device that will allow current to flow in one direction only.

DISC BRAKE: A hydraulic braking assembly consisting of a brake disc, or rotor, mounted on an axle, and a caliper assembly containing, usually two brake pads which are activated by hydraulic pressure. The pads are forced against the sides of the disc, creating friction which slows the vehicle.

DISTRIBUTOR: A mechanically driven device on an engine which is responsible for electrically firing the spark plug at a predetermined point of the piston stroke.

DOWEL PIN: A pin, inserted in mating holes in two different parts allowing those parts to maintain a fixed relationship.

DRUM BRAKE: A braking system which consists of two brake shoes and one or two wheel cylinders, mounted on a fixed backing plate, and a brake drum, mounted on an axle, which revolves around the assembly. Hydraulic action applied to the wheel cylinders forces the shoes outward against the drum, creating friction and slowing the vehicle.

DWELL: The rate, measured in degrees of shaft rotation, at which an electrical circuit cycles on and off.

ELECTRONIC CONTROL UNIT (ECU): Ignition module, module, amplifier or igniter. See Module for definition.

ELECTRONIC IGNITION: A system in which the timing and firing of the spark plugs is controlled by an electronic control unit, usually called a module. These systems have not points or condenser.

ENDPLAY: The measured amount of axial movement in a shaft.

ENGINE: A device that converts heat into mechanical energy.

EXHAUST MANIFOLD: A set of cast passages or pipes which conduct exhaust gases from the engine.

FEELER GAUGE: A blade, usually metal, of precisely predetermined thickness, used to measure the clearance between two parts. These blades usually are available in sets of assorted thicknesses.

F-Head: An engine configuration in which the intake valves are in the cylinder head, while the camshaft and exhaust valves are located in the cylinder block. The camshaft operates the intake valves via lifters and pushrods, while it operates the exhaust valves directly.

FIRING ORDER: The order in which combustion occurs in the cylinders of an engine. Also the order in which spark is distributed to the plugs by the distributor.

FLATHEAD: An engine configuration in which the camshaft and all the valves are located in the cylinder block.

FLOODING: The presence of too much fuel in the intake manifold and combustion chamber which prevents the air/fuel mixture from firing, thereby causing a no-start situation.

FLYWHEEL: A disc shaped part bolted to the rear end of the crankshaft. Around the outer perimeter is affixed the ring gear. The starter drive engages the ring gear, turning the flywheel, which rotates the crankshaft, imparting the initial starting motion to the engine.

FOOT POUND (ft.lb. or sometimes, ft. lbs.): The amount of energy or work needed to raise an item weighing one pound, a distance of one foot.

FUSE: A protective device in a circuit which prevents circuit overload by breaking the circuit when a specific amperage is present. The device is constructed around a strip or wire of a lower amperage rating than the circuit it is designed to protect. When an amperage higher than that stamped on the fuse is present in the circuit, the strip or wire melts, opening the circuit.

GEAR RATIO: The ratio between the number of teeth on meshing gears.

GENERATOR: A device which converts mechanical energy into electrical energy.

HEAT RANGE: The measure of a spark plug's ability to dissipate heat from its firing end. The higher the heat range, the hotter the plug fires.

HUB: The center part of a wheel or gear.

HYDROCARBON (HC): Any chemical compound made up of hydrogen and carbon. A major pollutant formed by the engine as a byproduct of combustion.

HYDROMETER: An instrument used to measure the specific gravity of a solution.

INCH POUND (in.lb. or sometimes, in. lbs.): One twelfth of a foot pound.

INDUCTION: A means of transferring electrical energy in the form of a magnetic field. Principle used in the ignition coil to increase voltage.

INJECTION PUMP: A device, usually mechanically operated, which meters and delivers fuel under pressure to the fuel injector.

INJECTOR: A device which receives metered fuel under relatively low pressure and is activated to inject the fuel into the engine under relatively high pressure at a predetermined time.

INPUT SHAFT: The shaft to which torque is applied, usually carrying the driving gear or gears.

INTAKE MANIFOLD: A casting of passages or pipes used to conduct air or a fuel/air mixture to the cylinders.

JOURNAL: The bearing surface within which a shaft operates.

KEY: A small block usually fitted in a notch between a shaft and a hub to prevent slippage of the two parts.

MANIFOLD: A casting of passages or set of pipes which connect the cylinders to an inlet or outlet source.

MANIFOLD VACUUM: Low pressure in an engine intake manifold formed just below the throttle plates. Manifold vacuum is highest at idle and drops under acceleration.

MASTER CYLINDER: The primary fluid pressurizing device in a hydraulic system. In automotive use, it is found in brake and hydraulic clutch systems and is pedal activated, either directly or, in a power brake system, through the power booster.

MODULE: Electronic control unit, amplifier or igniter of solid state or integrated design which controls the current flow in the ignition primary circuit based on input from the pickup coil. When the module opens the primary circuit, the high secondary voltage is induced in the coil.

NEEDLE BEARING: A bearing which consists of a number (usually a large number) of long, thin rollers.

OHM: (Ω) The unit used to measure the resistance of conductor to electrical flow. One ohm is the amount of resistance that limits current flow to one ampere in a circuit with one volt of pressure.

OHMMETER: An instrument used for measuring the resistance, in ohms, in an electrical circuit.

OUTPUT SHAFT: The shaft which transmits torque from a device, such as a transmission.

OVERDRIVE: A gear assembly which produces more shaft revolutions than that transmitted to it.

OVERHEAD CAMSHAFT (OHC): An engine configuration in which the camshaft is mounted on top of the cylinder head and operates the valve either directly or by means of rocker arms.

OVERHEAD VALVE (OHV): An engine configuration in which all of the valves are located in the cylinder head and the camshaft is located in the cylinder block. The camshaft operates the valves via lifters and pushrods.

OXIDES OF NITROGEN (NOx): Chemical compounds of nitrogen produced as a byproduct of combustion. They combine with hydrocarbons to produce smog.

OXYGEN SENSOR: Used with the feedback system to sense the presence of oxygen in the exhaust gas and signal the computer which can reference the voltage signal to an air/fuel ratio.

PINION: The smaller of two meshing gears.

CHILTON'S
AUTO BODY
REPAIR TIPS

Tools and Materials • Step-by-Step Illustrated Procedures
How To Repair Dents, Scratches and Rust Holes
Spray Painting and Refinishing Tips

With a little practice, basic body repair procedures can be mastered by any do-it-yourself mechanic. The step-by-step repairs shown here can be applied to almost any type of auto body repair.

TOOLS & MATERIALS

You may already have basic tools, such as hammers and electric drills. Other tools unique to body repair — body hammers, grinding attachments, sanding blocks, dent puller, half-round plastic file and plastic spreaders — are relatively inexpensive and can be obtained wherever auto parts or auto body repair parts are sold. Portable air compressors and paint spray guns can be purchased or rented.

Auto Body Repair Kits

The best and most often used products are available to the do-it-yourselfer in kit form, from major manufacturers of auto body repair products. The same manufacturers also merchandise the individual products for use by pros.

Kits are available to make a wide variety of repairs, including holes, dents and scratches and fiberglass, and offer the advantage of buying the materials you'll need for the job. There is little waste or chance of materials going bad from not being used. Many kits may also contain basic body-working tools such as body files, sanding blocks and spreaders. Check the contents of the kit before buying your tools.

BODY REPAIR TIPS

Safety

Many of the products associated with auto body repair and refinishing contain toxic chemicals. Read all labels before opening containers and store them in a safe place and manner.

• Wear eye protection (safety goggles) when using power tools or when performing any operation that involves the removal of any type of material.

• Wear lung protection (disposable mask or respirator) when grinding, sanding or painting.

Sanding

1 Sand off paint before using a dent puller. When using a non-adhesive sanding disc, cover the back of the disc with an overlapping layer or two of masking tape and trim the edges. The disc will last considerably longer.

2 Use the circular motion of the sanding disc to grind *into* the edge of the repair. Grinding or sanding away from the jagged edge will only tear the sandpaper.

3 Use the palm of your hand flat on the panel to detect high and low spots. Do not use your fingertips. Slide your hand slowly back and forth.

WORKING WITH BODY FILLER

Mixing The Filler

Cleanliness and proper mixing and application are extremely important. Use a clean piece of plastic or glass or a disposable artist's palette to mix body filler.

1 Allow plenty of time and follow directions. No useful purpose will be served by adding more hardener to make it cure (set-up) faster. Less hardener means more curing time, but the mixture dries harder; more hardener means less curing time but a softer mixture.

2 Both the hardener and the filler should be thoroughly kneaded or stirred before mixing. Hardener should be a solid paste and dispense like thin toothpaste. Body filler should be smooth, and free of lumps or thick spots.

Getting the proper amount of hardener in the filler is the trickiest part of preparing the filler. Use the same amount of hardener in cold or warm weather. For contour filler (thick coats), a bead of hardener twice the diameter of the filler is about right. There's about a 15% margin on either side, but, if in doubt use less hardener.

3 Mix the body filler and hardener by wiping across the mixing surface, picking the mixture up and wiping it again. Colder weather requires longer mixing times. Do not mix in a circular motion; this will trap air bubbles which will become holes in the cured filler.

Applying The Filler

1 For best results, filler should not be applied over ¼" thick.

Apply the filler in several coats. Build it up to above the level of the repair surface so that it can be sanded or grated down.

The first coat of filler must be pressed on with a firm wiping motion.

Apply the filler in one direction only. Working the filler back and forth will either pull it off the metal or trap air bubbles.

REPAIRING DENTS

Before you start, take a few minutes to study the damaged area. Try to visualize the shape of the panel before it was damaged. If the damage is on the left fender, look at the right fender and use it as a guide. If there is access to the panel from behind, you can reshape it with a body hammer. If not, you'll have to use a dent puller. Go slowly and work the metal a little at a time. Get the panel as straight as possible before applying filler.

1 This dent is typical of one that can be pulled out or hammered out from behind. Remove the headlight cover, headlight assembly and turn signal housing.

2 Drill a series of holes ½ the size of the end of the dent puller along the stress line. Make some trial pulls and assess the results. If necessary, drill more holes and try again. Do not hurry.

3 If possible, use a body hammer and block to shape the metal back to its original contours. Get the metal back as close to its original shape as possible. Don't depend on body filler to fill dents.

4 Using an 80-grit grinding disc on an electric drill, grind the paint from the surrounding area down to bare metal. Use a new grinding pad to prevent heat buildup that will warp metal.

5 The area should look like this when you're finished grinding. Knock the drill holes in and tape over small openings to keep plastic filler out.

6 Mix the body filler (see Body Repair Tips). Spread the body filler evenly over the entire area (see Body Repair Tips). Be sure to cover the area completely.

7 Let the body filler dry until the surface can just be scratched with your fingernail. Knock the high spots from the body filler with a body file ("Cheese-grater"). Check frequently with the palm of your hand for high and low spots.

8 Check to be sure that trim pieces that will be installed later will fit exactly. Sand the area with 40-grit paper.

9 If you wind up with low spots, you may have to apply another layer of filler.

10 Knock the high spots off with 40-grit paper. When you are satisfied with the contours of the repair, apply a thin coat of filler to cover pin holes and scratches.

11 Block sand the area with 40-grit paper to a smooth finish. Pay particular attention to body lines and ridges that must be well-defined.

12 Sand the area with 400 paper and then finish with a scuff pad. The finished repair is ready for priming and painting (see Painting Tips).

Materials and photos courtesy of Ritt Jones Auto Body, Prospect Park, PA.

REPAIRING RUST HOLES

There are many ways to repair rust holes. The fiberglass cloth kit shown here is one of the most cost efficient for the owner because it provides a strong repair that resists cracking and moisture and is relatively easy to use. It can be used on large and small holes (with or without backing) and can be applied over contoured areas. Remember, however, that short of replacing an entire panel, no repair is a guarantee that the rust will not return.

1 Remove any trim that will be in the way. Clean away all loose debris. Cut away all the rusted metal. But be sure to leave enough metal to retain the contour or body shape.

2 Grind away all traces of rust with a 24-grit grinding disc. Be sure to grind back 3-4 inches from the edge of the hole down to bare metal and be sure all traces of paint, primer and rust are removed.

3 Block sand the area with 80 or 100 grit sandpaper to get a clear, shiny surface and feathered paint edge. Tap the edges of the hole inward with a ball peen hammer.

4 If you are going to use release film, cut a piece about 2-3″ larger than the area you have sanded. Place the film over the repair and mark the sanded area on the film. Avoid any unnecessary wrinkling of the film.

5 Cut 2 pieces of fiberglass matte to match the shape of the repair. One piece should be about 1″ smaller than the sanded area and the second piece should be 1″ smaller than the first. Mix enough filler and hardener to saturate the fiberglass material (see Body Repair Tips).

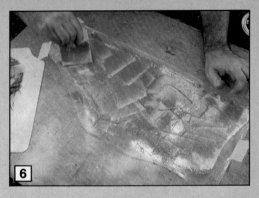

6 Lay the release sheet on a flat surface and spread an even layer of filler, large enough to cover the repair. Lay the smaller piece of fiberglass cloth in the center of the sheet and spread another layer of filler over the fiberglass cloth. Repeat the operation for the larger piece of cloth.

7 Place the repair material over the repair area, with the release film facing outward. Use a spreader and work from the center outward to smooth the material, following the body contours. Be sure to remove all air bubbles.

8 Wait until the repair has dried tack-free and peel off the release sheet. The ideal working temperature is 60°-90° F. Cooler or warmer temperatures or high humidity may require additional curing time. Wait longer, if in doubt.

9 Sand and feather-edge the entire area. The initial sanding can be done with a sanding disc on an electric drill if care is used. Finish the sanding with a block sander. Low spots can be filled with body filler; this may require several applications.

10 When the filler can just be scratched with a fingernail, knock the high spots down with a body file and smooth the entire area with 80-grit. Feather the filled areas into the surrounding areas.

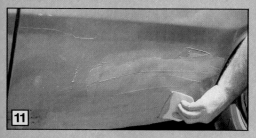

11 When the area is sanded smooth, mix some topcoat and hardener and apply it directly with a spreader. This will give a smooth finish and prevent the glass matte from showing through the paint.

12 Block sand the topcoat smooth with finishing sandpaper (200 grit), and 400 grit. The repair is ready for masking, priming and painting (see Painting Tips).

Materials and photos courtesy Marson Corporation, Chelsea, Massachusetts

PAINTING TIPS

Preparation

1 SANDING — Use a 400 or 600 grit wet or dry sandpaper. Wet-sand the area with a ¼ sheet of sandpaper soaked in clean water. Keep the paper wet while sanding. Sand the area until the repaired area tapers into the original finish.

2 CLEANING — Wash the area to be painted thoroughly with water and a clean rag. Rinse it thoroughly and wipe the surface dry until you're sure it's completely free of dirt, dust, fingerprints, wax, detergent or other foreign matter.

3 MASKING — Protect any areas you don't want to overspray by covering them with masking tape and newspaper. Be careful not get fingerprints on the area to be painted.

4 PRIMING — All exposed metal should be primed before painting. Primer protects the metal and provides an excellent surface for paint adhesion. When the primer is dry, wet-sand the area again with 600 grit wet-sandpaper. Clean the area again after sanding.

Painting Techniques

P aint applied from either a spray gun or a spray can (for small areas) will provide good results. Experiment on an old piece of metal to get the right combination before you begin painting.

SPRAYING VISCOSITY (SPRAY GUN ONLY) — Paint should be thinned to spraying viscosity according to the directions on the can. Use only the recommended thinner or reducer and the same amount of reduction regardless of temperature.

AIR PRESSURE (SPRAY GUN ONLY) — This is extremely important. Be sure you are using the proper recommended pressure.

TEMPERATURE — The surface to be painted should be approximately the same temperature as the surrounding air. Applying warm paint to a cold surface, or vice versa, will completely upset the paint characteristics.

THICKNESS — Spray with smooth strokes. In general, the thicker the coat of paint, the longer the drying time. Apply several thin coats about 30 seconds apart. The paint should remain wet long enough to flow out and no longer; heavier coats will only produce sags or wrinkles. Spray a light (fog) coat, followed by heavier color coats.

DISTANCE — The ideal spraying distance is 8"-12" from the gun or can to the surface. Shorter distances will produce ripples, while greater distances will result in orange peel, dry film and poor color match and loss of material due to overspray.

OVERLAPPING — The gun or can should be kept at right angles to the surface at all times. Work to a wet edge at an even speed, using a 50% overlap and direct the center of the spray at the lower or nearest edge of the previous stroke.

RUBBING OUT (BLENDING) FRESH PAINT — Let the paint dry thoroughly. Runs or imperfections can be sanded out, primed and repainted.

Don't be in too big a hurry to remove the masking. This only produces paint ridges. When the finish has dried for at least a week, apply a small amount of fine grade rubbing compound with a clean, wet cloth. Use lots of water and blend the new paint with the surrounding area.

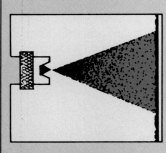

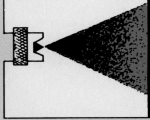

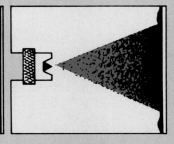

WRONG	CORRECT	WRONG
Thin coat. Stroke too fast, not enough overlap, gun too far away.	*Medium coat. Proper distance, good stroke, proper overlap.*	*Heavy coat. Stroke too slow, too much overlap, gun too close.*

PISTON RING: An open ended ring which fits into a groove on the outer diameter of the piston. Its chief function is to form a seal between the piston and cylinder wall. Most automotive pistons have three rings: two for compression sealing; one for oil sealing.

PRELOAD: A predetermined load placed on a bearing during assembly or by adjustment.

PRIMARY CIRCUIT: Is the low voltage side of the ignition system which consists of the ignition switch, ballast resistor or resistance wire, bypass, coil, electronic control unit and pick-up coil as well as the connecting wires and harnesses.

PRESS FIT: The mating of two parts under pressure, due to the inner diameter of one being smaller than the outer diameter of the other, or vice versa; an interference fit.

RACE: The surface on the inner or outer ring of a bearing on which the balls, needles or rollers move.

REGULATOR: A device which maintains the amperage and/or voltage levels of a circuit at predetermined values.

RELAY: A switch which automatically opens and/or closes a circuit.

RESISTANCE: The opposition to the flow of current through a circuit or electrical device, and is measured in ohms. Resistance is equal to the voltage divided by the amperage.

RESISTOR: A device, usually made of wire, which offers a preset amount of resistance in an electrical circuit.

RING GEAR: The name given to a ring-shaped gear attached to a differential case, or affixed to a flywheel or as part a planetary gear set.

ROLLER BEARING: A bearing made up of hardened inner and outer races between which hardened steel rollers move.

ROTOR: 1. The disc-shaped part of a disc brake assembly, upon which the brake pads bear; also called, brake disc.
2. The device mounted atop the distributor shaft, which passes current to the distributor cap tower contacts.

SECONDARY CIRCUIT: The high voltage side of the ignition system, usually above 20,000 volts. The secondary includes the ignition coil, coil wire, distributor cap and rotor, spark plug wires and spark plugs.

SENDING UNIT: A mechanical, electrical, hydraulic or electromagnetic device which transmits information to a gauge.

SENSOR: Any device designed to measure engine operating conditions or ambient pressures and temperatures. Usually electronic in nature and designed to send a voltage signal to an on-board computer, some sensors may operate as a simple on/off switch or they may provide a variable voltage signal (like a potentiometer) as conditions or measured parameters change.

SHIM: Spacers of precise, predetermined thickness used between parts to establish a proper working relationship.

SLAVE CYLINDER: In automotive use, a device in the hydraulic clutch system which is activated by hydraulic force, disengaging the clutch.

SOLENOID: A coil used to produce a magnetic field, the effect of which is produce work.

SPARK PLUG: A device screwed into the combustion chamber of a spark ignition engine. The basic construction is a conductive core inside of a ceramic insulator, mounted in an outer conductive base. An electrical charge from the spark plug wire travels along the conductive core and jumps a preset air gap to a grounding point or points at the end of the conductive base. The resultant spark ignites the fuel/air mixture in the combustion chamber.

SPLINES: Ridges machined or cast onto the outer diameter of a shaft or inner diameter of a bore to enable parts to mate without rotation.

TACHOMETER: A device used to measure the rotary speed of an engine, shaft, gear, etc., usually in rotations per minute.

THERMOSTAT: A valve, located in the cooling system of an engine, which is closed when cold and opens gradually in response to engine heating, controlling the temperature of the coolant and rate of coolant flow.

TOP DEAD CENTER (TDC): The point at which the piston reaches the top of its travel on the compression stroke.

TORQUE: The twisting force applied to an object.

TORQUE CONVERTER: A turbine used to transmit power from a driving member to a driven member via hydraulic action, providing changes in drive ratio and torque. In automotive use, it links the driveplate at the rear of the engine to the automatic transmission.

TRANSDUCER: A device used to change a force into an electrical signal.

TRANSISTOR: A semi-conductor component which can be actuated by a small voltage to perform an electrical switching function.

TUNE-UP: A regular maintenance function, usually associated with the replacement and adjustment of parts and components in the electrical and fuel systems of a vehicle for the purpose of attaining optimum performance.

TURBOCHARGER: An exhaust driven pump which compresses intake air and forces it into the combustion chambers at higher than atmospheric pressures. The increased air pressure allows more fuel to be burned and results in increased horsepower being produced.

VACUUM ADVANCE: A device which advances the ignition timing in response to increased engine vacuum.

VACUUM GAUGE: An instrument used to measure the presence of vacuum in a chamber.

VALVE: A device which control the pressure, direction of flow or rate of flow of a liquid or gas.

VALVE CLEARANCE: The measured gap between the end of the valve stem and the rocker arm, cam lobe or follower that activates the valve.

VISCOSITY: The rating of a liquid's internal resistance to flow.

VOLTMETER: An instrument used for measuring electrical force in units called volts. Voltmeters are always connected parallel with the circuit being tested.

WHEEL CYLINDER: Found in the automotive drum brake assembly, it is a device, actuated by hydraulic pressure, which, through internal pistons, pushes the brake shoes outward against the drums.

ABBREVIATIONS AND SYMBOLS

A: Ampere

AC: Alternating current

A/C: Air conditioning

A-h: Ampere hour

AT: Automatic transmission

ATDC: After top dead center

μA: Microampere

bbl: Barrel

BDC: Bottom dead center

bhp: Brake horsepower

BTDC: Before top dead center

BTU: British thermal unit

C: Celsius (Centigrade)

CCA: Cold cranking amps

cd: Candela

cm^2: Square centimeter

cm^3, cc: Cubic centimeter

CO: Carbon monoxide

CO_2: Carbon dioxide

cu.in., in^3: Cubic inch

CV: Constant velocity

Cyl.: Cylinder

DC: Direct current

ECM: Electronic control module

EFE: Early fuel evaporation

EFI: Electronic fuel injection

EGR: Exhaust gas recirculation

Exh.: Exhaust

F: Fahrenheit

F: Farad

pF: Picofarad

μF: Microfarad

FI: Fuel injection

ft.lb., ft. lb., ft. lbs.: foot pound(s)

gal: Gallon

g: Gram

HC: Hydrocarbon

HEI: High energy ignition

HO: High output

hp: Horsepower

Hyd.: Hydraulic

Hz: Hertz

ID: Inside diameter

in.lb.; in. lb.; in. lbs: inch pound(s)

Int.: Intake

K: Kelvin

kg: Kilogram

kHz: Kilohertz

km: Kilometer

km/h: Kilometers per hour

kΩ: Kilohm

kPa: Kilopascal

kV: Kilovolt

kW: Kilowatt

l: Liter

l/s: Liters per second

m: Meter

mA: Milliampere

mg: Milligram

mHz: Megahertz

mm: Millimeter

mm^2: Square millimeter

m^3: Cubic meter

MΩ: Megohm

m/s: Meters per second

MT: Manual transmission

mV: Millivolt

μm: Micrometer

N: Newton

N-m: Newton meter

NOx: Nitrous oxide

OD: Outside diameter

OHC: Over head camshaft

OHV: Over head valve

Ω: Ohm

PCV: Positive crankcase ventilation

psi: Pounds per square inch

pts: Pints

qts: Quarts

rpm: Rotations per minute

rps: Rotations per second

R-12: A refrigerant gas (Freon)

SAE: Society of Automotive Engineers

SO$_2$: Sulfur dioxide

T: Ton

t: Megagram

TBI: Throttle Body Injection

TPS: Throttle Position Sensor

V: 1. Volt; 2. Venturi

μV: Microvolt

W: Watt

∞: Infinity

<: Less than

>: Greater than

Index

Chilton's Repair & Tune-Up Guides

The Complete line covers domestic cars, imports, trucks, vans, RV's and 4-wheel drive vehicles.

RTUG Title	Part No.	RTUG Title	Part No.
AMC 1975-82 Covers all U.S. and Canadian models	7199	**Corvair 1960-69** Covers all U.S. and Canadian models	6691
Aspen/Volare 1976-80 Covers all U.S. and Canadian models	6637	**Corvette 1953-62** Covers all U.S. and Canadian models	6576
Audi 1970-73 Covers all U.S. and Canadian models.	5902	**Corvette 1963-84** Covers all U.S. and Canadian models	6843
Audi 4000/5000 1978-81 Covers all U.S. and Canadian models including turbocharged and diesel engines	7028	**Cutlass 1970-85** Covers all U.S. and Canadian models	6933
Barracuda/Challenger 1965-72 Covers all U.S. and Canadian models	5807	**Dart/Demon 1968-76** Covers all U.S. and Canadian models	6324
Blazer/Jimmy 1969-82 Covers all U.S. and Canadian 2- and 4-wheel drive models, including diesel engines	6931	**Datsun 1961-72** Covers all U.S. and Canadian models of Nissan Patrol; 1500, 1600 and 2000 sports cars; Pick-Ups; 410, 411, 510, 1200 and 240Z	5790
BMW 1970-82 Covers U.S. and Canadian models	6844	**Datsun 1973-80 Spanish**	7083
Buick/Olds/Pontiac 1975-85 Covers all U.S. and Canadian full size rear wheel drive models	7308	**Datsun/Nissan F-10, 310, Stanza, Pulsar 1977-86** Covers all U.S. and Canadian models	7196
Cadillac 1967-84 Covers all U.S. and Canadian rear wheel drive models	7462	**Datsun/Nissan Pick-Ups 1970-84** Covers all U.S. and Canadian models	6816
Camaro 1967-81 Covers all U.S. and Canadian models	6735	**Datsun/Nissan Z & ZX 1970-86** Covers all U.S. and Canadian models	6932
Camaro 1982-85 Covers all U.S. and Canadian models	7317	**Datsun/Nissan 1200, 210, Sentra 1973-86** Covers all U.S. and Canadian models	7197
Capri 1970-77 Covers all U.S. and Canadian models	6695	**Datsun/Nissan 200SX, 510, 610, 710, 810, Maxima 1973-84** Covers all U.S. and Canadian models	7170
Caravan/Voyager 1984-85 Covers all U.S. and Canadian models	7482	**Dodge 1968-77** Covers all U.S. and Canadian models	6554
Century/Regal 1975-85 Covers all U.S. and Canadian rear wheel drive models, including turbocharged engines	7307	**Dodge Charger 1967-70** Covers all U.S. and Canadian models	6486
Champ/Arrow/Sapporo 1978-83 Covers all U.S. and Canadian models	7041	**Dodge/Plymouth Trucks 1967-84** Covers all $^1/_2$, $^3/_4$, and 1 ton 2- and 4-wheel drive U.S. and Canadian models, including diesel engines	7459
Chevette/1000 1976-86 Covers all U.S. and Canadian models	6836	**Dodge/Plymouth Vans 1967-84** Covers all $^1/_2$, $^3/_4$, and 1 ton U.S. and Canadian models of vans, cutaways and motor home chassis	6934
Chevrolet 1968-85 Covers all U.S. and Canadian models	7135	**D-50/Arrow Pick-Up 1979-81** Covers all U.S. and Canadian models	7032
Chevrolet 1968-79 Spanish	7082	**Fairlane/Torino 1962-75** Covers all U.S. and Canadian models	6320
Chevrolet/GMC Pick-Ups 1970-82 Spanish	7468	**Fairmont/Zephyr 1978-83** Covers all U.S. and Canadian models	6965
Chevrolet/GMC Pick-Ups and Suburban 1970-86 Covers all U.S. and Canadian $^1/_2$, $^3/_4$ and 1 ton models, including 4-wheel drive and diesel engines	6936	**Fiat 1969-81** Covers all U.S. and Canadian models	7042
Chevrolet LUV 1972-81 Covers all U.S. and Canadian models	6815	**Fiesta 1978-80** Covers all U.S. and Canadian models	6846
Chevrolet Mid-Size 1964-86 Covers all U.S. and Canadian models of 1964-77 Chevelle, Malibu and Malibu SS; 1974-77 Laguna; 1978-85 Malibu; 1970-86 Monte Carlo; 1964-84 El Camino, including diesel engines	6840	**Firebird 1967-81** Covers all U.S. and Canadian models	5996
Chevrolet Nova 1986 Covers all U.S. and Canadian models	7658	**Firebird 1982-85** Covers all U.S. and Canadian models	7345
Chevy/GMC Vans 1967-84 Covers all U.S. and Canadian models of $^1/_2$, $^3/_4$, and 1 ton vans, cutaways, and motor home chassis, including diesel engines	6930	**Ford 1968-79 Spanish**	7084
Chevy S-10 Blazer/GMC S-15 Jimmy 1982-85 Covers all U.S. and Canadian models	7383	**Ford Bronco 1966-83** Covers all U.S. and Canadian models	7140
Chevy S-10/GMC S-15 Pick-Ups 1982-85 Covers all U.S. and Canadian models	7310	**Ford Bronco II 1984** Covers all U.S. and Canadian models	7408
Chevy II/Nova 1962-79 Covers all U.S. and Canadian models	6841	**Ford Courier 1972-82** Covers all U.S. and Canadian models	6983
Chrysler K- and E-Car 1981-85 Covers all U.S. and Canadian front wheel drive models	7163	**Ford/Mercury Front Wheel Drive 1981-85** Covers all U.S. and Canadian models Escort, EXP, Tempo, Lynx, LN-7 and Topaz	7055
Colt/Challenger/Vista/Conquest 1971-85 Covers all U.S. and Canadian models	7037	**Ford/Mercury/Lincoln 1968-85** Covers all U.S. and Canadian models of FORD Country Sedan, Country Squire, Crown Victoria, Custom, Custom 500, Galaxie 500, LTD through 1982, Ranch Wagon, and XL; MERCURY Colony Park, Commuter, Marquis through 1982, Gran Marquis, Monterey and Park Lane; LINCOLN Continental and Towne Car	6842
Corolla/Carina/Tercel/Starlet 1970-85 Covers all U.S. and Canadian models	7036	**Ford/Mercury/Lincoln Mid-Size 1971-85** Covers all U.S. and Canadian models of FORD Elite, 1983-85 LTD, 1977-79 LTD II, Ranchero, Torino, Gran Torino, 1977-85 Thunderbird; MERCURY 1972-85 Cougar,	6696
Corona/Cressida/Crown/Mk.II/Camry/Van 1970-84 Covers all U.S. and Canadian models	7044		

continued on next page

RTUG Title	Part No.
1983-85 Marquis, Montego, 1980-85 XR-7; LINCOLN 1982-85 Continental, 1984-85 Mark VII, 1978-80 Versailles	
Ford Pick-Ups 1965-86	6913
Covers all ¹/₂, ³/₄ and 1 ton, 2- and 4-wheel drive U.S. and Canadian pick-up, chassis cab and camper models, including diesel engines	
Ford Pick-Ups 1965-82 Spanish	7469
Ford Ranger 1983-84	7338
Covers all U.S. and Canadian models	
Ford Vans 1961-86	6849
Covers all U.S. and Canadian ¹/₂, ³/₄ and 1 ton van and cutaway chassis models, including diesel engines	
GM A-Body 1982-85	7309
Covers all front wheel drive U.S. and Canadian models of BUICK Century, CHEVROLET Celebrity, OLDSMOBILE Cutlass Ciera and PONTIAC 6000	
GM C-Body 1985	7587
Covers all front wheel drive U.S. and Canadian models of BUICK Electra Park Avenue and Electra T-Type, CADILLAC Fleetwood and deVille, OLDSMOBILE 98 Regency and Regency Brougham	
GM J-Car 1982-85	7059
Covers all U.S. and Canadian models of BUICK Skyhawk, CHEVROLET Cavalier, CADILLAC Cimarron, OLDSMOBILE Firenza and PONTIAC 2000 and Sunbird	
GM N-Body 1985-86	7657
Covers all U.S. and Canadian models of front wheel drive BUICK Somerset and Skylark, OLDSMOBILE Calais, and PONTIAC Grand Am	
GM X-Body 1980-85	7049
Covers all U.S. and Canadian models of BUICK Skylark, CHEVROLET Citation, OLDSMOBILE Omega and PONTIAC Phoenix	
GM Subcompact 1971-80	6935
Covers all U.S. and Canadian models of BUICK Skyhawk (1975-80), CHEVROLET Vega and Monza, OLDSMOBILE Starfire, and PONTIAC Astre and 1975-80 Sunbird	
Granada/Monarch 1975-82	6937
Covers all U.S. and Canadian models	
Honda 1973-84	6980
Covers all U.S. and Canadian models	
International Scout 1967-73	5912
Covers all U.S. and Canadian models	
Jeep 1945-87	6817
Covers all U.S. and Canadian CJ-2A, CJ-3A, CJ-3B, CJ-5, CJ-6, CJ-7, Scrambler and Wrangler models	
Jeep Wagoneer, Commando, Cherokee, Truck 1957-86	6739
Covers all U.S. and Canadian models of Wagoneer, Cherokee, Grand Wagoneer, Jeepster, Jeepster Commando, J-100, J-200, J-300, J-10, J20, FC-150 and FC-170	
Laser/Daytona 1984-85	7563
Covers all U.S. and Canadian models	
Maverick/Comet 1970-77	6634
Covers all U.S. and Canadian models	
Mazda 1971-84	6981
Covers all U.S. and Canadian models of RX-2, RX-3, RX-4, 808, 1300, 1600, Cosmo, GLC and 626	
Mazda Pick-Ups 1972-86	7659
Covers all U.S. and Canadian models	
Mercedes-Benz 1959-70	6065
Covers all U.S. and Canadian models	
Mereceds-Benz 1968-73	5907
Covers all U.S. and Canadian models	

RTUG Title	Part No.
Mercedes-Benz 1974-84	6809
Covers all U.S. and Canadian models	
Mitsubishi, Cordia, Tredia, Starion, Galant 1983-85	7583
Covers all U.S. and Canadian models	
MG 1961-81	6780
Covers all U.S. and Canadian models	
Mustang/Capri/Merkur 1979-85	6963
Covers all U.S. and Canadian models	
Mustang/Cougar 1965-73	6542
Covers all U.S. and Canadian models	
Mustang II 1974-78	6812
Covers all U.S. and Canadian models	
Omni/Horizon/Rampage 1978-84	6845
Covers all U.S. and Canadian models of DODGE omni, Miser, 024, Charger 2.2; PLYMOUTH Horizon, Miser, TC3, TC3 Tourismo; Rampage	
Opel 1971-75	6575
Covers all U.S. and Canadian models	
Peugeot 1970-74	5982
Covers all U.S. and Canadian models	
Pinto/Bobcat 1971-80	7027
Covers all U.S. and Canadian models	
Plymouth 1968-76	6552
Covers all U.S. and Canadian models	
Pontiac Fiero 1984-85	7571
Covers all U.S. and Canadian models	
Pontiac Mid-Size 1974-83	7346
Covers all U.S. and Canadian models of Ventura, Grand Am, LeMans, Grand LeMans, GTO, Phoenix, and Grand Prix	
Porsche 924/928 1976-81	7048
Covers all U.S. and Canadian models	
Renault 1975-85	7165
Covers all U.S. and Canadian models	
Roadrunner/Satellite/Belvedere/GTX 1968-73	5821
Covers all U.S. and Canadian models	
RX-7 1979-81	7031
Covers all U.S. and Canadian models	
SAAB 99 1969-75	5988
Covers all U.S. and Canadian models	
SAAB 900 1979-85	7572
Covers all U.S. and Canadian models	
Snowmobiles 1976-80	6978
Covers Arctic Cat, John Deere, Kawasaki, Polaris, Ski-Doo and Yamaha	
Subaru 1970-84	6982
Covers all U.S. and Canadian models	
Tempest/GTO/LeMans 1968-73	5905
Covers all U.S. and Canadian models	
Toyota 1966-70	5795
Covers all U.S. and Canadian models of Corona, MkII, Corolla, Crown, Land Cruiser, Stout and Hi-Lux	
Toyota 1970-79 Spanish	7467
Toyota Celica/Supra 1971-85	7043
Covers all U.S. and Canadian models	
Toyota Trucks 1970-85	7035
Covers all U.S. and Canadian models of pick-ups, Land Cruiser and 4Runner	
Valiant/Duster 1968-76	6326
Covers all U.S. and Canadian models	
Volvo 1956-69	6529
Covers all U.S. and Canadian models	
Volvo 1970-83	7040
Covers all U.S. and Canadian models	
VW Front Wheel Drive 1974-85	6962
Covers all U.S. and Canadian models	
VW 1949-71	5796
Covers all U.S. and Canadian models	
VW 1970-79 Spanish	7081
VW 1970-81	6837
Covers all U.S. and Canadian Beetles, Karmann Ghia, Fastback, Squareback, Vans, 411 and 412	

Chilton's Repair Manuals are available at your local retailer or by mailing a check or money order for **$14.95** per book plus **$3.50** for 1st book and **$.50** for each additional book to cover postage and handling to:

Chilton Book Company
Dept. DM
Radnor, PA 19089

NOTE: When ordering be sure to include your name & address, book part No. & title.